COMMUNITY
CORRECTIONS

To my wife, Penny, and our three children, Amy, Tiffany, and Adam.
I also dedicate this text to our granddaughter, Abigail. I am proud of
you all and consider it an honor to have each of you in my life.

COMMUNITY CORRECTIONS

ROBERT D. HANSER
University of Louisiana at Monroe

Los Angeles • London • New Delhi • Singapore • Washington DC

For information:

SAGE Publications, Inc.
2455 Teller Road
Thousand Oaks, California 91320
E-mail: order@sagepub.com

SAGE Publications Ltd.
1 Oliver's Yard
55 City Road
London EC1Y 1SP
United Kingdom

SAGE Publications India Pvt. Ltd.
B 1/I 1 Mohan Cooperative Industrial Area
Mathura Road, New Delhi 110 044
India

SAGE Publications Asia-Pacific Pte. Ltd.
33 Pekin Street #02-01
Far East Square
Singapore 048763

Printed in the United States of America.

Library of Congress Cataloging-in-Publication Data

Hanser, Robert D.
Community corrections / Robert D. Hanser.
      p. cm.
Includes bibliographical references and index.
ISBN 978-1-4129-5995-7 (pbk.)
    1. Community-based corrections I. Title.

HV9279.H36 2009
364.6′8—dc22   2008049621

This book is printed on acid-free paper.

09   10   11   12   13   10 9 8 7 6 5 4 3 2 1

Acquisitions Editor:	Jerry Westby
Associate Editor:	Lindsay Dutro
Editorial Assistant:	Eve Oettinger
Production Editor:	Karen Wiley
Copy Editor:	Teresa Herlinger
Typesetter:	C&M Digitals (P) Ltd.
Proofreader:	Scott Oney
Indexer:	William Ragsdale
Cover Designer:	Gail Buschman
Marketing Manager:	Christy Guilbalt

Brief Contents

Detailed Contents

Preface

This text is intended to provide the student with a fresh perspective on community corrections that is decidedly committed to the notion of offender reintegration. In this regard, this text is up-to-date with the current research and practices in the field of community corrections. Indeed, it would appear that the pendulum of correctional policy has shifted from one that is grounded in punitive measures to one that integrates a treatment perspective. The literature abounds in which this is quite evident, and this text is fully consistent with the current practices that have emerged.

Further, this text places a strong emphasis on partnerships between community corrections agencies and other agencies. Even more important is the specific attention given to the community itself—a necessary ingredient of any community corrections program. It is this emphasis on the collaborative nature of community corrections that sets this text apart from its predecessors. Rather than referring to other secondary resources, this text explicitly identifies and elaborates on collaborative efforts that currently exist around the nation. The integration of individual community members as volunteers and active citizens is also underscored, demonstrating that it is community members who must take responsibility and action in order to create a community that is safer for all who reside therein.

The emphasis on both treatment orientations and community partnerships emerges as a dual theme in nearly every chapter. This provides a sense of coherence and consistency throughout the text. In addition, this text contains chapters on issues related to diversity and its impact on both community corrections agencies and the communities where offenders are supervised. This, along with extensive detail on specific typologies or categories of offenders, gives depth and breadth to offender-related issues. Such elaboration is seldom found in most other textbooks on community corrections.

Likewise, this text places a strong emphasis on assessment and evaluation processes. Woven into various chapters is the need for sound assessment and classification protocols and procedures and their impact on both the security and treatment-related aspects of offender supervision. The early parts of the text clearly articulate the importance of effective assessment while also demonstrating the importance of issues such as the validity and reliability of instruments that agencies choose to use. Further, the last part of the text provides a strong argument for the use of evaluative research in the pursuit of continual improvement in the community supervision process. This last chapter does not appear in a vacuum; rather it is directly tied with other prior chapters so that the student can fully understand and appreciate the role of entry-level assessment and its impact on agency evaluation of offender outcomes. In between, the chapters offer specific detail on the case management and treatment planning processes and how effective assessment can greatly improve them.

Moreover, this text integrates the world of the practitioner with theoretical aspects. To be clear, this is not a theory text. It is every bit one that illustrates how the day-to-day practitioner conducts business in the community corrections segment of the criminal justice system. Yet at the same time, theoretical applications are made explicit to demonstrate to the student that contemporary punishment and supervision schemes are grounded in theories that are often otherwise overlooked. Indeed, this text shows that theory and the practical world do not have to be disjointed and disconnected from one another. Rather, each can serve to augment the other and in the case of this text, each aspect provides the student with a multifaceted understanding of *how* community corrections is implemented (reflecting the world of the practitioner) and *why* it is implemented in that manner (rooted in theoretical perspectives).

In addition, the role of technology has been highlighted in numerous chapters. Where many other texts might make mention of technological applications within the function of intermediate sanctions, this text provides such detail in a variety of chapters. The role of technology in the assessment and classification phase, the case management process, intermediate sanctions, and drug and DNA testing, as well as general supervision, are all addressed. This allows the student to see how community corrections has evolved into a profession that uses state-of-the-art technology and applications.

Finally, this text is also unique in one other critical aspect. The data, figures, tables, and various program examples are predominantly drawn from federal government documents and briefings. Thus, the data and programs selected are solid and tend to be of better quality than one might typically use. Federal research by the National Institute of Corrections abounds that examines many issues in community corrections, and the right to public domain of much of this material has allowed the author to integrate it within the pages of this text. This provides for rich data and examples that are guaranteed to aid in student learning. Further still, the sources have been subjected to rigorous scrutiny and consideration, ensuring that all information is valid and up-to-date.

APPROACH

The key defining approach to this text is one that illustrates how treatment and security aspects of community corrections can and do augment one another. The need for collaborative efforts where reintegration is the primary mode for reducing future recidivism is emphasized throughout. A strong practitioner emphasis is utilized so that students see exactly how community corrections processes occur. Further, the specific challenges of community corrections are discussed in great detail, providing the student with an in-depth understanding.

Significantly and perhaps uniquely, this text not only makes the point to connect treatment and security aspects of community correction, but also includes specific exercises where students themselves apply and synthesize the various concepts. These exercises help to augment the student's understanding of the practitioner world and make it necessary for the student to problem solve various scenarios and issues that face community corrections officials. Further, these exercises are directly tied to the material, yet provide scenarios that illustrate oblique problems so that students must extrapolate their readings to unique circumstances that require personal judgment and discretion. Thus, students using this text will not learn by rote but will instead learn through problem-solving exercises and through the application of what they have read.

In addition, this text includes numerous examples of different programs around the nation as a means of highlighting key points in each chapter. These examples serve to reinforce the points discussed throughout the chapters and also provide yet another view of the practitioner's world. This strong practitioner focus will ensure that, after reading this text, students will be familiar with the day-to-day challenges that face most practitioners in community supervision. The visual aids included throughout the text further illustrate for the student how supervision is conducted and what such supervision entails.

Finally, this text makes a point to present probation and parole in both a combined format—for cases where issues are similar for both types of supervision—and in a separate format where probation and parole are given individual and specific attention. This is done quite deliberately as a means of providing the student with both a comparison and a contrast of the two forms of supervision. For the most part, the two have more similarities than differences, but it is nevertheless important to make distinctions between them because of the differences in work that is required as well as the difference between offenders first entering supervision while on probation and those leaving prison under parole.

PEDAGOGICAL AIDS

There are a number of pedagogical aids that have been included in every chapter of this text. The primary goal of each of these aids is to enhance student learning and to ensure that the student synthesizes that learning and applies it to the modern world of community corrections. Through these added features, specific theories are identified and directly linked to a specific point in the community corrections setting. Also, cross-national perspectives are provided within each chapter to expose the student to applications that exist in other countries. This provides a view of community corrections that has, to this date, been lacking in most textbooks on this subject. The pedagogical features included in this book are listed below:

- At the beginning of each chapter is a set of learning objectives. These learning objectives serve as cues for the student and also provide for easy assessment of learning for the instructor. These points are germane to the chapter and prompt the student as to the information that will be covered. They also let the student know what is considered critical to the text readings.
- Each chapter includes Focus Topic boxes that provide additional insight regarding a specific point in the chapter. These Focus Topics typically help to add depth and detail to a particular subject that is considered important or interesting from a learning perspective. The inclusion of these boxes has been done with care and consideration to ensure that the material does indeed reinforce the learning objectives at the beginning of each chapter.
- Within each chapter, inserts known as Applied Theory sections are included. These inserts provide clear and focused application of a specific theory to a particular issue or set of issues in community corrections. This is an important feature because many textbooks fail to navigate the disconnection that seems to exist between the world of theory and the world of the practitioner. These inserts bridge the two worlds and also serve to highlight issues specific to the chapter from a theoretical perspective. This adds further reinforcement to the material and also serves to reinforce the learning objectives.
- At the end of each chapter, a list of key terms is included. These key terms serve the function of reinforcing specific knowledge that is applicable to the learning objectives at the beginning of each chapter. The terms are in bold throughout the text and are included in the glossary.
- At the close of each chapter are "What would you do?" exercises. These exercises present some sort of modern-day community corrections scenario that the student must address. In each case, a problem is presented to students, and they must explain what they would do to resolve the issue or solve the problem. This feature provides an opportunity for students to apply and synthesize the material from the chapter and ensures that higher-order learning of the material takes place.
- Each chapter includes an additional feature know as the "Applied Exercise." In some cases, these assignments require that the student interview practitioners in the field, while in other cases students may need to utilize specific tools or instruments (e.g., they might need to use of the Global Assessment of Functioning Scale to rank an offender's level of adjustment) when addressing an issue in community corrections. In each of these cases, the student is required to demonstrate understanding of that particular aspect of the chapter readings and must also demonstrate competence in using the information, techniques, or processes that he or she has learned from the chapter. These exercises often also require the student to incorporate information from prior

chapters or other exercises in the text, thereby building upon the prior base of knowledge that the student has accumulated throughout the text. Thus, the student's learning occurs in progression, building on prior learning.

- Within each chapter is a Cross-National Perspective segment. This component of the chapter provides a brief examination of a related topic in community corrections as it applies to a country other than the United States. In addition to a brief write-up on the subject, students are provided website information to read further on the cross-national topic, and they are also encouraged to consider the implications of the cross-national perspective through the use of Critical Thinking Questions at the end of the segment. This feature is quite distinct from other texts on community corrections and serves to broaden the student's view of the world of community supervision. These cross-national articles are included in the text's web-based study site along with other additional readings that address multinational perspectives in community corrections.
- A glossary of the key terms throughout this text is included at the end of the book. These key terms are necessary to ensure that students understand the basics of community corrections. Definitions are provided in simple but thorough language.
- A Web-based supplemental site is also available. This site features a number of electronic articles and resources that are organized by chapter. This allows students additional references for material relevant to each chapter and provides instructors with additional material or information for lectures or other activities. The Web-based study site is also designed to enhance courses that are offered in the online learning environment, providing instructors with video recordings or other visual aids that can enhance that medium of teaching and learning.

INSTRUCTOR SUPPLEMENTS

A number of Web-based features are included with this text. Among these are numerous exam questions, both objective and subjective in nature; Power-Point presentations; and a library of articles and references for anyone researching community corrections. This study site is designed specifically for instructors who may use this text in an online course in community corrections. In such cases, the additional Web-based materials will prove to be an invaluable resource.

Acknowledgments

A number of people have helped in the preparation of this book. I would like to thank them for their encouragement throughout the process of completing this project. In particular, I would like to offer my sincere thanks to Dr. Gene Scaramella of Ellis University, who was responsible for connecting me with Sage Publications, a connection that led to the contracting of this textbook. I would also like to thank Dr. Scott Mire of the University of Louisiana at Lafayette, who provided input and contributions to the research and evaluation elements of Chapter 15. I would also like to thank Mr. Howard Henderson of Sam Houston State University for his insights and contributions on community corrections processes within the pages of Chapter 11 of this text. Likewise, I would like to thank Ms. Amber Rawls and Ms. Cheryl Pringle, who both assisted in developing the Cross-National Perspectives for this text. Thanks also to Mr. Alton Braddock for proofing early drafts of the first few chapters of this text.

In addition, I would like to thank the following reviewers of the manuscript for their input and recommendations throughout the development of this text:

Gaylene Armstrong
Sam Houston State University

Natasha Frost
Northeastern University

Caroline Mitchell
Western State College of Colorado

Shannon Barton
Indiana State University

Kelly Gould
Sacramento City Community College

Alexandra Naday
Metropolitan State College of Denver

Gerald Bayens
Washburn University

Sharon Green
Louisiana State University Shreveport

John M. Paitakes
Seton Hall University

Jeb Booth
Northeastern University

Marie Griffin
Arizona State University

Robert Peetz
Midland College

Michael P. Brown
Ball State University

Patricia Joffer
South Dakota State University

Philip Quinn
University of Tampa

Martha Karin Dudash
Cameron University

Eric Metchik
Salem State College

Thomas Rutherford
West Virginia University

Last, I welcome any comments regarding this textbook or its ancillaries. Please feel free to contact me using any of the information below:

Robert D. Hanser, University of Louisiana at Monroe
700 University Avenue, Stubbs Hall, #208, Monroe, LA 71201
Phone: 318-342-1443
E-mail: hanser@ulm.edu

Definitions, History, and Development of Community Corrections

LEARNING OBJECTIVES

1. Define community corrections and understand the reasons for its emergence.

2. Identify early historical precursors to probation and parole.

3. Identify key persons in the early development of probation and parole.

4. Identify and discuss the various philosophical underpinnings associated with sentencing and the administration of offender supervision within the community.

5. Be aware of developments in community corrections from the 1960s onward.

INTRODUCTION

Community corrections is a term that brings many different thoughts to mind. The term itself can shift in meaning and perception from person to person. For instance, some people may view community corrections as consisting of only probation and parole, while others might see it as being more related to community service and other such programs. Still others tend to equate community corrections with being "easy" on crime. Certainly, the first two examples are (objectively speaking) actual tools used within the field of community corrections. However, the third example demonstrates that perceptions may negatively impact the notion of community corrections, even when the term is considered on a mere conceptual level. This is important because the perceptions that people have of community corrections will, in fact, have a direct impact on how effective community-based programs are likely to be.

In some respects, this harkens back to the "power of perception" phenomenon, a common point that is emphasized by psychologists and laypersons alike. This point is also consistent with the often touted "power of positive thinking" in that a positive outcome is more likely to be seen among community corrections agencies when the community holds a positive image of such forms of supervision. This is not to be confused with the idea that we are to sell an image of community corrections that is false or that we should ignore the drawbacks to such initiatives. Nor is this to say that we, as community members, should highlight the positive aspects of such programs. Quite the contrary, we do want to maintain an evidence-based practice in our community corrections programs. However, these programs are not ever likely to achieve their optimal outcome unless the community is involved with such programs, and yet the community is not likely to be involved unless some form of positive gain is seen to exist within that same community. Thus, a positive community perception is actually quite relevant and important for evidence-based programs.

With it being clear that community perceptions are important to the overall effectiveness of community corrections, this begs the question, how does the community envision a community corrections program and how would we define such a program? When examining any social phenomenon, it is important that investigators, researchers, and other inquirers achieve clarity on their issue of scrutiny. In other words, we must not only determine the notion of community corrections as a potentially viable response to crime; in doing so, we must also determine exactly what is meant by the term *community corrections.*

Schmalleger (2004) defines community corrections as "the use of a variety of officially ordered program-based sanctions that permit convicted offenders to remain in the community under supervision as an alternative to active prison sentences" (p. 445). Similarly, Champion (2002) cites Harris (2002) by stating that "community-based corrections is the broad array of correctional programs established at the community level that provide alternatives to incarceration" (p. 31). These two definitions seem very similar in nature, the primary implication being that community corrections is simply an alternative to the use of prisons. But consider the definition that is provided by Clear and Cole (2003), which states that community corrections is "a model of corrections based on the assumption that the criminal justice system should aim at reintegrating the offender into the community" (p. 544).

This last definition is substantially different from the prior two definitions for two reasons. First, the definition by Clear and Cole (2003) makes absolutely no mention of the fact that community corrections is an alternative to incarceration. Second, this definition contends that the primary aim of community corrections is to reintegrate the offender into the community; yet the other two definitions completely fail to even address the issue of offender reintegration. This is actually a very important point from which to start this text. Each of the three texts previously cited are premier textbooks dealing with criminal justice, basic corrections, and community corrections. Each of these definitions, while adequate, includes certain elements to the exclusion of others. This also demonstrates that perceptions of community corrections can (and do) vary among authors of renowned textbooks. These same texts ostensibly shape students' future perceptions of criminal justice in general and community corrections in particular.

The intent in pointing this out is not to criticize the various approaches to explaining community corrections. Rather, the point is to illustrate that there are indeed a variety of perceptions associated with community corrections. This is true among both laypersons and experts in the field. This also means that the current discussion pertaining to the definition of community corrections may not simply be a matter of semantics. Instead, the very definition of community corrections is a critical aspect of defining the area of study as well as the role of the practitioner. It is with this in mind that this text will utilize a hybrid definition of community corrections. For purposes of this textbook, **community corrections** *includes all non-incarcerating correctional sanctions imposed upon an offender for the purposes of reintegrating that offender within the community.* This definition is important for several reasons.

First, this definition acknowledges that community corrections consists of those programs that do not employ incarceration. Yet, this definition does not contend that these sanctions simply exist due to a need for alternatives to incarceration. This is a very important point that deserves elaboration. It is undoubtedly true that there is a need for alternatives to jail or prison simply due to the fact that both types of facilities tend to be overcrowded in various areas of the United States. In truth, the need for options to avoid further jail and prison construction is probably the main impetus behind the proliferation of community corrections programs that occurred during the late 1990s. Despite the prison boom that occurred, incarcerating strategies simply could not house all of the offenders that were processed during this time period.

Eventually, concern over such aggressive and expensive prison construction programs did lead to the exploration for alternatives to offender supervision. Community corrections provides alternatives at both the front and back end of the correctional system. With respect to front-end alternatives, probation has been used as a means of avoiding further crowding in jails and prisons. Indeed, many chief judges and court administrators are acutely aware of population capacities in the jails that are run by their corresponding sheriff's office. It would be foolish to think that such courtroom or criminal justice actors do not collaborate when determining aggregate sentencing patterns within their own local jurisdiction. At the back end of the correctional process, parole systems have continued to act as release valves for prison system populations, allowing correctional systems to ease overcrowding through the use of early release mechanisms that keep offenders under supervision until the expiration of their original sentence.

Thus, to say that community corrections provides an alternative to incarceration is not necessarily wrong, but it limits the intent and use of community corrections sanctions. This also further implies that, if there were enough prison space, community corrections might not exist. This is simply not the case, being that community corrections is often implemented in jurisdictions that do not have overcrowding problems. Rather, community corrections, in and of itself, holds value as a *primary* sanction, regardless of whether jail or prison space is abundant. In times past, this may not have been the case, such sanctions being restricted to a set of options only used in lieu of prison sanctions. However, it should instead be considered that the contemporary use of community corrections often exists as a first choice among sanctions and that these programs are now used because they have been shown to be more effective than sentencing schemes that are overreliant on incarceration. Thus, almost by accident, the criminal justice system has found that community-based programs actually work better than incarceration and are therefore the preferred modality of sanctioning in many cases of offender processing. This is a very distinct point, elaborating on the earlier definitions that were provided.

In essence, students should consider that it is now out of date to believe that these sanctions exist merely to serve as alternatives to incarceration. Through data-driven analyses of outcomes and comparisons in recidivism rates, it has been found that these programs are often superior in promoting long-term public safety agendas. This is largely due to the fact that these sanctions tend to work better with the less serious offender population, particularly those that are not violent. The nonviolent offender population happens to be the larger segment of those on community supervision. To be sure, jails and prisons do still have their place in corrections, but there are a large number of offenders that fare better in terms of recidivism if they are spared the debilitating effects of prison but are still made to be accountable for their crime to the community. This then derives a quasi-therapeutic benefit that leads to a long-term reduction in future criminality. This also leads into the second aspect of the community corrections definition that was provided by this text, that community corrections has a definite reintegrative component.

The reintegrative nature of community corrections is important from both society's perspective and the perspective of the offender. First, if the offender is successfully reintegrated, it is more likely that the offender will produce something of material value (through gainful employment) for society. The mere payment of taxes, coupled with a lack of further cost to society from the commission of further crimes, itself is a benefit extending to the whole of society. Further, offenders who are employed are able to generate payment for court fines, treatment programs, and victim compensation. None of these benefits are realized within the prison environment. Likewise, a truly reintegrated offender can provide contributions through effective parenting of his or her own children. This is actually a very important issue. Female offenders are often the primary caretakers of their children (with at least 70 percent of such offenders having children), while male offenders are often absent from the lives of their children (further adding to problems associated with father absenteeism). The social costs associated with foster homes are staggering, not to mention the fact that these children are likely to have a number of emotional problems that stem from their chaotic childhoods. Offenders that are reintegrated can stop this trend and can perhaps counter intergenerational cycles that persist in some family systems. This alone is a substantial social benefit that makes the reintegrative aspects of community corrections all the more valuable.

Additional social benefits might also come in the area of offender community involvement. Reintegrated offenders may be involved in religious institutions, volunteer activities, or even anticrime activities with youth that might be at risk of crime (prior offenders can provide insight on the hazards of criminal lifestyles in school or other settings). The potential benefits for society may not be apparent from a budgetary perspective, but society can reap enormous benefits in the form of relationships that build community cohesion. Further, prevention efforts can be aided through the input of prior offenders involved with various community programs. Thus, it is clear that there are financial, familial, and community benefits associated with offender reintegration that can be realized by society.

From the perspective of the offender, the potential benefits should be clear. Such offenders do not have their liberty as restricted as they would if incarcerated. Further, such offenders are still able to be in contact with family (particularly their children), and they are able to maintain meaningful connections with the community. This is exclusive of the fact that these individuals are spared the trauma and debilitating effects associated with prison life. Rather, such offenders are spared the pains of imprisonment, being able to develop relations with significant others, maintain contact with their children, pursue vocational and educational goals, and so forth. It is clear that such options are likely to be perceived as more beneficial by nonviolent offenders than a prison sentence might be. Thus, the reintegrative nature of community corrections holds value, in and of itself, regardless of the holding capacity of incarcerating facilities.

When talking about the development of community corrections, there are several historical antecedents that are important to understand. This chapter will provide the student with an examination of some alternatives to incarceration that existed in the early history of corrections and punishment sentencing. In offering this broad historical backdrop, it will be made apparent that early alternatives to incarceration had a therapeutic or reintegrative intent rather than a desire to save space or resources in correctional programs. Indeed, overcrowding was not a concern in the early history of corrections since there were no regulations regarding an inmate's quality of life and since deplorable conditions were (at one time) considered standard fare within a prison setting. Thus, the desire to save space or expenses was not of any appreciable concern when providing offenders with alternatives to incarceration.

Because probation was one of the earliest uses of genuine community supervision, some of the discussion that follows will center on the development of this sanction. As will be seen later in this chapter, probation is largely thought to be an invention of the United States. More important for this current section of Chapter 1 is the fact that probation was, in actuality, originally started for reintegrative purposes and was not initially intended to save jail or prison space. An argument for this point will be provided in the sections that follow. For now, suffice it to say that probation became a form of community supervision that was widespread, and the use of probation was grounded in benevolent intentions as opposed to concerns regarding the allocation of jail or prison space.

EARLY ALTERNATIVE SANCTIONS: SANCTUARY

One of the earliest forms of leniency was known as sanctuary. **Sanctuary** came in two forms, one that was largely secular in nature and the other that had its roots in Christian religion. The secular form of sanctuary existed through the identification of various cities or regions (most often cities) that were set aside as a form of neutral ground, safe havens from criminal prosecution. Accused criminals could escape prosecution by fleeing to these cities and maintaining their residence there. Though it might have been a bit difficult to reach these cities of sanctuary, they were widely known by the populace to be places of refuge for suspected criminals and provided a means for accused criminals to essentially "self-select" a banishment within these neutral regions. Incidentally, banishment was also a common punishment during the Middle Ages, but this sanction will be discussed later in the text. The basis for this form of sanctuary lies in the Christian Bible, where the book of Numbers, Chapter 35, verses 9 through 11 of the King James Bible, states that "the Lord spake unto Moses, saying, speak unto the children of Israel, and say unto them, When ye be come over Jordan into the land of Canaan, then ye shall appoint you cities to be cities of refuge for you."

Naturally, this was an alternative to the use of prison and provided the accused with options that they were able to formulate on their own. Sahagun (2007) notes that "these cities essentially were a way to prevent vigilante action against someone who had accidentally killed another person. But the refuge wasn't indefinite. The refugee was allowed to stay until he could face proper judgment by the community" (p. 1). Thus, it is clear that this type of sanctuary was mainly intended to protect the accused from capricious forms of punishment, but this also indicates that some crimes required mitigation efforts that eliminated the need for incarcerative sanctions.

Photo 1.1 Churches such as the one shown above may have been one source of temporary sanctuary for many offenders. Such practices occurred during a time when the separation of church and state had not yet emerged.

The second type of sanctuary began during the 4th century and was grounded in European Christian beliefs that appealed to the kind mercy of the church. Cromwell, del Carmen, and Alarid (2002) note that this type of sanctuary consisted of a place—usually a church—where the king's soldiers were forbidden to enter for purposes of taking an accused criminal into custody. In such cases, sanctuary was provided until some form of negotiation could be arranged or until the accused was ultimately smuggled out of the area. If, while in sanctuary, the accused confessed to the crime, he or she was typically granted abjuration. Abjuration required that the offender promise to leave England with the understanding that any return without explicit permission from the Crown would lead to immediate punishment (Cromwell et al., 2002).

This form of leniency lasted for well over a thousand years in Europe and was apparently quite common in England. Even if the accused did not confess to the crime as a means of seeking abjuration, he or she could still be granted sanctuary. Over time, however, specific rules were placed upon the use of this form of leniency. For instance, during the 13th century, felons that sought sanctuary could stay up to 40 days or, before the expiration of that time, could agree to leave the kingdom. If they remained past the 40 days, "they risked being forced out of sanctuary through starvation" (Sahagun, 2007, p. 1). Eventually, sanctuary lost its appeal in Europe and, "in the 15th century, several parliamentary petitions sought to restrict the right of sanctuary in England. In the next century, King Henry VIII reduced the number of sanctuaries by about half" (Sahagun, 2007, p. 1). From roughly 1750 onward, countries throughout Europe began to abolish sanctuary provisions as secular courts gained power over ecclesiastical courts. The process of eliminating sanctuary was a long and protracted one, and it took nearly 100 years before sanctuary ultimately disappeared as an option of leniency for accused offenders (Sahagun, 2007, p. 1).

EARLY ALTERNATIVE SANCTIONS: BENEFIT OF CLERGY

Benefit of clergy was initially a form of exemption from criminal punishment that was provided for clergy in Europe during the 12th century. This benefit was originally implemented for members of various churches, including clerics, monks, and nuns, who might be accused of crimes. This alternative to typical punishment required church representatives to be delivered to church authorities for punishment, avoiding criminal processing through the secular court system. When originally implemented, the ecclesiastical courts (church courts) were very powerful (particularly in regard to religious matters or issues that could be connected to them), and they had the power to enact life sentences, if so desired. This was, however, a rarity since the church clergy members involved in crimes (clerics, monks, nuns) were often purported to have religious convictions, moral considerations, or ethical binds that mitigated their various offenses.

Church authorities, being well versed in religious precepts and complexities, were better able to discern outright hedonistic bloodshed or wanton lust from other acts that may have resulted from simple lapses of judgment or spiritual dilemmas that might be at the heart of many of these crimes. In addition, the ecclesiastical courts viewed negative behavior as being more a result of sin, and therefore an offense against God, than an offense against men or the Crown. Given this fact and that biblical leanings toward repentance, forgiveness, and mercy might sometimes be offered as the underlying basis for sentencing, church clergy members were often given sentences that were less punitive and more reformative in nature.

Though this might seem to be an effort to simply integrate compassion into the sentencing process, benefit of clergy had its genesis in a feudal power struggle between the Crown and the Holy Roman Catholic Church in England (Dressler, 1962). During this period, King Henry II desired more control over the Church in England and wished to diminish the influence that the ecclesiastical church had on the decision-making powers of the Crown (Dressler, 1962). Much of this power was also rooted in the fact that the masses deferred to the Church and also revolved around the fact that the Crown utilized religion as a form of social control among a populace that was otherwise uneducated and potentially unmanageable. Thus religious constraints on behavior, and the belief that God was judging behavior even when the king could not himself observe and regulate it, aided in keeping much of the populace within due bounds of moral and legal constraints— at least on the surface.

It was the specific desire of Henry II to subject the clerics and monks of the church to the will of the King's Court (Dressler, 1962; Latessa & Allen, 1999). In doing so, the Crown would then hold dominion over the Church, and power would be centralized under a secular court controlled by the king. Thus, the benefit of clergy was the Church's attempt to thwart the efforts of King Henry II and to maintain power within England. This is interesting because it is an early example of how political power struggles can impact justice-making decisions. As will be seen in later chapters of this text, many of the programs that are implemented in both prison and community corrections systems are steeped in ideology or have their beginnings attributed to some form of political debate over crime and punishment. The benefit of clergy is a very early example of how ideology and public policy become intertwined and how both are shaped and crafted due to power struggles between opposing parties. This also demonstrates that justice, in its purest form, is manipulated by the underlying desires of those in power. Further, this illustrates that social forces can impact sanctions that are utilized on a widespread basis. This will be an important point in later chapters as well, demonstrating that history does indeed repeat itself and likewise making clear the fact that community corrections does not operate in a social vacuum.

Through benefit of clergy, ordained clerics, monks, and nuns were transferred to what was referred to as the Bishop's Court of the Holy Roman Catholic Church. To further illustrate the fairly manipulative nature of this court, consider the following quote by Dressler (1962):

When a member of the cloth, suspected of a crime, was brought into King's Court, his bishop could claim the dispensation for him. Thereupon, the charge was read to the cleric, but no evidence was presented against him. Instead, he gave his own version of the alleged offense and brought in witnesses to corroborate his testimony. With all the evidence against the accused expunged and only favorable witnesses testifying, it is hardly astounding that most cases ended in acquittal. (p. 7)

Though this form of leniency was initially reserved for church clergy members, by the 14th century it had been made available to all who were literate (Latessa & Allen, 1999). Judges in secular courts provided this option but required offenders to demonstrate that they were indeed literate. The test of literacy required that the offender read the text of Psalm 51 out loud in front of the judge. Psalm 51 was an especially appropriate chapter from the Christian Bible, as its verses specifically appeal to God for forgiveness and redemption from one's own transgressions (see Focus Topic 1.1). However, criminals being a fairly wily and crafty lot, they began to memorize the verse. Many criminals who were not literate at all, but were able to stand before a judge, looked at the page with Psalm 51 and recited the verses from memory, all without being able to actually read the verses in front of them. Assuming the criminals could master the verses—word for word—and could recite them when before witnesses, a lighter sentence was theirs to be had. Naturally, one could test their ability to read by requiring the accused to point at specific words within the text, and this is precisely what occurred in later years as judges became aware of the past deception that had occurred in their courts.

FOCUS TOPIC 1.1

AN APPEAL TO GOD THROUGH PSALM 51

Psalm 51 was often referred to as the "neck verse" because the reading of this verse by an offender could essentially save his or her neck from the gallows through the benefit of clergy. Psalm 51, verses 1 through 10, was particularly fitting for this purpose because the verses emphasized the desire for repentance and the need to have one's transgressions forgiven. From the King James version of the Christian Holy Bible, the verses follow:

1. Have mercy upon me, O God,
   According to thy loving-kindness:
   According unto the multitude of thy tender mercies
   Blot out my transgressions.

2. Wash me thoroughly from mine iniquity,
   And cleanse me from my sin.

3. For I acknowledge my transgressions,
   And my sin is ever before me.

4. Against thee, and thee only, have I sinned,
   And done this evil in thy sight
   That though mightest be justified when thou speakest,
   And be clear when though judgest.

5. Behold, I was shapen in iniquity;
   And in sin did my mother conceive me.

6. Behold, thou desirest truth in the inward parts;
   And in the hidden part thou shalt make me to know wisdom.

7. Purge me with hyssop, and I shall be clean:
   Wash me, and I shall be whiter than snow.

8. Make me to hear joy and gladness;
   That the bones that thou hast broken may rejoice.

(Continued)

(Continued)

9. Hide thy face from my sins,

And blot out all mine iniquities.

10. Create in me a clean heart, O God;

And renew a right spirit within me.

Psalm 51 was originally a request by King David of Israel for his God's forgiveness. King David had committed adultery with a woman named Bath-Sheba, who was married to one of King David's high-ranking generals. King David plotted against the loyal general, placing him in a battle where he was sure to be slain (and he was indeed killed) so that he could lie with the general's wife, unimpeded. Eventually, his sin was found out and King David was punished. He asked for forgiveness and according to Hebrew accounts, received forgiveness from God. This is a common tale used to demonstrate that any sin, regardless of how despicable, can be forgiven by God if one sincerely repents, and served as the basis behind the benefit of clergy used in Europe for centuries.

SOURCE: The American Bible Society. (2001). The Psalms 51. *The Holy Bible: King James Version.* Retrieved from http://www.bartleby.com/108/19/51.html.

Photo 1.2 Stan Davis (left), Brother Jim Fogerty (middle), and Willie J. R. Fleming all work in an area of Chicago known as Cabrini Green. This area has been plagued with high crime and has a disproportionate amount of it. Cabrini Green is known for having serious gang problems. These three men work with gang offenders, providing faith-based and community-based interventions. These men are prime examples of how church-based interventions work with modern-day offender populations.

However, most who were literate at this time were also financially well-off. Thus, this benefit tended to aid those who had power, meanwhile ignoring the plight of the poor who were more vulnerable. This was an especially important option given England's penchant for the death penalty during the centuries that followed. Benefit of clergy was thus a means of escaping a very tough sentencing scheme for minor crimes. Over time, the English criminal law did achieve a much better sense of parity or proportionality. Because of these changes, the benefit of clergy was effectively abolished in 1827 since it was no longer necessary to safeguard persons from an unwieldy and brutal sentencing structure.

The benefit of clergy was clearly not a means of saving prison resources, but was instead the result of a political power struggle between two opposing entities of social control in England. Further, even though this benefit was eventually extended to those who could demonstrate literacy, this tended to only include those persons that were wealthy or at least moderately well-off. With this in mind, it is unlikely that the clergy or the rich were among those most often processed through the court systems of England. Rather, it was typically the poor and the underclasses that were most often given incarcerative sanctions (not much different from today's socio-economic sentencing demographic). Moreover, concern for jail or prison conditions did not even exist throughout most of the centuries in which this option existed. Rather, there was actually no limit to the number of offenders that might be housed together, and early accounts of English prisons acknowledge the squalid conditions of these facilities. It is unlikely that the benefit of clergy would have been a necessary mechanism to alleviate overcrowding, pestilence, or disease within old English jails or prisons, since these deplorable conditions were simply viewed as part of the incarceration experience and therefore part of the offender's sentence.

EARLY ALTERNATIVE SANCTIONS: JUDICIAL REPRIEVE

Later, during the last part of the 1700s, it became increasingly common for judges in England to utilize an alternative method of punishment known as judicial reprieve. These were used at the full discretion of judges, in cases where they did not believe that incarceration was proportionate to the crime or where no productive benefit was expected. The judicial reprieve simply suspended sentences of incarceration as an act of mercy or leniency. Naturally, as might be expected, this option was reserved for offenders who had committed minor infractions of the law and who did not have prior records. Cromwell et al. (2002) note that while the offender was on reprieve, he or she retained liberties and freedoms. Upon the expiration of a specified period of time, the offender was then able to apply to the Crown of England for a full pardon.

In these cases, judges made decisions based on their own hunches as to the likelihood of offender outcomes, and this was regardless of the number of inmates in their local jail. In fact, jailers often received a substantial income from fees obtained through the provision of goods and services to inmates within their charge. In a literal sense, a jailer's income was enhanced when there were high numbers of inmates in the facility. The more inmates in a facility, the more income was produced for the jailer. Thus, it was not at all in the jailer's best interest to limit the number of inmates, particularly when one considers that there were no standards of care that jailers had to meet. Simply put, inmates could be crammed into jail facilities without any fear of public or court reprisal. Jailers thus had everything to gain and nothing at all to lose when overcrowding their jail facilities.

It is therefore clear that jailers would not have desired widespread use of reprieves since this would essentially block their income. Thus, when judges did use reprieves it was simply due to their own genuine concern for the inmate's welfare rather than pressure related to overfilled facilities. Cromwell et al. (2002) go so far as to note that judicial reprieves were a method by which judges "recognized that not all offenders are dangerous, evil persons" and thus sought to avoid prescribing the specified punishment when such punishment was simply out of sync with the judge's perception of the offender's temperament or demeanor (p. 27). This is important because it demonstrates that, at their base, reprieves were actually provided as a form of compassion in the hope that the offender would be deterred from criminal activity in the future. Such a perspective is nothing less than a rehabilitative perspective whereby the reintegration of the offender is given priority over mere desires for punishment.

EARLY ALTERNATIVE SANCTIONS: RECOGNIZANCE

Recognizance in the United States is often traced to the case of *Commonwealth v. Chase* (1830) in which Judge Thacher of Boston found a woman named Jerusha Chase guilty of stealing from inside a home (Grinnel, 1941). Ms. Chase pleaded her guilt but did have numerous friends that also pleaded for mercy from the court. This resulted in her release "at large" on her own recognizance until which time she was called to appear before the court (Begnaud, 2007). The accused was subsequently acquitted before the same court of another charge of larceny and was only sentenced for her prior 1830 crime (Begnaud, 2007; Grinnel, 1941). Cromwell et al. (2002) note that "recognizance came to be used often in Massachusetts as a means of avoiding a final conviction of young and minor offenders in hope that they would avoid further criminal behavior," adding that "the main thrust of recognizance was to humanize criminal law and mitigate its harshness" (p. 28). This again points toward the idea that many of the early alternatives to incarceration were implemented more for the reintegration of offenders than because of a concern over the population of the local jail facility.

Begnaud (2007) contends that this use of recognizance in the United States is the first antecedent to probation, given that the convicted offender was released into society but, if charged for a subsequent criminal act, could then be charged further for the original crime that led to the offender's initial contact with the court. Latessa and Allen (1999) support this contention by demonstrating that more and more aspects of modern probation began to appear also in the use of recognizance in England. This practice, also known as "binding over," involved the use of "a bond or obligation entered into by a defendant, who is bound to refrain from doing, or is bound to do, something for a stipulated period, and to appear in court on a specified date for trial or for final disposition of the case" (Dressler, 1962, p. 9; Latessa & Allen, 1999, p. 108). As with judicial reprieves, this alternative to incarceration was usually only used with offenders who had committed petty crimes. If the offender violated the terms of this agreement, the binding was claimed by the state and the offender might then face incarceration or some other form of punishment, often including physical sanctions (Latessa & Allen, 1999).

Latessa and Allen (1999) further note that this sanction has been thought to consist of the very beginnings of community supervision because it included the supervision of a sentence and provided conditional freedom that was leveraged against possible revocation of the offender's recognizant release. But it is generally considered premature to say that this sanction was the actual beginning of probation because it did not include official intermittent or structured supervision from an agent or representative of the court. Nevertheless, Latessa and Allen do point out (as does Begnaud, 2007) that the various elements associated with recognizance qualify the sanction as a noteworthy antecedent of probation, and for this reason the description of this sanction is placed just before the next section on the early history of probation.

THE BEGINNING OF PROBATION

While many of the traditions and means of addressing issues associated with crime and punishment originated in England, the United States did have its own novel inventions. Probation is one such invention, being an alternative to incarceration that is unique to the United States. **John Augustus,** a cobbler and philanthropist of Boston, is often recognized as the father of modern probation. During the time that John Augustus provided his innovative contribution to the field of community corrections, the temperance movement against alcohol consumption was in full swing. Augustus, being aware of many of the issues associated with alcoholism, made an active effort to rehabilitate prior alcoholics who were processed through the police court in Boston. While acting as a volunteer of the court, Augustus observed a man being charged for drunkenness who would have, in all likelihood, ended up in the Boston House of Corrections if it were not for Augustus's intervention. Augustus posted bail for the man, personally guaranteeing the man's return to court at the prescribed time. Augustus helped the man to find a job and provided him with the guidance and support necessary so that the defendant was able to become a functioning and productive member within the community. When the court ordered the return of the offender 3 weeks later, the judge noticed a substantial improvement in the offender's behavior. The judge was so impressed by the initial outcome that "he fined him only one cent and court costs, which were less than $4.00. The judge also suspended the six-month jail term" (Champion, 2002, p. 136). From this point in 1841 until his death in 1859, Augustus continued to bail out numerous offenders, providing voluntary supervision and guidance until they were subsequently sentenced by the court. During his 18 years of activity, Augustus "bailed on probation" 1,152 male offenders and 794 female offenders (Barnes & Teeters, 1959, p. 554; Latessa & Allen, 1999). His rationale centered on his belief that "the object of the law is to reform criminals and to prevent crime and not to punish maliciously or from a spirit of revenge" (Dressler, 1962, p. 17).

The above quote by Dressler is important because it again goes back to this chapter's initial point that community corrections (including, of course, probation) was just as much designed to reintegrate (another word for "reform" as used by Dressler in 1962) the offender as anything else. In fact, given this particular quote from Dressler, it might be concluded that issues of crowding within incarcerating institutions were not of any concern at all during the mid-1800s prior to the Civil War. After all, it is clear from the above passage that Augustus was primarily concerned about the malicious treatment of offenders or the desire for revenge that might perhaps have clouded society's vision. This contention is further supported by Champion (2002), who states that "Augustus, however, could not save everyone from incarceration. In fact, that was not his intention. He only wanted to rescue those offenders he felt worthy of rehabilitation" (p. 138). Thus, it was rehabilitation that Augustus ultimately sought to achieve, regardless of whether jails or houses of correction were considered humane. (In fact, many were very inhumane.)

Augustus was aware that jail and prison conditions were barbaric in many cases. Yet this still was not his primary reason for implementing his intervention. Rather, he selected his candidates with due care and caution, tending to offer aid to those who were first-time offenders. He also looked to their character, demeanor, past experiences, and potential future influences when making his decisions. Thus, whether you use the word reform, rehabilitate, or reintegrate, it is clear that the early intent of probation was to provide society with a person who was more productive after sentencing than he or she had been prior to it. This intent stood on its own merit and sense of purpose, regardless of jail or prison conditions that might have existed, thereby establishing the original mission of community corrections as a whole.

Photo 1.3 Alexander Maconochie is a key figure in much of early community corrections history. He was the primary person to develop a program of early release for inmates who were in custody on Norfolk Island.

THE BEGINNING OF PAROLE

Two primary figures are attributed with the development of parole: Alexander Maconochie and Sir Walter Crofton. Maconochie was in charge of the penal colony at Norfolk Island and Crofton directed the prison system of Ireland. While Maconochie first developed a general scheme for parole, it was Sir Walter Crofton who later refined the idea and created what was referred to as the ticket-of-leave. The **ticket-of-leave** was basically a permit that was given to a convict in exchange for a certain period of good conduct. Through this process, the convict could earn his own wage through his own labor prior to the expiration of his actual sentence. In addition, other liberties were provided so long as the convict's behavior remained within the lawful limits set by the ticket-of-leave system. This system is therefore often considered the antecedent to the development of parole.

In the 1600s and 1700s, England implemented a form of punishment known as *banishment* on a widespread scale. During this time, criminals were sent to the American colonies under reprieve and through stays of execution. Thus, the convicts had their lives spared, but this form of mercy was generally only implemented to solve a labor shortage that existed within the American colonies. Essentially, the convicts were shipped to the Americas to work as indentured servants at hard labor. However, the War of Independence within the colonies put an end to this practice, until 1788, when the first shipload of convicts was transported to Australia. Australia was the new dumping ground for convicts who were used as labor. The work was hard and the living conditions were challenging. However, a ticket-of-leave system was developed on this continent in which different governors had the authority to release convicts who displayed good and stable conduct.

In 1837, Alexander Maconochie, a captain in the Royal Navy, was placed in command over the English penal colony in New South Wales at Norfolk Island, which was nearly 1,000 miles off the eastern coast of Australia. The convicts at Norfolk Island were the worst of the worst, since they had already been shipped to Australia for criminal acts in England, only to be later shipped to Norfolk Island due to additional criminal acts or forms of misconduct they had committed while serving time in Australia. The conditions on Norfolk Island were deplorable, so much so that many convicts preferred to be given the death penalty rather than serve time upon the island (Latessa & Allen, 1999).

While serving in this command, Maconochie proposed a system in which the duration of the sentence was determined by the inmate's work habits and righteous conduct. Though this was already used in a crude manner through the ticket-of-leave process in Australia, Maconochie created a **mark system** in which "marks" would be earned by the convict for each day of successful toil. His system was quite well organized and thought out, being based on five main tenets, as described by Barnes and Teeters (1959):

1. Release should not be based on the completing of a sentence for a set period of time, but on completion of a determined and specified quantity of labor. In brief, time sentences should be abolished and task sentences substantiated.

2. The quantity of labor a prisoner must perform should be expressed in a number of "marks" which he must earn, by improvement of conduct, frugality of living, and habits of industry, before he can be released.

3. While in prison he should earn everything he receives. All sustenance and indulgences should be added to his debt of marks.

4. When qualified by discipline to do so, he should work in association with a small number of other prisoners, forming a group of six or seven, and the whole group should be answerable for the conduct of labor of each member.

5. In the final stage, a prisoner, while still obliged to earn his daily tally of marks, should be given a proprietary interest in his own labor and be subject to a less rigorous discipline, to prepare him for release into society. (p. 419)

Under this plan, convicts were given marks and moved through phases of supervision until they finally earned full release. Because of this, Maconochie's system is considered indeterminate in nature, with convicts progressing through five specific phases of classification. These phases included the following: (1) strict incarceration, (2) intense labor in forced work group or chain gang, (3) limited freedom within a prescribed area, (4) a ticket-of-leave, and (5) full freedom. This system, as devised by Maconochie, was based on the premise that inmates should be gradually prepared for full release. It is apparent that Maconochie's system utilized versions of intermediate sanctions and indeterminate sentencing. **Indeterminate sentencing** is sentencing that includes a range of years that will be potentially served by the offender. The offender is released during some point in the range of years that are assigned by the sentencing judge. Both the minimum and maximum times can be modified by a number of factors such as offender behavior and offender work ethic. The indeterminate sentence stands in contrast to the use of **determinate sentencing,** which consists of fixed periods of incarceration imposed on the offender with no later flexibility in the term that is served. This type of sentencing is grounded in notions of retribution, just deserts, and incapacitation. Due to the use of indeterminate sentencing and primitive versions of intermediate sanctioning, Maconochie's mark system is perhaps best thought of as a precursor to parole as well as the use of classification systems. In fact, the use of classification systems tended to be underdeveloped. Thus, Maconochie provided a guide in predicting likelihood of success with convicts, making him a man that was well ahead of his time.

However, Maconochie appears to have been *too far* ahead of his time; many government officials and influential persons in both Australia and England believed that Maconochie's approach was too soft on criminals. His methods of reform drew increasing negative publicity from Australian and English citizens who perceived the system as being too lenient on convicts. Ironically, this is not much different from today where the common consensus among Americans is that prisons and punitive sanctions are preferred forms of punishment. In contrast, Maconochie was fond of criticizing prison operations in England, his own belief being that confinement ought to be rehabilitative in nature rather than punitive (note that this is consistent with the insights of John Augustus and his views on the use of probation). Maconochie's ideas were not popular among government officials of the Crown nor with the general populace of England, and he ultimately was dismissed from his post on Norfolk Island as well as other commands for being too lenient with convicts. Nevertheless, Maconochie was persistent, and in 1853, he successfully lobbied to pass the **English Penal Servitude Act,** which established several rehabilitation programs for convicts.

The English Penal Servitude Act of 1853 applied to prisons in both England and Ireland. Though Maconochie had spearheaded this act to solidify, legalize, and make permanent the use of ticket-of-leave systems, the primary reason for this act's success had more to do with the fact that free Australians were becoming ever more resistant to the use of Australia as the location for banished English convicts. This act did not necessarily eliminate the use of banishment in England, but it did provide incentives and suggestions for more extensive use of prisons. This law included guidelines for the length of time that inmates should serve behind bars before being granted a ticket-of-leave and, according to Cromwell et al. (2002), maintained the following:

1. The power of revoking or altering the license of a convict will most certainly be exercised in the case of misconduct.

2. If, therefore, he wishes to retain the privilege, which by his good behavior under penal discipline he has obtained, he must prove by his subsequent conduct that he is worthy of Her Majesty's Clemency.

3. To produce a forfeiture of the license, it is by no means necessary that the hold should be convicted of a new offense. If he associates with notoriously bad characters, leads an idle or dissolute life, or has no visible means of obtaining an honest livelihood, and so on, it will be assumed that he is about to relapse into crime, and he will at once be apprehended and recommitted to prison under his original release. (p. 166)

It should be clear that the above guidelines are the basis of a general form of parole. As we will see in later chapters, the conditions that are mentioned in the English Penal Servitude Act of 1853 are also common to today's use of parole in the United States, though of course, there are many more technical aspects to the use of parole in today's society. However, the guidelines mentioned (particularly those in number 3 above) clearly demonstrate that the offender's early release is contingent on his or her continued good behavior and desistance from crime as well as fending off criminogenic influences. Because of this and other significant improvements in penal policies in England, as well as his contributions to early release provisions there, Maconochie has been dubbed the father of parole.

During the 1850s, Sir Walter Crofton was the director of the Irish penal system. Naturally, since the English Penal Servitude Act of 1853 was passed during his term of office, he was aware of the changes implemented in prison operations and he was likewise aware of Maconochie's ideas. Crofton used these ideas to create a classification system that proved useful and workable within the Irish prison system. This classification system utilized three stages of treatment. The first stage placed the convict in segregated confinement with work and training being provided to the offender. The second stage was a transition period during which the convict was set to the task of completing public work projects while under minimal supervision. During the third stage, presuming that the offender proved reliable, he was released on license (Dressler, 1962; Latessa & Allen, 1999).

In implementing this classification system, each inmate's classification level was specifically measured by the number of marks he or she had earned for good conduct, work output, and educational achievement. This idea was, quite naturally, borrowed from Maconochie's system on Norfolk Island. It is also important to point out that the Irish system developed by Sir Walter Crofton was much more detailed, with specific written instructions and guidelines that provided for close supervision and control of the offender, using police personnel to supervise released offenders in rural areas, and an inspector of released prisoners in the City of Dublin (Cromwell et al., 2002).

Release on license was contingent upon certain conditions, with violations of these conditions subject to the possibility of reimprisonment. "While on license, prisoners were required to submit to monthly reports and were warned against idleness and association with other criminals" (Latessa & Allen, 1999, p. 156). Thus, offenders released on license had to report to either a police officer or other designated person, they had specific requirements that they had to meet, they had to curtail their social involvements, and they could be again incarcerated if they did not maintain those requirements (Latessa & Allen, 1999). This obviously resembles several aspects of modern-day parole programs. In fact, it could be said that contemporary uses of parole in the United States mimic the conditions set forth by Sir Walter Crofton in Ireland.

Cross-National Perspective

The History of Probation in England

The Development of Probation in England: A Quick Chronological History

1876: Hertfordshire printer Frederic Rainer, a volunteer with the Church of England Temperance Society (CETS), writes to the society of his concern about the lack of help for those who come before the courts. He sends a donation of five shillings (25p) toward a fund for practical rescue work in the police courts. The CETS responds by appointing two "missionaries" to Southwark Court with the initial aim of "reclaiming drunkards." This forms the basis of the London Police Courts Mission (LPCM), whose missionaries worked with magistrates to develop a system of releasing offenders on the condition that they kept in touch with the missionary and accepted guidance.

1880: Eight full-time missionaries are in place, and the mission opens homes and shelters providing vocational training and develops residential work.

1886: The Probation of First-Time Offenders Act allows for courts around the country to follow the London example of appointing missionaries, but very few do so.

1907: The Probation of Offenders Act gives LCPM missionaries official status as "officers of the court," later known as probation officers. The act allows courts to suspend punishment and discharge offenders if they enter into a recognizance of between 1 and 3 years, one condition of which was supervision by a person named in the "probation order."

1913: The first newsletter of the National Association of Probation Officers records the association's first annual meeting at Caxton Hall in London on December 11, 1912. The newsletter reports the address given to the Grand Jury of the London Sessions in September 1912 by Robert Wallace, KC, who said that the calendar was one of the lightest in the history of the sessions. "Of 137 prisoners, 17 had been sent for sentence as 'incorrigible rogues' and 12 others were awaiting punishment. There were only nine women. There has been a steady diminution in the number of cases ever since the new method of dealing with offenders under the Probation of Offenders Act was adopted four years ago. Of those who had been dealt with in that way, very few had offended again."

1918: With juvenile crime increasing during and after the First World War, the Home Office concedes that probation should not be left to philanthropic or judicial bodies and that state direction is needed. The influential Molony Committee of 1927 stimulates debate about the respective roles of probation officers, local government, and philanthropic organizations. It encourages the informal involvement of probation officers in aftercare from both borstal [youth prison] and reformatory schools.

1938: The Home Office assumes control of the probation service and introduces a wide range of modernizing reforms. The legal formula of "entering into a recognizance" is replaced by "consent to probation." Requirements for psychiatric treatment are also introduced and it is made mandatory for female probationers to be supervised by women officers. LCPM concentrates on hostels for "probation trainees" and branches out into homes for children in "moral danger," sexually abused children, and young mothers.

1948: The Criminal Justice Act incorporates punitive measures such as attendance centers and detention centers, but the stated purpose of the probation order remains intact and is reaffirmed as "advise, assist, and befriend."

1970s and 1980s: Partnerships with other agencies result in cautioning schemes, alternatives to custody, and crime reduction, while changes in sentencing result in day centers, special program conditions, the probation order as a sentence, and risk of custody and risk of reconviction assessment tools.

2000: The Criminal Justice and Court Services Act renames the probation service as the National Probation Service for England and Wales, replacing 54 probation committees with 42 local probation boards and establishing 100% Home Office funding for the probation service. It creates the post of Director General of Probation Services within the Home Office and makes chief officers statutory office holders and members of local probation boards.

2004: The government publishes *Reducing Crime—Changing Lives,* which proposes to improve the effectiveness of the criminal justice system and the correctional services in particular. The National Offender Management Service is established with the aim of reducing reoffending through more consistent and effective offender management. The government proposes to introduce commissioning and contestability into the provision of probation services, which it says will drive up standards further among existing providers, and to enable new providers to deliver services.

2007: The Probation Service in England and Wales is 100 Years Old.

SOURCE: Adapted from Probation Board Association of England and Wales. (2007). *Probation centenary, 1907–2007.* Retrieved from http://www.probationcentenary.org/contactus.htm.

Critical Thinking Question

1. Discuss the commonality of early religious involvement in corrections and explain how that affected correctional thought in both the United States and England. Next, after reading the chronological history of probation in England, explain whether this religious emphasis continued or if it appears to have diminished over time. Is this the same as or different from developments in the United States? Explain your answer.

For more information about probation in the United Kingdom, visit the website www.probationcentenary.org/contactus.htm.

PHILOSOPHICAL BASIS OF COMMUNITY CORRECTIONS—BOTH PROBATION AND PAROLE

Within the field of corrections itself, four goals or philosophical orientations of punishment are generally recognized. These are retribution, deterrence, incapacitation, and rehabilitation. Two of these orientations focus on the offender (rehabilitation and specific deterrence), while the other orientations (general deterrence, retribution, and incapacitation) are thought to generally focus more on the crime that was committed. The intent of this section of the chapter is to present philosophical bases specifically related to community corrections and offender reintegration. However, it is useful to first offer a quick and general overview of the four primary philosophical bases of punishment. Each of these will be discussed in greater detail in Chapter 2 of this text, but a quick introduction to these concepts is provided here for student reference when completing the remainder of the current chapter.

Retribution is often referred to as the "eye for an eye" mentality, and simply implies that offenders committing a crime should be punished in a like fashion or in a manner that is commensurate with the severity of the crime that they have committed. In other words, retribution implies proportionality of punishments to the seriousness of the crime. **Deterrence** includes general and specific forms. **General deterrence** is intended to cause vicarious learning whereby observers see that offenders are punished for a given crime and therefore themselves are discouraged from committing a like-mannered crime due to fear of similar punishment. **Specific deterrence** is simply the infliction of a punishment upon a specific offender in the hope that that particular offender will be discouraged from committing future crimes. **Incapacitation** deprives the offender of liberty and removes him or her from society with the intent of ensuring that society cannot be further victimized by that offender during the offender's term of incarceration. Finally, **rehabilitation** implies that an offender should be provided the means to fulfill a constructive level of functioning in society, with an implicit expectation that such offenders will be deterred from reoffending due to their having worthwhile stakes in legitimate society—stakes that they will not wish to lose as a consequence of criminal offending.

Numerous authors and researchers associated with the field of community corrections have noted that the underlying philosophical basis of both probation and parole is that of rehabilitating offenders and reintegrating them into society (Abadinsky, 2003; Latessa & Allen, 1999). That is, of course, the general message of this chapter since an examination of the early uses of probation and parole has demonstrated that historically, these mechanisms of offender supervision were utilized with more concern given to the offender's likely reformation than to the population conditions of jails and prisons. It is clear that notable figures such as John Augustus (the "Father of Probation") and Alexander Maconochie (the "Father of Parole") were more concerned with the potential reformation of the offender when determining suitability of sanctions.

Latessa and Allen (1999) point out that the use of probation as a correctional sanction was largely in response to the punitive philosophy that had existed among the nobility and royalty of Europe and had been carried over to America. The earliest theoretical and philosophical bases for both probation and parole lie in the work of Cesare Beccaria's classic treatise entitled *An Essay on Crimes and Punishments* (1764/1983). Beccaria is also held to be the "Father of Classical Criminology," a field that was instrumental in shifting views on crime and punishment toward a more humanistic means of response. Among other things, Beccaria advocated for proportionality between the crime that was committed by an offender and the specific sanction that was given. Since not all crimes are equal, the use of progressively greater sanctions becomes an instrumental component in achieving this proportionality. Naturally, community-based perspectives that utilize a continuum of sanctions (Clear & Cole, 2003) fit well with the tenets of proportionality.

The key differences between earlier approaches to processing offenders (i.e., harsh and publicly displayed punishments) and the emerging reformation emphasis that occurred during the last part of the late 1700s were grounded in the way that offenders were viewed as well as the decided intent of the criminal law (Latessa & Allen, 1999). According to Latessa and Allen, "the focus shifted to dealing with individual offenders, rather than focusing on the crime that had been committed" (p. 111). The need for individualization of treatment and punishment began to be realized, with the tenets of classical criminology being central to the implementation of treatment and punishment schemes.

Classical criminology, in addition to proportionality, emphasized that punishments must be useful, purposeful, and reasonable. Rather than employing barbaric public displays (a deterrent approach in itself) designed to frighten people into obedience, reformers called for more moderate correctional responses. Beccaria, in advocating this shift in offender processing, contended that humans were hedonistic—seeking pleasure while wishing to avoid pain—and that this required an appropriate amount of punishment to counterbalance the rewards derived from criminal behavior. It will become clear in subsequent pages that this emphasis on proportional rewards and punishments dovetails well with behavioral psychology's views on the use of reinforcements (rewards) and punishments. Behavioral and learning theories will likewise be presented as the primary theoretical bases of effective community corrections interventions since they jibe well with the tenets of classical criminology, are easily assessed and evaluated, and can be easily integrated with most criminal justice program objectives. Finally, Siegel (2003) notes that classical criminological theory contained four basic elements:

1. In every society, people have free will to choose criminal or lawful solutions to meet their needs or settle their problems.

2. Criminal solutions may be more attractive than lawful ones because they usually require less work with a greater potential payoff.

3. A person's choice of criminal solutions may be controlled by his or her fear of punishment.

4. The more severe, certain, and swift the punishment, the better able it is to control criminal behavior (p. 108).

Though it is certain that there are exceptions to the above tenets, classical criminology does continue to serve as the basic underlying theoretical foundation of our criminal justice system in the United States, including the correctional components. It is indeed presumed that offenders can (and do) learn from their transgressions through a variety of reinforcement and punishment schedules that institutional and community-based corrections may provide. Not only was this presumed by John Augustus when implementing the prototypes of what would later be known as formal probation, but Alexander Maconochie and Sir Walter Crofton likewise held similar beliefs when using their mark systems and methods of classifying offenders.

Applied Theory | Classical Criminology, Behavioral Psychology, and Community Corrections

In addition to Cesare Beccaria, another noteworthy figure associated with classical criminology was Jeremy Bentham. Bentham is known for advocating that punishments should be swift, severe, and certain. This has been widely touted by classical criminologists and even by many modern-day criminologists who have leanings toward classical or rational choice theories on crime. Essentially, Bentham believed that a delay in the amount of time between the crime and the punishment impaired the likely deterrent value of the punishment in the future. Likewise, Bentham held that punishments must be severe enough in consequence as to deter persons from engaging in criminal behavior. Finally, Bentham noted that the punishment must be assured; otherwise the person will simply become more clever at hiding the crimes once he or she knows that the punishment can be avoided.

Current research supports some aspects of classical criminology, while refuting other points. In particular, it has been found that the certainty of the punishment does indeed lower the likelihood of recidivism (repeat offending). Likewise, the less time between the crime and the punishment, the less likely offenders will reoffend in the future. However, it has not been found to be true that severe punishment is more successful in reducing crime. In fact, there has been substantial historical research on the death penalty that seems to indicate that general deterrence is not achieved with the death penalty, even though it is the most severe punishment that can be given.

Further, research on the use of prisons has shown that they may actually *increase* the likelihood of future recidivism for many offenders. Obviously, this is counterproductive to the desire of the criminal justice system. While some offenders are simply too dangerous to have released into the community, others who are not so dangerous will ultimately be returning. Among those, the goal of any sanction should be to reduce the likelihood that they will commit crime—not increase that likelihood. The research of Smith, Goggin, and Gendreau (2002) provides evidence that the prison environment may simply increase the likelihood for recidivism among many offenders. Smith et al. (2002) conducted a meta-analysis of various recidivism studies and concluded that prisons could indeed be considered "schools of crime" (p. 21). Further, they found that the longer the term of imprisonment, the more likely offenders were to recidivate. Thus, severity of the punishment does not reduce crime and, in actuality, it does indeed increase the likelihood of future crime. Other studies substantiate this research.

(Continued)

This alone presents a valid argument against the unnecessary use of prisons, particularly when community corrections can provide effective supervision and sanctions without the reliance on prison facilities. Community corrections sanctions can be swifter in implementation, and they are much more certain in their application. For example, many offenders may be given a certain number of years in prison but will later be released early, reducing the certainty (and severity) that they will be held to serve their intended punishment. Further, the plea-bargaining system in the United States provides the opportunity for the convicted to avoid incarceration entirely, even though a prison sentence would have been given for the crime that they had committed. Clearly, the use of such pleas detracts from the certainty of the sentence.

In addition, overcrowding may increase the time it takes for an offender to be placed in prison, with law enforcement jail facilities holding the offender during the interim. Further, offenders are able to avoid the assumption of responsibility for their crimes when they are simply given a sentence and allowed to serve their time without being accountable to the victim or society. Community corrections sentencing, on the other hand, has a number of additional conditions and programs that often require that the offender make restitution, provide services, or pay fines to victims or the community (examples of these conditions will be presented in later chapters). Thus, the flexibility of this type of sanctioning provides an element of certainty that offenders will be held accountable, and these types of sanctions can be administered quite quickly.

In addition, many behavioral psychologists note that if punishment is to be effective, certain considerations must be taken into account. These considerations, summarized by Davis and Palladino (2002), are presented below:

1. The punishment should be delivered immediately after the undesirable behavior occurs. *This is similar to the "swiftness" requirement of classical criminologists.*

2. The punishment should be strong enough to make a real difference to that particular organism. *This is similar to the "severity" requirement of classical criminologists, but this point also illustrates that "severity" may be perceived differently from one person to another.*

3. The punishment should be administered after each and every undesired response. *This is similar to the "certainty" requirement of classical criminologists.*

4. The punishment must be applied uniformly, with no chance of undermining or escaping the punishment. *When*

considering our justice system, it is clear that this consideration is undermined by the plea-bargaining process.

5. If excessive punishment occurs or if punishment is not proportional to the aberrant behavior committed, the likelihood of aggressive responding increases. *In a similar vein and as noted earlier, excessive prison sentences simply increase crime, including violent crime.*

6. To ensure that positive changes are permanent, provide an alternative behavior that can gain reinforcement for the person. *In other words, the use of reintegrative efforts to instill positive behaviors and activities must be supplemented to counteract those that are criminal in nature* (pp. 262–263).

Hopefully, from the presentation above, it can be seen that there is a great deal of similarity between classical criminologists and behavioral psychologists on the dynamics associated with the use of punishment. This is important because it demonstrates that both criminological and psychological theory can provide a clear basis for how correctional practices (particularly community corrections practices) should be implemented. In addition, #2 above demonstrates the need for severity, but it illustrates a point often overlooked: severity of a punishment is in the eye of the beholder. For instance, some offenders would prefer to simply "do flat time" in prison rather than complete the various requirements of community supervision. This is particularly true for offenders that have become habituated to prison life. In these cases, the goal should not be to acclimate offenders to prison life, but rather to acclimate them to community life as responsible and productive citizens. Community corrections encourages this outcome and utilizes a range of sanctions that can be calibrated to be more or less "severe" as is needed by the individual offender. In other words, community corrections utilizes techniques from behavioral psychology and classical criminology in a manner that individualizes punishment for the offender. It is this aspect that makes community corrections a superior punishment and reintegration tool over prison. It is also for this reason that prison should be utilized only for those offenders who are simply not receptive to change or the assumption of responsibility for their crimes.

SOURCES: Davis, S. F., & Palladino, J. J. (2002). *Psychology* (3rd ed.). Upper Saddle River, NJ: Prentice Hall; Smith, P., Goggin, C., & Gendreau, P. (2002). *The effects of prison sentences on recidivism: General effects and individual differences.* Saint John, New Brunswick, Canada: Centre for Criminal Justice Studies, University of New Brunswick.

It is not at all surprising that these forefathers of community corrections were impacted by the work of Cesare Beccaria. Beccaria's treatise was highly regarded and publicized throughout Europe and the United States and predated each of these persons' own innovations. In fact, classical criminology and Beccaria's own thoughts on crime and punishment served as the primary theoretical and philosophical basis to all forms of community corrections that existed during their time. Further, as will be seen, the works of Beccaria, the tenets of classical criminology, the contentions of each of the father figures in the early history of community corrections, and the use of indeterminate forms of sanctioning as leverage and motivation in obtaining offender compliance, as well as the later developments in behavioral and learning psychology, all complement one another and are likewise congruent in nature. This then provides the primary set of theoretical and philosophical perspectives on community corrections for this text, thereby establishing a consistent connection between the past and present practice of community corrections.

As with probation, the underlying basis for parole also includes the tenets of both classical criminology and behavioral psychology. However, this contention has been debated, depending upon the point in history one is examining. For instance, Champion (2002) suggests that "parole's eighteenth-century origins suggest no philosophical foundation" (p. 129). However, it would seem that Champion's point is actually erroneous. Indeed, the very use of any form of indeterminate sanction suggests a belief that an offender's behavior can be shaped or modified through the use of incentives (rewards for good conduct or industrious labor). Thus, this text will continue through the remaining chapters with the notion that the original and primary philosophical underpinnings of both probation and parole were centered on a rehabilitative orientation of offender processing.

Champion (2002) does clarify this statement by adding that penological pragmatism operated through the use of early release during the 1700s prior to the advent of Maconochie's contributions. In essence, early release might have been chosen during this time to eliminate prison overcrowding. However, prison overcrowding was not the same issue that it is today, particularly when one considers that prisons were not widely used at the time and that banishment and transportation were mainstay forms of punishment. In addition, it is very important to provide a historical distinction between the mere use of early release and true precursors of parole. As noted in the previous historical section on parole, it was not until the mid-1850s that a true likeness to parole even emerged. Prior attempts had been used in England and in other areas of Europe (primarily Spain, France, and Germany), but these are not considered true versions of parole as we know them today.

Champion (2002) goes on to add that from 1850 onward into the 1900s, the influence of social reformers, religious leaders, and humanitarians upon parole as a rehabilitative medium were quite apparent. In addition, Champion notes that the rehabilitative uses of parole after the 1970s have been questionable. Indeed, just as Champion contended in 1990, the pendulum has swung to a form of societal retribution. This is particularly true when considering the prison boom that was experienced in the late 1990s and early part of this millennium. This modification of parole as being primarily oriented toward retribution has impaired its effectiveness to rehabilitate offenders released under such forms of supervision. It is of course undesirable to place the public in jeopardy due to offenders being released into the community, but it is also undesirable for prison crowding to be the deciding factor in determining whether an offender is likely to recidivate or be productive in society. In no case should public safety be compromised; the only consideration that should be given is whether the offender is genuinely likely to reform. Mixing the two concerns (likelihood of reform with concerns over prison overcrowding) impairs the assessment process and places the community in harm's way.

Champion (2002) provides an interesting presentation of the functions of parole by suggesting that there are both manifest and latent functions. According to Champion, manifest functions are specifically intended and are apparent to all who view the parole process. On the other hand, latent functions, while being important, are not quite so apparent as a genuine function of parole. The two primary manifest functions of parole are (1) the reintegration of parolees into society, and (2) the desire to deter future criminality. The "three latent functions of parole are (1) to alleviate prison overcrowding, (2) to remedy sentencing disparities, and (3) to protect the public" (Champion, 2002, p. 129).

This is an interesting analysis of parole for several reasons. First, the reintegration of parolees into society is not only considered a manifest function; it is also the first function that Champion lists (1990). This then supports the argument that parole, at its core, should be considered first and foremost a reintegrative tool. A second point of interest is the fact that Champion lists prison overcrowding as a latent function when, in fact, many practitioners would note that parole tends to serve as a release valve for currently overcrowded prisons. Indeed, it might even appear that Champion himself has changed to this view of parole since in 2002 he notes that community corrections primarily serves as an alternative to incarceration (see earlier sections of this chapter). However, this aspect of community corrections (being an alternative to prison) is indeed secondary in nature, and should not be considered at all when determining the likelihood of offender relapse. Finally, it is probably best to consider the desire to protect the public as a manifest function, and this function is automatically fulfilled if the offender is successfully reintegrated into the community. Indeed, the second manifest function listed by Champion (1990) should not be necessary (the desire to deter future criminality) if the offender is truly reintegrated.

Thus, community corrections (probation and parole) was initially implemented to reform or reintegrate the offender. Further, if assessment of likely offender reformation is accurate, then public safety will be automatically enhanced. The job of the criminal justice system in general and that of the correctional section in particular is public safety. When further dividing the correctional section of the criminal justice system between institutional and community-based corrections, it is perhaps best explained that institutional corrections seeks public safety through incapacitation while community corrections does so through reintegration. Both are tasked with public safety as the primary function, yet each goes about achieving such protection in a different manner. Thus, as with all criminal justice functions, protection of the public is paramount, and the primary purpose of community corrections is the reintegration and rehabilitation of the offender to achieve this goal.

If probation and parole are the pre- and post-incarcerative sanctions most frequently associated with community corrections, and if the philosophical basis for each is primarily one of reintegration or rehabilitation, then one must ascertain the specific theoretical approaches that should be used when achieving this function. Abadinsky (2003), in describing rehabilitation as the primary function of probation and parole, notes that there are three basic theoretical models. These are (1) the social casework model, (2) the use of reality therapy, and (3) behavioral or learning theory. This text will, for the most part, incorporate Abadinsky's theoretical perspective on probation and parole for two reasons. First, the author of this current textbook has noted in previous publications that clinical/mental health perspectives used in the community are the best choice to use when reintegrating offenders (Hanser, 2007b). Second, the author has previously pointed toward the importance of assessment and evaluation in improving current community-based correctional programs (Hanser, 2007b). Abadinsky also emphasizes these points when providing his own theoretical perspective on probation and parole.

SUGGESTED THEORETICAL APPROACH TO REINTEGRATION AND OFFENDER TREATMENT

According to Abadinsky (2003), social casework provides concrete services to persons in need as a means of solving problems. The importance of social casework in probation and parole starts with theory and extends into the very skills and professional training that helping professionals must have to do their jobs. These skills include effective interviewing, fact-finding in the offender's background, and the ability to identify and distinguish surface from underlying problems. Such skills aid the clinician in getting a good baseline of the offender's challenges to effective reintegration. With this in mind, Abadinsky notes that there are three key components practiced in social casework, which are as follows:

1. Assessment: Gathering and analyzing relevant information upon which a treatment and a supervision plan should be based (p. 295)

2. Evaluation: The organization of facts into a meaningful, goal-oriented explanation (p. 295)

3. Intervention: Implementation of the treatment plan (p. 295)

Assessment is intended to provide the clinician and the community supervision officer with a clear understanding of the client's current level of functioning. The presentence investigation report (PSI)—which will be discussed later in this text—is perhaps a very effective and pragmatic assessment, being a compilation of numerous areas of functioning that must be considered for each offender. This is also a good example of how supervision and treatment plans may work hand-in-hand to augment one another (Hanser, 2007b). Assessment includes the gathering of information from documents and through interviews with the offender as well as other persons that are familiar with the offender (Abadinsky, 2003). The need for effective assessment will be discussed in greater detail later in this text, but for the time being, it is sufficient to state that assessment serves as the foundation to everything else that follows, in relation both to treatment and to public safety. Thus, assessment is the cornerstone to addressing the manifest factor related to offender reintegration and the latent factor of public safety.

Evaluation is the process whereby assessment data is incorporated into the planning process to assist in goal setting for the offender. Perlman (1957) suggests that this phase of social casework include

1. The nature of the problem and the goals sought by the client, in their relationship to

2. The nature of the person who bears the problem, his or her social and psychological situation and functioning, and who needs help with his or her problem, in relation to

3. The nature and purpose of the agency and the kind of help it can offer or make available (pp. 168–169).

The evaluation plan takes into account both the processes and the desired outcomes for effective offender reintegration. These components must be clearly defined at the outset, and both require consistent monitoring throughout the entire period of offender supervision. The most effective form of evaluation design will include a pretest (once the offender begins supervision) and a posttest (when the offender has successfully completed his or her sentence) to determine progress that can be attributed to either interventions that are employed or supervision regimens that are maintained.

Finally, intervention involves activities, assignments, and routines that are designed to bring about behavior change in a systematic manner, resulting in goal-directed behavior toward the desired community supervision outcome. The specific relationship between the community supervision officer and the offender is actually quite important. One might be surprised to find that many offenders do develop some degree of affinity for their supervision officer. Naturally, the community supervision officer has authority over the client and must ensure that the client continues to meet the requirements of his or her supervision. Regardless of any collaboration between the offender and the officer, it is the officer's task to keep a close watch over the offender and ensure that compliance is maintained.

One of the most practical theoretical approaches to offender reintegration and treatment is the use of reality therapy. *Reality therapy* is based on the notion that all persons have two specific psychological needs: (1) the need to belong, and (2) the need for self-worth and recognition. Therapists operating from a reality therapy theoretical perspective seek to engage the offender in various social groups and to motivate him or her in achievement-oriented activities. Each of these helps meet the two psychological needs that are at the heart of most all human beings. Further, most therapists maintain a warm and caring approach, but reality therapy rejects irresponsible behavior. Therapists are expected to confront irresponsible or maladaptive behavior and are even expected to set the tone for "right" or "wrong" behavior. This is an unorthodox approach when compared with other theoretical perspectives in counseling and psychotherapy, since it is often thought that therapy should be self-directed by the client. Reality therapy encourages, indeed it expects, the therapist to be directive.

In addition, reality therapy has been used in a number of correctional contexts, both institutional and community-based. The tenets of reality therapy are complementary to community supervision where direct interventions are often necessary and where a client may have to be told that he or she has committed a "wrong" behavior. Finally, William Glasser, founder of reality therapy, has expressed a great deal of support for correctional agencies in general and for community supervision officers in particular, but he cautions against the excessive use of punishments to correct offender behavior, especially among juvenile offenders (note that this is consistent with classical criminological concepts). This is because punishment can often serve as a justification or rationalization for further antisocial behavior, particularly if it is not proportional to the offense (especially with technical offenses), and the criminogenic peer group will likely reinforce these faulty justifications. On the other hand, when a given penalty is actually proportional and is consistent with the listed sanctions, such countereffects do not seem to occur.

Finally, one primary theoretical orientation used in nearly all treatment programs associated with community corrections is *operant conditioning*. This form of behavioral modification is based on the notion that certain environmental consequences occur that strengthen the likelihood of a given behavior and that other consequences tend to lessen the likelihood that a given behavior will be repeated. A primary category of behavior modification occurs through operant conditioning. Those consequences that strengthen a given behavior are called *reinforcers*. Reinforcers can be either positive or negative, with **positive reinforcers** being a reward for a desired behavior. An example might be if we provided a certificate of achievement for offenders that completed a life skills program. **Negative reinforcers** are unpleasant stimuli that are removed when a desired behavior occurs. An example might be if we agreed to remove the requirement of wearing electronic monitoring devices when offenders successfully maintained their scheduled meetings and appointments for one full year without any lapse in attendance.

Consequences that weaken a given behavior are known as punishments. Punishments, as odd as this may sound, can be either positive or negative. A **positive punishment** is one where a stimulus is applied to the offender when he or she commits an undesired behavior. For instance, we might require the offender to pay an additional late fee if the person is late in paying restitution to the victim of his or her crime. A **negative punishment** is the removal of a valued stimulus when the offender commits an undesired behavior. An example might be when we remove the offender's ability to leave his or her domicile for recreational or personal purposes (placed under house arrest) if the offender misses any scheduled appointments or meetings.

The key in distinguishing between reinforcers and punishments is that reinforcers are intended to *increase* the likelihood of a *desired* behavior whereas punishments are intended to *decrease* the likelihood of an *undesired* behavior. In operant conditioning, the term "positive" refers to the addition of a stimulus rather than the notion that something is good or beneficial. Likewise, the term "negative" refers to the removal of a stimulus rather denoting something bad or harmful.

Operant conditioning tends to work best if the reinforcer or the punishment is applied immediately after the behavior (again, similar to classical criminology). Reinforcers work best when they are intermittent in nature rather than continual, since the offender must exhibit a desired behavior with a reward given at unpredictable points, thereby instilling a sense of delayed gratification (rather than instant gratification). Punishments, on the other hand, have been found to work best when they are in close proximal time to the undesired behavior (swift) and sufficient enough to prevent repeating the behavior (severe), and when there is no means of escaping the punisher (certain). These findings have been determined through empirical research and are consistent with the notions of classical criminology that were previously discussed. Finally, behavioral psychologists have found that excessive punishments can (and often do) breed hostility among subjects—specific hostility toward the punisher in particular as well as hostility that is generalized within the environment. Thus, this supports Beccaria's point that punishments should not be excessive but should be proportional to the crime. To do more may unwittingly create a more hostile future offender. (For further information on these points, refer to the Applied Theory box.)

PROBATION AND PAROLE FROM 1960 ONWARD

During the period from 1930 through the 1950s, correctional thought reflected what was then referred to as the "medical model," which centered on the use of rehabilitation and treatment of offenders. In general, support for the medical model of corrections began to dissipate during the late 1960s and had all but disappeared by the 1970s. The medical model presumed that criminal behavior was caused by social, psychological, or biological deficiencies that were correctable through treatment interventions. The 1950s were particularly given to the ideology of the medical model, with influential states such as Illinois, New York, and California falling under the treatment banner.

Ultimately, this line of thought was followed by a brief period where community-oriented interventions and reintegration efforts were given the most attention. Clear and Cole (2003) note that this period of correctional thought, known as the community model of corrections, was in direct response to the failings of the medical model that preceded it. This was a time of great social unrest, with prison riots taking place, the civil rights movement in full swing, and the Vietnam War being fought by drafted U.S. soldiers.

The reintegration era lasted barely 10 years, until the late 1970s, and advocated for very limited use of incarceration (only a small proportion of offenders being incarcerated with short periods of incarceration being most commonly recommended). Probation was the preferred sentence, particularly for nonviolent offenders. Indeterminate sentences were utilized and deinstitutionalization was the theme for this period of corrections. However, this era was short-lived and received a great deal of criticism. Indeed, the prior medical model of corrections had hardly come to a full conclusion before the community model was also being seriously questioned by skeptics.

Prior to the end of the community model of corrections, acting as a sort of harbinger of things to come, the 1970 Supreme Court case of *United States v. Birnbaum* (1970) made it clear that probation was a privilege and not a right. Though this ruling may seem to address an issue that, on the face of it, should have been obvious, it did help to solidify the fact that community corrections in general, and probation in particular, are options of leniency. In other words, probation—and parole as well—were considered discretionary means of processing offenders. In all cases, the rights of probationers and parolees are, in actuality, no different from those of incarcerated persons. It is simply due to the leniency of the courts that the offender is allowed to serve his or her sentence within the community. (See Focus Topic 1.2 for further information on the development of probation. See also Cross National Perspective for a time line of its development in England.)

Historical Developments in Probation

1841	John Augustus becomes the "Father of Probation."	1943	Presentence investigation reports formally created by federal probation system.
1869	First official probation program is developed in Massachusetts (the home of probation).	1956	Mississippi becomes the 48th state to formally establish adult probation.
1901	New York creates the first statute officially establishing adult probation services.	1965	The birth of "shock probation" occurs in the state of Ohio.
1925	Federal probation is authorized by Congress.	1979	Various risk/needs assessments are developed by the state of Wisconsin.
1927	Forty-seven states implement juvenile probation (all but Wyoming).	1983	Intensive Supervised Probation has its birth in Georgia.

Shortly following the case of *United States v. Birnbaum* (1970), public concern increased along with rising crime rates. The mid- to late 1970s saw a slowly emerging shift take place due to high crime rates that were primarily perceived as being the result of high recidivism rates among offenders. This skepticism about rehabilitation was brought to its pinnacle by practitioners that cited (often in an inaccurate manner) the work of Robert Martinson. Martinson (1976) conducted a thorough analysis of research programs on behalf of the New York State Governor's Special Committee on Criminal Offenders. He examined a number of programs that included educational and vocational assistance, mental health treatment, medical treatment, early release, and so forth. In his report, often referred to as the **Martinson Report**, he noted that "with few and isolated exceptions, the rehabilitative efforts that have been reported so far have had no appreciable effect on recidivism" (p. 22).

From this point forward, there was a clear shift from a community model of corrections to a **crime control model of corrections.** During the late 1970s and throughout the 1980s, crime became a hotly debated topic that often got intertwined with political agendas and legislative action. The sour view of rehabilitation led many states to abolish the use of parole. Indeed, from 1976 onward, more than 14 states and the federal government abolished the use of parole. The state of Maine abolished parole in 1976, followed by California's elimination of discretionary parole in 1978, and the full elimination of parole in Arizona, Delaware, Illinois, Indiana, Kansas, Minnesota, Mississippi, New Mexico, North Carolina, Ohio, Oregon, Virginia, and Washington (Sieh, 2006). In addition, the federal system of parole was also phased out over time. Under the Comprehensive Crime Control Act of 1984, the United States Parole Commission only retained jurisdiction over offenders that had committed their offense prior to November 1, 1987. At the same time, the act provided for the abolition of the Parole Commission over the years that followed, with this phasing-out period being extended by the Parole Commission Phase-Out Act of 1996, which extended the life of the Parole Commission until November 1, 2002, but only in regard to supervising offenders who were still on parole from previous years. Thus, though the U.S. Parole Commission continued to exist, the use of parole was eliminated and federal parole offices across the nation were slowly shut down over time period (See Focus Topic 1.3 for further information on various developments in parole.)

Historical Developments in Parole

1840	Maconochie creates his "mark system" in an Australian penal colony.	1976	The state of Maine abolishes parole.
1854	Sir Walter Crofton establishes the ticket-of-leave system in Ireland.	1984	The federal government abolishes granting additional forms of parole leniency.
1869	New York establishes indeterminate sentencing processes.	1996	The state of Ohio becomes the 11th state to formally abolish parole.
1870	American Prison Association publicly endorses parole.		

In addition to the eventual elimination of parole, many states implemented determinate sentencing laws, truth-in-sentencing laws, and other such innovations that were designed to keep offenders behind bars for longer periods of time. The obvious flavor of corrections in the 1980s was that of crime control through incarceration and risk containment (Clear & Cole, 2003). This same crime control orientation continued through the 1990s and even through the beginning of the new millennium, with an emphasis on drug offenders and habitual offenders. Also noted were developments in intensive supervised probation (ISP), more stringent bail requirements, and the use of "three strikes" penalties. The last half of the 1990s and on through the year 2000 saw a decidedly punitive approach to crime control. The costs (both economic and social) have received a great deal of scrutiny even though crime rates decreased in the first years of the new millennium. Though there was a dip in crime during this time, it is unclear if this was due to the higher rate of imprisonment or other demographic factors that impacted the nation.

AN OVERVIEW AND STATE-BY-STATE COMPARISON OF COMMUNITY SUPERVISION MODELS

States around the nation have varied methods of managing the organizational structure of their probation and parole programs. The National Institute of Corrections (NIC) has conducted extensive research on the organization of community supervision programs in the United States. The NIC interviewed the head administrator of each state agency to determine the structure of each program, with primary emphasis being given to the implementation of probation. The organization of probation service delivery is quite important to understand before progressing into any in-depth study of community corrections, for two key reasons.

First, probation is the single most common form of sanction used in correctional systems throughout the nation. Nearly 60 percent of all offenders in the United States are on probation, meaning that this sanction is much more common than prison sentences or the use of parole. Indeed, a total of 4,162,536 persons were on probation in 2005 compared with a mere 784,408 persons who were on parole (Glaze & Bonczar, 2007). Second, as was mentioned earlier in this chapter, the use of parole has slowly been reduced or outright abolished in many states (as well as in the federal correctional system).

This second point is not meant to imply that the paroled population of offenders in the United States is decreasing; quite the opposite is true. However, this group of offenders is only slightly larger than the group of those serving jail time—747,529 inmates in state jails—and is just over half of those offenders in prison, with 1,446,269 inmates serving prison sentences in the United States (Glaze & Bonczar, 2007). Thus, parolees make up only about 11 percent of the entire correctional population and only about 16 percent of the entire population under community supervision. When considering the total population under community supervision, clearly the overwhelming majority (roughly 84 percent) are on probation rather than parole.

Data from the National Institute of Corrections shows that the most common organizational structure for probation consists of a state-level executive branch agency to oversee probation services throughout the entirety of the state (Krauth & Linke, 1999). Roughly 26 states provide probation services through executive branch agencies associated with the state-level (rather than county-level) department of corrections (Krauth & Linke, 1999). In contrast, three states (Iowa, New York, and Oregon) provide probation services through county agencies (rather than state agencies) in the executive branch. In eight states (Colorado, Connecticut, Hawaii, Kansas, Massachusetts, Nebraska, New Jersey, and South Dakota), probation services are administered through the state-level judicial branch. In five states, local agencies in the judicial branch administer probation services (including Arizona, Illinois, Indiana, Texas, and West Virginia). Last, probation services are delivered through multiple organizational models in Minnesota, Ohio, Pennsylvania, and California (see Table 1.1). In the first three of these states, there is a combination of state executive branch and local executive agencies that provides services. In California, probation services are always delivered by local agencies, but these agencies may be either executive or judicial in nature, depending on the particular area of the state.

TABLE 1.1 Branch and Level of State Government Delivering Adult Probation Services

	Executive Branch		Judicial Branch	
	State Level	Local Level	State Level	Local Level
Alabama	X			
Alaska	X			
Arizona				X
Arkansas	X			
California***		X		X
Colorado			X	
Connecticut			X	
Delaware	X			
Florida	X			
Georgia	X			
Hawaii			X	
Idaho	X			
Illinois				X
Indiana				X
Iowa		X		

	Executive Branch		Judicial Branch	
	State Level	Local Level	State Level	Local Level
Kansas			X	
Kentucky	X			
Louisiana	X			
Maine	X			
Maryland	X			
Massachusetts			X	
Michigan	X			
Minnesota***	X	X		X
Mississippi	X			
Missouri	X			
Montana	X			
Nebraska			X	
Nevada	X			
New Hampshire	X			
New Jersey			X	
New Mexico	X			
New York		X		
North Carolina	X			
North Dakota	X			
Ohio***	X			X
Oklahoma	X			
Oregon		X		
Pennsylvania***	X			X
Rhode Island	X			
South Dakota	X			
Tennessee	X			
Texas				X
Utah	X			
Vermont	X			
Virginia	X			
Washington	X			
West Virginia				X
Wisconsin	X			
Wyoming	X			

SOURCE: Krauth, B., & Linke, L. (1999). *State organizational structures for delivering adult probation services.* Washington, DC: National Institute of Corrections.

*** Indicates a state with multiple service delivery structures.

Equally important when examining the organization of community corrections from state to state is determining whether probation (a front-end sanction) and parole (a back-end sanction) are administered together by the same agency or separately. It has been found that states exhibit a great deal of variety in terms of probation service delivery and the delegation of other types of supervision caseloads, such as with paroled offenders or juvenile offenders. In the majority of states, the probation and parole functions are fully integrated with one another (see Table 1.2 for a detailed comparison). In these states, officers usually have combined caseloads of both probationers and parolees. Only nine states have jurisdictions that deliver services solely to adult probationers.

In addition, adult and juvenile probation service delivery has been integrated in several states. These states include California, Colorado, Illinois, Indiana, Kansas, Nebraska, New Jersey, New York, South Dakota, and West Virginia. Another six states (Arizona, Minnesota, Ohio, Oregon, Pennsylvania, and Texas) combine adult and juvenile probation in some jurisdictions but not in others. Thus, there is a great deal of variety in supervision organizational structure from state to state when addressing adult and juvenile probationer caseloads.

TABLE 1.2 Adult Probation Agency's Responsibility for Other Community Corrections Functions

	Adult Probation & Parole	Adult Probation Only	Adult & Juvenile Probation
Alabama	X		
Alaska	X		
Arizona	Parole is abolished	X	X
Arkansas	X		
California	X		X
Colorado		X	X
Connecticut		X	
Delaware	X But parole is abolished		
Florida	X		
Georgia		X	
Hawaii		X	
Idaho	X		
Illinois	Parole is abolished		X
Indiana	Parole is abolished		X
Iowa	X		
Kansas	Parole is abolished		X
Kentucky	X		
Louisiana	X		
Maine		X	
Maryland	X		
Massachusetts		X	
Michigan	X		

	Adult Probation & Parole	Adult Probation Only	Adult & Juvenile Probation
Minnesota	X But parole is abolished		X
Mississippi	X But parole is abolished		
Missouri	X		
Montana	X		
Nebraska			X
Nevada	X		
New Hampshire	X		
New Jersey			X
New Mexico	X But parole is abolished		
New York			X
North Carolina	X But parole is abolished		
North Dakota	X		
Ohio	X But parole is abolished		X
Oklahoma	X		
Oregon	X But parole is abolished		X
Pennsylvania	X		X
Rhode Island	X		
South Dakota	X		
Tennessee		X	
Texas		X	X
Utah	X		
Vermont	X		
Virginia	X		
Washington	X		
West Virginia			X
Wisconsin	X		
Wyoming	X		

SOURCE: Adapted from Krauth, B., & Linke, L. (1999). *State organizational structures for delivering adult probation services*. Washington, DC: National Institute of Corrections.

Finally, in a number of states (Delaware, Minnesota, Mississippi, New Mexico, North Carolina, and Ohio), there is a combination of probation and parole services but these states have abolished parole in years past. This combination of both types of community service sanction simply reflects the fact that there are residual offenders whose parole sanction has extended past the date of parole abolishment, and their supervision has been combined with probation agency caseloads, thereby eliminating the need for a specific parole agency in that state. In other states where parole has been abolished, there is no combination of probation and parole services because no residual supervision has been necessary, or it has been completely phased out through some sort of alternate means (see Table 1.3).

TABLE 1.3   State Parole Board Appointments, Structure, Terms, and Functions

	Governor Appointed	Leg. Confirm.	Term Years	Number on the Board	F-Full or P-Part Time	Use of Parole Analysis
Alabama	X		5	5	P	NO
Alaska	X	X	5	5	P	NO
Arizona	X	X	5	5	F	YES(6)(7)
Arkansas	X	X		5 F, 2 P	F	
California	X	X	7	6	F	YES
Colorado	X	X	6	7	F	NO
Connecticut	X	X	4	15, 3 full	F/P	YES(6)
Delaware	X	X	4	5, 1 full	F/P	NO
Florida	X	X	6	3	F	YES(6)(7)
Georgia	X	X	7	7	F	YES(6)
Hawaii	X	X	4	3, 1 full	F/P	NO
Idaho	X	X	3	5	P	YES
Illinois	X	X	6	15	F	YES(7)
Indiana	X		4	5	F	NO
Iowa	X	X	4	5, 2 full	F/P	YES(8)
Kansas	X	X	4	4	F	NO
Kentucky	X	X	4	8	F	NO
Louisiana	X	X	11	7	F	NO
Maine						
Maryland	X	X	6	8	F	YES(9)
Massachusetts	X		5	7	F	YES(9)
Michigan	Dir. of Corr.		4	10	F	YES(7)
Minnesota	Dir. of Corr.					
Missouri	X	X	6	7	F	YES(6)(7)(9)
Montana	X	X	4	5	P	YES(6)
Nebraska	X	X	6	5	F	NO
Nevada	X		4	13, 7 full	F/P	YES(9)

	Governor Appointed	Leg. Confirm.	Term Years	Number on the Board	F-Full or P-Part Time	Use of Parole Analysis
New Hampshire	X		5	7	P	NO
New Jersey	X	X	6	15	F	YES(9)
New Mexico	X	X	6	9	P	NO
New York	X	X	6	19	F	
North Carolina	X		4	3	F	YES(6)(7)
North Dakota	X	X		6	P	
Ohio	Dir. of Corr.		life	9	F	YES(7)(9)
Oklahoma	1		4	5	P	YES(6)
Oregon	X	X	4	3	F	YES(6)(7)
Pennsylvania	X	X	6	9	F	YES
Rhode Island	X	X	3(12)	7, 1 full	P	
South Dakota	2	X	4	6	P	NO
Tennessee	X		6	7	F	YES(9)
Texas	X	X	6	18	F	YES(8)
Utah	X	X	5	5	F	YES(6)
Vermont	X	X	3	5	P	NO
Virginia	X	X	11	3	F	YES(9)
Washington	X	X	5	3	F	YES(6)
West Virginia	X	X	6	5	F	
Wisconsin	X	X	2(10)	7	F	NO
Wyoming	X	X	6	7	P	
US Parole Commission	President	X	6	5	F	YES(9)

SOURCE: Adapted from the *Parole Board Survey* produced by the Association of Paroling Authorities International. (2001). Retrieved from http://www.apaintl.org/en/aw_surveys.html.

1. Appointed by the Governor, one by Supreme Court, one by Court of Appeals

2. Two by the Governor, two by the Attorney General, and two by Supreme Court

3. Three years for the Chair and 2 for the members

4. Eight years for the Chair and 4 to 6 for the members

5. Full-time 5 years and part-time 3 years

6. Case reports writing and interviews

7. Hold probable cause hearings

8. Hold revocation hearings

9. Hold parole consideration hearings

10. The chair, 2 years; or others merit

11. At the pleasure of the governor

12. Chair is double appointment, 3 years as member and 2 years as chair

With respect to the administration and organization of parole boards, it is clear that there is a great deal of variation in their structure and implementation. Table 1.3 shows that state parole board systems select members through a variety of means (most typically including selection by the state's governor). The term of service for parole board members, the number of persons serving on parole boards, and the use of either part-time or full-time members greatly varies from state to state. The types of activities that each board may perform and the sources of information that each board may use also vary greatly. This demonstrates that there is a great deal of disparity throughout the United States among the top organizationally ranked decision-making bodies that decide on issues related to parole.

When we consider the variation in state implementation of the day-to-day supervision of parolees (i.e., as a separate function or when being combined with probation caseloads) and the variation that exists among parole boards themselves, it is clear that the entire organizational structure can be quite complicated. While this may appear to be the case, there is a great deal of similarity in the types of laws, forms of supervision, and regulations that are required throughout the nation. While each state naturally has the right and ability to administer community supervision functions in a manner that it finds most suitable, it will become clear that there are as many similarities between probation and parole programs around the nation as there are differences. As you progress through the remaining chapters, common trends and tendencies will become more apparent.

CONCLUSION

Community corrections has gone through a long and complicated process of development. Throughout this process, the specific purpose of community corrections has not always been clear. Indeed, many recognized experts, authors, and researchers offer competing views on the purpose of community corrections, resulting in much confusion and uncertainty related to the effectiveness of community-based sanctions. The importance of a clear definition as well as a clear rationale for the use of community corrections sanctions has been illustrated. Further, this chapter has traced the historical developments and philosophical precursors to both probation and parole. These developments help to make sense of the various challenges associated with community corrections sanctions and also provide guidance for their future use. Last, there is tremendous variety from state to state in regard to the community supervision process. The implementation of probation and parole comes in many shapes, forms, and methods, creating a rich yet challenging process of offender supervision in communities throughout the United States.

Key Terms

Augustus, John	General deterrence	Positive punishment
Benefit of clergy	Incapacitation	Positive reinforcers
Community corrections	Indeterminate sentencing	Recognizance
Crime control model of corrections	Mark system	Rehabilitation
Determinate sentencing	Martinson Report	Retribution
Deterrence	Negative punishment	Sanctuary
English Penal Servitude Act	Negative reinforcers	Specific deterrence
		Ticket-of-leave

"What Would You Do?" Exercise

You are the Chief Probation Officer of a large community supervision agency. You have several community supervision officers who work under you and it is a high-pressure job. You deal with several criminal and civil court judges at your courthouse and you are generally well liked and respected, by both the community supervision staff and the Chief Judge of your court. In the course of your duties, you have been asked to meet state legislators, various city officials, and a number of other important persons in state and local political arenas. Typically, the Chief Judge asks that you accompany her so that you can provide specific details on the community supervision process.

One reason for your attendance at a number of functions is the fact that the state is considering the allocation of substantial resources to offender reintegration projects. However, there are opponents of this development at the state level. Your Chief Judge is an advocate of treatment and reintegration, but she has spent most of her time lawyering and serving in her judgeship. As a result, she is actually not very conversant on historical or theoretical bases for community corrections. As it turns out, you have some knowledge of these dimensions of the community corrections field. (After all, you just read this chapter!)

The state officials are having a meeting and wish to formulate an underlying referendum that explains what reintegration is, why it is important, and how it ties into the historical context of corrections. Further, they want to develop some type of philosophical basis for the program before it is implemented. They want to have the underlying mechanisms in place before proceeding forward in considering funding opportunities. Your Chief Judge is well thought of among state-level bureaucrats, and she has specifically been invited to take part in this workgroup. She has asked you to come to this all-day work meeting and to formulate and bring with you a brief draft. Specifically, she wants you to address the following three points:

1. How reintegration ties into the historical context of corrections

2. The development of a philosophical basis for a reintegration program

3. The means by which offenders would be reintegrated, on a broad level. (Specifically, she would like you to discuss some of the mechanisms by which offenders might be motivated to succeed in a reintegration program.)

Naturally, you are honored to be asked to assist. You have indicated that you would generate the draft.

What would you do?

Applied Exercise

Match the following modern-day programs with their appropriate past ideologies or philosophy of origin.

Program	Ideology or Philosophy of Origin
1. A judge temporarily releases a defendant by stating, "You are released on your own recognizance."	A. Mark system
2. Laws that select specific types of offenders and provide enhanced penalties to ensure that they are effectively removed from society (i.e., habitual offender laws, three-strikes laws, etc.)	B. Ticket-of-leave
3. The use of "good time" for inmates in state prison systems allowing early release for good behavior	C. Negative punishment

(Continued)

(Continued)

Program	Ideology or Philosophy of Origin
4. Moving offenders through phases of supervision until they finally earn full release	D. Negative reinforcement
5. Removal of visitation privileges because an offender commits the undesired criminal behavior of child abuse	E. Indeterminate sentencing
6. Exacting a fine for undesired behavior	F. Commonwealth v. Chase
7. Removing the need for face-to-face office visits and extensive "check-ins" with the probation officer due to perfect compliance while on probation	G. Determinate sentencing
8. Providing substance abusers with certificates of graduation when completing an addiction treatment program	H. Positive reinforcement
9. Sentencing is grounded in notions of retribution, just deserts, and incapacitation with no flexibility in terms.	I. Positive punishment
10. Sentencing with variable terms, affected by the context of the crime and later offender behavior while serving the sentence	J. Incapacitation

Chapter 1 Applied Exercise Answer Key:

1. F	3. B	5. C	7. D	9. G
2. J	4. A	6. I	8. H	10. E

CHAPTER 2

Community Corrections

Public Safety Is Job One

LEARNING OBJECTIVES

1. Identify the four main purposes of punishment and explain how each serves as a guide in agency policy and practice.

2. Identify and apply key criminological and psychological theoretical perspectives to the community supervision process.

3. Know and explain how theory aids in meeting public safety objectives.

4. Understand and explain the complexities involved when setting offender caseloads for community supervision personnel, and explain the impact that this has on public safety.

5. Understand and explain how the use of volunteers can improve both public safety and reintegration efforts associated with community corrections programs.

INTRODUCTION

As was noted in Chapter 1, the definition of community corrections is one that is open to some degree of interpretation. Indeed, this definition varies from expert to expert but generally centers on the functions of relieving prison overcrowding or reintegrating the offender into society. However, this overlooks one key issue that must be considered: public safety. As this current chapter's title suggests, public safety is the number one job of community corrections. Without any assurance of public safety, community corrections agencies cannot possibly expect the community to support or provide assistance to any program that places offenders in the community. However, as was demonstrated in the previous chapter, enhanced public safety is actually a natural by-product of effective reintegration programs.

This point ties in well with the previous chapter for several reasons. First, if we overlook public safety, we presume that the use of prisons constitutes goals and objectives other than the protection of the public. Indeed, from a punishment perspective, the true reason that we incarcerate offenders is to provide graduated and proportional punishments that are measured by the total time of lost liberty that is inflicted. However, this presumes that incapacitation is not the primary objective of correctional incarceration. Thus, there is an inherent contradiction in correctional goals. On the one hand, prisons are thought to be primarily punishment oriented, while on the other hand, prisons are thought to be warehouses that prevent offenders from committing further acts of victimization. It would seem that many experts do not necessarily consider public safety as the primary purpose of corrections. In fact, as we have seen from the previous chapter, Champion (2002) goes so far as to state that public protection is a latent rather than a manifest goal of community corrections.

This text takes the opposite approach and instead notes that both public safety and offender reintegration should be considered manifest goals that are used in a synonymous fashion. The criminal justice system as a whole is given many tasks, but without doubt the public has an expectation that this system will seek to protect those it serves. Indeed, many law enforcement agencies use this very motto, "to protect and serve," as their creed in describing their social function. This most certainly is an explicit message of the self-proclaimed objective of such agencies.

However, clearly law enforcement, no matter how effectively it is administered, cannot prevent crime with 100 percent certainty, and community corrections personnel cannot guarantee that citizens will not be victimized by recidivists who are released into the community. Thus, a degree of risk is inherent to community supervision, and this requires that the public citizenry, as well as the criminal justice system, accept some accountability for the overall sense of public safety within a given community. This is not an unusual proposition. Consider that in old England, the term "hue and cry" was used to describe a process whereby community citizens were required to provide support for one another when it was clear that criminal victimization was occurring. Quinion (2007) offers a very clear and accurate description of how the ordinary citizenry were largely responsible for enforcing law and order:

> Our modern meaning goes back to part of English common law in the centuries after the Norman Conquest. There wasn't an organised police force and the job of fighting crime fell mostly on ordinary people. If somebody robbed you, or you saw a murder or other crime of violence, it was up to you to raise the alarm, the *hue and cry*. Everybody in the neighbourhood was then obliged to drop what they were doing and help pursue and capture the supposed criminal. If the criminal was caught with stolen goods on him, he was summarily convicted (he wasn't allowed to say anything in his defence, for example), while if he resisted arrest he could be killed. The same term was used for a proclamation relating to the capture of a criminal or the finding of stolen goods. The laws relating to hue and cry were repealed in Britain in 1827. (p. 1)

In the early days of official police formation in England, it was quite common for those with enforcement authority to enlist the aid of citizens, forming posses that would help bring offenders to justice. Slowly, over time, there was a sharing of duties between citizens and official authority, with an official organized police force eventually becoming a norm in England and the world as a whole. As the evolution of policing continued, police absorbed the responsibility for social order and thus assumed responsibility for civilian protection. The fact that hue and cry laws were repealed in Britain in the early 1800s demonstrates this shift in police-civilian functions. Thus, we have today the objective "to serve and protect" as part and parcel of the policing function.

Since community supervision officers provide an enforcement function—after all, their title includes the word "supervision"—this also means that such personnel must share a similar objective of protecting the public. However, unlike police, community supervision personnel are also required to at least remain receptive to the goals and objectives associated with the client's integration into the community. This naturally creates a bit of a paradox for the community supervision officer since the two perspectives (public safety and offender integration) often compete with each other.

Photo 2.1　North Delta Regional Training Academy (NDTRA) provides pre-service training for police and community supervision officers who are required to receive Peace Officer Standards and Training (POST). As will be discussed later, controversy abounds over whether community supervision officers should carry firearms. In states where they do carry such weapons, community supervision officers or juvenile probation workers may train alongside police cadets. In the Northeast Louisiana region, this is indeed the case and NDTRA provides this training. The author provides instruction at NDTRA on some occasions, training both police and community corrections personnel.

Because of the fact that police cannot be in all places at all times to ensure that crimes are prevented (indeed, much of policing is reactionary rather than preventative) and because community supervision officers have competing objectives, this text notes that public safety should be viewed as a shared responsibility between the criminal justice system and the community membership. However, the public will only place their faith in a system that convincingly demonstrates that it is genuinely interested in their own safety rather than the mere processing of offenders.

A publication by Mactavish and Winter (1991) illustrates the importance for community supervision managers to consider both community interests and offender requirements at the initial phase of annual development. Indeed, these authors point toward the fact that other agencies, civic groups, and volunteer sources may all be stakeholders in the community supervision process. This is shown in Figure 2.1.

The process of offender supervision is, quite obviously, carried out by the community supervision officer. However, on a communitywide level, the individual officer can only be responsible for his or her caseload and (perhaps) a few other auxiliary duties. If public safety is truly to be secured, this will require the involvement of many more stakeholders (persons having a shared interest in the safety of their community) than the probation or parole officer alone. The community, victims, local law enforcement, state institutions, social service agencies, and so forth, all must come together to ensure community safety. At the heart of the process is the community corrections agency and the community supervision officer. If the agency is provided with this interagency and communitywide support, the offender is then observed by and placed into human contact with numerous supervisory elements. This increases the extent to which the offender is under observation and also empowers the community to take an interest in this process.

This is actually similar to the point and purpose of community policing, where programs such as Neighborhood Watch, National Night Out, and other forms of police-citizen integration create a rapport between the community and the police agency while also extending the surveillance function of law enforcement. When other agencies and private citizens take an active interest in crime prevention efforts, there are fewer points of vulnerability in the community where offenders can commit crimes and evade detection. This same point extends to community supervision officers; thus, just as community policing has left its mark on modern-day police forces, the use of "community probation" should also be integrated into the process.

This suggestion takes us back in history to the days of the hue and cry, reaching back to the community for assistance in ensuring public safety beyond that secured by the individual probation or parole officer. This also suggests that both police and community supervision officers can and should make a concerted effort at working together in the supervision process. In fact, there are numerous examples nationwide where both types of agencies do just that (Hanser, 2007b).

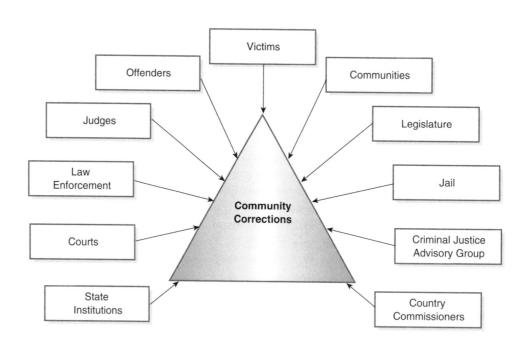

FIGURE 2.1 Community Corrections Stakeholders

SOURCE: Mactavish, M., & Winter, V. (1991). *The practical planning guide for community corrections managers.* Washington, DC: National Institute of Corrections.

However, just as was noted in Chapter 1, the definition of a given concept can greatly impact everything else that follows. Thus, when integrating various agencies or community members into the process, it is important to clearly and effectively determine the specific goals and objectives of the community supervision agency. Naturally, one would also want to ensure that these goals and objectives are disseminated to both agency and community members so that internal and external personnel are aware of the general intent, point, and purpose of decisions that are made by the agency. Roughly 20 years ago, Van Keulen (1988) clearly made this point in her "Statement of Program Goals and Objectives" for the Colorado Alternative Sentencing Programs by saying that

> the importance of developing and distributing a statement of clear and consistent program goals and objectives is often misunderstood by community service programs. Like reports that gather dust on bookshelves in every office, goals and objectives are often seen as "nice, but useless" extra work that has little to do with the business of running a community service program.
>
> Nothing could be further [from] the truth! Goals and objectives are a way of stating a program's philosophy or orientation. Developed in cooperation with the courts and the community served by the program, goals and objectives serve several practical purposes. Goals and objectives insure that everyone involved in the community service process is in general agreement about the purpose of the program. When issues arise that need to be resolved, the goals and objectives can then serve as a focal point of discussion. For example, if program goals and objectives are clearly punitive or restitutional, yet judges frequently vacate community service orders after reports of noncompliance, the program can reiterate the goals and objectives and request the court's cooperation in enforcing the orders. If there are consistent problems in meeting program objectives, the goals and objectives may need to be reexamined and possibly modified.
>
> Clear goals and objectives are also critical to the development of program policies and procedures. For example, if a program goal is incapacitation (perhaps as an alternative to jail), the program would be designed to monitor the physical whereabouts of participating offenders very closely to insure that the offenders are involved in court-approved activities such as paid employment, community service, or treatment.
>
> Goals and objectives also play a critical role in evaluation by providing a standard against which to measure the program's success. If the purpose of the program is to serve as an alternative to jail, the number of jail-bound offenders the program serves would be analyzed. If the program's focus is to provide labor to community agencies, the number of hours worked by offenders would be examined.
>
> Last, having a statement of goals and objectives will enhance your program's credibility by showing that careful thought has been given to what you are doing. (p. 1)

Continuing from our discussion in Chapter 1, Van Keulen (1988) demonstrates the reasons why clarity in definition, point, and purpose of a community corrections program is important. As Van Keulen notes, clearly articulated goals help to crystallize the agency's philosophical orientation regarding the supervision process. Underlying philosophical tenets of the purpose of punishments were at the heart of many historical changes that led to the emergence of probation and parole. Having a philosophical grounding that is clearly articulated translates to concrete guidance as to the specific actions that should be taken when an agency seeks to maintain consistency with the stated goals. Thus, the philosophical basis, as articulated by the agency's goal-setting process, determines everything that follows afterward from the agency, with all activities ideally being directed toward the fulfillment of agency goals and objectives (see Focus Topic 2.1 for detailed definitions of policies, activities, goals, and objectives). In addition, this clarity allows the agency to measure its effectiveness and to perform evaluative research to determine if its efforts are actually successful or if they are in need of improvement. This particular aspect will be covered in this text's final chapter, and it will then become clear that the process of community corrections comes "full circle" as the planning, implementation, evaluation, and refinement phases of agency operation are realized.

FOCUS TOPIC 2.1

WHAT ARE POLICIES, ACTIVITIES, GOALS, AND OBJECTIVES?

Policy: A governing principle pertaining to goals, objectives, or activities. It is a decision on an issue not resolved on the basis of facts and logic only. For example, the policy of expediting drug cases in the courts might be adopted as a basis for reducing the average number of days from arraignment to disposition.

Activities: Services or functions carried out by a program (i.e., what the program does). For example, treatment programs may screen clients at intake, complete placement assessments, provide counseling to clients, etc.

Goal: A desired state of affairs that outlines the ultimate purpose of a program. This is the end toward which program efforts are directed. For example, the goal of many criminal justice programs is a reduction in criminal activity.

Objectives: Specific results or effects of a program's activities that must be achieved in pursuing the program's ultimate goals. For example, a treatment program may expect to change offender attitudes (objective) in order to ultimately reduce recidivism (goal).

SOURCE: Bureau of Justice Assistance, Center for Program Evaluation. (2007). *Reporting and using evaluation results.* Washington, DC: Author. Retrieved from http://www.ojp.usdoj.gov/BJA/evaluation/sitemap.htm.

Van Keulen (1988) notes that community supervision agencies should consult with other local criminal justice agencies as well as social service agencies and personnel to develop a written statement that details the program's philosophy relative to the goals of sentencing. The guidelines that are developed should provide policies that are mutually shared, and these policy statements should be reviewed periodically so that timely modifications or refinements can be made when and if necessary. However, in her statement, Van Keulen also points toward the importance of theory when determining the goals of sentencing and, by extension, those of community corrections supervision. According to Van Keulen, current criminal justice theory holds that the goals of sentencing are the following:

1. Incapacitation (physical restriction to prevent further opportunities for lawbreaking)

2. Rehabilitation (changing the offender's behavior or circumstances to reduce the possibility of further lawbreaking)

3. Deterrence (discouraging the general public from lawbreaking by example)

4. Retribution (punishment of the offender to discourage further lawbreaking)

5. Restitution (compensation to the victim and/or community)

These same goals were explicitly pointed out in the last chapter, sans the philosophical basis of restitution. It is in this manner that Van Keulen (1988) provides a fitting modern-day example of how philosophical and theoretical underpinnings of community corrections programs are just as important today as they were in earlier times in history, when community corrections concepts were first being formed. Thus, Van Keulen provides an effective segue from Chapter 1 into our discussion that follows in which criminological and psychological-theoretical applications to community corrections are considered.

KEY CRIMINOLOGICAL AND PSYCHOLOGICAL-THEORETICAL PERSPECTIVES

It should be obvious at this point that an effective community correctional program will have a clear theoretical and philosophical grounding. However, theoretical applications may not always be clear in the day-to-day practice of community supervision. In addition, it is often easy to see how psychological theories or variables may come into play with offender behavior when seen from the vantage point of a therapist dealing with offender clients. However, the various sociological approaches may not always be so clear to the therapist. For the community supervision officer making offender home visits, the macro-level variables and theories dealing with neighborhood surroundings and other such considerations are very easy to see.

The specific applications of these perspectives to probation and parole may not be clear to most students. However, the philosophical underpinnings of punishment are important to understand since this will often shape official reactions to criminal offending. It is the point of this subsection to demonstrate the value of sociologically based theories when considering community corrections, and to further demonstrate how these theoretical underpinnings might intersect with underlying philosophical ideologies regarding punishment. This will then form the basis of future chapters that deal with the specific details of probation and parole.

One primary criminological theory to be introduced is **routine activities theory**. This theory is based on three simplistic notions. First, this theory holds that in order for a crime to occur, a motivated offender must be within the vicinity of a suitable target. Second, the likelihood of such an occurrence is directly impacted by the routine activities that both victims and offenders engage in. Third, the area of occurrence must be absent of capable guardians that might thwart criminal behavior (for example, police on patrol, physical lighting, or the presence of closed-circuit television [CCTV] cameras). With this in mind, some areas are more prone to criminal activity than others. Aside from the typical red light district or seedy parts of town, this might include various public festivities or shopping centers during holiday seasons in the year. The point here is that the areas where crime is more likely to occur may or may not be easy to identify.

Routine activities theory is actually quite applicable to both law enforcement and community supervision personnel. First, this theory accentuates the point that law enforcement must focus its attention on certain areas as "hot spots" for crime, for both crime prevention and response. Likewise, community supervision agencies are wise to restrict these areas from the general routine of offenders that are on probation or parole. In fact, community supervision agencies do this with great frequency. Some examples might be the restriction of offenders from having alcohol or being in establishments that primarily serve alcohol, restriction from school zones (particularly with child molesters), restrictions from certain areas of town known to be frequented by gang members (especially when the offender is a prior gang member), and so forth. In addition, electronic monitoring is used to track the movement and activity of these offenders, thereby thwarting the potential for encountering suitable victims when the offenders are unguarded.

Though it is of course the desire for most programs to reintegrate offenders in such a manner that they do not inherently wish to engage in illegal activity, these added mechanisms associated with the routine activities of the offender help to ensure public safety, meet the requirements for any incapacitation goals of the program, and also serve as "training wheels" that provide parameters of offender movement, optimizing the likelihood of treatment success by eliminating many factors that might otherwise jeopardize intervention programs.

Social learning theory and differential association theory are presented together because they have a common history, and many of their basic precepts are similar (Ronald Aker's social learning theory was spawned from Edwin Sutherland's differential association theory). As with differential association theory, social learning theory contends that offenders learn to engage in crime through exposure to crime as well as the adoption of definitions that are favorable to criminal activity (Lilly, Cullen, & Ball, 2007). While both theories contend that exposure to normative definitions that are favorable to crime commission can influence others to commit crime (through vicarious learning or reinforcement for repeating similar acts), social learning explicitly articulates the manner by which such definitions are learned by criminals. Differential association, on the other hand, does not clarify this point, and this is the primary distinction between the two theories.

Social learning theory essentially utilizes learning theory from the field of psychology to explain the process whereby offenders learn to commit crimes. This theory holds that crime tends to be learned through imitation and differential reinforcement. Differential reinforcement is nothing less than operant conditioning (as was presented in Chapter 1 of this text), based on the idea that an offender's behavior is shaped or conditioned by the rewards and punishments that he or she receives throughout the life span. Social learning likewise notes that offenders may learn criminal behaviors through vicarious reinforcement, being that individuals are thought to have the cognitive capacity to imagine themselves in the role of others. Potential criminals come to identify with the offender's circumstances and incorporate it into their own conceptions of themselves (Cullen & Agnew, 2003).

As was observed in the preceding chapter, components of social learning theory (i.e., the use of rewards and punishments) dovetail with other elements of community supervision or offender treatment regimens. The connection is quite obvious and basic, punishments being structured around the loss of liberty (i.e., jail time) and rewards being centered on the successful completion of expected activities (e.g., a certificate of completion for finishing a vocational training program). However, social learning and differential association also address the various nuances and influences that are reinforced by group reactions. One such example is that of gang offenders. Gang exit programs seek to remove the offender from the group pressure and influences of gang life because such groups provide constant definitions that favor the commission of crime. In most probation and parole supervision agreements, there are specified restrictions that prohibit the offender from having associations with key persons that are known to be criminogenic. Likewise, many probationers and parolees are cautioned from having associations with other persons under community supervision, unless such is specifically required by the court. These elements are practical responses to etiological elements noted in social learning and differential association theories. In addition to restrictions, many programs may require offenders to spend time completing community service as well as spend a specified amount of time with prosocial organizations (i.e., community, civic, and religious activities; educational programs; and so forth).

Subcultural theory is, to some measure, an extension of social learning theory when explaining the onset of criminal behavior. However, the key to subcultural theory lies in the idea that many individuals tend to simultaneously learn to commit crime in one location, and this results in crime rates becoming disproportionately high in such areas where criminal behavior is learned as a valued norm. This is a particularly relevant theory when considering the supervision or treatment of gang offenders (Valdez, 2005). According to Short and Nye (1958), subcultures are "patterns of values, norms, and behavior which have become traditional among certain groups," and they are "important frames of reference through which individuals and groups see the world and interpret it" (p. 296). This is a succinct and clear definition of subcultural theory and explains why subcultures are so integral to the production of crime.

Though this may seem simple and straightforward, the effects of subcultural influences are actually much more serious than might be initially thought. For instance, Valdez (2005) notes that in some areas of Chicago and Los Angeles, there are neighborhoods that are populated with intergenerational gang members. In other words, it is quite possible that multiple generations within the same family are members (or prior members) of a given gang. Gang membership in these neighborhoods is taught from one generation to the next, sometimes with the father in and out of prison, and sometimes even with the grandfather, father, and juvenile son all being members. This can also include wives and mothers who are either affiliated with the gang or in a corollary sister gang. Obviously, many of these offenders are in and out of jail or prison and therefore many find themselves under community supervision.

In such cases, it may be necessary to separate youth from these family systems or even the entire community, if they are to ever leave a life of crime and gang membership. Short and Nye (1958) point out that the subcultural gang discourages expression of conventional values and instead clings to "values which are given active support within the context of gang interaction, for example toughness and sexual prowess, [and which] are not conducive to conventional types of achievement" (p. 300). Similarly, Walter Miller (1958) proposes that such criminogenic behavior in subcultures is focused on a key concern with *trouble,* which for male offenders typically involves physical altercations or sexual conquests while also under the influence of drugs or alcohol; for female offenders, concern with trouble tends to revolve around risky sexual and drug-using behavior, with these women being as much victims as offenders (Hanser, 2007b).

Miller (1958) notes that in most cases, any desire to avoid troublesome behavior is based more on a concern for the legal consequences (often viewed more as a hassle than as a stigmatizing event) or other inconveniences than on concerns over the morality or healthiness of one's behavior. Such thinking would make the threat of a probation/parole violation hold some deterrent value. However, this is complicated by the fact that in many cases, a visit to the jail or serving a stint of time in a jail or prison facility can bring about a sense of general prestige among those associated with the subculture. In areas where inter-generational gang activity occurs, this may even be considered a rite of passage for many youth or young adults in the neighborhood. This is actually part and parcel of another aspect of Miller's analysis of the lower-class criminal subculture, a preoccupation with *toughness,* where members of this subculture demonstrate a lack of fear, a willingness to engage in aggressive or risky behaviors, and a sense of bravado that defies authority. In such cases, the community supervision officer will find clients resentful of controls, yet these same persons will tend to act in such a manner as to ensure that they are sanctioned shortly after they have been released. This becomes a display of their resistance to being controlled, adding credence to the concern with trouble, yet also demonstrating their toughness in coping with and overcoming authority's attempts to keep them within imposed parameters of behavior.

Yet another theory, **social disorganization theory,** also examines issues associated with norms in the community, but takes a slightly different perspective from that of subcultural theory. Social disorganization theory holds that "disorganized communities cause crime because informal social controls break down and criminogenic cultures emerge" (Cullen & Agnew, 2003, p. 6). Such neighborhoods lack the ability to provide the community support and cohesion necessary to fight the criminal elements that have taken over the neighborhood. One key distinction between this theory and subcultural theory is the idea that elements of the community or neighborhood are, in fact, law-abiding and wish to be rid of the criminal actors in their location. These individuals do not favor definitions that are supportive of criminal behavior, but they are unable or perhaps too intimidated to take any action to prevent such activity.

Photo 2.2 As a means of maintaining public safety, probation and parole officers may have to confiscate various types of contraband. Standing here is an officer who has confiscated both weapons and some elaborate drug paraphernalia while out in the field.

Social disorganization theory is important to understand for two reasons. First, these neighborhoods are probably not ideal areas for offenders to return to. However, offenders under community supervision often do return to these types of neighborhoods because their family or friends may be located in such an area. If they are to have any familial support and connection, they must rejoin these locations. If the family or social connections are, in fact, law-abiding and conducive to the offender's supervision and reintegration, then community supervision agents are usually hard-pressed to prevent such connections merely because other unsavory persons not connected to the family happen to coexist in the area. This is further complicated by the fact that the offender may have no other options and may seem to genuinely desire reform. Second, this theory demonstrates how preventative efforts and neighborhood improvement programs can aid in reducing initial criminal offending, the development of enmeshed subcultures in the area, and recidivism among returning offenders. More will be discussed on this particular aspect of theoretical application in the next section, but *at this point it should be understood that neighborhood variables greatly impact the outcome of community supervision programs.*

Given this fact, it becomes important for the community supervision officer to consider such motivations behind what are otherwise maladaptive behaviors (though in the offender's subculture, such behaviors are reinforced and have a sense of utility). Community supervision officers must then learn to walk a delicate tightrope in the use of punitive sanctions since there are pros and cons for both society and the offender when sanctions are either too light or too heavy-handed. Similar awareness among clinical treatment staff working with the offender should also be encouraged since this can help treatment staff to address ulterior motives and self-defeating behaviors that appear at first glance to be illogical, yet provide substantive reinforcement and emotional incentives.

The next theory to be examined is **strain theory/institutional anomie.** This theory denotes that when individuals cannot obtain success goals (such as money, status, and so forth), they will tend to experience a sense of pressure often called *strain.* Under certain conditions, they are likely to respond to this strain by engaging in criminal behavior. Merton (1938) and Messner and Rosenfeld (2001) note that this is often aggravated in American society by the continued emphasis on material (monetary) success and the corresponding lack of emphasis on the means by which such material accumulation is obtained. In other words, these authors contend that society in the United States emphasizes winning the game (of life) much more than how the game (of life) is played.

Abadinsky (2003) notes that the theory of anomie offers the community supervision officer numerous potential options to consider in the reintegration of offenders. First, the issue of aspirations may prove to be an area in need of attention. Offenders often have unrealistic goals and they are often not well-versed on goal-setting techniques. The ability to set realistic goals that can be accomplished, one step at a time, requires planning skills, a willingness to delay gratification, and the ability to stay committed to agreed-upon tasks. These are life skills that may not be possible (or practical) for the probation officer to teach. However, offenders can be enrolled in life skills training, workshops or seminars on effective decision making or planning, and so on.

In many cases, the aspirations of offenders exceed the ability level at which they can perform. Abadinsky (2003) notes that "in such cases, if anomie is to be avoided, the probation/parole officer must help the client to make a realistic assessment of the situation, and then assist him or her with achieving goals that are both constructive and reality based" (p. 312). Each offender should be encouraged, but the community supervision officer must ensure that the goals are actually obtainable, both for purposes of meeting expectations while on community supervision and to ensure that the offender does not unnecessarily experience a sense of dejection or hopelessness with his or her inability to meet agreed-upon goals. In addition, the community supervision officer must remain vigilant and receptive to the potential for discrimination in the workforce. Community supervision officers must maintain routine contact with employers to ensure that access to opportunity genuinely exists for the offender that chooses to work hard and to be industrious. Otherwise, the offender's overall likelihood of recidivism is increased, particularly when it is considered that employment is one of the chief correlates for offender success when on supervision. Prolonged or repetitive problems with employment discrimination impede the offender's reintegration and also place the community at further risk of future crime.

Another theoretical application that is relevant to community supervision is **labeling theory.** This theory contends that individuals become stabilized in criminal roles when they are labeled as criminals, are stigmatized, develop criminal identities, are sent to prison, and are excluded from conventional roles. In essence, the label of "criminal offender" or "convict" simply stands in the way of the offender reintegrating back into society. Such labels impair the offender's ability to obtain employment, housing, or other necessary goods or services to achieve success. Naturally, these forms of tracking and labeling often result from the need to ensure public safety (as with pedophiles) and thus are simply a necessary aspect of the punishment, incapacitation, and public safety objectives of many community corrections programs. However, it may be that these functions can be achieved in a manner that aids public safety while at the same time does not prevent the offender from achieving reintegration.

The desire to allow for public information of an offender's past errors (due to a need to achieve public safety) without undo blockage of the offender's ability to reintegrate has been directly addressed by labeling theory scholars. One particular labeling theorist, John Braithwaite, has provided a particularly insightful addition to the labeling theory literature that is specifically suited for the field of community supervision. In his work entitled *Crime, Shame, and Reintegration,* Braithwaite (1989) holds that crime is higher when shaming is stigmatizing and criminal activity is lower when shaming effects serve a reintegrative purpose. This contention obviously dovetails well with many of the points already covered in Chapter 1, and it should be equally obvious that Braithwaite's contention holds substantive appeal for treatment professionals working with offenders.

According to Braithwaite (1989), the negative effects of stigmatization are most pronounced among offenders who have few prosocial bonds to conventional society (such as family, religious institutions, or civic activities). This would place young males who are unmarried and unemployed at the greatest risk of being thrust further into criminality due to shaming effects. Because of lack of resources, connections, and general social capital, these offenders find themselves further removed from effective participation in legitimate society. Over time, these offenders will find that it is much easier to join criminal subcultures (whose members have faced similar impediments in access to legitimate opportunities), and they are provided tangible reinforcements from those subcultures for their activities. Thus, a cycle is created where a given segment of the offender population is further encouraged to repeat criminal activity simply due to the fact that other options have essentially been knifed away from their menu of community integration selections.

Community supervision officers often must contend with the effects of labeling since they impact the outcomes for offenders on their caseloads. Offenders may have great difficulty obtaining good job prospects, housing, and educational opportunities due to their previous criminal history. Community supervision officers must be receptive to this challenge. Many such officers do understand the hurdles involved and find it useful to develop relationships with social service agencies, employment services, businesses that are willing to hire the prior convicted, religious institutions, and other organizations in the community. This is an important element in enhancing the ability of an offender to reintegrate without the lure of further criminal involvement. It should also be noted that this labeling process can result in the offender internalizing a negative self-concept. (This is especially true with female offenders and with substance abusers.) When this occurs, it is likely that the offender will seek out other offenders similarly disposed for companionship, as these individuals will likely be within their own range of comfort. Since these individuals will not be able to relate to most persons in middle-class America (and since much of middle-class America will not likely relate to these offenders), it is less likely that interactions will prove rewarding for these individuals unless they are among others who are from a similar walk of life. In some respects, this can provide a sense of empathetic support (such as with AA programs) and mutual understanding. Community supervision programs must operate with this understanding, and officers must have caseloads that allow them to attend to the details of differentiating various social connections that the offender develops.

The last theory to be considered in this section is **feminist theory.** In recent years, there has been a noted increase in female offending and this has warranted a more detailed examination of the female offender population. Further, female offenders do tend to receive community supervision at a rate that is higher than that for the corresponding male population. This adds to the need for a theoretical application specific to female offenders under community supervision and will therefore be included in this current section.

The heart of the issue for feminist criminologists is the fact that traditional criminology has typically generated theories that are suited for the male population, with little or no regard for the corresponding female offender (Lilly et al., 2007). This has largely been true due to both a bias and oversight as well as the fact that female offending patterns have not tended to be nearly as common or severe as those of male offenders. However, as noted earlier, this is changing in today's society. Nevertheless, many of the variables and issues associated with female offending tend to differ from those of the male offender population. Issues related to being a primary caretaker of children, unequal access to job opportunities, adult victimization in domestically violent relationships, sexuality, gender-specific health concerns, and so forth, are all issues that tend to be more frequently relevant to the female offender than the male offender.

Feminist criminologists contend that female crime cannot be understood without considering gender. They contend that crime is shaped by the different social experiences of and power exercised by men and women (Lilly et al., 2007). These theorists note that patriarchy is a broad structure in our society that shapes gender-related experiences, essentially leaving women subservient to men. This is an important contention because in many cases, women engage in the selling of sex (prostitution), drug abuse crimes (often as a means of coping), and crimes of theft (particularly shoplifting or fraudulent check writing). In the vast majority of violent crimes, the situation is domestic and in retaliation for abuse by an intimate other.

In fact, female offenders do often experience a high level of victimization. Such victimization is usually either from a significant other or sexual in nature. In many instances, the crimes against these women are not reported. Consider as an example a female prostitute that is raped by a potential customer—being forced to engage in undesired sexual acts or being denied payment for her services. Though the act of prostitution might be illegal in a given jurisdiction (making the female an offender, of course), this should not overlook the fact that sexual activity without consent is rape, regardless of the woman's particular life choices. Often, prostitutes are not taken seriously when bringing such charges and this results in the underreporting of these types of crimes. Consider also that many women taking part in crime are involved with male partners who are also involved in criminal activity (consider again the nature of criminal subcultures). In such cases, the female is likely to engage either in petty offending (especially substance abuse) or in a role that supports her male counterpart (lying to cover for her partner, hiding goods, etc.). This alone places the woman in a vulnerable position. But consider that when domestic abuse issues emerge (very common among the offending subcultural population), it is highly unlikely that these women will call the police for support or intervention. Thus, many female offenders tend to have victimization patterns that occur throughout their adulthood.

It is important to note that the above examples do not even touch on issues related to prior childhood verbal, physical, or sexual abuse, common to many female offenders (particularly sexual abuse). These experiences are often at the hands of a male victimizer (especially in the case of childhood sexual abuse), and this alone tends to reinforce a patriarchal power dynamic in the household between the adult male molester and the childhood female victim. This is even true if the female "consents" to sexual activity (sometimes occurring in highly dysfunctional families) with the adult male (either a family member or an unrelated male in the household, e.g., the mother's boyfriend), since such consent is not legal and constitutes statutory rape. However, even though society defines this behavior as criminal, it nonetheless becomes socialized within the female's family experience and tends to be internalized by the female offender. Given the effects of labeling theory that will be evident if the female should exhibit subsequent promiscuous behaviors, it is clear that early familial experiences can start the initial process of gender stigmatization and are reinforced through social messages related to gender and sexuality that occur throughout the life span. This is a commonly observed trend among many women engaged in the illicit sex industry and among many substance-abusing female offenders.

Both community supervision officers and treatment professionals tend to be aware of many of these dynamics that exist among female offenders. During the past decade, a great deal of attention has been given to female offenders and the specific challenges that confront them. When attempting to reintegrate female offenders, feminist criminology not only brings a great deal of insight into female crime causation but also provides insight for persons providing treatment services for this population of offenders. This is even more important to mention when one considers that female offenders tend to be much more amenable to treatment than their male counterparts (Hanser, 2007b). In addition, feminist criminology provides fruitful groundwork in improving current programs that are designed for both supervision and treatment aspects of community correctional services with women offenders. Acknowledgment of these issues can result in lower recidivism, fewer social and collateral costs (such as with displaced children that are dependents of the female offender), and an enhanced sense of public safety (Hanser, 2007b). For more information on female offenders, students should refer to Chapter 14 of this text.

THE APPLICATION OF THEORY TO SPECIFIC ISSUES IN COMMUNITY SUPERVISION

The previous section has given some fairly specific connections between sociological or criminological theory and practices in community supervision. We will now take a step back and consider the theoretical applications that have been discussed in this chapter as well as those that were discussed in Chapter 1. When doing so, note that there tend to be two levels of theoretical explanation: the micro and the macro level of analysis. Micro levels of analysis explain or address singular issues in behavior and usually are centered on internal causal factors that are inherent to the individual offender him- or herself. These theories also tend to be more or less grounded within the fields of psychology or counseling and provide much of the basis for mental health interventions used with offender clients. Macro-level theories, on the other hand, often address group norms, behavior, and values, but do so in a manner that integrates variables from entire societies or civilizations. These theories tend to be more sociological in nature and are the basis for most traditional criminological theories. Neither theoretical perspective should be considered as superior to the other and neither should be used in a mutually exclusive manner.

With the above explanations, it is clear that theory is an important first ingredient for a successful community corrections recipe. But just as we have learned before, effective definitions and statements of one's goals are critical when determining what one seeks to accomplish. When treatment issues are of importance to the program, behavioral and cognitive-behavioral programs are among the most widely used theoretical orientations by correctional treatment specialists. This is true in a variety of treatment services ranging from substance abuse interventions to anger management programs, and including sex offender treatment services. The reason for this is simple and twofold: (1) these programs are easy to evaluate, and (2) these programs have been shown to work.

In criminal justice treatment programs, measurement of outcomes is important for a variety of reasons. It is vital to be able to clearly measure whether the offender is making suitable progress, and it is important to demonstrate to correctional agencies that the program does indeed result in some kind of observable improvement. The ability to clearly demonstrate progress and effectiveness is also necessary to grant-funding considerations that keep such programs fiscally viable. Thus, the clear means of identifying offender behaviors (i.e., recidivism, adherence to programs, etc.) when reinforcements or punishments are administered make this type of theoretical basis in therapy highly amenable to agency implementation and tracking.

Beyond the fact that these interventions are easy to define, measure, and evaluate, it has also been shown that they are quite effective. Such interventions have had demonstrated success with substance abusers, sex offenders, and mentally ill offenders (Barker, 2004). In particular, behaviorism and cognitive-behavioral approaches have been shown to be effective with comorbid disorders (two or more disorders that occur together) that include substance abuse and posttraumatic disorders, depression, or anxiety-related disorders (Barker, 2004). This is particularly encouraging since these types of disorders affect a substantial amount of the offender population. Further still, behaviorism, as presented by notables such as B. F. Skinner (the father of behavioral psychology), is based on the theoretical notions of objective observation. In other words, Skinner maintained that if one could not observe the behavior, then one could not suppose that any learning—aside from that observed—could be occurring (Barker, 2004).

Though cognitive and social learning theorists such as Albert Bandura did not agree with Skinner, this source of disagreement led to a wide variety of theoretical perspectives that were implemented in the treatment of offenders. Today, treatment programs tend to use elements of both behaviorism and cognitive-behavioral schools of thought. For example, faulty cognitions are subject to challenge in group and individual therapy sessions. Again, just as with strict behaviorist orientations, this type of therapy (cognitive-behavioral) has been and is currently used with a wide range of offenders including drug offenders, sex offenders, and domestic abuse offenders. The key point to understand is that theoretical perspectives from psychological and other mental health literature routinely shape the approaches that are used with specific offender populations.

Among micro-level theories, theoretical orientations associated with reality therapy are likewise instrumental to many treatment programs that provide services to the offender population. This perspective on human behavior was discussed earlier, in Chapter 1, but it is useful to again clarify some specific applications that have been noted among the offender population. This therapy has been used effectively with offenders and is well accepted among criminal justice practitioners because it emphasizes the offender's need to accept responsibility as well as avoid excuses and external blaming, and it does not look to the person's past to explain present behaviors. Reality therapy has been used in a number of group settings and group homes, including juvenile wilderness camps, adult halfway houses, batterer intervention groups, and substance abuse residential treatment facilities. Aside from the emphasis on personal responsibility for one's behavior, reality therapy also emphasizes the need for offenders to develop connections with others in society. Naturally, these connections are expected to be healthy ones with persons pursuing responsible lifestyles. This aspect of reality therapy serves to reinforce many other aspects of treatment programs, both clinical and otherwise, such as Alcoholics Anonymous or Narcotics Anonymous, which emphasize the need to accept responsibility for one's actions and also encourage their members to provide support for one another while in their recovery.

Among macro-level theories, the application of social disorganization theory has been particularly productive. Recent literature and developments in probation and parole have generated great interest in James Q. Wilson's "broken windows" contention, which holds that neighborhood areas that are not maintained (i.e., landscaping, lighting, painting, and housing conditions) effectively serve as areas that will draw crime into the region. This has had specific applications for community supervision in two regards. First, probationers and parolees that are at risk of recidivism will tend to be drawn to these areas since they are likely to be where other like-minded persons will reside or conduct illegitimate business. Second, community members will not tend to be active in these areas, thereby making the number of potential prosocial human contacts minimal.

In addition to the fact that socially disorganized areas tend to have substandard physical structures, there also tends to be a lack of effective informal social control within these areas. Where formal social controls include such elements of government as the police, the courts, and jails and prisons, informal social controls consist of families, religious institutions, civic organizations, peer groups, and other such norm-producing institutions that impact the day-to-day behavior of individuals but not through some form of formal sanction. In reality, it is most often informal social controls that shape our behavior since these tend to be more integrated into our daily lives, personal relationships, and belief systems. Because people in such communities lack a sense of informal cohesion, there is a more frequent reliance on formal forms of criminal justice intervention, which in turn further exacerbates the sense of conflict, chaos, and anarchy that may exist in such a community.

When agencies make a point to avoid releasing offenders into areas of the city that are considered hot spots for criminal activity, it is often because they have identified socially disorganized neighborhoods. In addition, placing halfway houses and residential treatment facilities in such areas is often avoided so as to limit offenders' access to (or temptation from) those influences that placed them in their current status of offending. As a result, some middle-class communities may find such facilities opened in their locale and may express a degree of displeasure with this. While such displeasure is understandable, it is the desire of the supervision agency to keep supervised offenders in regions or community locations that have better environmental and structural components, thereby providing the offender with superior support and enhanced overall routine human contact. In a simultaneous fashion, offenders are prevented or discouraged from frequenting less-than-suitable sections of a metropolitan area, particularly if they are supervised throughout their daily routine by a series of employers, volunteer coordinators, civic activity groups, and treatment specialists, as well as the community supervision officer him- or herself.

Another specific theoretical application that can be made to most community supervision processes is the concern over labeling and the integration of labeling theory. The most widespread and well-known integration of this theory is with juvenile offenders. Because these offenders are not typically considered as culpable as adult offenders and because they are often considered more amenable to treatment (being impressionable and not usually as hardened as adult offenders), there are specific aspects of the juvenile justice system that work to ensure that youth are not permanently stigmatized. When juvenile records are sealed or expunged, or when juveniles are given suspended sentences, this is part of the effort to avoid labeling the youthful offender.

As Neubauer (2002) notes, most aspects of the juvenile court proceeding are kept from public display. Neubauer goes on to add,

> This means that crime victims who are interested in what happens in their case, or ordinary citizens who are simply curious about what goes on in the courthouse, may freely attend sessions involving adults but not involving juveniles. In most jurisdictions it is illegal for law enforcement personnel or juvenile court officials to release the names of juveniles to the media. Moreover, even if the media indirectly is able to find out the names, journalistic ethics prohibit that information from being printed or broadcast. (p. 504)

It is clear from Neubauer's comments that the juvenile system desires that juvenile offenders not be easily identified and that the commission of their crimes be kept from general public knowledge. The reason for this is simply to ensure that juveniles are not hindered by social judgments based on their past offending, which is the main concern in regard to labeling theory. Thus, our entire juvenile justice system is based on the basic tenets of labeling theory, either directly or indirectly.

In another vein, the use of feminist theory has been found to be applicable to female offenders. Often, these women are encouraged in therapeutic programs to avoid unhealthy dependencies on men. Further, most treatment programs seek to empower these women to be as self-sufficient as possible. Likewise, there is a growing understanding that these women have been subjected to abuses and hardships that are mostly associated with the female gender. Programs that seek to address these issues are employing, at least in an oblique sense, aspects of feminist theory. Any program that attempts to empower women and to likewise minimize the female offender's dependence on her male counterparts can be thought of as having some element of feminist thought. Educating women on gender bias, patriarchy within family systems, and other such issues would fall under the umbrella of feminist interventions.

Last, restitution programs and methods of restorative justice would be consistent with Braithwaite's (1989) version of labeling theory that seeks to use shaming experiences in a constructive manner to promote offender reintegration. Hanser (2006, 2007a, 2007b) has demonstrated that such programs have been used with both violent and nonviolent offenders. Indeed, these approaches are ideal when used with female offenders that have children, some geriatric offenders, and juvenile offenders, as well as those offenders that present with mental illness (Hanser, 2007b). In addition, these same approaches have been useful with typically violent offenders such as sex offenders and domestic batterers, and this also has been true in nations outside the United States (Hanser, 2007a). The key to success is again the effective reintegration of the offender as the guiding principle in implementing these programs but only in conjunction with community involvement and support. Otherwise, these programs typically have dismal results that can backfire for advocates of such a form of offender processing. Naturally, this process requires that the community remain cognizant that the offender is, after all, a criminal but also not allow this to stigmatize the offender such that he or she cannot make productive efforts toward restitution for past infractions against the victim and the community.

In concluding this section on theoretical applications currently used in community supervision, it should be noted that no single theoretical perspective works with every client. Rather, therapists must constantly tailor the fit among theory, clinical issues, and the individual offender. Likewise, no single criminological theory will be applicable to every type of community or offender typology. Rather, again, theories are designed to explain a given range of criminal behaviors within the constraints of a set of theoretical constructs and variables. In all cases, theory is not reality and it is always to some degree artificial—otherwise, it would not be theory. However, it provides us with a paradigm and effective basis from which we can address abstract and complex issues in our social environment. Finally, as has been noted throughout this chapter, effective integration of criminological theory into community supervision responses requires the involvement of the entire community. This comes back full circle to the same point presented earlier in this chapter. Community supervision agencies cannot ensure public safety on their own. Rather, public assistance will be required if safety and effectiveness are to be optimized.

THE APPLICATION OF THEORY TO IMPROVE PUBLIC SAFETY

Community supervision programs around the United States, as well as community supervision experts, have pointed out the need for probation to "reinvent" itself (The Reinventing Probation Council, 1999). Among other contentions, these experts have long advocated for the increased use of community partnerships to fill the gaps in routine community supervision processes. This is consistent with the earlier recommendations in this chapter that emphasized a need for increased and enhanced community involvement as a means of securing public safety. Though very little of the literature connects this current contention with the past history of criminal justice, it is interesting to note that experts are coming back again to the contributions of the individual community member to aid in resolving many of the challenges that have been encountered by the criminal justice system.

However, the "broken windows" concept goes beyond simply asking for community volunteerism. It calls for the improvement and upkeep of communities that are not well kept or cared for. Such communities convey a sense of chaos and disorganization, and this opens the door to problematic populations that thrive in such conditions. The broken windows concept contends that neighborhood citizens can reduce crime, including recidivism, by improving the physical and structural elements of their community. This integrates both a crime prevention and a community supervision orientation. It also reflects what has been called a "community justice" approach to addressing crime (Clear & Cole, 2003).

Photo 2.3   Two parole officers discuss their schedule for the upcoming week in an effort to maximize their field and office work. They work as partners in supervising a specified area (called a zone) of the city.

Community justice is, in a general sense, a philosophy based on the pursuit of justice that goes beyond the traditional tasks of the criminal justice system—apprehension, conviction, and punishment (Clear & Cole, 2003). Community justice approaches seek to improve the quality of life in a given community, and this is especially the case for communities that have been hard hit by crime (consider, for example, gang-infested communities). In essence, there is a deliberate attempt to develop a sense of "collective efficacy" within the neighborhood (Cullen & Agnew, 2003). The term **collective efficacy** refers to a sense of cohesion within a given community where citizens have close and interlocking relationships with one another. These relationships tend to cement the community together, psychologically, sociologically, and perhaps even spiritually.

Collective efficacy is clearly the opposite of social disorganization. The process of taking a socially disorganized community and instilling a sense of collective efficacy is accomplished through a three-part strategy of justice that has been most aptly presented by Clear and Cole (2003). According to these authors, the means by which the formal criminal justice system can assist communities in reclaiming their communities, building collective efficacy, and integrating a community justice framework consists of environmental crime prevention efforts, the implementation and maintenance of community policing, and the use of restorative justice case processing.

Environmental crime prevention involves improvements of a community's structure and landscape to deter the likelihood of criminal offending in that given area. Target-hardening techniques are utilized to enhance the security of the area (e.g., more effective street and business lighting; ensuring that business/domicile entry points are visible from other locations; effective placement of landscaping, parking, or fencing; etc.). Such efforts can be implemented in very specific locations rather than throughout an entire city and can have impressive results. This stems from the fact that in some urban areas, nearly "70 percent of crime occurs in 20 percent of the city's locations" (Clear & Cole, 2003). This is an important point because it demonstrates that well-placed and targeted efforts can truly offset major areas of crime production.

Community policing is an approach to law enforcement that uses problem-solving strategies that involve community participants in the process. Community meetings, advisory boards, and other committee-based forms of civilian input are sought by both the police and the community supervision agency. Community policing seeks to encourage a sense of community involvement in an effort to build a rapport with the community. Programs such as citizens' police academies, National Night Out, and Neighborhood Watch all help to serve this function. In addition, police make themselves visible (both in uniform and otherwise) within the community as a means of integrating the officer staff with the law-abiding community it is tasked to serve and protect. Such an approach is preventative in nature and goes beyond the simple arrest of offenders. Further, this approach tends to build a list of investigative leads from law-abiding witnesses throughout the community that feel a sense of personal commitment to the officer or the agency. Ultimately, this type of rapport can greatly enhance security of the neighborhood and the degree of human contact that offenders under community supervision will receive in these communities.

Last, restorative justice approaches to offender sanctioning seek to restore the victim, the community, and the offender to a similar level of functioning to what existed prior to the commission of the criminal act. Restorative justice approaches require the offender to admit to the criminal behavior and demonstrate earnest and sincere remorse. Restitution is often made to the victim, and the victim provides direct input into the process. There are a number of such programs in the United States and around the world (Hanser, 2006). In all cases, the attempt is made to heal the damage that has been done to the victim and the community, and it is the specific charge that the offender perform the actions necessary to provide for this healing. More will be presented on restorative justice later in this text. For now, it is sufficient to note that this approach is consistent with other theoretical approaches (e.g., reality therapy, labeling theory, and so forth) and provides a good overlay to community empowerment programs.

Community justice approaches are based in the neighborhood and are focused on solving crime problems. Within these approaches, the incorporation of the community is a central tenet to success. Clear and Cole (2003) describe a general process of implementing a community justice orientation in a community as follows:

1. Crime-mapping is used to identify where criminal activity is most problematic.

2. Citizen advisory groups prioritize community concerns.

3. Working citizen partnerships between criminal justice agencies and citizen groups should be formed.

4. Integrated collaboration among police agencies, the court system, and community supervision agencies should be cultivated and information sharing should be emphasized.

5. Citizens and victims are encouraged to be involved in the sentencing and even the supervision process of the offender.

6. Community supervision of the offenders is designed to restore victims and the community.

7. In the process of restoring the victim and community, the offender is given community support to adequately reintegrate into the community (both emotionally and economically).

This seven-stage process, adapted from Clear and Cole (2003) but including modification as a means of refining its applicability to the current discussion, demonstrates the exact manner by which programs should be implemented within a community. It should be clear that community supervision personnel and agencies are likely to be at the center of such a process. Nearly all of these stages also utilize some form of theoretical basis, and this entire approach is intended to reintegrate the offender through a process of repairing the damage the offender has done to his or her victims and the community. Thus, this approach is much more comprehensive in nature, it improves supervision of the offender (more eyes are on the offender with increased community involvement), and the offender is made to be accountable for the criminal offense. Such an approach, grounded in a strong theoretical background, is practical to implement and is not, as critics might contend, soft on crime.

Routine Activities Theory: A Model Theory for Improving Public Safety

Of all the theories that have been discussed, it is perhaps routine activities theory that holds the most promise in enhancing public safety on a communitywide scale. As noted earlier, this theory simply contends that in order for a crime to happen, three variables must simultaneously converge: a suitable target, a motivated offender, and the absence of capable guardians. This simplicity in definition is exactly what is appealing since it succinctly defines yet also categorizes the three key elements that are part and parcel of any effective crime prevention program.

This theory's definition is also very well suited to the community justice model of community involvement. This likewise has direct implications for any community supervision agency that seeks to develop community involvement in the process of supervising excessive offender caseloads. Consider the connections among routine activities theory, community justice, and a community supervision program's desire to have a collaborative form of offender supervision. There are many similarities among the different mechanisms that each perspective would use. The three components of routine activities theory, the three components of a community justice model of intervention, and the "broken windows" notions associated with community supervision all share similarities that make them synonymous in many respects. To further illustrate the connections among all three of these theoretical and philosophical concepts and to also demonstrate how the community can be fully integrated into the process, consider the information in the Applied Theory box.

Hopefully, after an examination of the various connections among the three perspectives in the Applied Theory box, it will be clear how all three are interrelated. In addition, it can be seen that there are specific methods of implementation involving physical aspects of the neighborhood, the need for collaboration among agencies (particularly law enforcement and community supervision agencies), and the integration of community personnel that can fill many of the gaps that may exist between such collaborative efforts. This is an important point because it demonstrates the critical nature of community involvement. Such involvement can and should be reinforced by media support and highlighting of effective citizen participation—thereby demonstrating that community members are not being relegated to mere busywork—to further recruit more active citizen involvement, and also to demonstrate on a public level that the community justice model is a comprehensive and organized response to criminal offending in the community.

Routine Activities Theory	Community Justice	Community Supervision Agency
A suitable target	Policing outreach to the community and community education/awareness training on crime commission and methods of preventing victimization.	Implement "community probation" that mirrors community policing campaigns. Join police agency and educate/inform community about released offenders in the community.
	Self-defense classes. Crime prevention efforts such as Neighborhood Watch, Seniors and Law Enforcement Together (SALT), and domestic violence prevention efforts.	Implement community advisory groups on at least a bi-weekly basis. Provide names and numbers of key probation office personnel to notify if suspicious activity is noticed among known probationers or parolees.
	Use community policing to increase contact between citizens and police personnel.	Have community supervision officers visit citizens in neighborhood.
	More citizens will provide police with informal leads and information if they have a relationship with the agency personnel.	More citizens will provide community supervision officers with informal leads and information if they have specific and known means of making contact.
A motivated offender	Police detect, arrest, and apprehend offenders that are in the process of committing criminal acts or have committed such acts.	Community supervision officers and police officers should conduct as many conjoint "ride-alongs" as possible to increase collaborative efforts. There are even legal benefits to this type of collaboration; numerous examples exist throughout the nation.
	Police know most of the routine offenders by name and quite often see them recycle in and out of jail.	Many of these same offenders are on community supervision. Ensure that the correct level of intermediate sanction (i.e., standard probation vs. intensive supervision probation) is implemented with each of these offenders.
	The same repeat offenders (perhaps 10 percent of all offenders) commit well over half of all criminal acts throughout the nation.	Increase informal community contacts with these offenders. Ensure that there is an informal "chain of custody" from person to person in the community who have their eyes on this group of offenders.
A lack of capable guardians	Police cannot be everywhere all the time. Use target-hardening techniques to deter criminal activity from hot spot areas of the community. Use community initiatives to have better lighting, fencing, community landscaping projects, business facility design and layout, etc.	Community supervision officers cannot be everywhere all the time. Use technological tools more effectively and efficiently. Also, adjust surroundings so that less opportunity exists for the offender. For example, have halfway houses and residential treatment facilities near the probation agency or next to the police station!

Routine Activities Theory	Community Justice	Community Supervision Agency
	Use more data tracking such as Compstat to continually optimize placement of police personnel. ARC-GIS services and other such technological mapping devices should be implemented as often as is feasible. Naturally, training for effective use of equipment should be mandatory as well.	Use more GPS tracking when feasible. The agency must encourage staff to be fully competent with technological tools. Also, encourage effective (and legal) community communications through cell phone lists, e-mail chains, podcasts, and other informal yet expedient means of disseminating information regarding offenders in the community.

SOURCE: Based on Lilly, J. R., Cullen, F. T., & Ball, R. A. (2007). *Criminological theory: Context and consequences* (4th ed.). Thousand Oaks, CA: Sage Publications.

It is on this last point that this section will conclude. Agencies should utilize the media as a means of educating the public on the overall point and purpose of their comprehensive response to offending in the community. It is recommended that agency staff or even scholarly personnel that are involved with agency crime-fighting initiatives provide a literal overview of routine activities theory (a scaled-down version, of course), the community justice model, and the intent of community supervision agencies to maintain effective watch over known offenders. This last element of communication would disseminate the full concept and would serve as what Durkheim referred to as "social glue" among the law-abiding community. This sense of cohesion would improve the collective efficacy of the community, which would, in turn, improve public safety as members of the community develop a sense of connection and awareness of the broader goals of their criminal justice agencies. This would essentially come full circle to the points made earlier in this chapter while, at the same time, educating the community on the theoretical and philosophical foundations that shape the goals and objectives of various agencies involved with the supervision of offenders. In the process, it is hoped that citizens will begin to interpret crime in the community from a routine activities theoretical perspective, thereby giving them a clear and coherent means of understanding the crime phenomenon and the three-pronged means of responding to the threat of criminal behavior.

EXCESSIVE CASELOADS AND THEIR IMPACT ON COMMUNITY PROTECTION

While community support can and should be used to aid in the supervision of offenders on probation or parole, it still stands true that the central figure of authority in the process of community supervision is the individual probation or parole officer. The job of a community supervision officer (probation, parole, or otherwise) is stressful, placing numerous and diverse demands upon the professional working in such a role. Indeed, the workload can be difficult to quantify since much of the time allocated to various functions may not be easy to understand or operationalize. Nevertheless, the need to quantify expectations has resulted in an analysis of community supervision caseloads, the main issues involved with such a formal analysis being the number and type of offenders on one's caseload. It should be clear that if community supervision officers are stretched too thinly among the various offenders being supervised, the safety of the public is then compromised. Thus, the workload of a community supervision officer is directly linked to the safety

Photo 2.4 Probation officer Rosalyn Horton looks over her reports of checking an offender on her caseload during the penalty phase of the trial involving the abduction, rape, and murder of a child named Carlia Brucia. © Getty Images.

and security of the public. For this reason, caseload considerations have been (at least in a general sense) included in this chapter's discussion on public safety.

During the past two decades, the American Probation and Parole Association (APPA) has attempted to identify the ideal caseload for community supervision officers. The earliest official attempt to address this issue occurred in the early 1990s when a paper issued by the APPA recommended that probation and parole agencies examine staffing needs and caseload size within their own organizations (APPA, 1991; Burrell, 2006). Though this seemed to be a reasonable recommendation, it has been much harder to implement than might initially be imagined. The goal of determining the ideal caseload size has been an elusive one, complicated by multiple factors that are difficult to resolve or include in any specific equation.

Because of the diversity in size, structure, and geographical area covered by different agencies, as well as the diversity of offender typologies, it is difficult to provide any specific guidelines in determining ideal caseloads. Burrell (2006) points out that there are three specific reasons why it is difficult to put uniform standards on caseload sizes around the nation. These three points are as follows:

1. Not all offenders are alike: Offenders vary in their age, gender, offense seriousness, risk factors, and unique needs and challenges (e.g., mental illness, disability, and so forth).

2. Not all court/parole orders are similar: Judges vary greatly in regard to the terms and conditions that they tend to place on offenders.

3. Not all jurisdictions are the same: Statutory and policy issues may vary from area to area throughout the nation, and this can impact the nature of the community supervision officer's daily routine.

When considering prior attempts to reduce caseloads, the community supervision literature has a history that extends back to the 1980s. At that time, nearly all community supervision agencies utilized some form of (what was then) the newly designed intensive supervision probation or parole (ISP). Generally speaking, it was found that ISP was not effective with offenders that had committed misdemeanors or nonviolent crimes (Champion, 2002). In fact, the use of ISP tended to impair the successful completion of probation requirements for these offenders. However, ISP was shown to be much more effective than standard probation with high-risk, serious, or violent offenders on community supervision. This has led to some interesting developments in the community corrections field. Namely, hardcore offenders now receive more of a law enforcement style of supervision, while less serious offenders may be provided supervision that is likened to the casework model described in Chapter 1.

However, even among the ISP programs that were routinely evaluated during the 1980s and 1990s, there were a few agencies that took unique and effective approaches to implementing their programs. These agencies emphasized the use of data-driven, evidence-based approaches that also tended to include various treatment-oriented aspects in the program's design (Aos, Miller, & Drake, 2006; Burrell, 2006; Petersilia & Turner, 1993a). It was found that these ISP programs had more positive results, in terms of reducing crimes and technical violations as well as increasing the exhibition of prosocial behaviors such as gaining and maintaining employment, meeting court requirements, paying restitution, and meeting child support requirements (Aos et al., 2006; Burrell, 2006; Petersilia & Turner, 1993).

From the literature on this topic, a consensus model has slowly emerged throughout the United States as a result of input from experienced and thoughtful practitioners in the field of community supervision (Burrell, 2006). Though not necessarily ideal for all agencies, these generally agreed-upon recommendations provide a baseline from which other agencies can operate, comparing and modifying their own operations against the backdrop of the consensus that has emerged. To make these standards flexible and usable by agencies throughout the country, they are provided in terms of ratios of cases to officers and should be considered as upper-level ratios that should not be exceeded (Burrell, 2006). Burrell notes that "framing the standards as numbers not to be exceeded helps to reduce the chance that better staffed agencies will not be forced to allow caseloads to increase because of the standards" (p. 6). These cases are classified into broad categories based on criteria such as risk of recidivism, type of offense, or individualized needs. Table 2.1 provides the recommended caseload sizes. Classifying offenders on these relevant criteria is critical, as it ensures that offenders are correctly matched with the required level of supervision necessary to optimize their potential for completing their community supervision requirements (Burrell, 2006; Hanser, 2007b).

Hanser (2007b) has offered a strong argument for the implementation of valid, reliable assessment instruments, demonstrating that such tools are the critical first step in providing effective supervision of offenders. This allows agencies to allocate resources most accurately and effectively by eliminating the

TABLE 2.1 Recommended Caseload Sizes When Considering Type of Offender Case

Adult Caseload Standards	
Case Type	Cases to Staff Ratio
Intensive	20:1
Moderate to High Risk	50:1
Low Risk	200:1
Administrative	No limit? 1,000?
Juvenile Caseload Standards	
Case Type	Cases to Staff Ratio
Intensive	15:1
Moderate to High Risk	30:1
Low Risk	100:1
Administrative	Not recommended

SOURCE: Burrell, B. (2006). *Caseload standards for probation and parole.* Washington, DC: National Institute of Corrections.

likelihood of false positives and false negatives (Burrell, 2006; Hanser, 2007b), as well as to maximize public safety (Hanser, 2007b). According to Burrell, the "evidence suggests that staff resources and services should be targeted at intensive and moderate- to high-risk cases, for this is where the greatest effect will be had. Minimal contacts and services should be provided to low-risk cases" (p. 7). Burrell goes on to note that when examining recommendations such as those presented in Table 2.1, the first reaction from most administrators will be that many more staff will be needed to meet such recommendations. However, the reality is that this reallocation of staff would simply shift supervision staff to higher-risk offenders and away from those that are low risk (Burrell, 2006). It is in this manner that community supervision caseloads can be structured to optimize overall public safety while at the same time supporting the reintegrative aspects that serve as the basis for this text's underlying message. In this way, public safety is maintained as the primary focus of the agency, with treatment services and community volunteerism augmenting the primary goal of public safety.

USING THE COMMUNITY TO IMPROVE SAFETY: VOLUNTEERS AND NEIGHBORHOOD PROGRAMS

Since it is community support that is perhaps most needed when implementing a reintegrative approach to community corrections, community education is critical. Many community members may have no idea how specific treatment needs can directly impact the likelihood of offender reintegration. Further, these same people may not truly understand that offender recidivism as well as the future crime rate are directly impacted by the successful rehabilitation and reintegration of the offender.

For example, many citizens may not realize that a substantial number of offenders under community supervision are physically or mentally handicapped. Naturally, these offenders will experience difficulties finding jobs, particularly jobs that will at least pay the bills. Add to this the stigma of being a prior offender, and their chances in the job market are further diminished. However, employment is critical to successful offender rehabilitation and is thus critical to lowering their likelihood of recidivism. As it turns out, this is most often a necessary condition for offenders to remain on community supervision. Therefore, the offender, the employing community, and the agency must all meet each other on middle ground if the employability of offenders is to be realistically achieved. Community members and employers may not realize this and thus may incidentally miss an opportunity to reduce crime in their locale through the rehabilitation of offenders that would otherwise be productive.

Indeed, it is not uncommon for small business owners to be unaware of the state and federal tax incentives offered to employers that hire offenders. Naturally, if the offender is able to secure long-term employment, the individual will be better able to pay restitution to his or her victims and to probation departments. This then feeds back to the restorative justice concept, itself a part of the community justice perspective of enhancing public safety. It also means that victims and community members are stakeholders in the offender's ability to find gainful employment. Victims that desire compensation should therefore be supportive of efforts that put offenders to work. Otherwise, how else can the money for restitution be raised?

The point here is that the whole process works better if the community is involved. For example, consider a mentally challenged offender, having family involvement (if possible), with community involvement (certain churches, big brother/big sister organizations, the YMCA, and so forth) to check on the offender, and an employer that is able and willing to utilize such labor. The multiple forms of interconnections will ensure that the offender is properly supervised by informal networks of community members. These informal networks serve to ensure that the offender is conducting him- or herself in an appropriate manner and that the offender's likelihood of making restitution to the victim is increased. At the same time, the mentally challenged offender is provided social connections that can also benefit his or her mental health prognosis, making the benefit twofold.

The probation agency can oversee and coordinate much of this but will more importantly play the role of liaison between the victim and offender to ensure that all court conditions agreed upon by both the victim and the offender are met. It is expected that the community supervision agency will use its array of intermediate sanctions to supervise the offender. Among these techniques are such mechanisms as electronic supervision (including Global Positioning System devices), community service (which should be ideally linked to either the offense or the issues pertinent to that particular offender), and house arrest (except during times of employment or other mandated appointments or activities).

Community supervision agencies are also able to coordinate the activities of volunteers within their own agencies and throughout the community. This may seem like a potentially onerous task, but if one probation officer were to be solely in charge of coordinating volunteer efforts to supervise offenders, the payoff for the agency could be tenfold or greater. This is not simply wishful thinking; rather, these very types of programs have been successfully implemented throughout the nation for several years (see Figures 2.2 and 2.3, which introduce such programs from Hennepin County, Minnesota, and Los Angeles County, California).

 FIGURE 2.2 Promising Community Supervision Volunteer Programs—Hennepin County Department of Community Corrections

Hennepin County Department/Program: Department of Community Corrections

Division: Adult Probation

Location (Address) of the volunteer department site: A-302 Government Center

Program goal or mission: Promote public safety by expanding community partnerships, extending program services, and fostering teamwork and productivity among talented staff and volunteers.

Contact:

Tatiana Przytula

612-348-6893

tatiana.przytula@co.hennepin.mn.us

Mail Code 032

Opportunities for: Adults; Minimum Age 19

Types of opportunities: Ongoing, Corporate, Interns, Group

Shifts Available: Days, Evenings, Weekends

Client Populations: Families, Children, Adults, Seniors, Immigrants, Mental Health

Locations: Minneapolis, NW Suburbs, Western Suburbs, South Suburbs

Kind of work volunteers do:

Volunteers support staff in all areas of our work. Our social service work is oriented toward supporting positive change, which will in turn enhance public safety. Some work directly with our clients and other positions are more oriented toward computer work or research or monitoring of court-ordered conditions. We work with juvenile and adult offenders and families who are in the process of divorce. We work throughout Hennepin County. . . . in field offices, offices located with courts, or in institutions.

Application process for becoming a volunteer may include, but is not limited to, the completion of a volunteer application, background check, and interview process.

SOURCE: Hennepin County. (2006). *Adult probation volunteer opportunities.* Minneapolis, MN. Retrieved from http://wwwa.co.hennepin.mn.us/portal/site/HCInternet/menuitem.

RESERVE DEPUTY PROBATION OFFICER

The Reserve Deputy Probation Officer is a deputized volunteer who reports to, and is supervised by, a non-supervisor probation staff member. He or she has received special training in order to assist the probation staff member in a wide range of responsibilities, which may include direct involvement with juvenile and adult probationers. He or she is a highly motivated, skilled, and caring person who wants to serve the community as a part of the Los Angeles County Probation Department.

The Reserve Deputy Probation Officer is not a replacement for, or an alternative to, paid staff, but serves as a force multiplier that enhances existing resources.

STATUS OF RESERVE DEPUTY PROBATION OFFICER

The Reserve Deputy Probation Officer is a volunteer of the department deputized by the Chief Probation Officer to perform his/her assigned duties.

No Peace Officer Powers. The Reserve Deputy Probation Officer does not have peace officer authority and it not authorized with arrest, or search and seizure powers. Additionally, the carrying of firearms, other weapons, and handcuffs by the Reserve Deputy Probation Officer, including those who have an outside legal authority to do so, is not authorized.

TRAINING

Reserve Deputies will be required to complete a minimum of 75 hours of training course and a subsequent 6-month on-the-job training period. Reserve Deputies may also complete any designated training for assignments, which can require additional training or skills.

ASSIGNMENTS

A Reserve Deputy can work on weekdays, weekends, or evenings, serving a minimum of 16 hours per month. Reserve Deputies work under direct supervision of Deputized Probation staff in the supervision and investigation of adults and juveniles. They assist in Field Offices, Juvenile Halls, Camps, and some support service areas of the Probation Department.

Reserve Deputies also assist Deputized Probation staff in making home visits, field investigations, and monitoring conditions of probation. They serve at the will of the Chief Probation Officer, must observe all Department regulations, and do not fall within the framework of the civil service system.

SOURCE: Los Angeles County Probation Department. (2006). *Reserve deputy probation officer.* Downey, CA: Los Angeles County Probation Department. Retrieved from http://probation.co.la.ca.us/jobs/job_pdf/RDPOVOLUNTEER.pdf.

In addition, local police can enhance the supervision process without placing an extra burden on the police department staff by simply developing an effective Volunteers in Policing (VIP) program and providing these volunteers with the task of visiting the domiciles and communities of the offenders who are returned to the community. These groups can also demonstrate concern for the victim by making visits to the victim's domicile (if the victim is receptive to this) and just ensuring that satisfaction with the process has been obtained. Human visits of this sort, as opposed to some obscure survey, convey genuine human concern and provide the victim with another name and face to contact, rather than a survey form to fill out.

The additional benefit is that volunteers are given the opportunity to make a direct contribution to the justice system by working directly with the victims and offenders that are involved. This ensures that volunteers are utilized in a manner that is significant and should show the volunteer that his or her contribution is not taken lightly. Indeed, the police department is taking volunteers seriously in their desire to work in the justice system by involving them in a very important (yet fairly safe) and necessary task of "follow-up."

The use of Neighborhood Watch programs should be solicited since their members are often more than willing to observe and visit various locations to ensure that their locality is safe. Having these groups incorporated into the supervision process may be an additional way to further supervise the offender. Further, the members of this watch group, being members of the community where the offender resides, may likely know the offender and his or her family, and they may be in a position to provide supervision that is structured more as a genuine visit of concern (more as a relapse prevention than a "you're busted" visit) that may be perceived as helpful by the offender and his or her family.

Other forms of community involvement may include "corollary" forms of therapy that are not necessarily central to the offender's crime or even the supervision regimen, but are nonetheless adaptive activities from which the offender can benefit. For example, the offender may smoke cigarettes or may be overweight. In this case, the strong urging at the behest of the therapist to join a group for smoking cessation or weight control may not be directly relevant to the crime, but nonetheless is more beneficial than harmful for overall social integration purposes. This results in even more community members who supervise the offender, and the leaders of these programs can report progress to the therapist, who then increases the number of weekly human contacts that the offender has. Thus, on a social level, the offender is constantly under the watchful eye of community members who are addressing other needs of the offender. Therapists can provide another effective link that enhances therapeutic and supervision objectives simultaneously.

All of these mechanisms demonstrate that volunteers, employers, families, and probation departments can provide supervision that is comprehensive yet receptive to the challenges associated with the reintegrative process. This is important because the components of both care and supervision must be maintained. It is clear from the preceding examples that this requires participation from the community. This is a pivotal point to this chapter. Without support from the community, it will be unlikely that public safety can be assured.

Cross-National Perspective

The Use of Volunteers With Probation Agencies in Japan

In Japan, it is common practice that volunteers from the community provide services for the probation agency. These individuals are called Volunteer Probation Officers (VPOs). They are private citizens and they assist professional probation officers (PPOs), aid offenders of all ages to rehabilitate themselves at all levels in the community, and enhance crime prevention in the community. Legally, the VPOs are defined as non-permanent government officials. The activities of VPOs are generally classified into two categories: (1) rehabilitation aid activities and (2) crime prevention activities.

VPOs conduct the following rehabilitation aid activities based on the referral of the case from the Chief Probation Officer (CPO). The major rehabilitation aid activities are (1) to supervise and assist the probationers and parolees, (2) to inquire into the environment where an inmate in a correctional institution will live after release and to adjust any problems there, and (3) to conduct preliminary investigation into a candidate for pardon.

Regarding effective crime prevention, the establishment and maintenance of social/community support for offenders' rehabilitation cannot be emphasized too much. From this point of view, VPOs carry out many forms of crime prevention activities in the community with the close collaboration of probation offices, the Ministry of Justice, other national/local government ministries and agencies, schools, police, and other volunteers and voluntary organizations (NGOs) such as the Women's Association for Rehabilitation Aid (WARA) and the Big Brothers and Sisters (BBS) Association.

(Continued)

(Continued)

The actual number of VPOs has varied from 48,000 to 49,000 in this decade. There are 48,642 VPOs at present and the average age is 63.4 years. The proportion of females has increased to 24.0%. As to occupation, VPOs represent almost every sector of society. The largest group (44.5%) is composed of retired persons and company workers, followed by housewives (14.4%), those engaged in primary industries (12.4%) such as farming and fishing, and the religious profession (10.9%). Other individuals serving as VPOs include company owners, government officials, manufacturers, social workers, schoolteachers, medical doctors, and private lawyers (as of April 1, 2001).

Legally, the VPOs are defined as non-permanent government officials. Therefore, VPOs are entitled to obtain national compensation benefits when any bodily injury is inflicted on VPOs in the performance of their duties. However, they are not paid any remuneration for their services. The government may only pay the expenses incurred in discharging their duties, or a part thereof. In practice, the VPO is reimbursed a small amount of money for his or her expenses. The term of service of the VPO is 2 years with the possibility of reappointment. In practice, most of them are reappointed repeatedly for a number of years, because the duties of the VPO require long-term experience with much knowledge and skill regarding the treatment of offenders.

A VPO's character and personality substantially affect his or her role. Therefore, VPO law requires that a VPO should be (1) evaluated highly with respect to the character and conduct in the community, (2) enthusiastic and sufficiently available to work, (3) financially stable, and (4) healthy and active.

To recruit VPOs, the CPO of a probation office prepares a list of candidates based on the information gathered from various sources in the community. In effect, the list reflects, to a great extent, the opinion of representatives of the VPO Association. Further screening is made by a VPO Screening Committee, an advisory committee to the Ministry of Justice that is established in 50 locations corresponding to each probation office. This committee consists of representatives of the court, prosecution, the bar association, correctional institutions, probation and parole services, other public commissions in the community, and learned citizens. The Minister of Justice then appoints VPOs from the candidates who pass the screening process.

There are five types of systematic training courses for VPOs such as (1) Initial Training designed to provide essential knowledge and information for newly appointed VPOs, (2) Primary Training designed to provide practical knowledge of various procedures in supervision and other care for the offenders for VPOs with less than 2 years of experience, (3) Secondary Training designed to provide basic knowledge and skills regarding treatment methods for VPOs with between 2 and 4 years of experience, (4) Regional Regular Training designed too provide various kinds of knowledge and skills related to rehabilitation services for all VPOs, and (5) Special Training designed to provide special knowledge and skills regarding treatment methods for various types of offenders for VPOs selected by the director of the probation office.

SOURCE: Adapted from Sakai, K. (2002). *Community involvement and crime prevention in Japan: Extensive use of volunteer probation officers (VPOs)*. Torino, Italy: United Nations Interregional Crime & Justice Research Institute. Retrieved from www.unicri.it/wwk/related/pni/docs/2002/06_kunihiko_sakai.doc.

IMPROVING PUBLIC SAFETY: HOW INDIVIDUAL VOLUNTEERS CAN MAKE A DIFFERENCE

The following case examples are offered to demonstrate the reintegrative dimensions that can be realized through the use of simple volunteerism. In all three cases, the emphasis on public safety is never jeopardized, but is instead further enhanced. In addition, the offender develops an informal and genuine connection to the community, which serves to ultimately decrease the risk of recidivism while at the same time improving the offender's ability to contribute to his or her community of origin. Each of these examples was drawn from case highlights of community supervision volunteers as provided by the National Institute of Corrections' (2000) publication entitled *Misdemeanor Courts, Hope for Crime Weary America: Volunteer Mentoring in Misdemeanor Courts,* written by Judge Keith J. Leenhouts.

Example One: The Professional Volunteer

The defendant's name was Billy. He was convicted of simple assault and battery, a misdemeanor which violated the city's disorderly conduct ordinance.

Billy had a bad eye. It did not focus correctly. He did not appear to be honest. When he spoke to anyone, the eye did not make contact. It seemed to wander at about a 45 degree angle. Billy looked as though he was dishonest and deceiving.

During the pre-sentence investigation, Billy seemed to be evasive and dishonest, even to the retired volunteer investigators. They knew better, but were sure others did not evaluate Billy correctly. He looked dishonest and people saw him in that light. Billy was struggling.

Billy had a concerned mother. She was suspicious, and somewhat paranoid, but she was concerned about Billy. Ralph realized this was a plus, and said, "That gives us something to build on."

A new question arose for the young program. Would professionals help? The judge placed a call to an optometrist friend. "Would you see Billy? Would you help Billy? We have many volunteers who give us five to ten hours a month. We have seven retirees who give us full time to administer the program and to do pre-sentence investigations. Would you volunteer to see Billy?" The optometrist seemed surprised and even disappointed that the question needed to be asked. "Of course I will," he said.

Billy was assigned to a one-to-one volunteer. His toughest job was to convince Billy's mother that she would not get a bill from the optometrist. She was finally convinced, and Billy, for the first time, saw a doctor about his eye. The doctor found the eye was totally dysfunctional, and did him no good. It needed to be removed. Billy would see as well, perhaps even a little better, and he certainly would look better.

The mother, the one-to-one volunteer, and Billy agreed with the optometrist's diagnosis. The doctor then explained that he did not do such surgery and that it was a job for an ophthalmologist. The situation seemed rather bleak until he said that he knew a good ophthalmologist who owed him a favor. "Maybe he will do it as a volunteer," he offered. The ophthalmologist agreed that if Billy could get an artificial eye he would perform the surgery. The town's Lions Club agreed to purchase and furnish the artificial eye.

The surgery was performed successfully and Billy became a new man. He had been a high school dropout. He returned to school and got his diploma a year later. Probation was terminated and the case was dismissed. Billy faced life with a clean record which he had earned through community service and a very good probation record.

After Billy had been off probation for a year, he came back into court with a young lady. He excitedly introduced her to several of the volunteers. When he returned later he asked almost breathlessly, "What did you think of her?" The response was an enthusiastic approval—not that Billy needed it.

Billy was doing well in his job. He had completed high school and was taking some adult education classes. A college education seemed possible. And he was in love with a fine young lady. It looked like a happy ending was in store, but it was not to be. The night before his wedding, which the optometrist and his one-to-one volunteer were going to attend, Billy was a passenger in an automobile. There was an accident and Billy was killed.

Billy's last years were filled with hope, success, dignity, self-respect, and accomplishment because of the doctors and his one-to-one volunteer. Billy also gave the court a gift: the confidence that, if approached right, professionals will volunteer.

The next time the court felt the need for assistance from an eye doctor it contacted the optometrist, and almost apologetically said, "We need more help, but we don't want to call on you all the time. Do you have any fellow colleagues who might help?" His answer was, "Of course."

(Continued)

(Continued)

The optometrist wrote a letter to a number of his colleagues. He described what had happened and asked them if they would come to a meeting in the court. The judge did a follow-up letter. The optometrist then called all of those he had contacted by letter, urging them to come to the meeting. Nearly all of them attended the meeting and as a result some 15 offered their services. There was an ample supply.

The court readily agreed never to refer more than one case at a time to any optometrist. Each doctor agreed to work with one case at a time, and perform four evaluations a year. The court set up a well-administered and highly accountable procedure to keep broken appointments and lost time to a minimum.

A number of defendants needed eye exercises to help them overcome learning disabilities. Often the optometrist would train the one-to-one volunteer who would assist with the exercises. Their academic achievements were greatly enhanced when their vision improved. The inability to read had caused a lack of dignity, pride, and self-respect, which in turn had caused criminal behavior. Better vision and the ability to read were some answers.

The court had the same experience with dentists, medical doctors, lawyers, psychologists, psychiatrists, and other professionals. The court, which was willing to administer the program well and do careful follow-up, did not have to worry about not having money. It could provide all the professional services it needed. Slowly it dawned on the court. The answer is in our own backyard. The answer is not getting tax dollars. That can go to prisons, highways, space, and war. We have another, and better, answer. Volunteers!

SOURCE: Leenhouts, K. J. (2000). *Misdemeanor courts, hope for crime weary America: Volunteer mentoring in misdemeanor courts.* Washington, DC: National Institute of Corrections. Retrieved from http://www.nicic.org/Library/016295.

Example Two: Retirees—A Special Gift

The young judge found himself trying to coordinate and oversee the work of the eight professional counselors and some forty "ordinary folks" serving under their immediate guidance and supervision as role model–mentors. This, plus his judicial duties, was getting to be too much to do well. He needed help and thought of a family friend, a retiree, who loved young people very much. He called "Harry" and told him of his plight. Harry agreed to come into the court several hours each day as a volunteer and coordinate the effort. (The word "program" was still a bit of an exaggeration.)

A little office space was carved out and Harry would be present when each defendant was placed on probation with orders to report to one of the eight and a one-to-one volunteer, in addition to a fine or jail term. Harry would then type the probation order, orientate the defendant, and arrange and attend a meeting with all three of them a few days later.

As the caseload grew, Harry would meet regularly with the judge and tell him how things were going. The judge no longer met each month with the probationer, but only as needed in the opinion of Harry and the volunteers, who came to be known as direct service volunteers.

Harry followed each case very carefully. He would meet with the volunteers at least monthly and sometimes more often to review each case. The motto of the "program" was that everything had to be done with excellence. Nothing was left to chance. Harry, a retired purchasing agent and business executive, was the perfect man. He seemed to be everywhere and knew everything.

As the program grew, as related later, Harry needed help. He became the overall administrator and was joined by three other retired volunteers. One coordinated the one-to-one volunteers, Harry's first job.

Another coordinated the community service program, and the other the education and group programs. The four all "worked" full time. (They did not call it work since it was a labor of love, more like a hobby. As time went on, some were paid a small amount each month to supplement Social Security and other pensions, while others were never paid at all.)

They often joked that the court made them the second happiest people in town. They had a whole new outlook on life. They were needed and vital again. The only persons happier were their wives who took them "for better or worse, in sickness and in health," but NOT for lunch every day. The wives were even happier, they said with a smile.

The quest for excellence in accountability and administration was accomplished. As each person was placed on probation, the judge, based on the pre-sentence report which is described later, would indicate on a form all the services which were to be provided (mandatory at first) to each probationer. Harry would receive a copy on each sentencing day. The list of services grew and grew and included such things as one-to-one volunteers, group psychotherapy, AA, driver violator and alcohol and drug information schools, referral to various professional services, community service, etc.

Then each month the judge would meet with the four retirees for a six to seven hour session to review the cases on probation. In every case the questions were:

- what did we order?
- was it or is it being provided with excellence?

The program was highly accountable and very well administered.

The retired volunteers really took what was best described as an effort and made it into a program, the difference being high quality administration and accountability.

The methodology of accountability was simple and effective. Every active case was reviewed using the form used by the judge when sentencing the defendant. Then each case was checked as to the quality of services. Whatever follow-up was needed was done forthwith.

One of the volunteers who suggested this form of accountability was a business consultant. After the system had been in effect for some time, he reviewed it. His comment was interesting. "This is better accountability than any business I have ever consulted with over many years."

Of course, superb accountability is of little value without well-administered follow-up. This was done by the retirees with the cooperation of all the staff and volunteers.

The retirees usually related well to the probationers and when it happened, it was encouraged. Often the one-to-one volunteer would become a father image, and the retiree the grandfather image. Thus, while their main activity was administration and accountability, they never forgot the whole goal was to rehabilitate the offender, and that should always come first.

Once when a probationer came in to see his mentor-volunteer, the volunteer was discouraged. It had been about three months and the probationer was still in the initial stage of hostile, miserable confrontation. Then, suddenly one day the probationer appeared smiling and relaxed, and for the first time they chatted like friends. The one-to-one volunteer was amazed and asked what happened. The probationer replied, "I was walking down the hall and looked in at one of the offices and saw this old man. His face was so kind and gentle. It reminded me of my grandfather, the only one who ever really loved me. I decided if he was part of the program, it must be OK." He did well thereafter.

The retiree had not only made a program out of an effort, an organization out of hope, but also had added much to the goal of the program. Retirees: a precious gift.

SOURCE: Leenhouts, K. J. (2000). *Misdemeanor courts, hope for crime weary America: Volunteer mentoring in misdemeanor courts.* Washington, DC: National Institute of Corrections. Retrieved from http://www.nicic.org/Library/016295.

Example Three: Ordinary People Doing Extraordinary Things

Linda Larson was a very good wife and mother who was active in community affairs. She was an attractive and intelligent lady who had made a decision to be a homemaker while her children were young, and after they were grown, to seek challenging employment. Among her community activities, she decided to be a volunteer mentor to the court. She had been recruited by word of mouth by one of the original eight volunteers. Like all volunteers without experience and education in professional counseling, she received orientation and training and careful ongoing supervision and guidance.

Linda was assigned to a probationer named "Sally." Sally was a very strong and husky woman who weighed about 180 pounds. She was not fat, just big and strong. Sally had been involved in a fight with two other women. Sally was the aggressor. No real damage was done because the fight was stopped, and the police were called. Sally was arrested and brought to court on a misdemeanor charge: "Disorderly Conduct—Fighting." It was a violation of a city ordinance, not a state law, like most misdemeanors.

Sally pled guilty. It was her first offense in this court. She was fined and placed on probation. She was assigned to "Tom," one of the original eight professional counselors, and also to Linda.

Linda began meeting with Sally once a week. At first the meetings lasted the required one hour. Linda reported to Tom and told him the meetings were terrible. Sally would rant, rave, and scream for an hour and Linda would listen. That is about all that happened. Sally used a lot of obscenities and profanity. Linda listened. And she listened.

During the second month, the meetings got longer and longer as Sally began telling about her life. She had no knowledge or memory of her father. The only memory of her mother was when she was dropped off at an orphanage when she was a very young girl. She had grown up in orphanages and had been in juvenile institutions for juvenile offenses. She was now 24 and living with an ex-convict. They had two children. The family was very insecure and unstable. They had no friends or relatives to support and help them. They were struggling. Linda listened . . . and listened. She did what no professional probation officer had time to do. In two months she did some fifteen hours of listening. What she heard could be summarized in minutes, but it took many hours and Linda's understanding ear for Sally to be able to say it.

Still, Linda told Tom at the end of the second month, "I do not seem to be able to help. I just listen." Tom told Linda, "The awesome power of the listening ear is at work. Be patient. You are enhancing her dignity, you are gaining her confidence simply by listening. It is a new experience for Sally. No one has ever listened to her before. When someone like you with a home, family, and friends listens, it is a new experience for Sally. Keep listening and, when it is appropriate, offer assistance. Be a friend.

The meetings were longer now, once as long as three hours. Finally, after some 25 hours of listening, Linda sensed Sally was ready to hear the words Linda had been aching to say since their first meeting. She blurted them out. "If I can ever help you, day or night, call me." Not long after that Sally phoned Linda in the middle of the night. One of her children was sick and she had no idea what to do. Linda knew this was a critical moment in more ways than one. She immediately told Sally she would meet her at the hospital in an hour with her doctor.

The doctor stayed through the physical crisis. Linda stayed through the physical, and also the emotional crisis, which lasted much longer. Hours later, at the dawn of a new day, and the beginning of a new friendship, Sally told Linda, "You really do care. You are really a friend." After that they were able to get together as friends, and not necessarily in scheduled meetings. They would go shopping and do things they both enjoyed. Sally changed, and so did Linda. Friendship does that.

A year later the effect that one ordinary person could have on a probationer was affirmed. When she was dismissed from probation Sally said, "I used to dream of wealth and fame. Now all I want is to be a good wife and mother. I want to give my husband and children a good home. Just like Linda." And she did. Sally later moved to another state, but for many years she and Linda stayed in contact with each other. Sally made it.

This, and other cases seemed to prove that people with no specific training could, with proper support, guidance, and supervision, be very effective role models and mentors.

An idea which began with imagination was, with implementation, blessed with affirmation and confirmation.

Although much more had to be done, the basic idea was in place and ready to be expanded. The next hurdle seemed to be the development of a well administered and highly accountable program which would insure the day-to-day excellence of the efforts of some eight professional counselors–volunteers and about forty "ordinary people doing extraordinary things."

SOURCE: Leenhouts, K. J. (2000). *Misdemeanor courts, hope for crime weary America: Volunteer mentoring in misdemeanor courts.* Washington, DC: National Institute of Corrections. Retrieved from http://www.nicic.org/Library/016295.

CONCLUSION

It is important for community supervision agencies to have clear and well-articulated philosophical and theoretical bases when determining their goals and objectives. This text contends that the primary purpose of our correctional system is to ensure the public safety of society. With this in mind, goals and objectives set by agencies should be directed at achieving this purpose. When setting these goals and objectives, agencies should make a point to integrate input from community members. Collaborative goal setting that incorporates the assistance of other agencies as well as community citizens will be most effective in achieving those objectives that are most meaningful to the locale.

In addition, it is the contention of this chapter that public safety can be achieved through reintegrative efforts. However, the supervision function of probation and parole should never be jeopardized when attempting the reintegration of offenders. Rather, the nature of supervision should be changed to include more informal rather than formal types of human contact. This requires further assistance from the community, since probation and parole caseloads preclude the ability of agencies to effectively provide such human contact. Methods of including community members in the supervision process should be implemented. In many cases, community members are able to provide substantial assistance to reintegrative efforts with offenders. This means that the community member—long an inherent participant in the criminal justice process—becomes central to both reintegrative and public safety agendas. It is with the assistance of the community that probation and parole agencies are best able to set goals and objectives that are in line with public expectations, and it is with the assistance of the community that such agencies can best meet those expectations. In short, though public safety is job one, public safety is also a team effort.

Key Terms

Activities	Incapacitation	Retribution
Collective efficacy	Labeling theory	Routine activities theory
Deterrence	Objectives	Social disorganization theory
Environmental crime prevention	Policy	Social learning theory
Feminist theory	Rehabilitation	Strain theory/institutional anomie
Goal	Restitution	Subcultural theory

"What Would You Do?" Exercise

Jim is a convicted sex offender who has been placed on intensive supervised probation. As a condition of his probation, he is required to keep a sign on his front lawn that openly and very visibly states, "Convicted Sex Offender Lives Here." Over a 6-month period, he has met all of the terms and conditions of his probation in an exemplary manner. However, he has noted to you, his probation officer, that there is a group of youth that constantly pester him and yell at him, calling him names such as "scum," "dirtbag," "loser," and other worse names. Also, his neighbor across the street has vocalized that he would like to see Jim get arrested and sent to prison. One of the youth that has harassed Jim is the son of the neighbor across the street. Jim asks you if he has any recourse, since he believes that what the neighbor and the youth are doing is illegal.

For this exercise, explain how you would handle this situation. In doing so, indicate both the informal and formal steps that you might take to resolve this issue. In addition, explain which theoretical perspectives might apply to this scenario. Finally, which sentencing goals do you believe are the objective of Jim's sentence (i.e., rehabilitation, deterrence, retribution, etc.)? Explain your answer.

What would you do?

Applied Exercise

Linda is 32 years old and is a heroin addict. For several years, Linda worked as a topless dancer and also worked in the illicit sex industry. She had moved out of her mother's house when she was 16 and run away. She was never found by her family, and within a few months she was begun to prostitute herself as a means of self-support. Eventually, she landed a job as an exotic dancer (though she really could not "dance" at all), and from there her work as a prostitute was managed by the club owner. Though Linda often "serviced" the club owner, she became involved with Jack, a biker with the Hell's Angels. After a period of time, she became pregnant and gave birth to a daughter. Shortly after she became pregnant with Jack's baby, Jack was sent to prison for trafficking drugs. After Linda became pregnant again, the club owner would not let her dance on her shift, but he did take care of her, giving her a place to stay and the basic necessities, and having the other female dancers check on her. But of course, there was an exchange that took place as compensation.

After the birth of her second child, the responsibilities associated with mothering were simply too much. Linda was under enormous pressure and felt pushed and pulled in every direction. The club owner kept her over a barrel, demanding sexual favors along the way. Taking care of her baby was ever more difficult as a single parent with no real family support network, and she had a number of patrons that were constantly harassing her. Further, her drug use became more serious and she began using heroin on a routine basis.

Ultimately, the drug use veered out of control and she was arrested and convicted of illegally purchasing a Schedule II drug. She served several years in prison and now has been paroled out. While in prison and in therapy, she revealed that she had been molested by her father as a young child and by her stepfather as a teenager. She believes that her mother knew but simply chose to ignore the signs and symptoms. It is important to Linda that she resume contact with her 9-year-old daughter who is now in the custody of state child services.

In the scenario above, note which theories could be used to explain Linda's development and her involvement in crime. Then, explain from any variety of theoretical perspectives what you think would be an effective way of processing this offender.

CHAPTER 3

Assessment and Risk Prediction

LEARNING OBJECTIVES

1. Understand the importance of the PSI and why accurate information is critical to later supervision and treatment needs of the offender.

2. Understand basic concepts inherent to assessment.

3. Know the meaning of false positives, false negatives, true positives, and true negatives.

4. Understand the difference between static and dynamic risk factors.

5. Identify subjective and objective means of assessment and risk prediction.

6. Be familiar with the Wisconsin Risk Assessment and the flaws associated with that instrument.

7. Be familiar with the Level of Supervision Inventory—Revised, and understand the strengths associated with that instrument.

8. Understand the reasons why the MMPI-2 Criminal Justice and Correctional Report is presented as a premier instrument.

INTRODUCTION

Because of concerns with public safety, it is imperative that a correctional agency be as adept as possible at accurately assessing the future prognosis of any offender under its supervision. For the purposes of this text, the term **prognosis** refers to the likelihood that an offender will successfully reform and will refrain from further criminal activity. Thus, there is both a treatment component (reform) and a public safety component (likelihood of further criminal activity) contained within an offender's prognosis. Both must be considered simultaneously if the correctional agency is to fulfill its mission in a satisfactory manner.

The intake is the process that occurs when the offender is initially entered into the correctional system. This process is heavily tied to information obtained from the presentence investigation report (PSI) that the probation department will provide to the presiding judge of an offender's case. The **presentence investigation report** is the file that includes a wide range of background information on the offender. This file will typically include demographic, vocational, educational, and personal information on the offender as well as records on prior offending patterns and the probation department's recommendation as to the appropriate type of sentencing and supervision for the offender in question. In many respects, the PSI is the initial point of assessment, and it will often be utilized during assessment in the institutional setting or when the offender is officially placed under the jurisdiction of the probation department. Because the PSI is used in all community supervision agencies and because this is a centerpiece component of the probation process, we will now take a closer look at the PSI in the section that follows.

THE PRESENTENCE INVESTIGATION REPORT (PSI)

The primary purpose of the presentence investigation report is to provide the court with the necessary information from which a sentencing decision can be derived. The PSI is conducted after a defendant is found guilty of a charge (whether by pleading or court finding) but prior to the point of sentencing. During this point betwixt conviction and sentencing, the probation officer will complete the PSI, which will include extensive information pertaining to the offender. This information, along with a sentencing recommendation, will aid the judge who must ultimately fashion a sentence as well as any corollary obligations attached to that sentence.

Likewise, the PSI tends to serve as a basic foundation for supervision and treatment planning throughout the duration of the offender's sentence. This document will serve as a reference point for placing the offender in a variety of programs; it is used when the offender is on supervision and may serve as a guidepost for jail and detention facilities as well. The PSI will contain sundry amounts of information about an offender's background, including education, social and medical history, and work experience. In addition, an offender's file may contain a number of documents from a variety of professionals who provide services for the community supervision agency. Community supervision officers should make a point to keep the information as confidential as is realistically possible. Thus, free and open disclosure of the information should be discouraged.

Among other things, the PSI will contain information related to the character and behavior of the offender. This means that the probation officer's impressions of the offender can greatly impact the outcome of the PSI. The Federal Probation System has set forth some clear and simplified guidelines for completing the PSI. These guidelines are as follows:

1. Brevity: Avoid repetition. For clarity and interest, use short sentences and paragraphs without risking the ability to acquire information that is required.

2. Language: It is important to not take the offender's statements out of context. Also, direct quoting of the offender should be used if such gives a clearer picture of the situation or context.

3. Sources of information: PSI reporting officers should verify the facts contained in their report from some other source than the offender. If unverified information is included, it should be clearly designated as being unverified. It is important to note that unverified information can and does cause serious harm to the offender and can also negatively impact supervision or treatment programs in the future.

4. Technical words and phrases: The PSI reporting officer should use technical words and phrases only if they are commonly known among practitioners in the criminal justice or court system.

5. Style and format: The report should be kept as simple and direct as possible. Likewise, emotional appraisals and other such comments from the officer should not be included as content.

The PSI is typically conducted through an interview with the offender. Because the PSI information is largely obtained from the interview process, it is naturally important that community supervision officers have good interviewing skills. This cannot be overstated given the fact that community supervision officers are in contact with persons on a routine basis from whom they must collect and record information. Further, the community supervision officer will often conduct interviews with family members, employers, and so forth to validate the information received from the offender. It is of course important that the PSI contain reliable information that is relevant to the defendant's character, attitude, and activities. Thus, the presentence investigator must make a point to seek reliable sources, to verify information, and to corroborate all information with as many objective or external sources as is reasonably possible. The written report should include the full police report related to the criminal incident, the defendant's version of the incident, the victim's input related to the offense, and a complete background on the offender.

According to the American Probation and Parole Association (APPA), the PSI should reflect the background of the offender and should be as accurate and comprehensive as the probation department's resources will allow. In being comprehensive, a report should contain certain bits of information that are germane to effective sentencing and offender placement. According to the APPA, the specific items included in most reports are as follows:

1. A complete description of the offense and circumstances surrounding it, not limited to the aspects developed for the record as part of the determination of guilt

2. A statement from the victim and a description of the victim's status, the impact upon the victim, losses suffered by the victim, and restitution due the victim

3. A full description of any prior criminal record of the offender

4. A description of the educational background of the offender

5. A description of the employment background of the offender, including military record and his or her present employment status, financial status, and capabilities

6. The social history of the offender, including family relationships, marital status, interests and activities, residence history, and religious affiliations

7. The offender's medical history and, if desirable, a psychological or psychiatric report

8. Information about environments to which the offender might return or to which he or she could be sent should probation be granted

9. Supplementary reports from clinics, institutions, and other social agencies with which the offender has been involved

10. Information about special resources that might be available to assist the offender, such as treatment centers, residential facilities, vocational training services, special educational facilities, rehabilitation programs of various institutions in which the offender might be committed, special programs in the probation department, and other similar programs that are particularly relevant to the offender's situation

11. A summary and analysis of the most significant aspects of the report, including specific recommendations as to the sentence (A special effort should be made in the preparation of presentence reports not to burden the court with irrelevant and unconnected details.)

Figure 3.1 provides a good illustration of a typical PSI that may be submitted to a court prior to sentencing. When examining the PSI form from the state of Kansas, it is clear that most all of the information

Photo 3.1 Probation and parole officer Chris Byrd and a court attorney discuss some of the content in an offender's PSI before the sentencing judge appears in the courtroom. In some cases, negotiations may be arranged by various court actors depending on the circumstances of the crime and the offender.

recommended by the APPA is included. The form in Figure 3.1 is very well structured and largely provides this information in a standardized format. The typical PSI will also tend to have narrative components that are provided by the offender as well as others that are interviewed by the presentence investigator.

Many states have rules of confidentiality when gathering privileged information for the PSI as well as regulations regarding the disclosure of that information once it has been included in the final report. However, the conversations between the probation officer and the defendant are not considered privileged and such information may be subject to disclosure. In addition, when the conviction information is a matter of public record, probation officers may disclose this information to noncriminal justice agencies or other persons as long as this disclosure does not violate any agency regulations. As one might reasonably suspect, while in the course of their duty, probation officers may disclose an offender's information to criminal justice agencies on a need-to-know basis in most states. Courts will typically base their decision of disclosure on the type of crime that was committed as well as the probation officer's assessment of the offender's potential to harm other victims. Finally, most states do allow the probation officer to provide information or records to the offender's victims, but often these same records are not available to the general public.

In the 1949 case of *Williams v. New York* (337 U.S. 241), the U.S. Supreme Court upheld the confidentiality of the PSI. This is largely due to the perception of the Court that the presentence investigator is a neutral and detached party with no real vested interest in the punishment of the offender. Indeed, the probation officer was considered to be a helping professional rather than one in league with prosecutorial efforts. Nevertheless, many states do allow defendants to view their PSI and have even passed regulations requiring that defendants be given the chance to review their PSI and to refute its contents before the sentence phase begins.

In the federal probation system, the contents of the PSI are disclosed to the defendant, the defendant's legal counsel, and the prosecuting attorney. Likewise, since the passage of the 1984 Sentencing Reform Act, the content of the PSI has determined the parameters of sentencing. This means that the central nature of the PSI to the sentencing process has become a source of scrutiny by defendants since it is important to the future sentence and since it serves as the basis for participation in specific programs offered within a prison system or community supervision agency. In many cases, the PSI serves as the basis of classification within both institutional and community-based systems, and this is especially true in the federal system.

Thus, the PSI is a significant document for the offender, and its content must be closely guarded to ensure accuracy. From an assessment standpoint, this is an important consideration because this critical document is completed by one person (the presentence investigator) and thus allows for a great deal of discretion by that person. Given that this document will follow the offender throughout his or her sentence, it is perhaps one of the most important components of the community supervision process. The accuracy of information is critical to this stage of the community supervision process, and the information

FIGURE 3.1   Presentence Investigation Report in the State of Kansas

**2004 KANSAS SENTENCING GUIDELINES—PRESENTENCE INVESTIGATION REPORT
FACE SHEET**   7.04

Judicial District: _____	**OFFENSES**
County: _____	**NAME OF PRIMARY OFFENSE:**

NAME OF PRIMARY OFFENSE:
_____

K.S.A. No:_____ ☐ Felony ☐ Offgrid
☐ Misd. ☐ Nongrid

☐ Person ☐ Drug ☐ Attempt ☐ Conspiracy
☐ Nonperson ☐ Nondrug ☐ Solicitation

Case No: _____

Name: _____

A/K/A's: _____

D.O.B.: ___/___/___ **S.S.N. #:** _____

Age: _____ **K.B.L. No:** _____

Sex: ☐ Male ☐ Female **Race:** ☐ W ☐ B ☐ A.I. ☐ A

Ethnicity: ☐ Hispanic   ☐ Non-Hispanic

Address: _____
_____
_____

Citizenship: ☐ U.S.   ☐ Citizen of: _____

DETAINER OR OTHER CHARGES PENDING? ☐YES ☐NO

SUBJECT IN CUSTODY AWAITING SENTENCING?
☐ YES ☐ NO

begin _____ end _____

begin _____ end _____

IF OFFENDER WAS UNDER 18 YEARS OF AGE WHEN
CRIME(S) WAS COMMITTED AND WAS TRIED AS AN ADULT,
OFFENDER WAS:

☐ ADJUDICATED AS AN ADULT UNDER KSA 38-I636
☐ AUTOMATICALLY CONSIDERED AN ADULT
   BECAUSE OF A PRIOR FELONY

NAMES OF CO-DEFENDANTS, IF ANY _____
_____

NAME OF DEFENSE ATTORNEY: _____
_____

TYPE OF COUNSEL PRIOR TO SENTENCING:
☐ RETAINED ☐ APPOINTED ☐ SELF ☐ OTHER

NAME OF PROSECUTING ATTORNEY: _____
_____

NAME OF SENTENCING JUDGE: _____

DATE OF GUILTY PLEA
OR JUDGMENT: ___/___/___

DATE OF SENTENCING: ___/___/___

NAME OF PRESENTENCE INVESTIGATOR:
_____

DATE ASSIGNED   ___/___/___

DATE SUBMITTED: ___/___/___

Severity Level: ___   **Criminal History Score:** ___

Sentencing Range:

Standard   _____   ☐ Presumptive Prison
Aggravated _____   ☐ Presumptive Probation
Mitigated _____   ☐ Border Box
            ☐ Special Rule Applicable (see p. 4)

☐ Mandatory Drug Treatment ("SB 123")
☐ Drug Treatment with Court finding
☐ Not eligible for Drug Treatment due to criminal history

Postrelease Supervision Duration: ☐ 12 months ☐ 24 months
☐ 36 months ☐ 60 months ☐ No Postrelease - per K.S.A.
                                              22-3716 (e)

Probation Duration: ☐ 12 months   ☐ 18 months
☐ 24 months   ☐ 36 months   ☐ Other

NAME OF ADDITIONAL OFFENSE:
_____

K.S A. No: _____ ☐ Felony ☐ Offgrid
☐ Misd. ☐ Nongrid

☐ Person ☐ Drug ☐ Attempt ☐ Conspiracy
☐ Nonperson ☐ Nondrug ☐ Solicitation

Severity Level: _____ **Criminal History Score:** _____

Sentencing Range:

Standard   _____   ☐ Presumptive Prison
Aggravated _____   ☐ Presumptive Probation
Mitigated _____   ☐ Border Box
            ☐ Special Rule Applicable (see p. 4)

☐ Mandatory Drug Treatment ("SB 123")
☐ Drug Treatment with Court finding
☐ Not eligible for Drug Treatment due to criminal history

Postrelease Supervision Duration: ☐ 12 months ☐ 24 months
☐ 36 months ☐ 60 months ☐ No Postrelease - per K.S.A. 22-3716 (e)

Probation Duration: ☐ 12 months   ☐ 18 months
☐ 24 months   ☐ 36 months   ☐ Other _____

**KSG Desk Reference Manual 2004
Appendix D Page 1**

(Continued)

FIGURE 3.1 (Continued)

2004 KANSAS SENTENCING GUIDELINES—PRESENTENCE INVESTIGATION REPORT
FACE SHEET SUPPLEMENTAL PAGE

NAME OF ADDITIONAL OFFENSE:

K.S.A. No: _____ ☐ Felony   ☐ Offgrid
                                ☐ Misd.   ☐ Nongrid

☐ Person   ☐ Drug   ☐ Attempt   ☐ Conspiracy
☐ Nonperson   ☐ Nondrug   ☐ Solicitation

Severity Level: _____ **Criminal History Score:** ___

Sentencing Range:

Standard   _____   ☐ Presumptive Prison
Aggravated _____   ☐ Presumptive Probation
Mitigated   _____   ☐ Border Box

              ☐ Special Rule Applicable (see p. 4)

☐ Mandatory Drug Treatment ("SB 123")
☐ Drug Treatment with Court finding
☐ Not eligible for Drug Treatment due to criminal history

Postrelease Supervision Duration: ☐ 12 months ☐ 24 months
☐ 36 months ☐ 60 months ☐ No Postrelease - per K.S.A.
                                              22-3716 (e)

Probation Duration: ☐ 12 months   ☐ 18 months
☐ 24 months   ☐ 36 months   ☐ Other

NAME OF ADDITIONAL OFFENSE:

K.S.A. No: _____ ☐ Felony   ☐ Nongrid
                                ☐ Misd.   ☐ Offgrid

☐ Person   ☐ Drug   ☐ Attempt   ☐ Conspiracy
☐ Nonperson   ☐ Nondrug   ☐ Solicitation

Severity Level: _____ **Criminal History Score:** ___

Sentencing Range:

Standard   _____   ☐ Presumptive Prison
Aggravated _____   ☐ Presumptive Probation
Mitigated   _____   ☐ Border Box

              ☐ Special Rule Applicable (see p. 4)

☐ Mandatory Drug Treatment ("SB 123")
☐ Drug Treatment with Court finding
☐ Not eligible for Drug Treatment due to criminal history

Postrelease Supervision Duration: ☐ 12 months ☐ 24 months
☐ 36 months ☐ 60 months ☐ No Postrelease - per K.S.A. 22-3716 (e)

Probation Duration: ☐ 12 months   ☐ 18 months
☐ 24 months   ☐ 36 months   ☐ Other

NAME OF ADDITIONAL OFFENSE:

K.S A. No: _____ ☐ Felony   ☐ Nongrid
                                 ☐ Misd.   ☐ Offgrid

☐ Person   ☐ Drug   ☐ Attempt   ☐ Conspiracy
☐ Nonperson   ☐ Nondrug   ☐ Solicitation

Severity Level: ____ **Criminal History Score:** ____

Sentencing Range:

Standard   _____   ☐ Presumptive Prison
Aggravated _____   ☐ Presumptive Probation
Mitigated   _____   ☐ Border Box

              ☐ Special Rule Applicable (see p. 4)

☐ Mandatory Drug Treatment ("SB 123")
☐ Drug Treatment with Court finding
☐ Not eligible for Drug Treatment due to criminal history

Postrelease Supervision Duration: ☐ 12 months ☐ 24 months
☐ 36 months ☐ 60 months ☐ No Postrelease - per K.S.A. 22-3716 (e)

Probation Duration: ☐ 12 months   ☐ 18 months
☐ 24 months   ☐ 36 months   ☐ Other _____

NAME OF ADDITIONAL OFFENSE:

K.S A. No: _____ ☐ Felony   ☐ Nongrid
                                ☐ Misd.   ☐ Offgrid

☐ Person   ☐ Drug   ☐ Attempt   ☐ Conspiracy
☐ Nonperson   ☐ Nondrug   ☐ Solicitation

Severity Level: ____ **Criminal History Score:** ____

Sentencing Range:

Standard   _____   ☐ Presumptive Prison
Aggravated _____   ☐ Presumptive Probation
Mitigated   _____   ☐ Border Box

              ☐ Special Rule Applicable (see p. 4)

☐ Mandatory Drug Treatment ("SB 123")
☐ Drug Treatment with Court finding
☐ Not eligible for Drug Treatment due to criminal history

Postrelease Supervision Duration: ☐ 12 months ☐ 24 months
☐ 36 months ☐ 60 months ☐ No Postrelease - per K.S.A. 22-3716 (e)

Probation Duration: ☐ 12 months   ☐ 18 months
☐ 24 months   ☐ 36 months   ☐ Other _____

KSG Desk Reference Manual 2004
Appendix D Page 2

KANSAS SENTENCING GUIDELINES—PRESENTENCE INVESTIGATION REPORT
CURRENT OFFENSE INFORMATION

OFFICIAL VERSION:

DEFENDANT'S VERSION:

VICTIM'S INJURY / DAMAGE / STATEMENT(S):

TOTAL RESTITUTION _____

OWED TO   Name: _____
                Address: _____
                _____

                Amount: _____

                Name: _____
                Address: _____
                _____

                Amount: _____

                Name: _____
                Address: _____
                _____

                Amount: _____

                Name: _____
                Address: _____
                _____

                Amount: _____

                Name: _____
                Address: _____
                _____

                Amount: _____

STATEMENT(S):

(Continued)

FIGURE 3.1 (Continued)

RECOMMENDED PLACEMENT: [The following is <u>not</u> a recommendation regarding the appropriate disposition to be imposed in this case, but is provided as the court services or community corrections officer's professional assessment if the court places the offender on probation or orders some form of community sanction.]

_____ COMMUNITY CORRECTIONS   [Indicate the criteria from K.S.A. 75-5291(a)(2) met by this defendant qualifying him/her for placement in Community Corrections.]

_____ COURT SERVICES

☐ Mandatory Drug Treatment ("SB 123")
☐ (a)(2)(A) Listed grid box (Border box, level 6 H or I, level 7 C-I)

_____ DEPARTMENT OF CORRECTIONS

☐ (a)(2)(B) Downward dispositional departure (presumptive prison)
☐ (a)(2)(C) Seventy level 7 or higher sex offender
☐ (a)(2)(D) Condition violator
☐ (a)(2)(E) Scored "high risk or needs, or both"
☐ (a)(2)(F) Follows successful completion of a conservation camp program

OFFICER'S ASSESSMENT OF CONDITIONS OF PROBATION:

K.S.A. 21-4610 and;   [Check All That Apply]

☐ (Alcohol) (Drug) (Mental Health) evaluation (follow recommendations)
☐ (In) (Out) Patient (Alcohol) (Drug) (Mental Health) treatment (Follow recommendations of counselor)
☐ (AA) (NA) Attendance
☐ No possession or consumption of alcohol or illegal drugs
☐ Submit to random (Breath) (Blood) (Urinalysis) testing at request of C.S.O. at defendant's own expense
☐ Community Service Work [_____ Hours]
☐ (Gain) (Maintain) employment
☐ Notify the C.S.O. of changes in employment, residence and phone number
☐ No contact with (victim) (co-defendant)
☐ Educational program - (G.E.D.) (Vocational) (Higher Education)
☐ Curfew Restriction: _____
☐ Travel Restriction: _____
☐ OTHER _____
☐ OTHER _____
☐ OTHER _____
☐ OTHER _____
☐ OTHER _____

PLEASE CHECK ANY SPECIAL SENTENCING RULES APPLICABLE TO THIS CASE:

☐ Person Felony Committed with a Firearm – K.S.A 21-4704 (h) (Shall be presumed imprisonment)
☐ Aggravated Battery on an L.E.O. – K.S.A. 21-4704 (g) (Shall be presumed imprisonment) (6-H or 6-I)
☐ Aggravated Assault on an L.E.O. – K.S.A. 21-4704 (g) (Shall be presumed imprisonment) (6-H or 6-I)
☐ Crime Committed for Benefit of Criminal Street Gang – K.S.A. 21-1704 (k) (Shall be presumed imprisonment)
☐ Persistent Sex Offender – K.S.A. 21-4704 (j) (Shall be presumed imprisonment)
☐ Felony DUI (third) – K.S.A 21-4704 (i)
☐ Felony DUI (fourth or subsequent) – K.S.A. S-1567 (g)
☐ Felony Criminal Deprivation of Property / Motor Vehicle [Crime committed prior to July 1, 1999.] – K.S.A. 21-3705 (b)
☐ Felony Domestic Battery – K.S.A. 21-3412a (b)(3)
☐ Crime Committed While Incarcerated and Serving a Felony Sentence, or While on Probation, Parole, Conditional Release or Postrelease Supervision for a Felony – K.S.A. 21-4603d (f) (New sentence shall be consecutive – K.S.A. 21-4608
☐ Crime Committed While on Felony Bond – K.S.A. 21-4603d (f) (Crime committed on or after 7/1/99 may sentence to prison even if presumptive probation)
☐ Kansas Securities Act – K.S.A. 17-1267
☐ Extended Jurisdiction Juvenile Imposed – K.S.A. 38-1636
☐ Second or Subsequent Manufacture of a Controlled Substance Conviction – K.S.A. 21-4705 (e)
☐ Residential Burglary After a Prior Residential or Nonresidential or Agg. Burglary Conviction – K.S.A. 21-4704 (1) (Shall be presumed imprisonment)
☐ Second Forgery – K.S.A. 21-3710 (b)(3)
☐ Third or Subsequent Forgery – K.S.A. 21-3710 (b)(4)
☐ Mandatory Drug Treatment – K.S.A. 21-4729 (SB 123)
☐ Other _____

KSG Desk Reference Manual 2004
Appendix D Page 4

SOURCE: Kansas Sentencing Commission. (2004). _Kansas sentencing guidelines: Presentence investigation report._ Topeka, KS: Author. Retrieved from http://www.kspace.org/bitstream/1984/69/7/Appendix_D_2004_PSI_Form.pdf.

contained must pass the scrutiny of both the prosecution and the defense. Otherwise, this means of assessment/classification is greatly compromised. This point is illustrated in Section 32.1, subsections b through f of the U.S. Courts Sentencing Guidelines, which read as follows:

Presentence Investigation Report. The probation office shall prepare a presentence investigation report in every case unless the court finds that sufficient information exists in the record to enable the meaningful exercise of its sentencing authority pursuant to 18 U.S.C. § 3553. The probation office, during the presentence investigation, shall provide notice and a reasonable opportunity to defendant's counsel to attend any interview of the defendant.

Written Version of Facts. No later than fourteen (14) days following a plea or verdict of guilty, the government shall provide the probation office with a written version of the facts of the case, including all relevant conduct. The government shall provide, at a minimum, the probation office with the same discovery materials it provided to the defendant. The prosecutor assigned to the case and the primary case agent shall make themselves reasonably available to the probation office to answer any inquiries.

Disclosure of Presentence Investigation Report. No later than thirty-five (35) days prior to the scheduled sentencing date, the probation officer shall disclose the initial presentence investigation report to the parties. One copy shall be given to counsel for the government. Two copies shall be given to defense counsel, who shall give one copy to the defendant for review. Defense counsel shall ensure that the defendant has timely reviewed and understands the presentence report.

Objections to Presentence Investigation Report. No later than fourteen (14) days after receiving the initial presentence report, counsel for the government and counsel for the defendant shall deliver to the probation officer, and to each other, written objections of fact or guideline application to the initial presentence report. If counsel has no objections, counsel shall so notify the probation officer in writing. Delivery of said objections shall be made by mail, in person, or by facsimile transmission. A party waives any objection to the presentence report by failing to comply with this rule unless the court determines that the basis for the objection was not reasonably available prior to the deadline.

Revised Presentence Investigation Report and Addendum. If either party objects to the presentence report, the probation officer shall conduct such further inquiry as is necessary to attempt to resolve the objections raised.

This is an important point of discussion in relation to the PSI. Aside from the fact that the PSI will contain various information that is related to the supervision and treatment of the offender, the accuracy of the information is sometimes questionable and can actually impair the treatment outcomes of offenders. This is the primary concern in noting the use of the PSI. As will be seen in a later section of this chapter, other departments (e.g., in Travis County, Texas) have noted inefficiency in their presentence investigation process and have had to streamline and revamp their systems. Likewise, it will be seen in Chapter 4 that the completion of the PSI is a large part of the community supervision officer's job design, and the excessive paperwork associated with the PSI and other documentation serves as a primary source of stress for community supervision officers. Thus, given the extensive detail required for these reports and given the heavy caseload burden that many community supervision officers face, it is no surprise that information may not always be accurate and that these inaccuracies lead to poor assessments, supervision schemes, and treatment outcomes. Being that judges tend to rely on the recommendation of PSI investigators when determining their sentence, it is clear that the PSI is a critical aspect of the community supervision process from both a reintegration and a public safety perspective. More will be discussed regarding the PSI process later in this and other chapters. However, students should consider the following two example scenarios, presented by Michael Santos (2000):

Example One: Alfredo

Alfredo, an offender who was convicted of conspiracy to distribute cocaine, played a minor role in his offense. He allowed others to use his telephone to facilitate their drug transactions. Alfredo was not privy to the quantity of drugs being sold, nor to the number of transactions that took place over his telephone line. Yet the PSI report indicated over 20 kilograms of cocaine were sold and that all conspirators, including Alfredo, were equally culpable.

The sentencing judge, who had listened to all the testimony at trial, however, knew that Alfredo was a minor player in the conspiracy. He found Alfredo less culpable than the others and gave him a downward departure from the sentencing guidelines because of his minor role. The PSI, however, was never amended. As a result, in using the PSI as its reference point, the BOP classifies Alfredo as a serious offender and refuses him camp placement. Alfredo has tried to have his PSI amended several times during his confinement, but the judge has ruled the matter moot because Alfredo received the downward departure at sentencing.

This was Alfredo's first experience in the criminal justice system. He did not appreciate the significance of his PSI at sentencing and relied on his public defender to represent him in all matters. The public defender was successful in persuading the judge that the PSI inaccurately portrayed Alfredo as an equal participant in the conspiracy, but made no attempt to change the PSI itself. Accordingly, Alfredo was sentenced appropriately, but he serves his sentence in more severe conditions than other similarly situated offenders because his PSI remains inaccurate.

Alfredo has made efforts to show his case manager the sentencing transcripts where the judge clearly ruled that Alfredo was less culpable than the others and sentenced him accordingly. Such evidence is irrelevant to the BOP, however, as the PSI governs all classification decisions. Consequently, Alfredo serves his sentence in a higher-security facility and he may be denied access to half-way house placement toward the conclusion of his term.

Example Two: Rich

Rich pled guilty to an indictment charging several defendants with organized crime involving extortion and murder. Rich's role, however, was minor and he was sentenced to serve approximately five years as a result of his conviction; other codefendants who were charged on Rich's same indictment received sentences of life imprisonment.

Rich's probation officer conducted the presentence investigation for all defendants on the indictment. When Rich appeared for his interview, he was accompanied by his defense counsel. The defense counsel heard everything said during Rich's interview, and Rich was cooperative throughout the proceeding. When the report was completed and given to Rich and his attorney for review, however, it was clear that the probation officer had confused some of Rich's codefendants' recalcitrant statements and inappropriately applied them to him. The PSI indicated that Rich was involved in murders, domestic abuse, and drug sales. In fact, none of this information applied to Rich.

At the sentencing hearing, Rich's attorney succeeded in showing the clear error in the PSI. He ordered the PSI to be amended, and it was changed. Rich was sentenced appropriately.

When Rich reported to prison, however, he learned that his case manager was using the original, erroneously prepared PSI. Consequently, the case manager told Rich that he would never be eligible for camp placement and that he may not be eligible for halfway house placement either.

Rich contacted his attorney, who then initiated legal action to force the BOP to use the corrected version of the PSI. The court has thus far refused to grant the order, though, stating that such issues should have been resolved at the sentencing hearing. And as a result of Rich's attorney's error, he continues to serve his sentence under the misclassification wrought by an inaccurate PSI.

Though these are just two examples, many others abound. Further, such instances are even more likely to occur within state and county systems where community supervision caseloads are even higher and where turnover among staff is higher as well. Aside from understanding the basic information that is contained in a PSI, the fact that community supervision officers collect the information in the PSI, and the basic use of that information, the single most important factor for students to understand in regard to the PSI is that it is only as good as the investigator allows it to be.

THE BASICS OF RISK ASSESSMENT

Before we can begin a discussion on specific instruments and inventories, it is important that the student understand the underlying presumptions behind risk prediction. In any type of risk assessment, there are some common principles that tend to run consistently throughout. If these basic statistical considerations or methodological processes are not honored during the construction of an instrument, the instrument is likely to be flawed and will therefore be less accurate in prediction. This places the public at risk and also improperly classifies offenders, even when they are not in a position to be dangerous to the public. James Austin (2006) provides six basic suggestions for correctional officials who wish to know whether their instruments are effective. Most of Austin's comments center on the methodology that is utilized in constructing and testing the instrument, thereby relating to the validity and reliability of that given instrument. Austin provides a very good, hard-hitting description.

1. *Risk Assessment Instruments Must Be Tested on Your Correctional Population and Separately Normed for Males and Females.*
   Austin (2006) notes that when assessment tools are tested on the offender populations in one area of the nation, they may not be as relevant to offenders in another area. For example, take the state of Florida as compared with the state of Iowa. Is it likely that the correctional populations are similar? These issues should be considered, and agencies should use instruments that are essentially normed for, or tailored to the characteristics of, their own offender populations. As Austin notes, "in research terms this issue has to do with the 'external validity' of the instrument and the ability to generalize the findings of a single study of the instrument to other jurisdictions" (p. 1). Thus, if an instrument is normed for an offender population that is different from the one being examined, it is likely that the assessment will not be accurate.

   Further, male and female offenders are not the same. The issues leading to female offenders' criminality, the types of crimes committed, and their prognosis for treatment all tend to be different from male offenders. Thus, risk assessments for both types of offenders should also be different, yet in many cases they are not. At the very least, assessment tools must give appropriate weight to gender differences among offenders. Austin (2006) notes that "recidivism and career criminal studies consistently show that females are less involved in criminal behavior, are less likely to commit violent crimes, and are less likely to recidivate after being placed on probation or parole" (p. 1).

2. *An Inter-rater Reliability Test Must Be Conducted.*
   Austin (2006) contends that both an inter-rater reliability test and a validity test must be completed by independent researchers who have no monetary or political incentive in regard to the testing outcome. Though these terms may be alien to many undergraduate students of criminal justice (particularly if a student has not had a class in research methods), they are important to understand. As applied to our current discussion, inter-rater reliability has to do with the consistency of the results that are obtained from an instrument. It should consistently yield the same outcomes regardless of the person who is using the instrument, presuming that each person administering the assessment is competent in administering it.

3. *A Validity Test Must Be Conducted.*
   Likewise, instruments must be valid. Validity simply ensures that the instrument is actually measuring what researchers believe it is measuring. In some cases, instruments can provide measures that correlate with a

given issue, but the cause of that correlation may be due to some unknown factor. With respect to our current discussion, it is important that instruments actually measure recidivism (or perhaps reintegration, depending on our intent) rather than some other unknown variable. Consider that states' economic conditions may be stable or changing. Good economic conditions are associated with less offending. If an instrument in this area predicts less likelihood of recidivism among that area's offender population, how do we know whether this is due to actual characteristics of the offender or to transient economic conditions that could change a year after the offender is released? This issue must be addressed appropriately for accurate assessment.

4. *The Instruments Must Allow for Dynamic and Static Factors That Have Been Well Accepted and Tested in a Number of Jurisdictions.*

   The use of dynamic and static risk factors will be discussed in depth in a subsection that follows. Examples of dynamic risk factors include characteristics such as age, marital status, and custody level. These characteristics can and do change over time. Static risk factors include characteristics such as age at first arrest, crime seriousness, and prior convictions. Once established, these characteristics do not fluctuate over time.

5. *The Instruments Must Be Compatible With the Skill Level of Your Staff.*

   As noted in suggestion number 2 above, the accuracy of the assessment is also dependent on the skill of the person administering the assessment. Often, agencies use simple risk-assessment tools because these are easy for their staff to understand and administer with little need for extensive training. While on paper this may seem to be effective, and while it may appear that agency staff are using objective criteria effectively, they are often not trained to utilize more sophisticated instruments that have better levels of reliability and validity. Thus, instruments tend to be poor or, if the agency does utilize well-developed instruments, the staff may be poorly trained in their administration. Thus, even effective instruments can produce ineffective or inaccurate results. In addition, staff must have experience administering these instruments. Training alone is not sufficient, as there is no replacement for the self-assurance that comes with repetition.

6. *The Risk Assessment Must Have "Face Validity" and Transparency With Staff, Prisoners, Probationers, Parolees, and Policy Makers.*

   The instrument and the process of assessment must be understood and recognized as credible by all persons in the agency. Instruments that are only understood by "eggheads" and academics will never go over well with most practitioners. Further, if the instrument is perceived as being too "bookish" in nature and not applicable to the realities of the "street," so to speak, both practitioners and offenders will see the instrument as artificial and sterile, and not really able to probe the true reality of what an offender may (or may not) do. This can also be exacerbated by the presence of false positives (falsely predicting recidivism when it would not have occurred) or false negatives (failing to predict recidivism when it does later occur). False positives and false negatives will be discussed in more detail later in this chapter, but for now, the student should understand that a lack of "face validity" means that the instrument is not recognized as valid on its face, or at initial glance, by those who judge its ability to truly discern a set of characteristics. In this case, if the instrument appears to ask bogus questions or if the questions are asked in a naive manner, it will not be perceived as credible by practitioners and offenders alike.

FALSE POSITIVES AND FALSE NEGATIVES

Agency administrators tend to assume that their instruments are, in fact, valid and reliable and that their staff are able to effectively use these instruments. To some extent, these administrators are forced to operate under these assumptions, as alternatives may be unavailable or unacceptable. Further, these administrators operate under these assumptions when making release decisions. However, as has just been discussed, when instruments are not normed appropriately, do not possess appropriate degrees of external validity, or lack other forms of appropriate methodological rigor in their manufacture, they tend to generate either underpredictions of future criminality or overpredictions of the same. Moreover, individuals using their own subjective opinions will also tend to over- or underpredict criminality. These forms of error are important to understand, and it is in this manner that a false negative or false positive may be generated. The chronic occurrence of these two mistakes in risk prediction can lead to tragic consequences for society or costly expenditures for correctional agencies.

When decision makers are making release decisions for offenders, they will ultimately have to decide if the offender will be allowed out into the community or remain behind bars. There are some implications to these decisions that may not be readily apparent to the casual observer, and these implications, as well as the official professional terms associated with them, should be understood by the student.

First, when correctional decision makers predict that an inmate is not likely to reoffend (and is thus a good risk for community supervision), this is called a *prediction in the negative*. If in fact the offender is released on community supervision and does not commit any future offense, this is referred to as a *true negative*. This is because the prediction turns out to be true. Thus, the **true negative** implies that the offender is predicted to not reoffend and the prediction turns out to be true (see Table 3.1 for added clarity). However, if the agency personnel predict that an offender is likewise not likely to offend, but upon community supervision the offender commits some form of crime, this is referred to as a *false negative*. This is because the agency made the prediction in the negative (meaning it thought the offender would not reoffend), yet it turned out the prediction was false or incorrect. Thus, the **false negative** implies that the offender is predicted to not reoffend but the prediction turns out to be false.

On the other hand, if an offender is predicted to reoffend, this is referred to as a *prediction in the positive*. If the offender is predicted to reoffend but is allowed on community supervision due to the effectiveness of his legal representation or some other odd course of events, and he or she then later does in fact commit an offense, this is called a *true positive*. The **true positive** implies that the offender is predicted to reoffend, and this prediction later turns out to be true. However, if an offender is likewise predicted to be likely to commit a crime, but later the offender somehow is released into community supervision and is found to never reoffend, this would be a **false positive**. The prediction was in the positive, indicating risk of reoffending, yet it turned out to be false and thus not accurate.

Naturally, the true positives and true negatives are what agencies hope to obtain as often as possible. These are perfect predictions of offender behavior. However, things not being perfect, the false positive and false negative predictions are inevitable at some point. Because of this, there are a couple of key points that should be mentioned. First off, false positives are a "safe bet" for correctional prediction boards because if the offender is locked up, the offender simply cannot commit any further crimes in society. From this perspective, it is prudent to simply incarcerate as many offenders as possible (indeed, all of them, optimally speaking) to ensure public safety. However, this would be very costly and can result in excessive expenditures on prison systems that have inmates who are neither dangerous nor likely to repeat their criminal behavior. This also can essentially "create" recidivism, as those who would normally refrain from further criminality

TABLE 3.1	True/False Positives and Negatives in Offender Prediction	
	Offender Offends	*Offender Does **Not** Offend*
True Prediction	**True Positive**	**True Negative**
False Prediction	**False Positive**	**False Negative**

are placed in an environment where they can learn from and become socialized by other inmates, thereby increasing their incentive to reoffend in the future (students will recall this point made earlier in Chapter 1). Thus, overpredicting offender likelihood of recidivating is not a prudent long-term strategy and results in further overcrowding of prisons and ever more costs to taxpayers. By the same token, false negatives result in dangers to public safety and also damage the public perception of community corrections. Ironically, it is often due to the fear of committing a false negative that some correctional agencies may decide to deliberately make more false positives. No criminal justice professional wants to see people in the community get hurt because they commit a false negative, and no agency wants its credibility at risk due to incorrect predictions. Thus, agencies find themselves in a dilemma between the risk of making a false negative and the short-term safety of a false positive.

STATIC AND DYNAMIC RISK FACTORS

Not all risk factors are the same. Indeed, some risk factors are fairly permanent, or at least they occur due to no fault of the offender. Other risk factors, on the other hand, are solely due to the offender. Further, some risk factors are more suited for security, custody, and control of the offender, whereas others are more designed for treatment. Factors such as age at first conviction, gender, sex, and even disabilities or mental impairments are not caused by the offender and are also unlikely to change. These permanent factors are often referred to as *static risk factors*. Thus, **static risk factors** are characteristics that are inherent to the offender and are usually permanent in nature (Van Voorhis, Braswell, & Lester, 2000). These characteristics are often the best basis for security determinations. Opposite of the static risk factors are the *dynamic risk factors*. **Dynamic risk factors** are those characteristics that can change and are more or less influenced or controlled by the offender, such as employment, motivation, drug use, and family relations (Van Voorhis et al., 2000). These characteristics are often most useful to treatment providers but are not really a sound basis for security determinations because they have the possibility of changing when certain stimuli are presented in the offender's life. Figure 3.2, Risk Assessment Form for Juvenile Sex Offenders, provides an example of a risk assessment form that incorporates both static and dynamic scales for juvenile sex offenders. The student should note the specific subscales and the separate scoring sections for static and dynamic scores when examining this insert.

THE APPROPRIATE USE OF SUBJECTIVE AND OBJECTIVE ASSESSMENTS

If the offender is accurately assessed, then only those offenders who are a risk to public safety will be incarcerated. Indeed, those offenders who are a low risk for recidivism, or even those who are a high risk but are most likely to commit nuisance or nonviolent crimes, should not be placed in prison. This is because such forms of custody are very expensive and are designed mainly to prevent the offender from hurting others in society. Despite the common notion that the loss of liberty (the punishment) is the basis for the prison, such a punishment can in fact be fulfilled as well through house arrest or some other form of secure supervision that does not require the expense incurred by prison. Whether the offender is kept within the strict confines of his or her bedroom or the strict confines of a prison cell is not the main concern since both sufficiently restrict liberty. The only difference is that if the offender decides to violate the sentence and leave the confines of his or her bedroom, there is no one immediately there to prevent it, whereas in prison such an option is unlikely due to physical facility construction and the immediate reaction of prison staff who are available to respond with haste. Thus, it is the offender's likelihood to comply with the mandate of the sentence, not the actual restriction of liberty, that should be the criterion for deciding whether to

FIGURE 3.2   Risk Assessment Form for Juvenile Sex Offenders

Juvenile Sex Offender Assessment Protocol-II Scoring Form

Scoring Code: 0 = Stable; 1= Moderate; 2 = Severe

Sexual Drive/Preoccupation Scale

1.	Prior Legally Charged Sex Offenses	0	1	2
2.	Number of Sexual Abuse Victims	0	1	2
3.	Male Child Victim	0	1	2
4.	Duration of Sex Offense History	0	1	2
5.	Degree of Planning in Sexual Offense(s)	0	1	2
6.	Sexualized Aggression	0	1	2
7.	Sexual Drive and Preoccupation	0	1	2
8.	Sexual Victimization History	0	1	2

Sexual Drive/Preoccupation Scale Total: _____

Impulsive/Antisocial Behavior Scale

9.	Caregiver Consistency	0	1	2
10.	Pervasive Anger	0	1	2
11.	School Behavior Problems	0	1	2
12.	History of Conduct Disorder	0	1	2
13.	Juvenile Antisocial Behavior	0	1	2
14.	Ever Charged or Arrested Before Age 16	0	1	2
15.	Multiple Types of Offenses	0	1	2
16.	History of Physical Assault and/or Exposure to Family Violence	0	1	2

Antisocial Behavior Scale Total: _____

Intervention Scale

17.	Accepting Responsibility for Offense(s)	0	1	2
18.	Internal Motivation for Change	0	1	2
19.	Understands Risk Factors	0	1	2
20.	Empathy	0	1	2
21.	Remorse and Guilt	0	1	2
22.	Cognitive Distortions	0	1	2
23.	Quality of Peer Relationships	0	1	2

Intervention Scale Total: _____

Community Stability/Adjustment Scale

24.	Management of Sexual Urges and Desire	0	1	2
25.	Management of Anger	0	1	2

(Continued)

FIGURE 3.2   (Continued)

26. Stability of Current Living Situation	0	1	2
27. Stability in School	0	1	2
28. Evidence of Positive Support Systems	0	1	2

Community Stability Scale Total: _____

Juvenile Sex Offender Assessment Protocol-II Summary Form

Static/Historical Scales

1. Sexual Drive/Preoccupation Scale Score:
    (Add Items 1–8 [range: 0–16]) _____/16 = _____

2. Impulsive-Antisocial Behavior Scale Score:
    (Add Items 9–16 [range: 0–16]) _____/16 = _____

Dynamic Scales

3. Intervention Scale Score:
    (Add Items 17–23 [range: 0–14]) _____/14 = _____

4. Community Stability Scale Score:
    (Add Items 24–28 [range: 0–10]) _____/10 = _____

Static Score

(Add items 1–16) _____/32 = _____

Dynamic Score

(Add items 17–28) _____/24 = _____

Total J-SOAP Score

(Add items 1–28) _____/56 = _____

SOURCE: This assessment form was adapted from the following U.S. Government publication: Prentky, R., & Righthand, S. (2003). *Juvenile Sex Offender Assessment Protocol-II (J-SOAP-II) Manual*. Washington, DC: Office of Juvenile Delinquency and Prevention. Retrieved from http://nicic.org/Library/019361.

incur the added expense of a prison cell. Otherwise, financial resources are wasted and squandered unnecessarily on an offender that could have been just as severely punished for wrongdoings at a fraction of the cost.

It should be noted that assessment is also critical because those offenders who have a high risk of committing violent crimes should not be placed on community supervision. This nonetheless occurs due to jail and prison overcrowding, which then places institutions in the precarious position of choosing the "least dangerous" of the violent offenders when releasing to the public. This is a very risky position that no administrator relishes, and this is also the most common source of criticism leveled at community release programs. Ideally, these violent offenders should simply not be in the community at all. But given the reality of corrections in our society, such offenders should be given supervision that ensures they are under the constant watchful eye of a human supervisory authority so that immediate interventions can be provided just as if they were still within the prison facility itself. Regardless of the correctional system's situation, it is a strong recommendation of this text that *all security-level determinations be based solely on objective assessment instruments and that subjective criteria be avoided when issues of public safety are at stake.* This is prudent for agency and personnel liability purposes, and it provides the most mathematically precise, consistent, and effective means of protecting public safety. On the other hand, *when making determinations regarding treatment progress, the use of subjective criteria from the specific primary treatment provider should be utilized more than any other form of assessment.* These subjective criteria should consist of feedback from both the clinical and the security staff that have had substantial "face time" with the offender. It is important that the student understand the distinctions between the two types of assessment and the appropriate times for their use. These two types of assessment will be discussed at length in the following subsections of this chapter. As the student reads through these subsections, it is important to remember their most appropriate use that was just articulated above. This will prove to be a good guiding principle throughout the remainder of the readings for this chapter.

Thus, offender supervision processes revolve around two key forms of response to the offending population. These two responses are simply the goals of (1) incapacitation and (2) treatment. As defined earlier, **incapacitation** is the process of simply removing the offender from society so that he or she cannot cause further harm to the public. There is no goal beyond this, nor is there any implied retribution or desire to deter other offenders from committing crime. Such goals are too lofty to be pursued with most offenders, and this is especially true with most special needs offenders due to their unique challenges. On the other hand, *treatment* is the process whereby the offender is provided some form of intervention that will help him or her to function within society without resorting to criminal behavior. The student should make one key observation with each of these approaches. Both have the same goal of simply reducing the likelihood of future offending by that specific individual offender. In other words, each of these approaches has the same exact purpose (to prevent the offender from committing future criminal behavior), but each pursues this purpose in a different manner.

Subjective Assessment

One of the wisest investments for any correctional system desiring to ensure public safety is in the arena of assessment. More money and resources in assessment mean that the subsequent stages (diagnostic, recidivism prediction, classification) in the equation will also operate better, resulting in increased public safety as the ultimate answer. One method of assessment, the **subjective assessment process** of interviewing and observation, is an important yet less structured method of determining the security and treatment needs of the offender. This process entails the use of professionals who utilize their sense of judgment and experience to determine the offender's possible dangerousness, treatment needs, likelihood of responding to treatment, and likelihood of escaping. This is an important process that should not be overlooked. However, it should not be the primary form of assessment but should serve as an integral part of a "two-pronged" assessment process.

There are some drawbacks to this process, just as there are with any form of assessment. For one, the process is subjective, which means that the determination is based upon the impressions of an individual. Thus, these assessments are likely to vary from one professional to another. Second, these assessments can be lengthy in nature and will thus not be useful for large facilities that lack numerous well-qualified staff. Third, these forms of assessment require extensive skill from the staff, and they are therefore only as good as the personnel administering them. Such assessment forms can thus be very costly since only highly educated or well-trained staff will be able to utilize them.

To offset the potential capriciousness of a subjective assessment process, it is suggested that the use of a structured form of interview or observation process be utilized in all cases. A **subjective structured interview** is simply a process whereby an interviewer will ask a respondent a set of prearranged and open-ended questions so that the interview seems informal in nature (conversational), yet because of the prearranged questions, a structure evolves throughout the conversation that ensures that certain bits of desired data are gathered from the offender. These forms of interviews are useful since they guide clinicians and other staff who may conduct intakes. Further, the structure of these interviews provides for consistency and uniformity in record keeping, meaning that agencies can ensure similar criteria are considered despite the style and form of the individual interviewer. This provides a certain "baseline" of information against which all offenders are judged. Last, this type of interview ensures that even less-qualified staff can conduct an interview and that it will still contain the information considered critical for agency assessment.

Standardized interviews are designed to collect the same type of information from all the respondents. If it is a structured interview, all offenders are asked the same questions in the same order, and the answers are recorded in an identical manner (Drummond, 1996). In unscheduled interviews, the interviewer sometimes varies the sequence of the questions and the order of the topics, so that the data can be compared and summarized. The following are some of the advantages and disadvantages of the interviewing process, based on Drummond's work.

Advantages:

- Clients can be guided to answer items completely.
- Additional information or understanding can be pursued.
- Nonverbal behavior and cues as well as affective behavior and voice tone and pitch can be observed and noted. Again, this information should be noted only when the nature of the interview allows the clinician to focus on these behaviors as relevant.

Disadvantages:

- Success often depends on the skill of the interviewer to ask the right questions with the right timing and to correctly interpret the observations.
- The communication of some individuals is inhibited, and clients may simply be unwilling to answer certain questions. They will then either refuse to answer, or just provide a response that is a lie.
- The personality of the interviewer can greatly influence the outcome.

Drummond (1996) notes that even though the reliability and the validity of interviewing may be questionable, this is sometimes the only way possible to gather certain types of information. Further, the interviewer can reword questions, add questions, seek clarification of information provided, focus on topics of clinical interest, and so forth. This means that information obtained from such a process will likely be much more relevant to the specific clinical focus, and it also means that helping professionals will have richer information to work with when consulting the client's case file.

Objective Assessment

As noted earlier in this chapter, when making determinations about security levels (especially when community supervision is involved), it is strongly recommended that determinations be based solely on objective assessment instruments. However, there are a variety of specific assessment instruments employed by agencies throughout the United States. These types of objective assessments can range from behavioral checklists that staff complete after a brief period of observation; to paper-and-pencil tests completed by the offender; to assessment formats that characterize the offender's social, demographic, and criminal history (Van Voorhis et al., 2000). Regardless of the type of objective assessment (and some are better than others), it should *always be based upon the response of supervision staff and should never incorporate self-report data from the offender.* Further, input from the victim (for example, in programs that utilize a restorative justice element) should not be considered when making decisions to release to the community. Rather, the determination should be clearly restricted to objective mathematical "risk factor" criteria devoid of all other considerations (e.g., prison or jail overcrowding, desires of the victim, apparent sincerity of the offender, and so forth).

Perhaps one of the best-known risk assessment systems is the **Wisconsin Risk Assessment System.** During the 1970s, the state of Wisconsin sought to develop a risk assessment scale that would assess an offender's likelihood of further unlawful or rule-violating behavior. To achieve this goal, outcome measures were gathered that were based on arrests, misdemeanor convictions, felony convictions, absconding from probation or parole, technical violations, and so forth. After randomly selecting a construction sample, the criminal history and other characteristics of these offenders were entered into a series of statistical analyses to determine the combination of variables that would best predict future behavior of offenders. At the close of this process, 10 specific factors were identified, isolated, and weighted. Many of these same factors appear on most other risk assessment instruments as well.

In addition to these 10 risk factors, this scale includes an administrative policy override. This override consists of an additional factor regarding prior or current assaultive offense history that is weighted in such a manner as to automatically classify an offender as high risk if he or she possesses that factor (Connolly, 2003). These types of overrides are typically policy decisions that are made to classify all offenders with a certain characteristic (such as an assaultive offense history) as high risk, regardless of whether the statistical analysis determines that variable to actually be an indicator of likely recidivism. This is designed to address the consequences associated with that offender's potential criminal behavior rather than the actual likelihood of committing a crime. Thus, if an offender has a stable job with no prior criminal history but he is convicted of a violent sex offense, he may not score high in likelihood of reoffending, but if he were to reoffend, the injury to the community from his crime would be considered too potentially dangerous to place the community at risk (Connolly, 2003).

This form of structured assessment has become the prototype for many probation and parole systems. Staff members use this instrument to score probationers on the predictors contained on the list, and at this point they classify them into high-, medium-, or low-risk categories (Van Voorhis et al., 2000). The items that are included on this list are all statistical predictors of likely failure while on probation. These predictors are all based on previous probation histories among probationers and on the premise that the best predictor of future aggregate probationer behavior is prior aggregate behavior. As a result of tracking probationers over time, this instrument has been able to find those factors that are associated with failure and success while on probation. Some of the factors that are examined include the following:

1. Number of address changes in the last 12 months

2. Percentage of time employed in the last 12 months

3. Alcohol consumption problems

4. Other drug consumption problems

5. Offender attitude

6. Age at first conviction

7. Number of prior periods of probation/parole supervision

8. Number of prior probation/parole revocations

9. Number of prior felony convictions

10. Type of convictions or prior adjudications

An illustration of the Wisconsin Risk Assessment scale, as used in the state of Pennsylvania, is provided in Figure 3.3. This example gives the student a clear view of each of the 10 factors used by the model as well as the administrative override variable. Connolly (2003) notes that even though the Wisconsin Risk Assessment is one of the most commonly used instruments among agencies, there is very little comprehensive research that has been conducted on its predictive accuracy. However, based on the research that does exist, there is considerable reason to question the validity of this assessment instrument. The fact that this scale is so widely used but has not been truly validated may be one reason for many of the prediction error rates that have been found to occur throughout the nation. Unfortunately, textbooks on community corrections often present the Wisconsin Risk Assessment scale but do not go into detail as to its validity as an instrument. This is a serious oversight and should be fully addressed within the field of community corrections.

Connolly (2003) conducted one of the most comprehensive examinations of risk assessment instruments in her dissertation at the University of Texas at Austin. Connolly's examination was of such caliber as to be funded by the United States Department of Justice. In her evaluation of the Wisconsin Risk Assessment scale, she includes research that clearly demonstrates the ineffective nature of this instrument. For example, one study by Harris (1994) examined a sample of adult felons on probation. This study sought to compare the predictive accuracy of the Wisconsin Risk Assessment with the Client Management Classification (CMC) as well as a combination of the two instruments. Overall, Harris found that the Wisconsin Risk Assessment instrument had high prediction error rates, thus demonstrating this instrument's lack of validity. In another study by Yacus (1998), the Wisconsin Risk Assessment scale and the Wisconsin Needs Assessment scale were examined for accuracy in the classification of adult felons in the state of Virginia. This study utilized a sample of 13,011 adult probation and parole offenders that were placed on supervision. Yacus also found high classification error rates for the Wisconsin Risk Assessment. As can be seen in Table 3.2, the results of both studies demonstrate some clear concern for the continued use of this instrument.

When examining Table 3.2, it can be seen that the study by Harris (1994) shows the false positive error rate to be very high (43%), which means the instrument tends to overpredict that offenders will fail on community supervision due to a resulting revocation of their probation or parole status. On the other hand, the Yacus (1998) study examines the likelihood of probation success. In this study, a true positive is generated when an offender is predicted to be successful and turns out to actually be successful in completing his or her probation. Conversely, a true negative for this study occurs when an offender is predicted to fail and does, in fact, fail. From the data in Table 3.2, it can be seen that the Wisconsin Risk Assessment instrument

TABLE 3.2 Predictive Accuracy of Wisconsin Risk Assessment (in Percentage)

Study	False Positive	False Negative	True Positive	True Negative	Error Rate
Harris (1994)	43	3	13	41	54.5
Yacus (1998)	22	12	57	9	34

FIGURE 3.3 Wisconsin Risk Assessment Scale

RISK ASSESSMENT

NAME—LAST, FIRST	PROB. NO. X–	DPO	CL NO.	AO
DATE OF GRANT	EXPIRATION	DATE OF ASSESSMENT	BY	

		SCORE
Number of Address Changes in Last 12 Months: ___ (Prior to the offense)	0 None 2 One 3 Two or more	_____
Percentage of Time Employed in Last 12 Months: __ (Prior to the offense)	0 60% or more 1 40%–59% 2 Under 40% 0 Not applicable	_____
Alcohol Usage Problems: _____ (Prior to the offense)	0 No interference with functioning 2 Occasional abuse: some disruption of functioning 4 Frequent abuse: serious disruption: needs treatment	_____
Other Drug Usage Problems: _____ (Prior to the offense)	0 No interference with functioning 1 Occasional abuse: some disruption of functioning 2 Frequent abuse: serious disruption, needs treatment	_____
Attitude: _____	0 Motivated to change; receptive to assistance 3 Dependent or unwilling to accept responsibility 5 Rationalizes behavior; negative; not motivated to change	_____
Age at First Conviction: _____ (or Juvenile Adjudication)	0 24 or older 2 20–23 4 19 or younger	_____
Number of Prior Periods of Probation/Parole Supervision: _____ (Adult or Juvenile)	0 None 4 One or more	_____
Number of Prior Probation/Parole Revocations: ____ (Adult or Juvenile)	0 None 4 One or more	_____
Number of Prior Felony Convictions: _____ (or Juvenile Adjudications)	0 None 2 One 4 Two or more	_____
Convictions or Juvenile Adjudications for: _____ (Include current offense.)	2 Burglary, theft, auto theft, or robbery	_____
Convictions or Juvenile Adjudications for: _____ (Include current offense.)	3 NSF checks or forgery	_____
	TOTAL	_____

SOURCE: Zhan, X., & La Paz, C. (1990). *The evaluation of the Wisconsin classification system as it applies to the Los Angeles probation population.* Downey, CA: Los Angeles County Probation Department. Retrieved from http://www.nicic.org/pubs/1990/008749.pdf.

overpredicts that offenders will be successful. Each of these studies examines the instrument from an opposing vantage point. One study examines the instrument from the point of predicting that offenders will fail (Harris, 1994), while the other studies the prediction that offenders will succeed (Yacus, 1998). In both cases, the Wisconsin Risk Assessment is found wanting, though of course the results are more significant in the Harris study than in the Yacus study.

Clearly, some serious questions have to be asked in regard to this tool, particularly since its predictive accuracy has not been established. In addition, the overprediction of offending should be considered a serious flaw since this costs needless tax dollars, results in overstuffed prison systems, and is likely to expose offenders to environments that may actually increase the likelihood of reoffending. (As implied in Chapter 1, prison is sometimes equated to an educational camp for career criminals.) One key ingredient to this overprediction may be the use of administrative overrides. The use of these mechanisms creates enhanced likelihoods of false positives regardless of what the statistical analyses may otherwise indicate. This may explain much of the inaccuracy involved with the Wisconsin Risk Assessment and indicates that the system might be improved if such mechanisms were more carefully considered.

Another area of concern regarding the Wisconsin Risk Assessment revolves around problems with inter-rater reliability of the instrument. In brief, inter-rater reliability is simply a research term that describes the likelihood that multiple persons rating an instrument will derive similar ratings of that instrument. For a high inter-rater reliability to occur, a larger number of diverse rating experts must have similar judgments in reference to a given variable (such as the likelihood of an offender to continue using drugs). It is clear from past research that the Wisconsin Risk Assessment does not facilitate strong inter-rater reliability and thus indicates that the subjectivity of the rater can negatively impact the outcomes of the instrument. Indeed, the question related to the offender's attitude leaves a great deal to the discretion of the interviewer (ranging from 0 to 5), and attitude itself is a somewhat subjective concept. In addition, questions related to alcohol and drug usage also leave room for discretion that can be faulty. Different raters may rate the same offender(s) inconsistently, and this will then weaken the instrument's predictability (Connolly, 2003).

Since we have determined that reintegrative treatment is a necessary component of any community corrections strategy to reduce recidivism, it stands to reason that variables associated with reintegration must also be considered in the assessment process. In fact, it is often the case that the specific needs of the offender are intertwined with future recidivism. For example, a female offender that is unable to find suitable employment may resort to prostitution to make ends meet (particularly if she has one or more children to care for). In a similar vein, that same offender may have a drug habit that, when left untreated, can result in further offending to sustain it. Likewise, mentally ill offenders may have medication or treatment needs to aid them in maintaining emotional balance. Without such needs being met, the likelihood of future offending is increased. Therefore, when discussing assessment, an additional distinction must be presented. This distinction rests between the understanding of risk-principled assessment and needs-principled assessment of offenders on community supervision.

With **risk-principled assessment,** the main concern revolves around the protection of society. Within the treatment scheme, the risk-principled assessment system will ensure that hardcore offenders are not in the same treatment regimen as less serious offenders. This may seem to be a topical distinction, but it can be critical to long-term success. For instance, in an anger management program, an offender that has problems with verbal abuse and verbal explosiveness may not benefit from being in an anger management group that has a majority of offenders who are severe domestic batterers. This would be even truer if these assaultive offenders had some form of personality disorder to further interfere with their success. In this case, it is likely that the success of the offender with verbal anger problems might actually be impaired by repeat exposure to these other offenders. These offenders could therefore ruin any positive prognosis for change that the offender might have. In essence, the treatment program could ironically make the offender worse than he was when he started! Though many students may be skeptical, this does in fact frequently happen in many community health service provider agencies. The same could be true in various substance abuse treatment groups and programs, and any other treatment regimen that mixes offenders at various levels of therapeutic recovery.

Further still, research has shown that intensive correctional treatment programs are more successful with high-risk offenders than with low-risk offenders. Thus, it does not pay to place low-risk offenders in programs designed for high-risk offenders, and this could actually lower their likelihood of success due to negative influence from other high-risk members. Therefore, treatment programs should distinguish between risk principles in their assessment and future placement of offender clients. Indeed, according to Van Voorhis et al. (2000), the risk principle notes that low-risk offenders tend to do more poorly as a group on intensive treatment than if they had not been assigned to an intensive correctional intervention. Van Voorhis et al. go on to add that the treatment implications of the risk-principled assessment are as follows:

Identify the high-, medium-, and low-risk offenders.

Direct intensive treatment efforts (not just intensive security and supervision) to high-risk offenders.

Think carefully about intensive treatment interventions for low-risk offenders.

The above three points clearly enunciate the importance of the risk-principled assessment and are specifically relevant to special needs offenders such as domestic batterers, differing types of sexual offenders (adult and juvenile, pedophile and rapist), substance abusers, mentally disordered offenders, and so forth.

Needs-principled assessment, on the other hand, is more concerned with factors specific to the effective treatment and reintegration of the special needs offender. Thus, **needs-principled assessment** deals with the subjective and objective needs of the offender to maximize his or her potential for social reintegration and to reduce the likelihood of future recidivism. Needs-principled assessment takes into account factors such as substance addiction, medical assistance, mental health issues, job development, educational attainment, physical disabilities, and relationships with family or peers. The needs-principled assessment consists mostly of dynamic risk factors, but it will assess offenders based less on whether they possess a certain risk factor and more on the severity of that need or the seriousness of the affliction. For instance, substance abusers whose primary addiction problem revolves around pain relievers may be substantially different from those who abuse to have an elevated mood. Though all are addicts, the type of drug and the type of addiction severity may again warrant differing levels or types of treatment for the offender.

Needs-principled assessment is also multifaceted in nature and goes beyond looking at the main risk characteristic of concern. For instance, a substance-abusing offender may have a wide range of other needs such as the settlement of legal issues, the maintenance of employment, and resolution of family-of-origin conflicts. Each of these issues is not specifically related to the offender's drug addiction but each one, if not properly addressed, can impair the offender's likelihood for further recovery. Rather, the failure to address one of these corollary needs can result in the likelihood of relapse since it is commonly known that drug offenders often resort to drug use during times of stress. Thus, the multifaceted nature of needs-principled assessment involves examining the offender's global likelihood of reintegration.

Many agencies classify their offenders according to their likely risk of recidivating as well as their identified needs. Aside from the desire to improve the likelihood of reintegration, the use of needs assessments also provides a measure to indicate the amount of time and effort that a community supervision officer will spend on a given case in relation to his or her overall caseload. In addition, the use of needs assessments forces qualitative reviews of the offender's progress that go beyond simply determining if he or she has evaded detection for a technical violation or criminal action. The use of needs-based assessments and resulting classification schemes will be discussed further in Chapter 8, Needs-Based Case Management and Case Planning, since needs assessments are directly related to the casework model of community supervision. As noted in prior chapters, the casework model of supervision is the primary orientation of offender supervision that is supported by this text. Figure 3.4, Assessment of Client Needs, is provided as an early view of a commonly used needs-assessment scale. This same figure, along with others, will be provided in more detail in Chapter 8. It is hoped that students will keep the current discussion in mind when they begin their reading of Chapter 8, thereby creating a sense of familiarity and continuity in regard to material that is presented throughout the text.

RECIDIVISM PREDICTION

Recidivism prediction is built on the information derived from the presentence interview. It is at this point that correctional personnel attempt to determine the risk involved with allowing the offender to be placed under community supervision. One key quasi-objective clinical inventory that is used to determine offender suitability is the **Level of Supervision Inventory—Revised (LSI-R).** This inventory was created by Don Andrews and James Bonta, and it has been found to be highly predictive of recidivism among a variety of correctional offender clients (Van Voorhis et al., 2000). The LSI-R is administered by case managers/counselors or mental health professionals. The assessment process includes a semi-structured interview. As with the Wisconsin Risk Assessment System, the LSI-R provides for reassessments of an offender's risk score. Reassessment of risk scores can be useful when assessing program effectiveness as well as facilitating program release decisions. In fact, it was found that the LSI-R predecessor, the LSI, was a better predictor of parolee recidivism than the Wisconsin Risk Assessment System. In a study by O'Keefe, Klebe, and Hromas (1998), it was found that initial classification levels based on the Wisconsin Risk Assessment indicated that 98 percent of offenders scored in the maximum supervision range. Similar to the previously discussed research by Connolly (2003), these researchers concluded that the Wisconsin system is strongly influenced by raters and may lead to overclassification (O'Keefe et al., 1998). With overclassification, a waste of money occurs due to more expensive security measures being used with offenders that do not require such extensive maintenance.

According to Andrews and Bonta (2003), the LSI-R inventory is a quantitative survey of offender attributes and their situations relative to supervision levels and treatment decisions. Designed for offenders age 16 and older, the LSI-R inventory aids in predicting parole outcome, success with offenders in halfway houses and aftercare facilities, and probation recidivism. This inventory consists of 54 items that are based on legal requirements, and it includes relevant factors needed for making decisions about security risk levels and the likelihood of treatment success (Andrews & Bonta, 2003). The LSI-R is designed for probation and parole officers, to assist them with decisions about probation and parole placement, security level classifications, and possible treatment progress.

The LSI-R screening version (LSI-R:SV) consists of eight items selected from the full LSI-R. Like the full version, the LSI-R:SV samples both risk and needs, and the item content reflects four key risk factors: criminal history, criminal attitudes, criminal associates, and antisocial personality pattern (Andrews & Bonta, 2003). In addition, the LSI-R:SV examines other factors such as employment, family,

FIGURE 3.4   Assessment of Client Needs

Pennsylvania Board of Probation
and Parole   **ASSESSMENT OF CLIENT NEEDS**

Client Name	(Last)	(First)	(MI)	Parole No.	SID No.
Release Date	(Month, day, year)	Agent Name		Date	

Select the appropriate answer and enter the associated weight in the score column. Higher numbers indicate more severe problems. Total all scores. If client is to be referred to a community resource or to clinical services, check appropriate referral box.

ACADEMIC/VOCATIONAL SKILLS   **REFERRAL SCORE**

−1 High school or above skill level	0 Adequate skills; able to handle everyday requirements	+2 Low skill level causing minor adjustment problems	+4 Minimal skill level causing serious adjustment problems	☐ _____

EMPLOYMENT

−1 Satisfactory employment for one year or longer	0 Secure employment; no difficulties reported; or homemaker, student or retired	+3 Unsatisfactory employment; or unemployed but has adequate job skills	+6 Unemployed and virtually unemployable; needs training	☐ _____

FINANCIAL MANAGEMENT

−1 Long-standing pattern of self-sufficiency; e.g., good credit rating	0 No current difficulties	+3 Situational or minor difficulties	+5 Severe difficulties; may include garnishment, bad checks or bankruptcy	☐ _____

MARITAL/FAMILY RELATIONSHIPS

−1 Relationships and support exceptionally strong	0 Relatively stable relationships	+3 Some disorganization or stress but potential for improvement	+5 Major disorganization or stress	☐ _____

COMPANIONS

−1 Good support and influence	0 No adverse relationships	+2 Associations with occasional negative results	+4 Associations almost completely negative	☐ _____

EMOTIONAL STABILITY

−2 Exceptionally well adjusted; accepts responsibility for actions	0 No symptoms of emotional instability; appropriate emotional responses	+4 Symptoms limit but do not prohibit adequate functioning; e.g., excessive anxiety	+7 Symptoms prohibit adequate functioning; e.g., lashes out or retreats into self	☐ _____

ALCOHOL USAGE

0 No interference with functioning	+3 Occasional absue; some disruption of functioning	+6 Frequent abuse; serious disruption; needs treatment	☐ _____

(Continued)

FIGURE 3.4 (Continued)

OTHER DRUG USAGE

0 No interference with functioning	+3 Occasional substance absue; some disruption of functioning	+5 Frequent substance abuse; serious disruption; needs treatment	☐ _____

MENTAL ABILITY

0 Able to function independently	+3 Some need for assistance; potential for adequate adjustment; mild retardation	+6 Deficiencies severely limit independent functioning; moderate retardation	☐ _____

HEALTH

0 Sound physical health; seldom ill	+1 Handicap or illness interferes with functioning on a recurring basis	+2 Serious handicap or chronic illness; needs frequent medical care	☐ _____

SEXUAL BEHAVIOR

0 No apparent dysfunction	+3 Real or perceived situational or minor problems	+5 Real or perceived chronic or severe problems	☐ _____

RECREATION/HOBBY

0 Constructive activities apparent	+1 Some constructive activities	+2 No constructive leisure-time activities or hobbies	☐ _____

AGENTS IMPRESSION OF CLIENTS NEEDS

−1 Minimum	0 Low	+3 Medium	+5 Maximum	☐ _____

Total: _____

SOURCE: Pennsylvania Board of Probation and Parole website: http://www.pbpp.state.pa.us/pbpp/site/default.asp.

and substance abuse. The items included in the LSI-R:SV not only contribute to its predictive validity, but they also include information that is important to offender treatment planning (Andrews & Bonta, 2003). Each of these items is rated either "yes/no" or "0–3" (0: a very unsatisfactory situation with very clear and strong need for improvement, to 3: a satisfactory situation with little or no need for improvement).

It should be noted that the LSI-R is not intended to replace the professional judgment of the correctional worker. Rather, an objective risk-needs assessment enhances professional judgment, adds to the fairness of offender assessment, and alerts correctional staff to the need for a fuller offender risk-needs assessment (Andrews & Bonta, 2003). Research with the LSI-R shows that scores on the instrument have predicted a variety of outcomes important to offender management. Among probation samples, LSI-R scores have predicted violent recidivism and violations while under community supervision. In assessments of incarcerated offenders, scores have predicted such varied outcomes as success in correctional halfway houses and institutional misconduct (Andrews & Bonta, 2003).

Andrews and Bonta (2003) make it clear that the LSI-R is designed for use as a screening instrument in busy intake settings where, due to time constraints and insufficient staff resources, a

Photo 3.2 This laptop has GPS tracking software loaded and is used to keep tabs on offenders of different classification levels throughout the local community. In addition to classification information, this software can determine the area of the city in which the offender is located (the zone), whether the offender has a curfew requirement, and whether he or she is required to wear a bracelet strap. All of these aspects (as well as other custody and security features) are noted at the bottom of the screen.

complete LSI-R assessment may not be feasible for everyone. The LSI-R also provides a summary of the static and dynamic risk factors that may require further assessment or further intervention from agency personnel.

In addition, the LSI-R fits a rather specific type of treatment model. As a risk-prediction inventory, the LSI-R fits best with programs that are based on clear cognitive-behavioral and social learning treatment modalities. This is not a problem, however, because most treatment programs in the criminal justice system are based on such orientations. But if clinicians desire an accurate assessment of the offender's likelihood of reforming, they must keep in mind that the LSI-R has limits that are grounded in cognitive-behavioral approaches. Van Voorhis et al. point out that most research on cognitive-behavioral and social learning approaches is showing that this modality is the most effective, overall, when dealing with the offender population. Thus, the LSI-R is ideally suited and designed for those programs that utilize the most effective modalities. The LSI-R therefore dovetails nicely with these programs and lends further validity to the nature and intent of therapeutic treatment programs in the criminal justice field.

THE CONFLUENCE OF ASSESSMENT, CLASSIFICATION, AND STAFF ATTITUDES IN DETERMINING PROGRAM EFFECTIVENESS

In the state of West Virginia, an ingenious study took place in 2006 that examined the use of effective assessment and classification systems implementing the LSI-R. The evaluation's rigor alone would have been sufficient for inclusion as a Focus Topic in this chapter. However, the researchers, Stephen M. Haas, Cynthia A. Hamilton, and Dena Hanley, also examined the effects of staff culture and attitudes toward reentry and rehabilitative orientations. Specifically, these authors examined West Virginia's implementation of the West Virginia Offender Reentry Initiative (WVORI). They point out that research consistently shows that correctional staff can have a strong influence on the predicted success or failure of a program that is implemented by a correctional agency. This is an important aspect of the classification process that is rarely (if ever) considered as a variable in assessment or classification systems. It may well be that staff attitudes could explain some of the variance that exists between predicted offender outcomes and those that ultimately occur.

Thus, this research points to an underexplored area of assessment and treatment planning that may be applicable to any number of correctional programs. Some of the results these researchers found are as follows:

1. Programs or interventions that depart substantially from the principles known to inform effective correctional programming are much less likely to observe reductions in recidivism.

2. Given that staff, such as case managers, counselors, and parole officers, interact with prisoners on a daily basis, they can determine the success or failure of any initiative undertaken by a correctional organization.

3. The identification of appropriate service and level of supervision after release should be contingent upon the accurate assessment of offender risk and needs.

4. Research has consistently shown that objective risk and needs assessments, based on statistical probabilities, more accurately predict the level of risk than personal or staff positions.

5. The success of a program can be significantly hampered by individual attitudes, and personal opinions toward the new strategy and the implementation of that strategy may be responsible for the success or failure of a new initiative.

6. Older organizations, with strong institutionalized organizational cultures, and larger organizations with more layers of bureaucracy, have more difficulty with communication and coordination.

7. Conflict between individual values of the staff and the values of the organization negatively impacts implementation strategies.

8. Detachment between staff work routines and organizational values translates into role conflict. Role conflict produces stress and job dissatisfaction, contributing to a negative organizational culture.

9. Organizational culture drives staff behavior and knowledge of what is valued in the organization.

10. Staff tended to support the WVORI when they were supportive of rehabilitation, were more human service oriented, liked to work with others, liked their jobs, were empathetic toward inmates, and believed the department was committed to staff training and professional development.

11. A large majority of correctional staff were found to have a punitive orientation toward inmates, did not believe in the efficacy of rehabilitation, and were not oriented toward a human service career.

12. The initial report concluded that a substantial change in the human orientation of staff and greater support for rehabilitative efforts may be necessary for achieving greater support for reentry initiatives among correctional staff.

This study is important because it illustrates that the predictions of offender behavior can be mitigated or aggravated by the actions of supervision and treatment staff within an agency. This observation is not, in and of itself, particularly astute. However, the fact that this was specifically linked to the assessment and classification process makes this research innovative and very useful. Further, these factors are important both for the prognosis of individual offenders and when evaluating agency outcomes. These authors, through this research approach, have found a common linchpin between individual offender treatment planning and agency evaluation outcomes. Because of this, it is perhaps a good recommendation that future classification systems take into account data input regarding the agency staff and its organizational culture, since these factors are seldom assessed and they have direct bearing on the success or failure of offenders who are released to community supervision.

SOURCE: Haas, S. M., Hamilton, C. A., & Hanley, D. (2006, July). *Implementation of the West Virginia Offender Reentry Initiative: An examination of staff attitudes and the application of the LSI-R.* Charleston, WV: Mountain State Criminal Justice Research Services.

THE LINK BETWEEN THEORY AND RISK PREDICTION

Connolly (2003) notes that in order for significant improvements in risk prediction to occur, instruments will need to be better grounded in theory. Specifically, actuarial prediction models to be used with serious offenders should be directly based on the discoveries made by research that empirically tests the ability of theories to explain and predict crime. Many students fail to appreciate the important connection between theoretical explanation of crime and our ability to predict crime. In essence, theory is nothing less than a macro-level form of assessment. What many laypersons and even experts in the field may not realize is that many variables used to predict criminal behavior in theoretical tests are identical to those used in assessment instruments. Thus, there is a direct relationship between the research of theorists and the potential for improvement of risk assessment instruments. Indeed, as theoretical research continues, fertile ground is created for further refinement of instruments that use the same or similar variables. However, most current models are based on their simple ability to predict the likely outcome, rather than their ability to explain the reason for criminal or noncriminal behavior (Connolly, 2003). This is problematic, particularly when one considers that needs-assessment variables are more related to explaining why recidivism might occur, and these variables are critical to the ultimate success of offender reintegration. Consider the point made by Krauss, Sales, Becker, and Figueredo (2000), who state,

> Probation risk assessment and other forms of risk assessment have become exclusively based on prediction rather than explanation of behavior. Actuarial assessment instruments are, by and large, atheoretical, and consequently, do not effectively examine the causes of the behavior that the instruments are designed to predict. Present methods of probation risk assessment simply highlight individuals who are high risks for recidivism, without explaining why these individuals are more likely to recidivate. (p. 92)

Explaining the "why" behind criminal behavior can improve the treatment prognosis for most offenders (incorporating a needs-based approach that is best addressed through a casework model), which in turn improves their likely reintegration. While there is no single best theory to explain all crime, there are some common starting points that lend themselves well to risk prediction. When considering these starting points, Connolly (2003) notes that the most promising research with direct application to the construction of adult offender risk prediction is based on one of the following three criminological theories: the general theory of crime, or self-control theory, by Gottfredson and Hirschi;

the age-graded theory of informal social control by Sampson and Laub; and social learning theory by Ronald Akers.

Gottfredson and Hirschi's self-control model suggests that people differ in their simple will to refrain from criminal behavior. Simply put, a more disciplined person will be less likely to commit crime. Correspondingly, individuals with low self-control are more likely to exhibit criminal behaviors. One application of Gottfredson and Hirschi's (1990) self-control theory to predicting adult criminal offending used a six-factor, 24-item scale that had been used in various studies with a variety of subpopulations (Connolly, 2003). A comprehensive test of this scale was conducted on a cross-cultural sample of 8,417 adolescents from four different countries (Vazsonyi, Pickering, Junger, & Hessing, 2001), who were administered the 24-item scale. One of the significant findings of the study is that the scale is predictive of deviance, with a risk-seeking or high sensation–seeking life view explaining up to 25 percent of the potential causes of continued criminal behavior. Connolly notes that the scale has also performed well in numerous other studies as well. For instance, Alarid, Burton, and Cullen (2000) tested five measures of social control: marital attachment, attachment to parents, attachment to friends, involvement, and belief. The social control variables of attachment to parents, involvement in conventional activities, and belief in the law were all significantly correlated with future criminal behavior. Further, these predictors could be pinpointed to the specific type of crime that is likely for a given offender. For example, marital attachment only impacted and reduced the likely involvement in property crimes, while attachment to peers was positively correlated with criminal activity.

Sampson and Laub's (1993) theory extends the concepts of social control into adulthood. The authors emphasize the quality and nature of informal social ties rather than simply noting that such exist. For example, merely being employed is not necessarily as effective an indicator as knowledge of the offender's desire to keep that job. Connolly (2003) points out that "adult risk prediction instruments frequently include the basic construct of social control variables, however, they fail to go to the next step in measuring the quality and strength of the social ties" (p. 156). Rather than simply noting if an offender has a job, it may be equally important to know about the stability of the job (seasonal, temp, and so forth), the type of work, and the work habits of the offender. Such factors have been found to be important in predicting future recidivism, with low job stability making an offender 5 times more likely to carry out a future criminal behavior (Connolly, 2003).

Finally, social learning theory has not been as widely tested in recent years as self-control theory. However, Alarid et al. (2000) tested the correlation among individual definitions of crime, others' definition of crime, and criminal friends with the likelihood of criminal behavior. All three of these associations were found to be statistically significant, directly correlating with drug and property offenses as well as violent offenses. As has been noted in earlier chapters of this text, social learning theory is the primary theoretical orientation that is thought to extend the concepts of the classical school of criminology. In addition, this theoretical perspective lends itself well to the social casework model that is a primary theme of Chapter 8, later in this book.

The previous research demonstrates the usefulness of theory and its connection to risk prediction. "Constructing adult risk prediction models that are grounded in theory is a direction the field of criminology needs to take if any substantive gains in predictive power of these instruments are likely" (Connolly, 2003, p. 156). Researchers and agencies wishing to improve adult risk-prediction scales would thus be wise to incorporate the quantitative research that has proliferated within the field of criminological theory.

Though this chapter makes it clear that theory aids in explaining the "why" behind criminal offending, students should also understand that the "why" also aids in predicting future criminal behavior. This is an important point because many people may not be aware that criminological research examines variables that are quantified, measured, and examined for significance in likely criminal behavior. This is nothing less than a form of prediction.

The primary difference between purely theoretical research and pure risk prediction is that theoretical research starts with a hypothesis that is designed to test the efficacy of a theory in explaining criminal behavior, while on the other hand, risk prediction presumes these variable-based hypotheses are correct and uses them to predict the likelihood of criminal behavior in the future. It is in this manner that the two are interconnected, one with the other, in a circular relationship. Indeed, as practitioners use risk-prediction devices, the effectiveness of these instruments will be established and, over time, will validate (or disprove) the theoretical bases that were initially used during their construction.

Risk prediction instruments are the practical outcome of widespread criminological and psychometric research. In other words, these instruments tend to combine findings from a wide range of theoretical approaches, with the single-minded purpose of predicting recidivism. Thus, these instruments are a composite of a variety of theoretical components, ideally mixing and matching various constructs from multiple theoretical perspectives in a manner that optimizes prediction (leading to true positives and true negatives) and minimizes the likelihood of error (false negatives and false positives) in the risk assessment process.

SOURCE: Lilly, J. R., Cullen, F. T., & Ball, R. A. (2007). *Criminological theory: Context and consequences* (4th ed.). Thousand Oaks, CA: Sage Publications.

BETTER DIAGNOSIS: THE NEED FOR IMPROVED ASSESSMENT

The information for this section is largely drawn from the work of Tony Fabelo and Geraldine Nagy (2006), two widely respected authorities on correctional research in the state of Texas. Much of the material supporting this section was produced by the JFA Institute in Washington, D.C., and is derived from the federal publication entitled *Better Diagnosis: The First Step to Improve Probation Supervision Strategies*. As the authors of that publication, Fabelo and Nagy note that without a diagnosis of offenders along risk and criminogenic factors,

> it is very difficult to: (a) distinguish offenders along characteristics that identify their supervision needs; (b) guide judges in setting appropriate conditions of supervision; (c) guide probation administrators in designing differentiated supervision strategies; (d) provide probation officers with reliable information to formulate and implement effective supervision plans; and (e) devise clear outcome expectations for different populations. (p. 4)

Though this statement may seem fairly straightforward and deceptively simple, it fully captures the essence and importance of assessment.

Fabelo and Nagy (2006) conducted a comprehensive examination of assessment processes in Travis County, Texas (the county that includes the state's capital, Austin). They found that the assessment processes used at that time faced the following issues:

1. PSI officers did not develop PSI's that followed a comprehensive, standardized interview protocol, nor did they integrate the results from a risk assessment and case classification into their final diagnosis.

The PSI's were essentially "biographies" characterized by long narratives developed by the PSI officers following a general interview guideline. It was found that these narratives were potentially affected by the different writing styles and predispositions of the officers when interpreting the offender's responses to open-ended interviews.

2. Assessment tools were in place but were not properly used. For example, the risk assessment in that county was typically done after the PSI was completed by the assigned field officer during an "initial interview" with the offender. Consequently, risk levels were not considered during the setting of conditions or the assignment of cases.

3. The PSI officer would make recommendations to the judge, but in many cases the conditions of probation were not well-coupled with the supervision requirements.

4. A large number of requests were observed to modify the conditions of supervision after an offender was placed on probation. This was interpreted as being the result of not having a clear diagnosis of the offender at the point of adjudication, thereby undermining the match of the conditions of supervision to the appropriate supervision strategies.

5. It was found that the paperwork to request supervision modifications required a substantial amount of time and effort. This was in addition to the roughly 8 to 10 hours to complete the general PSI. Further, other assessments such as those associated with substance abusing offenders took another 2 to 3 hours. (As has already been noted in Chapter 2 and as will be discussed in Chapter 4, the excessive paperwork associated with the community supervision officer's job causes a great deal of stress and generates inefficiency in agencies.) Moreover, these assessments often required multiple visits by the offender to the agency before they were completed. This tended to create additional burdens on community supervision staff as well as on other administrative personnel.

Figure 3.5 summarizes the main issues that were addressed during Travis County's reform process to rectify problems with its assessment process. The five previous observations from Fabelo and Nagy (2006) tie in with this illustration. The assessment process and challenges with the integration of the PSI process are illustrated in Figure 3.5.

From the noted deficiencies in the assessment process used by Travis County, it became clear that the assessment, diagnosis, and classification process would require substantial improvements, particularly in regard to the use of the PSI. Through the use of a committee of probation experts, officials, and seasoned practitioners, a number of improvements were generated to the process. It was found that a wide range of forms were used as part of the assessment process. In fact, nearly 40 forms were used, and this entailed nearly 100 pages of content when completing the process. Figure 3.6 illustrates the number and type of forms that were used by the Travis County system, and this was also reflective of what many other counties in Texas used. These forms were categorized as (a) interviews, questionnaires, data collection; (b) assessments and screenings; (c) movements and referrals; (d) consent forms; and (e) ending evaluations and exit reports.

When examining this process, experts in Travis County observed that much of this paperwork either was not related to the overall cohesive program of community supervision or duplicated the information included on other forms. In essence, much of the paperwork was either not necessary at all or redundant. Further, it was found that many of the forms could easily be collapsed down into single forms of combined administration. This is actually a very important point from both an assessment and an individual practitioner perspective. Further elaboration is necessary to clarify both of these points.

First, the use of excessive paperwork creates a disorganized form of offender assessment. What may seem to be comprehensive is, in actuality, overstuffed with information that may not even be closely examined

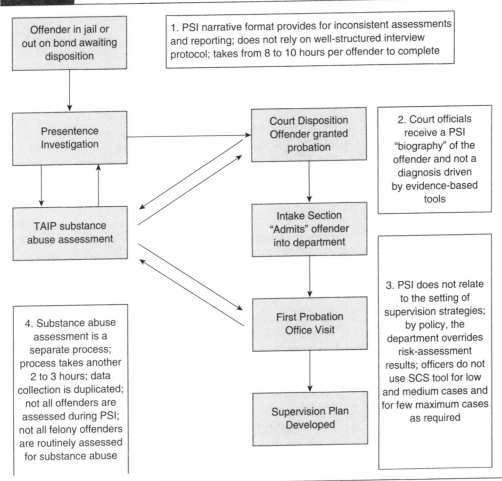

SOURCE: Adapted from Fabelo, T., & Nagy, G. (2006). *Better diagnosis: The first step to improve probation supervision strategies.* Washington, DC: The JFA Institute.

when it is understood by agency personnel that forms are redundant or unrelated to the true process of setting a supervision strategy. Such a system detracts from the information that is included, since this information gets buried in the redundancy or lack of pertinence. If this occurs, it can easily lead to human error when already overworked community supervision staff are expected (unrealistically) to incorporate all of these sundry details into a genuine assessment. While a comprehensive report is indeed desired, it is important that agencies not increase the strain on already tired and sore eyes that must pore through volumes of information that may, in the real world of supervision, simply get lost in the shuffle. Thus, all paperwork should be relevant to primary concerns with supervision and treatment strategies and should be centralized to key forms as much as possible. This will improve the use of the information that is collected, thereby contributing to an enhanced sense of efficiency and improved public safety.

Second, it will be seen in Chapter 4 that excessive paperwork happens to be one of the most common sources of stress and burnout among community supervision officers. This problem should not be taken lightly. Keeping knowledgeable and committed staff within an agency is critical to that agency's performance and is therefore critical to the community's safety. If community supervision officers are to be

FIGURE 3.6 Forms Used in Travis County PSI and Intake Process

Interviews, Questionnaires, Data Collection

Diagnostic Presentence Information
Intake Setup Form
Victim Interview Guide
Caseload Assessment Form
Vendor Financial Study
Staffing Sheet
Initial Interview Questionnaire
SMART Psycho-social Interview

Assessments and Screenings

Substance Abuse Evaluation (SAE)
SASSI Screening
Adult Placement Education Tool
Strategies for Community Supervision (SCS)
Wisconsin Risk Assessment
Static 99 Assessment for Sex Offenders

Movements and Referrals

Internal
  Felony Court
  Referral
  Diagnostic Assessment
  Checklist
  Intake Assignment Form
  Missed Appointment Notice
  General Orientation to Comm Supv
  Pre-employment Program Form
  Things to Bring to an Initial CSCD General Referral Form

External
  Request to Reset Sentencing Date
  Wishing to Proceed Out of State
  Ignition Interlock

Consent Forms

Release of Confidential Info
TAIP Consent Forms
TAIP "No Harm" Client Contract
SMART Consent Forms
Travis County Consent Forms

End Product Reports

Presentence Investigation Report
Risk Assessment (Perkins only)
Supplemental Information
TAIP Admission Approval Form
Recommended Conditions of Probation
Offender Supervision Plan

SOURCE: Adapted from Fabelo, T., & Nagy, G. (2006). *Better diagnosis: The first step to improve probation supervision strategies.* Washington, DC: The JFA Institute.

expected to maintain human face-to-face contact with their offender caseload, they must not be burdened with paperwork that is irrelevant or redundant. Otherwise, agencies will continue to grapple with turnover due to job stress (often cited as being caused by paperwork expectations that compete with time demands from other aspects of the job). As will be seen in Chapter 4, this is an often-cited issue of frustration for community supervision officers and is therefore worthy of serious consideration.

Travis County experts noted that overall, the process was disjointed. To make this point even more clear, it was found that the PSI was considered an assessment report, in and of itself. While this does hold some appeal given the comprehensive nature of the PSI, it is not necessarily read or examined by judges. In fact, most judges make their decision regarding supervision based on the guidance of the Chief Probation Officer. Though the Chief Probation Officer may be familiar with the material in the PSI, the PSI itself may lack key objective assessment criteria that are completed at later periods in the supervision process (students should remember that these assessments may require multiple visits to the agency before they can be completed), and the supervision decision is therefore based on subjective determinations of the PSI officer. When considering this evaluation of the Travis County assessment and classification system, Fabelo and Nagy (2006) noted the following:

> In effect, there was no reliable diagnosis that could be used by the Courts to identify conditions of probation supervision that would best match the supervision and treatment needs of offenders based on the risk posed to the community or their particular criminogenic needs. (p. 7)

Results such as the above are counter to the purposes of reintegration and do not improve community security. In essence, the above statement sums up what every community supervision agency should strive to avoid. With this in mind, this text again contends that assessment and classification are critical to effective casework, and that the casework approach is crucial for any reintegrative program—reintegration being part and parcel of any program that achieves a lasting effect of recidivism reduction.

Photo 3.3 An intake and classification worker enters information that will aid in determining an offender's eventual classification level, both in the jail and later on community supervision.

AGENCY-CREATED ASSESSMENT INSTRUMENTS

Frank Domurad, a prior Director of Staff and Organizational Development with the New York City Probation Department, provides insight on the benefits of creating one's own assessment scale rather than using one already available such as the Wisconsin Risk Assessment. In the case of New York City, this approach was a practical means of addressing noted deficiencies in that city's assessment scheme. However, it should be made clear that in most cases, agencies are advised to utilize assessment instruments that have been validated and found reliable. Generally, the more studies that exist to examine a given scale, the more refined its use and perhaps its revised construction is likely to be. This is an important point that cuts to the basis of overall assessment effectiveness for the agency. If the assessment scale is faulty or inappropriately normed, then everything that follows in the agency is not likely to work well either.

Domurad (2000) notes New York City's need for an assessment instrument that focused on rearrest of violent offenders in their probation population. Interestingly, he also points out that those agencies "interested in protecting public safety by positively changing their client's criminal behavior had to pay particular attention to the mantra of risk, needs, and responsivity" (p. 11). This demonstrates that even though Domurad seeks to focus on predicting rearrest of violent offenders, his (and presumably the New York Department's) intent was to achieve lower crime rates by reintegrating offenders through needs assessments and responsive means of working with the offender population. That is, of course, the approach this text has taken, and thus Domurad validates the notion that the best means of lowering long-term recidivism is through reintegration of the offender.

Nevertheless, the reality is that not all offenders will successfully reintegrate. In such cases, community corrections agencies have a duty to ensure the protection of the community. Thus, agencies must focus their resources on the skillful selection of factors facing offenders that place them at the greatest risk of reoffending. With this in mind, it was considered a priority that agencies target probationers with the highest likelihood of physically harming others in the community. In other words, New York City specifically sought to predict which offenders would have a higher likelihood of committing a violent crime than others. Domurad (2000) notes three steps to the assessment creation process that proved to be extremely important when trying to improve such predictions. These three steps are listed below.

1. Confront the policy decisions embedded in such a process as openly and forthrightly as possible. Domurad (2000) makes it clear that this is especially important when selecting the criterion variable or the item that is the outcome being predicted. Though the likelihood of "violent rearrest" may be the primary outcome of concern, defining this result is more complicated than people may realize. Simplistic definitions, such as those that might be obtained from the Uniform Crime Reports, do not suffice in capturing all the images of violent rearrest that might come to mind (such as the nuances involved with family violence, for instance). In addition, this point made by Domurad indicates his savviness when dealing with various criminal justice stakeholders, being that executive staff, practitioners, interest groups (such as domestic violence advocates), and other external stakeholders may have their own legitimate agendas to consider. Agencies often must consider these various vantage points since, as we have seen in Chapter 2, the community itself may be interwoven with the supervision process as well as being an external recipient of the good (or bad) service delivery that a community supervision agency may provide.

An additional observation should be pointed out, one that is not necessarily raised by Domurad but that dovetails nicely with the previous point. When examining an assessment scale, the policy decisions embedded in it may actually be much more important than simply being receptive to the various actors that are affected. Consider again our discussion of the Wisconsin Risk Assessment. As you may recall, the last item of this instrument asks whether the offender has committed an assaultive offense within the last 5 years. Further clarification indicates that such an offense would involve the use of a weapon, physical force, or the threat of force. While it is of course a good step to consider—and give added weight to—violent criminal behaviors, the use of this administrative override (as Connolly has called it) has some questionable outcomes for agencies, the offender, and society. As was noted earlier in this chapter, it is likely that this override is responsible for much of the overprediction that occurs with the Wisconsin Risk Assessment.

In addition, agencies should consider if such a criterion is well tailored to their own region of the United States. Consider that the Wisconsin Assessment is normed on offenders that may not be reflective of an agency in another state such as California or Florida. This is particularly true when looking at the differences in racial and cultural diversity of the latter two states. Therefore, an instrument may have different levels of predictive ability in different areas of the United States.

Further, agencies may find it prudent to modify such administrative overrides to their own specific needs or observed patterns in criminal offending. For instance, should such an item include violent offenses during the last 5 years? Or would 7 years or even 10 years be more appropriate. On the other hand, a term of 5 years may be a bit too long; thus it may be that 3 years or 4 years would more accurately predict likely outcomes of committing a violent crime while at the same time reducing the rate of overprediction. This is a very important point for agencies to consider before they arbitrarily adopt the number "5" as an automatic time period. In other words, 5 years should not be a "set in stone" period of time for determining if prior violent offending adequately ties in to the prediction scheme.

Last, the definition used in the Wisconsin Risk Assessment states that the offense "involves the use of a weapon, physical force, or the threat of force." This may or may not be a sufficient definition for agencies to employ when determining violent rearrest. Agencies may want to divide such a definition into multiple parts, such as the distinction between an actual act of violence and one that is a threat but that was never acted upon. Consider, for instance, a telephone threat made in anger but where the offender does not follow up on the threat, or when an offender threatens to assault another offender that has stolen something from him or her, and so forth. These instances, when compared with an offender that has, for example, committed a violent act of sexual assault, a stabbing during a domestic dispute, or a shooting during a gang altercation, should not be coded in a similar fashion. It is also noteworthy to point out that the Wisconsin Risk Assessment requires a simple "yes" or "no" response to the administrative override that is included. This is a ludicrous means of addressing this variable since, as was just pointed out, there are degrees of violence in both the length of time since its occurrence and the level of lethality involved. The use of a binary scale creates a deceptive outcome that forces the assessment rater to either ignore minor acts of violence (not a good option if you want to improve public safety) or include minor acts of violence with a weighting that is identical to heinous acts that have been committed; such an option makes no sense whatsoever if one desires an accurate prediction.

Rather, it may be that administrative overrides, being the result of agency policy decisions that are included in the assessment instrument itself, should be modified to better accommodate the range of possibilities that occur in the real world of offending. For instance, the use of an ordinal scale (e.g., 1 to 15 years) would allow raters a range of values to choose from, which could then be used to reflect the time since the last violent offense (e.g., 6 months ago, a year ago, 4 years ago, or 10 years ago) and would also allow the rater to consider the lethality of the offense (e.g., a threat by phone, a mutual assault between two rival gang members, a sexual assault, or perhaps a murder). In addition, the number value would not have to remain at a maximum of 15 but could be increased to, say, 20 or even higher for more serious offenses.

The point to this discussion is simply that this variable requires substantial forethought and attention by agencies. The simple adoption of some criterion that has not been tailored to a state's population or particular response to criminal offending may lead to overprediction or even underprediction, depending on the scale that is selected. When considering public safety, it is violent crime that generates the most concern. After much discussion and debate, New York City settled on a definition of a "violent" offense that included the following: homicide, assault, sex offenses, kidnapping, serious burglary, arson, robbery, endangering the welfare of a child, and the use of firearms and other dangerous weapons (Domurad, 2000). As Domurad notes, "it was not your usual garden-variety list, but one that suited the risk we were most interested in managing in terms of our agency's mission" (p. 12). This statement speaks specifically to the concern with the administrative override employed with the Wisconsin Risk Assessment and likewise illustrates that community supervision objectives may indeed vary from state to state and even from community to community within a given state. With this in mind, agencies should closely consider their own administrative policy decisions as they apply to their own assessment schemes.

2. Select experts whom you know and trust to construct your instrument. Domurad (2000) notes that agencies should use experts that are familiar with the agency itself. The more collaborative and ethically insightful such an expert may be, the better. For example, experts who are on an agency's community board, steering committee, or other such governance body will be more informed of the agency's mission and its own perceived purpose. Further, nuances related to agency culture, community relations, local community population demographics, and community norms are likely to be much better understood and appreciated by such experts. Domurad states that "your developers need to view the project not just as an exercise in statistical model construction; they also need to understand and make transparent the policy decisions that are required at every step of the way and to explain the ethical, as well as the practical, consequences of such decisions" (p. 13). This is very important to note, since many experts in the ivory tower of academia often lose sight of the real-world implications of their instrument designs, removed as they are from the real-world fallout that later might ensue and not held accountable to the community for such outcomes.

However, agency administrators do not often enjoy such a cloistered existence and must therefore seek experts who understand that consequences and ramifications occur for the agency well beyond the mere construction and even application of a created assessment device. To further illustrate this point, Domurad notes the following:

> Risk instruments have a tremendous impact on human beings, whether they are potential victims or known offenders. There will always be error in any effort at human prediction. False negatives will result in harm to the public when a crime is committed. False positives will result in unwarranted intrusions on the part of the state into the lives of clients, intrusions that, ironically, may actually increase the very recidivism you are seeking to prevent. How many of each of these errors you will tolerate as a result of the operation of your assessment instrument is a matter of policy as well as "objective" scientific practice. Any experts who pretend differently are probably not worth hiring. (p. 13)

This statement clearly addresses this issue from both an agency and a public safety perspective. Indeed, it may well be that the agency's outcome will not look as good on paper, even though it has improved the safety of the community that it serves. As pointed out, more offenders may be found to be engaged in criminal activity and thus there may be a lower rate of offenders that finish their supervision requirements (thus increasing recidivism). Though this may not make probation or parole seem effective, it does translate to improved community safety and also ensures that only those offenders that are truly reintegrated are allowed to carry forth within the community. This is, by all accounts, a therapeutic as well as a public safety success.

3. Create administrative and staff ownership of the process. Domurad (2000) points out that in many cases, executive-level supervisors may have little if any knowledge regarding the actual statistical or methodological bases of most assessment instruments. Because of this, it is important that such supervisors collaborate with those persons that are tasked with creating such an instrument. Administrators should be educated on the basics of instrument design as well as the pros and cons associated with different options that may be considered. This training should be given prior to the actual design of the instrument so that a baseline of knowledge is possessed by all parties. This will ensure that administrators are aware of the impact of design decisions prior to the introduction of various decisions that may be emotionally or politically laden.

In addition, input from individual probation officers simply should be mandatory. After all, these persons will utilize the instrument on a day-to-day basis. As much as possible, the instrument should be designed to be practitioner-friendly. With input from those that are in the field, different approaches to administration can be considered that ensure that the entire process is as smooth and workable as possible. Further, training on administration should be designed with the input of practitioners as well, since it is likely that a "train the trainers" type approach will be taken whereby agencies provide instruction on the instrument's use through in-house training. The instrument must be amenable to the working requirements of the community supervision officer and, as has been discussed before in this chapter, should be clearly relevant to risk-prediction purposes. The instrument should also not be redundant with other instruments or forms that assess the same variables unless such duplicity is specifically desired as a cross-validation check within the agency assessment process. As discussed in this chapter and again in Chapter 4, excessive paperwork is a prime source of stress and burnout among community supervision officers; the instrument designed by an agency should be of such a nature as to generate no more paperwork than is necessary and, if possible, should eliminate paperwork that would otherwise be redundant. The need to reduce forms and paperwork was demonstrated in the section that discussed improvements to the PSI and assessment processes in Travis County, Texas (this chapter's prior subsection), highlighting the fact that such excesses can truly impair the effective functioning of an agency and its ability to assess and place offenders on the agency caseload.

Finally, integration of input from administrators and general practitioners is important because the design of the instrument will have to navigate both the "purist" approach to risk prediction and the "realistic" approach that remains central to the world of the practitioner. Ensuring that the instrument is statistically and actuarially sound is of course the primary key to accuracy, but if an agency wishes to ensure that such a high-quality instrument is also used in a high-quality fashion, then input from practitioners is necessary and the effective training of administrators and practitioners is simply a mandatory requirement as well. In no circumstances can either of these aspects be overlooked, since one dimension (the actuarial component) consists of the substantive content of the assessment and the other (the practitioner's day-to-day use of the instrument) consists of the procedural dimension of the assessment. Both are mutually dependent on one another if the assessment process is to be optimized, making each essential to effective assessment and future public safety outcomes.

The results of the New York City Probation Department's efforts are illustrated in Figure 3.7, ASR Case Classification and Assignment Instrument, and Figure 3.8, ASR Case Classification and Assignment Instrument Guidelines. The acronym "ASR" stands for "Adult Supervision Restructuring," which indicates that supervision levels are restructured or are based on results from the administration of this scale. This is an additive scale instrument whose variables, such as age, criminal history, and current offense, are static risk factors (discussed earlier in this chapter) and are thus not likely to change due to the offender's situation or exhibited behaviors (Domurad, 2000). This instrument is used for the purposes of initial assessment and classification. The scale's primary predictive component is age, and this variable is directly subtracted from the total value derived from the summation of the other six variables. Thus, the greater the offender's age, the less the likelihood that he or she will be placed on high-risk supervision (Domurad, 2000).

Domurad notes that the ASR assigns offenders into one of the two following categories:

High-Risk Enforcement Track (23 points or above): Within this track there are three subgroups. The first subgroup consists of interventions using cognitive-behavioral techniques for male adolescents and young men between the ages of 16 and 20. The second subgroup consists of individualized supervision and case management and also utilizes cognitive-behavioral interventions. The last group focuses on relapse prevention and is the least at-risk group among those scoring over 23 points (many scoring 24 or 25 points and therefore barely exceeding this threshold criterion).

Low-Risk Special Conditions Track (under 22 points): Offenders in this category may be assigned appended conditions of probation, depending on the determination of the judge and the circumstances of the case, or they may be placed on an automated reporting track if their ASR score is particularly low.

Domurad (2000) points out that there are specific policy decisions that act as administrative overrides, regardless of the numerical score that is obtained by the offender. These are considered exceptional circumstances and might include cases involving current or prior child abuse, sexual abuse, or domestic violence. In these cases, the offender is placed on high-risk Amber alert, regardless of the actuarial assessment outcome. In addition, offenders that are considered "high profile" may be placed on enhanced supervision, regardless of the actuarial assessment that is obtained.

Finally, Domurad (2000) notes that preliminary indications have confirmed the efficacy of the ASR. In one evaluation, the New York City Probation Department studied probationers sentenced in Manhattan over a 3-month period who were subsequently rearrested for a violent offense within 6 months to 9 months of being placed on probation. "The odds in favor of a rearrest for a violent crime in general were 2.3 times greater for a high-risk than a low-risk case and 2.1 times greater for violent felony rearrests alone" (p. 15). This shows that the ASR has sufficient discriminant predictive ability to correctly and effectively categorize offenders.

FIGURE 3.7   ASR Case Classification and Assignment Instrument

ASR CASE CLASSIFICATION AND ASSIGNMENT INSTRUMENT

CASE NUMBER: _____   CASE NAME: _____

NYSID NUMBER: _____

I. ASR CASE CLASSIFICATION INSTRUMENT   SCORING

1. Defendant is eligible for a Probation sentence.   <u>32</u>

2. How many victims were physically injured in the instant offense?   _____ × 6 = ___

3. How many prior misdemeanor arrests does the offender have for offenses against persons?
                                                             _____ × 1 = ___

4. Does the offender have any juvenile arrests?   No = 0 Yes = 11   ___

5. Is the current or any prior arrest for a violent offense?   No = 0 Yes = 19   ___

6. Is the offender a Youthful Offender?   No = 0 Yes = 11   ___

                                                           Subtotal of Items 1–6   ___

7. What is the offender's age?   (Subtract from subtotal)

                                       Classification Score   _____

II. ASR TRACK UNIT ASSIGNMENT CRITERIA

Classification Score is 23 or above, and:

1. Offender is male, 20 years of age or less, speaks English, and is not developmentally or psychiatrically disabled.

   Assign to Enforcement Blue

2. Offender does not meet Blue Criteria

   Assign to Enforcement Amber

1. There is a Court ordered special condition of Probation, such as a fine, restitution, community service or participation in a treatment program.

   Assign to Special Conditions

2. Offender has no special conditions.

   Assign to Reporting

3. There are exceptional circumstances:

   (a) Current or prior history of child abuse, sexual abuse, domestic violence:

      Assign to Amber

   (b) Probationer has completed STAR:

      Assign to Green

   (c) "High Profile"[1] case:

      Assign to Green With BC Approval

III. ASR ASSIGNMENT

Case Assigned to _____ Track/Unit   P.O. _____

Date Completed: _____ Completed by: _____

                                    (P.O. Name and I.D. No.)

The examples in Travis County, Texas, and in New York City both demonstrate that agencies find the need to revamp their systems when faced with challenges to public safety. Both agencies have sought to improve their assessment schemes. This is an important statement because it indicates that when a system

FIGURE 3.8 ASR Case Classification and Assignment Instrument Guidelines

---

ASR CASE CLASSIFICATION AND ASSIGNMENT INSTRUMENT GUIDELINES

Score each of the items in Section I as they apply to the offender using the definitions included below. Add items 1 through 6. Subtract the offender's age to obtain the ASR Classification Score. Refer to Section II, ASR Track/Unit Assignment Criteria, to determine the correct assignment. Record the ASR assignment in Section III.

I. ASR CASE CLASSIFICATION INSTRUMENT

Item 1.   Include the Score of 32 points for every case legally eligible (at PSI stage) or received on Probation (supervision stage).

Item 2.   Multiply the number of individuals who are reported to have suffered a physical injury in the instant offense by 6 and enter the **result** on the appropriate line.

Item 3.   Misdemeanor crimes against persons are defined as: Assault 3 (120.00), Menacing 2 (120.14), Menacing 3 (120.15), Hazing 1 (120.15), Reckless Endangerment 2 (120.20), Sexual Misconduct (130.16), Sex Abuse 3 (130.55), Sex Abuse 2 (130.60), Unlawful Imprisonment 2 (135.05), Coercion 2 (135.60.(1), Endangering the Welfare of a Child (260. IO), Endangering the Welfare of an Incompetent Person (260.25), Criminal Possession of a Weapon 4 (265.01).

Item 4.   Include any juvenile arrest regardless of the disposition of the case.

Item 5.   The following are defined as violent offenses: assault, homicide, sex offenses, kidnapping, burglary 1st and 2nd, arson, robbery, endangering the welfare of a child, and firearms and other dangerous weapons.

Item 6.   Has the Court made a Youthful Offender adjudication at sentencing?

Item 7.   Enter the Offender's age at time of sentence and subtract from total value of Items 1 through 6. **The result is the classification score.**

II. ASR TRACK/UNIT ASSIGNMENT CRITERIA

Cases with a Classification Score of 23 or above will be assigned to the Enforcement Track.

Cases with a Classification Score of 22 or below will be assigned to either Special Conditions or Reporting Tracks unless there are exceptional circumstances as described in Item 3 in this section.

III. ASR ASSIGNMENT

Use the criteria in Section II to assign the case to the appropriate Track or Unit. P.O. assignment is to be made by consulting the appropriate **Unit** Supervisor.

15

SOURCE: Domurad, F. (2000). *So you want to develop your own risk assessment instrument.* New York: New York City Probation Department. Retrieved from National Institute of Corrections Library at http://www.nicic.org/pubs/1999/period160.pdf.

is faulty, agencies should perhaps start from the beginning: assessment. Assessment is the foundation of any smoothly operating supervision agency. A good assessment instrument and good assessment processes only need one additional ingredient: good staff. As was noted earlier, having an effective and streamlined assessment process can help with the retention of quality staff (since this reduces burnout), and the ability to predict violent offenders' behavior allows the agency to better allocate its resources so that public safety is held at a premium.

The Adult Actuarial
Risk Instrument (AARI)—A Model Risk Assessment Instrument From Australia

Max Maller of the Crime Research Centre of the University of Western Australia and Richard Lane of the Department of Justice of Western Australia presented a paper highlighting a newly developed risk-assessment system. This system was named the Adult Actuarial Risk Instrument (AARI), and this computer-aided program was developed over 5 years by the Crime Research Centre. The AARI was designed using data that spanned 17 years, from 1984 to 2000. The data used when norming and designing this instrument consisted of over 620,000 arrests that included dynamic and static risk factor information. Information such as sex, arrest cardinality (position in the offender's arrest career), age at arrest, race, and most-serious offense are some examples of the common data utilized. The AARI system continually iterated over time through a process that includes new data and archiving of outdated data. In addition, the AARI included a "Case Needs" assessment that contained ratings for eight domains: 1. Occupation, 2. Marital/family, 3. Associates/social interaction, 4. Alcohol use, 5. Substance use, 6. Community functioning, 7. Personal/emotional orientation, and 8. Attitude.

The AARI was created to better identify high-risk offenders. Previous risk-assessment tools in Australia had problems because the data chosen had only dealt with a small group of offenders during a particular time, thereby lacking external validity. Further, many of these instruments were not always reliable over a longer period of time. The AARI is an example of how actuarial models are used throughout the world to predict offender recidivism. Specifically, the student should note the following points regarding this assessment instrument developed in Australia:

1. Miller and Lane (2002) refer to the Wisconsin Risk Assessment System and the Canadian Level of Supervision Inventory when discussing the creation of the AARI. This demonstrates that researchers and practitioners around the world face similar problems and that, as a whole, they tend to learn from one another even if oceans stand between them.

2. The AARI is developed from the integration of police data, prison data, and community supervision data or information. This means that there are multiple dataset observations of the offender and thus, the data is likely to be more valid in determining risk of offenders since there are multiple points of observation within the justice system.

3. Miller and Lane (2002) note that the AARI accounts for the fact that substantial differences in rate and type of offending occur between male and female offenders. This naturally reiterates the points made earlier in this chapter by Austin (2006), who noted that these two populations should not be assessed similarly.

4. The AARI uses a needs-based assessment as well as the typical variables used to predict recidivism. As Miller and Lane (2002) point out, this distinguishes "between risk control—those constraints and sanctions placed on an offender to ensure that he/she remains less likely to reoffend while under supervision; and risk reduction—the effort to achieve a permanent reduction in the offender's likelihood of reoffending" (p. 2). Thus, needs-based variables aid in allocating supervision resources so as to reduce likely future offending, rather than simply predicting it. It should be noted that though the correlation between actuarial risk and case-needs scores was not strong, a positive correlation between the two was nonetheless found to exist.

The AARI has proven to be highly accurate, and the Case Needs inclusion has helped prioritize those situations where changes are needed, even with individual offender cases. This instrument is also useful as a case management planning tool, and is thus able to enhance reintegrative efforts among those individuals who are most likely to reoffend. Students are encouraged to read the entire article by Miller and Lane (2002) found at http://aic.gov.au/conferences/probation/maller.pdf, since this instrument is an excellent cross-national example of both a recidivism prediction instrument and a case-needs assessment instrument.

SOURCE: Miller, M., & Lane, R. (2002). *A risk assessment model for offender management*. Paper presented at the Probation and Community Corrections: Making the Community Safer Conference convened by the Australian Institute of Criminology and the Probation and Community Corrections Officers' Association Inc., Perth, Australia. Retrieved from http://aic.gov.au/conferences/probation/maller.pdf.

Critical Thinking Questions

1. What are some of the perceived benefits to having a more accurate risk-assessment instrument? What are some of the problems?

2. Does the Case Needs supplement sufficiently address external factors in risk assessment?

For more information, visit the website http://aic.gov.au/conferences/probation/maller.pdf.

CLASSIFICATION

As has been addressed in earlier chapters, the presumption of this text is that recidivism can be more effectively reduced by ensuring that reintegrative efforts are maximized for offenders in the community. As was just pointed out, risk assessment of offenders is often simultaneously tied to their specific treatment needs. This means that security and treatment needs are not always easy to untangle from one another. Because of this, agencies must not only determine the general risk level of the inmate or offender on community supervision, but must also correctly "match up" the offender's treatment plan with the level of supervision determined by the LSI-SR and other risk-prediction tests and procedures. One primary tool used in corrections is an instrument known as the MMPI-2, which is the most widely used objective test instrument in corrections. The **MMPI-2** is an objective personality adjustment inventory test that can be given to large numbers of offenders at the same time or individually as desired. The MMPI-2 has 567 true/false questions that require the offender to be able to read at the sixth-grade level. Further, the MMPI-2 has been restandardized and is on tape for blind, illiterate, semiliterate, or disabled individuals. It is important to stress that the MMPI-2 is primarily a clinical tool used for detecting mental health disorders among abnormal populations.

This test has a number of "subscales" within it. These subscales are a series of questions that are embedded and camouflaged within the 567 total questions and are dispersed at random points within the test. The questions are all designed to measure specific points of interest, to provide a multi-profile view of the offender's personality. However, the MMPI-2 is very effective with the manipulative offender population because of three specific subscales that are included. These subscales of interest are the Lie (L), Infrequency (I), and Correction (K) scales.

The Lie or "L" scale consists of 15 items (out of 567 total) such as "I never get angry." The scale indicates whether the client is consciously or unconsciously presenting him- or herself as a perfectionist. The "I" scale consists of 64 questions (again, out of 567) but does not measure a trait. Because the items are answered in a deviant direction by less than 10 percent of those who take the test, a high score indicates that the offender has endorsed a large number of serious psychological items. For offenders, this may be an attempt to look bad on the test, or they may be confused or even having delusions (this is especially likely with mentally ill offenders). Last, the "K" or Correction scale measures defensiveness as a test-taking attitude. The scale has 30 items that cover a wide range of content areas. Low scores usually indicate a deliberate attempt to appear bad, but sometimes a self-critical offender (an addict, some pedophiles, or an offender that feels remorse) may endorse responses that indicate pathological tendencies.

In addition to the MMPI-2, the **MMPI-2 Criminal Justice and Correctional Report** is based on decades of research and is designed to more closely fit the outcome data from the MMPI-2 to a classification scheme (Megargee, 2004). The MMPI-2 Criminal Justice and Correctional Report (MMPI-2 CJCR) is perfectly suited to "match up" the offender's treatment plan with the level of security and serves as an additional double check when making security decisions from the LSI-SR. This report is used in conjunction with the MMPI-2 to provide information pertaining to the offender's needs assessment, risk assessment, and program planning within a correctional agency. The report is designed to identify those offenders who may suffer from thought disorders, serious depression, and substance abuse problems. It identifies those that may need mental health treatment as well as those that are most likely to be hostile, predatory, bullied, or victimized while incarcerated. This report also includes predictor items related to self-injury and suicide.

The MMPI-2 CJCR system was developed by Edwin Megargee and is fashioned around the well-regarded **Megargee Offender Classification System.** This system of classification is known to provide solid empirical support for classification and placement decisions. The Megargee System is especially effective in assisting criminal justice practitioners to deal with an offender population that is increasingly including the mentally ill or disordered offenders within its ranks. Further, the Megargee System has been reported to effectively classify 90 to 95 percent of the MMPI-2 profiles encountered in most probation, parole, and institutional correctional settings. In fact, one federal institution used the system as a guide in providing offender cell assignments and found that this process resulted in a 46 percent reduction in serious violence within that institution (Megargee, 2004). The Megargee Offender Classification System is the basis for the MMPI-2 CJCR. The results from this report can be used to support important management, treatment, and programming decisions. This includes the ability to do the following:

- Reliably classify offenders at initial intake of incarceration to support important supervision and treatment issues
- Identify offenders who may present less risk to the system, possibly allowing a downgrade in security level and improvement in placement on community supervision
- Better understand an offender's background, attitudes, and abilities to determine if the individual will benefit from substance abuse treatment, mental health programming, and other services
- Identify offenders who may do well in prison work programs based on their educational and vocational abilities
- Address readiness of offenders to leave the institution and to assist in developing effective aftercare programs
- Accurately evaluate and reclassify offenders over the course of their supervision to support programming or treatment decisions

The MMPI-2 CJCR also consists of nine behavioral dimensions that compare offenders to other offenders rather than to the general outside population to ensure that results are correctly normed. The following is a list of these behavioral dimensions:

1. Apparent need for further mental health assessment or programming

2. Apparent leadership ability, dominance

3. Indications of conflicts with or resentment of authorities

4. Likelihood of positive or favorable response to academic programming

5. Indications of socially deviant behavior or attitudes

6. Apparent need for social participation, extroversion

7. Likelihood of mature, responsible behavior; positive response to supervision

8. Likelihood of positive favorable response to vocational programming

9. Likelihood of hostile or antagonistic peer relations

Further, the MMPI-2 CJCR also identifies nine possible areas relevant to the offender. This provides treatment staff with indicators of difficulties that the offender may face. As with the other report components, the offender's problems are normed against a population of other offenders to ensure that comparisons are similar and that the test is valid for the offender population. The nine problem areas identified are as follows:

1. Difficulties with alcohol or other substance abuse

2. Manipulation or exploitation of others

3. Thought disorders

4. Overcontrolled hostility

5. Family conflict or alienation from family

6. Depressive affect or mood disorder

7. Awkward or difficult interpersonal relationships

8. Anger control problems

9. Tendency to get sick/ill frequently

When taken together, the MMPI-2 and the MMPI-2 CJCR provide a comprehensive means of classifying offenders based on both mental health and criminal justice categories of concern. The use of the LSI-SR serves as an initial predictor of recidivism, and it is desirable to have one single instrument strictly for this purpose. The MMPI-2 and the MMPI-2 CJCR both go beyond mere recidivism prediction by including mental health and security classification determinations. The process described in this chapter would provide for optimal assessment, security, and treatment of offenders placed on community supervision. Simultaneously, the offender would also gain excellent treatment programming from a system that would address specific areas identified as possible "problem areas" in their effective reintegration.

CONCLUSION

The collection of information is an important first step in the intake and assessment process. It is critical that community supervision officers ensure that information included in the PSI is accurate, since this document affects sentencing, later supervision levels, later treatment program participation, and release decisions that follow. In fact, it could be said that the PSI is a combined subjective and objective assessment document, and it is therefore fitting that it is discussed from an assessment or classification perspective.

Both subjective and objective assessments should be used when making security and treatment decisions for special needs offenders. However, security decisions should be based solely on objective risk-prediction criteria, while treatment decisions should be based more upon subjective structured interviews and clinical diagnoses so as to capitalize upon the expertise of the clinician. The Wisconsin Risk Assessment System was presented as the recommended objective assessment scale for security-based decisions, while the use of subjective structured interviews based upon the *DSM-IV-TR* diagnosis criteria were recommended for purposes of treatment. The Level of Supervision Inventory—Revised (LSI-R) was presented as the preferred instrument at the recidivism-prediction stage due to its utility with large populations, its quantitative aspect, the ease with which practitioners may use the instrument, and its ability to directly link with programs based on cognitive-behavioral treatment. (Most dealing with special needs offenders will use some variety of cognitive-behavioral intervention.)

The problems and pitfalls associated with false positives and false negatives were noted to provide a general overview of the problems associated with inaccurate assessment in correctional systems. This demonstrates that it is assessment that provides the basic building blocks to the success of community corrections as a whole. The MMPI-2 and the MMPI-2 Criminal Justice and Correctional Report were presented as the premier tools for effective classification of offenders based on their self-reported pathology and a variety of behavioral dimensions and problem areas that were identified. These tools are specifically designed to be consistent with the Megargee Offender Classification System, which is presented as a top-quality classification system for utilization by any agency that has a substantial population of special needs offenders.

Key Terms

Dynamic risk factors

False negative

False positive

Incapacitation

Level of Supervision Inventory—
Revised (LSI-R)

Megargee Offender Classification System

MMPI-2

MMPI-2 Criminal Justice and
Correctional Report

Needs-principled assessment

Presentence investigation report

Prognosis

Risk-principled assessment

Static risk factors

Subjective assessment process

Subjective structured interview

True negative

True positive

Wisconsin Risk Assessment System

"What Would You Do?" Exercise

You are the chief probation officer in a small community supervision agency in the rural part of your state. Your own particular state does not centralize probation services. Instead, each county is responsible for funding and implementing its own community supervision programs. You have talked with the chief judge of the county and you both have decided to implement a more standardized form of offender classification within the agency. The chief judge explains that she wants you to spearhead the design of such a classification system.

The chief judge explains that money is limited but some is available. Your task is to create an assessment and classification system for your agency that is based on elements of other standardized assessment or classification tools that exist. Further, the chief judge says that she can probably get funding for at least one scale of your choosing, but you will need to determine the price for that scale. Thus, your task is to develop an assessment and classification system for your agency and identify one scale that you would purchase to augment your own agency-made system of assessment.

For this project, you are to conduct online searches and find one of the standardized scales mentioned in this chapter. You must find the company that produces that scale and also find the cost of that scale on the open market. Be sure to cite and reference your source in APA format. Next, you are to outline the steps that you would take to produce your own agency-created assessment instruments. Since you are a chief probation officer, it is a good thing that you read current literature on community supervision issues. As such, you just completed reading this chapter of your textbook, and you may use the information from this chapter to guide you in completing your task, but you should be specific when outlining your plan. Further, the chief judge wants you to explain why you would choose those particular processes. With that in mind, you must clearly detail the process and explain the actions that you decide to take.

What would you do?

Applied Exercise

Complete the following questions as if you were constructing a PSI for Juan:

Juan is a Mexican American youth who has just turned 17 years of age. He lives in Los Angeles with his mother and two brothers. Juan's father is currently in prison for trafficking drugs and is not expected to be released for several more years. Juan has recently been convicted of committing simple battery of another youth. Police information indicates that Juan is suspected of being a member of a local street gang, and police believe that Juan's offense was gang-related.

This is Juan's first offense, and Juan does not have the appearance of being a hardened youthful criminal. Further, Juan is known to occasionally talk with Father Miguel, a local priest of the Catholic Church in the area. Juan has been noted to respect Father Miguel's guidance and advice; however, Juan's brothers do not hold similar respect for the Church. In fact, one of Juan's brothers is a known gang member.

At school, Juan is basically a quiet teen; he has a girlfriend, Miranda, who was expelled from school at one point due to drug use on school grounds. Juan has been labeled as having a math and reading learning disability by the school system. He is fully bilingual but does not excel at school regardless of whether the curriculum is in Spanish or English.

Juan's mother works hard at a local grocery store. She comes from the area and, upon asking, you learn that most of the men in her family of origin were or currently are affiliated with the Mexican Mafia. Juan's mother, however, has never had any official contact with the criminal justice system and has a completely clean record. She attends the same church that Father Miguel presides over and she is also active with a variety of church groups.

Students should complete this application exercise as a mini paper that explains the scenario and then addresses each question throughout. Total word count: 1,200 to 2,000 words.

Students: You know that there are many other things that you need to include in Juan's PSI, and you know that the information above is important. With this in mind, answer the following questions:

1. What points of information do you think are most critical from the information noted above?

2. Who would you talk with first when conducting the PSI? Who would be second and third on your list? Explain why.

3. What other issues would you seek to determine when constructing the PSI? How would you go about determining them?

4. How likely do you believe it is that Juan will recidivate?

5. Would you recommend Juan for probation or some sort of institutionalization? Explain your answer.

CHAPTER 4

The Role of the Practitioner

LEARNING OBJECTIVES

1. Identify the qualifications, nature, and work of probation officers.

2. Identify the qualifications, nature, and work of parole officers.

3. Identify key sources of stress for community supervision officers.

4. Explain the different roles and approaches of community supervision officers when addressing the interests of public safety and offender reintegration.

5. Identify the qualifications, nature, and work of correctional treatment specialists.

6. Identify the sources of stress for correctional treatment specialists.

7. Explain how the efforts of community supervision officers and correctional treatment specialists work to enhance and complement one another.

INTRODUCTION

No text on community corrections would be complete without a thorough discussion on the nature of the job and function of community corrections personnel. After reading this chapter, it should be clear to the student that the job of a probation officer is quite stressful and challenging, and at the same time, it does not pay nearly as well as many other professions. Further still, the qualifications for probation officers tend to be fairly high, at least in relation to the demands and pay that are associated with the position. This is truly an unfortunate paradox within the criminal justice system, since it is the probation officer that supervises the lion's share of offenders in the correctional system.

Because of the stress involved with probation work (or for that matter, with any community corrections employment), there is a great deal of turnover in the field. Naturally, this can have negative effects on the correctional system since personnel with expertise are even harder to keep. This can impact the service delivery that agencies are able to provide, and in some respects, it is likely to affect outcomes among offenders on community supervision. Indeed, the prognosis for recidivism can be impacted (at least in part) by the longevity of the probation officer and his or her demeanor on the job.

Thus, the content of this chapter is more than a simple orientation to probation and parole work. This chapter also presents an aspect of the field that is critical for students and others in society to understand. Indeed, society should be grateful for these personnel since it is they, as well as police personnel, who are largely responsible for keeping our communities safe from known criminals. Interestingly, most community supervision departments pay lower salaries than do police agencies in their same region. This tends to be true across the board, in terms of starting, midcareer, and managerial salaries.

Finally, it should be pointed out that a good deal of the information in this chapter regarding the nature of probation and parole officer work comes from a federal government source known as the *Occupational Outlook Handbook, 2006–07 Edition* from the U.S. Bureau of Labor Statistics. This source is freely available to people in the United States and provides one of the most comprehensive and accurate descriptions of job functions available. Students are encouraged to pursue this source when looking for employment in the criminal justice field or related fields. The information in the *Occupational Outlook Handbook* tends to be accurate and is directly published by the U.S. government.

TASKS AND NATURE OF WORK FOR PROBATION OFFICERS

Probation officers (also called community supervision officers), quite naturally, supervise those offenders that are placed on some form of probation and spend more time monitoring the activities of these offenders than anything else. Probation officers most frequently maintain this supervision through personal contact with the offender, the offender's family, and the offender's employer. This point alone is worth expounding upon since the very nature of the word "contact" has changed greatly during the last decade. Prior to the 1990s, it was not uncommon for many probation officers to treat their job as if it were mainly a desk job. In these cases, probation officers would tend to stay within the familiar surroundings of their office and would simply require the probationer to visit during an agreed-upon appointment. Though this was an easy way of maintaining contact with probationers, it did not ensure that probationers were being appropriately supervised and it did not give the probation officer a true feel for the probationer's contextual experience and lifestyle routine. Though probation officers during this time might have conducted frequent phone contacts with employers and other such persons, this still did not give the probation officer sufficient perspective as to the family life and personal aspects of the probationer's lifestyle that might be important, from both a public safety and a reintegrative standpoint.

During the mid-1990s, this type of probation became commonly termed "fortress probation" among many experts in the field, so named because the probation officer would essentially sit within his or her "fortress" (the office), waiting for the probationer to approach him or her. Over time, there was a deliberate push to ensure that probation officers spent time in the field and that field visits were commonly conducted. This also led to a change in the work hours that many probation officers had become accustomed to. Indeed, because it was the intent to keep a more random and closer eye upon the offender, probation officers found themselves conducting visits in the evenings and even on weekends. No longer was probation a Monday through

Photo 4.1 Probation and parole officer Monica Below conducts an informal interview while working her caseload. Interviews like the one seen here are conducted routinely in the office, with alternating days being worked in the office and in the field. Officer Below was once a graduate student of the author and now works full time as a community supervision officer.

Friday, 8:00–5:00 job. This has had substantial impact on the field and on the work expectations of probation officers in particular, and community supervision in general.

In addition to making contact with the offender through a combination of field visits and officer interviews, probation officers make routine contact with the offender's therapist(s), often having therapeutic reports either faxed or delivered to their office. These reports, providing the clinicians insight as to the offender's emotional progress and mental health, can be very important to the probation officer's assessment of the offender's progress. Typically, probation officers will work in what is called a casework fashion (recall this orientation from Chapter 1). This means that probation officers may coordinate job training, substance abuse counseling, community service involvement, and other elements of the offender's reintegration process. In addition, offenders that are on electronic supervision require that the probation officer know how the equipment operates, and the officer may be required to use such equipment to track the offender during odd points of the day or night. For instance, supervision officers may drive by the probationer's home at night using electronic monitoring devices to ensure that the offender is actually present at his or her home (indicated via electronic anklets that may be worn by certain offenders). Officers may also receive morning reports from automated "phone checks" that require the probationer to provide voice verification that he or she is at home during certain times in the evening. These are some of the functions performed by probation officers when fulfilling the public safety element of probation.

One other function of the probation officer ties in with the local court. In many cases, the probation officer will be tasked with investigating the background of the offender and writing what are known as presentence investigation reports (PSI's, covered in the previous chapter). While doing this, probation officers may review sentencing recommendations with the offender and even (perhaps) with his or her family. Note that this is in addition to any other arrangements that might be made throughout the plea bargaining process between the offender's counsel and counsel from the prosecutor's office. In some cases, probation officers may also be required to testify in court as to their findings and recommendations. They also will attend hearings for offenders on their caseload and will often update the court on the offenders' efforts at rehabilitation and compliance with the terms of their sentences.

A large portion of a probation officer's time is spent completing PSI's. As noted in the last chapter, the investigative time that it takes to complete these detailed and comprehensive reports should not be underestimated. Probation officers must verify employment, confirm the nature of relationships listed in the report, amass educational and vocational records, and complete interviews with family members (when applicable), and they must also often obtain statements from victims and witnesses. In addition, various records such as the police report, prior mental health service case notes, court records, and the like must be gathered before the preparation of the PSI can truly begin. These various tasks naturally take up a great deal of time that may often go unaccounted for since these tasks are not easy to observe, monitor, and measure in terms of work productivity analyses. Further, many jurisdictions (particularly in rural regions) may not have much in the way of staff office support, and this makes the entire process even more difficult to organize and maintain. Since this is often the case, probation officers typically type up their own PSI's, meaning that they spend a substantial amount of time at a computer, making it understandable why the "fortress probation" mentality might indeed be tempting. Given the volume of paperwork and the emphasis on field visits, it is clear that probation officers tend to work long hours that may not be clearly or explicitly covered by their salary.

Aside from the completion of PSI's, probation officers can have very large caseloads. As you may recall, this was a specific concern in Chapter 2, since it impacts the public safety of the community. However, this is also a prime source of stress for many probation officers. Technological tools can assist the probation officer in maintaining heavy caseloads, with computers, telephones, and fax machines being common working tools of probation. In fact, probation officers may conduct business from their own home via telephone or computer-based communications and form-submission processes. Naturally, this can result in a blurring of distinctions between time off the job and time at work, sometimes further compounding the stressful elements of the job.

The daily working conditions for probation officers are safer when in the office, but can also be fairly dangerous when conducting field visits. Some of the offenders that are on a probationer's caseload may be more dangerous than their arrest record or actual conviction may indicate. Further, these offenders may still (in violation of their probation) continue to maintain contact with other associates who are more prone to violence than is the probationer. In many instances, the probationer may have to conduct fieldwork in high-crime areas.

This point should not be taken lightly, and it is unlikely that the average person can understand the true contextual feeling that is associated with such an experience when conducting casework. Often, members of the community may display negative nonverbal behavior toward the probation officer and may be evasive if the officer should happen to ask questions about the offender in their own neighborhood. In fact, in many cases, persons living next to the probationer may not disclose anything because they are also at cross-purposes with the law. In addition, family members are not always happy to have the probation officer visit the home and, while complying with the requirement, may openly resent the intrusion. Finally, from time to time, the probation officer may make unannounced visits only to find the probationer in the company of unsavory sorts or involved in acts that are criminal in nature or in violation of his or her probation (e.g., drinking alcohol, trafficking drugs, or discussing various criminal opportunities). All of these issues can lead to some dangerous occurrences. This is even truer when one considers that most probation officers do not carry a firearm. The issue of firearm protection is a controversial one and will be discussed later in this chapter. However, it is safe to say at this point that there is a safety concern when meeting probationers on their own turf.

In addition, the travel may be quite extensive if the probation officer works in a large rural area. Some jurisdictions can be quite large, requiring substantial time on the road to reach probationers. The road time that may be involved can further exacerbate the stress, since these same officers will likely have numerous court-imposed deadlines, along with PSI's and other paperwork to complete, creating an even heavier caseload. Though probation officers are thought to generally work a 40-hour week, the reality is that they may work much more than this, especially during crime-prone seasons of the year. Add to this the fact that most probation officers are technically on call 24 hours a day to supervise and assist offenders or deal with agency concerns, and it becomes clear that work in probation is not a "cookie cutter" style of employment from day to day.

Though this work can be stressful, many probation officers do find the work rewarding. This is particularly true when probationers are successful on their probation and turn their lives around. Also, there tend to be solid benefits from working with local government agencies, as well as other perks that may not be available at other jobs. All in all, the work of a probation officer requires a person who is intrinsically rather than extrinsically motivated by his or her work. This means that people likely to carve a successful career out of probation work will tend to thrive on the challenge of the job, as well as the inherent reward of knowing that their work contributes to the reform of persons that may be in need and that their services contribute to society in a meaningful manner. Such people will need to believe this at a deep personal level, regardless of what community members may (or may not) believe regarding the point and purpose of probation.

PAY AND DEMOGRAPHICS OF PROBATION OFFICERS

One interesting aspect of probation work is the fact that the majority of probation staff tend to be female— roughly 57 percent or more, depending on the area of the United States (Champion, 2002). This is substantially different from fields such as law enforcement, where male officers predominate; women constitute less than 15 percent of the entire policing community (Shusta, Levine, Wong, & Harris, 2005). This is perhaps partly due to the nature of probation as compared with law enforcement and the particular skills women bring to the job. In the policing field, women have been found to be highly effective in defusing conflict situations or using a less contact-prone means of response. Shusta et al. note that female police officers are inherently more suited to facilitating cooperation and trust in stressful contact situations and that they are less prone to using excessive force. Likewise, there are fewer citizen complaints reported against female officers. Though these observations are related to female police officers, these same characteristics would be well suited to probation work, given the fact that probation has a reintegrative and supportive role with offenders on the officer's caseload.

On the other hand, most probation officers also tend to be Caucasian. This can be an important issue when one considers the fact that there is a disproportionate minority representation on most client caseloads. Given that there is such a lack of minority representation among probation officers, diversity-related training is all the more necessary and important in cultivating a rapport between community supervision personnel and those on community supervision. An abundance of literature has examined issues related to therapist–client interactions when the two are of different racial or ethnic groups. Generally, the prognosis in mental health research does not tend to be as good as when there is a degree of matching or when specific training and consideration is given for racial or cross-cultural issues. Since community corrections has a reformative element, it is not unreasonable to presume that such observations could be equally true among probation officers and their probationers.

Last, most probation officers have a college degree. That means that this group as a whole is a bit more educated than much of the general workforce. This might mitigate some of the cross-cultural differences since probation officers will be more likely to have exposure to diverse belief systems, ideas, and concepts. Further, this may also help to mitigate job dissatisfaction and stress, since higher-educated people tend to, in general, be motivated by more than external reward (Robbins, 2003). Somewhat supporting this is the fact that several studies have found that probation work in general tends to be enriching and challenging, requiring more of an emphasis on problem-solving skills that are likely to mesh well with high-functioning and educated persons. From this, it is clear that probation work is becoming more professionalized and has been likened to an art where probation officers must be skilled at matching security and treatment issues with the particular offender's needs (Champion, 2002). This, along with the helping aspects of the profession (despite the supervisory components), is likely to appeal to educated females that seek a professional track in their careers.

As of midyear 2004, the median annual earnings of probation officers was $39,600. The middle 50 percent of probation officers earned between $31,500 and $52,100 per year. Those within the lowest 10 percent of payment earned less than $26,310, and the highest 10 percent earned more than $66,000. As would be expected, higher wages are found in urban areas of the country, and also tend to be found in states that have a higher standard of living (Bureau of Labor Statistics, 2008).

ROLE CONFUSION, STRESS, AND BURNOUT RELATED TO THE JOB OF PROBATION OFFICERS

As noted in prior chapters, there is a dichotomy or duality of purpose that is associated with community corrections. On the one hand, the probation officer is expected to essentially act as a law enforcement agent, supervising and monitoring the offender. In this capacity, it is the charge of the probation officer to check on the probationer, interviewing and even interrogating him or her. Obviously, this serves an important public safety function, but this naturally impairs the sense of rapport that such officers are able to build with the offender. This sense of rapport is integral to any reintegrative approach, and, as we have seen in Chapters 1

Photo 4.2 They say a picture is worth a thousand words. In this case, body language of the community supervision officer demonstrates the tension and stress that can take its toll on officers.

and 2, the reintegrative process perhaps serves as the best means of ensuring that offenders refrain from future criminality. Thus, there are competing interests that are inherent to the community corrections process. While this has already been mentioned, what has not been considered is the effect that this dichotomy of purpose has upon the community supervision officer.

The competing interests associated with probation (and parole, for that matter) have been found to cause a great deal of stress and uncertainty for many supervision officers. Indeed, ambiguity and uncertainty tend to generate stress for most persons because it is simply human nature to desire a sense of control or mastery over one's environment. Amidst ambiguous and competing messages, this sense of mastery or security is difficult to achieve. This then leads to a competing professional identity among probation officers. This has been termed *role identity confusion* and is a primary source of burnout among community supervision officers.

Role identity confusion occurs when an officer is unclear about the expectations placed upon him or her as the officer attempts to juggle between the "policing" nature of the work and the "reform" orientation to the work. If the agency is unclear or sends contradictory messages (such as noting that attention should be given to each offender's needs to prevent recidivism, yet weighing officers down with excessive caseloads), then the stress level for the officer is increased. Thus, in some agencies, the officer must strive to utilize both approaches so that the multiple overt and covert expectations of the agency may be fulfilled.

The stress associated with probation work has become a serious issue of concern to agencies and should likewise be of concern to most communities. Public safety is directly impacted if officers are stressed to the point that supervision is not as effective as it otherwise would be. Finn and Kuck (2003) conducted one of the most comprehensive examinations of stress among community supervision personnel to date. In their report to the U.S. National Institute of Justice, they found that when considering stress associated with probation, there are three frequent and severe sources of stress: high caseloads, excessive paperwork, and unreasonable deadlines.

Officers report that high caseloads create more stress for them than any other single aspect of their work. There is objective evidence to substantiate these officers' feelings (Finn & Kuck, 2003). While there is no officially recommended maximum caseload number for probation and parole officers (a lot depends on the types of offenders they supervise), the average regular adult supervision caseload for probation officers in 1999 was 100 offenders (Finn & Kuck, 2003). But even this "average" caseload size vastly understates the number of offenders the typical officer supervises, because not all probation employees or even line officers supervise offenders.

Next to high caseloads, paperwork is the most significant source of stress for many officers. The study mentioned above found that paperwork was the most frequently mentioned of six sources of stress for federal probation officers (Finn & Kuck, 2003). Even when extensive Management Information Systems have been introduced into an agency, the workload is not significantly reduced. Further, the introduction of technology tends to bring its own unique set of problems, as unwieldy data entry screens and outmoded databases prove to be equally onerous challenges for officers and supervisors.

Having to meet deadlines—many of them unexpected—is the third most common and serious source of stress for officers. Many officers must meet a variety of immutable deadlines, many of them unpredictable.

For example, court hearings can cause interruptions in the officer's workload, particularly if one of the officer's supervised offenders is arrested. Once this happens, the officer must quickly prepare associated paperwork to get the arrest report finished prior to the hearing deadline; meanwhile, the officer's other work gets backlogged.

High caseloads, excessive paperwork, and deadlines, while distinct sources of stress, typically combine to have widespread and frustrating results. This makes it difficult for many officers to find the time to supervise their caseloads properly (Finn & Kuck, 2003). Essentially, "many officers find that they are so burdened by huge caseloads that they are unable to help probationers and parolees avoid recidivating and thereby protect the public" (Finn & Kuck, 2003, p. 20). Roughly half of all probation officers in one notable survey reported that there was insufficient time to complete assigned and essential tasks of their job (Whitehead, 1986). The more recent Finn and Kuck study provided additional support for these earlier findings, noting that federal probation officers identified insufficient time for their workload as the most frequent cause of stress.

Beyond caseloads, paperwork, and deadlines, Finn and Kuck (2003) also discovered that the following six issues were particularly stressful for community supervision officers:

1. *Lack of promotional opportunities:* Many probation officers have few options for promotion and feel stuck in their current service capacity.

2. *Low salaries:* Many officers report that the low salaries they are paid contribute to their work-related stress. Because of their inadequate pay, many officers are forced to seek additional outside employment. Working lengthy hours can, of course, impair the officer's ability to function at optimal levels when supervising offenders.

3. *Danger to officers* (see Focus Topic 4.1): The danger of assault, typically experienced during field contacts, is a significant source of stress for some officers. In a survey of federal probation and pretrial service officers, almost all (96 percent) expressed concern for their personal safety when making field contacts; almost 9 percent had experienced physical assaults (Lowry, 2000).

4. *Changing or conflicting policies and procedures:* These frustrating policies and procedures tend to come from two sources. First, different judges may request different information and set different priorities, creating a lack of uniformity in the agency's operations. Second, probation and parole agencies may have their own conflicting or changing regulations.

5. *Personal accountability for offenders:* Sometimes officers feel that the community, the media, or agency administrators hold them personally accountable for an offender's misconduct or criminal behavior while under their supervision. This may be a serious concern in some states, particularly when legislation has given just cause for such concern. For instance, in Washington State, the passage of the Offender Accountability Act provides legal recourse for victims of crime committed by recidivists by allowing personal liability lawsuits against state community corrections officers responsible for supervising those offenders. In addition, many conscientious supervision officers may feel personally responsible for their offenders' criminal behavior simply because they care about protecting the public and feel embarrassed to have an offender under their supervision harm the public.

6. *Courts and judges:* In some cases, officers have voiced concern that the court system does not give adequate weight to the officers' reports. Interestingly, some supervision officers also express concern for perceived leniency on the part of the courts. This likewise adds stress to their own job and can undermine their motivation to maintain effective supervision.

It is clear that the job of a probation officer has many challenges and associated stressors. This may paint a bleak picture for those considering such a line of employment. However, it should be pointed out that many officers successfully complete entire careers within this aspect of the criminal justice system. Further, the job of probation officer does provide many invaluable opportunities to network within the community. Probation officers tend to be central figures in their community, particularly if a community probation model is implemented within the agency. In such a capacity, an officer can see the direct impact he or she has upon his or her own community, thereby making an observable social contribution that is rarely achievable in other service functions.

FOCUS TOPIC 4.1

HOW DANGEROUS IS IT TO BE A PROBATION OR PAROLE OFFICER?

Surveys of State parole or probation officers in New York, Pennsylvania, Texas, and Virginia have found that between 39 and 55 percent of probation or parole officers have been the victims of work-related violence or threats at some time during their careers (National Center for Victims of Crime, 1998).

In Pennsylvania, 38 percent of the total probation/parole workforce in the State have been victimized (e.g., assaulted, threatened, intimidated) at least once during their careers. Half of officers who actively supervise cases were victimized. Of the most serious incidents, 24 percent took place in an offender's or someone else's home, 22 percent in agency offices, 9 percent on the telephone or by mail, and 11 percent on the street. Almost 38 percent of the victimized officers reported being shaken up emotionally by the incident, with 11 percent experiencing physical symptoms such as headaches and stomach aches (Parsonage & Bushey, 1987).

Many probation and parole officers think their work has become more dangerous. There are good explanations for this perception. The increase in drug use and the severity of the type of drug among offenders on caseloads have resulted in individuals that have little hesitation in choosing to use violence (Brown & Maggio, 1997). More generally, people sentenced to probation and released on parole are more serious offenders than in the past in terms of seriousness of criminal acts, prior records, and drug abuse histories (Finn & Kuck, 2003). A second reason for the perception of increased danger is that roughly 72 percent of community supervision agencies have created increased expectations for field visits with officers spending more time in challenged neighborhoods and/or dangerous areas of a community than was the case in previous years. Naturally, field work tends to be the most dangerous aspect of a supervision officer's line of work (McCoy, 2000). In 2003, for example, New York City probation officers were authorized to carry handguns because of a new policy that required an increased number of officers to make field visits (Finn & Kuck, 2003).

SOURCE: Quoted verbatim from Finn, P., & Kuck, S. (2003). *Addressing probation and parole officer stress.* Washington, DC: National Institute of Justice.

EDUCATION, TRAINING, AND QUALIFICATIONS FOR PROBATION OFFICERS

The field of community corrections in general and probation in particular has undergone a shift toward increased professionalization. Organizations such as the American Probation and Parole Association (APPA) as well as the American Correctional Association (ACA) have been instrumental in developing the field of community corrections into a professionalized form of service delivery. This has led to a number of on-site training conferences, correspondence, and online in-service training opportunities. While many states do not necessarily certify their probation or parole officers, some states do have various forms of certification that credential the skills of qualified professionals. For instance, the states of Illinois and Louisiana have a certification option for correctional workers, which is known as the Certified Criminal Justice Professional (see Focus Topic 4.2). This certification, while not specific to probation and parole officers, is ideally suited for such workers since it requires a working knowledge of court procedures, casework, correctional supervision, and treatment planning. Most all of the skills for this certification dovetail with the requirements for probation and parole officers.

THE CERTIFIED CRIMINAL JUSTICE PROFESSIONAL (CCJP)

The Certified Criminal Justice Professional credential defines the minimum acceptable standards for treatment professionals working in criminal justice settings (i.e., law enforcement, judicial, corrections, probation/parole, etc.) and recognizes that treatment of addiction in a criminal justice setting is a specialty field that requires performance by competent professionals. Individuals who seek this certification must be knowledgeable of both the criminal justice and substance abuse treatment systems.

The link between drug abuse and involvement in criminal behavior is well documented. Reports estimate that more than a third of inmates in State and Federal Correctional Facilities committed crimes while under the influence of drugs. This certification is a direct response to the increasing statistics and sets a baseline standard for treatment professionals working in criminal justice settings and providing an array of services to drug-involved offenders.

Important principles in regard to this credential:

1. This certification, which is based on a combination of competence and knowledge about addiction work in the field of criminal justice, includes academic achievement and specialized training in criminal justice work.

2. Authority for this certification comes from professionals working in the field of alcohol and drug abuse counseling who share a common concern for standards of competency.

3. Application for this certification is entirely voluntary.

Experience:

The experience requirement is 6,000 hours (three years) of supervised work experience for a Certified Criminal Justice Addictions Professional. Supervised work experience is defined as paid or voluntary professional experience providing direct service to individuals involved in the criminal justice system (e.g. law enforcement, judicial, corrections, probation/parole, etc.). Supervised work experience must be in the International Certification & Reciprocity Consortium, Inc. (IC&RC/AODA) Criminal Justice Addictions Professional performance domains [as follows]:

Domain #1—Dynamics of Addiction and Criminal Behavior; Domain #2—Legal, Ethical, and Professional Responsibility; Domain #3—Criminal Justice System and Processes; Domain #4—Screening, Intake, and Assessment; Domain #5—Case Management, Monitoring, and Client Supervision; Domain #6—Counseling

SOURCE: Certification Examining Board. (2004). *Certified Criminal Justice Professional (CCJP)*. Baton Rouge: Louisiana Association of Substance Abuse Counselors and Trainers. Quoted verbatim from http://www.lasact.org/pdf/CCJP%20Inquiry%20Packet.pdf.

For the purpose of recruitment, there are some basic background qualifications listed in the *Occupation Outlook Handbook*. The background qualifications for probation officers vary by state, but generally a bachelor's degree in criminal justice, social work, or a related field is required for initial consideration. Though this was not always the case in times past (some states allowing for less education when combined with experience), this is increasingly becoming the norm in most all states. Some employers may even require previous experience in corrections, casework, or a treatment-related field, or a master's degree in criminal justice, social work, psychology, or a related discipline.

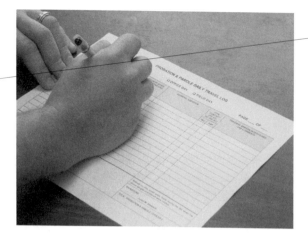

Photo 4.3 In this photo, a probation and parole officer begins to fill out a daily travel log. Community supervision officers often alternate days in the field with those spent in the office. While out in the field, they will drive to and from the sites where their offender caseload must be visited. This log is used to record the distances and time traveled for each officer.

According to the *Occupation Outlook Handbook*, applicants are also usually administered a written, oral, psychological, and physical examination. Given the concern with job stress that is inherent to this field of work, it is no surprise that changes in screening mechanisms have been observed during the hiring phase (Champion, 2002). Indeed, according to Champion, practices "have changed to include psychological interviews and personality assessment inventories for the purpose of identifying those most able to handle the stress and psychological challenges of probation and parole work, with less emphasis on physical abilities" (p. 354). This demonstrates that agencies are aware of the unique challenges with this type of work and wish to identify those persons hearty enough to withstand the pressures. This is of course a wise and prudent move on the part of agencies from the standpoints of liability, public safety, and employee–agency relations. Effective recruitment and selection at the outset can prevent a host of problems that would likely be encountered by supervisors and agency leaders in the future.

Beyond recruitment and selection considerations, probation officers are also required to complete a training program sponsored by their particular state of employment. In some states, this may be similar to a police academy method of training. Indeed, many states essentially certify probation or parole officers as peace officers, though their specific jurisdiction remains with persons on community supervision rather than general law enforcement in the community. In such cases, officers must maintain qualifications that are identical to peace officers in that state, including handgun proficiency, physical standards, and completion of in-service training. This type of training is especially true in states that have centralized training programs or that combine probation and parole into one agency function. One concern with this model of training is that much of the academy-level training is more specific to policing than to community supervision.

However, this drawback can be greatly offset if agencies follow with sufficient on-the-job training and utilize effective mentoring between senior community supervision officers and those just graduating from the academy. In fact, when states utilize standard police academy forms of instruction, it can be an instrumental means of creating camaraderie between policing professionals and community supervision professionals. As was pointed out in Chapter 2, such forms of collaboration should be specifically sought by agencies. Further, this provides the community supervision officer with a much more comprehensive and in-depth understanding of his or her law enforcement function. Moreover, as just noted, when local agency field offices provide a well-structured period of follow-up on-the-job training along with effective professional mentoring, the probation or parole officer will generally be more prepared for the challenges associated with his or her new function. Add to this an emphasis on in-service professional training through the APPA and the ACA, as well as an emphasis on obtaining eventual certification as correctional treatment specialists, and it is clear that such individuals are likely to be very well suited for their line of work.

During this period of mentoring, many agencies will have new probation officers work as trainees or on a probationary period for up to one year before being given a permanent position. This allows the agency to further assess the fit of the new hire with the agency and the line of work required. This prudent move can prevent many long-term problems likely to occur during later stages of that person's employment. In addition, many agencies will have several levels of probation or parole officers (see Figure 4.1), which can

FIGURE 4.1 Parole Officer Career Ladder

TEXAS DEPARTMENT OF CRIMINAL JUSTICE PAROLE DIVISION	
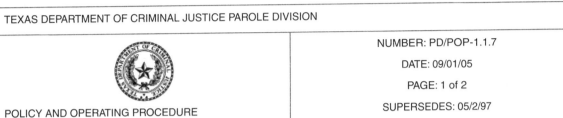	NUMBER: PD/POP-1.1.7
	DATE: 09/01/05
	PAGE: 1 of 2
POLICY AND OPERATING PROCEDURE	SUPERSEDES: 05/2/97

SUBJECT: PAROLE OFFICER CAREER LADDER

AUTHORITY: TEX GOV'T CODE ANN. §§ 76.005, 508.113

PURPOSE: To establish criteria for Parole Officer career advancement in the Texas Department of Criminal Justice Parole Division (TDCJ-PD)

PROCEDURE:

I. The entry level position for Parole Officers is Case Manager I (salary group B04) unless the applicant possesses one or more years of relevant experience, as discussed in the position description, and qualifies to be hired as a Parole Officer I (salary group B06). Applicants possessing relevant experience shall document the amount of experience on the State of Texas Application.

II. ADVANCEMENT FROM CASE MANAGER I TO PAROLE OFFICER I

The criterion for advancement to Parole Officer I is one year of experience as a TDCJ Parole Case Manager I performing in a satisfactory manner as indicated by performance assessments at the level of "meets standards" or higher in all essential functions on the employee's most recent Annual Performance Evaluation. The experience needs to be continuous; breaks in service longer than 30 calendar days will not count toward the experience requirement.

III. ADVANCEMENT FROM PAROLE OFFICER I TO PAROLE OFFICER II

The criterion for advancement to Parole Officer II is two years of continuous experience (with no breaks in service for more than 30 days, as described in section II above] as a Parole Officer I performing in a satisfactory manner, as indicated by performance assessments at the level of "meets standards" or higher in all essential functions on the employee's most recent Annual Performance Evaluation.

IV. Employees against whom disciplinary action has been taken may not advance to higher Parole Officer career levels until disciplinary penalties have been satisfied. Additionally, time spent on disciplinary probation or suspension will not count toward the career path experience requirements.

Effective September 1, 2005, if an employee meets the criteria established in Personnel Directive (PD) 72, *Employee Salary Administration,* Section III D the employee may be eligible to have the prior months of disciplinary probation restored.

V. The following procedures apply to any individual who was previously employed by TDCJ-PD in a career ladder position and is either rehired or transfers back to a career ladder position from another TDCJ position.

A. If a former employee is re-hired or transfers back to a career ladder position within 12 months of leaving the position, he or she may return at the same level in the career path occupied at the time of leaving.

B. If a former Case Manager I or Parole Officer I is re-hired or transfers back later than 12 months after leaving the position, he or she must return according to the guidelines for entry-level caseworkers and Parole Officers. Eligibility for subsequent advancement in the career ladder will be calculated in accordance with the criteria applicable to newly-hied personnel (i.e., only experience after the re-hire date is applicable to subsequent advancement in the career ladder).

C. If a former Parole Officer II is re-hired or transfers back later than 12 months after leaving the previous position, he or she must return as a Parole Officer I. However, only one year of experience as a Parole Officer I after the re-hire date will be required before the employee becomes eligibe to advance to Parole Officer II, provided that all the job performance criteria in section IV are satisfied.

D. A current employee of TDCJ of the Board of Pardons and Paroles who previously occupied the position of Parole Officer II and who occupies a position higher than a Parole Officer II may request and, if approved by the Section Director, receive a voluntary demotion to Parole Officer II level, provided that the employee meets the minimum qualifications.

SOURCE: Texas Department of Criminal Justice—Parole Division. (2005). *Parole officer career ladder.* Austin, TX: Author.

provide additional compensation as well as recognition of competency in the field. Indeed, agencies that do not have varying levels of staff classification should seriously consider adopting such a program, regardless of whether the compensation is greatly adjusted, since there is an inherent and intrinsic reward associated with the mere acknowledgment of the employee's expertise by the organization. This can go a long way in motivating and retaining experienced staff within the agency.

Entry-level probation officers should be in good physical and emotional condition. Most agencies require applicants to be at least 21 years old and, for federal employment, not older than 37 (Bureau of Labor Statistics [BLS], 2008). In many jurisdictions, individuals that have been convicted of a felony may not be eligible for employment in this occupation. Familiarity with the use of computers is typically expected, given the increasing use of computer technology in probation and parole work (BLS, 2008). Likewise, it is expected that candidates be knowledgeable about laws and regulations pertaining to community supervision, though of course, much of this information will be provided during both the formal and informal training process. Probation officers should have strong writing skills because they are required to prepare many reports. In addition, a graduate degree in a related field such as criminal justice, social work, counseling, or psychology can aid an employee in advancing into supervisory positions within the agency (BLS, 2008).

Community corrections agencies will also tend to have multiple levels of community supervision supervisors. Skill sets associated with supervisors of community corrections agencies can be quite demanding and can consist of a wide array of competencies ranging from the hiring of staff and coordination of training to offender case management, and even including the maintenance of interagency community relationships (see Figure 4.2). This last competency is directly related to much of the discussion in Chapter 2, where the need for community involvement in goal setting, volunteering, and offender assistance was specifically highlighted. In addition, the need for interagency collaboration (also highlighted in Chapter 2) is also critical to the success of any type of case management and therefore is germane to the reintegrative process. As noted before, reintegrative approaches are more likely to get the offender to internalize incentives and values that will encourage the person to regulate his or her own behavior (rather than relying on external controls) and therefore desist from criminogenic lifestyles. It is imperative that supervisors in community corrections adopt this viewpoint and impart this to their subordinate employees, building an agency culture that is reintegrative in nature. Thus, this area of competency (as well as others) is exceedingly important to the agency and the community.

TASKS AND NATURE OF WORK FOR PAROLE OFFICERS

First, it is important to note that parole differs from probation in some very distinct ways. The offender on parole has served a portion of his or her sentence in a correctional facility. This alone can have an impact on the type of security that must be maintained as well as the issues associated with reintegration. In these cases, the offender will likely need more support services since he or she has been subject to the effects of **prisonization.** For the most part, probationers have only served brief stints in jail and therefore do not tend to suffer the same level of emotional shock when introduced back into the free world. For the ex–prison inmate, it may have been years since the offender has seen his or her area of origin, family members, or friends. Spouses may have abandoned the person, he or she may be cut off from family, and progress in society may have drastically changed workforce requirements or other issues.

Latessa and Allen (1999) note that in one study, it was found that parole officers tend to review their caseloads in an effort to identify the presence of offenders that seem unpredictable or irrational. These offenders are likely to be more dangerous and in need of added supervision since they do not respond to threats or promises made by the supervision agency in a rational manner. In this regard, it would seem that parole officers tend to view their role as being primarily concerned with public safety.

FIGURE 4.2 Community Corrections Professional III

> **COMMUNITY CORRECTIONS PROFESSIONAL III**
> . . . manages community corrections programs by supervising staff and interacting with courts, clients, and other agencies in order to offer safe alternatives to incarceration.

Duties ⟵

A	Supervise Staff ⇒	A-1 Schedule staff	A-2 Delegate responsibilities	A-3 Monitor quality of work daily	A-4 Motivate and recognize staff	A-5 Facilitate supervision meetings
B	Maintain Interagency/ Community Relationships ⇒	B-1 Complete and provide courts and other agencies with documents	B-2 Serve as a referral to community resources	B-3 Inform supervising agencies of pertinent information	B-4 Collaboration/ coordinate with community/other agencies	B-5 Provide training to other community agencies
C	Develop, Implement, and Maintain Programs ⇒	C-1 Assess need for programs	C-2 Locate and coordinate available resources	C-3 Create programs	C-4 Implement programs	C-5 Monitor programs
D	Provide Case Management ⇒	D-1 Gather client information	D-2 Create/update client records	D-3 Contact clients regularly	D-4 Assess/evaluate client needs	D-5 Develop and implement case plans
E	Recruit and Hire Staff ⇒	E-1 Initiate hiring processes	E-2 Screen application	E-3 Schedule and contact interviews	E-4 Access candidates and offer positions	E-5 Conduct background investigation and check references
F	Coordinate Training ⇒	F-1 Identify training needs	F-2 Develop curriculums	F-3 Establish training logistics	F-4 Recruit and prepare trainers	F-5 Generate training schedules
G	Develop and Revise Policies and Procedures ⇒	G-1 Identify areas to be addressed	G-2 Conduct research	G-3 Revise/review existing policies and procedures	G-4 Write policies and procedures	

(Continued)

FIGURE 4.2 (Continued)

Duties

H	Continue Professional Development ⇒	H-1 Attend annual training (minimum of 40 hours per year)	H-2 Maintain competence on new computer programs	H-3 Attend conferences and seminars	H-4 Read related literature	H-5 Track new legislation
I	Administer Budget ⇒	I-1 Analyze current budget	I-2 Justify budget request	I-3 Monitor budget	I-4 Project future budgetary needs	

NOTE: Duty bands J and K are performed only by specialized Community Corrections Professional IIIs. Duty band K is only performed by CCP IIIs in juvenile facilities.

J	Perform Board Commissioner Process ⇒	J-1 Gather client information	J-2 Create and update client records	J-3 Assess and evalutate client needs	J-4 Determine case disposition	J-5 Complete and disseminate paperwork
K	Maintain Detention Facility ⇒	K-1 Provide emotional/ physical safety and security	K-2 Maintain security of facility	K-3 Supervise daily programming/ schedule	K-4 Attend to basic needs/requests of clients	K-5 Administer medication

Traits & Attributes

Patient/tolerant
Empathic
Organized
Self-motivated
Ethical/honest
Resourceful
Positive
Dependable/reliable
Flexible
Independent
Analytical
Decisive
Disciplined

Knowledge & Skills

Knowledge of:
State revised statutes
Children's code
Administrative order
Constitution
Criminial procedures
Pretrial law
Court proceedings
Secruity
Agency's organizational structure
Agency's mission/goals
Human behavior
Cultural awareness/diversity
Substance abuse
Domestic abuse dynamics
Probation abuse dynamics

Skills in:
Verbal written communication
Computer literacy
Leadership
Crisis resolution
Organization
Teaching
Mediation
Supervision
Interviewing
Self-defense
First aid and CPR
Working in teams
Listening
Fingerprinting
Using security devices
Using office equipment

SOURCE: National Institute of Corrections. (2006). *Community Corrections Professional III.* Longmont, CO: Author.

In many states, such as Colorado, Louisiana, and elsewhere, community parole officers are also Peace Officer Standards Training (POST) certified. As with the training for probation officers discussed previously, much of the training for this certification is similar to that provided to law enforcement. Parole officers must maintain offender records, and they often must maintain automated information systems that manage inmate records.

Unlike probation officers, parole officers almost always work for the state, and they do not answer to a judge or set of judges. The parole officer is an extension of the correctional system and is therefore overseen by the executive branch of the government. This makes for a less stressful situation, since there is usually more uniformity in operations for parole officers. Also, parole officer caseloads tend to be lighter than those assigned to probation officers, though parole officer caseloads are still challenging and are often considered too heavy to manage. Also keep in mind that all of the offenders on a parole officer's caseload will have committed more serious offenses than would be the case for probation officers.

Essentially, the work of a parole officer is very similar to that of a probation officer, and it is perhaps for this reason that the functions are combined among several state systems. Nevertheless, parolees are a distinct group from probationers and in many states they are supervised separately. Even though this may be true, the tasks performed by both types of supervisors are fairly similar. Consider the job description of adult parole officers in the state of Kansas, provided by the Kansas Department of Corrections (2005), as shown below:

> This is work in the case management and rehabilitation of individuals who have been released on parole by the Kansas Parole Board from a correctional institution and individuals on parole or probation in Kansas under the terms and conditions of the Interstate Compact. Work involves the performance of professional field work in communicating with and providing assistance to adult parolees and Compact clients with an assigned geographical area. Under the direction of a Parole Officer II or under the supervision of a Parole Supervisor, provides direction and counsels an assigned caseload of adult offenders to assist such clients in understanding and meeting requirements placed on them. Work includes assisting clients with personal, social, financial, family, employment or psychological problems. Participates in working with various community service agencies and law enforcement authorities in establishing and coordinating community projects that will serve to enhance the rehabilitative process and reintegration of the offender into the community. (p. 1)

This is a very good overall description of an adult parole officer's function within a defined parole agency. Beyond the tasks listed in this general description, parole officers in Colorado, Kansas, Louisiana, New Mexico, Pennsylvania, and elsewhere may conduct a pre-parole investigation (PPI) for the purpose of determining the suitability of an inmate's proposed parole plan. Such an investigation may include an examination of the proposed living conditions, the type of community surroundings, the plans for employment, and input from regional law enforcement, as well as explanations from the person that has agreed to sponsor the parolee. This is somewhat similar to the presentence investigation (PSI) described in Chapter 3 when we examined the job functions of probation officers.

In addition, just as with probation officers, parole officers make personal contact with the parolees on their caseload, though there is often a great deal of caution associated with this aspect of the supervision process. This is especially true in the states of Kansas and Texas where lower-ranking parole officers are given less discretion when conducting their jobs. In these cases, low-ranking parole officers (such as the Level I parole officer mentioned in the previous quote from the Kansas Department of Corrections) may be assisted or directed by a higher-ranking parole officer, particularly when field visits or other tasks are conducted in high-danger areas of the state.

Though many parole officers view themselves as performing an enforcement function, many find themselves addressing issues such as marital discord, financial troubles, housing challenges, placement with vocational or educational training, and referral for mental health counseling, as well as providing appropriate referrals to community service agencies for the previously mentioned issues as well as others that may emerge. This resembles the casework function noted in earlier parts of this chapter and in Chapter 1—specifically, keep in mind Abadinsky's social casework model. These parole officers will take reports from the parolees themselves and will also verify the validity of these reports by checking with employers, family, and other sources that have contact with the parolee.

As would be expected, the parole officer, by virtue of his or her job assignment, assumes responsibility for the proper maintenance of the offenders assigned to his or her caseload and is expected to ensure that offenders comply with the rules and regulations of their parole requirements. When violations are detected, these officers will be required to complete incident reports for major violations of parole conditions, but they may exercise some degree of discretion in the case of technical violations (violations that do not result in a new criminal offense but are noncompliant actions). It is the parole officer that typically makes the decision to issue a warrant for parole violations that result in the offender being sent back to prison.

Parole officers, like probation officers, will frequently make regular and special home visits to the offender's domicile. The parole officer will also visit the parolee's family members, sometimes in separate circumstances and sometimes with the parolee present during the visit. As noted with probation officers, this can be an unpleasant experience even if the family is welcoming and compliant. In many cases, the neighborhood will be able to identify the parole officer (particularly if he or she is driving a state-owned vehicle with state markings) and, in criminogenic neighborhoods, local community members may consider the parole officer's presence to be a bother or intrusion. In addition to field visits, parole officers may visit prison facilities for the purpose of establishing personal contact with prospective parolees that will soon be released. Such decisions will often be made by what is referred to as an institutional parole officer (called a facility parole officer in the state of New York), who is tasked with assessing inmates within the prison system and making determinations of suitability to present to the state parole board. In other cases, prison classification personnel may make this determination and will fill the role that institutional parole officers would perform.

Applied Theory   Critical Criminology and Community Supervision

The basic tenets of critical criminology are that inequality in power and material wealth help to create conditions that lead to crime. Critical criminologists contend that capitalism and the effects of the market economy are particularly prone to generating criminal behavior. This is largely due to the extreme inequality that impoverishes a large amount of the population. This also makes the less affluent groups open to exploitation and economic abuse at the hands of those who are more powerful. Thus, criminal behavior, according to conflict criminologists, has its etiology in the disparities between the rich and the poor, with the rich using their power and influence to dominate, subordinate, and exploit the poor.

Though it is not the role of the community supervision officer to right the wrongs of society, it would be useful for such practitioners to be aware of the economic structures that impact society and that may also impact how an offender sees

his or her plight. Most high-crime areas of the United States are also areas that are impoverished, consisting of populations that live in poverty and have great difficulty competing in the legitimate economy. Many of these high-crime regions, including those that offenders may return to once they are released on community supervision, offer few legitimate employment opportunities. Due to the lack of monetary resources in the community, other social services and opportunities will be likewise limited. The populations in these areas may also have had poorer access to education, medical care, and other services that impact the quality of life for community members.

In such communities, there may be a culture of poverty, with little legitimate hope of breaking out of the economically debilitating circumstances. This culture is far removed from that of middle-class America, though middle-class American youth may emulate the ghetto culture or sensationalized versions of such life that are portrayed by Hollywood and the media. This is unfortunate because it ensures that middle-class youth will not truly understand the pains of poverty, instead idealizing many of the negative criminogenic influences in such communities. Further, it labels, stereotypes, and reinforces the notion that poverty-ridden communities are criminogenic and even normalizes this so that youth in such communities accept this as their lot in life. Thus, the external portrayals exacerbate the problem. Incidentally, the portrayal of such underprivileged communities is done at the hands of rich and powerful media moguls, recording companies, and executive decision makers, all of whom fit within the upper-class and affluent society.

From these formulated expectations and due to the inequality of resources, the poor are again victimized as they are corralled into believing in and accepting a fundamentally unfair system. In addition, they are told through media accounts that the life of crime is perhaps their most viable bet to achieve parity within a system of economic *dis*-parity. It is with this in mind that police and other government agents are seen as being in league with "the man" who serves as a nefarious and obscure mastermind behind the lower class's woes. Such communities may also have family systems that teach children to fear police or to be disrespectful to police. Naturally, this extends to other government agents of the criminal justice system as well. Thus, the community in general and the offender in particular may actually hold the community supervision officer to be an agent of such inequalities.

This results in resentment that can build between the probationer and community supervision officer, and this also can create a chasm between the community and the agency. This resentment may have little to do with the crime committed and the actual supervision provided by the officer; it may instead be primarily due to years of underclass socialization that has conditioned the offender to see

government agents as part of a system that deliberately and methodically seeks to exploit the poor and underprivileged. Thus, an understanding of economic disadvantages, potential institutionalization, and marginalization to an inferior or subordinate role in society can aid the community supervision officer in developing a rapport with the community and his or her clientele. An understanding of these factors that impact crime-prone and underserviced communities can help community supervision officers who find themselves engaged in correctional case management services for people from such neighborhoods. This knowledge is also useful for correctional treatment specialists, who must understand the latent and manifest mistrust of treatment providers that is inherent in much of the underclass.

Community supervision officers and correctional treatment providers cannot single-handedly repair these communities. Further, these professionals cannot necessarily change the subculture of resentment and mistrust that may exist within some of these communities. But they can encourage involvement in community development and stabilization projects and they can be cognizant of the serious limits that face probationers and parolees who come from such communities. Agencies must work with people in such communities who are receptive to forming multi-agency partnerships, citizen volunteer groups, and the like. Above and beyond all else, such agencies and agency members must emphasize a sense of respect for the community in general, since this sense of mutual respect is what has particularly been lacking. An emphasis on community concern may help to take the sting out of the intergenerational resentment and distrust that may exist in such communities, allowing agency members to slowly change community attitudes and culture over the years that follow.

SOURCE: Lilly, J. R., Cullen, F. T., & Ball, R. A. (2007). *Criminological theory: Context and consequences* (4th ed.). Thousand Oaks, CA: Sage Publications.

Some states, such as Texas and New York, may rely heavily on institutional parole officers. In Texas, institutional parole officers are primarily involved with making assessment determinations regarding parole suitability rather than eligibility. These officers use various assessment instruments to weigh both static and dynamic factors (see our Chapter 3 discussion of these factors) associated with the inmate's risk of recidivating. At this point, "institutional Parole Officers compute a Parole Guidelines Score (which combines assessed risk and severity classification factors) online and document the results in a Decision Summary Form, which is transmitted electronically to members of the Board of Pardons and Paroles along with each inmate's case file. Board members then vote electronically to grant or deny parole" (Texas Board of Pardons and Paroles, 2001, p. 1). This same or a similar process (whether electronic or otherwise) tends to be used in most other states where institutional parole officers are used.

Finally and critically, parole officers will usually be expected to maintain an open line of communication with the law enforcement community in the area. This is similar to the functions of probation officers but also reflects the need for collaborative functions between agencies, as discussed in Chapter 2. However, this is an especially important function for parole officers, particularly in areas where released offenders may be prior or—unbeknownst to correctional staff—current gang members. Because gang offenders tend to recycle in and out of prison systems—going into the community, committing an offense, getting placed back in prison, and then again being paroled—this can have a revolving-door effect observed both by parole officers and police officers that routinely arrest and rearrest these offenders.

This relationship between the parole officer and the police agency is specifically enunciated in Colorado's description of duties for their Community Parole Officers. Specifically, the Colorado Department of Corrections (2006) notes,

> The Community Parole Officer is a liaison with local law enforcement and particularly with anti-gang units. Most YOS offenders are gang affiliated and the ties and values of the gang culture [have] proven to be very strong and destructive. Gang intervention is ongoing and is confronted immediately and directly. Gang behavior and associations are not tolerated. Coordination with the local law enforcement gang units is critical in understanding and interdicting the gang culture, its influence, and also serves to enhance the safety of the youth offender and officer.

This demonstrates that coordination of parole officers with local law enforcement is critical to effective supervision. As has been noted throughout earlier segments of this chapter, such coordination is particularly important with gang offenders, both juvenile and adult, and in those communities where gang membership may be a norm. Parole officers may also be instrumental in overseeing gang-exit programs so that youth can safely and permanently break away from gang membership. Regardless, it is clear that parole officers (typically called aftercare officers when dealing with juvenile offenders) must work closely with police in cases where this is beneficial or a necessity. This also fits with the self-image that parole officers tend to have of themselves where their primary function is one of enforcement, ensuring compliance among their parolee caseload.

EDUCATION, TRAINING, AND QUALIFICATIONS OF PAROLE OFFICERS

For the most part, the education and qualifications of parole officers are similar (if not identical) to those of probation officers. Parole officers typically must have a bachelor's degree in criminology, criminal justice, social work, psychology, counseling, sociology, or some other related field. In addition, many areas of the nation (such as the state of New York) also require 3 to 5 years of relevant work experience in casework or some other related area of employment. Most states specify that parole officers must be at least 21 years of age and also require the applicant to successfully pass a civil service examination.

Naturally, candidates must prove eligible through a full background investigation and psychological screening. Depending on the specific state, the psychological screening can be quite extensive. Consider the state of Ohio where a series of three personality tests are given to prospective parole officer candidates along with an in-depth interview. The assessment process is conducted by contract psychologists that determine whether to recommend the candidate for employment, recommend with reservations, or (when the applicant is not suitable) not recommend the applicant for any future employment whatsoever.

Training for parole officers, as for probation officers, can vary. In states where probation and parole are combined, the training is similar to that of probation officers. Often this may include undergoing paramilitary or law enforcement styles of training (such as in Louisiana where such officers are POST certified). In states where parole functions are not combined with probation, training can still require that parole officers be peace officer certified (as with the state of Texas where officers are TCLEOSE certified). In other states (such as Ohio), parole officers are expected to be distinct from peace officers and thus are not given that type of training.

Finally, as mentioned earlier, there is a growing emphasis on the professionalization of community corrections that includes both probation and parole. The APPA and the ACA have been instrumental in advocating for continued training on everything from the use of technological equipment to understanding unique needs associated with specialized offenders. It is expected that this tendency will continue into the future as community supervision becomes an increasingly important function of the overall criminal justice system.

WHEN PROBATION AND PAROLE ARE COMBINED INTO ONE DEPARTMENT

In many states, probation and parole functions are combined. You may recall from your readings in Chapter 1 that numerous states have abolished parole, though some residual offender caseloads may exist from before the abolition of this sanction. The point in mentioning this fact is to illustrate that parole has had a diminished influence on community corrections research, literature, and training developments, being that probationers greatly outnumber parolees across the nation and parole is not even a continued practice in 19 states. Thus, probation and parole services are often provided simultaneously, being a combined function in several states. In such states, it is the probation function that tends to consume most of the activities of community corrections agencies.

Also, the qualifications, functions, and type of work conducted for both probation and parole officers are very similar in most respects. This should have been clear from the discussions of probation and parole officers in the first half of this chapter. It is with this idea in mind that the remaining section of the chapter will progress. There are numerous issues that similarly confront probation and parole officers, and because of this, as well as the similarity in functions that they perform, many texts and professional journals refer to these practitioners simply as "PO's." Throughout the remainder of the text, the term **community supervision officer** will be used interchangeably with the terms probation officer or parole officer to identify persons that work in community supervision agencies and perform the duties typically associated with probation or parole officers. The exceptions to this use of the term will occur in Chapters 6 and 7 where specific reference is made to either probation officers exclusively (Chapter 6) or parole officers exclusively (Chapter 7). Even in these cases, reference may still sometimes be made by using the term *community supervision officer*.

As noted earlier, community supervision officers often have heavy caseloads and this can impair their ability to effectively supervise offenders. Though community supervision officers with caseloads restricted only to parolees tend to have smaller caseloads (as mentioned earlier), only a minority of officers are assigned caseloads solely consisting of parolees. Thus, it is clear that caseload issues are a serious source of stress for the majority of community supervision officers, and it should also be clear that the management of this caseload may require certain means of adaptation by community supervision officers. In this regard, it has been found that community supervision officers approach their jobs from different vantage points, based on their own perceptions of their particular role in the community corrections process. This again ties into the dichotomy between the competing emphases on public safety and offender reintegration.

Daniel Glaser conducted research on parole officers and the orientation from which they approach their job. The research that Glaser (1964) conducted will be utilized in this text to provide a general framework for all community supervision officers, both probation and parole. Basically, Glaser contended that community supervision officers operate at differing points along two spectrums: offender assistance and offender control. These two spectrums work in seeming contradiction with one another, as they each tend to put officers at cross-purposes when trying to balance their job as reformer and public safety officer. Four basic categories emerge that describe the officer's general tendency when supervising offenders. Table 4.1 illustrates both the Offender Assistance and Offender Control spectrums as well as the four resultant categories of officer supervision styles.

Paternal officers use a great degree of both control and assistance techniques (Clear & Cole, 2003). They protect both the offender and the community by providing the offender with assistance, as well as praising and blaming. This type of officer can seem sporadic at times. These officers are impartial regarding the concerns of the offender or the community; this is just a job that they do. Indeed, these officers may be perceived as noncommittal by taking the community's side in one case, then the offender's in another. The officers do not tend to have a high degree of formal training or secondary education, but they are generally very experienced and thus are able to weather the difficulties associated with burnout within the field of probation.

Punitive officers see themselves as needing to use threats and punishment in order to get compliance from the offender. These officers may also view the offender as a "lower class" of individual and are likely to see punitive methods of control as the only type of mechanism that the offender population will or can understand. They will likely have a morally judgmental view of their caseload. These officers will place the highest emphasis on control and protection of the public against offenders, and they will also be suspicious of offenders on their caseload. This suspiciousness is not necessarily wrong or unethical, as this is part and parcel of the supervision of offenders; however, these officers may in fact never be content with the offender's behavior until they find a reason to take some form of punitive action. In other words, the view is that those on the caseload are doing wrong but they are just not getting caught. The officer knows this to be true and makes it his or her duty to ensure that the offender gets away with as little as possible. Naturally, human relations between this officer and his or her caseload are usually fairly impaired and strained.

The **welfare worker** style of supervision describes officers who view the offender more as a client than a supervisee on their caseload. Welfare workers believe that ultimately, the best way they can enhance the security and safety of the community is by reforming the offender so that further crime will not occur. These officers will attempt to achieve objectivity that is similar to that of a therapist and will thus avoid judging the client. They will be most inclined to consider the needs of their offender-clients and their potential capacity for change. Welfare workers tend to view their job as more a therapeutic service than a punitive service, though this does not mean that they will not supervise the behavior of their caseload.

TABLE 4.1   Role Orientations of Community Supervision Officers

Assistance Spectrum	Control Spectrum	
	High	Low
High	Paternal Officer	Welfare Worker
Low	Punitive Officer	Passive Agent

SOURCE: Glaser, D. (1964). *The effectiveness of a prison and parole system.* Indianapolis, IN: Bobbs-Merrill.

Rather, the purpose for their supervision is more likened to the follow-up screening that a therapist might provide to a client to ensure that he or she is continuing on the directed trajectory that is consistent with prior treatment goals.

The **passive agent** tends to view his or her job as just that—a job. These officers generally do as little as possible and they do not have passion for their jobs. Unlike the punitive officer and the welfare worker, they simply do not care about the outcome of their work so long as they avoid any difficulties. These individuals are often in the job simply due to the benefits it may have as well as the freedom from continual supervision that this type of job affords.

Clear and Cole (2003) note that it is debatable whether officers would best be served using one consistent type of approach or if they should attempt to use each orientation when it seems appropriate. Thus, the community supervision process can be greatly impacted by the approach taken by the community supervision officer. Further, agencies can transmit a certain tendency toward any of these orientations through policies, procedures, and informal organizational culture, or even through daily memos. The tone set by the agency is likely to have an effect on the officer's morale and subsequently his or her approach to the supervision process.

On the other hand, some agencies may be very clear about their expectations of community supervision officers. In this case, if the agency has a strict law-and-order flavor, the officer may be best served by utilizing the approach of a punitive officer to ensure that he or she is a good fit with agency expectations. In another agency, the emphasis might be on a combined restorative/community justice model coupled with community policing efforts that are designed to reintegrate the offender. In an agency such as this, the officer may find that a welfare worker approach is the best fit. Thus, the culture of the community service organization will have a strong impact upon the officer's orientation, and if the officer's personal or professional views are in conflict with the organizational structure, the likelihood of effective community supervision is impaired. This is an important point because it again comes back to the sense of stress that is encountered by most community supervision workers.

Beyond the other stressors mentioned earlier in this chapter, it has been found that much of the stress for community supervision officers is organizationally generated (Finn & Kuck, 2003). Indeed, it is common for officers to feel that their agency is the primary source of their stress, including the lack of consistency in priorities and orientations that are emphasized. Most telling is the fact that it tends to be the agency rather than the offender population that is the most reported source of stress for community supervision officers (Finn & Kuck, 2003). The specific organizational culture and the manner in which the organization treats its employees can be very important to ensuring that quality employees are retained and that turnover (which is generally high in community supervision agencies) is minimized. Excellent research on organizational culture within community supervision agencies was conducted in 2006 by the National Institute of Corrections. This research, led by Stinchcomb, McCampbell, and Layman (2006), points toward the impact that an agency's culture can have on individual officer performance and the agency's approach toward the completion of the job requirements.

Organizational culture is basically the personality of an organization. Just as an individual's personality consists of behavioral tendencies, organizational culture defines and reinforces behaviors that are acceptable and fails to reinforce (or even perhaps punishes) those that are not acceptable. Essentially, organizational culture defines how tasks are approached in a particular agency. Naturally, some officer typologies on the control spectrum and the assistance spectrum (see Table 4.1) may not fit with certain agencies. This can seriously impact agency effectiveness, employee turnover, and offender outcomes.

Agencies that overemphasize a paramilitary approach, place distance between officers and supervisors, emphasize liability evasion, fail to give frequent positive reinforcers, and are control oriented will tend to have less loyalty among personnel, higher rates of employee absence, and high rates of turnover (Champion, 2002; Latessa & Allen, 1999). Employee longevity will likely be less than would otherwise exist, and valuable experience will tend to be lost. Thus, when and where possible, agencies should be amenable to the means of coping that individual officers may take to adapt to their dichotomous roles of law enforcer and caseworker.

FIREARMS AND THE COMMUNITY SUPERVISION OFFICER

Similar to the preceding discussion, the agency's emphasis on law enforcement functions can be seen in its policy orientation toward the use of firearms. However, there are two competing means by which agency firearm usage can be interpreted. On the one hand, it may indicate an agency with an orientation based on offender control and the enforcement of supervision requirements. On the other hand, an agency's firearm usage can be interpreted as a desire to ensure that officers are protected and that they feel safe in some of the criminogenic areas that they must travel through when conducting their field visits.

As noted earlier in Chapter 2, public safety is considered "job one" of this text. From this author's standpoint, the community supervision officer constitutes part of the public and the community and, therefore, deserves to have as many security options available as he or she may find suitable. Thus, the use of firearms by community supervision officers is perhaps a necessary ingredient to ensuring their own safety. It is also the contention of this text that this does not necessarily clash with the reintegrative aspects of community corrections. In fact, the use of firearms should be an irrelevant issue if offenders are not committing actions that would require an officer to unholster his or her weapon.

Critics of such a policy would be well served to keep in mind three key points. First, the use of firearms by community supervision personnel has more to do with the officer's personal safety than with being a means of obtaining offender compliance. Offender compliance is most often achieved through the power to arrest, and few critics would contend that community supervision officers should have that power stripped from their repertoire of options.

Second, even in those cases where firearms might be used to obtain offender compliance, this is simply an aspect of the public safety charge to which community supervision agencies must be receptive and accountable. This is no different than the responsibility police officers assume when they agree to "serve and protect" the public, and this is the same charge for the community supervision officer as well. In addition, it is clear that in many states, community supervision officers (CSO's) already obtain the same entry-level recruit training that peace officers obtain (including firearms practice and proficiency), and thus it seems more than reasonable to have such CSO's armed with an agency-approved firearm. In fact, it is the contention of this text that community supervision officers deserve the same respect accorded to standard peace officers. It would seem to be nearly a professional slight for agencies to prevent officers from carrying a firearm, particularly when they have been trained to do so, and even more so when one considers that they must come into contact with serious offenders during field visits.

Third, many community supervision officers in general, and especially those that supervise parolees, view their function as primarily involved with enforcement. This is telling of the agency culture that is likely to surround such officers, and this is also a statement of how the officer perceives his or her role in the community. With this in mind, it may be consistent with both community supervision officers' self-perceptions and the agency climate to include firearms among the officers' tools of the trade. Evidently, this is the general line of thought in many state agencies around the nation, as Table 4.2 demonstrates. The clear majority of states have some sort of allowance for carrying firearms (at least with adult probation and parole officers), though there is still a large minority of states that do not make such an allocation.

	Probation		Parole	
	Adult	*Juvenile*	*Adult*	*Juvenile*
Alabama	Y	N	Y	N
Alaska	Y[1]	N	Y[1]	N
American Samoa	—	—	—	—
Arizona	Y[1]	Y[1]	Y[1]	N
Arkansas	Y[2]	N	Y[2]	N
California	Y[3]	Y[3]	Y[2]	Y[2]
Colorado	N	N	Y[2]	N
Connecticut	N	N	Y	N
Delaware	Y[2]	Y[4]	Y[2]	Y[4]
District of Columbia	N	N	N	N
Florida	Y[1]	N	Y[1]	N
Georgia	Y[2]	N	Y[2]	N
Guam (probation only)	Y[2]	Y[2]	—	—
Hawaii	N	N	N	N
Idaho	Y[1]	Y[1]	N	Y[1]
Illinois (parole only)	Y	Y	Y	Y
Indiana	Y[5]	Y[5]	Y[1]	Y[1]
Iowa	Y	N	Y	N
Kansas	N	N	Y[3]	N
Kentucky	Y[1]	N	Y[1]	N
Louisiana	Y[2]	Y	Y[2]	Y
Maine	Y	N	Y	N
Maryland	N	N	N	N
Massachusetts	N	N	N	N
Michigan	Y	N	Y	N
Minnesota	N	N	N	N
Mississippi	Y[1]	N	Y[1]	N
Missouri	Y[1]	N	Y[1]	N
Montana	Y	N	Y	N
Nebraska	N	N	N	N
Nevada (adult only)	Y[2]	Y[5]	Y[2]	N
New Hampshire	Y[2]	N	Y[2]	N
New Jersey	N	N	Y[2]	—
New Mexico	Y[1]	N	Y[1]	N
New York (probation only)	Y[5]	Y[5]	Y[2]	N

TABLE 4.2   Arming of Probation and Parole Officers in 2006

(Continued)

TABLE 4.2 (Continued)

	Probation		Parole	
	Adult	Juvenile	Adult	Juvenile
North Carolina	Y[3]	N	Y[3]	N
North Dakota	Y[2]	N	Y[2]	N
Northern Mariana Islands	—	—	—	—
Ohio	Y[5]	Y[5]	Y[2]	N
Oklahoma	Y[2]	N	Y[2]	N
Oregon	Y[5]	N	Y[5]	N
Pennsylvania	Y[5]	Y[5]	Y[5]	Y[5]
Puerto Rico	—	—	—	—
Rhode Island	N	N	N	N
South Carolina (juvenile p/p only)	Y	N	Y	N
South Dakota	N	N	Y	N
Tennessee	N	N	N	N
Texas	Y[5]	N	Y	N
Utah	Y[2]	N	Y[2]	N
Vermont	N	N	N	N
Virgin Islands	N	N	N	N
Virginia (adult only)	Y	Y	Y	Y[5]
Washington	Y[3]	N	Y[3]	N
West Virginia	Y[1]	Y[1]	Y[7]	Y[1]
Wisconsin	N	N	N	N
Wyoming (adult only)	N	N	N	N

SOURCE: American Probation and Parole Association. (2006). *Adult and Juvenile Probation and Parole National Firearm Survey* (2nd ed.). Lexington, KY: Author.

1. Optional
2. Mandatory
3. Based on job specifications
4. Only for those supervising serious juvenile offenders
5. Based on county
6. Subject to judicial authorization
7. Intensive supervising and absconder program officers only

Finally, it should be noted that probationers and parolees can be dangerous. As was seen earlier in this chapter, probation and parole officers in New York, Pennsylvania, Texas, and Virginia all have reported dangerous circumstances associated with their jobs. The percentage of respondents reporting dangerous conditions (see again Focus Topic 4.1, How Dangerous Is It to Be a Probation or Parole Officer? for specific details) was substantial enough to seemingly justify the need for firearms among community supervision officers. Though this text's orientation is one geared toward reintegration of

TABLE 4.3   Most Serious Offense of Adults on Probation

Most Serious Offense	Total	Felony	Misdemeanor
(Total Number of Probationers)	2,595,499	1,479,504	988,033
Violent Offenses	17.3%	19.5%	13.5%
Homicide	0.7	1.0	0.2
Sexual assault	3.6	5.6	0.4
Robbery	1.9	3.2	0.0
Assault	9.2	7.6	11.1
Other violent	2.0	2.1	1.7
Property Offenses	28.9%	36.6%	18.2%
Burglary	5.8	9.7	0.3
Larceny/theft	9.9	11.1	8.5
Motor vehicle theft	1.4	2.0	0.4
Fraud	7.2	9.6	4.2
Stolen property	1.7	2.3	0.9
Other property	2.7	1.9	3.8
Drug Offenses	21.4%	30.7%	7.8%
Possession	9.8	13.1	4.6
Trafficking	9.7	15.4	1.6
Other/unspecified	1.9	2.3	1.4
Public-Order Offenses	31.1%	12.1%	59.6%
Weapons	2.3	2.5	2.1
Obstruction of justice	2.2	1.3	3.3
Traffic	4.7	0.9	10.2
Driving while intoxicated	16.7	5.2	35.2
Drunkeness/morals	2.1	0.5	4.5
Other public order	3.0	1.7	4.3
Other	1.3%	1.0%	1.2%

SOURCE: Bureau of Justice Statistics. (1998). *Sourcebook of criminal justice statistics 1998*. Washington, DC: Author.

offenders, it would be a very naive outlook to ignore the fact that some offenders are not only resistant to such opportunities but are also an outright danger to society and to those that supervise them. As the information in Table 4.3 demonstrates, a fair number of offenders (nearly 1.5 million) are on community supervision for felony-level crimes, and among those offenders, almost 20 percent have committed some type of violent crime such as homicide, sexual assault, robbery, assault, or some other type of violent offense. This alone should be sufficient grounds for community supervision officers to carry firearms, at least for those with offenders on their caseloads that committed felony offenses. However, even the misdemeanant offenders include some violent offenders. Moreover, there is a large dark figure of crime among these offenders in that offenders on supervision have probably committed numerous other offenses that were never detected prior to (and perhaps even during) their stint on community supervision. It is likely that some of their activities did entail acts of violence, but these acts never were (and never will be) detected by the criminal justice system. It is because of all of these considerations that this text takes a definitive stand on community supervision officers' use of firearms, and it is also the contention of this text that such an approach, whereby officer safety is placed as a top priority, does not impair an integrative orientation toward community supervision. This contention is held to be true so long as the agency's organizational culture supports such an outlook as part of its organizational mission.

NATURE OF WORK FOR TREATMENT PROFESSIONALS

As with the previous job and occupational descriptions given for probation and parole officers, much of the information regarding correctional treatment specialists will be drawn from the *Occupation Outlook Handbook* provided by the federal government. Correctional treatment specialists work in a variety of settings that range from jails and prisons to probation or parole agencies, and everything in between. Thus, these specialists can also be found in the various types of halfway houses, residential treatment facilities, and other such treatment-oriented intervention programs. Most typically, these professionals work with inmates to develop their release plans or treatment planning goals. These specialists also work with offenders in setting therapeutic goals and in ensuring that offenders meet the treatment requirements associated with their sentence.

Correctional treatment specialists that work within institutions will evaluate the progress of inmates and will develop case reports that are provided to the parole system. These case reports can have significant influence on release decisions from the parole board. In addition, correctional treatment specialists plan education and training programs so that offenders can improve their job prospects when released. Further, it is the correctional treatment specialist that often provides specialized counseling and psychotherapy related to a variety of issues such as anger management, substance abuse counseling, or sexual abuse/offender counseling. These types of interventions may be provided in a group counseling format or in an individual counseling form of service delivery.

Photo 4.4 Dr. Hanser stands in his office and describes abusive patterns of behavior as being rooted in faulty cognitions and socialization. While explaining this, he has found a resource to provide to a client.

Correctional treatment specialists often write offender treatment plans and clinical summaries for each offender on their caseload. This duty is performed whether the offender is in a facility or on community supervision. The correctional treatment plan will tend to include both short- and long-term goals that the offender agrees to complete. In addition, strengths and weaknesses associated with the offender will be taken into consideration as a means of assisting the individual in maximizing his or her skills and abilities while at the same time moderating the offender's cognitions and behavior to overcome weaknesses that might make him or her prone to relapse or recidivism.

The specific duties of a correctional treatment specialist have been very succinctly outlined and described by the Federal Bureau of Prisons (BOP) in job announcements and other such descriptions. According to the typical job announcement released by the BOP in 2007, there are six specific duties of a correctional treatment specialist. These six duties are listed below:

1. *Case Work:* The incumbent, in preparation of diagnostic studies, is responsible for collecting, interpreting, and evaluating factual information reflecting developmental and circumstantial factors for the assigned caseload of inmates. The incumbent is assigned full professional responsibility for cases presenting a wide range of problems; there are no limitations as to the difficulty of the services performed.

2. *Group Counseling:* The incumbent independently conducts group guidance sessions of a varying nature. During the sessions, different group techniques are applied to help the inmate understand the basic problems and to assist in functioning in a more acceptable manner.

3. *Individual Counseling:* Individual sessions vary in methods and intensity relevant to the individual's problems. They may focus on helping the individual offender understand and live within the complex family circumstances and assist him in developing new adjustment techniques. Helps the offender to understand, accept, and work within the bounds of authority.

4. *Liaison:* The incumbent acts in a liaison capacity with other units and institutional employees on matters concerning inmate behavior. He or she is responsible for interpreting and making critical judgments to institutional and other agency staff concerning the inmate's program and desired objectives. In this function, is required to have a thorough knowledge of the inmate's entire program. Serves as the primary liaison with the U.S. Parole Commission in reporting the inmate's program progress.

5. *Reports and Correspondence:* Prepares special progress reports for such consideration as parole, transfer, and restoration of forfeited good time, and makes appropriate recommendations. Corresponds with attorneys, judges, probation and parole officers, and other professionals regarding the inmate's case.

6. *Community Contacts:* Routinely deals with community resources to secure information and develop release plans. In order to serve the offender's needs, the incumbent coordinates the use of other professional disciplines. In doing so, routinely mediates with other jurisdictions and influences the public attitude and acceptance of parolees. These contacts require initiative, independent professional judgment, and skill to maintain good public relations and accomplish casework objectives.

Before proceeding further, there are a few points that should be made in regard to the six duties that have just been enumerated. First, it is important to note to the student that each of these duties complements those associated with community supervision officers. Indeed, the duties above are quite similar, except for the individual and group counseling activities. Though probation and parole officers undoubtedly act as sounding boards for offenders (being a layperson's form of individual counseling), they do not tend to perform clinical work. Nevertheless, the correctional treatment specialist's other functions are quite similar to what officers generally are expected to do on a routine basis. Thus, the role of the correctional treatment specialist is complementary to that of the community supervision officer, and vice versa.

Second, as can be seen, the casework function of correctional treatment specialists is synonymous with the social casework function that was noted earlier in Chapter 1. Indeed, Chapter 1 points toward Abadinsky's (2003) description of social casework skills, which include the three key components that follow: (1) assessment, which consists of gathering and analyzing relevant information upon which a treatment and a supervision plan should be based; (2) evaluation, which consists of the organization of offender facts into a meaningful goal-oriented explanation; and (3) intervention, which results in the implementation of the treatment plan. It is clear that the functions of the correctional treatment specialist listed by the BOP entail each of the three key components of social casework noted by Abadinsky.

Third, the discussion relating to reality, behavioral, and cognitive-behavioral therapies provided in Chapter 1 also gives the student guidance on the specific mechanisms used by correctional treatment specialists when conducting group or individual counseling with offenders. Here again, we see a very visible connection between intervention orientations in Chapter 1 and the specific duties that are listed for correctional treatment specialists in the current chapter. Thus, it is important for the student to realize that many of the principles associated with treatment and supervision tend to be interlocking and overlapping in nature.

Fourth and last, the correctional treatment specialist is expected to act as a liaison with other agencies and is also expected to maintain community connections beyond his or her own agency. This of course dovetails with many of the contentions noted in Chapter 2 where it was clearly presented that community supervision officers must engage in collaborative efforts with persons from other agencies. In addition, the correctional treatment specialist's need to maintain community connections also mirrors the points made in Chapter 2 where it was suggested that community supervision agencies maintain a close relationship with the community itself. Specific examples of community programs that use volunteers as well as examples of specific volunteer scenarios made it clear that this is an important dimension of effective community corrections; likewise, when examining the duties of correctional treatment specialists, it is clearly also an important dimension of their work. In short, the functions of the correctional treatment specialist are complementary to those of the community corrections officer, and should be taken as an added and integral component of the reintegration process.

RECORD KEEPING, CASE NOTES, AND ADMINISTRATIVE DUTIES WITH THE COURTS

Perhaps one of the best-kept secrets in the therapeutic professions, though undoubtedly understood by all therapists, is that there seems to be an unending need to document all actions that take place. Correctional treatment personnel must keep case notes of their sessions, and these must contain enough details so as to be useful during a therapeutic session. These case notes will typically include the therapist's own impressions, issues disclosed by the client, and any other issues of importance during the therapeutic encounter.

These notes are not impervious to court exposure, and, in some cases, treatment specialists are required to hand over their case notes to the courts. Likewise, treatment specialists may be required to report certain criminal activities that are disclosed by clients, since state laws may have reporting requirements that supersede the normal bounds of confidentiality. These are important issues to consider, since it is often the case that offenders will have numerous other criminal behaviors for which they are responsible, many of which go beyond the crime that eventually resulted in a criminal sanction being placed upon them. Naturally, this has implications for the bonds of trust that offenders may have with treatment specialists and again demonstrates how the power dynamics between the offender-client and the correctional therapist may be impaired by what is ultimately an enforcement function associated with most all types of staff employed in the correctional environment.

Finally, the workload associated with administrative duties should not be underestimated. Often, state and federal governmental oversight programs require any number of forms and documents on offenders, and the correctional caseworker must maintain these records. This may include medical challenges or histories, substance abuse issues and detox records, employment information, family information, criminal records, and any other type of necessary administrative maintenance. In addition, some treatment specialists may work on a correctional team with other therapists or caseworkers. In these cases, it is common for such groups to meet at least weekly to discuss the progress of offenders on their caseload. Such coordination of resources and personnel can improve the quality of the treatment program, but such an approach can be more time-consuming and challenging in its implementation.

TYPES OF TREATMENT PROVIDERS IN THE COMMUNITY CORRECTIONS SYSTEM

There is a public perception that most correctional treatment staff are employed through federal, state, or local government (see example in Focus Topic 4.3). Much of this perception probably stems from the fact that most institutions are themselves the property of various levels of government and are correspondingly run by these forms of government. However, this perception, though largely accurate, does not take into account the growing number of private correctional facilities throughout the nation. Likewise, many halfway houses and residential treatment facilities are privately owned or nonprofit.

FOCUS TOPIC 4.3

QUALIFICATIONS FOR CORRECTIONAL TREATMENT SPECIALISTS WITH THE FEDERAL BUREAU OF PRISONS

Qualifications: All applicants must possess a four-year degree that included at least 24 semester hours in the behavioral or social sciences or a combination of education and experience that included at least 24 semester hours in the behavioral or social sciences, and that provided applicants with knowledge of the behavioral or social sciences equivalent to a four-year degree. Courses such as sociology, correctional administration, criminal justice, government/political science, psychology, social work, counseling, and other related social or behavioral science courses can be used to satisfy the 24 hour requirement. In addition to the basic qualifications, applicants at the GS-09 level must possess 2 years of progressively higher level graduate education leading to a Master's Degree or possess one year of specialized experience equivalent to at least the GS-07 level that was gained in casework in a correctional institution or in another criminal justice setting; counseling in any setting, provided it required diagnostic or treatment planning skills to achieve specific social or occupational goals; or work treating persons in need of social rehabilitation. Applicants at the GS-11 level must possess the basic qualifications as well as 3 years of progressively higher level graduate education leading to a Ph.D. or one year of specialized experience equivalent to at least the GS-09 level. All graduate education must demonstrate that it provided the knowledge, skills, and abilities necessary to do the work.

SOURCE: Federal Bureau of Prisons. (2007). *BOP career opportunities: Correctional Treatment Specialist (Case Manager) GS 10 1–9/GS 11.* Quoted verbatim from http://www.bop.gov/jobs/job_descriptions/case_manager.jsp.

Indeed, during the past few years there has been a trend toward the use of faith-based programs, which are nonprofit in nature, spiritually based, and often residential in nature. These programs often work with pre-release and post-release offenders in an effort to facilitate the reintegrative effort. These facilities, though nongovernmental in nature, tend to operate from budgets that receive some form of government subsidy or grant funding. In addition, these facilities (particularly those that address substance abuse issues as a primary mission) tend to engage in the full range of correctional treatment planning. The intake, assessment, intervention, and referral process is just as comprehensive (and sometimes more so) as in those programs administered by local, state, or federal governments.

Beyond this, there is also a growing trend to contract out for the delivery of counseling services with private agencies or corporations. This trend has occurred at all levels of government and may even occur in some private treatment settings. The point to this is that the clinician can sometimes be either a temporary employee or one that is paid per client case. Aside from any concerns about the effectiveness of treatment delivery from such a variety of staff (an issue that will be discussed in later chapters), it has become the case that a number of different types of treatment staff may fill the role as a correctional treatment specialist. The only key similarity may lie in the fact that all have a therapeutic objective when performing their assigned duties within the agency. Further still, state laws often have different distinctions among types of therapeutic providers and the level of credential or license that they must hold. For instance, while a person may be *certified*, this is not the same as licensure. **Certification** implies a certain level of oversight in that a minimum standard of competency exists, but it is **licensure** that provides the legal right to see clients and accept third-party billing. Third-party billing is when insurance companies, employment assistance programs, or state programs are billed to reimburse the therapist. Obviously, this is important for the therapeutic practitioner working in private practice or in a nonprofit but private facility. In addition, not all mental health specialists can give assessment tests. Many of the tests (such as the MMPI-2) discussed in the next chapter require a fully licensed psychologist with a Ph.D., whereas other tests may have little or no minimal criteria other than training to administer and score the test.

The student should realize that when community supervision agencies contract with various providers, they must be cognizant of the abilities and limitations that these service providers have. Clearly, the more trained and educated the clinician, the more costly he or she is likely to be. Thus, agencies must be aware of what or whom they are networking with; it is not a fiscally sound decision to pay a full-blown psychologist for something that a counselor with a certification can do, perhaps just as well and for a much lower cost. Obviously, when deciding to add better assessment scales to their program, they must factor in the cost of paying a highly qualified mental health professional, such as a psychologist who is trained in psychometrics.

The following is a brief list of the types of therapeutic treatment professionals that most agencies are likely to work with either full time or on a contract basis:

Counselors—These professionals typically have training in particular areas, such as substance abuse treatment. They tend to deal with very specific populations that have specific problems. However, many counselors have a master's degree and full licensure; these counselors are referred to as Licensed Professional Counselors.

Social Workers—These individuals might only have a bachelor's degree, but most practicing social workers have a master's degree in social work. Their knowledge of social support systems, organizations, and groups (e.g., community aid organizations, support groups) along with their background in psychological interventions distinguish their fields of competence.

Psychologists—These practitioners have doctorates in psychology and typically have extensive education or experience in research, theories of human behavior, and therapeutic techniques. In addition to therapy and counseling, they specialize in the administration of psychological tests and assessments.

Psychiatrists—These are medical doctors. These individuals are typically only involved with the criminal justice system during times when inmates must be subdued with medicine or when seriously disturbed persons are involved. Their ability to prescribe medication for anxiety, depression, anger, and other disorders distinguishes them from the other three categories of mental health provider.

CHALLENGES TO THE WORK OF A CORRECTIONAL TREATMENT PROVIDER

Similar to the issues associated with community supervision officers, it would seem that correctional treatment specialists are also impacted by the effects of stress. Often, correctional agencies are stressful environments, in and of themselves. Caseloads are large, just as they are for probation and parole officers, though the nature of the work is not identical to that of supervision officers. In addition to the stress associated with the excessive caseloads, the knowledge that a substantial number of clients will not benefit from the treatment efforts provided can be somewhat defeating for many treatment specialists.

Another challenge that tends to be more common to correctional counseling than other types of counseling is the fact that caseloads are not only large but also very diverse. Indeed, the majority of inmates and offenders on community supervision are generally either African American or Latino. On the other hand, the majority of treatment *staff* tend to be Caucasian. This calls for the increased need for culturally competent treatment staff, but such competencies are much harder to develop than might seem initially apparent. For instance, there can be language barriers (such as with the Latino population in the Southwest and Southern United States, as well as Illinois and New York, or the Asian inmate population in California), or there can be issues of historical and institutional racism (such as with the African American population of the Untied States), or there can be cultural misunderstanding and stereotypes that occur from staff toward the inmates as well as those that are projected from inmates to the therapist. (Inmates and offenders also have their own biases and misunderstandings among themselves.) Issues regarding race and racism are further compounded by the fact that many offender-clients in state facilities will have come from lower socioeconomic backgrounds, this adding to the sense of powerlessness and deprivation that these individuals will experience. Likewise, racism can be a supercharged issue within prison facilities; the fact that most inmate gang allegiances are based on racial lines provides some idea of how important this key issue can be in the correctional setting. Such issues can undermine the ability of an unprepared treatment specialist to effect any positive change in his or her clients. More detailed information related to diversity and cultural competence in the community corrections context will be provided later, in Chapter 14.

In addition, the prison environment is not typically ideal for treatment programs. The prison subculture can undermine treatment efforts, particularly in state institutions. Beyond the inmate subculture, security staff may be distrusting of treatment personnel, and many may see such staff as "soft" on the inmate population or as being easily conned by inmates. In most cases, this is a simple lack of understanding on the part of custodial staff who presume that treatment staff do not realize the offender population is frequently manipulative. Indeed, such a naive treatment professional would be a hazard in regard to public safety concerns, and it is likely that he or she would impair the true efforts of most treatment regimens since accountability is a common theme. Nevertheless, there is often a schism that exists between treatment and security staff (particularly in state facilities), and this can be a source of substantial stress for many correctional treatment specialists.

Another key challenge associated with correctional treatment is the issue of building a genuine rapport with clients. This is impaired in institutional settings simply due to the setting itself. Consider that when participating in a group counseling session within an institutional setting, inmates will discover confidential information about one another. There is often a fear that such information will be shared with other inmates outside of the session, so many offenders in group therapy will simply refrain from disclosing. This is a very real and serious impediment to such activities since some information can be quite embarrassing and even dangerous to the inmate making the disclosure, placing him or her in a position of vulnerability in an environment from which there will be no immediate or short-term escape. Thus, many group sessions tend to stay focused on topical issues and result in few serious disclosures or exercises in empathy building.

In both institutional and community-based settings, the limits and boundaries on confidentiality may preclude any genuine connection between the treatment specialist and the offender-client. Correctional treatment staff should be sure to clearly note the limits on confidentiality prior to engaging in any therapeutic relationship. However, this ethical practice often has the unintended effect of placing the offender on guard in the relationship and, once again, the sense of trust is compromised. This can lead to further stress and frustration for correctional treatment specialists that genuinely hope to see positive change from clients and, over time, can lead to a sense of pessimism as the outcomes turn out to be increasingly dismal with each passing year of employment at the facility. Indeed, if a correctional treatment specialist stays at a facility long enough, he or she may see paroled inmates recycle back from the community to the facility, leaving the therapist with a dubious sense of occupational success.

Cross-National Perspective

The Effect of Homelessness on Probationers and Probation Officers in Ireland

The effects of homelessness are devastating, no matter what country, or under what context. For probation and parole officers, homelessness can add to the ambiguity of their job assignment and it can add stress to their day-to-day experiences. Homelessness makes an already difficult job even more difficult since probation officers know that homeless individuals are unlikely to desist from further criminality; they simply have few other options. Several problems can arise when an offender on probation or parole is homeless, including the probation officer spending excessive amounts of time trying to locate the offender or not being able to locate the offender at all. In addition, a homeless offender may not be able to comply with certain conditions of his or her parole or probation. Homelessness itself is a risk factor for criminal behavior. To combat this problem, the Irish government has implemented a plan known as the Homeless Offenders Strategy Team (HOST).

HOST has established several strategies to help prevent homelessness among offenders. The first strategy is giving special attention to those most at risk of becoming homeless, and instituting preventative programs. Such risk factors include age, race, substance abuse, or psychiatric issues. In addition, HOST helped create a Prisoner Information Booklet, which includes information about housing, welfare, and money matters. HOST has also worked to arrange transitional housing for offenders, and to develop partnerships with local agencies that can provide essential services. These aspects of HOST resemble a case management approach to improving the prognoses of homeless offenders on community supervision.

While the problem is not completely eradicated, the Irish government has made several successful steps to prevent offenders from becoming homeless and possibly reoffending.

As a note to students, the issues of homelessness, recidivism, and the role of the community supervision officer are interconnected to the points illustrated in the Applied Theory box in this chapter, Critical Criminology and Community Supervision, because problems with homelessness and criminality further highlight the link between impoverished economic circumstances and criminal behavior. Though the circumstances may not be identical in Ireland to those in the United States, this nonetheless illustrates how access to economic resources can greatly impact recidivism among offenders on a community supervision officer's caseload. Finally, this cross-national perspective also underscores the case management function of community supervision officers. It is clear that community supervision personnel in Ireland must also grapple with corollary social issues that affect their offender caseload. More information on case management functions in community supervision will be provided later, in Chapter 8 of this text.

SOURCE: http://www.probation.ie/pws/websitepublishing.nsf/Content/HOME.

Critical Thinking Questions

1. Should homelessness be a concern for parole and probation officers? Why or why not?

2. Would such a program in the United States be effective, or does the smaller size of Ireland give it an advantage?

For more information regarding the Irish probation system, visit the following website: http://www.probation.ie/pws/websitepublishing .nsf/Content/HOME.

CONCLUSION

The nature of work for probation and parole officers tends to be very similar, and often both of these functions are combined. Given the similarity between these two types of offender supervision, it has become common to refer to these professionals as PO's or, more appropriately, community supervision officers. The work of community supervision officers is highly stressful, can be dangerous, and is not well compensated. However, the work itself can be challenging and is ideally suited for persons seeking intrinsic motivators related to a sense of social contribution. This intrinsic sense of motivation can be equally enhanced or impaired by the officer's own perceptions of his or her own role as a community supervision agent as well as the organizational culture of the agency to which the officer must report. Each of these factors can "make" or "break" the individual community supervision officer's career, commitment, and sense of purpose.

The dual emphases on public safety and offender treatment are perhaps even further illustrated with the introduction of the correctional treatment specialist. The correctional treatment specialist places more primary emphasis on treatment aspects of offender processing but is expected nevertheless to provide accurate assessments of the offender's suitability for pre-release. In addition, these professionals may offer an array of casework services in an effort to provide a holistic approach to reintegration. Many of the efforts of correctional treatment specialists are challenged by the very nature and social culture of corrections, both institutional and community-based. Nevertheless, the duties of correctional treatment specialists tend to be very similar to those noted for community supervision officers, demonstrating that at all levels and in all capacities, efforts geared toward obtaining enhanced public safety through effective offender reintegration are the most appropriate means of approaching a community corrections program.

Key Terms

Certification

Community supervision officer

Counselors

Licensure

Passive agent

Paternal officers

Prisonization

Psychiatrists

Psychologists

Punitive officers

Role identity confusion

Social workers

Welfare workers

"What Would You Do?" Exercise

Consider the following scenarios where probation officers explain routine stress in their day-to-day work environment:

"I can have somebody's file pulled because they are a higher-risk person and I want to focus on his supervision and service needs, and then the 16 stupid things that I shouldn't have to be dealing with at all come walking in the door. At the end of the day, I realize that the one person I really should've been spending time with didn't get any time. That frustrates me because, let's face it, those are the cases that potentially are going to blow up in your face."

"Most probation officers' lives are kind of chaotic due to the size of our caseloads and the nature of who we have to deal with. It's hard not to reduce everything to self-preservation, routing people without getting in-depth, just to survive. On a personal level, I think most officers stay pretty closed up—like police officers. What do you do—go home and tell your wife or husband about the child abusers and rapists you saw in the office today? It's difficult for officers not to carry their work home, and yet difficult not to be able to talk about it there."

"In small communities, we are all interconnected. It brings a different kind of accountability. You can't just go home and forget about it because your neighbors are the people on your caseload or know your clients."

"You feel intense pressure because you have such a responsibility to the community. These high-risk offenders pose such a potential threat to public safety that you feel pressure to find the right treatment for this person and to make sure that they're getting something out of it."

SOURCE: The above scenarios have been adapted from Section 4: Addressing Secondary Trauma from the Center for Sex Offender Management training curriculum, Office of Justice Programs, U.S. Department of Justice. Retrieved from http://www.csom.org/train/trauma/4/4.htm.

Additional Scenario Information:

As it turns out, your Chief Probation Officer is always coming up with new ideas for the agency. He comes up to you and says, "Hey, I was reading some stuff online just a while ago about this concept called secondary trauma, and basically the notion is that probation officers with difficult client caseloads are likely to also suffer from a form of indirect trauma from having to deal with all of their cruddy crap," and after clearing his throat he goes on to add, "Well, I got to thinking that this stuff undoubtedly affects everyone's stress levels and all." After clearing his throat once again and displaying a rather wry grin, he finishes by saying, "So, since you have kind of been stressed yourself, I thought it might be good if you were to design a stress management/secondary trauma program for our staff."

He looks at you and says, "Thanks, I really am glad to have you on this!" and walks down the hallway to his office.

Students: Explain how you might design a self-care, stress management, or secondary trauma regimen for your agency. Be detailed and specific and explain how you would provide this training. In addition, you may find it helpful to conduct research of your own on this issue. If you do so, be sure to cite and reference your source materials in APA format.

What would you do?

Applied Exercise

Probation officers have not typically carried firearms while on duty in your jurisdiction. However, you have recently been placed on a task force that is charged with determining whether this would be a wise move for probation officers in your state of operation. This task force's project, known as the *Probation Officer Handgun Initiative,* has been formed in reaction to a spike in assaults on probation officers that has occurred in several high-crime areas of your state. In fact, one probation officer was shot and killed while doing a home visit. This entire incident has sparked substantial media attention, and many public activists and politicians have spoken on this issue. At the current time, reactions are mixed on the issue, but it is expected that the determinations of your task force will be instrumental when officially responding to the public. Because of the intensity of the issue, you have been given a very short amount of time to formulate an answer. You are expected to provide a balanced, well thought out, and organized analysis of the issue that can guide law and policy makers when deciding upon this issue.

Note that the instructor can either assign this as an individual project or as a group project for three or four students. In either case, students should complete this application exercise as a mini paper that is submitted to their instructor. Total word count: 1,200 to 2,000 words.

Legal Liabilities and Risk Management

INTRODUCTION

Throughout the remainder of this text, students will notice that this chapter will be referred to on a fairly regular basis. If there is any one chapter that is critical for both administrators and general practitioners alike, it is this one. Knowledge of liability law is very important for what should be intuitively obvious reasons. However, it should also be noted that risk management activities are also central to the good administration of a community supervision agency. Such activities make the world of difference between an agency under good stewardship and one that is plagued with internal and external problems.

In addition, much of the information for this chapter has been derived from a handful of sources. Most of these sources are federal government documents that allow for the free use of their content without copyright concern or infringement. Though this is, quite naturally, a wonderful benefit to researchers and writers in the field of criminal justice, it is not necessarily the free access to material that is the basis for the use of these identified documents. Rather, it is the sheer expertise of the persons who generated these government publications that has led to the heavy use of their works. Indeed, the mere fact that this information is disseminated through the federal government lends credibility to its accuracy and pertinence. With this in mind, one work by del Carmen, Barnhill, Bonham, Hignite, and Jermstad (2001) is an invaluable and exhaustive resource when discussing the issue of liabilities with probation and parole officers.

The current chapter will utilize the information provided by del Carmen et al. to a great extent when deriving various mainstream aspects of liability.

The means by which liability may ensue are many. First, liability issues can occur at both the state and the federal levels of government. Second, this liability, though most often civil, can be criminal as well. In most cases, the sources of liability are not restricted to community supervision officers but often serve as the basis of liability for any actor who is employed by the state. Nevertheless, just as with other practitioners that act under "color of law" (a term we will expound upon later in this chapter), community supervision officers typically incur potential liability due to their role as agents of the state (*state* being used in a general sense to cover local, state, and federal government). In addition, the types of liability may include a variety of forms and may come from multiple sources. For instance, civil and even criminal liability can emerge, and a community supervision officer can be subject to both state and federal levels of civil liability, depending upon the circumstances. For the purposes of this chapter, we will first begin with state-level forms of liability and will progress to the federal level.

STATE LEVELS OF LIABILITY

Civil liability under state law often is referred to as "tort" law. A **tort** is a legal injury in which the action of one person causes injury to the person or property of another as the result of a violation of one's duty that has been established by law (del Carmen et al., 2001; Neubauer, 2002). Torts can be either deliberate or accidental in nature. A deliberate tort refers to an act that is intended to have a certain outcome or to cause some form of harm to the aggrieved. On the other hand, an accidental tort would generally be one that is committed out of negligence with the intent of harm being nonexistent. These types of state law liability exist for all public servants, and this of course includes community supervision officers. Likewise, it is clear from this very brief description that community supervision officers can be held liable for damages to either property or a person and that this liability can occur whether the act is intentional or unintentional.

Intentional Torts

According to *Black's Law Dictionary,* an **intentional tort** is one in which the actor was judged to have possessed intent or purpose to cause injury, whether expressed or implied. This means that an intentional tort has numerous components, all of which must be proven by a plaintiff if the suit is to prevail. The components of an intentional tort that must be proven are as follows:

- The act was committed by the defendant.
- The act was deliberate and can be shown to be such due to the fact that the defendant had to have known of the potential consequences of the act.
- The resulting harm was actually caused by the act.
- Clear damages can be shown to have resulted from the act.

A hypothetical example might be a scenario where Parole Officer X conducts a home field visit to a parolee's house. While in the house, the parole officer assaults the parolee and says, "I can reach out and touch you anytime and if you say anything about it, I will have your parole revoked." The parolee is injured, has to go to the doctor for internal injuries, and decides to disclose the source of his injuries. In this case, the parole officer has obviously committed an intentional tort. The assault was committed by Parole Officer X (the defendant in this case), the assault was obviously on purpose and Parole Officer X was clearly cognizant of his actions, and clear damages in the way of physical injuries occurred as a direct result of the assault.

It is clear that the above hypothetical scenario was a *physical tort* action. The physical assault itself makes this evident. It should be made clear that physical tort actions can consist of a number of actions that are not as severe as an outright assault but that might nonetheless constitute a physical damage to the person or his or her property. For example, false arrest, where the person is illegally arrested while also in the absence of a warrant, and false imprisonment, where the person is illegally detained after arrest, both constitute grounds for a physical tort yet are not the typical assault or battery circumstances (i.e., excessive use of force) that come to mind with physical torts. Other types of physical torts might involve the person's property. These torts would need to be intentional (such as breaking an offender's property as a means of intimidating him or her) if this was not to be considered an act of negligence. Though the list could go on into eternity, perhaps it is sufficient to say that there are many avenues of potential liability when considering physical torts alone.

When considering *nonphysical torts,* the list of potential liability issues grows even larger. This is particularly true with community supervision personnel. The reason for this is actually quite simple. Though physical contact and restraint is frequent between custodial staff and inmates in jails and prisons (resulting in more per capita issues revolving around the use of force), it is not near as commonly needed between community supervision officers and their client caseload. Rather, community supervision officers are required to keep large amounts of personal information organized and confidential (remember, in particular, our discussion in Chapter 3 regarding PSI information), and they are entrusted with a great deal of latitude and discretion while conducting their duties. Most of the community supervision officer's duties include the exercise of effective communication skills with his or her clients. Because of the dynamics involved in this type of supervision, physical torts will tend to be less likely with community supervision officers than with custodial staff. When coupled with the increasing need to be mentally fit for the challenges associated with community supervision processes, it is clear that a whole set of stressors associated with this job make nonphysical torts much more likely than physical torts for most community supervision officers.

For the community supervision officer, there are several specific types of offenses or damages that might fall under nonphysical torts. These might include defamation, invasion of privacy, misrepresentation of facts, malicious prosecution, and wrongful death. Likewise, acts that cause harm to a person's reputation, privacy, and overall emotional well-being can all be grounds for nonphysical tort as well. Because this area of liability is most common among community supervision officers and because the categories of potential tort liability are so broad, it is necessary to expound on many of these concepts to ensure that the student has a clear understanding of each potential source of liability. Though the following discussion will not be exhaustive, it will highlight the more common areas of liability that community supervision officers face in their day-to-day functions.

First, **defamation** is an invasion of a person's interest through his or her reputation. In order for this to occur, some form of *slander* or libel must have occurred against the aggrieved individual. Many students use the term slander loosely but often have an unclear understanding of that term. Because of this, we will break these terms down further within the context of defamation to ensure clarity of understanding. *Slander* is any oral communication that is provided to another party (aside from the aggrieved person) that lowers the reputation of the person that is discussed and, when taking all of the facts and circumstances together, is such that at least a substantial minority of a given community would find such facts to actually be damaging to that person's reputation. Thus, the aggrieved and/or the community supervision officer do not serve as the arbiters in determining this criterion; rather, it is the perception that others have when hearing this information that determines whether it is slanderous. On the other hand, written forms of information that tend to diminish an aggrieved person's reputation would be called *libel,* not slander (and this is where many students have loose or even incorrect understanding of the terms). In such cases, it must be clear that the parties reading this information did indeed understand the material, and the information must cause a negative perception of the person, thus generating a negative reputation. As with slander, this must be demonstrated as an outcome that would impact at least a substantive minority of the community population.

Naturally, there is some fluidity in determining whether slander or libel has occurred. In fact, slander is very difficult to prove without any other corroborating evidence than the aggrieved person's testimony. Though extreme cases could exist where a community supervision officer repeats slanderous information about an offender on community supervision to numerous persons in the community, creating the opportunity for multiple points of testimony and thus causing damage to the offender's reputation among a sizable number of persons in the community, this is not likely to occur with untrue statements or circumstances. On the other hand, libel may actually reach a fair number of people in a much more expedient fashion through a printed source that is widely copied and distributed among numerous people. This is also more easily proven since it is, after all, in writing for all to see at points in the future. However, community supervision officers do tend to be careful with what they put into writing, particularly if such records may be used outside of their own agency, thus making this less common than one might think. Regardless, the fact of whether the information is true or untrue is actually critical to determining slander or libel. Indeed, any proof that a statement's content is true is an absolute and irrefutable defense against slander or libel. This is the case regardless of how damaging a statement may be (del Carmen et al., 2001). Thus, as long as community supervision officers ensure that their information is, as a matter of material fact, true and accurate, they do not need to worry about being found liable for defamation.

Invasion of privacy is a general term that involves multiple forms of action and legal concepts. Aside from the commonly understood issue of interfering with a person's reasonable right to privacy (the actual right to privacy itself being fluid in nature), invasion of privacy can also occur if the aggrieved can show that there is some form of encroachment or damage to their very personality. Both of these aspects are related to the right to essentially be left alone (del Carmen et al., 2001). These areas of concern might include (1) an intrusion into the aggrieved person's private affairs or violation of his or her seclusion, (2) publication of facts that are arranged or stated in such a manner as to portray the person in a false light, and (3) the public disclosure of private facts about the aggrieved person. For community supervision officers, this might occur when communication of some incident in their client's private life occurs in an unauthorized context. This can also include other behaviors related to surveillance, such as "peeping" or spying, taking unauthorized photographs of the offender, or the unauthorized hiring of other persons to conduct such acts on behalf of the community supervision officer.

The next category, infliction of emotional distress, refers to acts (either intentional or negligent) that lead to emotional distress of the client. Emotional distress can occur due to words alone, gestures, or conduct. In the context of community supervision officers, tactics that bully or abuse the client would fall within this category. Even words alone can involve liability, depending on the circumstances and context, such as a situation where the community supervision officer causes verbal insult to the offender client while in public. However, one simple incident, though not likely to be in adherence to agency policy, typically does not incur liability unless the situation can be shown to be "extreme" and "outrageous" (del Carmen et al., 2001). In other cases, it may be that the emotional distress must be profound enough to cause physical symptoms or injuries (e.g., accidental injuries due to worry/anxiety from mental abuse, heart attack, ulcer, or post-traumatic stress disorder that results in nightmares and self-injurious behavior). In other cases (depending on that state's laws), the outrageous conduct of the community supervision officer may, in and of itself, be sufficient grounds for liability, regardless of whether injuries can be proven (del Carmen et al., 2001).

The next area of potential nonphysical liability involves the misrepresentation of facts. In order for liability to be incurred through the **misrepresentation of facts**, the community supervision officer must provide some sort of false representation of either a past or present fact that is used in a decision-making outcome related to the offender. The very nature of community supervision makes personnel working in this field fairly vulnerable to this possibility. Community supervision officers must routinely provide facts (again, consider the PSI from Chapter 3) and compile information and also may find the need to share this information with authorized agencies or persons. The welfare of the client often hinges on the accuracy of the PSI and the probation/parole officer's effective discretion when releasing this information. Naturally, community supervision officers are open to liability when they deliberately generate injurious falsehoods and, whether detected or not, are breaking the law and are in violation of most all agency rules.

The last area of nonphysical tort that will be discussed is that of malicious prosecution. **Malicious prosecution** is when a criminal accusation is made by someone that has no probable cause, and when he or she generates such actions for improper reasons. In such cases, the accused must be, as a matter of material fact, innocent of the charges that were made. Take for instance a scenario where Parole Officer X is talking with a female parolee on his caseload. The female parolee is attractive and Parole Officer X knows that before serving prison time, the female parolee was an exotic dancer and an active prostitute. Parole Officer X propositions her for sex. Parole Officer X states that he will help the parolee to get further recommendations to receive custody of her children from a current foster home where the children reside; if the parolee does not consent to sexual relations, Parole Officer X threatens to charge her with prostitution as well as soliciting an officer of the court (the implication being that Parole Officer X will tell the judge that the female parolee propositioned *him* for positive recommendations in exchange for sexual favors). The female parolee refuses to comply with the request and Parole Officer X files criminal charges against her for prostitution and soliciting/bribing an officer. Unbeknownst to Parole Officer X, a private investigator hired by the female parolee was hidden in the room and recorded the entire conversation on video and audio. The female parolee was ultimately found to be innocent of the charges and, in turn, charged Parole Officer X with malicious prosecution. Parole Officer X lost his job and the female parolee sued the agency, later settling out of court.

Negligence Torts

The next primary category of state tort is those that are acts of negligence. In many cases, these types of torts are filed by persons that are injured by the criminal behavior of probationers or parolees that recidivate while under supervision. Presumably, these plaintiffs contend that the agency and its staff have neglected their duty to ensure the safety of the public. In the vast majority of cases, these suits are not actually won, particularly if the community supervision officer has adhered to agency policy. Most agencies have sufficient policy safeguards to ensure that an adequate good-faith attempt is made at public safety and, presuming that the officer follows policy, liability is not likely to be incurred. Nevertheless, this area of concern can be troublesome since it is never pleasant to be faced with the prospect of a lawsuit. This can (and does) add to the stress of the community supervision officer, with lawsuits being yet another contributor to the high rate of burnout.

It is important to have a clear understanding of what negligence is, and is not. For the purposes of this text, **negligence** is defined as doing what a reasonably prudent person would *not* have done in similar circumstances, or failing to do what a reasonably prudent person *would* have done in similar circumstances. Essentially, negligence is the failure to exercise the same degree of caution, foresight, and good judgment that any other reasonable person would have in a similar situation. One key point to keep in mind is the term "reasonable person." This is a common term used by the U.S. Supreme Court in a variety of cases. Though this term does not have a specific definition, it does provide a general criterion against which liability can be assessed. Nevertheless, it can be seen that there is a great deal of fluidity with this concept. Aside from the vague conceptualizations associated with such general definitions, the following minimal conditions are typically required to establish a case of negligence:

1. A legal duty is owed to the aggrieved person.

2. A breach of that duty must have occurred, whether by the failure to act or by the commission of action that was not professionally sufficient to fulfill that duty.

3. The aggrieved can demonstrate that an injury did occur.

4. The person with the duty owed to the aggrieved person committed the act (or lack of action) that was the proximate cause of the injury.

In addition, there are three general classifications of negligence; these are slight, gross, and willful negligence. **Slight negligence** is the failure to exercise the standard of care and attention that highly conscientious and attentive persons might use. Thus, slight negligence can be considered an accidental lapse of judgment, typically from someone who ordinarily does exercise due caution in the performance of his or her duties. **Gross negligence** is a failure to exercise the standard of care and attention that is even less than that which would be expected from someone who was already careless in his or her duty. Thus, persons committing gross negligence are truly derelict in their duties, falling short of those who are already careless and haphazard in the fulfillment of their duty. Last, **willful negligence** occurs when the person commits an act that is in flagrant disregard of consequences that are probable and that he or she was most assuredly able to foresee.

In most all cases, no true liability will be found for slight negligence, the only exceptions being those instances where the offense is one where the agent is held *strictly liable* (strict liability offenses are those where no culpability is required for the person to be guilty of the offense, such as with traffic offenses, or even statutory rape). Though the commission of slight negligence may violate policy or procedure that the agency has set, and though the employee may (or may not) be subject to internal disciplinary action, there is no damage or wrong that has been inflicted upon a person or his or her property so as to rise to the level of being legally liable for remuneration or compensation. Naturally, liability can and does attach for both gross and willful negligence. However, it should be clear that all three types of negligence have fairly broad and open definitions. This is actually quite problematic because the results in determining liability may not always be uniform or consistent. While this is true among judges that are tasked with providing their own subjective input, this is especially true with juries who tend to be less well versed in the law or standards of accountability. This creates some inconsistencies in the classification of negligence offenses and the corresponding awards for damages that ensue. Despite this, even among juries, the tendency is to consider the seriousness of the charge in correlation to the gravity of the damage that has been incurred by the aggrieved party.

Photo 5.1 Judge Wilson Rambo sits in his court and poses for a photo. Judge Rambo hears a variety of cases and works in processing a number of offenders who are sent through the community's drug court.

Liability Under Section 1983 Federal Lawsuits

This avenue for civil redress is one of the most frequently used by persons seeking damages from the government. Though there is substantial history associated with this particular form of liability, this text will delve right into the substantive issues associated with Section 1983 (42 U.S.C. § 1983) liabilities. Essentially, there are two simple requirements that must exist in order for liability to be imparted to a person so charged:

1. The person charged (the defendant) acted under color of state law.

2. The person charged violated a right secured by the Constitution or by federal law.

Both of these requirements need some bit of explanation. First, the term "color of state law" must be clarified. This term simply means that the actor committed the behavior while under the authority of some form of government. In this case, the term "state" is meant to imply government in general, regardless of the level of government (i.e., local, state, or federal) that is associated with the agency. Thus, local jailers, county probation officers, and state parole officers all act under the color of state law when they are performing their duties in the employment of their respective agencies. This liability does not, however, apply during their off-time "normal" lives. In further clarifying this concept, del Carmen et al. (2001) note that anything that a community supervision officer does in the performance of his or her regular duties and during the usual hours of employment is considered to fall under the color of state law. In contrast, whatever this same person does as a private citizen during his or her off hours falls outside and beyond the color of state law.

Though specific mention has been made regarding local-, county-, and state-level agents, it should be noted that federal agents can also be held liable under the basic tenets of Section 1983. Thus, federal probation officers can be held liable by this federal statute that was initially intended to govern lower levels of government. Often, however, when federal agents are sued for violation of a constitutional or federally protected right that occurred while under the color of state law, this process may be referred to as a *Bivens* suit. This is because it was the U.S. Supreme Court case of *Bivens v. Six Unknown Agents* (1971) that clarified this avenue of liability for federal agents.

Likewise, the case of *Richardson v. McKnight* (1997) has made it clear that private individuals that are under contract with a public agency may be held liable just as if they are public servants because they are, in fact, acting under the color of state law. This would naturally include persons with private companies that provide PSI work and other such functions that are sometimes contracted out in some areas of the nation. This can also include private medical staff, mental health professionals, and other such actors if they are under contract or work for the community supervision agency.

Next, in order for a Section 1983 claim to prevail, the defendant (in this case, the community supervision officer) must have violated either a constitutional right or a right that is created or protected by federal law. Note that when considering Section 1983, this only applies to those rights guaranteed by the United States Constitution (not a state constitution), and it also only applies to rights secured by federal (not state) law. Thus, if a probation or parole officer conducts an illegal search of an offender (a 4th Amendment right) or if he or she inflicts cruel or unusual punishment (freedom from this is protected under the 8th Amendment), he or she can be held liable under a Section 1983 lawsuit. Similarly, if a federal law is passed providing certain rights or protections to individuals, a community supervision officer may not violate that right or protection without subjecting him- or herself to liability. In our previous examples with Parole Officer X, it was found that he had assaulted a parolee while saying "I can reach out and touch you anytime and if you say anything about it, I will have your parole revoked." This assault resulted in physical injuries to the parolee, which were grounds for an intentional tort. This excessive use of force is *also* sufficient grounds to be a violation of the parolee's 8th Amendment protections against cruel and unusual punishment. Thus, Parole Officer X is liable under Section 1983 as well.

However, in other cases, it may not be so clear whether an infraction rises to the level of a constitutional violation. Likewise, the Supreme Court case law regarding community supervision is a bit scant in comparison to prison case law and case law related to policing. Thus, there may be a lack of uniformity and clarity in interpretation of the fine-line distinctions in federal protections, and this may vary from one circuit court to another. Therefore, it is very important that community supervision officers stay abreast of the legal rulings and developments in their own circuit area. Regardless, the overall general concepts and protections do, for the most part, have similarities throughout the nation since they all have a constitutional basis.

Also, it is important to note that both of the two elements previously noted must be present. If either is lacking, then there simply is no liability under Section 1983. However, as was noted just previously in regard to Parole Officer X, the officer can be held liable under some other form of legal protection, such as under state tort law, or the penal code, or other possible ordinances or laws. In such cases, Section 1983 protections will not apply. For instance, Parole Officer X goes to a local club on the weekend and becomes inebriated. While in his drunken stupor, he gets into an altercation with another person at the club and is sued by the club owner and the person that was assaulted. While he is indeed likely to be found liable for damages, he was not acting under color of state law (being off duty during this time) and is therefore not liable under Section 1983.

While Section 1983 suits can be effective for aggrieved parties that have had their constitutional or federally protected rights violated, it should be made clear to the student that this actually creates a limiting effect on the use of Section 1983. Indeed, when reading about liability issues, it can seem as if state actors are constantly in danger of liability and that the risk is high that they will make a mistake that ultimately holds them liable for some type of tort or Section 1983 suit. Actually, this is not true at all for the vast majority of community supervision officers, particularly if they are prudent and attentive to their duties and the processes that must be utilized (i.e., agency policies and procedures) when carrying out those duties. There are many protections and limitations that actually safeguard the public agency, and community supervision officers enjoy these protections.

In regard to Section 1983 itself, it is important to point out that violations of an offender's rights do not automatically become a constitutional or federal issue. Rather, as del Carmen et al. (2001) put it, "the violation must be of constitutional proportion" (p. 34). Though there is some degree of ambiguity in determining what exactly is (and is not) an issue of constitutional proportion, it does underscore the fact that most cases that will incur federal liability must be serious—perhaps even "unusually serious" according to del Carmen et al.— if they are to be considered sufficient grounds for a Section 1983 suit. Simple words, threats, gestures, and even actual pushes or shoves do not automatically constitute a civil rights violation (del Carmen et al., 2001; Weisz & Crane, 1977). However, the U.S. Supreme Court case of *Morrissey v. Brewer* protects the offender's rights during parole revocation hearings, making such actions clear violations of a constitutional right.

In addition, it should also be pointed out that agencies can be held liable in some circumstances if they allow certain policies or customs to exist within their jurisdiction. In *Monell v. Department of Social Services* (1978), the U.S. Supreme Court held that local units of government can be held liable for an unconstitutional action by an officer if it occurred in adherence to a policy or custom that had been set in that agency. The specific definitions of a policy and especially those of a *custom* have been fluid and subject to much interpretation in a number of cases. The key thing to remember with this ruling is that this applies only to local governments, not state or federal governments. However, defenses that are common for state and federal levels of government have changed over time, and it could be, in future years, that concern for an organizational culture that reinforces customs in violation of the offender's rights could extend to state or federal agencies as well.

Last, courts have applied this ruling to many local agencies around the United States, and, in some states—such as Colorado, Georgia, and Washington—probation officers may be employed as *municipal probation officers*. In these specific cases, it is perfectly feasible that the rulings in *Monell* would or could apply since municipalities are local forms of government. This distinction is seldom noted in discussions related to liability but is an important point for community supervision officers that are so employed. This is especially the case if these officers find themselves working in an environment that has accepted norms or customs that are not consistent with federal protections or if the agency does not ensure that employees are maintaining adequate levels of ethical behavior.

FORMS OF IMMUNITY AND TYPES OF DEFENSE

One key protection for community supervision officers, as agents of the state, is potential immunity from tort suits. Official immunity is a term that refers to being legally shielded from suit. Official immunity is granted to those professions that must be allowed to, at least in the majority of circumstances, actively pursue their duties without undue fear or intimidation. Otherwise, law enforcement, correctional, and judicial professionals simply could not fulfill their duty correctly. However, official immunity comes in a number of different forms, reflecting the different levels of responsibility and liability associated with different functions in the justice system. For the purposes of this text, students need only discern between *absolute immunity* and *qualified immunity*.

Absolute immunity exists for people who work in positions that require unimpaired decision-making functions. Judges and prosecutors have this type of immunity since their jobs require that they make very important decisions regarding the livelihood of persons in their courts; these decisions must be made free of intimidation or potential recrimination and therefore these court actors enjoy absolute immunity when carrying out their responsibilities. This type of immunity is also referred to as judicial immunity, in some cases, as it is usually reserved for judicial officers of the court rather than those who fulfill an executive function.

For typical community supervision officers, protection through immunity is typically referred to as qualified immunity. **Qualified immunity** requires that the community supervision officer demonstrate three key aspects prior to invoking this form of defense against suit: (1) the community supervision officer must show that he or she was performing a discretionary act, not one that was mandated by agency policy; (2) the community supervision officer must have been acting in good faith, that is, holding the sincere belief that his or her action was correct under the circumstances; and (3) the community supervision officer must have acted within the scope of his or her designated authority. Thus, most community supervision officers do not enjoy the same level of immunity as their colleagues in the judicial arena since they have to demonstrate the grounds for their possession of immunity. However, there is one key exception; in the Fifth and Ninth Circuits, community supervision officers are given immunity when completing presentence investigation reports (PSI's) due to the fact that this is more of a judicial function than an executive function and also because courts tend to request PSI's from community supervision agencies so that judicial sentencing can occur.

In addition, in most cases, higher-level officials that must make judgelike decisions are considered to be performing judicial functions that warrant absolute immunity. One key example would be most state parole boards that are tasked with granting parole, making release recommendations, or conducting revocation hearings for parolees that recidivate or commit technical offenses. Though exact particulars may vary from state to state, parole board members tend to have absolute immunity when performing the aforementioned functions.

This brings us to an additional consideration that shields community supervision staff/personnel from liability. The public duty doctrine of tort law holds that in general, community supervision officers are not liable for failing to protect a member of the public from injuries inflicted by an offender on their caseload. This is because general functions of public safety and security are owed to the public as a whole but not necessarily to any one individual in particular. Though it would seem that community supervision officers would be liable to the public (particularly in light of this text's discussion in Chapter 2), the simple truth is that, for the most part, they are not. This concept is aptly explained by del Carmen et al. (2001), who state,

> Injured members of the public file lawsuits against probation/parole officers and departments because they link the injury caused by probationers or parolees to negligent supervision or failure to revoke probation or parole. The public assumes that, had the offender been properly supervised and had the probation/parole been revoked upon violation of conditions, the injury could have been prevented. Logical as this thinking may be, it generally has no basis in law. The reality is that, were it not for the protection against civil liability given by the public duty doctrine, nobody would ever want to be a police, probation, or parole officer. These are high-risk occupations that profess public protection as a part of their mission, yet they hardly have any control over what the public or their supervisees do vis-à-vis the public; therefore, they are protected against civil liability. (p. 25)

Despite the fact that agencies are not liable for recidivism from offenders under supervision, the issue of public safety is still considered very important to community supervision agencies. In fact, many have adopted more of a law enforcement model than a casework model. The emphasis on supervision is taken very seriously by community supervision agencies, and it is highly unlikely that any such agency would be calloused toward the community's safety. Yet, all of this emphasis occurs among these agencies even though they are not liable for keeping the public safe as a whole. Thus, it is clear that agencies have a sincere desire to simply be of service to the public, evidenced by the fact that so much effort is put into the security aspect of community supervision, even though they are not liable should they fail to be able to provide a perfect safety scorecard to citizens in the community.

This lends support to the points made in Chapter 2 regarding the fact that community safety can only be obtained with the help of the community itself. Probation/parole officers cannot, all by themselves, ensure or guarantee safety for the community. These individuals are frequently overloaded with their caseloads and cannot guarantee any better forms of security considering agency resources and normal human limits. The public duty doctrine, just explained earlier in the block text, makes this clear and provides support for the involvement of the community if supervision of offenders in the community is likely to be improved.

Finally, while it is true that there is no guarantee of safety to the public as a whole, supervision agencies and supervision officers may be liable when a special relationship exists between the person being protected and the community supervision agency/officer. Though these are a minority of cases, they do occur from time to time. For instance, if a community supervision officer knows that a crime—especially a violent crime—is likely to be committed by an offender on his or her caseload, and if the officer has the means to prevent it, but negligently fails to do so, this may incur liability. One clear area where this would be likely is in cases of domestic abuse, particularly if the offender were on supervision for crimes of domestic abuse and especially if the crime were again perpetrated against the original victim of his abuse. In such a case, it is likely to be considered negligence if the community supervision officer has knowledge of the crime's likelihood but fails to act. Another situation that might constitute a special relationship is when the offender is given a specific order from the court, such as when a pedophile is ordered to stay away from school zones, and the offender does not comply with this order. If the community supervision officer knows that this is occurring and he or she does not act, liability can be incurred. Though these special relationships can occur, they are very rare, and, in the overwhelming majority of the cases, officers respond to these situations and harm is prevented. Beyond their rarity and the tendency for officers to respond in such events, it is not always easy to determine that special relationships actually exist since these are determined largely on a case-by-case basis according to the circumstances. However, aside from this special relationship exception, the public duty doctrine holds community supervision officers free from liability in ensuring public safety and security. If the case were otherwise, the nation would probably not be able to employ persons in the community supervision field, thus requiring the use of more prisons and further expense due to the false positives that this would essentially generate.

Beyond the initial forms of liability protection (i.e., qualified immunity and the public duty doctrine) that are afforded community supervision officers, there are some defenses that officers can raise on their own behalf. First among these is the good faith defense. The **good faith defense** essentially buffers a community supervision officer from liability in Section 1983 cases (not state tort cases), unless the officer violated some clearly established constitutional or federal statutory right that a reasonable person would have known to exist. This basic premise was established in the U.S. Supreme Court case of *Harlow v. Fitzgerald*, in which the Court added that judges may determine both the law and whether that law was clearly established at the time that the action had occurred. Thus, even if a law has been passed that makes the officer's conduct illegal or questionable, if it is new, obscure, or relatively unknown, community supervision officers may not be held liable. It can then be concluded that if reasonable public officials were able to substantially differ on the legality of a given supervision officer's actions, that officer would most likely be entitled to qualified immunity. Finally, it should be mentioned that the good faith defense is an affirmative defense and thus must be invoked by the defendant (the community supervision officer) who has the burden of proof to establish the good faith claim.

Because of this defense and due to other court cases since *Harlow*, it is clear that community supervision officers must be well versed on the constitutional and federal rights of offenders. In addition, this knowledge must be constantly updated for two key reasons. First, rulings by the various circuit courts (and occasionally the U.S. Supreme Court) are always developing and federal laws go through revisions, making it a very real likelihood that the officer's duties can be affected. Second, officers are only human and do not remember all of the complex nuances of the law after an initial introduction to a given set of guidelines. Rather, repetition helps to reinforce this knowledge to ensure that liability issues stay at the forefront of the supervision officer's mind when under the stress of his or her routine and non-routine functions. In addition, the *Harlow* case has also placed a responsibility on community supervision agencies to ensure that their policies are updated and that they keep their officers informed on legal updates that occur. In fact, agencies are well served if they do this and, of course, document the fact that such information has indeed been disseminated to members of the agency.

Photo 5.2 A state employee prepares to take the stand and provide testimony. In cases where employees of agencies must go to court, they are "sworn in" prior to the question-and-answer process that occurs in a court proceeding.

From the previous discussion of both state tort and Section 1983 forms of lawsuit, it is clear that the issue of good faith is important. The notion that the officer acted in good faith (the sincere belief that his or her action was appropriate) is important to establishing qualified immunity against state tort suits. Likewise, as with the *Harlow* ruling, good faith (genuine attempt to follow well-established federal laws and citizen rights) also serves to protect community supervision officers from Section 1983 lawsuits. It is the same term, *good faith,* but its application to the two types of lawsuit (state tort and Section 1983) is different. Because students often find the differences in state tort law and federal protections under 42 U.S.C. Section 1983 a bit confusing, and because the terminology regarding good faith defenses is similar in appearance but different in actual application, students are encouraged to examine Table 5.1 for further clarity in classifying each type of legal redress and its particular parameters.

TABLE 5.1 Comparing State and Federal Lawsuits Against Community Supervision Officers

State Tort Cases	*Federal Section 1983 Cases*
Based on state law.	Based on federal law.
Plaintiff seeks money for damages.	Plaintiff seeks money for damages and/or policy change.
Usually based on decided cases.	Law was passed in 1871.
Usually tried in state court.	Usually tried in federal court.
Public officials and private persons can be sued.	Only public officials can be sued.
Basis for liability is injury to person or property of another in violation of a duty imposed by state law.	Basis for liability is violation of a constitutional right or of a right secured by federal law.
Good faith defense usually means the officer acted in the honest belief that the action taken was appropriate under the circumstances.	Good faith defense means the officer did not violate a clearly established constitutional or federal right of which a reasonable person should have known.

SOURCE: Adapted from del Carmen, R. V., Barnhill, M. B., Bonham, G., Hignite, L., & Jermstad, T. (2001). *Civil liabilities and other legal issues for probation/parole officers and supervisors.* Washington, DC: National Institute of Corrections.

INDEMNIFICATION, REPRESENTATION, AND TYPES OF DAMAGES

When community supervision officers are faced with lawsuits (whether state or federal), the issue of legal representation is an automatic concern. This issue, as well as that of indemnification (payment for court costs), is one that varies greatly from state to state. As a general rule, most states around the nation are willing to provide assistance in civil cases, but this is not always true when the charges are criminal in nature. While it is typical for states to cover financial costs associated with civil proceedings, many do not do this automatically, and this makes it likely that officers will occasionally face such instances without any financial assistance from their place of employment—a scary thought indeed.

Most states do cover an officer's act or failure to act in civil cases, provided it is determined that the incident occurred within the scope of the officer's employment. In some cases, this may also require a good faith element where it can be reasonably shown that the officer did act in good faith within the scope of his or her duty. However, the particular way each state defines good faith, for purposes of deciding whether to cover an employee in a suit, may vary. For instance, good faith may be seen as simply not being grossly negligent, while in other states, good faith may be held as not having violated a state rule or law. In still other states, the definition may stay with the notion that the officer believed that the act was proper and appropriate under the circumstances. This all of course contrasts with the use of good faith in Section 1983 suits where good faith is clearly defined. In most cases, however, if the officer's behavior was within state guidelines, the officer will be represented by that state's attorney general. That said, the attorneys general in all states have a wide degree of discretion in choosing whether to defend an officer faced with a civil suit. If it should turn out that the "AG" (as the attorney general's office is sometimes called) does not agree to defend the officer, that individual will have to retain private counsel at his or her own expense.

The student should consider the implications of this decision that go beyond the mere fact that the employee will have to obtain his or her own form of legal representation. Indeed, if the state does refrain from defending an employee, this can be perceived as a negative statement by the judge (or worse yet, the jury) that is assigned to the particular case. Though this information is not necessarily disclosed during proceedings in many states, it is plausible that judges (and perhaps some jury members) may be aware of the case and the fact that the representing counsel is not in the employ of the state attorney general's office. This would then raise suspicion for many that were knowledgeable of how such systems are intended to operate. Regardless of whether such information does or does not prejudice the judge or jury, it would be quite discomforting to know that your agency has declined to defend your actions that are about to be examined in a court of law.

However, once the issue of representation is resolved, the last issue of concern tends to revolve around the payment of legal costs. Most typically, when state tort cases are involved, both the plaintiff (in this case, it would be the offender) and the defendant (the community supervision officer) would pay their own attorney's fees, and this would remain so, regardless of the case outcome. Thus, even if the community supervision officer is found innocent of the allegations made by the offender, the officer will still likely have to pay his or her own court costs if it is a state tort case. To remedy these concerns, some officers may opt to purchase their own professional liability insurance, but they will typically be required to pay the premium themselves, and, in some states, they may not even be able to purchase such insurance if there are no companies operating to underwrite the policy.

If, on the other hand, the case is a civil rights case, it would most likely be filed under Section 1983. In civil rights cases, the Civil Rights Attorney's Fee Awards Act of 1976 provides that courts may award payment of legal fees to the plaintiff (usually the offender) if the individual's allegations prevail (or win) in a suit involving a person's civil rights or rights dictated by federal statute (del Carmen et al., 2001). Such payment even extends to cases that are settled out of court or that result in some sort of decree. Conversely, if the community supervision officer (as the defendant) prevails in such a case, this act allows him or her to then claim attorney's fees from the plaintiff (the offender), so long as the officer can show that the offender's suit "was frivolous, unreasonable, or unfounded" (del Carmen et al., 2001, p. 46).

Most states have some sort of indemnification policy, but this does not necessarily mean that the state will automatically compensate the officer. In most all cases, the officer must have acted within the scope of his or her duty, and the defining factors in determining the scope of an officer's duty can vary greatly from state to state. In addition, many states place a limit on the amount that will be reimbursed or paid. This also varies from state to state, but if the award in court exceeds this amount, then the officer will be required to pay the difference.

Finally, most all civil cases (particularly tort cases) seek to obtain monetary damages. The amount can vary greatly, depending on the type of injury, the type of tort that is found (i.e., gross or willful negligence), and the severity of that injury. Most often, these financial awards come in the way of **compensatory damages,** which are payments for the actual losses suffered by a plaintiff (typically the offender). In some cases, **punitive damages** may also be awarded, but these monetary awards would be reserved for an offender that had been harmed in a malicious or willful manner by agency staff; however, these damages are often added to emphasize the seriousness of the injury or to serve as a warning to other parties that might observe the case's outcome. The type of award for civil rights cases under Section 1983 suits can also vary greatly and often is similar to those under tort law. As with tort cases, the specific award may depend on the circumstances of the case or the nature of the right that has been violated.

However, it is common for Section 1983 cases to also result in other types of remedies that go beyond financial awards. These remedies are typically geared toward agencies rather than individual officers, though both financial damages and additional awards can be made. One such non-monetary award that is occasionally granted is the **declaratory judgment,** which is a judicial determination of the legal rights of the person bringing suit (Neubauer, 2002). An example might be a suit where a probationer sues for violation of certain due process safeguards during revocation proceedings. A court may award a declaratory judgment against the agency to ensure that future offenders under supervision are afforded the appropriate safeguards established by prior Supreme Court case law. In addition, courts may employ injunctions against an agency. An **injunction** is a court order that requires an agency to take some form of action or to refrain from a particular action or set of actions (Neubauer, 2002). While injunctions are not as common in community corrections settings as they are in institutional corrections settings, they still remain as a potential remedy, particularly when federal civil rights or federal statutes are violated.

LEGAL ISSUES OF DISCLOSURE
WITH PRESENTENCE INVESTIGATION REPORTS

Students may recall that the issue of presentence investigation reports was discussed at length in Chapter 3, demonstrating the importance of these documents. As mentioned in that chapter, the U.S. Supreme Court held that the PSI is confidential in nature in the case of *Williams v. New York,* due to the perception of the Court that the presentence investigator is a neutral party with no vested interest in the punishment of the offender. However, the Federal Rules of Criminal Procedure require federal judges to disclose to either the defendant or the defendant's counsel the presentence information relied upon in sentencing. The only information that is not required for disclosure is diagnostic information or opinions that could undermine rehabilitation program efforts if the information were disclosed. In addition, information obtained based on a promise of confidentiality or that which might, if disclosure were to occur, result in any type of harm to the defendant or other persons is also restricted from disclosure. Importantly, offenders have no right to the disclosure of a codefendant's PSI.

Generally speaking, courts will release information that was used as a basis for determining the offender's sentence. In addition, some states mandate that the information in the PSI may be given to counsel without any such disclosure to the offender him- or herself. In essence, the offender's counsel may be given access to the information with clear instructions that the information is not to be released to the client. Though this is not often done, it is important to understand the parameters that surround an offender's rights. In fact, the U.S. Supreme Court has not found it necessary to consider the constitutional parameters regarding disclosure of PSI content, being content to leave this to legislatively set guidelines such as those set by the Federal Rules of Criminal Procedure. Similar to the federal government, states also tend to require the disclosure of PSI information to defendants, taking it upon themselves to bear the burden of ethical and fundamentally fair disclosure to the accused.

Aside from the disclosure to the defendant, there is the additional concern of disclosing the PSI content to third parties. Most often, the third-party question revolves around victim access to the offender's PSI records. Further, there are few if any specific statutes that require the PSI to remain confidential after the offender has been sentenced. In fact, several states have explored this exact issue. States such as Arizona, Louisiana, and Montana have addressed the issue of third-party disclosures. At this time, Arizona does allow the crime victim to inspect the PSI report once it has been made available to the defendant. The state of

Louisiana has a similar statute that allows both the victim and the victim's designated family members to view the contents of the PSI. In Montana, prosecutors are allowed to disclose the contents of the PSI report to the victim. Thus, in different states, the process may be different, but in most cases the victim does have access to the offender's records.

One additional issue regarding liability, PSI's, and community supervision officers has to do with the officer's legal standing when completing the report. This is perhaps the most relevant issue for the day-to-day probation or parole officer. It has been examined in numerous federal and state courts, and it is very clear that community supervision officers are given absolute immunity when completing these reports. This must of course be nearly mandatory if one expects the community supervision officer to be able to complete this function of the job. When one considers the excessive paperwork, the number of offenders on standard caseloads, and the fact that the completion of PSI's is one of the more time-consuming functions within a community supervision agency, it is clear that absolute immunity is warranted. Again, this is a practical matter, if nothing else. The job simply could not get done if the situation were otherwise, and it is doubtful that anyone would agree to take on the task if one could routinely be held liable for honest mistakes that were made under such working conditions.

This last note regarding honest mistakes is also an important point. The provision of absolute immunity does not extend to cover cases where it is found that the discrepancies in the report are due to some sort of malice or intended ill will on the part of the community supervision officer. In such cases, the officer is liable and the offender that is sentenced on the basis of that report has basically had his or her right to due process violated (thus raising a Section 1983 issue). The officer is then liable under both state law and regulations (this violation constituting a tort) and under federal law. Last, it should be pointed out that even in cases where information is false but due to an honest mistake on the part of the officer, the offender's right to due process has still been violated, but in such a case the officer acted within the scope of his or her duty and would be presumed to have sincerely believed that the information was true and correct. This would also exempt the officer from federal liability since the absolute immunity acts as a full shield from suit, presuming (again) that no hurtful intent existed.

The last issue to be discussed in this section addresses the use of PSI's and parole. This is brought up because, in most cases, classification workers—staff who determine housing and job assignments—in a prison system, as well as institutional parole officers, tend to refer back to the PSI when making critical decisions regarding the placement of offenders in programs within prisons (as discussed in Chapter 3) and when making determinations regarding parole eligibility. In such cases, the key question for the offender revolves around the issue of due process (as per the 14th Amendment) when decisions impact his or her liberty interests. When an offender is incarcerated, his or her liberty interests are severely diminished and, because of this, the due process issues become considerably different from when the offender was a "free world" citizen being tried for an offense. (We will discuss due process issues, as established in *Wolff v. McDonnell,* for inmates and offenders on community supervision later in this chapter.) Thus, the more pressing issue for this immediate discussion is whether such offenders actually have a legitimate liberty interest in the first place. From a purely constitutional perspective, the answer is a simple and resounding "no, they do not have any such liberty interest." The case of *Greenholtz v. Inmates of the Nebraska Penal and Correctional Complex* makes this clear.

In *Greenholtz,* it was found that due process does not apply to parole release proceedings unless there is a specific state law (no such federal law exists) that virtually creates an expectation that parole will be granted. Such a law would have to have clear language that establishes parole as an expectation to which an inmate is entitled if such were to be considered a point of fact. If such does indeed exist, then that state has created a liberty interest for its inmates where none had existed before. It is not clear why a state would desire to make such a provision, but nonetheless, this is the requirement if a liberty interest is to be established.

However, even in such a case, the associated due process safeguards for such proceedings would then need to be granted and established by state statute or administrative regulation since this is not, after all, a right that was secured or protected by the U.S. Constitution or by federal law. This means that access to various inmate files, such as PSI's, will be dependent upon the statute that regulates such proceedings or procedures.

LIABILITY OF PAROLE BOARD MEMBERS FOR VIOLATION OF SUBSTANTIVE OR PROCEDURAL RIGHTS

For the most part, it is clear that parole boards are not typically liable for violations of substantive or procedural rights when determining initial parole decisions. This should not be confused with decisions during parole revocation hearings. During revocation hearings, the Supreme Court case of *Morrissey v. Brewer* clearly establishes a number of rights related to due process through a prompt informal inquiry before some form of impartial hearing officer. However, initial decisions to grant parole are simply a privilege to which an inmate has not constitutionally secured a right. Though inmates do not have a right to parole, they do have a right to not be discriminated against on the basis of race, religion, sex, creed, and so forth, when such determinations are being made. One case, *United States v. Irving,* was filed under Section 1983 in the Seventh Circuit. In this case, the offender alleged systematic racial discrimination against African American inmates with respect to parole board decisions for release. Interestingly, the circuit court did hold that the parole board members themselves had absolute immunity when faced with such a suit. However, the Seventh Circuit noted that the offender could still sue for declaratory relief (essentially requesting an injunction that the parole board change their practices) due to the fact that the court did find evidence that tended to demonstrate discrimination on the part of the parole board.

Thus, it may be that individual parole board members are immune from liability when performing their functions. Yet, on the other hand, offenders do still retain certain civil rights under the 14th Amendment that must be honored by parole boards just as they must be honored by custodial corrections officials. This is a reasonable point since, after all, the desire to eliminate bias and discrimination among government officials was the reason that Section 1983 forms of redress were created. Just as prison officials must provide constitutional treatment of prisoners, so should parole-granting bodies.

One additional point of interest regarding parole board liability should be mentioned. It revolves around the rights of offenders that are released on parole, only to later find out that such a release was a mistake on the part of the parole board. While such instances are not common, they have occurred frequently enough to be ruled on by more than one federal court. Indeed, two lower courts have held that the protections in *Morrissey* also confer some substantive protections for inmates that are mistakenly released. In both *Ellard v. Alabama Board of Pardons and Paroles* and *Kelch v. Director, Nevada Department of Prisons,* it was determined that once a state confers a right to be released, the inmate's due process rights go beyond the contours set by *Morrissey.* Indeed, it was determined that the granting of freedom places substantive limits on a state's power to reincarcerate an inmate that has been mistakenly released. In the *Ellard* case, it was held that a mistakenly released inmate could not be reincarcerated unless the release violated some sort of state law and this departure from state law substantially undermined that state's penological interests (see the U.S. Supreme Court case *Turner v. Safely* for a discussion on legitimate penological interests). A similar ruling was found in the *Kelch* case as well, demonstrating a consistency among circuit court rulings and supporting the point that parolees do not have a right to parole, prior to the parole-granting decision. However, this changes when they are actually released on parole, with *Morrissey* protections affecting revocation proceedings for those legitimately on parole, and a subsequent expectation of parole surfacing when offenders are mistakenly and prematurely released from the prison environment by parole board officials.

When considering the procedural elements of the parole-granting process, it is important to remember that parole boards are given a great deal of discretion that is statutorily granted to the parole board body. Indeed, it was held in *Partee v. Lane* that parole boards enjoy absolute immunity from Section 1983 suits when processing requests for parole. In other federal cases, it is equally clear that parole boards are considered to have absolute immunity when making decisions that grant, deny, or revoke parole. For instance, in *Walker v. Prisoner Review Board*, it was found that the board did have absolute immunity for its official actions. This was despite the fact that the board had not allowed the inmate to have access to critical files relevant to his parole determination, and that the district court found this to be a violation of the inmate's civil rights. In such cases, inmates have a right to another parole board hearing or determination, and some form of injunctive determination may be imposed against the parole board, but the board members themselves cannot be held legally liable for these actions. The *Walker* case was, in actuality, only a district court–level case, but this court correctly pointed to the Seventh Circuit's precedent that has held parole board review functions to be adjudicatory in nature, and thus absolute immunity was considered to extend to board members just as it does to judges.

PAROLE BOARD LIABILITY FOR RELEASED OFFENDERS THAT RECIDIVATE

This issue has been partially addressed earlier in this chapter. Specifically, it is the public duty doctrine that holds that community supervision personnel (including parole board members) are not liable for failing to protect a member of the public from injuries inflicted by an offender on community supervision. As noted before, this is because general functions of public safety and security are owed to the public as a whole but not necessarily to any one individual. However, one might ask, does this change when the decision makers are tasked with protecting the entire public when making the ultimate decision to release or not to release?

The answer is both "yes" and "no." When considering these answers, it is important that the distinction between tort cases and Section 1983 cases is kept squarely in mind. Currently, some federal circuit courts have indicated that liability can occur in cases where gross or reckless negligence is found *(Grimm v. Arizona Board of Pardons and Paroles)*. While there is no concrete answer as to when members are reckless or grossly negligent in granting parole release, courts have tended to consider the standard of duty that is owed by parole boards as well as the predictability of the potential danger (del Carmen et al., 2001). This is a rather nebulous set of criteria that ultimately is decided by the circumstances of each case. Thus, it is possible for state parole boards to be found liable for their release decisions if they are shown to have committed reckless or gross negligence where the standard of duty to the public is broadened by that state's own laws to create potential liability to individuals, and where the danger that occurs is judged to be foreseeable. Despite this possibility, it is rare that such suits are ever successful.

The unlikely success of these suits is exemplified in the case of *Santangelo v. State,* where it was found that the release decision did not include a rigorous or even suitable examination of the parolee's background or character (del Carmen et al., 2001). No psychological or psychiatric reports were utilized in this release decision. Further, prior to being released, the release decision-making body never interviewed the parolee nor had he appeared before the releasing body for any reason other than to have the conditions of his release explained to him. This offender ultimately ended up raping a woman who subsequently brought suit against the state. However, it could not be proven that the releasing body would have made a different releasing determination if such precautions had been implemented, and, since liability for negligence requires that the negligent actions must be shown to be the cause of the injury, it was found that the releasing body was not liable.

Beyond state-level parole boards, the Fifth Circuit court also found that federal agencies could be sued via tort claim (just as with state torts) through the Federal Tort Claims Act. In *Payton v. United States,* the U.S. Parole Commission was itself sued via tort claim for releasing what should have been an obviously dangerous inmate who later kidnapped, raped, and murdered three women (del Carmen et al., 2001). However, the Fifth Circuit held that the decision to release was discretionary and thus fell under the realm of judicial absolute immunity.

Another case—perhaps the most important case on this issue—was decided by the U.S. Supreme Court. The case of *Martinez v. California* involved a 15-year-old girl who was murdered by a parolee only 5 months after he was released from prison. The offender also had a history of sexual offending. The parents of the girl brought suit under Section 1983, and this case eventually reached the U.S. Supreme Court. The Court held that the parole board members were not liable under federal law because, among other things, the parole board was not aware that a particular person (remember the "special relationship" exception to the public duty doctrine), as distinguished from the larger general public, was in any special danger. Further, the parole board's decision was not a proximate cause of the girl's death; in other words, the girl's death was too remote a possibility for the parole board to know that such might occur. Therefore, it was found that the parole board members could not be held directly responsible under a Section 1983 suit.

FOCUS TOPIC 5.1

SEX OFFENDER REPORTING LAWS AND COMPLICATIONS WITH MANDATORY COMMUNITY NOTIFICATION INITIATIVES

In 2006, Congress passed the Adam Walsh Act as a means of revamping sex offender supervision. This law was named after a young boy in Florida who was abducted, sexually victimized, and later murdered and dismembered. The law was created and passed due to the efforts of Adam's father, John Walsh, who is now the host of a television show called America's Most Wanted. Other parents of children who had been sexually victimized and murdered were also involved in establishing this law. This act was established to accomplish the following:

1. Expand the National Sex Offender Registry: This act integrates information in state sex offender registry systems and ensures that law enforcement has access to the same information across the United States, helping to prevent sex offenders from evading detection by moving from state to state. Data drawn from this comprehensive registry is made available to the public (The White House, 2006).

2. Strengthen federal penalties for crimes against children: This act imposes tough mandatory minimum penalties for the most serious crimes against children. It also provides grants to states to help them institutionalize sex offenders who have shown they cannot change their behavior and are about to be released from prison (The White House, 2006).

3. Make it harder for sexual predators to contact children on the Internet: The act authorizes new regional Internet Crimes Against Children Taskforces that will help law enforcement officials combat crimes involving the sexual exploitation of minors on the Internet (The White House, 2006).

The Adam Walsh Act has substantially broadened the scope of sex offender reporting and has increased the penalties against sex offenders. This law divides sex offenders into three tiers. The first tier, Tier One sex offenders, is for the least serious of offenses and requires 15 years of registration.

Tier Two sex offenders include those guilty of offenses that are punishable by more than 1 year in prison and include serious abusive contact, coercion and enticement, transportation with intent to commit a sexual crime, or sex trafficking. Tier Two offenders must register for 25 years. Tier Three sex offenders are those that commit aggravated forms of sexual abuse or abusive contact with a minor under the age of 13 years. These offenders must register for life due to the harshness of their offenses and/or the age of their victims. The registry process does allow for reductions in time required if offenders have clean records for a specified amount of time.

Currently, the federal law requires adults and some juveniles convicted of specified crimes that involve sexual conduct to register with law enforcement agencies. These laws have typically been referred to as "Megan's Laws" in the United States in tribute to a child victim, Megan Kanka, who was kidnapped, raped, and murdered. The crime against this child was committed by a repeat sex offender, and it drew national attention, eventually serving as the impetus behind these laws. The laws established public access to registry information, in most cases using online registries that provide a former offender's criminal history, current photograph, current address, and other information such as place of employment. In many states, everyone who is required to register is included on the online registry. While these laws seem to make sense on the surface, there are some challenges that exist with their implementation.

Naturally, these registration laws are intended to prevent the possibility of additional crimes by these offenders, particularly sex-based crimes. However, the incidence of stranger-based sexual assaults on children by offenders who have had prior documented sex offenses is actually quite low. Thus, the use of these laws as prevention tools for future juvenile sex offenders is actually quite limited. In fact, most sexual crimes against children occur at the hands of family members or acquaintances. Indeed, the perpetrator is known to the child in over 90 percent of the sex crimes perpetrated against children (Human Rights Watch, 2008).

Further, these laws are based on the notion that most sex offenders will commit similar crimes in the future, if the opportunity should arise. However, regardless of the media hype and political agendas of persons advocating for these laws, nearly three quarters of all sex offenders do not commit another sex offense (Human Rights Watch, 2008). For juvenile sex offenders in particular, the likelihood for recidivism is even lower. In the United States, the rationale for the registry laws is often centered on concerns with violent

sex offenders; however, the laws are so poorly written in some states that a vast number of offenses may be included within the required registry (Human Rights Watch, 2008). In some cases, the offenses included may be minor and not even truly related to an actual sex assault. As an example, in some states, kids that expose themselves as a prank and people who have urinated outside are required to be reported on the sex offender registry. Even more common in many states is the reporting of teens who have had consensual sex with one another, with one being perhaps 2 or 3 years older than the other. Consider the following example:

> Brandon was a senior in high school when he met a 14-year-old girl on a church youth trip. With her parents' blessing, they began to date, and openly saw each other romantically for almost a year. When it was disclosed that consensual sexual contact had occurred, her parents pressed charges against Brandon and he was convicted of sexual assault and placed on the sex offender registry in his state. As a result, Brandon was fired from his job. He will be on the registry and publicly branded as a sex offender for the rest of his life. (Human Rights Watch, 2008, p. 5)

These types of situations have occurred in numerous U.S. states and point toward the need to be more careful and thoughtful when implementing this type of legislation. This is especially true when considering the use of online registries that make the person's status a public affair. Further, in many cases, the narration given on such websites does not explain the context of the offense, making it impossible for website visitors to distinguish between truly dangerous juvenile sex offenders and those who may have committed an offense like the example just presented. Given that these youth are required to register for years and sometimes even for their lifetime, this issue is very important to resolve. It would seem that while sex offender reporting laws placate the desires of the public, they are in fact mired in a number of issues that make their application somewhat complicated. In such situations, one has to wonder about the civil rights of offenders such as Brandon (in the example above) and whether future judicial outcomes might modify the ability of states to enforce such liberal forms of reporting.

SOURCES: Human Rights Watch. (2008). *No easy answers: Sex offender laws in the U.S.* New York: Author; The White House. (2006). *Fact sheet: The Adam Walsh Child Protection and Safety Act of 2006.* Washington, DC: Office of the Press Secretary.

THE USE OF OBJECTIVE INSTRUMENTS
AS A SAFEGUARD FROM LIABILITY

As has become quite clear, parole board members are largely insulated from liability when performing their discretionary acts of release determination. So long as parole board members maintain a judicial function and these discretionary acts are within the purview of this function, no liability issue will likely emerge. Indeed, any community supervision official or agent, when performing judicially related functions, is likely to be given absolute immunity. This has, of course, been made clear throughout this chapter and is one of the reasons that probation officers enjoy such immunity when completing their PSI reports. Further, the use of discretion is authorized and legally protected for parole board members due to their responsibilities reflecting a judgment or judicial function.

The use of such discretion, however, is not equally protected for probation or parole officers and the agency supervisors that must make decisions regarding the enforcement of probation or parole conditions related to revocation. It is important to point out that individual probation or parole officers do not have to worry about potential liability issues related to decisions to release. The reason for this is simple: individual officers are not tasked with this responsibility. Rather, it is the court judge that will make such decisions regarding probation, and it is the parole board/committee or other such post-incarcerative releasing body that will be given this function. All of these individuals who have such discretionary powers are granted absolute immunity.

However, probation or parole officers may make another type of discretionary decision that addresses the offender's likelihood to be supervised in the community. This occurs when officers must make discretionary decisions to revoke an offender's probation or parole. Though this is not necessarily a decision that the individual officer will make alone, it still requires a degree of discretion that can perhaps open up the possibility of liability for the officer. Consider, for example, a situation where the offender commits a minor infraction and the probation officer (aware that the local jail is already overcrowded and also having a general idea of the probationer's supervision ethic) decides to provide a warning and to strengthen some of the sanctioning restrictions on the offender. If this same offender should again commit some criminal act (regardless of whether it may be similar to the previous violation), this can place the supervision officer in a position where a lawsuit or at least questioning of his or her judgment may take place from members of the general public. For the most part, as we have noted, community supervision officers will be granted qualified immunity in these circumstances (presuming that they acted in good faith within the scope of their duty).

However, the officer making such recommendations may indeed be called to task and may be denied qualified immunity in some cases where the circumstances warrant it. Though this may be a moot issue in situations where revocation automatically requires that the offender be reincarcerated, offenders are often simply given stricter conditions for their current community supervision sentence. This can be an issue in some cases where qualified immunity is concerned. This is particularly true considering that qualified immunity is extended for those cases where a discretionary act (not a mandatory act based on agency policy) is at issue and where the officer must indicate sincere belief that his or her action was correct under the circumstances.

In these specific cases, officers would be well-served to base their discretionary decisions on the results of any objective assessment tools that are available. Because the officer will have no true policy, per se, to rely upon and because a sincere belief in the correctness of his or her action will be an issue, the use of such instruments, based on the findings of other assessment professionals, can substantially bolster the officer's determination and can add a great degree of confidence to his or her decisions. Though this is a specialized set of circumstances and limited use of these instruments, it can make a considerable difference in those instances where qualified immunity may not be assured for the officer. This can also serve as a substantial area of consideration for juries and judges that must make decisions regarding liability should the officer find himself or herself in court. The use of objective assessment indicators (as students should recall from their readings in Chapter 3) can provide the officer with additional protection to shield him or her from being found liable. Further, knowledge of these assessment tools and their outcomes can provide additional ammunition when supervision officers seek to have certain modifications added or required for a particularly problematic offender under their supervision. Community supervision officers should strive to become fairly conversant in the use of these tools since this knowledge can bolster their decisions regarding offender community supervision revocation. Further, even if this knowledge does not prove necessary as a means of protection from liability, this knowledge helps to improve the day-to-day competence of the officer. This in itself is a laudable goal.

Photo 5.3 This photo provides a view of a law library that has been created for inmates in a large regional jail. Many times when offenders sue state agencies, they may use resources such as the law library.

PROBATIONER AND PAROLEE CASE LAW REGARDING DUE PROCESS DURING REVOCATION

Essentially, there are two primary cases that establish due process rights for probationers and parolees. The first case to emerge was *Morrissey v. Brewer* (1972), which dealt with revocation proceedings for parolees (Clear & Cole, 2003). The second case was *Gagnon v. Scarpelli* (1973), which extended the rights afforded to parolees under *Morrissey* to offenders on probation as well (Champion, 2002; Clear & Cole, 2003). Basically, the *Morrissey* Court ruled that parolees facing revocation must be given due process through a prompt informal inquiry before an impartial hearing officer. The Court required that this be accomplished through a two-step hearing process when revoking parole. The reason for this two-step process is to first screen for the reasonableness of holding the parolee, since there is often a substantial delay between the point of arrest and the revocation hearing. This delay can be costly for both the justice system and the offender if it is based on circumstances that do not actually warrant full revocation. Specifically, the Court stated that some minimal

> [i]nquiry should be conducted at or reasonably near the place of the alleged parole violation or arrest and as promptly as convenient after arrest while information is fresh and sources are available. . . . Such an inquiry should be seen as in the nature of a "preliminary hearing" to determine whether there is probable cause or reasonable ground to believe that the arrested parolee has committed acts that would constitute a violation of parole conditions. (*Morrissey v. Brewer,* 1972, p. 485)

The Court also noted that this would need to be conducted by a neutral and detached party (a hearing officer), though the hearing officer did not necessary need to be affiliated with the judiciary and this first step did not have to be formal in nature. The hearing officer is tasked with determining whether there is sufficient probable cause to justify the continued detention of the offender.

After the initial hearing, the revocation hearing would follow. It is interesting to note that the Court was quite specific on how the revocation hearings were to be conducted (del Carmen et al., 2001). During this hearing, the parolee is entitled to contest charges and demonstrate that he or she did not, in fact, violate any of the conditions of his or her parole. If it should turn out that the parolee did, in fact, violate the parole requirements but that this violation was necessary due to mitigating circumstances, it may end up that the violation does not warrant full revocation. The *Morrissey* court specified additional procedures for the revocation process that include the following:

(a) Written notice of the claimed violation of parole;

(b) Disclosure to the parolee of evidence against him;

(c) An opportunity to be heard in person and to present witnesses and documentary evidence;

(d) The right to confront and cross-examine adverse witnesses;

(e) A "neutral and detached" hearing body, such as a traditional parole board, members of which need not be judicial officers or lawyers; and

(f) A written statement by the fact finders as to the evidence relied on and reasons for revoking parole (*Morrissey v. Brewer*, 1972, p. 485).

The *Morrissey* case is obviously an example of judicial activism (much like *Miranda v. Arizona*) that has greatly impacted the field of community corrections. The Court's clear and specific guidelines set forth in *Morrissey* have created standards and procedures that community supervision agencies must follow. Rather than merely ensuring that revocation proceedings include a just hearing and means of processing, the Court laid out several pointed requirements that have continued to be relevant and binding to this day. While these specific requirements have been modified to meet a variety of circumstances that may not lend themselves to the strictest observance of the above procedures, the general spirit of the above requirements has been honored. For instance, there is a great deal of variation from state to state in how offenders are provided written notice of their violation, and, when notice is not able to be given because the offender cannot be located, failure to deliver notice does not result in a violation of the offender's constitutional rights. Likewise, the right to confront witnesses can be foregone if the hearing officer specifically finds good cause for not allowing such confrontation. Thus, a sense of pragmatism has since developed in regard to the requirements established by *Morrissey*, with the general principles outlined by the Court still being considered the gold standard of revocation proceedings, even today.

The next pivotal case dealing with revocation proceedings and community supervision is *Gagnon v. Scarpelli* (1973). In the simplest of terms, the U.S. Supreme Court ruled that all of the requirements for parole revocation proceedings noted in *Morrissey* also applied to revocation proceedings dealing with probationers. However, this case is important because it also addressed one other key issue regarding revocation proceedings. In *Gagnon v. Scarpelli*, the Court noted that offenders on community supervision do not have an absolute constitutional right to appointed counsel during revocation proceedings. Such proceedings are not considered to be true adversarial proceedings and therefore do not require official legal representation (Champion, 2002). Nevertheless, the Court did note that some cases may warrant such representation when and if the offender can provide a substantive claim that shows he or she did not commit the violation in question or when mitigating circumstances are involved that may impact the decision of the revocation body. Thus, the Court basically held that there is no absolute right to counsel for offenders facing revocation proceedings. But, depending upon the circumstances, such representation may be offered on a case-by-case basis as determined by the circumstances.

It should be pointed out that there is a great deal of variation from state to state as to the specific standard of proof required to revoke parole. Some jurisdictions may require only slight evidence while others require a preponderance of the evidence. Likewise, the *nature* of the proof necessary for revocation may also vary.

Some states rely on the community supervision officer's testimony as the sole or primary basis of revocation while others may not allow this to be sufficient without additional corroborating evidence of violation being produced by the officer. Nevertheless, del Carmen et al. (2001) note that community supervision officers should remain cognizant of the fact that their testimony or evidence may also be useful in court as later rebuttal evidence, for the purpose of impeachment, or to demonstrate the offender's state of mind. Further, if a community supervision officer does not have personal knowledge of a given act that might lead to revocation, it is unlikely that the officer's testimony will be sufficient to demonstrate the commission of a violation. But prior arrests, prior criminal history, risk-prediction instruments, or clinical assessments (related to relapse) can be used to prove the likelihood of the community supervision officer's testimony. Thus, here again objective assessment or risk-prediction data may prove useful in adding validity to an officer's testimony when supervising a probationer.

Cross-National Perspective

Extracts of the European
Rules on Community Sanctions and Measures

The following excerpt is taken from the *Handbook for Probation Services: Guidelines for Probation Practitioners and Managers*, published by the United Nations Interregional Crime and Justice Research Institute. This document provides guidelines on probation for various nations throughout the European Union. The content of this particular Cross-National Perspective consists of several rules and guidelines that are enumerated and mandated for probation agencies across the entire continent of Europe.

Legislative Framework

Rule 20 There shall be no discrimination in the imposition and implementation of community sanctions and measures on grounds of race, colour, ethnic origin, nationality, gender, language, religion, political or other opinion, economic, social or other status, or physical or mental condition.

Rule 21 No community sanction or measure restricting the civil and political rights of an offender shall be created or imposed if it is contrary to the norms accepted by the international community concerning human rights and fundamental freedoms. These rights shall not be restricted in the implementation of the community sanction or measure to a greater extent than necessarily follows from the decision imposing this sanction or measure.

Rule 22 The nature of all community sanctions and measures and the manner of their implementation shall be

in line with any internationally guaranteed human rights of the offender.

Rule 23 The nature, content and methods of implementation of community sanctions and measures shall not jeopardise the privacy or the dignity of the offenders or their families, nor lead to their harassment. Nor shall self-respect, family relationships, links with the community and ability to function in society be jeopardised. Safeguards shall be adopted to protect the offender from insult and improper curiosity or publicity.

Rule 24 Any instruction of the implementing authority, including in particular, those relating to control requirements shall be practical, precise and limited to what is necessary for the effective implementation of the sanction or measure.

Rule 25 A community sanction or measure shall never involve medical or psychological treatment or procedures which are not in conformity with internationally adopted ethical standards.

Rule 26 The nature, content and methods of implementation of a community sanction shall not involve undue risk of physical or mental injury.

Rule 27 Community sanctions and measures shall be implemented in a way that does not aggravate their afflictive character.

Rule 28 Rights to benefits in any existing social security system shall not be limited by the imposition or implementation of a community sanction or measure.

(Continued)

(Continued)

Legal Framework

Rule 30 The imposition of community sanctions and measures shall seek to develop an offender's sense of responsibility to the community in general and the victim in particular.

Rule 31 A community sanction or measure shall only be imposed when it is known what conditions or obligations might be appropriate and whether the offender is prepared to co-operate and comply with them.

Rule 32 Any conditions to be observed by the offender subject to a community sanction or measure shall be determined taking into account both his individual needs of relevance for implementation, his possibilities and rights as well as his social responsibilities.

Rule 33 Notwithstanding the issue of the formal document conveying the decision on the community sanction or measure imposed, the offender shall be clearly informed before the start of the implementation in a language he understands and, if necessary, in writing, about the nature and purpose of the sanction or measure and the conditions or obligations that must be respected.

Rule 34 Since the implementation of a community sanction or measure shall be designed to secure the co-operation of the offender and enable him to see the sanction as a just and reasonable reaction to the offence committed, the offender should participate, as far as possible, in decision-making on matters of implementation.

Rule 35 The consent of an accused person should be obtained before the imposition of any community measure to be applied before trial or instead of a decision on a sanction.

Rule 36 Where the offender's consent is required it shall be informed and explicit. Such consent shall never have the consequence of depriving the offender of any of his fundamental rights.

Community Service Orders

Rule 66 The kind and amount of information about offenders given to agencies which provide work placements or personal and social assistance of any kind shall be defined by, and be restricted to, the purpose of the particular action under consideration. In particular, without the explicit and informed consent of the offender, it shall exclude information about the offence and his personal background, as well as any other information likely to have unfavourable social consequences or to constitute an intrusion into private life.

Rule 67 Tasks provided for offenders doing community work shall not be pointless, but shall be socially useful and meaningful and enhance the offender's skills as much as possible. Community work shall not be undertaken for the purpose of making profit for any enterprise.

Rule 68 Working and occupational conditions of offenders carrying out community work shall be in accordance with all current health and safety legislation. Offenders shall be insured against accident, injury and public liability arising as a result of implementation.

Rule 69 In principle, the costs of implementation shall not be borne by the offender.

Professional Staff

Rule 37 There shall be no discrimination in the recruitment, selection and promotion of professional staff on grounds of race, colour, sex, language, religion, political or other opinion, national, ethnic or social origin, property, birth or other status. Staff recruitment and selection should take into account specific policies on behalf of particular categories of persons and the diversity of offenders to be supervised.

Rule 38 The staff responsible for implementation shall be sufficiently numerous to carry out effectively the various duties incumbent upon them. They shall possess the qualities of character and the professional qualifications necessary for their functions. Norms and policies shall be developed to ensure that the quantity and quality of staff are in conformity with the amount of work and the professional skills and experience required for their work.

Rule 39 The staff responsible for implementation shall have adequate training and be given information that will enable them to have a realistic perception of their particular field of activity, their practical duties and the ethical requirements of their work. Their professional competence shall be regularly reinforced and developed through further training and performance reviews and appraisals.

Rule 40 Professional staff shall be appointed on such a legal, financial and working-hours basis, that professional and personal continuity is ensured, that the employees' awareness of official responsibility will be developed and that their status in relation to conditions of service is equal to that of other professional staff with comparable functions.

Rule 41 Professional staff shall be accountable to the implementing authority set up by law. This authority shall determine the duties, rights and responsibilities of its staff and shall arrange for the supervision of such staff and assessment of the effectiveness of their work.

Note that this excerpt is a reprint of information from the source document below. This source document may be freely reprinted provided the source is acknowledged.

SOURCE: Klaus, J. F. (1998). *Handbook for probation services: Guidelines for probation practitioners and managers.* Rome, Italy: United Nations Interregional Crime and Justice Research Institute. Retrieved from http://www.unicri.it/wwk/documentation/probation/docs/Probation_handbook.pdf.

Critical Thinking Questions

1. Consider the rules listed above. How are the guidelines and expectations similar to those for agencies in the United States? How are they different? Be sure to explain your answers.

2. From reading the international rules for the implementation of probation in Europe, what do you believe is the philosophical intent behind them?

Applied Theory   Labeling Theory and Legal Issues/Liabilities

Lilly, Cullen, and Ball (2007) point out that it is the social reactions of the public and of state officials toward offenders that have the greatest causal effect on an offender's further recidivism. This means that when labeling is severe enough, it can entrench persons in their criminal identity. This can especially be true for serious offenders such as sex offenders, who are given a stigma-producing label that follows them throughout society. If such labeling processes do indeed entrench these offenders in a life of criminal behavior, then the labeling process is counterproductive. However, if the labeling process is grounded in therapeutic intent, this is similar to the notions espoused by John Braithwaite in his classic work entitled *Crime, Shame, and Reintegration* (1989). In this work, Braithwaite emphasizes that offenders must be given stakes in conformity, for otherwise they are shut off from the community and are further encouraged to maintain their association with deviant criminal subcultures. This is precisely what community corrections seeks to avoid.

As will be noted later in this chapter, *Kansas v. Hendricks* (1997) determined that extended forms of punishment are constitutional so long as their basis is in treatment. The ruling in *Kansas v. Hendricks* would also include additional terms and conditions of community corrections sentencing, such as those which shame the offender: for example, the use of sex offender registration, requiring notification signs in the offender's front yard, or perhaps the use of special license plates that identify cars owned by sex offenders. The use of various reintegrative shaming techniques, as proposed by Braithwaite, comports perfectly with the decision made by the Supreme Court in its ruling in *Kansas v. Hendricks.* However, the question then centers on whether these additional conditions of probation or parole are grounded in therapeutic intentions.

Essentially, this again demonstrates that aside from legal considerations, the general point and purpose to corrections (including community corrections) is the reintegration of offenders. Legal liabilities are important for practitioners in the field, and that is why they are covered in this text. However, these liabilities usually exist to facilitate one of two different goals: to safeguard the constitutional rights of offenders, or to ensure public safety. Indeed, when examining most liabilities that safeguard the offender's rights, an argument can be made that the reintegrative process would be moot without these protections. Liabilities for staff are meant to encourage a certain standard of behavior and accountability among community correctional personnel. Such standards improve the possibility of offenders desisting from crime, providing clear boundaries and expectations for those being supervised as well as those who do the supervising.

SOURCE: Lilly, J. R., Cullen, F. T., & Ball, R. A. (2007). *Criminological theory: Context and consequences* (4th ed.). Thousand Oaks, CA: Sage Publications.

LEGAL ISSUES WITH COURT SHAMING
AND THE USE OF POLYGRAPH EXAMINATIONS

This last section seeks to examine some of the offender rights or agency liability issues associated with two specific practices used in community supervision—the use of offender shaming and the use of polygraph examinations. Regarding the use of both of these supervision techniques or conditions, a specific appeal to public safety and to reintegration can be made, though this may not be readily apparent to the student or layperson. This section is provided to demonstrate how these two competing interests (public safety and offender reintegration) can actually work hand-in-hand to justify the use of techniques that might, on the face of it, seem purely punitive. In addition, it is important to understand that these approaches have been validated by the courts as being legally permissible and constitutionally sound.

Consistent with ideas presented in Braithwaite's (1989) work entitled *Crime, Shame, and Reintegration*, the use of shaming techniques with offenders has been thought to shame the offender into behavioral change while also notifying the community of the offender's particular propensity. Many of these public notification laws are implemented with various sex offenders or other violent types of offenders, and they are intended to enhance community safety. In addition, these techniques improve the likelihood that the offender will be more closely watched by the community, thereby deterring the offender from further criminal behavior and (hopefully) reducing the risk of relapse or recidivism. Thus, many jurisdictions contend that the use of shaming techniques further rehabilitation/reintegration goals of community supervision by "deterring the offender from committing future crimes of the same nature as the one for which he or she was convicted" (del Carmen et al., 2001). While most lower courts have held that the use of shaming techniques does not violate the 8th Amendment's restriction against cruel and unusual punishments, this issue has not been ruled upon by the U.S. Supreme Court.

However, it is likely that these types of programs will, if ever examined by the High Court, be found constitutional, particularly if agencies maintain that these conditions of supervision are implemented for a treatment-related function rather than a punitive one. Indeed, the 8th Amendment prohibits cruel and unusual punishment, but it does not prohibit unusual therapeutic modalities (or even cruel therapeutic modalities, for that matter). In fact, the 8th Amendment does not (and cannot) speak to matters of treatment interventions because these are presumed to be benevolent functions that are contrary to punitive techniques. Though this may seem to be a fine-line technicality, it actually has relevant Supreme Court precedence in the case of *Kansas v. Hendricks* (1997), where the Court ruled that it was indeed constitutional to civilly commit a sexual predator beyond his sentence of incarceration. The rationale for this was that the civil commitment was to allow the offender additional rehabilitative services, and to protect society until the offender was cured of his mental abnormalities. The civil commitment was therefore considered a benevolent form of detention that was not construed as having a punitive element. Because of this, the 8th Amendment simply did not apply to this case.

The use of shaming conditions of parole can have a similar purpose. It is clear that the common connection between the two circumstances (the use of shaming techniques with a community supervision sentence and civil commitment of offenders beyond their sentence) is that there is both a treatment-related justification on the one hand, and a concern for public safety on the other. This common connection is important because it demonstrates a legal thread that has been a theme throughout previous chapters: the role of community corrections is geared toward both reintegration of the offender and the protection of the public.

This same line of thought has been used to legitimize the use of polygraphs (lie detectors) when supervising sex offenders. For the most part, state courts have held that either one or all of the following reasons are sufficient to justify continued use under the U.S. Constitution: (1) the instrument is used to augment treatment processes, (2) such tests are used as tools to ensure offender compliance with supervision requirements, and/or (3) the tool is used to detect the commission of additional crimes (de Carmen et al., 2001). While there is no clear or complete consensus on each of these purposes from state to state, Hanser (2007b) notes that the use of these tools is both beneficial and necessary to ensure that treatment programs with repeat sex offenders are successful. The use of such leverage, while appearing to be grounded in punishment, is actually an effective way to monitor accountability and to circumvent potential relapse. Thus, it is the contention of this text that these instruments serve a therapeutic purpose and that they are therefore constitutionally valid.

CONCLUSION

As shown in this chapter, concerns with liability can be quite complicated. The types of suits that can be brought forward, both state and federal (as well as those that are either tort or civil rights based) provide avenues of redress that have numerous similarities and differences, each being suited to different circumstances that offenders may wish to bring forward. Understanding these types of suits, and the grounds upon which they may be filed, is important for all practitioners within the field of community supervision. Community supervision officers do enjoy some degree of immunity to lawsuits that may be brought forward, but this form of immunity tends not to be as certain as the absolute immunity that is afforded to judges or parole boards. The only exception to this is when community supervision officers are tasked with the completion of a PSI, in which case community supervision officers enjoy the same absolute immunity given to judges and parole board members. Because of this, it is important that community supervision officers understand issues related to liability and that they understand the parameters associated with their qualified immunity protection.

In addition, the public duty doctrine of tort law shields most all community supervision personnel from liability for recidivate acts that probationers or parolees may commit. All in all, it is clear that such actions are beyond the control of parole boards, judges, and community supervision officers. In fact, it would seem that community supervision agencies exercise a level of care for public safety that exceeds the minimal level typically required by precedent or federal law. While offenders on community supervision do have some rights that must be honored before their probation or parole may be revoked, the risk of liability for most community supervision officers that make mistakes during revocation proceedings is likely to be slight. Last of all, it has been seen that various added conditions of a community supervision sentence, such as shaming techniques or the use of polygraphs, have not been found to be unconstitutional. In fact, so long as agencies emphasize the therapeutic (rather than punitive) value of these added conditions, it is likely that these various added sanctions will survive any legal question that may arise in the future.

Key Terms

Absolute immunity	Injunction	Punitive damages
Compensatory damages	Intentional tort	Qualified immunity
Declaratory judgment	Invasion of privacy	Slight negligence
Defamation	Malicious prosecution	Tort
Good faith defense	Misrepresentation of facts	Willful negligence
Gross negligence	Negligence	

"What Would You Do?" Exercise

Jimmy Ray had been in a relationship with Jenny Kay for nearly 5 years. Both persons had chronic problems with alcoholism and led a very rough-and-tumble lifestyle. The two lived together but had not made plans to marry. Both had kids from other marriages, and Jimmy paid an exorbitant amount in child support. Jenny's kids sometimes lived with their father and sometimes stayed with her, but usually the father kept them throughout the years because Jenny was usually either too drunk or too hungover to take care of them.

Jimmy worked construction and Jenny worked at a local diner. Aside from going to work, the two would drink a variety of beer, whiskey, and tequila beverages any time they had the chance. Both engaged in rough "play" from time to time and were seen sometimes "gently hitting" each other. One night, things got very rough and they had engaged in mutual batteries of each other's person. However, Jenny ended up the worst off and spent the night in the hospital. Jimmy Ray spent the night in jail.

After getting out of jail, Jenny would not talk to Jimmy at first. Then she became angry with him. She began seeing another man, Bobby Dean, who told Jimmy that he would beat Jimmy to a pulp if he caught him talking to Jenny ever again.

Soon after getting out of jail, Jimmy was placed on probation. He was classified as a domestic abuser and was sentenced to 3 years of probation and community service at a local thrift shop that generated money for battered women, and he was required to attend group therapy for alcoholics twice a week as a condition of his probation.

When Jimmy found out about his community service assignment, he explained his concerns about the particular place of business. The thrift shop was one that Jenny routinely shopped at, sometimes to buy clothes for her kids (when they were with her) and sometimes just for leisure. Jimmy explained that he did not want to have inadvertent contact with Jenny and asked if he could do his community service at another location.

The probation officer, Officer Hardy, told Jimmy, "Look, she can go wherever she wants to go to shop," and while pointing at Jimmy, he said, "There are people all around and she will not do anything. You just mind your own business and it will be fine."

The probation officer added, "I think that you just do not want to do the community service at a ladies' thrift store and that you are still upset about this domestic abuse case sticking to you," and while looking into Jimmy's eyes, Officer Hardy said, "That's it, isn't it? You're too proud to do community service over there, huh?"

Jimmy explained that he was not worried so much about Jenny, but that her new boyfriend, Bobby Dean, was a really rough man and that Bobby would most likely antagonize Jimmy. In fact, he noted that Bobby would probably try to pick a fight with Jimmy and humiliate him at the thrift store.

Officer Hardy responded by saying, "Well, we can cross that bridge if we even get to it. Besides, you should have thought about this kind of stuff before you went drinking and beating on women."

Two weeks later, Jimmy was working at the thrift store and by all accounts had been doing an adequate job. However, Jenny stopped in and on the first day said nothing. On the following day, she went in, saw Jimmy, and tried to talk with him. Jimmy told her to quit being a tease, and he went to another area of the store. Jenny got mad at his remark and left. Two witnesses, employees of the thrift store, observed the incident. After about 30 minutes, Jenny arrived back in the store with Bobby Dean. Bobby verbally assaulted Jimmy and, without any hesitation, punched Jimmy in the face. Bobby and Jimmy then got into an altercation that ended with Jimmy being taken to the hospital.

Police arrived at the scene and, based on witness testimony, arrested Bobby Dean. Jenny Kay was nowhere to be found at the time the police arrived. Jimmy was taken to the hospital and treated for moderate injuries. The police called Jimmy's probation officer and notified him of the circumstances. The police decided not to press charges against Jimmy and did not issue him a citation because the employees of the thrift store made it clear that he was simply trying to not get beaten any worse than had already happened. In fact, the employees were now afraid to have Jenny come to the store in the future since she had brought this upon everyone.

Jimmy did not have medical insurance and was now stuck with an expensive medical bill. He also could not work for a couple of days and lost some pay. The doctor's information validated the extent of his injuries.

Jimmy went to a lawyer and filed suit against Officer Hardy for gross negligence and also filed a Section 1983 suit citing violation of his 8th and 14th Amendment rights.

Instructor: Note that this assignment is perfectly suited for a group activity. Students can be divided into groups and can discuss the case, providing their input and voting among themselves before providing you with their final answer.

Students: You are on the jury as Officer Hardy faces a federal suit filed by Jimmy and his attorney. Explain if Officer Hardy is actually liable and in doing so, identify the specific legal criteria that justify your determination.

What would you do?

Applied Exercise

Consider the public duty doctrine and the fact that release decision-making bodies (i.e., judges and parole boards) are not usually held legally liable for their decisions when releasing or supervising offenders in the community. In addition, consider the various constitutional rights afforded offenders through cases such as *Morrissey v. Brewer* and *Gagnon v. Scarpelli* (due process protections), *United States v. Irving* (equal protection), and *Martinez v. California* (test of the public duty doctrine under Section 1983). In addition, consider the various types of intentional and negligence-based torts that exist to protect the offender from personal damages inflicted by supervision officers or other community corrections personnel.

From the fact that community corrections personnel are not typically liable to the public (as put forth in the public duty doctrine) and given that community corrections personnel can be held liable if they violate the offender's civil rights, rights to due process, or rights to privacy through the security of presentence investigation data, or if they commit a personal injury against the offender (i.e., they violate tort law), determine whether the current system is more in favor of offender rights or public safety. In making your argument, be sure to identify how these legal mechanisms are useful in implementing a reintegrative approach to community supervision processes. Likewise, explain how public safety may (or may not) be compromised in the current system. Students should complete this application exercise as a mini paper that is submitted to the instructor. Total word count: 1,200 to 2,000 words.

CHAPTER 6

Specific Aspects Related to Probation

LEARNING OBJECTIVES

1. Understand the probation organization, primarily at the county and state levels of government.

2. Be aware of the objectives and advantages of probation.

3. Understand the future potential of private probation agencies.

4. Understand the importance of the PSI.

5. Understand the importance of the various courtroom actors when setting terms and conditions of probation.

6. Be cognizant of basic issues involved with probation evaluation.

7. Know the various forms of alternative probation sentences.

8. Understand various factors associated with the revocation of probation.

INTRODUCTION

Probationers are criminal offenders who have been sentenced to a period of correctional supervision in the community in lieu of incarceration (Glaze & Bonczar, 2007). During the past few years, the overall population growth of probationers has continued; however, the rate of that growth has progressively slowed over the past several years. For instance, in 2005 the probation population grew by only 0.5 percent, or 19,070 probationers; this is the lowest rate of growth that has been seen in 26 years. Nevertheless, the probation population accounted for approximately half of all growth in the overall correctional population throughout the nation (Glaze & Bonczar, 2007). Probationers continue to account for the largest proportion of persons under corrections supervision, with 58 percent of all convicted offenders being on probation. At the close of 2005, the total probation population, including state and federal probationers, was 4,162,536 (Glaze & Bonczar, 2007). Figure 6.1 illustrates the growth in the probation population in relation to other correctional population categories (i.e., jails, prisons, and parole).

181

FIGURE 6.1 Number of Persons Under Adult Correctional Supervision by Type of Supervision Between 1990 and 2005

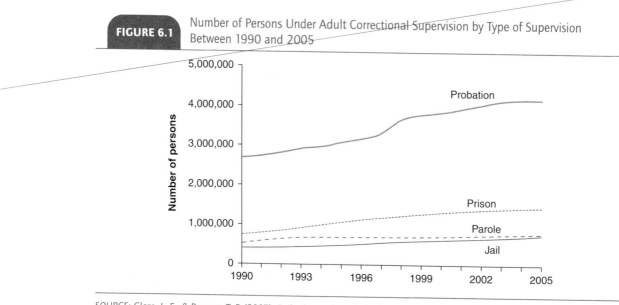

SOURCE: Glaze, L. E., & Bonczar, T. P. (2007). *Probation and parole in the United States, 2005.* Washington, DC: U.S. Department of Justice.

Again, though probation has experienced the largest amount of growth among the correctional population, it has nevertheless experienced a slowdown in that growth. In fact, during 1990 the overall proportion of probationers, when combining probation, jail, prison, and parole populations, was roughly 61 percent. Thus, not only has the probationer population grown at a slower rate during the past few years, but the other categories of the correctional population have experienced a correspondingly higher rate of growth since 1990, with proportions of jail and prison inmates rising during the past 15 years (Glaze & Bonczar, 2007). Specifically, jail inmates have risen from 9 to 10 percent of the overall correctional population and prison inmates have risen from 17 to 20 percent. Thus, as a whole, the institutionalized population has gone from being roughly 26 percent of the total population to about 30 percent (Glaze & Bonczar, 2007). This differential increase of 4 percent is what accounts for the 4 percent proportional decrease in the probation population. Amidst this growth in the institutionalized population, the parolee population has remained relatively stable and has not changed greatly (this is discussed in more detail in the following chapter). Figure 6.2 illustrates that after a sharp spike in growth in the probation population in 2001, that population has declined in each successive year thereafter.

Table 6.1 provides an overview of the numbers of probationers in the top 10 states with the largest probation populations. The 10 states with the highest rates of supervision and the 10 states with the lowest rates are also covered in Table 6.1. Interestingly, only half of the states with probation populations that rank in the top 10 also rank in the top 10 for the highest rate of growth, these states being Massachusetts, Michigan, New Jersey, Ohio, and Texas. During the year 2005, the state of Mississippi had the highest rate of growth (17 percent), followed by West Virginia and Wyoming. Across the nation, 32 states reported an overall increase in their probationer populations (Glaze & Bonczar, 2007).

Among the probation population, almost 1 out of 4 (23 percent) are female offenders. Nationwide, women represented a slightly larger percentage of the probation population in 2005 than during the 10 years prior. This represents a slow but steady growth pattern within the female offending population. Further, more than half of all probationers are Caucasian, almost a third are African American, and one-eighth are Latino American. Persons of other racial orientations comprise about 2 percent of all probationers in the United States.

FIGURE 6.2 Annual Increase in Probation Population, 1995–2005

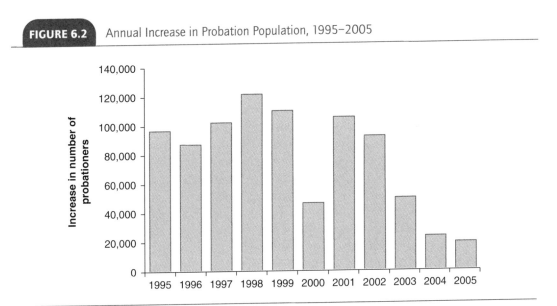

SOURCE: Glaze, L. E., & Bonczar, T. P. (2007). *Probation and parole in the United States, 2005.* Washington, DC: U.S. Department of Justice.

TABLE 6.1 Probation Among Notable Ranking States

10 States With the Largest Probation Populations	Number Supervised	10 States With the Highest Rates of Supervision	Persons Supervised per 100,000	10 States With the Lowest Rates of Supervision	Persons Supervised per 100,000
Texas	430,312	Massachusetts	3,350	New Hampshire	457
California	388,260	Rhode Island	3,091	West Virginia	533
Florida	277,831	Minnesota	2,988	Utah	578
Ohio	239,036	Delaware	2,828	Nevada	709
Michigan	178,609	Ohio	2,745	Kansas	723
Pennsylvania	167,561	Indiana	2,583	Maine	776
Massachusetts	165,365	Texas	2,580	Virginia	788
Illinois	143,136	Michigan	2,350	North Dakota	791
New Jersey	139,091	Washington	2,155	New York	810
Indiana	121,014	New Jersey	2,117	South Dakota	899

SOURCE: Glaze, L. E., & Bonczar, T. P. (2007). *Probation and parole in the United States, 2005.* Washington, DC: U.S. Department of Justice.

Overall, roughly 50 percent of all probationers are convicted of a felony offense, with the misdemeanor population consisting of 49 percent. The remaining 1 percent have been convicted of other types of offenses, such as city ordinances, county codes, and so forth. As Glaze and Bonczar (2007) indicate, the largest body of the probation population has been convicted of some form of drug-related violation (28 percent), followed by DWI (15 percent) and larceny/theft (12 percent). Though most probationers are on probation for nonviolent offenses, 3 percent are serving for sexual assault, another 6 percent are serving for some form of domestic violence, and 10 percent are on probation for miscellaneous assault convictions (Glaze & Bonczar, 2007). Thus, about 1 in 5 probation offenders has committed an act of violence, and among these, many are not extreme acts. The remaining offenses tend to be fairly evenly distributed and include crimes such as fraud, burglary, and minor (but probably repetitive) traffic violations (Glaze & Bonczar, 2007).

Not all probationers are required to report to their probation officer. Indeed, a certain proportion are simply kept on caseloads administratively and are checked periodically, required to pay fees during the set amount of time, and so forth. So long as no word of violation is received or detected by other agencies, these offenders finish out their probation with relative ease. In 2005, roughly 7 in 10 probationers were under active supervision, being required to regularly report to a probation authority in person, by mail, or by telephone (Glaze & Bonczar, 2007). This means that roughly 30 percent of all probationers were on inactive administrative caseloads. The percentage of probationers required to report regularly has declined steadily, from 79 percent in 1995 to 70 percent in 2005 (Glaze & Bonczar, 2007). In addition, roughly 10 percent of all probationers absconded during 2005. Though these individuals are still on probation caseloads, their whereabouts are completely unknown. This is a concern, as it means there are roughly 400,000 probation absconders across the nation. The rate of probation absconders has, during the past decade, slightly increased from 9 percent to 10 percent and indicates a general need for improved methods of security for probationers.

Finally, while the total state probationer population is 4,114,864 (as of 2005), the total federal probation population is a minuscule 26,602 (Glaze & Bonczar, 2007). Thus, in comparison, the total population of federal probationers is less than 1 percent of the number that comprises state-level probation. To make the point even further, federal probation decreased by 6.6 percent in 2005, indicating that the use of federal probation is much less frequent than is the case for state probation (Glaze & Bonczar, 2007). Moreover, many of the services of federal probation officers are associated with pretrial functions. Thus, federal probation is not a central aspect of the overall probation picture around the nation and therefore will be discussed sparingly throughout this chapter and text. Rather, this chapter will focus on the other 99 percent of the probationer population and the systems that are responsible for their supervision.

MODELS OF PROBATION ADMINISTRATION

The specific means by which probation operates can vary considerably depending upon the level of government from which it is administered. Correctional systems, including community supervision components, can be very different from state to state. Students will recall from Chapter 1 that some discussion was given to this fact. A bit more discussion on the organizational aspects of probation will be provided here, since this greatly impacts the operations of probation services within a given jurisdiction. One key characteristic involves the degree of centralization that exists within an agency. Indeed, adult probation in one state may be administered by a single central agency, by a variety of local agencies, or by a combination of the two (as noted in Chapter 1). When considering local levels of administration, agencies may operate at the county or even municipal level. However, these supposedly smaller jurisdictions should not be underestimated. Consider, for example, the probation departments in New York City where felony and misdemeanor caseloads are larger than those of many entire state systems.

Further, probation services are delivered through one of two mechanisms: the executive or the judicial branch of government. In both cases, the probation agency will oversee the individual's compliance with conditions of his or her probation supervision. With this in mind, probation agencies administered through the executive branch may be part of the larger state correctional system, or they may exist as an entirely separate system. In addition, these agencies may operate at local levels of government but, again, may be included within areas of government associated with the executive (enforcement) functions of government. While the sentencing courts, in these cases, may require probation agencies to provide reports on the subsequent supervision of the offender, the probation agencies are themselves outside of the judicial process.

On the other hand, probation agencies that are administered through the judicial branch work directly with the court system itself. In these cases, state and local courts will enforce compliance with the terms of probation through court judgments. In the process, court administrative offices or designated staff monitor various aspects of the probation process. Functions such as the collection of fees or fines, victim restitution, court-ordered child support, and so forth are fulfilled through personnel that are tasked via judges or judicial administrators.

Those who support the operation of probation services in the judicial branch contend that probation is more responsive to the courts when it is administered by the judiciary (Abadinsky, 2003; Nelson, Ohmart, & Harlow, 1978; Peak, 1995). Moreover, when probation personnel and court personnel operate in close proximity, an automatic feedback loop develops, thereby optimizing the performance of the dispositions that are given. In addition, the court will have better insight as to the challenges involved with administering probation supervision (Abadinsky, 2003; Nelson et al., 1978; Peak, 1995). With this in mind, it is then likely that judges would be more receptive to the needs and concerns of the probation agency, particularly since the agency would work in tandem with (and directly under) the supervision of the judiciary. This would also allow for better discretionary operations, since the probation staff would not be members of an outside agency but instead would be aligned with the specific purposes of the court (Abadinsky, 2003; Nelson et al., 1978; Peak, 1995). Figure 6.3 provides an example of a probation department that is operated at the county level under a specific judicial court.

On the other hand, there are also those that oppose the operation of probation services in the judicial branch, noting several disadvantages. First, judges are trained in matters of legal interpretation rather than administration and are typically not appropriately equipped to administer probation services. Second, when under judicial control, services to persons on probation may receive a lower priority than services to the judge, such as with presentence investigations. Third, probation staff tend to be assigned to a variety of duties by judges, some of which are not related to probation but are instead intended to address other demands upon the courthouse. Fourth, the courts tend to be adjudicatory in nature and are therefore not oriented to a service style of operation. This then undermines the reintegrative nature of probation, a major aspect of this text's presentation of the subject. Fifth, placing probation in the executive segment of state government would allow for better coordination of service provision and for budgetary considerations. Sixth, the centralization of probation services within the executive branch allows for a coordinated continuum of services to offenders, thereby improving reintegrative efforts. Seventh and last, other human service agencies as well as institutional correctional systems tend to be placed in the executive branch as well (Abadinsky, 2003; Nelson et al., 1978; Peak, 1995). Therefore, probation would be in a better position to coordinate with these agencies. Thus, as one can tell, there is an equally compelling argument for probation departments to be administered through the executive segment of state government as there is for administering them through the judicial branch.

Consider further that in many cases, the administration of probation may be determined by the seriousness of the offense. For instance, felony offenses may be supervised by state-level personnel, while misdemeanor cases may be supervised by local governmental probation agencies. In Michigan, for example, adult felony probation is administered through the state department of corrections while adult misdemeanor probation is administered through the local district courts.

Juvenile probation adds a whole new dimension of organizational considerations. Indeed, over half of all juvenile probation agencies are administered at the local level. To illustrate, juvenile probation may be provided through a separate agency or through a subdepartment of the large adult probation system. In over a dozen states, juvenile probation services are split, with the juvenile court administering services in urban jurisdictions and the state administering such services in rural areas. Some states have a statewide office of juvenile probation that is located in the executive branch (Siegel, Welsh, & Senna, 2003).

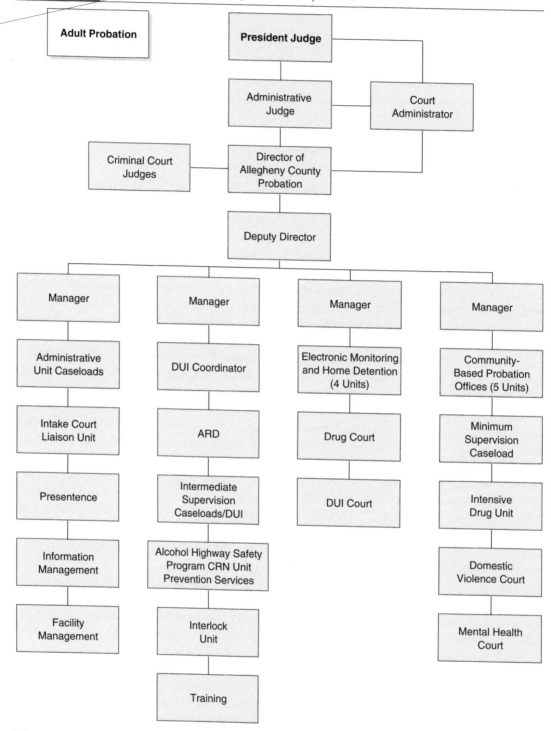

Example of a Local-Based Probation Organization That Is Under The Direction of a Judicial Court: The Allegheny County Probation Department

Adult Probation

President Judge

Administrative Judge

Court Administrator

Criminal Court Judges

Director of Allegheny County Probation

Deputy Director

Manager

Administrative Unit Caseloads

Intake Court Liaison Unit

Presentence

Information Management

Facility Management

Manager

DUI Coordinator

ARD

Intermediate Supervision Caseloads/DUI

Alcohol Highway Safety Program CRN Unit Prevention Services

Interlock Unit

Training

Manager

Electronic Monitoring and Home Detention (4 Units)

Drug Court

DUI Court

Manager

Community-Based Probation Offices (5 Units)

Minimum Supervision Caseload

Intensive Drug Unit

Domestic Violence Court

Mental Health Court

SOURCE: Allegheny County Probation Department. Retrieved from http://www.alleghenycourts.us/downloads/organization%20charts/adult_probation.pdf. Copyright © 2008, Fifth Judicial District of Pennsylvania Allegheny County Probation Department.

Last, Abadinsky (2003) notes that probation systems can be separated into six categories, with states having more than one system in operation simultaneously. The six categories of operation are as follows:

1. Juvenile: This includes separate probation services for juveniles that are administered through county or municipal governments, or on a statewide basis.

2. Municipal: These are independent probation agencies that are administered through lower courts or through the municipality itself.

3. County: The probation agency is governed by laws or guidelines established by the state, which empowers a county to operate its own probation agency.

4. State: One agency administers a centralized probation system that provides services throughout the state.

5. State combined P & P: Probation and parole services are administered together on a statewide basis by a single agency.

6. Federal: Probation is administered nationally as a branch of the courts.

The above categories of operation are of course reminiscent of Chapter 1 in which it was demonstrated that the organization of community supervision agencies typically revolved around the particular level of government at which a probation agency was administered. Much of the research on the organization of probation points toward the fact that probation would, in the most practical sense, be best administered through an executive segment of governmental administration. Moving probation within the executive segment of government requires that probation be operated from a centralized managerial scheme that would then naturally be administered at the state level (Peak, 1995). The coordination of centralized, state-run probation systems tends to be much better and also allows for better integration of overall services (Nelson et al., 1978; Peak, 1995). While administrators will be more removed from the rank-and-file probation officer staff, the uniformity of services, elimination of widespread disparity in supervision, and the improved integration of services with other social service agencies is thought to offset concerns related to this type of administration (Peak, 1995).

OBJECTIVES AND ADVANTAGES OF PROBATION

As was noted in previous chapters, the two primary objectives of community supervision—or more specifically, probation—are to protect the community from further criminal behavior (recidivism) while also reintegrating the offender. These two goals are complementary, though they may seem to operate at cross-purposes. The means by which these competing goals are met is determined on a case-by-case basis where the granting of probation is a highly individualized process. This allows the judge and the probation agency to provide the appropriate balance between these competing objectives so as to best address the specific conditions surrounding an offender. Naturally, the individualized nature of probation leads to some degree of variability and also requires a more detailed approach to supervising cases.

Latessa and Allen (1999) note that even though probation tends to have this individualized approach, there are several advantages to probation that are generally recognized among probation experts. According to Latessa and Allen (1999), these advantages are as follows:

1. The use of community resources to reintegrate offenders who are thus forced to face and hopefully resolve their individual problems while under community supervision.

2. Fiscal savings over imprisonment.

3. Avoiding prisonization, which tends to exacerbate the underlying causes of criminal behavior.

4. Keeping an offenders' families off local and state welfare rolls, or at least reducing the amount of needed assistance.

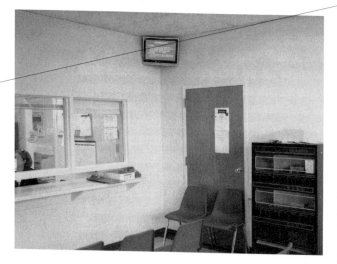

Photo 6.1 The lobby outside of a probation and parole office can be seen. Probationers/parolees check in at the window and wait for their probation/parole officer to come forward to meet them. Note the screen in the corner. This screen lists the various conditions of community supervision and includes a voice recording, ensuring that offenders are reminded about the various conditions of probation or parole.

5. A relatively successful process of correcting offending behavior, depending on the type of offender and the specific jurisdiction.

6. A sentencing option that can permit selective incapacitation of those that genuinely require displacement from the community (p. 173).

While the disadvantages of probation naturally include the fact that offenders are able to reoffend in society since they are not incarcerated, it is the general notion that this can be minimized effectively enough so as to ensure that the advantages to the public outweigh the disadvantages. The points above demonstrate that probation saves the public a great deal of money and resources, when used correctly. The last part of the previous statement is particularly important, since a poor or haphazard use of this sentence can result in physical, emotional, and economic costs to the public.

Understand that this argument is not presented as ideological support for the probation sanction. The mere fact that probation is used in approximately 60 percent of all sentences demonstrates that it has a great deal of utility. It is not the intent of this text to prove or disprove whether probation should be used. However, its use as leverage during negotiated pleas that are sought by the prosecutor, the range of special conditions that can be applied, and the types of treatment approaches that can be pursued make this sanction indispensable to the criminal justice system. In fact, students must understand that whether this is good, bad, or indifferent, the American criminal justice system simply could not operate without the existence of the probation sanction. This is a reality people often fail to see, believing instead that the justice system "ought to" do one thing or the other in an effort to eliminate what is perceived as a weak response to crime.

However, probation is a reality that is here to stay and is necessary. This is similar to the reality of plea bargaining. In the vast majority of cases (upward of 90 percent of all cases), the final sentence is the result of a plea between the prosecution and the defense counsel. This is of course arranged before the judge even begins sentencing. The use of plea bargaining is a critical element of our adversarial system of justice. In fact, plea bargaining occurs because of our emphasis on an adversarial system where both parties present their evidence, refute the evidence of the other party, and are generally expected to engage in a competitive process that allows judges or juries to sift through this parade of evidence (both real and testimony based) as a means of obtaining a truthful conviction.

The process just described is, quite naturally, a fairly involved one that can be quite costly and time-consuming. The process of *voir dire* (jury selection) alone can be quite complicated, and this is the beginning of the larger process that is required if a case is destined to go before a jury. Even if the case is to be decided by a judge (without the use of a jury), the cost entailed for the district prosecutor and the defense counsel can be quite burdensome. Thus, plea bargaining allows both parties to "cut to the chase," so to speak, allowing for a negotiated sentence that saves a considerable amount of time, money, and inconvenience for both the prosecution and the defense. This also allows the defendant the opportunity to avoid the most severe penalty possible, yet ensures that the courtroom is not tied up with frivolous antics in defense of the individual's case; this is demonstrated by the fact that the vast majority of cases that do go to court end with the defendant being found guilty and given a sentence that is much more severe than if he or she had taken a plea from the prosecutor.

Thus, the plea bargaining process provides the prosecution with leverage over the defendant. Similarly, the use of probation sentences provides both the prosecution and the defense with a series of options that can be negotiated. For instance, the prosecution may require that a defendant receive 6 months of drug treatment, get anger management therapy, provide restitution to the victim, and undergo intensive supervision if the charge is to be reduced. The defense counsel may then counter with the offer that the defendant be required to attend only 3 months of drug treatment, get anger management help, provide restitution to the victim, and have standard probation supervision with electronic monitoring (thereby maintaining security over the offender but eliminating the number of face-to-face contacts that the offender is required to maintain throughout the week). The defense counsel may also contend that this flexibility is necessary so that the defendant will be able to continue his or her employment, a necessary ingredient for the probation sentence and a necessary requisite if the offender is to pay the required restitution to the victim. Both parties can, from this point forward, negotiate the terms and conditions that seem reasonable under the circumstances.

The previous scenario is quite common in the United States court system. In fact, it is the norm, and this is known to any person that has had extensive experience in large court systems throughout the United States. Further, there is one additional advantage to the use of probation as a sentence, particularly during the plea bargaining phase. The advantage concerns the victim. In times past, the victim was not necessarily a party that was considered in plea negotiations. Often, the main focus given to the victim during sentencing revolved around restitution which, in many cases, might be administered through a victim's compensation fund, removing the victim from the direct process of adjudication. However, the new emphasis on victimology and victims' rights has ensured that elements such as victim impact statements, probation officer follow-ups with the victim, and victim input throughout the supervision process are considered both during the plea bargaining phase and during subsequent offender supervision while on probation. Likewise, the variety of probation sanctions allows for better compensation to victims, while innovations with mediation, restorative justice, and other types of community and victim involvement have resulted in better account-ability of offenders to the victims that were directly impacted by their criminal behavior.

If we did not have the probation sanction, none of this would be possible. The student of community corrections should make a point of keeping this in focus. Without this flexibility in the criminal justice system, options would be limited and the ability to provide restitution to victims would be much more difficult. Further, offenders in prison would not be likely to generate any true benefit for victims and would, in all likelihood, simply end up exacting a higher cost from society while at the same time failing to assume direct accountability to the victims of their crime(s). Thus, the benefit of community corrections to ensure offender accountability cannot be ignored.

Moreover, it is again important to remember that prison space is limited and also that prison space is not intended to actually serve a productive use. From an incapacitation perspective, prison space is simply meant to warehouse an offender. Indeed, prisons are not good environments for the reintegration of offenders and, in actuality, they tend to breed attitudes conducive to criminality among the offending population. Thus, the economic considerations (rather than rehabilitative ideals) should be primary when allocating prison space. Simply put, treatment is most effectively utilized in the community setting, because the effects of **prisonization** are avoided and because most social services are typically better administered in the community. Intensive prison treatment programs tend to be much more costly and have not been proven to work better than or even as effectively as those administered in the community. Thus, from a strictly fiscal and administrative point of view, institutional treatment programs are less desirable than community-based programs.

Once the question of public safety has been determined (if the offender cannot be safely released on community supervision, then the point regarding economics is probably moot), this leads to the notion that economic considerations should be the primary determining factor in allocating prison resources. Probation is an essential component of the system if finite correctional resources are to be adequately managed. In fact, the correctional system and the court system are both dependent on the use of this sanction, since jail space and prison space are both typically limited. Tables 6.2 and 6.3 illustrate the cost-effectiveness of community supervision sanctions when compared with prison sanctions.

Table 6.2 provides information from the state of North Carolina regarding the costs involved with different levels of offender supervision. It is clear from the information in this table that community supervision sanctions are much more cost-effective. Indeed, even if one were to place an offender on intensive supervised probation (ISP) costing $11.47 a day, and if the offender were also placed on electronic house arrest costing $7.92 a day, along with additional community service requirements costing only $.73 per day, as well the use of a fully integrated system of community partnerships (similar to that discussed in Chapter 2) for another $9.58 per day, the total daily cost is only $29.70. This comes well under the $50.04 daily cost that is required for minimum custody within a prison facility—a very important point, especially when drug offenders and other nonviolent offenders are among those being processed. In such cases, it is highly likely that a complete community supervision package will be just as effective as a prison sentence where minimal levels of security and supervision are maintained. Further, the types of comprehensive services given to the inmate are likely to be much better in community-based programs (an issue that will be discussed in more depth later on). Finally, the use of a full contingent of community supervision mechanisms can maintain security while at the same time allowing the offender to work and provide additional restitution to victims or state-run compensation programs. When inmates are in prisons, they are not as likely to be able to provide any meaningful restitution.

Thus, it is clear that these types of programs have substantial economic benefits, but it is also clear that along with this saving of tax dollars, these offenders (when correctly assessed and classified) are able to be far more productive to society and more accountable to the victims of their crimes if they are made to fulfill their sentence in the community. Naturally, there will be exceptions to this since some offenders will simply refuse to work or to comply with various requirements necessary for their sentence. In these cases, community supervision is not an appropriate sanction. However, in the majority of cases, offenders (particularly nonviolent ones) will comply at least at a bare minimum.

TABLE 6.2 The Costs of Incarceration and Community Supervision in the State of North Carolina

Specific Sanction and Cost of Sanction
State of North Carolina

Type of Sanction	Cost per Day	Cost per Year
Prison: Close Custody	$80.19	$29,269
Prison: Medium Custody	$65.17	$23,787
Prison: Minimum Custody	$50.04	$18,265
Community Supervision/Standard Probation	$1.83	$668
Intensive Probation	$11.47	$4,187
Electronic House Arrest	$7.92	$2,891
Community Service Work Program	$.73	$266
Criminal Justice Partnership Program	$9.58	$3,497

SOURCE: North Carolina Department of Correction. (2003). *Cost of supervision, fiscal year 2001–2002.* Retrieved from http://www.doc.state.nc.us/dop/cost/cost2002.htm.

TABLE 6.3	The Costs of Incarceration and Community Supervision in Federal Programs, 2004		
	*Imprisonment in Bureau of Prisons Facility**	*Community Correction Centers**	*Supervision by Probation Officers***
Daily	$63.57	$55.07	$9.46
Monthly	$1,933.80	$1,675.23	$287.73
Annually	$23,205.59	$20,102.75	$3,452.72

SOURCE: Administrative Office of the United States Courts. (2005). *Newsletter of the Federal Courts, 37*(5). Washington, DC: Author. Retrieved from http://www.uscourts.gov/ttb/may05ttb/incarceration-costs/index.html.

* Costs provided by the Federal Bureau of Prisons
** Costs provided by the Office of Probation and Pretrial Services

The cost-effectiveness of community supervision is also a compelling argument at the federal level, as Table 6.3 demonstrates. While the imprisonment of inmates in the Bureau of Prisons (the federal prison system) costs $63.57 per day, supervision by federal probation officers costs only $9.46 per day. Most federal inmates or offenders are, in fact, nonviolent, and this makes the use of probation a much more appealing option for the federal system.

From the information just discussed, it should be clear that community-based sanctions have a very practical function within our criminal justice system. The use of probation is, in the simplest of sentences, a functional approach to supervising the many offenders who are processed through the criminal justice system. Probation works well as leverage for prosecutors when negotiating pleas, is much less expensive than using overcrowded jails or prisons, provides more direct compensation for victims, and also provides better intervention services for the majority of offenders. Given these realities, it should be clear to the student that our current criminal justice system simply could not operate without the use of probation. The fact that roughly 60 percent of all convicted offenders in the United States are on probation attests to the fact that, like it or not, probation is a pragmatic reality of criminal justice in America, and that it is probably here to stay for quite some time to come.

PUBLIC AND PRIVATE PROBATION AGENCIES

A good deal of attention has been given to public probation agencies and their services to the community, but no true mention has been made regarding the increased use of privatized probation services. This issue is of no small import, as several states utilize private companies for community supervision of offenders on probation. **Private probation** is the same as other forms of probation but is administered by privately owned and operated companies that contract with courts to supervise misdemeanor cases. As an example of how widespread the use of private probation has become, consider that the state of Georgia passed legislation in the early 1990s that required various municipalities and counties to use alternative probation services as the state's Department of Corrections phased out its own supervision of probationers in many jurisdictions. As a result, Georgia established the County and Municipal Probation Advisory Council to create rules and regulations regarding contracts or agreements for the provision of probation services through private providers. The state reserves the right to deny, suspend, or revoke a company's right to operate, and it conducts routine audits of companies providing such services (Office of the Auditor, 2007).

As with much of the corporate world, the state of probation, when administered under private corporations, tends to experience rapid change and continual development. To gain an understanding of how quickly the private arena of corrections can change, consider that in May of 2005, the private company Maximus bought out another company, National Misdemeanant Private Probation Operations (NMPPO), as part of an acquisition agreement (Maximus, 2003). NMPPO serviced more than 31,000 misdemeanant clients in over 200 courts and agencies each week. Maximus, one of the nation's largest government services companies, providing state and local governments with program management, consulting, and information services, had over 5,300 employees located in more than 245 offices across the United States and even in other countries. NMPPO, the company purchased by Maximus, had made public claims of a 90 percent probation completion rate, with 90 percent of fines, fees, and restitution collected. This would make probation a high-profit business that also generates revenue for the community and provides full compensation to victims. Maximus, through its acquisition of NMPPO, would be equipped to provide programming for offenders, including treatment groups, drug and alcohol testing, and education classes. NMPPO had operated several nonresidential programs for misdemeanants that included various forms of offender assessment, case management, and enforcement/supervision. Software used by NMPPO collected and maintained accurate and comprehensive information on probationers, their payment status, the court-ordered conditions that are required, and their progress and history while on supervision (Maximus, 2003).

Then, in October of 2006, a company named Providence Service Corporation bought out Maximus, acquiring all of the assets of the correctional services business affiliated with Maximus (Providence Service Corporation, 2006). Providence Service Corporation noted that its annual revenue was estimated to be around $8 million, and the chief executive officer for that company, when commenting on the acquisition of Maximus, stated that "this acquisition further expands our human services delivery platform and will enable us to introduce probation services in those states where we operate that have privatized probation," adding,

> The number of felony arrests in America makes it impossible for most court jurisdictions to provide probation supervision for minor offenders. The acquired business has a great track record with its payer base and we believe will create a replicable service in many of our existing markets. The fit of human services staff and probation staff side by side should also be well received by our mutual payers. (Providence Service Corporation, 2006)

As of 2006, Providence Service Corporation maintained over 100 contracts, providing privatized misdemeanant probation services in the states of Georgia, Tennessee, South Carolina, Florida, and Washington (Providence Service Corporation, 2006). It should be clear that the world of private probation is one that is experiencing high growth and is constantly changing.

In Athens-Clarke County, Georgia, roughly 2,100 misdemeanant offenders are on probation during any given month. Private probation companies are contracted to supervise nearly 95 percent of the low-risk probationers in the dual-county region. The local government of Athens-Clarke supervises the remaining offenders that are in the community. Generally, the private probation corporations in Athens-Clarke supervise offenders with convictions for crimes such as DUI, underage possession, marijuana possession, shoplifting, criminal trespass, and (when violent) simple battery.

As has been noted in prior chapters, the majority of offenders on probation are nonviolent, and the examples provided from Athens-Clarke reflect this fact. This then makes a strong case for the use of privatized probation services since, for the most part, public safety is genuinely not an issue. Though this is not meant to trivialize crimes that are nonviolent in nature, it does demonstrate that outsourcing may be a viable alternative to managing the burgeoning caseloads of many community supervision agencies. Further, the standard of supervision can be (and is) maintained through state audits, ensuring that companies provide suitable levels of follow-up with offenders. Given that companies have an obvious incentive to collect program fees, fines, and other monetary requirements from probationers, it is highly likely that private companies would provide appropriate follow-up and routine services. In addition, the level of accountability, at least in terms of economic accountability, is likely to be further improved since these companies desire to generate profits from the fees and fines of the probationers under their supervision. This has direct benefits for the community and the victim that is compensated. Since most all of these offenders are nonviolent and since most forms of victimization are likely to be property-related in nature, this can be a particularly productive alternative with low-risk and nonserious offenders.

If the points just presented are indeed true, then it would seem that the main question to be resolved is whether private probation services are able to adequately sustain themselves while maintaining public safety. A direct examination of the viability of a private probation company was provided by an Athens-Clarke audit of private probation services. Table 6.4 provides a financial breakdown of the cost of services to maintain a total caseload of 2,100 probationers while staying within compliance of the regulations promulgated throughout the state of Georgia. The staffing estimates given in Table 6.4 assume that the senior probation officer would also provide a supervisory function but would maintain a caseload that would be roughly half that of the other probation officers in the private agency. The chief probation officer would have no caseload, focusing instead on the supervision elements of the agency. In addition, $75,000 would typically be required to cover rent, training, vehicle replacement, and other mundane costs. The total cost would then typically be around $571,000 annually to supervise roughly 2,100 offenders in Georgia. In Athens-Clarke County, municipal and state court probationers pay a monthly supervision fee of $39.00, with $30.00 being retained by the supervising agency and the remaining $9.00 being sent to the Georgia Crime Victim Compensation Program. Table 6.5 depicts the potential revenue that could be generated from supervision fees collected from the 2,100 average monthly probationers supervised by private probation companies, at varying rates of collection. From the figures presented in Tables 6.4 and 6.5, it can be determined that collection rates of probation supervision fees would typically need to approach 75 to 80 percent. The collection rates that current private companies achieve in Athens-Clarke County tend to meet or exceed this minimal level of income.

It should also be pointed out that, in actuality, the private probation companies in Athens-Clarke do not actually supervise 2,100 offenders; they supervise closer to 2,000 since, as noted before, these companies supervise roughly 95 percent of the dual-county offender population. This means that the caseloads of probation officers would be around 230 offenders. While these caseloads may seem large, they are actually

TABLE 6.4	Projected Staffing Requirements to Supervise 2,100 Monthly Misdemeanant Probationers by Private Probation Companies in Athens-Clarke County, Georgia	
Position Title	Number Required	Salary & Benefits
Chief Probation Officer	1	$55,864
Senior Probation Officer	1	$49,444
Probation Officers	8	$318,528
Accounting Technician	1	$36,284
Administrative Secretary	1	$36,284
Total	12	$496,404

SOURCE: Office of the Auditor. (2007). *Probations services for Athens-Clarke County state and municipal courts: Report to the mayor and commission.* Athens-Clarke County, GA: Unified Government of Athens-Clarke County.

TABLE 6.5 Estimates of Annual Revenue from 2,100 Monthly Misdemeanant Probationers Currently Supervised by Private Probation Companies in Athens-Clarke County, Georgia

Collection Rate →	70%	75%	80%	85%	90%
Estimated Annual → Revenue	$529,200	$567,000	$604,800	$642,600	$680,400

SOURCE: Office of the Auditor. (2007). *Probations services for Athens-Clarke County state and municipal courts: Report to the mayor and commission.* Athens-Clarke County, GA: Unified Government of Athens-Clarke County.

near to the standards recommended by Burrell (2006) in Chapter 2 of this text (the recommended ratio being 200 to 1 for low-risk adult offenders and well past this for cases that are only under administrative supervision for exceedingly minor offenses). In addition, collection rates tend to exceed the minimal rates necessary to be cost-effective. Thus, the likely overall picture is one where caseloads are a bit lower than initially projected while revenue is a bit higher than would be necessary to maintain solvency. If the claims made by NMPPO during its buyout by Maximus are at all near accurate, collection rates would likely be somewhere between 88 and 90 percent. As it turns out, Maximus is, in fact, one of the private probation companies that delivers services to Athens-Clarke County in Georgia. Thus, if the estimates provided by the county are accurate, the overall cost of supervising 2,100 misdemeanant offenders on probation might be around $571,000 in the state of Georgia and in other states that have a similar economic base. Likewise, if the probation officers did indeed supervise approximately 250 offenders, with the senior probation officer supervising roughly 100 to 125 probationers, a full caseload of 2,100 offenders could be supervised within the regulations set by the state of Georgia. From this point, if one were to conservatively use the claims by NMPPO and estimate an 85 percent collection rate (well under the 90 percent that was publicly claimed by NMPPO), total revenue would be around $642,000 annually. When subtracting $571,000 for total costs of running the agency, a net gain of roughly $71,000 is realized. This basically equates to a 12 percent profit off the costs that would annually be budgeted for running the agency. If the claims of NMPPO were indeed accurate (and there is some indication that they might be), then the actual gross income would be $680,000 with a net income of about $109,000 annually. This would indicate an approximate 19 percent profit.

While the overall dollar profits may not sound like much, it should be considered that these programs are also paying salaries that are on a par with other similar professionals throughout the nation. In fact, the pay scales indicated in Table 6.4 would actually be at the upper range of pay, especially for the southeastern portion of the nation. Indeed, job announcements in 2007 for Probation Officer I and II positions have starting annual salaries of about $30,027, while private probation officers receiving salaries according to Table 6.4 would have approximate salaries of $39,750 per year (calculated by taking $318,000 total allocated funds from Table 6.5 and dividing by 8 probation officers). Thus, private probation officers would receive roughly a third more pay than would state- or county-level probation officers.

Though this picture may provide an overly optimistic view of private probation services, it does seem to demonstrate that outsourcing of probation services may become more common in the future. From the information just presented, it would seem that such services provide better collection rates of compensation for victims, provide substantially more pay for probation staff employed in the agency, and have caseloads that are relatively close to recommended levels for low-risk and administratively supervised probationers (Burrell, 2006). All the while, the agency itself generates a profit margin that is likely to range from 12 to 19 percent, depending on the circumstances. While these figures will likely vary from region to region and from year to year, they demonstrate the viability of private probation services.

Further, caseload management could be improved in these circumstances since some relief could be provided by hiring combinations of assistant probation officers and part-time officers (roughly $20,000 could cover another 120 offender cases, ensuring that caseloads do not exceed 230 offenders throughout the agency). The Cross-National Perspective box offers an interesting example of the use of assistant probation officers in the nation of South Africa. It is worth mentioning that similar types of probation personnel are utilized in various parts of the United States, including Georgia. On the other hand, private companies could simply raise the probation fee by a mere $4.00 per month per probationer (at an 85 percent collection rate for 2,100 offenders, this would generate an additional $85,000) to hire two additional officers (at which point caseloads would be right at 200 low-risk offenders per officer, exactly within suggested levels). The point is that, with just some adjustment in charges, personnel allocation, collection rates, or accepted profit margins, private companies can provide supervision services that are well within the recommended caseload levels, thereby avoiding burnout of employees while providing salaries that are well above average in their respective locations. And, as just pointed out, victims are all the better compensated while the community benefits from the lack of tax expenditures on probationer supervision.

Beyond the benefits noted above, it would be reasonable to consider the level of quality of private probation personnel. States can and do set standards that are equal to or exceed those required of state-level probation or parole personnel. For instance, in the state of Georgia (Georgia being our state of reference for this current subsection), the Official Code of Georgia Annotated (O.C.G.A.) Section 42-8-102 and Rule 503-1-.21(b) specifically articulate minimal personnel standards that Georgia courts and private probation agencies must adhere to when signing contracts for private probation services. Such contracts typically include the following requirements, at a minimum:

> *Officer Qualifications and Training.* Contractor shall employ competent and able personnel to provide the services to be rendered hereunder and to appropriately administer the caseload. All probation officers shall be at least twenty-one (21) years of age and have the educational qualifications as required by Section 42-8-102 of the Official Code of Georgia Annotated. All probation officers shall also comply with the orientation and continuing education

training required per annum under the same Code Section. No person who has been convicted of a felony will be employed by Contractor as a probation officer.

Criminal History Check. Contractor shall have a criminal history records check made of all probation officers and certify the results to the County and Municipal Probation Advisory Council. (State of Georgia, 2007, p. 3)

Thus, it is clear that all qualification or training requirements for private probation officers are equal or similar to those required of public probation officers. Further, it should be pointed out that private companies have much more latitude in hiring and firing decisions than do public service agencies, and therefore may make more expedient and effective decisions regarding personnel retention when qualifications or professional performance criteria are an issue. The fact that these private agencies provide more income to their probation officers (at least in

Photo 6.2 In many states, when offenders are placed on community supervision they are fingerprinted. In this photo, a probation and parole employee trains another community supervision worker on the proper process of obtaining offender fingerprints and identification.

Georgia, or more specifically, in Athens-Clarke County) also means that it is likely these companies are able to recruit quality personnel to their ranks.

While private probation supervision is not meant to be construed as a panacea for the challenges that face state or county probation systems, it does demonstrate that such an option may be viable in the right circumstances. Certainly, cost-related figures presented in this section would be quite different in other states such as California or New York, but it would be presumed that revenue collected would be similarly inflated. In addition, programs such as those discussed would not necessarily be ideal for all supervision levels, though, at least hypothetically, more serious offenders could be supervised effectively by private agencies that have state-of-the-art technology and equipment. Naturally, costs would increase, fees would then increase, and overall profitability might go down, but regardless, the use of private agencies provides a set of opportunities that should not be overlooked.

Cross-National Perspective

The Development of the Assistant Probation Officer Position in South Africa

The first curriculum developed by University of Cape Town's (UCT) social development department for training assistant probation officers has been handed over to the national Department of Social Development. The 2-year course is the first of its kind in South Africa and a novel development in the history of probation practice internationally. The curriculum will be circulated to all relevant institutions for their comment. It is anticipated that once it has been approved by the South African Qualifications Authority (SAQA), it will be introduced at training institutions throughout the country. The program will train up much-needed assistant probation officers to ease the load of probation workers in the correctional services.

The drafting of the curriculum was a collaborative team effort, headed by a task team with UCT's Dr. Roland Graser (project convenor), colleague Patrick Smith, and the Provincial Administration of the Western Cape's Ruwayda Carloo and Dr. Stan de Smidt (Department of Social Services and Poverty Alleviation). "The assistant probation officers program had taken us 8 months to develop, including a national consultation workshop with probation coordinators from all the provinces," Graser said.

The undergraduate certificate qualifications originated amidst stark national statistics that reveal a disquieting increase in crime and delinquency in the Nation of South Africa. Prisons are overpopulated by 156 percent. "Of particular concern is the detention of awaiting-trial children," said Graser in his report. "We realized there was an urgent need to develop the occupational category of assistant probation officer to help address the problem of delinquency and manage the situation more humanely." The need for the

job of assistant probation officer has been advocated by the Probation Advocacy Group for a number of years.

With the design of this new professional position, the Probation Advocacy Group sought to ensure that assistant probation officers possessed sufficient knowledge of theory, concepts, and propositions that underlie probation practice. "Candidates need knowledge-guided practice," Graser added, "a familiarity with a host of related principles, focusing on the nature and manifestation of crime in South Africa, assessment and intervention of cases, criminal law, restorative justice, the criminal justice system, the courts, the prisons and nongovernmental organizations active in criminal justice, as well as the services, structures, and resources in probation practice. These officers must learn what motivates them to act antisocially. And in a multi-cultural society like South Africa, its important assistant probation officers are able to relate to the cultural context they operate in. This is vital when presenting community-based programmes," Graser noted.

The 2-year curriculum provides occupation-specific information for trainees that is also coordinated with the Department of Social Development at UCT. In addition to the practical elements of training, the curriculum addresses the following during the 2 years of study:

1. Probation practice and probation practitioners

2. Crime and South African society

3. Assessment and intervention

4. Values and principles of probation

5. Crime prevention policy and practice

6. Policy and legislation
7. The criminal justice system
8. Service structures and resources in probation

This is a comprehensive curriculum, particularly when one considers that this position is for an assistant probation officer as opposed to a full-fledged probation officer. However, assistant probation officers do not need a college degree, and this is the reason this curriculum is so in-depth. In regard to the new position's curriculum, Graser stated, "we believe this curriculum represents a milestone in the transformation and professionalization of probation practice." The use of assistant probation officers can extend the reach of probation supervision services in a cost-efficient manner that also ensures that appropriate training is provided to employees. Thus, this South African innovation may hold substantial promise for probation systems in the United States and elsewhere, demonstrating how multinational innovations can impact the development of community supervision programs that are local in nature.

SOURCE: Adapted from UCT News. (2004, October 4). Probation curriculum a first. *UCT News Archives, 23.29.* Cape Town, South Africa: University of Cape Town. Retrieved from http://www.news.uct.ac.za/mondaypaper/archives/?id=4762.

Critical Thinking Question

1. How might the use of assistant probation officers help to improve public safety? Can you see any drawbacks to using assistant probation officers?

For more information about the assistant probation officer curriculum, visit the website www.news.uct.ac.za/mondaypaper/archives/?id=4762.

THE SENTENCING HEARING AND THE PSI REVISITED

While procedures vary from region to region, a sentencing phase will be conducted at some point during the processing of a criminal conviction. At this point, the defense counsel can have an impact on the overall process for the offender. Defense counsel may include having a private presentence investigation conducted at the defendant's expense; filing a sentencing memorandum with the court that highlights mitigating factors that might be favorable to the defendant; and even providing advice on the defendant's interaction with the probation staff that conduct the PSI (in particular, providing the names and addresses of persons favorable to the defendant), while challenging any inaccurate, incomplete, or misleading information that may end up in the PSI report. This last function of the defense counsel is actually quite critical. As one may recall from Chapter 3, the PSI will follow the defendant well beyond the mere sentencing decision-making process. Indeed, the PSI will be used to classify the offender if he or she should be incarcerated and will also be used in future decisions regarding the supervision issues within the community. Thus, verification of the PSI's validity is crucial to the welfare of the defendant and prevents the creation of scenarios that make an already bad situation worse.

From the standpoint of the community supervision officer, the two most important sections of the PSI are the evaluation and the recommendation. There is typically a high degree of agreement between the probation officer's recommendations and the judge's decision when sentencing. However, it is unclear whether the probation officer simply suggests sentences that are consistent with a certain judge's personality or professional leaning, or if the judge actually tends to modify his or her decision making in favor of the probation officer's own judgment and impressions. Neubauer (2002) points out yet another possibility that may have little to do with the probation officer or the judge, but instead involves other actors within the courtroom. Neubauer speculates that probation officers may (in actuality) have no influence on the judge's decision making due to the effects of plea bargaining arrangements. He presents the possibility that the plea bargaining process has actually supplanted the role of the probation officer, as the defense counsel and the prosecutor make their own terms regarding sentencing agreements. This is not to infer that the probation officer is left out of the process, but rather that the prosecutor and the defense will, in most cases, collaborate with the probation officer prior to the time when the PSI is submitted to the court. However, this collaboration may result in an after-the-fact justification of a sentence that is agreed upon. In such a case, the probation officer's impact is minimal, with his or her input being used to simply cement a form of justice that is not so much individualized as it is negotiated within an adversarial system.

On the other hand, it is likely that those completing the PSI have at least some impact on the justice process, since their own narrative will affect subsequent outcomes that extend beyond the initial sentencing phase. Prosecutors and defense counsel are both aware of this and are not necessarily able to impact the input of the probation officer aside from the recommendations that are officially made to the judge. Proof of the fact that the PSI plays an important role both in the sentencing phase and in subsequent outcomes lies in the fact that if a defendant can afford such services, the defense counsel may purchase private services to construct a supplemental PSI to be considered by the court. Latessa and Allen (1999) note that "because most attorneys are not trained in behavioral sciences, retaining a 'correctional expert' has been suggested as a more plausible approach and, although there are ethical issues involved, it appears that a social scientist can serve an important role in the sentencing process" (p. 189).

While privately obtained PSI's are allowed in several states as well as the federal court system, they are not frequently used. They tend to be expensive, and there is a great deal of duplication in information between the privately constructed report and the report constructed by the probation agency. However, the private PSI can effectively argue on behalf of an offender and can also make suggestions that might not otherwise get included into the state-constructed PSI. In addition, the information in the private PSI may be used to refute or modify contentions made in the report provided by the probation agency. Though this may not affect the actual sentence, it can on rare occasions be of later use in classification or treatment decisions.

Applied Theory   General Strain Theory, the Offender, and the Probation Officer

General strain theory, developed by Robert Agnew, is based on the premise that persons experience strain when they are not able to obtain success goals that they desire. These goals can entail money, status, and even relationships. In some cases, persons may resort to criminal activities to alleviate this strain or to obtain their desired goal. However, strain is not caused only by the failure to achieve one's goals, often referred to as *goal blockage;* it can also occur when some type of *undesired stimulus* presents itself, or just as important, when some *valued stimulus* is taken away from the offender.

This theory, though not complicated, is important for probation officers to understand, since most reasons that offenders give for their crimes reflect the basic tenets of this theory. This is then important both from a sanctioning level (determining the type of sanction to give an offender) and from a treatment planning perspective for helping professionals.

As an example, consider a young adolescent male named Tom who has limited access to quality higher education opportunities and has poor job prospects. He has a girlfriend named Kim, whom he likes very much, but she is impressed with material goods. Kim has recently started talking about how bored she is since they cannot go out frequently due to a lack of money. Tom is worried about keeping Kim's interest. He cannot see any immediate rewards from education or employment opportunities. In order to maintain his relationship with her, he decides to engage in the burglary of a local business where money is sometimes kept and where goods are pawned. Tom commits the burglary, which is later reported in the local paper, and tells nobody about his activity. The police do not find any sufficient evidence and the business writes off the loss. Tom secures enough money to keep his girlfriend occupied through the months ahead, thereby achieving his desired goal.

Naturally, one can see that a degree of reinforcement also occurs with this example. Just as important, one should keep in mind that the goal of keeping the girlfriend is the reason for the youth's burglary, not his desire to accumulate money for personal greed. If Tom had been caught, it would be good for probation officers and treatment specialists to know the reasons behind the criminal activity. Treatment aspects might address self-esteem issues as well as healthy relationships, while the probation officers might pay attention to the youth's future choice of peers and significant others.

To continue with our example, Tom later marries Kim. At an early age, they have a child together, Tom gets a full-time job, they get an apartment, and Kim stays home to take care of the child. During this time, finances are tight and the relationship sours. Further, a new gentleman moves into the apartment unit right next door. Tom comes home early from work one day and finds the other man in his living room talking with Kim. While neither person is apparently engaged in anything inappropriate, it is clear from the laughter that Tom hears (prior to entering his apartment) that the two are having a very good time joking and talking with one another. Tom enters and the other man, named Kevin, thanks Kim for letting him borrow some cooking ingredients, excuses himself, and exits the apartment. Later that day, Tom sees Kevin in the parking lot and confronts him. He punches Kevin in the face repeatedly, pushes Kevin against a vehicle and says, "You stay away from my wife or I will kill you," followed with "If you say anything to anyone, I will break your legs. You keep quiet and stay away, you hear?" This is where Tom experiences strain due to the presentation of a negative stimulus; in this case, the negative stimulus is Kevin, and Tom resorts to violent crime in response to the presentation of Kevin in his life.

Kevin never does say anything, but he talks with the landlord about moving to another unit. He gives a bogus reason for the move but secretly wishes to put distance between himself and Tom. While moving to the other unit, Kim sees that Kevin has bruises and cuts on his face (from Tom punching him) and bemoans the fact that Kevin is moving to another section of the complex. She later notices that Tom has cuts on his knuckles and she asks him point-blank, "Tom, did you beat Kevin up?" to which Tom says, "Huh-uh, why would

you ask such a thing?" Kim knows that Tom is lying, and she tells him that she is leaving him. She tells him, "I am going to go stay with my parents for a while. I am taking baby Jade with me."

Tom gets mad because he is about to lose a valued stimulus. As a result, he corners Kim in their bedroom, pulls her hair back and grabs her throat with his other hand. He tells her, "If you ever leave me or if I ever catch you with another man, I will kill you," followed with "You won't even know that it is coming when I do it." Tom has again resorted to violent crime, but this time it is to avoid the loss of a valued stimulus.

The scenarios just presented also demonstrate how the same type of criminal activity (i.e., violent behavior) can be used for different stimulus concerns. In one case, the presentation of a negative stimulus is the antecedent, whereas in the other it is the possible loss of a valued stimulus. In addition, Tom's sense of strain, throughout his lifetime, has led to a variety of crimes, namely burglary and assault and battery, as well as a domestic assault and battery. Thus, strain theory can explain a diverse array of criminal behaviors, and probation officers will often find it beneficial to understand the circumstances that precede a crime, particularly when they construct presentence investigation reports. Though there are many other theoretical approaches to explaining criminal behavior, general strain theory (GST) provides a versatile means of analyzing and categorizing the drives behind such behavior. Whether they know it or not, offenders are often engaged in behaviors that, at their base, verify the notions that are commonly espoused by GST. For the probation officer or correctional treatment specialist, this and other theories provide a coherent rationale for quantifying or categorizing the range of criminal behaviors that they observe.

SOURCE: Lilly, J. R., Cullen, F. T., & Ball, R. A. (2007). *Criminological theory: Context and consequences* (4th ed.). Thousand Oaks, CA: Sage Publications.

THE COURT AND THE ROLE OF THE JUDGE: SETTING CONDITIONS FOR SUPERVISION

According to Neubauer (2002), the public perceives the judge as the principal decision maker in criminal court. But, in actuality, the judge often is not the primary decision maker in regard to an offender's sentencing or probation conditions. This is not to say that the judge does not have ultimate authority over the court, nor is it meant to imply that judges have a diminished sense of importance when presiding over their court. Rather, Neubauer demonstrates the collaborative nature of the various courtroom actors when processing offender caseloads. Throughout this process, judges will often voluntarily defer to the judgment of other members of the court, namely prosecutors, defense attorneys, victims' rights groups, or the probation agency.

During a typical day in criminal court, judges may accept bail recommendations offered by the district attorney, plea agreements that are struck by the defense and the prosecution, and even sentences recommended by a probation officer (though there is some debate as to the actual weight given to the probation officer's recommendation, at least in some courts). The main point is that, although judges do of course retain their power over the courtroom, they often share influence over the adjudication process with a variety of courtroom actors. This is an informal process that often takes place among courtroom actors that, when working together over time, have come to know each other in both a professional and a semipersonal sense (Neubauer, 2002).

Further, there are some challenges that can emerge when judges do not allow the input of other courtroom actors. For instance, the defense counsel and the district attorney may negatively impact the docket scheduling and case processing by requesting continuances for cases or by not having witnesses available when their presence is required. This is particularly true in large municipal jurisdictions where judges may feel pressure from the court administrator or the chief judge of the court to maintain a case-processing pace similar to that of most other judges in the courthouse. Indeed, if the delays are routine or excessive, the judge may be transferred to less desirable assignments (such as traffic violations or juvenile court) within the courthouse system (Neubauer, 2002).

Though other actors may be able to cause some problems in the courtroom, it is nevertheless clear that the judge ultimately has the real authority and is vested with the ability to use that authority to gain courtroom compliance. If, in the mind of the judge, actors in the courtroom are not behaving in a way that is conducive to courtroom operations, the judge can put pressure upon the prosecutors and defense counsel through a number of mechanisms that place both parties in uneasy positions. Judges can be sticklers for detail and for timekeeping. They can sift through every administrative detail, ask annoying questions, and openly rebuke one or both parties in front of a public audience. All of these techniques may be employed to ensure that the courtroom actors stay in compliance.

Finally, Neubauer (2002) notes that in larger court jurisdictions, a technique of judge selection may be common. Through a process of implementing motions of continuances and motions for a change of judge, defense attorneys may maneuver to have their case heard by a judge that is expected to be the most receptive to the offender's plight. Though judges strive to remain within common guidelines in decisions and rulings, the fact of the matter is that they tend to differ in terms of the sentences that are given, the manner by which they oversee their courtroom, and the number of cases that they have pending (Neubauer, 2002). An understanding of these tendencies can aid both the defense and the prosecutor in achieving a more favorable outcome consistent with their own particular desires.

Aside from each of the points just noted, the setting of conditions can actually be agreed upon prior to the judge's formal sentencing. Though the bargaining process may of course impact the final outcome of the probationer's sentence, the length of probation, and the conditions of that probation, the judge is always free to require additional conditions as he or she sees fit. The conditions that may be required are quite lengthy; some of the more commonly required conditions are noted as follows:

1. Refrain from associating with certain types of people (particularly those with a conviction) or frequenting certain locations known to draw criminal elements.

2. Remain sober and drug free; refrain from using or being in possession of alcohol or drugs.

3. Obey restrictions on firearm ownership or possession.

4. Obey requirement to pay fines, restitution, and family support that may be due.

5. Be willing to submit to drug tests as directed by the probation officer or representatives of the probation agency.

6. Maintain legitimate and steady employment.

7. Refrain from obtaining employment in certain types of vocations (e.g., an embezzler would be restricted from becoming a bookkeeper, or a computer hacker from working with automated systems).

8. Maintain a legal and legitimate residence with the requirement that the probation officer is notified of any change in residence prior to making such a change.

9. Obey the requirement that permission be requested to travel outside of the jurisdiction of the probation agency or to another state.

10. Refrain from engaging in further criminal activity.

Many of the conditions that are listed above may be statutorily authorized by state legislators as a means of validating their application to probation sentences. This is reflective of the fact that most legislators desire some degree of uniformity and consistency in the supervision requirements and process. However, as was noted in Chapter 5 of this text, judges still may call for innovative and even controversial conditions to be added for certain probationers. This is certainly the case with sex offenders and other violent criminals. To date, these requirements have not been invalidated by the U.S. Supreme Court, and it is unlikely that they ever will be invalidated if a convincing argument can be made that these conditions aid in the treatment process of the offender.

Regardless of the judge's own discretion regarding probation conditions, most states have at least some statutorily required conditions for probation sentences, but these may vary considerably from state to state (del Carmen, Barnhill, Bonham, Hignite, & Jermstad, 2001). Some states have only a few such requirements, while others have an extensive list that clearly requires judges and probationers to structure probation sentences according to a certain prescribed template of conditions. Further, and related to the use of discretionary conditions imposed by judges, some legislators may also clearly note that judges are to be given deference in assigning specialized conditions on certain types of offenders; this is especially true with sex offenders or substance abuse offenders (these offenders, the terms and conditions of their supervision, and therapeutic programming will be discussed in later chapters of this text).

Abadinsky (2003) notes that the American Probation and Parole Association (APPA) "recommends that the only condition that should be imposed on every person sentenced to probation is that the probationer lead a law-abiding life during the period of probation" (p. 39). The APPA instead notes that other conditions should be left to the purview of the probation officer who should primarily be responsible for setting conditions that are consistent with the circumstances of each case. Generally speaking, the APPA indicates that, aside from providing deterrent conditions to the commission of future recidivism, conditions should by and large be minimal. Further still, del Carmen et al. (2001) note that in general, "a special condition of probation or parole is invalid only if it has all three of the following characteristics: (1) has no relationship to the crime, (2) relates to conduct that is not in itself criminal, and (3) forbids or requires conduct that is not reasonably related to the future criminality of the offender or does not serve the statutory ends of probation or parole" (p. 77). Thus, it is clear that if put to the test, judges have a great deal of discretion and latitude when assigning conditions to an offender on probation. So long as the condition has some relation to the crime or to the ability of the agency to monitor for potential future recidivism, the condition is almost certain to be considered valid if it is later challenged.

PURPOSE OF PROBATION, EVALUATION, AND COMPLIANCE WITH CONDITIONS OF PROBATION

As noted in earlier chapters of this text, the purpose of probation is to reintegrate offenders into society, thereby improving public safety as offenders become less inclined to reoffend. Since our purpose is fairly well understood and defined, it becomes important to ask if programs do, in fact, achieve these intended outcomes. Earlier chapters have pointed toward prior research that demonstrates the viability of community supervision. However, how do we determine if our programs are successful? How exactly do we define our outcomes and measure them? These questions will be answered later, in Chapter 15, when we discuss evaluation and research within community corrections. Comprehensive explanations will be given at that time. Nevertheless, it is useful at this point to note how agencies might determine if they are able to keep offenders within compliance. Further, it is useful to know exactly what is meant by being "in compliance."

As noted earlier, one primary means of determining success is simply to note if offenders have recidivated. This is one of the simplest means of determining success in community supervision agencies. But the definition of offending lends itself to some degree of interpretation. For instance, should it be classified the same if one offender relapses with alcohol and is found to be drunk and disorderly, and another offender is caught burglarizing a home? Certainly, on the face of it, the offenses are not the same. Indeed, being drunk and disorderly may not be considered as serious as burglary. But consider that both offenses could be symptomatic of drug addiction; perhaps the first offender is an alcoholic who cannot seem to control his addiction (suffering from relapse and the corresponding behaviors associated with such difficulties), and in the other case, the offender might be a heroin addict who was simply seeking something of material value as a means of supporting his habit. Neither offense was violent; however, it is possible that either offense could have turned violent at any point. What if the drunk and disorderly offender had been antagonized, startled, or himself assaulted? What if the homeowner had walked in on the burglar/heroin addict while his withdrawal symptoms and discomfort were at their height? In desperation, would he have attacked the homeowner? Might the homeowner have attacked the burglar? It is clear that the circumstances of an offense are important considerations.

Further, what if an agency has two offenders that are both pedophiles and one of the offenders is later arrested for molestation while the other offender is arrested for shoplifting. Naturally, both acts are illegal and both are criminal, but is the level of recidivism the same? Should we be equally concerned about each act? These scenarios demonstrate the difficulty that can be involved with determining the effectiveness of community supervision and actual levels of compliance. Granted, offenders know that they are not supposed to commit criminal offenses, but if a convicted pedophile were never to commit another act of molestation while on supervision, yet he was found to have committed an act of shoplifting, it may well be that the supervision process was not an absolute failure. In some cases, certain types of recidivism may be the primary issue of concern and, assuming that other offenses are minimal and that they are not as serious as the primary offense of

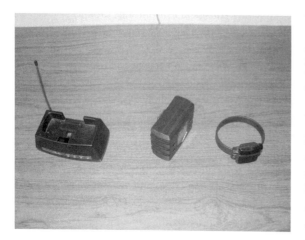

Photo 6.3 The equipment in this photo is used for GPS tracking. In some cases, equipment has specialized functions such as the emission of alarms or noises that can be sounded by a community supervision officer from a distance. When an offender cannot be found physically or when he or she enters a restricted or off-limits area, an alarm can be emitted by the probation officer merely pushing a button, even from a distance of several miles. The noise can be deafening and serves as a deterrent for most offenders and as a warning to community members.

concern, it may be that supervision was at least partially successful. This is a very difficult notion to sell to the public, however.

Further complicating the picture is the fact that some conditions of probation result in what are often called technical violations. **Technical violations** are actions that do not comply with the conditions and requirements of a probationer's sentence, as articulated by the court that acted as the sentencing authority. Technical violations are not necessarily criminal, in and of themselves, and would likely be legal behaviors if the offender were not on probation. For instance, a condition of a drug offender's probation may be that he or she stay out of bars, nightclubs, and other places of business where the selling and consumption of alcohol is a primary attraction for customers frequenting the establishment. Another example might be if a sex offender is ordered to remain a certain distance from schools. For most citizens, going to nightclubs or setting foot on school grounds is not a violation of any sort, and neither of these acts is considered criminal. However, for the probationer, this can lead to the revocation of his or her probation.

A number of other behaviors also can be technical violations. Additional examples might include the failure to attend mandated therapy, failure to report periods of unemployment, failing to complete scheduled amounts of community service, and failing to show up for routine appointments with the probation officer. Though these violations may be substantially different from those that carry a new and separate criminal conviction, they still carry the weight of a revocation and may be counted in recidivism measures in some agencies (Champion, 2002; Latessa & Allen, 1999). These indicators are obviously not comparable to a variety of criminal behaviors that offenders might commit.

Champion (2002) notes that the most commonly used measures of recidivism for probationers are reconvictions, reincarcerations, and probation revocations. Further, Champion cites Boone (1994), who provides some very useful and pragmatic suggestions that clarify the use of recidivism outcomes in generating program evaluation and research. According to Boone, agencies should

1. Standardize the definition of recidivism.

2. Refrain from using recidivism as the sole outcome measure for agency effectiveness.

3. Define alternative outcome measures for the evaluation of supervision effectiveness.

4. Encourage researchers, evaluators, and supervision personnel to use appropriate outcome measures to evaluate program performance.

The suggestions above are perhaps idealistic, since recidivism is likely always to play a key role in determining agency effectiveness. Moreover, recidivism rates are used by many different competing parties that have an incentive to define the concept according to their own specialized needs (Champion, 2002). However, if agencies simply aim for these goals, making the best effort possible, it is likely that a great degree of clarity can be achieved when determining if offenders are improving and if the public is safer. Likewise, Champion correctly notes that "the public as well as stakeholders definitely need to be educated concerning various ways of measuring agency success or effectiveness" (p. 558). This is a very good point, since it is to the community that probation agencies must make their appeal for support. As has been mentioned in prior chapters, the involvement of the community is critical for the improvement of community supervision services. In one manner of speaking, a cycle might emerge where agency involvement produces education on the notions of success or effectiveness for probation agencies; in a similar manner, community education efforts can work to further encourage continued and improved community involvement.

REDUCTION OF TECHNICAL VIOLATIONS OF PROBATION: A CASE EXAMPLE FROM CONNECTICUT

In July 2004, Connecticut passed legislation targeting prison overcrowding. Under the terms of the new law, the State of Connecticut Judicial Branch was required to develop a comprehensive strategy to reduce the number of incarcerations resulting from technical violations of probation. This resulted in a four-point response to reduce technical violations, which included the following:

1. *Reducing caseload size.* A reduction in caseload size was a key ingredient in the plan to reduce probation violations. The average caseload in 2000 was about 250 cases per probation officer. With the addition of new officers, the average caseload has been reduced to approximately 125. Through appropriate triaging of cases by risk and adding more probation officers in FY 2007, the agency aspires to have caseloads of fewer than 100 per officer.

2. *Modify policies on response to noncompliance.* The agency relies on written policy as a means of guiding field officers' work. As part of the four-point strategy to reduce technical violations of probation, the policy on response to noncompliance was amended to improve the handling of technical violators of probation. This policy had been first established to ensure that probation officers respond to all incidents of noncompliance in a consistent manner that is directly related to the risk level of the offender and the severity of the violation.

3. *Implement a special program for inmates with split sentences, to reduce the number and intensity of technical violations during the initial period of probation.* The Probation Transition Program (PTP) is provided for split-sentence inmates being released from Department of Correction custody to probation supervision. The PTP targets inmates who have terms of probation following their discharge from the Department of Correction, including those discharging at the end of a sentence from a correctional facility, a halfway house, parole, transitional supervision, or a furlough. The goal of the PTP is to increase the likelihood of a successful probation period for split-sentence probationers.

4. *Implement a special program for technical violators of probation, to reduce the number of probationers sentenced to incarceration.* The Technical Violation Unit (TVU) program targets probationers whose supervising officers have determined that a technical violation of probation warrant is imminent. The goal of the TVU is to reduce the number of probationers sentenced to incarceration as a result of technical violations.

During the probationer's first 30 days in the unit, the probation officer reviews the most recent LSI-R and may reassess him or her. The officer develops a case plan and makes referrals for services to address the offender's assessed needs. Services are often delivered at the local Alternative Incarceration Center (AIC), through funds appropriated to expand the center's existing services for delivery to TVU probationers. A TVU officer and the probationer have at least one face-to-face meeting per week, as well as home or field contacts as needed. During the next 30 to 60 days in the unit, the probationer receives services from one or more treatment providers. Face-to-face contacts occur at least twice per month, and home and field contacts continue as needed. Probationers are seen at least weekly by support staff at the AIC and by representatives of treatment programs.

During the final phase of the program, the TVU probation officer prepares to transfer the offender out of the unit. Face-to-face and home/field contacts continue as needed. The officer prepares a discharge summary, and a discharge meeting is held with the probationer. If the probationer has stabilized, he or she is transferred back to a regular caseload. If the probationer continues to violate the conditions of probation and fails to make progress in the program, a warrant is prepared following a case review with the Chief Probation Officer.

The PTP and TVU special probation programs are similar in that lower caseloads give the officer an opportunity to have more frequent contact and involvement with the probationer. Veteran probation officers were selected to staff these programs. They were encouraged to be innovative, to make use of enhanced community-based services, and to spend the time that a smaller caseload provides to work directly with probationers and their families in the community. To increase their effectiveness, officers and service provider staff received intensive training to bring the principles of cognitive-behavioral change to their daily casework. Courses included Motivational Interviewing, Criminal Thinking, Motivational Enhancement Therapy, Reasoning and Rehabilitation, and Case Planning and Management.

Programs such as these are becoming increasingly important as jails and prisons continue to be filled past their intended capacity. As will be seen in the following chapter (Chapter 7), problems with parolees committing technical violations have been given specific attention due to overcrowding in the Arkansas prison system. The current program—designed to reduce the number of offenders being sent to jail or prison for technical violation—simply addresses the same problem that will be noted in Chapter 7, yet this problem is addressed at the front end of the process (probation) rather than later (parole).

SOURCE: Hill, B. J. (2003). *Four-point strategy reduces technical violations of probation in Connecticut.* Whethersfield, CT: National Institute of Corrections Information Center.

ALTERNATIVE PROBATION METHODS

The variety of sanctions available to probation agencies is what gives probation its strength. Indeed, the flexibility in sentencing options with probation as well as the ability to individualize sanctions to specific offenders or offenses are what make probation so well-suited for reintegrative efforts. This continuum of sanctions is also what allows probation agencies to find suitable levels of supervision for different types of offenders, thereby aiding in the public safety element as well. This section of the chapter is designed to acquaint the student with some of the sanctions used in probation agencies.

First and most obviously, the sanction of **standard probation** is the basic form of supervision that is administered by most agencies. This type of sentence is actually little more than a baseline starting point for sanctioning. In reality, standard probation is not considered as an appropriate form of supervision for any but the least serious of offenders. Though probation officers are required to oversee the offender's compliance with the various conditions of his or her probation, standard probation tends to have little face-to-face supervision of offenders. Typically, probation officers will have high caseloads if most of their probationers are on standard probation. Though this text has tended to recommend approximate caseloads of 200 offenders on standard probation for every probation officer, it is not at all unusual for the number of offenders on a probation officer's caseload to greatly exceed this in urban jurisdictions. This often is not due to any fault of the agency but is simply based on the reality that there are so many offenders and so few probation officers.

Further, standard probation is typically the type that the community has in mind when forming the perception that probation is soft on crime. This is because of the comparatively lax forms of contact between the probation officer and the probationer. In many cases, the probationer may be free to simply contact his or her probation officer through a phone call. Likewise, the requirements attached to this type of probation are, quite naturally, much less stringent than other forms of probation. In the majority of cases, strict security is not necessary for probationers who have been given this type of probation. However, serious problems can develop when charges are pleaded down (especially if violent criminal charges are pleaded down to lesser or nonviolent offenses). In this case, some offenders may be on standard probation when they should be—due to the nature of the offense—on a stricter form of supervision. This can naturally end up compromising the security of the public. However, this is also a problem that the probation agency may inherit, with little ability to modify the situation until some sort of violation or other cause is provided to warrant an increase in supervision. When the offender is on standard probation, the terms are so lax that these offenders may recidivate and remain undetected, unless an actual arrest takes place. This particular dilemma is what has perhaps contributed the most to the negative public perception of probation.

Beyond the use of standard probation, there are a number of more secure sanctions that can be used to enhance public safety and the reintegration of the offender. The following is a list of various alternative probation methods that are commonly utilized:

Probation With Community Service and Restitution—This sanction requires the offender to provide a certain number of designated hours of free labor to a given cause determined by the court. The sanction also includes restitution, which is a stated amount of money that the offender must pay to the victim or to a state victim fund. It is the recommendation of this text that community service and restitution be used in *every single case* where an identified victim is involved, including cases involving juvenile offenders. This means that the sanction should be combined with those that are listed below.

Intensive Supervised Probation (ISP)—This form of sanction is usually viewed as the most effective alternative to imprisonment. Officer caseloads typically do not exceed 40 offenders. This sanction, because of its emphasis on security, has been found to be particularly suited for more serious offenders. The model for ISP was first established in Atlanta, Georgia, and this is the model used for this chapter and text. Specifically, this type of supervision consists of the following:

1. Five face-to-face visits between the probation officer and the offender per week
2. A minimum of 132 hours of community service
3. A set curfew
4. Mandatory employment (which should be required in all cases)
5. A weekly search for any new arrests
6. Automated tracking of arrests using a state crime information system
7. Frequent yet random testing for drugs or alcohol

This form of supervision is conducted by a team that consists of a probation officer if the caseload is 25 or under, or two assistant probation officers (surveillance officers) if there are 40 cases or more. In Georgia, this program is used to divert low-risk offenders from prison, typically nonviolent property offenders and drug abusers.

Day Reporting Centers—These are treatment facilities that offenders are required to report to on a daily (or near daily) basis. They are similar to residential treatment facilities except that offenders on intensive supervision are not required to stay overnight. In some states, these day reporting centers are designed so that offenders attend 8- to 10-hour intervention and treatment classes. The optimal programs are those that have an array of classes, such as relapse prevention, educational development, individual counseling, group counseling, structured bibliotherapy where clients complete their assignments as homework and return them each day for discussion in class, and so on. The point is that the offender is immersed in a treatment regimen that accomplishes three key tasks:

1. The offender is supervised on a face-to-face basis.
2. The offender is kept busy and thus cannot be out on the street offending.
3. The offender is forced to comply with treatment, and as we know from our earlier readings, a certain amount of this will eventually be processed by the offender, even if he or she is resistant.

Home Confinement With Electronic Monitoring—This form of sanction is used instead of incarceration for persons on community supervision. This is the most restrictive form of community supervision without actual incarceration and has also been used with offenders who have violated the terms of prior forms of community supervision. Most programs utilize this type of supervision for a period of 2 to 6 months. Home confinement with electronic monitoring should be utilized for much lengthier periods when used with adult pedophiles, rapists, or domestic batterers that present a long-term risk of violence.

Home confinement combined with electronic monitoring is an effective alternative to prison because the offender is watched closely, yet the cost of supervision is only a fraction of what the cost of a prison sentence would be. A variety of methods may be used to maintain the electronic monitoring. One is the use of **programmed contact systems** that have randomly programmed times during the day and night when an automated system calls the offender's house. The offender is required to repeat certain words and phrases, at which time a voice analysis determines if it is truly the offender who has answered the phone. If the phone is not answered, or if it is found that it is not the offender who answers, then community supervision personnel are alerted. Other versions use visual verifications where a picture is taken and automatically sent via installed equipment.

Home Confinement and Global Positioning System (GPS)—This form of supervision uses a series of satellites to monitor and locate offenders. The Florida Department of Corrections first initiated this program to track probationers in real time at any point during the day or night (Champion, 2002). This system is far superior to any other program of supervision because it ensures that probation officers have near-instantaneous notification of an offender's violation of his or her community supervision. With this system, supervision officers can track an offender with a computer system and can even tell which street the offender is on in any part of the country. Further, these programs can be set up to detect areas of inclusion or exclusion according to the limits of offender travel. Thus, if an offender enters a certain area that is restricted, the supervision officer is instantly notified (Champion, 2002).

Residential Treatment Home—Such facilities are designed to house the offender, but the offender is not ordered by the court to stay at the facility. In fact, these facilities may also have "day students" who use the facility as a day reporting center. The only difference is that offender-clients stay at the facility full time (sleep overnight). The offender may still be allowed to go to work or leave for weekend family visits, and so forth, but treatment staff determine when and where this is appropriate for the client. These facilities may have some clients who are court-mandated along with other clients who participate voluntarily. The point is that this is a treatment facility, and offenders have many more liberties to come and go throughout the day, have visitors, and engage in personal activities than they would in a halfway house, a jail, or a prison. These facilities are quite often run by nonprofit, private agencies and operate on a local community level. Most all of these facilities offer some sort of substance abuse counseling, and many of these programs are primarily based upon substance abuse recovery issues.

Official Halfway House—A halfway house is a residential setting for offenders who are court-ordered to stay at the facility while on community supervision. Also, offenders who are exiting prison will often be required to stay at one of these facilities. It is important to note that the restrictions on free movement are likely to be more than those of the residential treatment home. These facilities may be used for probation and parole violators as well, particularly while jail or prison systems are full. Most of these offenders will also have some form of community service requirement. In addition, substance abuse counseling is most often a service that offenders will be required to obtain.

Boot Camps—These are short-term forms of incarceration in an environment that is similar to basic training in the military. They are primarily used with youthful offenders and are intended to have an emphasis on disciplining the offender. This type of sentence consists of a short but very intensive period of incarceration that is highly structured and includes physical training and numerous educational classes, therapeutic groups, drills, chores, and other forms of prosocial activity. Generally speaking, the research on boot camp effectiveness has had mixed results, at best (Champion, 2002; Clear & Cole, 2003).

Split Sentencing—This is a procedure through which a judge will sentence the offender to a fixed period of incarceration that is followed by an additional fixed term of probation supervision. Felony-level offenders are more likely to receive split sentences than misdemeanants.

Shock Probation—This typically consists of placing an offender in prison and later releasing him or her on probation at some unknown date and time. The shock of incarceration is expected to have a deterrent impact on the offender with a corresponding sense of gratitude when the offender is released from the facility to probation. Some authors also contend that the "shock" in shock probation revolves around the surprise associated with the offender's eventual release to probation (Champion, 2002). Regardless of the source of shock, the fact that the offender does not know the length of time that he or she will serve a sentence under incarceration is thought to further add to the deterrent value, producing a therapeutic desire to refrain from behaviors that will likely place the offender in prison again.

The above list of sanctions has been presented from the least to the most restrictive. In most cases, the use of a higher, more restrictive sanction subsumes the requirements of all the lower sanctions. Therefore, except in cases where it is unproductive, each sanction will also include the terms and conditions of the one before it. Thus, the probation arena has a variety of responses available, and this provides a range of options that exist both at the sentencing stage and even later if probationers violate the terms and conditions of their initial probation sentence. For example, probationers that are placed on standard probation and who prove later to do poorly on this sanction can then have that probation completely revoked or, as is often the case, the probationer can be placed on intensive supervised probation. If, by some chance, the probationer should continue to have difficulties staying in compliance, home confinement, electronic monitoring, and the use of day reporting centers may prove to be effective options. In addition, therapeutic obligations (especially drug treatment) or community service requirements may be modified or increased. If the offender should again prove intractable, he or she can be placed on shock probation. At this point, if the offender should be so stubborn as to persist in offending, it is certainly safe to say that a long-term prison stint may be the only option available to ensure the protection of the community.

As has been discussed before, the use of correspondingly tougher sanctions can be mitigated or aggravated by the specific types of probation violation. Generally, the prior convictions and the current charge facing an offender tend to carry the most weight among practitioners when determining the outcome for offenders on community supervision. Naturally, recidivists that commit violent offenses are most likely to receive some form of incarceration. In fact, there may be little use of further intermediate sanctions, but such offenders may instead be (appropriately) placed in prison for a long-term period. However, nonviolent offenders, particularly misdemeanant offenders, may be persistently processed and reprocessed through various forms of probation supervision, particularly if they have a series of nuisance crimes or minor infractions. While this may be aggravating for the public, the actual social costs incurred from such offending tend to be slight, and the use of expensive custodial sanctions is completely ineffective, both in terms of economics and in terms of likely productive outcomes for the victim, the offender, or society. In these cases, a perpetual form of supervision will be required for the offender that continues to engage in petty (and occasionally not-so-petty) offenses that require invasive supervision within their lives, the simple reality being that the offender may be incapable of changing (or unwilling to change) his or her own life course habits and lifestyle.

Regardless of the rationale behind observed cases of recidivism, the use of progressive sanctions is considered a strength of probation. These sanctions provide definite benefits to the justice system, a degree of creativity, individualized sentencing, and flexibility for a system that is already strapped. Likewise, as noted in Chapter 1, these sanctions have been shown to be effective, though as we have just discussed, the specific definition of effectiveness may be hard to determine in many cases. Effective or ineffective, useful or not, there is a hard reality with which even the most ardent supporter of community corrections must contend: some offenders will simply not be amenable to probation and will therefore need to be restricted from continuing their sentence under such a sanction. It is with this in mind that we turn our attention to the revocation process itself, with a brief discussion of this type of proceeding.

PROBATION REVOCATION PROCEDURES

This last section of the chapter addresses revocation from a nonlegal standpoint, since Chapter 5 has already covered the legal requirements and offender rights associated with revocation. This discussion is intended to present the use of revocation as a sanction and a component of the probation process in circumstances where offenders are not able to complete their given probation sentence. Previous research demonstrates that roughly 4 in 10 probationers fail to successfully complete the initial requirements of their probation (Bonczar, 1995; Glaze & Bonczar, 2007; Clear & Cole, 2003). Further, the most frequent reason that revocation hearings are initiated is the probationer's failure to maintain contact with his or her probation officer. Of those probationers that must have a disciplinary hearing, the most frequent reason tends to be absconding or the previously mentioned failure to contact their probation officer. Other reasons may include an arrest or conviction for a new offense, failure to pay fines/restitution, or failure to attend or complete an alcohol or drug treatment program (Bonczar, 1995). Among probationers that have revocation hearings initiated against them, almost half may be permitted to continue their probation sentence. For those that are allowed to continue, they will almost always have additional conditions imposed on them, and their type of supervision will typically be more restrictive (Bonczar, 1995; Clear & Cole, 2003).

In addition, some areas of the nation are more prone to revocation than others. Certain counties or communities may be more criminogenic in nature and will therefore tend to have more offending as well as more serious offenders that are processed through the local justice system. In such cases, it should not be surprising that probation departments in these areas will have higher rates of revocation proceedings that are generated. For example, consider a region where multiple neighborhoods are infested with gang activity. In these cases, the probation department is likely to have numerous gang offenders on the caseload as well as individuals that are peripheral to the gangs in that area. The recidivism rates for these individuals tend to be high, and it is therefore more likely that a probation department in this vicinity will contend with higher rates of revocation than would departments in other areas of the nation.

Generally, revocation proceedings are handled in three stages. First, the **preliminary hearing** examines the facts of the arrest to determine if probable cause exists for a violation. Second, the **hearing stage** allows the probation agency to present evidence of the violation while the offender is given the opportunity to refute the evidence provided. Though the agency (or the local government) is not obligated to provide an attorney, the offender does have the right to obtain legal representation, if he or she should desire. Third, the **sentencing stage** is when a judge either requires that the offender be incarcerated or, as in many cases where the violation is minor, stipulates that the offender continue the probation sentence but under more restrictive terms.

Finally, it is not uncommon for offenders to have some sort of hearing or proceeding throughout their term of probation. The longer the period of probation, the more likely it is that this will happen. Nevertheless, many do eventually finish their probation terms. For those offenders that complete the terms of their probation (eventually meeting all of the requirements), termination of the sentence then occurs. These offenders are free in society without any further obligation to report to the justice system. At this point, their experience with community corrections ends, presuming that they lead a conviction-free life throughout the remainder of their days.

CONCLUSION

The institution of probation is one that is integral to our correctional system. As has been discussed, probation is complementary to our current adversarial system that results in a negotiated form of justice. Further, private probation companies have emerged as a viable option to address the nation's burgeoning probation population. Though privatization is no panacea to cope with the challenges of probation, private companies can provide services that are equally effective as public probation, with added benefits that are not realized among many public probation agencies (e.g., higher salaries for probation staff, cost-effectiveness, and competitive caseloads).

Likewise, the use of probation allows our justice system to implement a great degree of flexibility, in terms of both the conditions associated with a sentence and the specific type of probation that can be given to an offender. The various types of probation can also provide numerous options for those that must supervise probationers and enforce the conditions of probation sentences. Having these various means of implementing probation sentences also brings to question the effectiveness of these sanctions. Though specific and comparable comparisons are not easily found, some basic characteristics of probation can be standardized to provide more effective evaluative information for future policy makers. The use of this evaluative process can be an effective guide for future probation agencies, both when enforcing probation terms and when making critical decisions at revocation proceedings. From this chapter, it is clear that there are many aspects of the probation sanction that work together to provide a unique blend of options for the justice system. These same aspects are continually examined as practitioners and scholars seek to improve the ability of probation agencies to achieve the two primary goals of public safety and offender reintegration.

Key Terms

Boot camps

Day reporting centers

Hearing stage

Home confinement and Global Positioning System

Home confinement with electronic monitoring

Intensive supervised probation (ISP)

Official halfway house

Preliminary hearing

Prisonization

Private probation

Probationers

Probation with community service and restitution

Programmed contact systems

Residential treatment home

Sentencing stage

Shock probation

Split sentencing

Standard probation

Technical violations

"What Would You Do?" Exercise

You are the chief probation officer in a small county. You often work closely with the chief judge of the courthouse. Recently, in your jurisdiction, a number of crimes have occurred. In addition, the offenders who committed these crimes often have complicated issues and problems. This has made it hard for you to determine your sentence recommendation for each offender. Nevertheless, you have to make some form of recommendation. With this in mind, you consider the offender cases that you will have to examine, and you consider the range of sanctions that you can recommend. At some point, you will need to pair each case with one of the sentencing recommendations that are typically available.

Instructor: Note that there are no specifically correct (or incorrect) answers indicated. It is not important that the student pick any particular sanction. While some sanctions will naturally be better choices than others, the truth is that there is a great degree of variety among the selections. The main point to this exercise is to simply get students to contemplate the various sentences presented in the chapter and to consider what they might do if they had to make a sentencing recommendation.

Students: Consider the following vignettes below, and then explain which sanction you would recommend. The choices of sanctions are listed below the case vignettes. You may use each choice more than once. In fact, you may repeat the use of a sanction as often as you think appropriate. Also, you are not required to use all of the sanctions listed, and there is feasibly more than one right answer to each of the scenarios. For this assignment, you must answer the question, "What would you do?" when having to make a recommendation for each of the vignettes below.

CASE VIGNETTES

Vignette #1: A gang offender who is 20 years old and is violent. He has a prior conviction for assaulting other persons in the gang world. This time, he is being charged with minor assault.

Vignette #2: A female prostitute with substance addiction that has HIV and suffers from depression regarding her plight. She has a 5-year-old son, and it is found that she was a victim of childhood sexual abuse. She is being charged for prostitution; this is her third charge.

Vignette #3: A male offender who is 40 years old and has been arrested for domestic abuse of his wife. He has been charged twice before for assaulting his wife and served one jail term. In the other case, his wife dropped the charges and the district attorney did not follow through on a domestic abuse charge.

Vignette #4: A male offender who is 57 years old with dementia, who is also an opiate addict due to the need for relief from severe back and neck pain. Upon the recent death of his wife, he assaulted several family members who were arguing over where he would now stay.

Vignette #5: A drug addict who cannot seem to quit heroin on his own. He has committed two counts of burglary as a means of gaining valuables to support his drug habit.

Vignette #6: A schizophrenic and paranoid-delusional offender who has been homeless most of his life. He is an alcoholic with cirrhosis of the liver.

Vignette #7: A young female offender who has committed an act of shoplifting. She did this on a dare from her friends who often compete with one another to see who can accumulate the most "five-finger discounts" when they visit the local mall.

Vignette #8: A mentally handicapped 14-year-old boy who molested his 8-year-old female cousin. He had found some pornography that his older brother had hidden under the couch, and he wanted to show his cousin how the pictures worked.

Vignette #9: Three teenaged boys who vandalized an elderly woman's home. The teens spray-painted messages on the sides of her house and broke several keepsakes in her front yard.

Vignette #10: A bored housewife who wrote a couple of checks that did not clear. She has no criminal record and simply went on a spending spree without paying attention to the money in her family's account.

The sentences you may choose from are as follows:

Boot camp

Day reporting center

Home confinement with electronic monitoring

Home confinement with Global Positioning System (GPS)

Intensive supervised probation (ISP)

Official halfway house

Probation with community service and restitution

Residential treatment home

Shock probation

Split sentencing

Standard probation

What would you do?

Applied Exercise

Students must conduct either a face-to-face or phone interview with a probation officer who currently works in a community corrections setting. The student must set up a day and time with that practitioner and interview him or her to gain the officer's insight and perspective on several key questions related to work in the field of probation supervision. Students must write the practitioner's responses as well as their own analysis of those responses, and submit it by the deadline that is set by their instructor. It should be written in the form of a mini paper that addresses each of the points below. Total word count: 1,400 to 2,100 words.

When completing the interview, students should ask the following questions:

1. What are the most rewarding aspects of your job in probation?

2. What are the most stressful aspects of your job?

3. What is your view on treatment and reintegration efforts with offenders?

4. What are some challenges that you have in keeping track of your caseload?

5. Why did you choose to work in this field?

6. What type of training did you receive for this line of work?

7. What would you recommend to someone who was interested in pursuing a similar career?

In addition, students should ensure that their submission has appropriate spelling and grammar throughout.

Last, students are required to provide contact information for the person interviewed. Please have students obtain the following information from the probation practitioner they interview. While you will probably not need to contact the officer, it may become necessary in order to validate the actual completion of an interview.

Name and title of probation officer: _____

Community supervision agency: _____

Practitioner's phone number: _____

Practitioner's e-mail address: _____

Name of student: _____

CHAPTER

7

Specific Aspects Related to Parole

LEARNING OBJECTIVES

1. Know and understand the basics regarding state parole, its organization, and its administration.

2. Be able to discuss the parole selection process, factors influencing parole decisions, and factors considered when granting and denying parole.

3. Know some of the subjective and objective inputs (including both victim impact statements and the Salient Factor Score) that are included in the parole decision-making process.

4. Demonstrate knowledge of the entire supervision process, from pre-release planning to the successful termination of parole supervision.

5. Be aware of the common conditions of parole, and understand how parole effectiveness can be refined and adjusted to better meet supervision requirements that are based on the offender's behavior.

6. Understand how restorative justice paradigms can organize victim input and participation in the justice process, offender accountability in the reintegrative process, and community involvement in the supervision process.

INTRODUCTION

As discussed in previous chapters, parole is a function that has been eliminated at the federal level and has also been eliminated in many states throughout the nation. Nevertheless, a substantial number of inmates are released on parole throughout the United States, with some still serving sentences under the outdated federal system. Parole can be defined as the early release of an offender from a secure facility upon completion of a certain portion of his or her sentence. As of 2005, the nation's parole population included 784,408 offenders, with mandatory releases from prison due to state statutes or good time provisions accounting for nearly 51 percent of these (Glaze & Bonczar, 2007). This is important because it reflects the fact that discretionary releases have declined. In fact, as Figure 7.1 demonstrates, discretionary releases by parole boards have steadily declined from 55 percent in 1980 to 22 percent in 2004. Contrast this against the fact that mandatory parole releases have continued to increase since 1980, and it is clear that states are (by and large) relying more on legislative enactments than they are the actual discretion of parole board members when it comes to early release of offenders.

The state of parole and the characteristics of the population serving under that sanction have gone through some noticeable fluctuations and changes. For instance, while the parolee population has continued to grow each year from 1980 to 2005, this sanction experienced the highest rate of growth between 1980 and 1990, during which time the number of entries to state parole supervision more than tripled, from 113,400 to 349,000 parolees. These state parole entries continued to rise during the 1990s, while parole discharges also increased. An overall growth pattern in the number of parolees released in the community continued to occur. However, during the years 2000 to 2005, the number of state parole cases that entered the parole phase of supervision consistently exceeded the number of parolees that exited the system. All in all, the average percentage increase in state parolees has only been around 1.7 percent annually (see Table 7.1). From this, it can be seen that the rate of growth in the parolee population has been very slight, and this correspondingly means that state systems and state parole officers typically do not find themselves inundated with parolee caseloads. Table 7.2 provides an overview of the numbers of parolees in the 10 states with the largest parole populations. The 10 states with the highest rates of supervision and those with the lowest rates are also covered in this table.

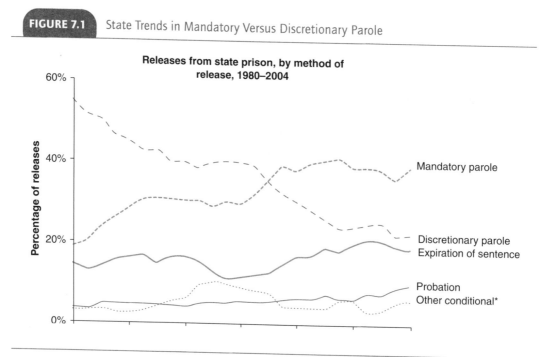

FIGURE 7.1 State Trends in Mandatory Versus Discretionary Parole

SOURCE: Glaze, L. E., & Bonczar, T. P. (2007). *Probation and parole in the United States, 2005*. Washington, DC: U.S. Department of Justice.

NOTE: Data are from the National Prisoners Statistics (NPS-1) series.

*Other conditional releases include: provisional releases, supervised work furloughs, releases to home arrest or boot camp programs, conditional pardons, conditional medical releases, or unspecified releases.

TABLE 7.1 Growth in State Parole Linked to Entries

Year	State Entries	State Exits
2000	441,600	432,200
2001	445,600	439,100
2002	436,300	420,000
2003	459,100	440,500
2004	465,500	448,800
2005	480,300	469,300
Average annual percent change 2000–05	1.7%	1.7%

SOURCE: Glaze, L. E., & Bonczar, T. P. (2007). *Probation and parole in the United States, 2005.* Washington, DC: U.S. Department of Justice.

TABLE 7.2 Parole Among Notable Ranking States

10 States With the Largest Parole Populations	Number Supervised	10 States With the Highest Rates of Supervision	Persons Supervised per 100,000	10 States With the Lowest Rates of Supervision	Persons Supervised per 100,000
California	111,743	Pennsylvania	787	Maine	3
Texas	101,916	Arkansas	782	Florida	34
Pennsylvania	75,732	Oregon	766	Rhode Island	41
New York	53,533	Louisiana	712	North Carolina	47
Illinois	34,576	Texas	611	Nebraska	50
Louisiana	24,072	California	421	North Dakota	57
Georgia	22,851	Missouri	414	Massachusetts	73
Oregon	21,499	South Dakota	414	Virginia	78
Michigan	19,978	Wisconsin	365	Mississippi	90
Ohio	19,512	New York	364	Delaware	92

SOURCE: Glaze, L. E., & Bonczar, T. P. (2007). *Probation and parole in the United States, 2005.* Washington, DC: U.S. Department of Justice.

Among the parolee population, roughly 1 out of 8 (or about 12 percent) is a female offender. During the past decade, the proportion of female parolees has increased from 10 percent to 12 percent, making this a 20 percent increase in the proportion of female offenders represented in the parolee population. In addition, the percentage of parolees that are African American tends to be around 40 percent, with a slight downward trend having been noted during the past decade or so (in 1995, African American offenders made up 45 percent of the parolee population). In contrast, the proportion of Caucasian offenders has increased during the past several years, to 41 percent of the overall parole population. Roughly 18 percent of all parolees nationwide are Latino, with another 2 percent from other racial categories. Finally, the largest percentage of parolees were convicted of drug offenses, with 37 percent of the total parole population having some drug-related conviction. A quarter of all parolees had committed violent offenses, while another quarter had property offenses. Table 7.3 provides an examination of the United States parole population by offense.

As with probation, parole has differing levels of supervision. Roughly speaking, one can divide parole conditions into those that require active supervision and those that do not. Active supervision requires parolees to routinely report to their parole officer through personal contact, via mail, or by telephone. Active supervision is used with roughly 83 percent of all parolees, and this statistic has remained stable over time. On the other hand, parolees on inactive status are still carried on the caseload, but they are not required to report to their parole officers. Only about 4 percent of all parolees are placed on this type of release, making this a small group of offenders who are the least likely to pose any serious public safety risk. In addition, roughly 7 percent of all parolees have absconded during a given year. During the past 10 to 12 years, the percentage of parolees that have successfully met the conditions of their parole sentencing requirements has remained stable at around 45 percent. However, this is lower than the rate of success that probationers have; probationers successfully completed the terms of their probation sentence in about 60 percent of all cases.

MODELS OF PAROLE ADMINISTRATION

The administration of parole tends to be much less complicated than the administration of probation. Peak (1995) notes that there are few studies concerning the organization, administration, or other aspects regarding policy and practice of parole. At the point of writing this text, Peak's (1995) observations were still true, but that is not so surprising. Simply put, there is little need for such an examination because parole is for the most part a static process throughout the nation. Aside from the fact that many states and the federal government have eliminated the official use of parole, no other major or sweeping changes in parole administration have occurred in decades. As was noted at the beginning of this text in Chapter 1, probation and parole functions are combined in many states throughout the nation. Thus, among those states that

TABLE 7.3	Parolee Characteristics by Type of Offense	
Type of offense	2002	2005
Violent	24%	25%
Property	26	25
Drug	40	37
Public order	. . .	6
Other*	10	7

SOURCE: Glaze, L. E., & Bonczar, T. P. (2007). *Probation and parole in the United States, 2005.* Washington, DC: U.S. Department of Justice.

NOTE: 2002 was the first year data for type of offense were collected.

. . . Not available.

*In 2002 public order offenses were reported among other offenses.

have retained parole, most have combined it with probation. When added with those states that have eliminated parole altogether, it becomes clear that there are few occasions when parole administration occurs as a truly stand-alone function. Thus, much of the information from Chapter 1 and the information pertaining specifically to probation in Chapter 6 will equally apply to this chapter as well. Rather than reading a repeat of that information, the student should simply keep in mind that there are substantial similarities between the two forms of supervision.

Another point regarding the administration of parole is that it is much simpler to understand than is the administration of probation. This is because in all cases where parole exists, it is administered by one single agency throughout the state. Thus, unlike probation, there are not multiple agencies or overlapping jurisdictions when administering parole, and this is true in all of the states across the nation. Though there can be some confusion with the choice of terms and vernacular, the word *parole* in this textbook strictly refers to *post-incarcerative release from prison,* not release from jail. The releasing from these two different environments should not be confused.

Generally speaking, there are three basic services that tend to be provided by a parole agency. These are parole release, parole supervision, and executive clemency (Peak, 1995). Among various states that have abolished parole, parole officers still exist and continue to supervise these offenders (though again, a number of states have simply combined this function with the probation apparatus). Also, many states and even the federal government may award early release due to the use of "good time" incentives, and this may also result in post-incarcerative community supervision that is not at the discretion of a parole board. In these cases, the release dates are projected based on legislatively set time lines and standards and simply act as a release valve for prisons. Though the supervision in the community comes on the heels of an offender being incarcerated, it is typically not referred to as parole. Further, this type of release is for much shorter periods of time than is parole, particularly due to truth-in-sentencing laws and mandatory minimums that have been passed in several states and by the federal government. In 1973, the National Advisory Commission on Criminal Justice Standards and Goals (NACCJSG) succinctly identified two basic models for administering parole services. Though this information may seem dated, the student is once again reminded that since the period of time when many states abolished parole or consolidated it with probation, there have been no serious changes in parole administration or organization. Thus, the two models identified by the NACCJSG still stand today as the only true models of parole administration. These two models are as follows:

1. **Independent Parole Administration Model:** This is where a parole board is responsible for release determinations from prison as well as overseeing the supervision processes of offenders that are released on parole (or good time). This type of administration is independent of any other state agency, and the board reports directly and only to the governor of the state.

2. **Consolidated Parole Administration Model:** This is where the parole board is a semi-autonomous agency that is connected (and perhaps subservient) to a larger agency or governmental body. This larger organization will typically oversee the entire spectrum of correctional services, particularly the prison system. Supervision of persons on parole falls under the leadership and authority of that state's chief correctional executive officer (i.e., the commissioner or the director of corrections) with the parole board having no authority to direct post-incarcerative supervision.

In both of the above models, probation services will sometimes be combined with parole services, just as has been discussed in prior sections of this text.

In addition, Peak (1995) points to the President's Task Force on Corrections, which summarized arguments for each of these models. Both arguments will be presented so that the student can compare and contrast the rationales behind each type of system. According to the President's Task Force on Corrections, benefits of the independent model of parole administration are as follows:

1. The parole board is in the best position to promote the notion of parole to aid in achieving public support for the use of this sanction.

2. Since the board is accountable for parole failures, it should be allowed to operate in a position where it can effectively supervise parolees.

3. The parole board can better evaluate and adjust the system of supervision since it is closer to problems associated with offenders released into the community.

4. An independent parole board in charge of its own services is in the best position to frame its own budget and operating expenses.

On the other hand, arguments for the consolidated model also exist. In providing a balanced presentation, the President's Task Force on Corrections summarized the arguments for combining parole services and prison institutions into a single agency. These arguments are as follows:

1. The correctional process is a continuum, and all staff should be under a single administration rather than being divided to ensure optimal efficiency and effectiveness.

2. A consolidated correctional department will have a consistent administration that will better oversee staff selection and supervision and will thus be better able to refine and perfect the services rendered by its staff to the community.

3. Parole boards are ineffective in performing administrative functions. The primary focus of the parole board should be on release decision making rather than on routine issues related to community supervision personnel. Indeed, most parole board members have never even worked in the field of corrections, being instead selected due to a variety of political factors and considerations.

4. Community-based programs can best be handled by a single centralized administration.

Photo 7.1   For most offenders, release on parole means leaving a living space like the one shown in this photo. Many community members may not realize that there is a great adjustment that occurs as offenders leave such restrictive living conditions to live in an open social setting that has a broad array of choices.

There have been critics and advocates for both models of parole administration. Critics of the independent model note that it tends to be indifferent to—or perhaps aloof from—institutional programs and that the parole board, when operating under this model, tends to place too much emphasis on concerns that do not dovetail with the needs or concerns of institutional corrections. On the other hand, critics of the consolidated model have noted that the parole board tends to be subjected to pressure and coercion from institutional management and institutional concerns regarding crowding and other issues that should be restricted to appropriate risk-assessment processes (recall the discussion in Chapter 3). As can be seen, there are pros and cons to both forms of administration. Regardless, parole boards, when used at all, should be administered independently to ensure that release decision making and risk prediction are as pure as possible rather than being contaminated by political concerns or other issues that do not hinge on the characteristics of the offender him- or herself.

Parole Officers in Canada

Driving up to the warehouse at 8 PM on a Thursday night, the parole officer hopes his client will be hard at work inside. So far, every meeting with the client has gone well, as have the meetings with the parolee's employer. But this is an unscheduled meeting, and the probation officer knows a good start by someone on parole doesn't always mean the virtuous behavior will continue.

"I don't like it when the guys return to jail," explains Rob Christensen. "It can be a very [defeating] feeling. When you do see someone come out and succeed, it's very good." In his nine years on the job, the Calgary parole officer has seen his share of successes and failures. Regardless of what happens from case to case, though, his main goal remains to help offenders released from prison do well in the community while protecting the public at the same time.

It's a busy and demanding job. And like other careers within law enforcement, [it] comes with its good and its bad, especially because parole officers must maintain constant contact with all aspects of the parolees' lives. "You see some really terrible stuff in the files and you have to deal with these people professionally," Christensen said. "You're always looked at as the bad guy when all you're trying to do is help the guy. And it can be confrontational at times." But, for him, there are many pluses as well. "I like the interaction with all the different characteristics of people. I like helping when I can and the law enforcement side of things."

Working for Corrections Canada as a parole officer in the community, Christensen's duties see him travel throughout the city meeting those on parole in their homes and at their jobs. Parole officers must also try and meet employers, family, friends, and others in regular contact with the parolee to ensure everything is on the straight and narrow, or to find a way to get more help to the parolee. This could include something such as enrolling the parolee in a substance abuse program. As all these matters are legal issues, parole officers spend plenty of time taking notes and completing paperwork in the office as well.

The law always held an attraction for Christensen, who originally contemplated applying for the RCMP [Royal Canadian Mounted Police] while he was in college. "I was looking at law enforcement of some sort," he said. But the thought of moving all over the country held little appeal. In discussing his future with others, someone suggested applying at the Bowden penitentiary. He did, was accepted, and began work as a federal corrections officer in 1989 and worked his way up the ladder. (Provincial corrections officers deal with those who receive sentences of less than two years.) He spent six years as a parole officer in the institution before moving to Calgary.

He now puts in a regular work week of 40 hours, but the days and times of his shifts may vary. Parole officers are paid on a sliding scale up to about $63,000 a year. Knowing the ins and outs of parole, however, is but a small part of what's required in a parole officer. Christensen said a parole officer needs solid communication skills, patience, and strong interpersonal skills. "You need to be able to interact on a professional level and a personal level. You have to be able to read people in a hurry."

Parole officers have been around for decades and that's likely to continue, Christensen said. And he offered this advice to those considering this line of work: "Don't feel like you can change the world and don't feel like you can change everybody. Take the satisfaction from the ones [you] do."

SOURCE: Sproxton, M. (2002). *Parole officers constantly deal with the good and bad.* Retrieved from http://www.nextsteps.org/steps/dec02/mirror.htm.

Critical Thinking Questions

1. In what ways do the functions of parole officers in Canada seem similar to those in the United States?

2. From the information in the article, does it appear that parole considerations in Canada operate as more of a punitive model or a reintegrative model?

FEDERAL PAROLE: A REMNANT OF THE PAST

The United States Sentencing Commission was created in 1987 and promulgated a set of sentencing guidelines that were officially instituted within the federal system. As a result of this legislation, parole for federal inmates was officially abolished, but the use of supervised release from federal prisons was not in fact entirely eliminated. While official parole and the use of parole boards no longer exist within the federal justice system, the modified version of early release is afforded some federal inmates based on requisites related to sentence completion. However, this form of early release is administered by the sentencing court for a given inmate, similar to community supervision under probation. In the federal system, the court has the authority to impose sanctions on released inmates if they violate the terms or conditions of their supervision.

Federal parole will not be discussed in detail within this text. As students may recall from Chapter 6, the number of federal offenders on probation is minuscule in comparison to those in state offender populations. Likewise, the parole population in the federal system is much smaller than in those states that continue to use parole. In 2005, there were 89,589 federal offenders on parole or early release while there were 682,263 state offenders on parole throughout the nation. Though the difference in numbers is not nearly as stark as the differences for probation populations (see Chapter 6), it is nonetheless substantial, with the federal population consisting of approximately 13 percent of what is found in state populations. Further, when considering the fact that parole was officially abolished some 20 years prior to the publication of this text, it seems that further coverage of a small and remnant vestige of the past is not needed.

THE FINANCIAL ASPECTS OF PAROLE

As has been discussed in other parts of this text, the use of community corrections yields substantial savings advantages when compared with incarceration. The advantages hold true for the use of parole just as with probation. Indeed, the state of Nebraska (as well as other states) notes that when comparing parole supervision and incarceration, it is clear that even the most stringent forms of parole are more cost-effective. The lower costs are associated with the reduction in the need for secure facility settings as well the fact that parolees pay their own housing, food, and medical expenses. In such cases, the primary budgetary items associated with parole administration are simply those of paying for personnel, vehicles, and equipment.

To provide a clear idea of the difference in costs, consider the state of Idaho. In the Idaho corrections system, the cost for housing one inmate for one day in prison is $55.00, compared with the very low cost of $4.00 per day for those on community supervision. Thus, parole costs only a fraction of what imprisonment entails. States could therefore literally save millions of dollars each year if they were to use parole more frequently when inmates are eligible. However, it is important that the financial cost-cutting aspects are not allowed to cloud the judgment of those working in a parole system. Students must remember what has been stated throughout this text, that public safety is "job one," and community corrections holds a responsibility to ensure that the public is made as safe as is reasonably possible. Thus, if state correctional systems decide to increase the use of parole, they may find it more prudent to use more structured and intensive forms of parole supervision. More intensive forms of parole, such as those that use electronic tracking or GPS surveillance, more frequent field visits from parole officers, day reporting, and intensive treatment program participation, will be more costly. But even in these cases, the cost is usually no more than $20.00 to $25.00 a day, compared with the $55.00 cost noted by the state of Idaho for holding someone in prison for a day.

In addition, as presented in other sections of this text, prolonged imprisonment can and does *increase* the likelihood of recidivism. This is compared with the resounding fact that, when implemented in a sound and effective manner, community corrections (including parole) produces *lower* recidivism rates. According to the Florida Correctional Commission, it stands to reason that if, in fact, parole does reduce recidivism, the savings are even greater when one considers the avoided cost of future incarcerations. Thus, there may be significant cost savings when using intensive supervised parole that go beyond the simple comparison of daily costs to house and supervise offenders. In fact, this long-term realization should be the true philosophical basis for implementing a more widespread use of parole, since this long-term effect is what essentially eliminates criminality and reforms the offender. In other words, the most cost-effective situation is one where neither supervision nor incarceration is necessary at all. Presuming that parole works better for the genuine reform of offenders, it would stand to reason that this option provides the greatest hope of achieving circumstances where states can safely say that no further supervision is necessary for a given offender. Such circumstances are, therefore, the most cost-effective outcomes for which one could hope.

Nevertheless, states around the nation find themselves considering the increased use of parole or early release due to problems with prison overcrowding (see Figure 7.2). State correctional systems may find it difficult to house the influx of offenders when their budgets are not increased to accommodate this continual flow of new inmates. The state of Arkansas is a very good example of how prison overcrowding has become a basis for the expansion of parole options. Indeed, in 2001, the Arkansas Board of Correction and Community Punishment implemented an accelerated parole scheme to release over 500 inmates, citing the need to free prison and jail space due to the state's record-breaking incarcerated population. The state's system was so backlogged that there were over 1,000 state inmates who were being held in county jails due to a lack of prison space ("Arkansas Speeds Parole," 2001). This same problem has been noted in other areas of the nation, such as Maricopa County, Arizona.

The state of Arkansas, in dealing with the overcrowding issue, lowered the security level of many cellblocks and facilities from maximum to medium security and from medium to minimum security, since lower levels of security require fewer officers to supervise these inmates. In 2001, the state had a high number of correctional officer vacancies and simply could not effectively supervise its inmate population. It is clear that the policies implemented—artificially lowering inmate security levels—were dangerous and were not based on the security of the institution or society but were instead based on economics ("Arkansas Speeds Parole," 2001).

As noted before, this is a dangerous game to play and fails to live up to the notion that "public safety is job one," a primary tenet of this text. Further, students may recall from Chapter 1 that the original purpose of community corrections was not to alleviate jail or prison overcrowding. Indeed, there were no legal protections for the incarcerated during the early correctional history of the United States or Europe. The true purpose of community corrections was consistent with that set forward by Alexander Maconochie and Sir Walter Crofton: to reform those offenders who showed sufficient motivation and likelihood to be reformed. The entire point and purpose of both probation and parole were reformation of the offender. This was even true for those persons who served their sentence in early penitentiaries, where it was the goal that offenders seek penitence for their crimes through introspective reflection and spiritual contemplation of their wrongdoings. The point is that while it is understandable that state agencies may resort to more use of parole, it is important that they not do so simply because of financial incentives.

As Chapter 3 demonstrated, correctional systems must adhere to scientifically valid risk-assessment processes when determining if inmates are eligible for parole. This determination must not be affected by financial concerns lest its validity be contaminated. If this contamination of the scientifically validated process is allowed, public safety is compromised, all in the interest of saving money and alleviating prison overcrowding. This is precisely what happens in a number of states when dangerous offenders are set loose under haphazard supervision schemes, sometimes resulting in heinous crimes against members of society. This also (quite understandably) reduces public support for parole and actually embitters many members of society against the idea of early release. Regardless of dollars that can be saved, state officials must keep this in mind if they wish to avoid putting their citizenry in jeopardy. Also important for any politician is the desire to avoid embarrassment and scandal, an all-too-certain by-product of any media-catching criminal incident that happens during the politician's tenure in office. Thus, it is in the best interests of state political officials (not just correctional officials) to pay closer attention to their correctional system budgets to ensure that those who should remain in prison do so, and to likewise ensure that those who have a greater likelihood

FIGURE 7.2   Parole Population Increases and Decreases by State (2002)

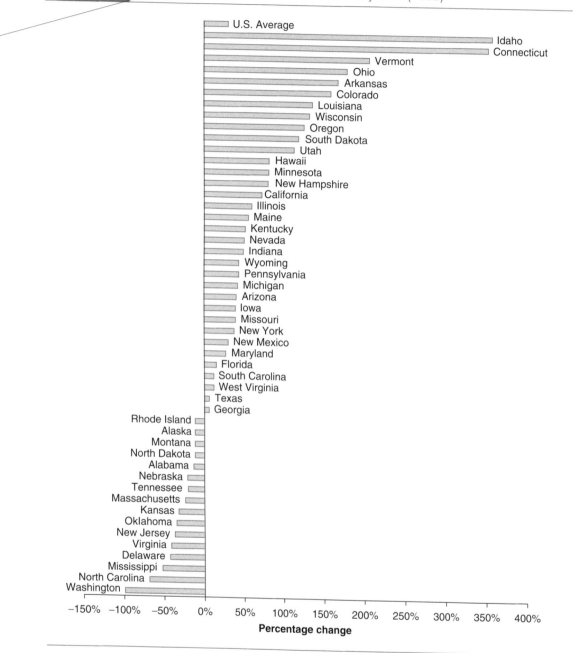

SOURCE: Travis, J., & Lawrence, S. (2002). *Beyond the prison gates: The state of parole in America.* Washington, DC: Urban Institute Justice Policy Center.

for reform are correctly identified and given the appropriate means for pursuing that reform. The best means of doing this is by obtaining the most effective system of statewide risk prediction that money can buy. Such a system will pay for itself 10 times over, both in dollars that are saved and in the reduction of public victimization that would otherwise occur.

Almost as if the state of Arkansas anticipated such criticism being leveled at its 2001 decisions to restructure its corrections system, the state implemented plans that emphasized rehabilitative efforts during the year that followed. These plans relied on drug court and community facilities for parole violators and included funding for a 300-bed facility for sex offenders ("Arkansas to Emphasize Rehabilitation," 2002). Such programs demonstrate that officials with the state of Arkansas understood the connection between reformative efforts and lowered recidivism. The fact that Arkansas sought to avoid reincarceration of those already on parole demonstrates three points that are fundamental: (1) non-dangerous parolees are better off in the community than in prison; (2) the public is better off if non-dangerous parolees are not sent back to prison; and (3) specialized forms of treatment must be given for offenders who have specialized criminal tendencies, such as with the sex offender population.

Photo 7.2   Parole also means that offenders will have many more options than might be encountered in a dayroom such as the one shown in this photo.

What is also important is that these implemented processes did not allow for more expedient release of offenders from prison. Rather, quite intelligently, the state of Arkansas focused on those who were already in the community and had good prospects of reform. The goal in this case was undoubtedly to continue their path to reform and, in the process, refrain from further crowding the state prison system through the reincarceration of these identified parolees. This is an especially good policy if parolees commit technical violations or minor forms of crime. In addition, the separation of sex offenders into a specialized facility allows these offenders the possibility of genuine change that is not obstructed by a prison subculture that tends to continually victimize these types of offenders. Such subcultures aggravate the mind-set of many sex offenders and can create a worse offender than the one who originally entered the prison facility.

THE GRANTING OF PAROLE

In most states, offender cases are assigned to various individual parole board members who are tasked with reviewing them so they can formulate their initial recommendations. The recommendations that they provide are typically honored and accepted as written. Most states that follow this process will have a formal hearing where parole board members may share their views. When the parole hearing is conducted with the offender seeking parole, all members involved with the decision may be present or just one member may be present. It is not always the case that all parole board members will meet with the inmate seeking parole; instead this may be modified considerably from what is typically presented on television. Last, when parole hearings are conducted, the board may convene at the facility where the inmate is located (requiring the board to travel), or the inmate may be brought to the board, wherever the board is located (in many cases, the state capitol).

The process and guidelines for parole selection vary considerably from state to state. Some have a minimum amount of time that must be served. Others may have stipulations based on the types of crimes that were committed in the past. Naturally, some states may have both of these criteria as well as others to regulate the parole process. However, the actual decision by any parole review decision-making body is often one that was made with a great deal of discretion. Indeed, it would appear that parole boards are influenced by a wide variety of criteria, many of which are not necessarily noted by statute or official agency guidelines. Institutional infractions, the age of the offender, marital status, level of education, and other factors may all weigh into the parole board's decision making.

Naturally, one of the key concerns with granting parole is the probability of recidivism. To a large extent, the prediction process has been little better than guesswork. For decades, the development of prediction devices has continued with an attempt to standardize risk factors. Psychometric tools and statistical analyses have ultimately rested upon actuarial forms of risk prediction. In most cases, it is the objective use of statistical risk prediction that turns out to be more accurate than that which allows for individual subjectivity. There are of course some exceptions, since the context surrounding the statistical data may be important and may provide alternate explanations as to why a certain set of numbers or statistical outcomes may have been obtained. However, as discussed in Chapter 3, this often simply results in the overprediction of likely reoffending, which is costly to prison systems and may contribute to overcrowding.

Parole mechanisms can serve as release valves for prison systems that become overstuffed with offenders. When this occurs, there may be a need for a certain amount of offender releases, and parole boards may have to make tough decisions that do not necessarily comport with the formal risk assessment described above, which is based on a standardized instrument. This is where the difficulty tends to occur, and it demonstrates why it is counterproductive for standardized risk-assessment instruments to overpredict likelihood of reoffending (as with the Wisconsin Risk Assessment scale). On the other hand, subjective decision making is a necessary evil that is also fraught with peril, resulting in mispredictions that ultimately lead to serious mistakes in determining an offender's likelihood to recidivate.

There are other factors that also affect the decision to grant parole. For instance, an inmate may (on a standardized instrument) have a high likelihood of reoffending, but the type of reoffending may be of a petty nature. In such instances, parole boards may decide to grant parole despite the fact that the offender is not considered a good risk based on a pure analysis of whether he or she will or will not reoffend. Thus, it is clear that the specific type of reoffending is also an important consideration among parole board personnel. As just noted, this may be an especially important consideration when parole boards are aware that the state's prison system is overcrowded and that a certain number of releases will assist prison administrators in maintaining their prison population levels within required guidelines. It is better to release a person likely to relapse on drugs or alcohol or that may commit some form of shoplifting than it is to release someone likely to commit some form of violent crime. It is with this next-best-solution approach that parole boards may be compelled (though not legally required) to make their releasing decisions.

Though not specifically germane to a community corrections course or textbook, it is important for students to appreciate the problems associated with prison overcrowding that go beyond the financial aspects of parole, as discussed earlier in this chapter. Administrators in state prison systems are required by a variety of federal rulings and mandates not to exceed their intended capacity of inmates that may be held within the various facilities that comprise that system. Individual prisons and other types of correctional facilities must (and do) pay close attention to the number of inmates within their custody as compared with the maximum number that are allowed to be kept within their facility. Various federal court rulings during the 1970s and 1980s penalized many state prison systems and essentially forced these systems to honor a variety of civil rights standards when incarcerating inmates. Thus, the issue of overcrowding is not something that can be taken lightly by prison administrators, and state systems resort to a number of alternatives to alleviate this overcrowding. Some states are better than others at finding innovative means of housing or supervising offenders. Among those states that still do use parole, it is an unquestionable fact that this option is one of the means by which state prison systems resolve their overcrowding problems, meaning that these state correctional systems rely on their community corrections system to augment and support their institutional correctional system. Thus, parole boards may play a key role in bridging these two components in an effort to ameliorate challenges facing a state correctional system.

The fact that parole boards may play such a critical linchpin role should not be underestimated. They may, in fact, be under some pressure to assist the overall state system. Further, consider that these boards are often constructed by the governor of a given state. In some cases, state politics and state priorities may come into play, affecting the decision making in some parole board cases. This is particularly true when the parole board's administration is consolidated rather than independent in nature (as was discussed earlier in this chapter). In times past, parole boards were subject to differing degrees of corruption or disparity in decision making due to the influences of political or other concerns. While this is an issue that warrants attention even today (as a degree of ethical oversight is always good to have), the point to this section is not to insinuate that parole boards are given to capricious decision making. Rather, the point is to demonstrate that parole boards do not operate in a complete vacuum. The influences of the surrounding contextual reality are inevitable, and these influences come from a number of directions. Indeed, prison wardens, state offices, victims, the parolee's family, and the public media may all have an impact upon the discretion that is employed by parole board members, individually and collectively.

Other points that may lead to premature release of offenders may be more relevant to the individual offender's circumstances. For instance, the offender may have been convicted when very young but may have committed a very serious crime (e.g., a multiple shooting) that carried a very lengthy sentence. It may be that the parole board simply considers the maturation of that offender and, as much of the criminological research demonstrates, considers that the offender is less likely to reoffend and that the individual is more likely to remain crime free in the later years of his or her life. In addition, an occasional situation may develop where the offender considered for parole has extenuating circumstances such as an ill or dying family member that is close to the offender, or perhaps children of the offender that are in need of parental contact. In these cases as well, the parole board may grant priority in releasing that offender from incarceration while noting that appropriate levels of community supervision should be maintained. Finally, there are various circumstances where offenders are given compassionate release. Hanser (2007b) notes that this is one option given to numerous inmates that are terminally ill. Hospice programs and other forms of medically related release programs have been implemented in a number of states, even those that typically adopt a hardened stance on crime and offender processing (Hanser, 2007b).

One of the key factors that may be held against offenders seeking parole is their behavior while within the institution. Inmates that have had continual infractions, especially violent ones, are quite naturally not likely to receive parole. Latessa and Allen (1999) note that parole boards are very sensitive to public criticism and thus are likely to be very reluctant to release any offender that has potential to commit an act of violence, even if there is only a very small likelihood that violent recidivism might occur. Just one incident can generate substantial public media attention and thus acts as a strong deterrent to releasing such offenders. This may be the case even if all other indicators show that the offender is highly likely to be successful on parole.

SUBJECTIVE AND OBJECTIVE INDICATORS IN PAROLE DETERMINATIONS

While Chapter 3 has provided an overview of subjective and objective characteristics associated with risk prediction, this subsection serves as a reminder to students that both contextually and statistically based factors are used when making decisions to release or to reincarcerate. In fact, subjective factors, such as terminal illness, likelihood of completing treatment programs, impressions during interviews, and so forth, have been talked about during earlier segments of this chapter as well. These factors undoubtedly come into play when making determinations. Students may recall from Chapter 3 that the use of subjective and objective indicators may be separated according to different purposes. This chapter will also follow along that notion, with the contention that all public safety determinations should be based solely on objective assessment instruments and that subjective criteria be avoided when issues of public safety are at stake. For parole boards that are sensitive to bad publicity from the media, reliance on mathematically precise, consistent, and effective means of protecting public safety provides board members with a quantifiable rationale for their decisions. Further, as was noted in earlier segments of this chapter, statistical models tend to be more accurate than subjective models of risk prediction. While there will be some degree of overprediction of the likelihood of recidivism, this will nonetheless minimize the amount of error that is made by the board and the amount of corresponding criticism that is leveled at the board. On the other hand, as noted in Chapter 3, when making determinations regarding treatment progress, the use of subjective criteria from the specific primary treatment provider should be utilized more than any other form of assessment. Many of the issues in determining offender genuineness and effective completion of treatment goals will require individual observation that cannot be adequately appraised by some form of standardized process. Thus, subjective indicators should only be considered after the board has objectively determined that the offender is a safe release risk.

Naturally, from our discussion in the prior subsection, this is not the case with many parole boards. In fact, parole boards may actually release offenders that are likely to reoffend but whose likely crimes are not expected to be serious in nature. Further, parole boards (as noted earlier) may release for other reasons such as terminal illness and so forth. These all lead to exceptions in a process that tends to overpredict (remember that many instruments are prone to false positives). The point to this discussion is that both subjective and objective indicators have their own primary roles yet, at the same time, overlap one another in their uses. Indeed, though objective indicators may provide one recommendation, subjective or contextual issues may simply be used to override the statistical risk assessment that is utilized. On the other hand, there may be cases where the contextual or subjective observations seem to indicate that an offender is genuinely making an effort to reform, but due to the nature of the prior offense and the mathematical risk calculations that are generated, the offender may be denied parole. Thus, both types of indicators have their time and place, and each tends to enhance the other in some offender cases, yet each one can serve to override the other type of indicator when other types of offenders may be involved. This demonstrates that a balancing act exists when using both types of indicators and points toward the need for sound judgment and the use of effective discretion among parole board members.

Other types of contextual information may also be used by parole boards, providing yet an additional layer of subjective influence in the release process. One example is the inclusion of victim participation. Prior to an offender's early release, it is common practice for states to notify the victim, if the victim desires to know. Figure 7.3, Victim Notification Request Letter, provides an example of the information that a correctional agency will maintain in an effort to ensure that victims are appropriately notified prior to an offender's release from prison. Once notified, numerous states also allow these victims or members of the victim's family to appear before the parole board prior to an offender's release. These persons, along with others that may be permitted to provide written statements, are allowed to share their thoughts and feelings regarding the offender's release. This is typically referred to as a **victim's impact statement**, where the victim is able to express his or her own views on the appropriateness of the parolee's release and is also allowed to voice a sense of trauma and victimization that resulted from the criminal actions of the offender. The actual impact that these statements have on parole boards has not been well studied. However, the fact that the use of such statements has become widespread, along with the modern emphasis on victims' rights, indicates that parole boards do consider these powerful and moving statements in their decision making, at least to some extent.

FIGURE 7.3 Victim Notification Request Letter

VICTIM NOTIFICATION REQUEST LETTER

RECORDS ADMINISTRATOR
DEPARTMENT OF CORRECTIONS
PO Box 5911
(605) 367-5190 OR (605) 367-5140

This request for notice
involves: _____
(Offender Name—Please Print Clearly)

1. Are you a victim or a sentencing judge of this offender? ❑ YES ❑ NO

2. Do you believe you are under threat of physical, emotional or financial harm from the offender? ❑ YES ❑ NO

3. If you answered "Yes" to questions 1 or 2, your request for notice will be kept confidential and you have a choice of two notification options.

4. If you did not answer "Yes" to either question 1 or 2, you may only request option 2.

❑ Option 1 (**Complete Notice**): You will be noticed if/when the following activities occur with this offender:

Discharges his/her prison sentence	Is granted a furlough
Is placed on minimum custody status	Escapes
Is removed from minimum custody status	Is returned to custody following an escape
Is placed on work release	Is released to parole or suspended sentence
Is removed from work release	Is returned to prison as a parole or suspended sentence violator
Dies	

❑ Option 2 (**Release Notice**): You will be notified when the offender:

Discharges his/her prison sentence	Is released to parole or suspended sentence
Dies	Is returned to prison as a parole or suspended sentence violator

5. Print your name, address and telephone number so that you may be contacted. You will be sent a letter confirming your notification request.

_____

Name

_____

Address

_____

Home Phone (Area Code/Number)   Work Phone (Area Code/Number)

Signature: _____

Date: _____

SOURCE: South Dakota Department of Corrections. (2003). *Victim notification request letter.* Sioux Falls, SD: Author.

Parole boards also use a variety of objective indicators. As noted earlier in this chapter, many of the subjective and objective criteria used in probation determinations are also used in parole settings; covering these various mechanisms again would be redundant. Indeed, the various forms of assessment noted in Chapter 3 have been presented in a comprehensive manner and include most all instruments that are used by both probation and parole. However, one scale that is typically used for parolees was not covered in Chapter 3. This is the *salient factor score,* which has been used by the U.S. Parole Commission (though federal parole was abolished, some early release mechanisms still remain) and some states around the nation. This instrument enjoyed widespread use for years due to its practicality and simplicity in administration. The **salient factor score** measures offender risk along six items, each of these being measured with a value ranging from 0 (zero) to 3 with inverted indications of risk (meaning that the lower the number, the higher the likelihood that the offender will recidivate).

The information that follows is drawn from 28 CFR Part 2 of the U.S. Parole Commission, as presented by Edward F. Reilly, Jr. (2002), chairman of the U.S. Parole Commission. The items included in the salient factor score are as follows:

Item A: Prior Convictions (0 to 3 points)—All convictions/adjudications (adult or juvenile) for criminal offenses (other than the current offense) that were committed prior to the present period of confinement are counted. According to 28 CFR Part 2, conduct resulting in diversion from the judicial process without a finding of guilt (e.g., deferred prosecution, probation without plea, or a District of Columbia juvenile consent decree) should not to be counted when scoring this item (Reilly, 2002).

Item B: Prior Commitments (0 to 2 points)—According to 28 CFR Part 2, this item includes confinement in adult or juvenile institutions, community corrections centers, and other residential treatment centers (e.g., halfway houses and community treatment centers). Item B does not include foster home placement. Confinement in a community corrections center or other residential treatment center should only be counted when it is part of a committed sentence. Confinement in a community corrections center or other residential treatment center when imposed as a condition of probation or parole should not be counted nor should self-commitments for drug or alcohol treatment (Reilly, 2002).

Item C: Age (0 to 3 points)—This item is quite detailed. (1) If the offender was 26 years of age or more at the commencement of the current offense and has three or fewer prior commitments, a score of 3 should be given; (2) if the offender was 26 years of age or more at the commencement of the current offense and has four prior commitments, a score of 2 should be given; (3) if offender was 26 years of age or more at the commencement of the current offense and has five or more prior commitments, a score of 1 should be given; (4) if the offender was 22–25 years of age at the commencement of the current offense and has three or fewer prior commitments, a score of 2 should be given; (5) if the offender was 22–25 years of age at the commencement of the current offense and has four prior commitments, a score of 1 should be given; (6) if the offender was 22–25 years of age at the commencement of the current offense and has five or more prior commitments, a score of 0 should be given; (7) if the offender was 20–21 years of age at the commencement of the current offense and has three or fewer prior commitments, a score of 1 should be given; (8) if the offender was 20–21 years of age at the commencement of the current offense and has four prior commitments, a score of 0 should be given; and last, (9) if the offender was 19 years of age or less at the commencement of the current offense with any number of prior commitments, a score of 0 should be given (Reilly, 2002).

Item D: Recent Period Being Commitment Free (0 points or 1 point)—This refers to being commitment free for a period of 3 years or more. Specifically, parole staff should count backward 3 years from the commencement of the violation behavior—including new criminal behavior (Reilly, 2002).

Item E: On Community Supervision at the Time of Offense (0 points or 1 point)—According to 28 CFR Part 2, the term "parole" includes parole, mandatory parole, supervised release, conditional release, or mandatory release supervision (i.e., any form of supervised release), while the term "confinement/escape status" includes institutional custody, work or study release, pass or furlough, community corrections center or other residential treatment center confinement (when such confinement is counted as a commitment under item B), or escape from any of the above (Reilly, 2002).

Item F: History of Heroin/Opiate Dependence (0 points or 1 point)—This item is fairly straightforward. However, 28 CFR Part 2 holds that if the offender was 41 years of age or more at the commencement of the current offense and the total score from items A–E is 9 or less, the score should be a 1. On the other hand, a score of 0 is given if the offender was less than 41 years of age at the commencement of the current offense or if the total score from items A–E is 10 (Reilly, 2002).

After considering all of the points listed in items A through F, scores for each are obtained and summed. The total of the scores is then used to assess the offender's likelihood of recidivism (Champion, 2002; Torres, 2005). The maximum number of points on the salient factor scale is 10, with a score of 8, 9, or 10 representing a low risk of recidivism and thus indicating a good candidate for parole. Table 7.4 provides a clear presentation of the scoring outcomes of the salient factor scale.

In addition, federal parole officers would use this score when determining the level and type of supervision that the offender would be given. Parolees with scores of 9 or 10 might be given minimal levels of supervision, while those with scores of, say, 3 or below would be given very strict levels of intensive supervision (Torres, 2005).

The salient risk factor score has been popular because of its utility and ease in administration. Though this is certainly a plus for agencies choosing to adopt a particular tool for assessment, this does not necessarily speak for the validity or reliability of this instrument. While the six factors of the salient risk factor score are relevant to recidivism and thus possess a good degree of face validity, this instrument has been normed on federal offenders (typically, federal inmates are not convicted of nearly as many violent offenses as state inmates), and it is therefore unlikely that it would be effective in predicting recidivism with these offenders (depending on the state, of course). Thus, to some extent, the external validity is questionable, depending upon the region of the United States and the particular type(s) of offenders involved (i.e., male or female, mentally ill, and so forth). This flies in the face of our prior discussion in Chapter 3, where it was made clear that effective assessment tools must be normed on the population to which they are administered and that such tools must have (at a minimum) strong inter-rater reliability and good face validity.

Further, the instrument does not consider other variables that may perhaps mitigate, contradict, or offset the six factors that are included. In addition, this instrument does not screen for general drug abuse or addiction, but instead restricts the focus of the examination to heroin and opiates. This is unlikely to be optimally effective since stimulant drugs such as cocaine, crack, and methamphetamine also correlate with criminal behaviors. This instrument does not seem to consider these and other drugs to be worthy of being coded or included as items. Thus, the assessment provides only a piece of the overall recidivism puzzle and

TABLE 7.4	Scoring of the Salient Factor Scale
Sum of Scores	Likely Success on Parole
8–10	Very Good
6–7	Good
4–5	Fair
0–3	Poor

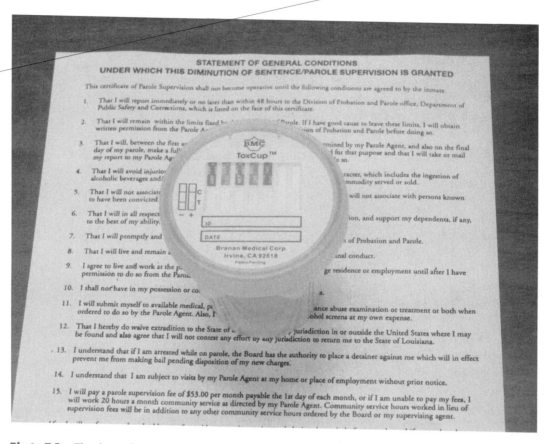

Photo 7.3   The sheet of paper underneath this urinalysis cup clearly identifies the conditions of an offender's parole. In this case, the parole officer is making it clear that the offender is expected to remain drug free by placing the urinalysis specimen cup directly on top of the list of parole conditions.

is not necessarily reflective of the vast drug-abusing offender population. This is a pretty serious oversight when one considers that over half of all offenders test positive for drugs or alcohol at the point of arrest (Hanser, 2007b).

In reality, the salient factor score is composed of variables that are the most basic of predictors, and therefore the instrument is only valid or reliable along a few specific criteria. This instrument, when placed in the balance, is definitely found wanting. Though parole boards may implement this instrument in their release decision making, it was not presented in Chapter 3 due to the fact that this author does not view this instrument as a premier assessment tool and (unlike the Wisconsin Risk Prediction Scale) its use is not as widespread as it once was.

PRE-RELEASE PLANNING AND INSTITUTIONAL PAROLE OFFICERS

Institutional parole officers, often referred to as case managers, will work with the offender and a number of institutional personnel to aid the offender in making the transition from prison life to community supervision while on parole. The profession of institutional parole officer was presented earlier, in Chapter 4, but the actual function of that individual was not given adequate elaboration to demonstrate the crucial role these professionals play in the reintegration process. They are often referred to as caseworkers as well as institutional parole officers, denoting their reintegrative role in the parole process and the fact that this professional's job function follows the theoretical casework tenets that were presented in Chapter 2. Thus, this professional serves both a security function (assessing suitability for parole) and a reintegration function (providing casework services inside the prison and providing networks that extend beyond the prison). Much of the information presented in this section regarding pre-release planning and the role of the institutional parole officer follows information from the state of Oklahoma's Pre-release Planning and Re-entry Process guidelines (Jones, 2007).

During pre-release planning, prison staff will work together to provide a bridge of services that connects the offender to the outside world. A great deal of work can go into the planning and preparation for an inmate's exit from prison. Students may recall from Chapter 4 that institutional parole officers often engage in assessment determinations regarding offender parole suitability rather than eligibility. However, that chapter did not explain the tasks and functions of the institutional parole officer once it has been determined that an inmate is both eligible and suitable for parole. This section will shed some light on the other aspects of the institutional parole officer's job and function, since these professionals provide a linking-pin function between the prison world and the outside community.

Upon determining that an inmate is suitable for parole, the institutional parole officer will begin the pre-release planning process that attends to the offender's transition from prison to the community. This process typically begins about 6 months prior to release and involves a shift from institutional case planning to individual community preparedness. Further, a range of wrap-around services are provided. **Wrap-around services** are those services provided to offenders transitioning to the community with the aid of a team of support individuals that may include the offender's family, clergy, social service workers, probation or parole officers, and so forth. Essentially, these services provide multi-agency networks that are maintained to aid the offender in his or her community transition and aftercare needs. Prior to exiting the prison, the goal of a good reintegration program should be to ensure that the offender has the support, information, and contacts necessary to begin anew during the initial 3- to 6-month period after leaving the prison. Even small details must be attended to, such as providing offenders with essentials like proper clothing and shoes that are appropriate for the season and are not marked as being inmate clothing, proper identification, and appropriate referrals to community agencies that can assist with other services.

As noted in Chapter 2, the use of one or two personable and involved volunteers can make a substantial difference in assisting the offender. Indeed, if such a volunteer were able to assist with some of the more mundane issues that emerge from simple day-to-day living, a world of difference can be made. Moreover, if that volunteer should go so far as to be a genuine friend to the soon-to-be-released inmate, this can provide further emotional support that will greatly improve the prognosis for the released offender (see multiple examples at the end of Chapter 2). If the offender should be so fortunate, it often happens that the institutional parole officer will maintain contact with this volunteer as well.

Throughout the process, agency administration will track the offender's progress, keeping a careful eye during the 6 months prior to release. At this point, the offender may experience problems with anxiety due to nervousness over his or her imminent freedom, the responsibilities of the outside world, and the effects of prisonization inside the facility. A good pre-release program will address these issues in advance, preparing the inmate psychologically for release. Aside from their initial entry into prison, this period prior to release is often one of the most stressful points for the inmates coping with prison life, since so much of their future is unexpected and they will be held to expectations that they have not had to meet in years.

Various forms and checklists will be completed during this time as interviews are conducted as part of the review case plan that notes the offender's approach toward release. These interviews will seek to identify various needs that the offender might have upon release. As you may recall from Chapter 3, needs-based assessment instruments perform this function and are used to determine an offender's treatment needs. These instruments will be covered in more depth in Chapter 8 that follows, when our focus is given to case management and case planning (the functions that are most relevant to institutional parole officers as well). Identified needs can be many but often include a program the offender did not complete while in prison, such as educational plans or substance abuse treatment programs. Other needs may be related to the payment of restitution, ensuring transportation, making provisions for child support, or other issues that are relevant to that offender. According to Jones (2007) and the state of Oklahoma's Department of Corrections, the pre-release plan must, at a minimum, include the following:

- The proposed residence of the offender or referral to temporary housing
- Information regarding the offender's financial obligations and identification of the proposed employment, provision of a referral to assist in locating employment, or identification of the means by which the offender will lawfully support him- or herself
- Program referrals for any aftercare needed as a result of programs completed while incarcerated or for services to satisfy an identified need that was not addressed while incarcerated

Beyond this, staff should note any unique circumstances in the pre-release plan that might provide challenges to the successful reintegration of the offender. This will typically be included in the Adjustment Review and will also be included with what is often referred to as the Offender Accountability Plan. This plan addresses the need for restitution, the need to respect the rights and privacy of prior victims, and any particular arrangements that have been made with the victim, as well as provisions that might be included to ensure the offender's responsibility to the community at large.

To demonstrate the multifaceted nature of this initial casework process, professionals in the community will be contacted so that appropriate referrals can be made, as deemed appropriate (Jones, 2007). The Oklahoma Department of Corrections provides that the following individuals be contacted during this stage of the releasing process:

1. A coordinator of clinical social work, who will ensure that proper discharge-planning activities, resources, and support are available for offenders with serious mental illness and offenders with other complicated or chronic medical problems. The coordinator will troubleshoot, monitor, and evaluate discharge plans.

2. A designated discharge planning nurse or a qualified mental health staff person, who will work with this social worker to screen for physical fitness and mental health issues associated with the offender.

3. Chaplains, who may provide coordination for faith-based and community assistance to any offender that requests such assistance. This may even include housing, employment opportunities, or spiritual counseling. These services are completely voluntary and are provided only at the offender's request. If the offender should desire such assistance, the chaplain will work with the facility staff and the faith-based community to provide resources and support for the offender during his or her period of reintegration.

4. Education and career services personnel, who should provide offenders with information to assist in reentry efforts including recommendations, referrals, and other resources that may be necessary and that may not already have been addressed in an Individualized Education Plan or job placement process prior to release (particularly if the offender will seek to change jobs later upon release).

5. Facility treatment program personnel, who will ensure that an aftercare plan is developed for those offenders completing treatment.

6. Probation and parole staff, who will naturally be contacted to provide assistance with local resources in the community and to ensure that the offender is an expected addition to their caseload.

7. Outside social service agencies, that will typically be encouraged to work with offenders prior to release through individual meetings in addition to special visits or presentations and workshops.

The actual day of release is an important milestone for the offender and is actually critical to the offender's successful reintegration. This should be treated as more than a nostalgic moment; the seriousness of the new challenge ahead should be kept in focus. Activities should focus on the last few tasks that are required for the seamless transition to the community. In addition, the offender should be provided a portfolio of the various services available, requirements of parole, and so forth, allowing the offender to keep the information and requirements organized. Organizational skills may be somewhat impaired given the newness of the release experience and the likely euphoria that will be experienced.

Last, Torres (2005) points out that although release from the prison facility can be a euphoric experience, it can also subsequently result in unexpected disappointment and frustration for the offender. Torres provides an insightful description of the psychological challenges associated with the offender's reintegration as the individual navigates between his or her past life prior to incarceration and the future life the offender now faces:

> The parolee's memories of family, friends, and loved ones represent snapshots frozen in time, but in reality, everyone has changed, moved away, taken a new job, grown up, or perhaps most disappointingly have become almost strangers. The attempts to restore old relationships can be very threatening and eventually disappointing. In addition, the presence of almost complete freedom after years of living in a structured, confined prison setting can also add tremendous stress to adjusting to the open community where the offender must now assume major responsibilities of transportation, obtaining a driver's license, finding a job, reporting for drug testing, and so on. If married, with children, the spouse may unrealistically expect the offender to immediately begin providing financial relief to the family that perhaps has endured financial hardships while the breadwinner was away. Other barriers to success include civil disabilities that prohibit the felon from voting . . . and most importantly, from being employed in certain occupations. (p. 1125)

Institutional parole officers are cognizant of the situation that faces upcoming parolees. They must ensure that the offender has the full range of support that is necessary to face what can actually be a traumatic adjustment. The offender will come to grips with issues that most people do not consider, making the experience of release sometimes bittersweet. Offenders may or may not realize the full range of emotional experiences they will have upon release, and it is the job of the institutional parole officer, among other duties and responsibilities associated with the offender's release, to ensure that appropriate support for coping is provided to the offender who may be disappointed or overwhelmed by his or her experience.

SUPERVISION FROM BEGINNING TO END OF SENTENCE

The community supervision process begins when the offender is placed on the caseload of a parole officer. This initial point of community supervision is referred to as the case assignment and will typically be handled according to either the offender's particular type of criminal activity (i.e., sex offender, gang-related offender, etc.) or the geographic location of the offender. For the most part, it is the geographic location where the offender intends to reside that first determines the agency and the likely parole officer that he or she receives. This is particularly true in rural areas or in small towns that do not have enough supervision officers to allow for highly specialized caseloads. However, urban areas will further segment geographical regions by the type of offense, with parole officers that have received specialized training overseeing specialized offender types.

Overall, the use of geographic considerations assist both the offender and the supervision officer since the amount of travel time is reduced. In rural jurisdictions, the caseload may be smaller to account for the added travel time that will be required as offenders are located in far-flung areas of the parole region. These factors are balanced against the type of offender, with specialized offenders being classified by their specific needs or security requirements. These requirements may naturally limit the offender's range of options in the community, will likely require that more activities be performed, and will produce additional work for the parole officer. Thus, this factor will also come into play when determining caseload and the work that is entailed with that particular offender caseload.

At this point, the initial interview is conducted. This is an important first meeting between the parole officer and the offender, typically occurring in the agency office of the parole officer. This can be a time of serious discomfort for the offender, as he or she is likely to be anxious in regard to his or her release, and many of the common sights, sounds, smells, and so forth will be new again to the offender's senses. (In prisons, sensory deprivation tends to occur as offenders lose contact with many of the familiar stimuli that we take for granted in our day-to-day lives.) The parole officer should naturally keep this in mind as the offender begins to acclimate, but, at the same time, the offender must be made to understand that the terms and conditions of parole begin the instant that he or she is released. For the offender, the initial impression of his or her parole officer can be very important when the offender attempts progress toward reintegration. Both the offender and the parole officer will seek to appraise one another. From the offender's perspective, questions may be of the following sort: Is he or she going to be a jerk? Will he or she always ride me, even when it is not necessary? Is he or she streetwise or a fool? For the parole officer, questions may be along the following lines: Is this offender going to be a hardhead? Will this offender lie to me? What is the likelihood that this offender will take this seriously? Though the parole officer will have a great deal of information related to the offender, this does not necessarily ensure that the offender will not relapse on drugs, slip back into prior relationships with criminogenic associates, and so forth. Likewise, this initial meeting has imbalanced dynamics, since the parolee probably knows nothing about the parole officer. This undoubtedly adds to the offender's overall anxiety throughout the initial interview process.

The mutual appraisal process, though informal to a large extent, is an important first step in the process of relationship building. Though the parole officer will be required to lay out the "house rules," so to speak, of the parole process, the manner by which he or she does this can convey a number of indicators and cues to the parolee. The parolee, having little background information related to the parole officer, will likely watch the person's nonverbal actions very intently and will also be likely to home in on voice tone and inflection in an attempt to get a general feel for the parole officer's persona and intent when supervising the parolee. It is therefore not surprising that the offender may be distracted by these observations while the parole officer is asking questions or addressing various mundane issues associated with the beginning of the supervision process.

The parole officer will explain the parameters of parole supervision during this time, including details such as the number of check-ins that are required per week, the types of check-ins that are required (i.e., personal office visit, phone, or mail), and likely field visits that the officer will make to the parolee's residence or place of employment. Additional restrictions or obligations required by the offender's particular circumstances (e.g., protective orders for spousal abusers, prohibition to enter school grounds for child molesters, avoiding certain familiar persons such as prior gang affiliates, etc.) will be discussed. In most cases, parole officers will have studied the file of the parolee in advance to ensure that nothing is overlooked. As a means of developing rapport, it is recommended that such officers ask about topics that are meaningful to the offender. The parole officer should do this in a relaxed and unstructured manner so that the inquiry does not seem to be an interrogation but rather one designed to allow both parties to connect on a personal level.

Once the parole interview has been completed, the parolee may find himself or herself at a bit of a crossroads, upon reflection. Though it would naturally be presumed that the parolee has considered his or her situation prior to exiting prison, the parolee now is faced with the reality that he or she is actually in prison and must start making active and motivated efforts to succeed in a world that is much less structured than that of the prison and where temptation is much more prevalent. The parolee may be faced with doubts, concerns, and worries that are not known by most persons observing him or her. For instance, what if his or her prior "good time friends" begin to emerge? What if he was a member of a gang and is approached by his old gang members? What if the offender faces financial setbacks? And so forth.

The manner in which the parole officer handles this first interview can actually set the tone for the relationship with the newly released offender. This is particularly true if the offender genuinely does not wish to return to prison. If the offender is willing to make a genuine effort, the parole officer would be wise in cultivating this sense of motivation. Thus, the parole officer should strive to provide a sense of empathetic concern, support, and sincere willingness to aid the offender in successfully completing the requirements of his or her parole. This initial experience can be quite uplifting for offenders on parole and can keep them from feeling isolated or in a position of increased vulnerability. On the other hand, if the parole officer exhibits a pessimistic or jaded demeanor, this is naturally likely to generate negative feelings from the parolee. Further, it is likely that an air of distrust will develop, with the parolee having a negative view of the future parole experience. Abadinsky (2003) notes that the two roles of enforcement and reintegrative acceptance should not necessarily be viewed as contradictory. This text maintains the same consistent theme throughout.

Thus, parole officers are reminded that their role is to facilitate reintegrative efforts. Given that the completion rate of offenders on parole is around 45 percent (as noted earlier in this chapter), there is obviously much room for improvement since it is clear that many offenders return to prison. Providing a supportive relationship is less likely to aggravate the circumstances of the parolee and is more likely to be of constructive benefit to the parolee's overall approach to community supervision. Parole officers must still, quite naturally, enforce the terms and conditions of the parolee's sentence, and, ironically, many parolees understand and expect this. Thus, the parole officer does not need to be "soft" on the parolee but rather, the parole officer needs to be balanced in his or her approach. Conduct that does not shirk supervision requirements yet also acknowledges the parolee's efforts is perhaps the best means of operation for both the parole officer and the parolee.

As the supervision experience continues over time, the parole officer should provide enough time to effectively relate with the offender and his or her family (Abadinsky, 2003). The use of home visits not only allows the parole officer to carry out supervision functions but also gives the officer the opportunity to meet the parolee's family members or significant other, thereby gaining a better understanding of the offender's life and context. When visiting a parolee's home, it is important that the officer take reasonable measures to ensure the confidentiality of the visit, when and where this can be done. In many cases, the neighborhood may already be aware of the parolee's status as an offender. For the sake of reintegrative efforts, it is best that officers not make a public display of the visit and that they draw as little attention as necessary. This is especially true when offenders have children in their home. The point is that the home visit is not intended to be stigmatizing, but is instead an opportunity to conduct a simple security check while also developing a rapport with the offender and his or her family or significant others.

Despite this, in many cases the parole officer may be known by multiple members of the community, particularly if the visit is conducted within a criminogenic area of the community (keep in mind that many parolees will return to neighborhoods that are crime prone, since this may have been their own community of origin). In such cases, the officer should simply normalize the visit and seek to ensure that the visit is amicable and productive. This is even true if the officer happens to see multiple community members that are watching from a distance. Indeed, it may even be that hostile eyes are set upon the officer. The parole agency and the parole officer may be viewed as invaders of the neighborhood. This is an experience that probation and parole workers experience routinely. In fact, this is also a common experience for many social workers who are employed in child protective services and other such agencies that are designed to intervene in people's lives. Keep in mind that there are some common correlates that occur with prior inmates. Many are poor (being that there is a disproportionate number of poor people in prison compared with wealthy and middle-class offenders), and many are minority members (African American males in particular being disproportionately represented in prison systems in the United States). In a number of cases, the parolees and the neighborhoods they tend to be drawn from will often have these dynamics as well. Given that the majority of community supervision officers (including parole officers) are Caucasian, a number of cross-cultural issues are relevant to effective rapport building as well. Though the officer may not be able to address the negative community sentiments directly, the officer should make a point to be courteous and respectful when moving through the community since, as has been noted before in this text, the ultimate goal of community corrections is to aid and enlist the support of the community in reintegrating the offender.

CONDITIONS OF PAROLE

The terms and conditions for parolees, in most cases, are identical to many of those included for offenders on probation. For instance, the state of Oklahoma requires parole fees of $40 at a minimum from offenders. This must be paid each month to offset various costs associated with supervision. This state also clearly demarcates the potential outcomes if an offender violates the terms of his or her parole, providing a list of potential outcomes that include additional levels of supervision, reintegration training, addition of day reporting centers, weekend incarceration, nighttime incarceration, intensive parole, jail time, and incarceration. This is similar to probation when offenders violate the terms and conditions of their supervision. If possible, the offender will be kept on supervision (depending on the nature of the violation) but will experience a graduated set of increasingly restrictive sanctions and requirements that will become additional conditions of his or her parole. Because this aspect of parole is so similar to that associated with probation, and because the issues related to terms and conditions have been fully discussed in Chapter 6 as well as Chapter 5 (addressing legal issues related to the setting of terms and conditions of community supervision), there is no need to provide further discussion. The general point here is to simply note that conditions of parole tend to be very similar to other forms of community supervision, but that these parole conditions have much more uniformity and consistency throughout the nation when compared with probation and other types of supervision. Again, the similarity between conditions of parole and those of probation should not be surprising since many agencies combine both functions and since both types of supervision may occur under the same officer. Figure 7.4 provides an example of some of the terms and conditions of parole in the state of Connecticut. The terms and conditions, for the most part, tend to be very similar from state to state. In addition, the use of additional conditions (such as noted in number 14 of Figure 7.4) that are unique to the offender are not as frequently used aside from additional fines or community service, unless the offender happens to be in a specialized category of population types (such as sex offenders), but even in these cases, restrictions tend to be similar to those required of other sex offenders.

As mentioned, terms and conditions of parole tend to have much more consistency across the nation when compared with probation. This should not be surprising since, as we have seen, parole is administered from a single agency in each state, and there are not hundreds of independent judges throughout the country that are setting conditions for this type of community supervision (as with county-based probation).

State of Connecticut
Board of Pardons and Paroles
Statement of Understanding and Agreement

CONDITIONS OF PAROLE

Name _____ CJIS No. _____ Release on or After _____

1. **RELEASE DIRECTION.** UPON RELEASE, YOU WILL REPORT TO YOUR ASSIGNED PAROLE OFFICER AS DIRECTED AND FOLLOW THE PAROLE OFFICER'S INSTRUCTIONS. YOU WILL REPORT TO YOUR PAROLE OFFICER IN PERSON, BY TELEPHONE AND IN WRITING WHENEVER AND WHEREVER THE PAROLE OFFICER DIRECTS.

2. **LEVELS OF SUPERVISION.** YOUR PAROLE OFFICER WILL ASSIGN YOU TO ONE OF SEVERAL LEVELS OF COMMUNITY SUPERVISION, DEPENDING UPON YOUR CIRCUMSTANCE. THESE LEVELS OF COMMUNITY SUPERVISION MAY INCREASE DEPENDING UPON CHANGES IN CIRCUMSTANCES AT THE DISCRETION OF THE PAROLE OFFICER, AND MAY INCLUDE RESIDENTIAL PLACEMENT, ELECTRONIC MONITORING, CURFEW, AVOIDANCE OF SPECIFIC GEOGRAPHICAL AREAS AND AVOIDANCE OF SPECIFIC SOCIAL CIRCUMSTANCES OR INDIVIDUALS.

3. **RESIDENCE.** YOU WILL LIVE IN A RESIDENCE APPROVED BY YOUR PAROLE OFFICER AND YOU WILL COORDINATE ANY CHANGES IN YOUR PLACE OF RESIDENCE THROUGH YOUR PAROLE OFFICER BEFORE MOVING. YOUR PAROLE OFFICER HAS THE RIGHT TO VISIT YOUR RESIDENCE AT ANY REASONABLE TIME.

4. **EMPLOYMENT.** YOU WILL SEEK, OBTAIN AND MAINTAIN EMPLOYMENT THROUGHOUT YOUR PAROLE TERM, OR PERFORM COMMUNITY SERVICE AS DIRECTED BY YOUR PAROLE OFFICER. YOUR PAROLE OFFICER HAS THE RIGHT TO VISIT YOUR PLACE OF EMPLOYMENT OR COMMUNITY SERVICE AT ANY REASONABLE TIME.

5. **MARITAL/DOMESTIC STATUS.** YOU WILL KEEP YOUR PAROLE OFFICER INFORMED OF ANY CHANGES IN YOUR MARITAL OR DOMESTIC STATUS.

6. **FIREARMS PROHIBITED.** YOU WILL NOT USE, OR HAVE IN YOUR POSSESSION OR CONTROL, FIREARMS, AMMUNITION, OR ANY OTHER WEAPON OR OBJECT THAT CAN BE USED AS A WEAPON.

7. **SUBSTANCE ABUSE AND TREATMENT.** YOU WILL PARTICIPATE IN AN ADDICTION SERVICES EVALUATION AND TREATMENT AS DEEMED APPROPRIATE. YOU WILL FOLLOW THE INSTRUCTIONS OF THE PROGRAM STAFF AND YOUR PAROLE OFFICER AND WILL NOT MAKE ANY CHANGES WITHOUT THE EXPRESS PERMISSION OF THE PROGRAM STAFF AND YOUR PAROLE OFFICER. YOU WILL ALSO SUBMIT TO RANDOM URINALYSIS FOR THE BALANCE OF THE PAROLE TERM.

8. **MENTAL HEALTH TREATMENT.** YOU MAY BE REQUIRED TO PARTICIPATE IN A MENTAL HEALTH SERVICES EVALUATION AND TREATMENT AS DEEMED APPROPRIATE. YOU WILL FOLLOW THE INSTRUCTIONS OF THE PROGRAM STAFF AND YOUR PAROLE OFFICER AND WILL NOT MAKE ANY CHANGES WITHOUT THE EXPRESS PERMISSION OF THE PROGRAM STAFF AND PAROLE OFFICER.

9. **DRUGS PROHIBITED.** YOU WILL NOT USE, OR HAVE IN YOUR POSSESSION OR CONTROL, ANY ILLEGAL DRUG, NARCOTIC OR DRUG PARAPHERNALIA.

10. **TRAVEL.** YOU WILL NOT LEAVE THE STATE OF CONNECTICUT WITHOUT PRIOR PERMISSION OF YOUR PAROLE OFFICER.

11. **OBEY ALL LAWS. REPORT ANY ARREST.** YOU WILL OBEY ALL LAWS, AND TO THE BEST OF YOUR ABILITY, FULFILL ALL YOUR LEGAL OBLIGATIONS, INCLUDING PAYMENT OF ALL APPLICABLE CHILD SUPPORT AND ALIMONY ORDERS. YOU WILL NOTIFY YOUR PAROLE OFFICER WITHIN 48 HOURS OF YOUR ARREST FOR ANY OFFENSE.

12. **GANG AFFILIATION.** YOU WILL NOT ASSOCIATE OR AFFILIATE WITH ANY STREET GANG, CRIMINAL ORGANIZATION OR WITH ANY INDIVIDUAL MEMBERS THEREOF.

13. **STATUTORY RELEASE CRITERIA.** YOUR RELEASE ON PAROLE IS BASED UPON THE PREMISE THAT THERE IS A REASONABLE PROBABILITY THAT YOU WILL LIVE AND REMAIN AT LIBERTY WITHOUT VIOLATING THE LAW AND

(Continued)

FIGURE 7.4 (Continued)

THAT YOUR RELEASE IS NOT INCOMPATIBLE WITH THE WELFARE OF SOCIETY. IN THE EVENT THAT YOU ENGAGE IN CONDUCT IN THE FUTURE WHICH RENDERS THIS PREMISE NO LONGER VALID, THEN YOUR PAROLE WILL BE REVOKED OR MODIFIED ACCORDINGLY.

14. **ADDITIONAL CONDITIONS.** YOU ALSO MUST ABIDE BY THE FOLLOWING CONDITIONS.

FAILURE TO COMPLY WITH THESE CONDITIONS MAY RESULT IN THE REVOCATION OF PAROLE, AND, IF APPLICABLE, THE LOSS OF GOOD CONDUCT CREDITS EARNED WHILE IN PRISON.

I HAVE READ OR HAVE HAD READ TO ME, IN MY PRIMARY LANGUAGE, THE CONDITIONS OF PAROLE RELEASE. I FULLY UNDERSTAND MY OBLIGATIONS AND AGREE TO COMPLY WITH THESE CONDITIONS OF RELEASE ON PAROLE. IN ADDITION, I UNDERSTAND THAT THESE CONDITIONS SHALL APPLY TO ANY TERM OF SPECIAL PAROLE FOR WHICH I MAY HAVE BEEN SENTENCED TO SERVE.

Parolee	Date	Witness	Date
For the Board of Pardons and Paroles	Date	Hearing Location	Date

SOURCE: State of Connecticut Board of Pardons and Paroles. (2008). Retrieved from http://www.ct.gov/doc/lib/doc/pdf/paroleconditions.pdf.

EVALUATION OF COMPLIANCE AND MODIFICATIONS TO PAROLE

As with the discussion in regard to the evaluation of probation compliance in Chapter 6, the primary means of determining success of parole is simply by determining if offenders have recidivated. Indeed, as was pointed out with the Salient Risk Factor Scale, the central focus given to the prediction of success tends to be the simple likelihood of recidivism. But, as noted earlier, this provides a very singular measure of risk prediction that does not necessarily define the type of recidivism likely to occur, nor does it take into account other mitigating variables that place the offender at risk.

In a similar fashion, it may be a bit shortsighted to simply focus on "yes" and "no" categories of reoffending. As noted in Chapter 6, the definition of reoffending can be quite fluid, and, as was also pointed out in that chapter, one act of recidivism is not necessarily equal to all others. So, with the variability of potential infractions (and considering again the issue of technical violations, as discussed with probation), there should also be variability in the types of response. As it turns out, there typically is quite a bit of variability in options. As noted in our brief discussion on the terms and conditions of parole in the previous section of this chapter, states such as Oklahoma provide for a variety of options, such as increases in the levels of supervision (e.g., going from standard parole to intensive parole, the use of GPS tracking, and so forth), the use of day reporting centers, the requirement of extra treatment (such as for substance abuse relapse), weekend incarceration, evening incarceration, and so forth.

The use of partial incarceration actually has a dual benefit. It is able to work as a sanctioning tool and, at the same time, a preventative tool. Indeed, it may well be that there are certain points in the day or the week when the offender is more at risk of reoffending, such as on Friday and Saturday evenings. Aside from the punitive aspects associated with the brief period of incarceration, such sanctions can be seen as tools that prevent the offender from engaging in criminal behavior. This might be used for a variety of offenders, such as substance abusers who tend to have strong urges toward relapse during evening hours or on weekends. This might even include those who are trying to avoid associations with prior friends who still engage in criminal activity (such as prior gang associates). The offender is essentially prevented from the physical ability to relapse while in custody and is shielded from other criminals that may continue to exert pressure on him or her to rejoin the criminal subculture. Indeed, an offender facing such peer pressure (a very relevant issue for juveniles on probation) or perhaps potential threats can essentially be removed from these influences while at the same time "blaming the man" for imposing this restriction on his or her freedom. In this way, the offender can have a way "out" for his inability to maintain contact with gang members, making it the system's fault rather than his own. This will then reduce or eliminate the likelihood that his peers will judge him negatively or consider him to be traitorous. Thus, such forms of parole modification can actually aid the offender's reintegration into the community while simultaneously assisting his or her attempt to pull out of the influences of other criminals or prior gang members.

Though this may seem a bit odd as a form of therapeutic intervention, it is consistent with other gang-exit strategies that exist (Hanser, 2007b). This is a particularly useful tool if the offender cannot (or will not) consider moving to another area or location. The offender may wish to remain in the current location due to the presence of nearby family and other friends, or perhaps due to the fact that the offender's only source of housing or place of employment is located in a particular area. Thus, the issues can be complicated, and examples such as these again demonstrate how both punitive and reintegrative approaches may actually be one and the same in many cases. The use of evening and weekend incarceration is very similar to the use of **intermittent sentences** in probation, which are simply sentences that require some form of temporary confinement at intermittent periods of an offender's sentence. The key difference here is that it is the parole agency that has applied this type of sanction, a modification of the initial sentence, most often as a response to some sort of detected violation of the offender's initial parole agreements.

As with probation, offenders on parole may have a number of requirements or conditions of their supervision that, if not met, can result in a technical violation. Consider again Figure 7.4 that provides some examples of the terms and conditions of parole in Connecticut. Conditions 7 and 8 require offenders to comply with any substance abuse treatment or mental health treatment requirements that might be relevant to their particular circumstances on supervision. Offenders that fail to meet these requirements might incur a technical violation of their parole, at which point other sanctions might be added. Though naturally the sanctions to be added can be those that restrict liberty (as with the use of evening and weekend confinement), they can also include requirements that are reintegrative in nature. For instance, the offender may be required to attend a life skills course that teaches time management, or reintegration training, or a variety of therapeutic courses at a more restrictive day reporting center. Again, this demonstrates how punitive and reintegrative responses tend to dovetail when administering parolee supervision.

Finally, the use of additional fines may also be imposed, depending on the type of violation. Fines are used extensively in community supervision sanctions and can be adjusted over the duration of an offender's supervision. However, offenders just trying to start anew while on parole often lack the true ability to pay such fines. Further, efforts to collect fines can be strained since community supervision cannot be revoked by an offender's inability to pay his or her fines. Thus, fining of offenders, though a plausible option in some circumstances, may not be a good solution in many cases. On the other hand, community service can be used to effectively sanction offenders. In fact, rather than fining offenders a specific dollar amount, it is perhaps best to look at community service as a form of bartered fine where a set amount of time and labor is exchanged for monetary compensation. The use of community service also enhances a number of therapeutic or reintegrative goals, since this type of service engages the offender in prosocial activities.

Champion (2002) notes that the use of community service aids in encouraging offender accountability. Further, community service provides a means by which the parolee performs a function for the state or the community. The specific type of service to be performed is at the discretion of the parole board (if assigned at the beginning of the parole sentence) or the parole agency, depending on the circumstances. Various forms of building maintenance, highway cleanup, or grounds maintenance may be required as community service. While Champion contends that the use of community service is based more on retribution than rehabilitation, he notes in a following section that offenders in New Jersey may aid with such programs as the March of Dimes Walk-a-Thon, Community Food Banks, and Goodwill establishments when completing their community supervision requirements. In theses cases, it would seem that the emphasis is more on a sense of giving to the community than on retribution. Indeed, providing services for such philanthropic causes would seem to be the epitome of community involvement and also seem to have a definite reintegrative approach. Thus, community service is perhaps one of the most ideal sanctions for parolees since it allows for the accounting of the offender's whereabouts while at the same time providing the offender with the ability to engage in a way that contributes to the community (as opposed to criminal activity that takes from the community).

This is not to say that there is no retributive element to community supervision, but it does imply that retribution is probably not the primary underlying philosophy that is best suited for community supervision. Indeed, Champion (2002) notes that "the element of retribution is strong" when talking about community service, but he further states that "it is believed by some observers that through community service, offenders are better able to understand the significance of the harm they inflicted on others by their criminal acts" (p. 316). It is upon this point that the current author wishes to elaborate, considering this an important point for community supervision in particular and for parole modification in general.

It would seem that any type of activity that builds a sense of understanding of the victim's perspective and the harm done to the victim is a form of empathy building. Indeed, at its basic level, the ability to understand and identify with the feelings or circumstances of others is the quintessential meaning of empathy. The building of empathy is obviously a therapeutic goal, and it is therefore used in many treatment programs as a precursor to additional progress within the regimens of mental health interventions. The use of empathy building and the identification of harm done to victims is specifically sought out in treatment programs for sex offenders (Hanser, 2007a). Such approaches are a common and frequent technique in these and other programs where the offender has harmed an identified victim.

Further still, as Abadinsky (2003) has noted, the approach used by the parole officer—being either positive and optimistic about the potential for reform or pessimistic and instilling a negative set of dynamics into the officer–parolee relationship—can set the tone and thereby influence whether a genuine attempt toward reintegration is made by the parolee. Abadinsky advocates that parole officers should attempt to provide a positive approach as a means of facilitating better chances of success for the offender that seeks to complete his or her parole requirements in a successful manner. This does not seem consistent at all with a retributive outlook but instead seems completely consistent with one that is reintegrative in intent. Granted, it is clear that parole officers must enforce the conditions that are set by parole boards, but this is not an issue of retribution (an "eye for an eye" mentality); rather, it is simply a means of ensuring compliance.

The entire point and purpose to parole are to allow some form of leniency due to the good behavior of the offender. It makes little sense to contend that one should take an offender out of a prison environment (the most restrictive and ostensibly the most retributive form of sanction that we have aside from the death penalty) and place him or her in the community as a means of emphasizing the desire for retribution. In fact, this would seem to be completely backwards. Therefore, sanctions such as community service should not be seen as retributive, but instead they should be viewed through the lens of reintegration, such a perspective being the primary orientation of this entire textbook's presentation of community corrections.

Finally, other modifications to parole may impose stricter forms of security over the offender, such as more frequent contacts each week, the use of restrictive electronic supervision, and so forth. Some of these might be considered retributive in nature since they impede the offender's liberty while at the same time requiring nothing therapeutic or prosocial on the part of the offender. Simply put, these mechanisms ensure that parole personnel are able to maintain supervision over the offender, and they keep the offender from being completely free to commit further violations that might evade detection.

PAROLE REVOCATION PROCEEDINGS

No discussion pertaining to parole (and particularly an entire chapter on the subject) would be complete without at least noting some of the issues associated with the revocation of that sentencing option. As discussed in Chapter 5, revocation is often a two-stage process, initially set forth in the U.S. Supreme Court ruling of *Morrissey v. Brewer* (1972). The first hearing is held at the time of arrest or detention and is one where the parole board or other decision-making authority will determine if probable cause exists in relation to the allegations against the parolee that are made by the parole officer. The second hearing is then tasked with establishing the guilt or innocence of the parolee. During this hearing, the parolee is entitled to a modified version of due process, namely being provided with written notice of the alleged violations, disclosure of evidence to be used against him or her (similar to discovery), the right to be present during the hearing and to provide his or her own evidence, the right to confront and cross-examine witnesses, the right to a neutral and detached decision-making body, and the right to a written explanation of the rationale for revocation.

One interesting development in response to revocation procedures is that of the parole revocations officer. In some states, such as South Carolina, the **parole revocations officer** is primarily tasked with the routine holding of preliminary parole revocation hearings by reviewing allegations made by parole officers against parolees. These hearings are administrative and not nearly as formal as those held by a judge in a true court of law. Typically, the proceedings in these courts are routine in nature, but some situations may have rulings and findings of fact that vary. Though most hearings are not complicated, a degree of discretion is required on occasion when determining if the evidence has been presented well or if the violation requires a true revocation of parole, as opposed to more restrictive sanctions. The position of parole revocations officer does not require formal legal training but instead simply requires that the hearing officer know the laws and regulations surrounding that state's parole system.

While the issue of legal liabilities was addressed in Chapter 5, issues surrounding the role of parole revocations officers were not discussed. In *King v. Simpson*, the U.S. Supreme Court ruled that parole officers and parole revocation officers have absolute immunity when acting in a quasi-judicial or prosecutorial role. The initiation of parole revocation proceedings and the task of presiding over those meetings are considered quasi-judicial in nature. Thus, the parole revocation officer is likely to have absolute immunity in the vast majority of functions that he or she performs (Cromwell, del Carmen, & Alarid, 2002).

Cromwell et al. (2002) point out that that the process of revocation is actually a bit more complicated and takes longer than many people realize. Indeed, Burke's (1997) research found that the average time required to complete the revocation process, from the point of violation detection to the disposition by the parole revocation decision-making body, was anywhere from 44 to 64 days. When taken in total with the safeguards afforded parolees during the revocation process, and the fact that many are returned to some more stringent form of parole (rather than prison), there is clearly an effort to work with offenders on parole. It is clear that, whenever possible, only dangerous offenders or those that simply will not comply with their conditions are returned to prison. Further, this demonstrates that parolees do, in many cases, have the time to formulate their defense or to prove that they are indeed working in earnest to meet their supervision requirements, despite violations that might be detected. The main point to these last few statements is that there is minimal likelihood that parolees experience revocation due to capricious and arbitrary reasons. Rather, the system of post-incarcerative supervision is quite balanced in many respects, particularly when one considers that these offenders are, after all, prior convicted felons.

Regardless of whether the decision-making body consists of the parole board itself or a parole revocations officer, there are situations where the offender may be entitled to some form of legal counsel. In *Gagnon v. Scarpelli* (1973), it was held that parolees do have a limited right to counsel during revocation proceedings, as determined by the decision-making person or body over the proceedings and decided on a case-by-case basis. This is, of course, relevant only to those circumstances where the parolee contests the allegations of the parole officer, and counsel is obtained at the parolee's own expense; there is no obligation on the part of the state to provide such representation.

Applied Theory	Braithwaite's Crime, Shame, and Reintegration as Related to Parole

Unlike most labeling theorists, Braithwaite (1989) does not suggest noninterventionist approaches when addressing offenders. Rather, he holds that shaming is necessary for social control and the offender. However, the important issue is what follows shaming: reintegration or stigmatization. Reintegration is essential because shamed individuals are considered to be at a turning point in their lives. It is at this point where the offender can either become reacquainted with society or find him- or herself further entrenched in the criminal subculture. Quality social relations provide the means through which offenders are given the forgiveness and support needed to become members of the community (Lilly, Cullen, & Ball, 2007).

According to Cullen and Agnew (2006), "restorative justice programs most closely mirror Braithwaite's admonition to meld shaming with reintegration" (p. 277). Restorative justice programs seek to restore and heal the victim, repair the damage to the community, and reintegrate the offender after he or she has made a commitment to the victim. From this point, "repentant offenders potentially are granted a measure of forgiveness by victims and are reaccepted by their family and community" (p. 277). These attempts at shaming and further reintegration provide much more effective alternatives to stigmatizing sanctions that are used in the criminal justice system.

In this chapter, the mention of reintegration is particularly important since these offenders will be coming back into the community after serving years in prison. In addition, the "measure of forgiveness" that Cullen and Agnew refer to is also important, since this will be a necessary ingredient if offenders are to have a chance at reintegrating into the community. Thus, Braithwaite's (1989) work specifically applies to the reintegration of paroled offenders and explains that although reconnection with the community is the primary goal, there is a shaming element that is both proper and necessary. In other words, there must be a genuine consequence to aberrant or illegal behavior if the learning mechanisms are to take place.

However, once those consequences have been meted out and once the offender has experienced the full impact of those consequences, society has an ethical obligation to cease and desist from applying additional consequences to the offender; not to do so is unethical, disproportional, and unproductive. In fact, excessive consequences that go beyond the norm are likely to produce more crime.

Given that there are serious labeling implications for ex-cons well after they have served their term in prison, it is clear that the consequences continue to follow them well after they have completed the duration of their sentence. This is true even after they finish their parole or early release obligations when coming out of prison. Further, these additional consequences affect the prior offender's ability to obtain jobs and necessary resources to function in society. Because of these additional consequences, the punishments may seem excessive and it is therefore to be expected that recidivism rates would be high.

The primary point to Braithwaite's work is that a shaming process is indeed necessary and this shaming process should be public and should hold the offender accountable. However, once that process of accountability has been fulfilled, society must then assume the burden of reintegrating the offender back within the community. Otherwise, we should not be at all surprised when individuals turn back to criminal behavior. In fact, when we fail to offer the chance for reintegration, we essentially have contributed to the recidivism. As a society, it could be argued that if we continue to add consequences beyond the sentence and if we do this with the knowledge that this is likely to increase recidivism, then we essentially make a knowing choice that encourages further criminality among those in need of our support and guidance.

SOURCES: Cullen, F. T., & Agnew, R. (2006). *Criminological theory: Past to present* (3rd ed.). Los Angeles: Roxbury; Lilly, J. R., Cullen, F. T., & Ball, R. A. (2007). *Criminological theory: Context and consequences* (4th ed.). Thousand Oaks, CA: Sage Publications.

VICTIMS AND RESTORATIVE JUSTICE

In recent years, there has been a continued emphasis on the use of restorative justice techniques within the United States criminal justice system. This is perhaps due to the corresponding victims' rights movement as well as the emergence of the field of victimology. Likewise, there has increasingly been a desire for accountability among offenders, regardless of whether they receive incarceration. Indeed, in times past (particularly during the rehabilitative model and the medical model eras of corrections), victims were for the most part overlooked. Rather than having a system that sought to repair the damage to the victim, the primary emphasis of our justice system was to find the offender and to ensure that the individual received his or her punishment. While punishment may indeed be rightfully in store for offenders, this did little to ameliorate the plight of the victim.

Ideally, the full reintegration of the offender requires that he or she be fully accountable for his or her transgressions and that reparations be made directly to the victim or the victim's family, not some amorphous agency that collects a monetary fine and payment. Naturally, if the victim does not wish to have such services, this desire should of course be primary and the wishes should be respected. Indeed, Lehman et al. (2002) note that any "victim-centered" approach to reentry partnerships must recognize the "us and them" feelings that victims may have about offenders, but simultaneously they must also account for the fact that victims would prefer to have a voice in issues that affect their own livelihood. Because of this, Lehman et al. contend that the victim impact statement is a critical component to restorative justice approaches, both from the perspective of the victim and from that of offender reintegration (see Focus Topic 7.1).

FOCUS TOPIC 7.1

VICTIM IMPACT STATEMENT IN THE STATE OF IOWA

Victim Impact Statement (915.21)

1. A victim may present a victim impact statement to the court using one or more of the following methods: A victim may file a signed victim impact statement with the county attorney. This filed impact statement shall be included in the presentence investigation report. If a presentence investigation report is not ordered by the court, a filed victim impact statement shall be provided to the court prior to sentencing.

   a. A victim may orally present a victim impact statement at the sentencing hearing, in the presence of the defendant, and at any hearing regarding reconsideration of sentence.

   b. If the victim is unable to make an oral or written statement because of the victim's age, or mental, emotional, or physical incapacity, the victim's attorney or a designated representative shall have the opportunity to make a statement on behalf of the victim.

2. A victim impact statement shall include the identification of the victim of the offense, and may include the following:

   a. Itemization of any economic loss suffered by the victim as a result of the offense. For purposes of this paragraph, a pecuniary damages statement prepared by a county attorney pursuant to section 910.3 may serve as the itemization of economic loss.

   b. Identification of any physical injury suffered by the victim as a result of the offense with detail as to its seriousness and permanence.

   c. Description of any change in the victim's personal welfare or familial relationships as a result of the offense.

   d. Description of any request for psychological services initiated by the victim or the victim's family as a result of the offense.

   e. Any other information related to the impact of the offense upon the victim.

SOURCE: Iowa Department of Corrections. (2007). *Victim services.* Des Moines, IA: Author. Quoted verbatim from http://www.doc.state.ia.us/VictimServices.asp.

The definition used for restorative justice in this chapter is borrowed from researcher and advocate Thomas Quinn from his interview with the National Institute of Justice in 1998 (cited in Lehman et al., 2002). Specifically, restorative justice is a term for interventions that focus on restoring the health of the community, repairing the harm done, meeting the victim's needs, and emphasizing that the offender can and must contribute to those repairs. Restorative justice considers the victims, communities, and offenders (in that order) as participants in the justice process. These participants are placed in active roles to work together to do the following:

- Empower victims in their search for closure
- Impress upon offenders the real human impact of their behavior
- Promote restitution to victims and communities

The use of restorative justice principles holds promise with parolees because they are often individually tailored to the victim and, at the same time, they are likewise tailored to the offender. Specific acts of redemption are required of the offender to meet his or her sentencing requirements, and these acts are derived from the agreed-upon contract established by the victim and the offender. Thus, this reintegration plan heals the victim, the offender, and the community, and thereby ensures that all parties work in congruence rather than conflict. Bazemore and O'Brien (2002) note that there is now significant evidence that restorative justice practices can have a significant impact on recidivism (Umbreit, Coates, & Vos, 2002). They contend that the overwhelming majority of the research shows that such programs either cause improvements in certain areas of offender reformation or, at the worst, work just as well as other traditional programs. This approach helps to inform and educate the community about the specific issues facing offenders.

Hanser (2007a) has also shown that the use of restorative justice can be quite effective, even with higher-risk offenders on intensive forms of community supervision, presuming that appropriate safeguards are utilized. Hanser's analysis examined the use of restorative justice with domestic abusers and sex offenders, comparing this type of approach in the United States and Canada. He concluded that restorative justice principles can augment both community involvement in the supervision process (recall Chapter 1) and offender accountability. Though Hanser makes it clear that restorative justice is no panacea, it does nevertheless provide a viable option, particularly when offenders are making genuine efforts to successfully complete their parole sentence. With this in mind, Hanser provides three specific recommendations that are expected to improve public safety, offender reintegration, and the plight of the victim. They are as follows:

1. **Concerns for the victim(s) must remain paramount:** This is not to say that such considerations are not given primary concern in most programs, but there is typically strong resistance to the notion of using such approaches for perpetrators and victims of certain crimes such as those associated with domestic violence. The resistance to these approaches is largely centered on concern for the victim's welfare and safety. If the safety of the victim is at all compromised by a restorative justice approach, then such an alternative form of processing domestic violence cases should simply not be allowed (Hanser, 2007a). This is perhaps the strongest argument against a restorative justice approach. Thus, safety planning practices for victims, appropriate security measures (both during and after the dialogue with the offender), and other pragmatic methods of ensuring victim safety will have to be fully implemented if such approaches are to be acceptable with violent offenders. Likewise, various power dynamics between the perpetrator and the victim will need to be identified and addressed to ensure that victims are not intimidated, manipulated, or exploited during or after the process (Hanser, 2007a, 2007b).

2. Vigorously and publicly address the perception that restorative justice practices are "soft" on crime: Specifically, jurisdictions should consider public bulletins, media campaigns, and citizen training programs to disseminate knowledge of the potential benefits of a restorative justice approach in the community. The public must be made fully aware that offenders processed through restorative justice processes are held accountable for their crimes. The fact that many victims tend to report more closure, compensation, and sense of satisfaction from these approaches will also be important if this type of orientation is ever likely to obtain full support in the United States. This recommendation augments the points made in Chapter 2 where both community education and community involvement are imperative in optimizing offender supervision and public safety.

3. High-risk offenders will need to be appropriately identified and supervised: This seems to reflect the same concern noted in the first recommendation. However, this goes a step further since it lies more with the function of community supervision agencies than with restorative justice programs. In other words, community supervision programs will need to correctly assess offender dangerousness (which points toward the need for effective assessment and classification processes) and will likewise need to use intensive forms of supervision that are likely to be technologically enhanced, such as with GPS tracking and other such modern innovations (Champion, 2002; Schmidt, 1994). These and other forms of tight supervision have been shown to be more effective for high-risk offenders than less rigorous supervision schemes (Champion, 2002; Hanser, 2007b; Schmidt, 1994). Conversely, intensive forms of supervision have been shown to be counterproductive for low-risk populations (Champion, 2002; Hanser, 2007b). Thus, intensive supervision schemes will need to be well integrated as an adjunct backdrop to any restorative justice program that processes violent offenders.

CONCLUSION

This chapter demonstrates that the use of parole concerns state-level offenders more than it does federal offenders. Likewise, it is clear that the organization and administration of parole systems, unlike probation, tend to have more similarities than differences when compared on a state-by-state basis. Likewise, it has been made clear that there are a number of subjective and objective forms of assessment that go into the parole decision-making process. One subjective element that is not often considered as part of the assessment process in many textbooks on community corrections is the use of victim input via the victim impact statement. The use of this information is becoming more important over time, and the inclusion of this input also dovetails well with a restorative justice approach. Likewise, the salient factor score has been presented, with updates from 28 CFR Part 2 included. Though this measure has been used extensively in the federal system, there are some pitfalls to the instrument that may make it less effective with state offenders throughout many areas of the nation, particularly since state inmates tend to be considerably different from federal inmates.

The parole supervision process has been discussed, with substantial emphasis being given to the rapport that is developed between the parole officer and the parolee. The importance of this relationship cannot be overemphasized, as it can be instrumental in setting the tone of a reintegrative experience rather than one that is punitive in nature. Though parole officers must naturally enforce the terms and conditions of parole, they do have a degree of discretion in relation to that enforcement, and they also have a great deal of choice in how they approach the supervision process. The individual parole officer stands second only to the parolee him- or herself in terms of the impact he or she can have on that parolee's success or failure on parole. Regardless of the parole officer's orientation, it is ultimately the parolee that is responsible for his or her behavior, and, if that behavior is not kept in compliance, revocation proceedings will likely be generated against the parolee. These proceedings progressively increase the sanctions against the parolee, up to and including reincarceration of the offender.

Last, restorative justice approaches have been presented as a useful paradigm in which victim input can be maximized while at the same time supporting reintegration efforts for offenders. However, restorative justice approaches must be grounded in the reality of the practitioner, not the theorist, and must have a strong supervision element that ensures the safety of the public. In addition, the use of community service, restitution, and other such mechanisms of compensation emphasize offender accountability. It is the clear contention of this text that such forms of accountability are not punitive (contrary to the claims of other researchers and authors), but that they are actually rehabilitative or reintegrative in nature, if implemented correctly. This then demonstrates that such sanctions are consistent with restorative justice approaches that seek to reintegrate the offender. In a like manner, victim impact statements used in the parole decision-making process and the supervision process are also consistent with restorative justice paradigms. The last component—the community—has been presented as a critical component in the community supervision process in prior chapters and demonstrates again the utility that restorative justice holds for parole in particular and community supervision in general.

Key Terms

Consolidated parole administration model

Independent parole administration model

Intermittent sentences

Parole

Parole revocations officer

Restorative justice

Salient factor score

Victim's impact statement

Wrap-around services

"What Would You Do?" Exercise

You are a state parole officer who has been active in various aspects of offender reentry. You currently work and live in a medium-sized community. On occasion, your supervisor asks you to serve on community committees and advisory boards as a means of both increasing partnerships in your area and extending the sources and abilities of your own agency. Recently, you have been asked to serve with a group of agencies—some state-level, some county-level, and many of them private or nonprofit in nature. This group has been referred to as the Community Reentry Initiative (CRI) among those in your area. The group has had very good success in creating employment opportunities for parolees in the community, and this has been a great help in reducing recidivism. This group has also had some success in obtaining affordable housing for offenders who do not have a place to stay.

At this point, the CRI has decided to implement a restorative justice component in their efforts. This will require contact with prior victims as well as their consent in participating in the process. This is likely to provide a challenging aspect to the project. However, all victims must be allowed to provide their input in the process as offenders are paroled into the community and integrated into the restorative justice process.

While at the meeting, it becomes clear that many people look to you as an expert on reentry issues. In fact, as time goes on, several members suggest that a subcommittee be constructed to begin the development of the restorative justice program. At the close of the meeting, you are asked to lead this subcommittee.

However, there has been a recent backlash among community members who do not favor offender reentry initiatives in their own community. In fact, some citizens have gone to city hall to protest the implementation of these initiatives.

Naturally, you are a bit uneasy with this responsibility, but you know that your supervisor would be disappointed if you did not agree to help with this task. Your supervisor is very progressive and is fond of saying, "Change is good, so let's have more good by making more change!" So, with no real time to consider the implications, you hesitantly agree to accept the position as head of the subcommittee.

Now, at this point, you want to help but do not know exactly what you should do. Your subcommittee consists of two local religious leaders, a police officer assigned to the neighborhood stabilization team, a victim's rights advocate from a local domestic violence facility, a low-ranking person from a local television station, a social services supervisor, a classification specialist who is employed by the prison that is in the region, and a counselor from a local substance abuse treatment facility. Your supervisor in your parole agency encourages you to help this group and even offers to give you a half-day off each week so that you can spend time in support of this initiative.

What would you do?

Applied Exercise

Students must conduct either a face-to-face or phone interview with a parole officer or other parole specialist who currently works in a community corrections setting. The student must set up a day and time with that practitioner and interview him or her to gain that person's insight and perspective on several key questions related to work in the field of parole supervision. Students must write the practitioner's responses, as well as their own analysis of those responses, and submit their draft by the deadline that is set by their instructor. Students should complete this application exercise as a mini paper that addresses each of the points below. Total word count: 1,400 to 2,100.

When conducting the interview, students should ask the following questions:

1. What are the most rewarding aspects of your job in parole?

2. What are the most stressful aspects of your job in parole?

3. What is your view on treatment or reintegration efforts with offenders?

4. What are some challenges that you have in keeping track of your caseload?

5. Why did you choose to work in this field?

6. What type of training have you received for this line of work?

7. What would you recommend to someone who was interested in pursuing a similar career?

In addition, students should ensure that their submission has appropriate spelling and grammar throughout.

Last, students are required to provide contact information for the parole practitioner. Please have them obtain the following information from the parole practitioner that they interview. While you will probably not need to contact them, it may become necessary in order to validate the actual completion of an interview.

Name and title of parole officer: _____

Parole agency: _____

Practitioner's phone number: _____

Practitioner's e-mail address: _____

Name of student: _____

CHAPTER 8

Needs-Based Case Management and Case Planning

LEARNING OBJECTIVES

1. Know and understand the background and basic components of the case management process.

2. Be able to describe the reasons that a client needs assessment is important.

3. Compare and contrast case management and caseload assignment models.

4. Understand common aspects of classification within the case management context.

5. Understand how automated innovations in case management classification have integrated the case management, caseload assignment, and treatment planning functions.

6. Have a clear sense of the screening process in treatment planning.

7. Understand the importance of treatment planning to the reintegration process.

INTRODUCTION

Case management as a function is relatively new in the mental health field. For the most part, this is the source from which case management, as applied to community corrections, is derived. According to Enos and Southern (1996), the term *case management* began to appear in the common treatment literature during the mid- to late 1970s. Other sources have also confirmed this to be the era during which case management emerged (Monchick, Scheyett, & Pfeifer, 2006), noting that case management is "seen as a way to connect clients with multiple needs to an increasingly complex social service delivery system" (p. 5). This is an apt description of the process. Monchick et al. point out that case management has traditionally focused on the holistic needs of clients, with particular attention given to basic needs, such as those related to food, shelter, medical services, employment, and basic safety. These various factors all work together to provide a person with stability—the very stability that is missing from the lives of most offenders.

During the 1930s, federal legislation in regard to social security and other forms of social aid served as the impetus for programs that required the processing of persons through organized systems of welfare and support. As a means of effectively organizing the client case flow while also coordinating services from a number of agencies, the beginnings of the case management system began to emerge. However, the first direct and deliberate connection between networks of social assistance and the use of case management was likely presented by Froland, Pancoast, Chapman, and Kimboko (1981). These authors called for more active and overt links among a variety of social support systems for clients. Enos and Southern (1996) claim that this is perhaps the primary notion of case management. They further note that from the 1990s onward, case management has generally been thought of as a "bridge and a system of networks resulting in the coordination and distribution of informal and formal services on behalf of someone in need" (p. 24).

THE HISTORY AND EVOLUTION OF CASE MANAGEMENT

Because Enos and Southern (1996) provide such a clear overview of the development of case management, this subsection will borrow greatly from their work. Indeed, their text entitled *Correctional Case Management* could be considered a premier resource when attempting to discuss any form of case management within the community corrections context. The true and direct forms of case management evolution, according to Enos and Southern, can be primarily traced to the work of Jones (1953), Stanton and Schwartz (1954), Goffman (1961), and Cumming and Cumming (1962). These authors were concerned about the welfare of patients in mental hospitals, and their works served as harbingers of the deinstitutionalization movement in the United States. A trend from hospitalization to community release was first set in motion in 1955, with nearly 559,000 mentally ill patients who were housed in state mental hospitals being progressively released over time (National Institute of Justice, 1998).

The work of Goffman (1961) portrayed mental hospitals as being ineffective environments for therapeutic intervention. Indeed, they were portrayed more as warehouses where an emphasis on security and control through sedation and operant punishments was the primary modality of operation. This is not too different from a prison environment, and it was this specific image that Goffman had intended to portray. Mental institutions were seen as being mostly custodial and relying upon physical and medical methods of behavior control with their patients. Treatments such as electroconvulsive shock therapy, insulin therapy, and lobotomies were known to exist. Likewise, the staff in these facilities were not well trained, and standards were much different (less rigorous) from what they are today. Enos and Southern (1996) even go so far as to point out that "in most mental health hospitals in the 1950s, there existed an inverse relationship between the amount of education and training compared with the amount of time spent in therapeutic encounters with the patients" (p. 25). Thus, there were significantly fewer contacts made with trained mental health personnel than there were with general custodial staff at most mental health facilities. This is not entirely unusual due to the fact that there are generally fewer persons who are fully trained as clinicians within the social service industries. On the other hand, the majority of activities throughout a patient's life (e.g., recreational or educational within a facility) do not necessarily require the expertise of a fully trained and qualified mental health clinician. However, it was found that the correctional staff were the *least* trained of all staff, and that these staff had the most contact with patients throughout their stay in secure facilities. This would indeed be problematic because such poorly trained persons would be very unlikely to respond appropriately to problems that might emerge during routine activities. Mental illness does not selectively present itself when clinicians are available, meaning that symptoms undoubtedly manifested while routine custodial staff were all that were available to lend assistance. Add to this the lack of extensive background checks for staff during this era, and it is easy to see why problems were pervasive.

This situation changed during the 1960s, but sadly it was due to an increased reliance on tranquilizing drugs. The education of staff increased mostly as a result of the higher number of nurses that were required to administer these drugs to a largely sedated population. The actual quality of care and service delivery was still not appropriate; much of the client population was simply placed in a zombie-like state of existence, eliminating the need for any truly productive intervention system.

Since the 1960s, the total number of persons housed in public psychiatric hospitals has consistently dropped in number despite the fact that the United States population (and the mentally ill population as well) has grown considerably since that time. Thus, more people are mentally ill, but fewer and fewer of them are placed in secure facilities. Rather, these individuals are returned to the community. It is because of this shift in treatment that the case management system of organizing client services emerged.

Jones (1953) is credited as being the founder of the community psychiatry approach. Often, the term *therapeutic milieu* is used in relation to his work, demonstrating Jones's receptivity to the environment that surrounds the client and the impact of that environment on the client's

Photo 8.1 This hospital once used a variety of case management and mental health interventions that would now be considered outdated. As research and evaluation continues, older facilities and outdated modes of intervention are refined and improved. A newer facility now exists not too far from this original site.

therapeutic progress. Jones contended that the traditional hospital setting could and should be changed into a therapeutic treatment milieu, rather than one reflecting custodial concerns. The primary orientation of such restructured facilities would be centered on the implementation of treatment goals and progress. This would require that all staff (not just mental health staff) change their paradigm of operation, requiring support from the administrative functions to ensure that custodial staff understood the terms and conditions of their job. In addition, the physical facility would need to be changed to reflect a therapeutic (as opposed to sterile) environment. Enos and Southern (1996) further clarify Jones's intent by stating that "Jones meant that the hospital setting needed to become transformed into a humanistic and democratically oriented setting in which the patients could try out new behaviors and skills in order to learn how to come to grips with reality" (p. 26). At this point, during the 1970s, hospitals began to change the sensory environment to one of warmth, and staff were indoctrinated to be more receptive to the point of intervention rather than being responsible only for security considerations. This naturally led to an era of job design and is perhaps associated with the emergence of the paraprofessional in the field of human services.

The work of Stanton and Schwartz (1954) is also credited with the rise of the case management model due to an emphasis on client input into their own treatment program. These authors also noted that both mental health and social interactions occurred in facilities, thereby pointing toward the oblique aspects of a client's experience in structured treatment programs. They note the anti-therapeutic nature of most facilities, contending that such programs actually made clients less mentally healthy in many cases. The primary cause of this was inherent to the structure and organization of the programs in most mental health hospitals. In changing the structure and organization of the mental health hospital, the culture of staff and the integration of various rank-and-file staff into the treatment process were considered important.

Other authors of the same period, such as Cumming and Cumming (1962), reflected this general trend toward integration of a mental health perspective among the rank-and-file staff. This led to more democratic means of programming between mental health professionals and the general staff. General staff were essentially empowered to aid in the behavior change process—no longer was this thought to be the strict domain of psychologists or psychiatrists. This resulted in a blurring of distinctions regarding the function of service workers, many of whom were not licensed but provided aid with mental health intervention programs nonetheless. Significantly, these staff had the most contact with the client, and thus they were in a better position to effect positive change and reinforce behavior consistent with the treatment regimen. Enos and Southern (1996) summarize the importance of this shift in professional operation thus:

> The reality of the inverse correlation between increasing levels of training and experience, and the amount of contact with clients, could be exploited in order to increase the efficiency of therapeutic services by increasing the training of the paraprofessional staff, and by utilizing them as primary therapists rather than as custodial services personnel. (p. 26)

This statement certainly points toward the emergence of the paraprofessional, being grounded in the wisdom that such individuals have the most routine contact with (and potential influence upon) the client. This also demonstrates that treatment options progressively extended beyond the direct purview of the highly trained psychiatrist or psychologist and extended to other persons who could fill gaps that would otherwise occur in any comprehensive program designed to address multiple needs of the client. This is important because it was the precursor to the case management system, fueling a need for more personnel who were qualified at the level necessary to provide a specific service, while not being overqualified for that function. Such an orientation maximized the use of human resources among intervention personnel and, when brought together in a group, allowed better services to more clients than could otherwise be delivered by prior methods.

The trend toward integrating paraprofessionals continued, coupled with a decrease in the use of secure mental health facilities. As the mentally ill clients were released into the community, it became clear that some sort of assistance would be necessary for these persons, as this was well beyond the ability or scope of practice for psychiatrists and psychologists who could not have routine community contact with large numbers of clients. Such an effort would prove to be both unwieldy and very costly. Rather, it was again the paraprofessional who became important in the follow-up coordination of care for those released during the deinstitutionalization movement. Deinstitutionalization, then, with its emphasis on outpatient services, required a new method of service delivery, leading to the rise of the case management method (Enos & Southern, 1996).

During the time that these changes took place, one key piece of legislation was particularly important to correctional counselors (Enos & Southern, 1996). This was Public Law 89-793, which addressed community care rather than imprisonment for substance abusers. This law also emphasized a holistic approach to treatment and further cemented the notion of a multifaceted method of intervention. Because this law shifted treatment to community approaches and also recommended a broad range of services, the orientation toward case management perspectives continued to emerge. Further legislative developments occurred and in 1975, Public Law 94-63 was passed. This was referred to as the Public Health Service Act Amendment and Special Revenue Sharing Act of 1975 and was the genesis for modern-day case management approaches, emphasizing the need for outreach efforts and coordination as a means of providing comprehensive health care and mental health services to those that were served (Enos & Southern, 1996).

More recently, the work of Monchick et al. (2006) describes the use of case management for the flow of offenders seeking drug treatment. In the community corrections field, this is a particularly important application because drug problems are often at the heart of an offender's difficulties; the tendency to relapse is often directly related to recidivism rates. Walsh (2000) presents four general case management models, these being the *broker/generalist model*, the *strengths-based perspective*, the *assertive community treatment method*, and the *clinical/rehabilitation method*. None of these models works in a completely unique manner; each has functions and purposes that overlap the others. Any agency utilizing case management processes must find the right balance among these models as determined by the needs of its clients and the resources that are available to the agency and the surrounding community. A brief presentation of each model is subsequently provided.

Broker/Generalist Case Management. Narrow in scope of action, the broker/generalist model focuses primarily on rapid linkage and referral. The case manager provides limited direct services, other than the initial assessment to determine service needs, service referrals, and occasional monitoring of service provision. Where resources are scarce, this model allows for the provision of a limited number of services to the greatest number of participants.

Strengths-Based Perspective Case Management. Case management in the strengths-based model involves assisting clients in examining and identifying their own strengths and assets as the vehicle for resource acquisition and goal attainment. The case manager helps the client identify his or her strengths and assets, supports the client in defining goals, and helps identify ways the client's strengths can be used to reach these goals. The case manager provides support to the client so that he or she may assert direct control over his or her search for resources, such as housing and employment (Rapp, 1998).

Assertive Community Treatment Case Management. Assertive community treatment is an intensive case management model with low caseloads and frequent, community-based contact with clients. The model is grounded in a multidisciplinary team approach where all team members share the caseload and work together to provide proactive services, assertive outreach, and strong advocacy to clients. The case management team provides many services to the client directly and, if referring to an outside agency, carefully monitors the relationship between the client and the service provider(s) (Bond, Salyers, Rollins, Rapp, & Zipple, 2004).

Clinical/Rehabilitation Case Management. In this approach to case management, those providing case management services deliver the clinical treatment as well, providing both in an integrated manner. The case manager in this model has the primary responsibility for providing therapeutic intervention, including therapy, counseling, skills teaching, and other rehabilitative interventions along with case management services (Anthony, Cohen, & Farkas, 1990).

These four approaches to case management will be referred to from time to time throughout the chapter. As we progress further, it will become clear that elements of each case management model are used in community corrections. Further, the more reintegrative the program, the more integral is the case management function. Given that this text's function is one that advocates reintegration of offenders, the student should understand that case management serves as the organizational backbone behind all offender reformation efforts. It is the case management process that ties the community and the community supervision agency together, as was discussed in Chapter 2. Indeed, the case management system works in tandem with the community supervision officer's caseload assignment, and it also integrates the use of volunteers, as covered in Chapter 2. See Focus Topic 8.1 for the specific duties and activities of a case manager.

THE ROLE OF THE CASE MANAGER

1. The case manager is responsible for outreach activities in order to identify community social problems, and in order to bring at-risk individuals into helping services systems.

2. The case manager conducts assessments of the client and of his or her problematic situation.

3. The case manager develops a plan for remediation of the problems in social or psychological functioning.

4. The case manager is responsible for identifying and keeping a record of programs and services in the community.

5. The case manager is responsible for linking the client to the needed service providers in the community.

6. The case manager monitors and evaluates the client's participation in the programs and services.

7. The case manager maintains liaison with other professionals and with other agencies in the community, and works collaboratively with them on behalf of the client.

8. The case manager provides supportive counseling services to the client's family and to other persons in the community who may have an impact on the client.

9. The case manager advocates on behalf of the client with respect to the development of needed resources in the community.

10. The case manager provides supportive counseling services to the client, including crisis-oriented services.

Before proceeding further, it is important to distinguish between two key concepts: caseload management and case management. For this text's purposes, **case management** *is the process whereby an offender is provided fully comprehensive and coordinated services* that address the offender's vocational, social, educational, and mental health functions. All aspects of the offender's needs, including basic medical, housing, and food accommodations, are provided within this coordinated program of service delivery, the goal being to help the offender become a fully functioning member of society. The previous description is what we mean when we refer to case management in this text. The student is encouraged to refer to Figure 8.1 for an illustration of the case management model that demonstrates the interrelated nature of multiple actors in the process.

Caseload management, on the other hand, *is the process that we use to assign supervision workloads to community supervision officers.* This takes into account the number of offenders, the security risk of those offenders, and the specialized needs they may have. The more serious the security risk or the more profound the needs, the more intensively that offender must be supervised,

Photo 8.2 The Rays of Sonshine facility is a faith-based drug treatment program. Case management principles are routinely applied as offenders are guided through the recovery process.

FIGURE 8.1 Case Management Model of Offender Reentry

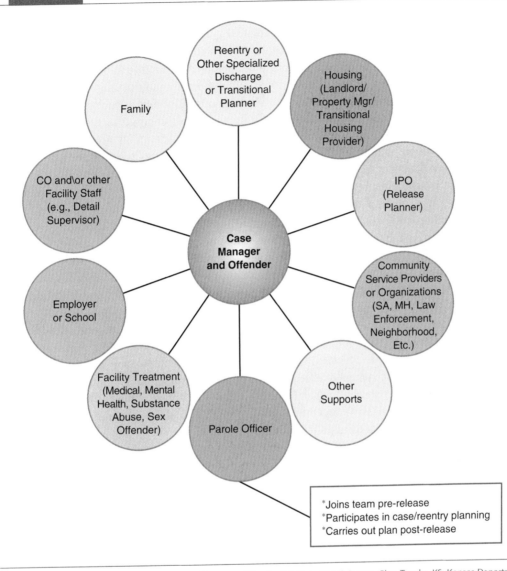

SOURCE: Kansas Department of Corrections. (2006). *Kansas Offender Risk Reduction & Reentry Plan*. Topeka, KS: Kansas Department of Corrections.

resulting in fewer offenders in a caseload, under a balanced system of caseload management. Naturally, lower security risks and fewer specialized needs of offenders would result in more such offenders being on a community supervision officer's caseload.

CLIENT NEEDS ASSESSMENT

Obviously, the needs of the offender are primary in the process of case management. However, the needs of the offender are not just balanced against considerations of security risk; they are also counterbalanced by the resources that are available to the agency and the community. The effective use of resources is critical for both the agency and the community because this can optimize overall recidivism outcomes. In addition, the effective use of resources ensures that the budget maintains integrity. Last but just as important, the effective use of resources optimizes the number of offenders that are given appropriate assistance, thereby enabling the reintegrative process to be optimized. One primary aspect of accomplishing this has been through a process of offender classification. If existing resources are to be appropriately matched to offenders, and if future resources are to be intelligently planned (i.e., based on systemwide profiles and projections), then classification data gathering, recording, and initial decision making become critical. Existing technology and accumulated professional experience can make classification an effective tool of correctional management.

The failure to provide a reasonable level of "matching" of needs and programs has come under scrutiny both in prison conditions suits and in professional corrections. Court findings have addressed the harm that often results when offenders are indiscriminately housed in overly restrictive facilities and when needed services or special management is not provided. Correctional officials are also recognizing the financial and internal management implications of failing to realistically assess offender risk and special needs. For example, maximum security space, which is disproportionately costly, warrants very judicious use. The early identification of needs often can prevent deterioration—physical, psychological, and social—that may occur if left unchecked. From a humane point of view, deterioration of an offender is always costly. From a management perspective, unmet needs have widespread and predictable side effects regarding recidivism.

Parallel challenges exist in the areas of offender needs, management practices, and service provision specifically related to custody and security. The offender needs assessment is critical to the overall reduction of recidivism. In fact, the typically high recidivism rates during the first year to 3 years of offender release from prison likely has to do more with a failure to address needs than anything else. In their research over 20 years ago, Clements, McKee, and Jones (1984) noted that one of the most serious challenges to effective program delivery is the development of effective objective screening devices. The authors pointed out that with such instruments, staff are able to apply standardized criteria that are uniformly weighted to identify the relative demands for services. Without this level of objectivity, it is less likely that all offenders who exhibit symptoms of need would be uniformly attended to.

The work of Clements et al. (1984) is important for two reasons. First, their claims related to needs assessment are completely true and accurate even today. The needs assessment process is critical both to aiding the offender and to the budgeting and scheduling of the agency's resources. This dual factor is important in its own right, but it also dovetails with the goals of case management that were just discussed. As a means of matching the offender needs with the various services in a coordinated and comprehensive fashion (see again Figure 8.1), the initial needs assessment serves as the basic foundation of the entire case management process. Indeed, without knowledge of the offender's needs, there can be no effective case management to implement. Thus, the case manager must have a starting point—a baseline—from which to start and from which services are identified that will be of benefit to the client. The needs assessment is that starting point, and from there, the case manager progresses, identifying the most important needs first and addressing them in priority rank order.

As just noted, some needs will be more important (or more necessary) than others for a particular offender. The severity of needs is used as the criterion for rank ordering or prioritizing the case management process and (naturally) ties in to the treatment planning process as a whole. Because severity of a need is critical to understanding the order of service delivery for the client, the use of objective criteria is necessary for the development of scales to determine the severity of need to be used. This is an effort to ensure that the most efficient allocation of scarce resources goes to those offenders that have the greatest need. Further, the use of standard screening techniques also helps to ensure that the agency meets its responsibility of providing each offender with the opportunity for self-help in addressing deficiencies.

The second reason that the work of Clements et al. (1984) is so important is that their work (specifically written with the correctional population in mind) clearly points toward the need for effective assessment and classification instruments and processes. This is a very important aspect of this current text, and Clements et al. show that this has been true in the field of reintegration for over two decades. Assessment and classification are of course critical in multiple areas of offender processing, not just in those areas related to security. The utility of instruments for non-security objectives is a primary point to this chapter, as the remainder of the text will move away from a focus on security to one based on offender reintegration strategies.

Just as with the need to clarify our definition of case management (especially when compared with caseload), it is perhaps important to also clarify what is meant by the terms *need* and *assessment*, particularly as they relate to each other from the perspective of needs assessment rather than security assessment. A *need* is generally defined as follows:

1. A lack of something requisite, desirable, or useful

2. A condition requiring relief

3. A pressing lack of something essential

Clearly, this definition is highly dependent on criteria; that is, one has to decide ahead of time on the conditions, states, or behaviors that are "requisite, desirable, useful, or essential" or that require "relief." In this context, "need" implies deficit. Such deficits may characterize an individual across a variety of settings, or be problematic (or even recognizable) only in a highly particular situation. Those identifying a need carry some obligation to respond to it—practically, socially, legally, or ethically. This sense of responsibility, and the sometimes elaborate structures that go with it (e.g., guidelines for hospital care), vary widely and reflect the degree of importance given to a particular need or set of needs.

Moreover, needs exist in degrees along a continuum from the barely perceptible to the glaringly obvious. One can have minor or monumental needs or deficits. The determination of the nature and degree of need arises from some type of assessment.

The term *assessment* is defined as follows:

1. Appraisal; estimation

2. A determination of importance, size, or value

Given these two basic definitions, we can easily see how the term *needs assessment* has become so widely used. Without assessment, the concept of need remains highly abstract or becomes limited to only the most obvious, critical, and popular areas. We do not suggest that the idea of need should extend into every trivial dimension of human concern. Rather, the process of needs assessment must provide both the tools to determine a given need and a context in which to judge its importance (Clements et al., 1984). With both the terms *needs* and *assessment* defined, we can now provide a working definition for needs assessment. For this text's purposes, the term **needs assessment** will refer to those aspects of offender classification that seek to identify or determine the condition or state of individuals relative to some preestablished functional criteria. These criteria may relate to more concrete attributes of adjustment (such as physical or psychological health); to behavioral skills that involve practical functioning (e.g., academic or vocational competence); or to more complex social situations in which deficits are measured relative to particular environments, conditions, or demands (e.g., vulnerability, personal/social skills).

TABLE 8.1   Levels of Assessment of Needs

Level or Type of Need	Scope	Decision or Function
Intake Screening of Needs	Basic needs	Initial assignment, management, and basic referral decisions
Dispositional Needs Assessment	Specific program areas	Assignment to group or offender category for specific foci of intervention
Intensive Needs Assessment	Priority areas of need	Individualized treatment planning for the offender

SOURCE: Clements, C. B., McKee, J. M., & Jones, S. E. (1984). *Offender needs and assessment: Models and approaches.* Washington, DC: National Institute of Corrections.

When considering the appraisal of an offender's needs, it is important to distinguish among successively refined levels of assessment. Each level of assessment involves a more specific focus and a more individualized evaluation of the offender. This then allows for refined matching between the needs of the offender and the specific services or interventions that are given.

As demonstrated in Table 8.1, the refinement of the classification process correlates with the level of assessment. At a primary level, **intake screening of needs** should result in a series of judgments that subdivide offenders into broad categories of basic needs or deficits. This then points case managers in the general direction for referral of offenders to generalized service areas. From the first level of analysis, the **dispositional needs assessment** provides additional information within one or more given need dimensions regarding the specific program or treatment that would benefit the offender. Finally, more **intensive needs assessment** would result in highly detailed intervention plans within a priority need area. Each level of assessment may require, in turn, the increased involvement of professionals who network with the community supervision agency, such as those representing job placement programs, educational institutions, medical services, or mental health treatment facilities. Another view of assessment levels sees the process as a "funnel" (Clements et al., 1984). Clements et al. describe such an outlook most aptly in the following excerpt:

> Different techniques are required, depending on the stage of assessment. At a wide mouth of the funnel, screening procedures may be employed to determine which persons would profit from treatment. Since a large number of people usually undergo screening, these procedures should be relatively inexpensive in terms of both cost and time. . . . Once the client has been selected, a broad range of information should be gathered. . . . Interviewing, self-report questionnaires, ratings by others, and self-monitoring may be techniques particularly appropriate for this broad assessment. Eventually, the assessment funnel narrows and more specific information is sought . . . [through] techniques [which] may include observations in naturalistic situations, self-report questionnaires, self-monitoring, physiological measurement, intelligence or achievement testing, or behavioral by-products. (p. 17)

Students should look ahead in the chapter to Figure 8.2 for an example of a classification form related to the classification of multiple offender needs. Multiple forms and tools such as that figure may be required, just as the excerpt above indicates. Further, it should be remembered that all people change over time; they also change as they encounter new experiences. This includes offenders as well. For better or worse, the offender is likely to have experienced some form of insight or addition to his or her repertoire of memories and experiences. This means that a person's needs do not stay the same. Some needs disappear, other new needs emerge, and others become either more or less severe over time. Thus, the needs assessment should not be viewed as a "one shot" exercise, but instead as a continual process of refinement that is repeated throughout an offender's supervision sentence. Naturally, there may be points at which repeat needs assessments are conducted, but they nonetheless should be updated regularly throughout a sentence of supervision that lasts for several years.

Thus, again, the needs assessment process is not limited to any one time, place, or stage in an offender's passage through the community supervision process. The basic principles of good assessment when determining offender needs would include the following:

1. Detecting critical needs that would be problematic in any setting (e.g., acute illness).

2. Identifying deficits or needs that may have influenced or been part of a pattern of law violation (criminality) or which may interfere with successful reintegration (e.g., drug abuse, impulse control, vocational deficits) (see Figure 8.2 for an example of a basic needs assessment scale).

3. Determining offenders' deficits, needs, traits, or behaviors that influence their adjustment or management while in prison (e.g., vulnerability, personal/social skills).

4. Serving broader human needs, e.g., for structure, activity, support, privacy, and so forth. Each purpose is usually associated with a different approach to assessment and intervention. Typically, these diverse needs are addressed by different agencies throughout the community.

Reliability and Validity of Needs Assessment Scales

As was true in Chapter 3 regarding risk assessment and prediction, the reliability and validity of needs-based assessment tools is important. The student should refer back to that chapter for a discussion on the various types of validity and reliability related to assessment scales. Though the primary focus in Chapter 3 was on assessment tools related to security classifications, all of the essential assumptions are equally applicable to any needs assessment. With this said, students should keep the following points in mind as we close our discussion on the needs assessment process.

The assessment system should use highly reliable information, instruments, and techniques. Any substantial investment of time and resources is best served by using only those techniques or instruments that can be consistently administered. The goal is to achieve a degree of uniformity that tends to yield comparable information from case to case. Moreover, officials, when relying on particular instruments or tests, must consider their inherent reliability characteristics. Finally, assessments should be conducted in settings and under conditions that are most conducive to obtaining full and accurate information.

Methods should be used that are specifically valid for and relevant to the assessments and decisions being made. A given instrument or method is not inherently valid; its relevance must be established for each specific purpose for which it is to be used. Needs assessment must move away from "shotgun" approaches in which information of widely varying reliability and validity is all fed into the "black box" of classification. In most instances, we need to limit sharply the generalization of information (or predictions) to those individual behaviors or conditions that have some known relationship to the assessment instrument or method.

FIGURE 8.2   Initial Offender Classification Assessment of Needs

Exh. 1

**INITIAL INMATE CLASSIFICATION
ASSESSMENT OF NEEDS**

NAME _____   NUMBER _____

Last   First   MI

CLASSIFICATION CHAIRMAN _____   DATE _____/_____/_____

TEST SCORES: _____   _____   _____

I.Q.   Reading   Math

NEEDS ASSESSMENT: Select the answer that best describes the inmate.

HEALTH:

1 Sound physical health, seldom ill

2 Handicap or illness that interferes with functioning on a recurring basis

3 Serious handicap or chronic illness, needs frequent medical care

_____ code

INTELLECTUAL ABILITY:

1 Normal intellectual ability, able to function independently

2 Mild retardation, some need for assistance

3 Moderate retardation, independent functioning severely limited

_____ code

BEHAVIORAL/EMOTIONAL PROBLEMS:

1 Exhibits appropriate emotional responses

2 Symptoms limit adequate functioning; requires counseling, may require medication

3 Symptoms prohibit adequate functioning; requires significant medication or intervention, may require separate housing

_____ code

ALCOHOL ABUSE:

1 No alcohol problem

2 Occasional abuse, some disruption of functioning

3 Frequent abuse, serious disruption, needs treatment

_____ code

DRUG ABUSE:

1 No drug problem

2 Occasional abuse, some disruption of functioning

3 Frequent abuse, serious disruption, needs treatment

_____ code

EDUCATIONAL STATUS:

1 Has high school diploma or GED

2 Some deficits, but potential for high school diploma or GED

3 Major deficits in math and/or reading, needs remedial programs

_____ code

VOCATIONAL STATUS:

1 Has sufficient skills to obtain and hold satisfactory employment

2 Minimal skill level, needs enhancement

3 Virtually unemployable, needs training

_____ code

SOURCE: Clements, C. B., McKee, J. M., & Jones, S. E. (1984). *Offender needs and assessment: Models and approaches.* Washington, DC: National Institute of Corrections.

Assessment approaches must provide for the potential for change across time and settings. Some individual needs may be relatively static (e.g., physical disability) and may require a fairly constant response or management or environment. Still other needs can be seen as recurring (e.g., exercise), thus requiring a continuing level of programming. Of more concern here, however, are those needs that are responsive to some degree of remediation or change. Since such changes should be measurable, follow-up assessments should be planned. Also, we must recognize that an individual's needs (especially in the interpersonal areas) may vary across settings. Clearly, then, descriptive labels should rarely be assigned to offenders on a permanent basis.

Cost-effectiveness is a commonsense, practical concern. A very expensive system or an approach yielding little useful information is an obvious—and thankfully rare—waste of resources. A reduction in costs can be accomplished, for example, by developing a referral system in which only selected offenders are given higher-level diagnostic assessments (e.g., for specific educational prescriptions). Effectiveness (often the forgotten side of the formula) can be enhanced through some of the principles cited above, for example, by selecting only reliable and valid assessment instruments. Moreover, the effectiveness of needs assessment becomes moot if inadequate and insufficient management and treatment options exist.

Mental Illness and Classification: The *DSM-IV-TR*

According to Carbonnell and Perkins (2000), mental health assessments attempt to answer questions about how and why people think, feel, and behave in the manner that they do. Issues pertaining to stress, emotional coping, ability to solve problems, and so forth may all be the focus in these types of assessments that ultimately may lead to some form of diagnosis. While these forms of mental health assessment may seem to be specific to psychopathology, it should be noted that many diagnostic factors related to psychopathology arise when dealing with the criminal offender. Indeed, there is an inflated representation of mental illness among offenders in prison and on community supervision (Bartol, 2002). Further, it is estimated that close to 30 percent of all offenders in maximum security institutions may have an antisocial personality disorder (Ashford, Sales, & Reid, 2002). Likewise, conduct disorder, oppositional-defiant disorder, and attention-deficit/hyperactivity disorder are highly represented among child and juvenile offenders. Dementia is encountered among the elderly offender population. Various mood and substance abuse disorders are found among those offenders with communicable diseases. In fact, it is thought that the majority of inmate offenders have some form of substance abuse problem (Bureau of Justice Statistics, 1999). This is not so surprising, since over 50 percent of inmates report that they had used drugs or alcohol at the time of arrest for the sentence they were serving (Bureau of Justice Statistics, 1999). Further, approximately 73 percent of federal and 83 percent of state prison inmates noted that they had abused substances within the 12-month period prior to incarceration. Fully 70 to 80 percent of all offenders are thought to have some form of substance abuse problem (Bureau of Justice Statistics, 1999). Since substance abuse disorders are considered diagnosable, mental health again becomes central to the assessment and diagnosis of the offending population.

Each of the above listed disorders or mental health issues is included within the *DSM-IV-TR*, which is the common vernacular for the ***Diagnostic and Statistical Manual of Mental Disorders***, 4th edition, text revision. This text is often referred to as the "bible" of mental health clinicians and diagnosticians. The *DSM-IV-TR* allows mental health practitioners to label, or diagnose, an individual (in this case, an offender) so that the individual can be better categorized for further treatment interventions. This is a necessary process when attempting to match the client with the correct treatment modality. Further, as will be seen in subsequent chapters, many special needs offenders will qualify for two, three, or more diagnoses, making them dual or *comorbid* in their diagnosis. This means that the proper diagnosis of special needs offenders can be quite complicated. In spite of this complexity, the *DSM-IV-TR* diagnostic categories provide important information when developing treatment plans for the offender.

The *DSM-IV-TR* criteria applied to a case are all based upon the judgments of the practicing clinician. This determination will therefore have a high degree of subjectivity that can only be balanced if the clinician is adequately trained to work with the offender population. But, presuming the clinician is adequately trained and experienced, this process of diagnosis can be very effective. Naturally, this process of diagnosis also ties in to the previously discussed structured interviews and observations. The clinician should be skilled at this process, and, ideally, the same person conducting the initial subjective structured interview should also be responsible for applying any diagnoses from the *DSM-IV-TR*. In fact, this should be a requirement among all quality mental health providers.

The *DSM-IV-TR* is a *multiaxial* system in that it involves an assessment of the offender on several different "axes." Each axis refers to a different area of content information that can assist a clinician in planning treatment for an offender, and it can also aid in the prediction of the treatment outcome with that offender. There are five axes included in the *DSM-IV* multiaxial classification, as shown below:

Axis I Clinical Disorders
    Other Conditions That May Be a Focus of Clinical Attention

Axis II Personality Disorders
    Mental Retardation

Axis III General Medical Conditions

Axis IV Psychosocial and Environmental Problems

Axis V Global Assessment of Functioning

The use of this multiaxial system facilitates comprehensive and systematic evaluation while paying attention to various mental disorders and general medical conditions, psychosocial and environmental problems, and the offender's overall level of functioning. This approach thus examines the many facets of the offender that might otherwise be overlooked if the focus were on assessing a single presenting problem.

This section of the chapter will provide a brief discussion of the various axes and their corresponding disorders. No in-depth discussion of each individual disorder will be provided. Rather, it is the purpose of this chapter to simply acquaint the student with the *DSM-IV-TR* and to demonstrate how this clinical guide is organized. The main point is to give the student a clear and specific idea of how offenders with mental health issues are ultimately diagnosed.

Axis I consists of clinical disorders or conditions that may be the focus of clinical attention. The disorders included in this category are as follows:

1. Disorders diagnosed in infancy, childhood, or adolescence (excluding mental retardation)

2. Delirium, dementia, amnestic, and other cognitive disorders

3. Mental disorders due to a general medical condition

4. Substance-related disorders

5. Schizophrenia and other psychotic disorders

6. Mood disorders

7. Anxiety disorders

8. Somatoform disorder (Briquet's syndrome)

9. Factitious disorders

10. Dissociative disorders

11. Sexual and gender identity disorders

12. Eating disorders

13. Sleep disorders

14. Impulse-control disorders not otherwise classified

15. Adjustment disorders

The **Axis II** category includes both personality disorders and mental retardation. This axis is also sometimes used to note maladaptive personality characteristics and defense mechanisms that the offender may use to avoid disclosure. These disorders are placed on a separate axis to ensure that symptoms from the personality disorders are not convoluted with the symptoms of those disorders in Axis I. Thus, such a structure ensures organization and accuracy of the clinical diagnosis. The disorders included in this category are as follows:

1. Paranoid personality disorder

2. Schizoid personality disorder

3. Schizotypical personality disorder

4. Antisocial personality disorder

5. Borderline personality disorder

6. Histrionic personality disorder

7. Narcissistic personality disorder

8. Avoidant personality disorder

9. Dependent personality disorder

10. Obsessive-compulsive personality disorder

11. Mental retardation

The **Axis III** category includes general medical conditions that are potentially relevant to the understanding or management of the individual's mental disorder. Typically, Axis III considerations are frequent among those offenders possessing communicable diseases and among geriatric offenders. A partial list of general medical conditions included in this axis is shown below:

1. Infectious and parasitic diseases

2. Diseases of the nervous system and sensory organs

3. Immunity disorders

4. Diseases of skin, musculoskeletal, and connective tissue

5. Diseases of the digestive, circulatory, and respiratory systems

The **Axis IV** category includes psychosocial problems that can aggravate diagnosis, treatment, and prognosis of an offender's mental disorders. A psychosocial or environmental problem may be a negative life event (financial problems, loss of employment), an environmental difficulty or deficiency (such as being in prison), familial or other interpersonal stress (such as divorce), inadequate social support (no family or reliable friends), or other problem related to the overall context in which the offender's issues have developed. The following individual problems are key examples included within the Axis IV category:

1. Problems with primary support groups

2. Problems related to the social environment

3. Educational problems

4. Occupational problems

5. Housing problems

6. Economic problems

7. Problems with access to health care services

8. Problems related to interaction with the legal system/crime

The last category, **Axis V,** deals with the overall functioning of the individual and is often referred to as the "GAF Scale"—Global Assessment of Functioning Scale. This scale is useful in tracking the clinical progress of an individual in global terms, using a single quick measure. The GAF Scale rates psychological, social, and occupational functioning. Its criteria are listed on Table 8.2.

The GAF Scale can be a useful mechanism for assessing the general functioning of an offender. This scale can be utilized as a supplemental screening device during structured interviews with mental health professionals. While it is informal in nature, it helps to augment other objective forms of assessment such as the Wisconsin Risk Assessment System. The GAF Scale likewise accounts for both static and dynamic risk factors (as discussed in Chapter 3) that are likely to be important for clinicians and community supervision staff alike. Though it is not expected that community supervision staff will necessarily rank order offenders using this scale, they should still be familiar with this rating system. In many cases, an offender's GAF score will be included in PSI reports, and this means that case managers and community supervision officers should consider this information as they become familiar with the offender's supervision challenges. If nothing else, it is useful for community supervision staff to understand how mental health personnel have ranked the offender, since this helps such probation/parole personnel to be informed about the perceptions of other practitioners involved with the offender's overall reintegration process.

CASELOAD ASSIGNMENT MODELS

The **model of caseload delivery** has to do with the process whereby offenders are initially assigned their community supervision officer. This is often determined by the agency size and the number of offenders under the agency's jurisdiction. Some models of caseload delivery may use a form of random offender assignment, or they may base the assignment on the geographical location of offenders to make the task of face-to-face supervision easier for the community supervision officer. However, other issues such as organizational culture and agency intent can affect the manner by which offenders are assigned to a given caseload. As the reader might recall, the caseload issue was discussed earlier in this chapter regarding caseload management, and in Chapter 6 regarding probation officers. In those discussions, the focus revolved around the workload

TABLE 8.2	Global Assessment of Functioning (GAF) Scale

Score	Narrative Level of Functioning
100–91	Superior functioning throughout most all activities, no serious problems with life adjustment issues; the person is specifically identified by others as having numerous positive qualities; the person has no apparent mental health symptoms.
90–81	A lack of symptoms, or few if any do exist. Overall, good functioning in all areas of life demands; the person is involved in a diverse array of activities, has good social skills, is generally happy with his or her life circumstances, and has few problems in social interactions.
80–71	If symptoms do appear, they are transient and within the normal range of expectations (for instance, displaying some frustration with day-to-day challenges); only slight impairment of social skills, work performance, or school performance.
70–61	A few mild symptoms such as mild depression or sleeping problems, or perhaps some difficulties in social interactions, work performance, or school performance. Generally, adequate functioning with at least some close and personal relationships.
60–51	Symptoms are in the moderate range such as a flat or bland affect or the visible display of nervousness or anxiety. Person has moderately effective social skills, moderate work and school performance. Individual has few friends and has somewhat routine conflicts at work and/or school.
50–41	Individual suffers serious symptoms such as with suicidal thoughts, severe obsessions, or criminal activities in response to impaired functioning. Will be very prone to have social skills deficits, and/or problems with work or school performance. Typically has no friends and is unable to maintain employment.
40–31	This individual may have some problems in identifying reality; communication processes are impaired, and the individual will likely have deficits in social skills, job functioning, and school performance. Family relationships will tend to be strained, abusive, or conflicted. Mood and adjustment problems will be clear to others near the individual.
30–21	Individual suffers from severe symptoms such as delusions or hallucinations. Has serious deficits in communication, discretionary judgment, and/or the ability to function in life (stays in bed all day, no job, home, or friends).
20–11	Individual is in danger of self-mutilation or suicide. Individual is dangerous to others, [is prone to] unexpected displays of violent behavior. Individual may fail to maintain minimal personal hygiene or may have severely impaired social skills.
10–1	Continual and serious danger of hurting self or others. Individual may be consistently unable to maintain minimal personal hygiene, or may be at risk for a serious suicidal act with death being a very likely outcome.
0	Information not sufficient.

SOURCE: Reprinted with permission from the *Diagnostics and Statistical Manual of Mental Disorders, Text Revision, Fourth Edition,* (Copyright 2000). American Psychiatric Association.

associated with various caseload assignments. For instance, a community supervision officer with a handful of hardcore offenders is likely to have a similar overall workload to a community supervision officer with numerous small-time offenders on his or her caseload. (The intensity of the supervision status of each offender typically determines the amount of work that is required to supervise that offender.) Finding an equitable match in officer workload and keeping things in equilibrium can be difficult. Unlike our previous discussions of this topic, however, the concern with caseload assignments here is more focused on ensuring that offender needs are met than on addressing the workload of community supervision officers.

Champion (2002) identifies three different types of caseload management models as follows: the *conventional model,* the *conventional model with geographic consideration,* and the *numbers game model.* A brief overview of each will be provided, simply to ensure comprehension. However, additional sections of this chapter will discuss more recent and advanced innovations related to case management and will also reemphasize the importance of assessment in the case management process.

The **conventional model** of case management involves the random assignment of offenders to community supervision officers. This model of case assignment results in officers having a mix of different types of offenders, which has pros and cons in developing equity in workload among officers and in optimizing service coordination for offenders. Champion (2002) notes that the conventional model is probably the most frequently used model in the United States. This model is simple to use because in reality, it is not even a model. It is simply assignment of offenders using a list of officers. There are no other logistical considerations, and offenders are assigned as they emerge. Though this is perhaps the most commonly used method of case assignment and management, it is somewhat haphazard in application and requires that a community supervision officer act as a "jack-of-all-trades" in many respects. This can be dangerous for community safety when some of these offenders should be given more specialized supervision to optimize both security and treatment outcomes. This method of case management is also likely to be more stressful than others for community supervision officers, since they essentially must learn to "do it all" and since their workload is determined more by luck and happenstance than a methodical and balanced approach based on evidence-based principles.

The **conventional model with geographic consideration** is common in many areas where it can be practically implemented. A prime determinant of this model is the amount of time that officers must spend traveling to various locations during their day-to-day routine of checking on offenders. This model has benefits for both the officer and the agency, since the officer's time traveling is minimized and since the agency can optimize the work efforts of the officer. Eliminating excessive travel time also provides the officer with more time for the visit itself and for the reams of paperwork that the officer must contend with. Students may recall from Chapter 4 that the backlog of paperwork was a notable source of stress. Thus, the consideration of geographic dispersal of an officer's caseload can help to reduce the stress of the job; this should undoubtedly improve morale of community supervision officers in the agency.

The next model is what Champion (2002) refers to as the numbers game model. The version of the **numbers game model** for this text consists of one where the agency defines a desired caseload per officer (such as 40 offenders), and the agency makes its hiring decisions based on this formula. For example, an agency employs seven community supervision officers and has a total of 400 offenders to supervise. This agency desires to have officer caseloads of 40 offenders per officer. The agency would need to hire three more officers to meet its caseload objective. This type of model is more useful for agency administrators than it is for the individual community supervision officer or the offender. Naturally, agencies will pick caseloads within their own budgetary considerations and, as such, the emphasis is on simply ensuring that numbers are distributed evenly, the only question being the specific number- per- officer that will be set by the agency. This approach is not too different from the conventional model, but it does ensure that the agency routinely addresses the caseload issues since hiring decisions are directly linked to the caseload assignment process itself.

The Specialized Needs Caseload Model

Generally speaking, the specialized needs caseload model is used when dealing with offenders in need of specialized services or treatment (Champion, 2002). Naturally, if and when it is possible, it would also be beneficial if the agency were to structure the caseload to be as geographically realistic as possible so that the supervision officers could reasonably make their visits. The **specialized needs caseload model** pertains to community supervision assignments of offenders who share common specialized needs such as substance abuse, sex offending, a given set of disabilities, and so on. This model is a derivative of the specialized caseload model presented in other works (see, for example, Champion, 2002). With this model, the officer assigned to these offenders will have special skills or training related to these needs.

Further, supervision officers will typically have a close rapport with the therapists and the treatment program that is utilized. Indeed, the supervision officer and the therapist should have a close working relationship, even if this is largely conducted by phone. Informal ties between the two should be fostered by both agencies, and supervisors on both ends could accommodate work schedules so that both are able to occasionally have lunch or other meetings with one another. The main idea is that the two work together as a team. The importance of these collaborative relationships between persons in various agencies was discussed in Chapter 2 and has been emphasized throughout various segments of this text. In order for specialized models to be correctly implemented, collaboration between different service providers is mandatory.

STANDARDS OF CLASSIFICATION

Students will recall that Chapter 3 provided an extensive discussion on security classification systems. This same information will be important for the purpose of this current chapter due to the fact that many of the treatment considerations will be tied to security considerations based on past offender behavior. As noted in Chapter 3, once the security risk of the offender on community supervision has been determined, the next step is to correctly "match up" the offender's treatment plan with the level of supervision determined by the Level of Supervision Inventory—Revised (LSI-R). Chapter 3 made it clear that this text advocates for the use of the MMPI-2 Criminal Justice and Correctional Report (MMPI-2 CJCR), since it is perfectly suited to "match up" the offender's treatment plan with the level of supervision and serves as an additional double-check when making security decisions from the LSI-R. Students will recall that this report works in conjunction with the MMPI-2 to provide information pertaining to the offender's needs assessment, risk assessment, and program planning within a correctional agency. This report identifies offenders who may suffer from thought disorders, serious depression, and alcohol and substance abuse and may need mental health treatment, as well as those that are most likely to be hostile, predatory, bullied, or victimized while incarcerated. The report also includes predictor items related to self-injury and suicide. Because of these elements, it is an effective clinical tool, particularly for treatment determinations.

This chapter seeks to move from the sole consideration of security needs to those of treatment. As such, an emphasis on case management has been presented so that students can observe the marriage that must take place between security and treatment functions if reintegration is expected to be successful. Since a sound assessment is the basic foundation to creating a strong marriage between these two spectrums of offender processing, the MMPI-2 Criminal Justice and Correctional Report and the Level of Supervision Inventory—Revised are presented as the premier standard in instrument selection for treatment and security concerns, respectively. For additional details regarding these instruments and the reasons for their selection, students are encouraged to review Chapter 3 in detail.

Though assessment is critical to overall success in treatment planning, it is only the first step. The next challenge is taking the data that is obtained from a variety of assessments and actually implementing it in the treatment process. This can be much more difficult than it may first appear. Consider that treatment specialists will have a considerable number of assessment tools, surveys, and other measures that they must keep track of. In addition, these professionals have the typical sundry array of forms, records, and so forth that other persons in community corrections tend to amass. While it is easy to collect this information and

Photo 8.3 As seen in this picture, case management systems tend to be automated in today's world of community supervision. A case management specialist prepares to examine offender records and make determinations regarding their cases, services received, and their performance while on community supervision.

place it in some offender file, it is another matter to be able to organize that information in a manner such that it can be applied to the treatment process itself. Thus, the connection from assessment to intervention can be difficult to make. If this connection is not made, then the data from the assessment becomes lost and serves no useful function. Further, this also means that treatment implementation will be less informed; the less that assessment data is used, the more likely that treatment programs will be misguided. This naturally results in ineffective programs and will also impair treatment outcomes for the program. It is with this in mind that attention is given to the case management classification process, with one program being showcased as the optimal solution in bridging assessment to the real world of case management, security classification, and treatment planning. This system is known as the Matrix, which is an intranet-based management system developed by Iowa's Sixth Judicial District Department of Correctional Services. More on this system is provided in the section that follows.

Case Management Classification— Presentation of a Model System

Problems associated with determining community supervision officer caseloads and workloads have been discussed earlier in this chapter and in Chapter 6. Likewise, Chapter 3 provided an extensive overview of the assessment and classification process associated with risk prediction and the assignment of levels of security. In addition, this chapter (as well as Chapter 3) has emphasized the need for effective case management within a treatment planning context. Each of these aspects of the offender supervision process is critical to the agency's success in monitoring its offender population and in improving overall outcomes. However, it is difficult to envision how all of these aspects are brought together as a collective whole, providing a comprehensive and yet cohesive process to identify the requirements and needs of offenders, the agency, and community safety. This process can be disjointed if not organized together and blended in such a manner as to ensure that all areas are addressed and that none are forgotten or overlooked in the process. As it turns out, there is an answer to this challenge, and Iowa's Sixth Judicial District Department of Correctional Services has provided that answer through a means that is data driven and evidence based in nature. Because of this, that system's model—which integrates all of these elements within one automated, computerized, and fully comprehensive program—will be presented. This system is known as the Matrix, and at this point we will turn our attention to the Matrix as a method of resolving the challenges of establishing a comprehensive case management classification process.

The Matrix, an intranet-based management system developed by Iowa's Sixth Judicial District Department of Correctional Services, is designed to address risk, need, and responsivity. The primary mission of the Matrix is to assist the officer, the agency, and the court in selecting the most desirable intermediate sanction or the least restrictive alternative to incarceration, commensurate with community safety, to control or change offender behavior. The Matrix automates the process of identifying appropriate options, based on risk, need, and responsivity, and presents those options to agents along with a range of information for decision support. It is also helping the district to develop protocols for delivering effective services while using resources wisely, and it provides administrators with useful information for agencywide resource allocation.

The Matrix synthesizes data from several assessment tools, such as the Level of Supervision Inventory (LSI-R) and the Iowa Classification System, and uses these data to plot a position for each offender on a 16-cell matrix grid. The staff psychologist in the Client Services Unit can provide further assessment using the HARE Psychopathy Checklist—Revised (PCL-R) to test for such factors as aggressiveness, and other assessment results are included as needed. For example, Matrix data also identify offenders who are high-risk limit setters and those who may have gang ties or other antisocial issues such as those described by Andrews and Bonta (1999). Additional data used include demographics, criminal history, and supervision status (see Figures 8.3 and 8.4).

The Matrix consists of two axes: risk (control) and need (treatment). The instrument operates on the principle that, to supervise offenders, one must assess both areas and use that information in developing a supervision and treatment strategy. Four levels are possible on each axis: low, moderate, elevated, and high. From this point, the offender population is broken into 4 major groups and 16 subgroups. Specific control and treatment options available to offenders in each subgroup are presented to agents via Matrix screens. The screens provide users with a range of case management interventions consistent with the offender's risk level and criminogenic needs (or dynamic risk factors). Matrix placements are fluid, enabling offenders to move up and down on both axes depending on their response to supervision. Generally, such movement occurs after an offender has successfully completed programming or in response to violating behavior.

The Matrix interfaces with a database to provide agents with data on offender success rates, program effectiveness, client profiles, and other information. By inputting information unique to the individual offender, the officer can match programming to the offender profile, thus maintaining the principle of responsivity. In working with a particular offender, the officer simply examines the system as displayed on the computer screen to find the supervision and treatment strategies available for working with offenders assigned to a given grid cell (see Figure 8.5). Buttons on the left margin of the computer screen provide links to additional information, such as potential responses to violation that may be appropriate for offenders in

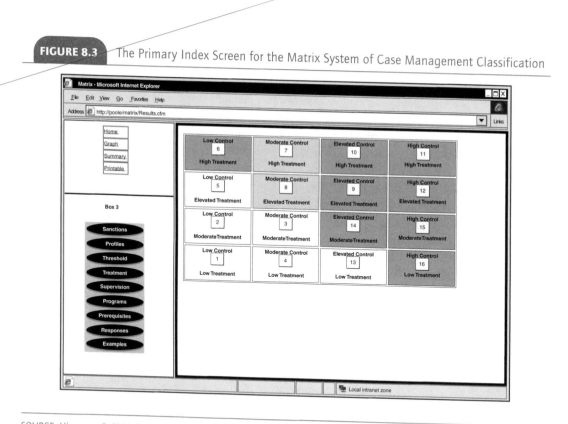

SOURCE: Hinzman, G. (2000). The Matrix: Matching the offender with treatment resources. *Topics in Community Corrections,* 2000 annual issue, 17–22.

a given grid placement, thresholds for response, and so forth. Staff select the appropriate option(s) for treatment or supervision based on the offender's case management history and available resources. These resources include diagnostic and treatment services for persons with attention-deficit/hyperactivity disorder (ADHD) and those dually diagnosed with substance abuse and mental health behavioral problems. Once an option is selected, the Matrix automatically displays the aggregate success rate for the option as applied in other Sixth District cases at the same grid level.

In addition, one can access common definitions of terms as well as a bibliography of research material related to the specific program options via the Matrix screen. For example, an officer exploring the use of the LSI-R could check the bibliography and find in Andrews and Bonta's (1999) work the "big four" factors related to antisocial issues. The Matrix also facilitates the development of protocol and policy to provide the best practice for managing scarce resources. For example, in addition to identifying a continuum of sanctions, the Matrix also suggests a continuum of treatment. The subtle benefit of developing a protocol for a continuum of treatment is that staff are not required to "ratchet up" responses to an offender's failure to comply. In fact, one of the assessments incorporated into the Matrix is the University of Rhode Island Change Assessment (URICA), which measures readiness for change. The Matrix also allows the agency to establish response thresholds and appropriate responses for all violating behaviors.

The Matrix offers the ability to use an assessment-driven response to move offenders up or down on a continuum of sanctions or a continuum of treatments to provide for public safety and identify an appropriate response to risk and need. It also makes possible the development of an objective and equitable protocol for moving offenders within a range of treatments and sanctions as well as providing an objective criterion for revocation responses. Although further development is still under way, the Sixth District has field-tested the Matrix during the past year and has been very satisfied with its success. The Sixth District has charted Matrix

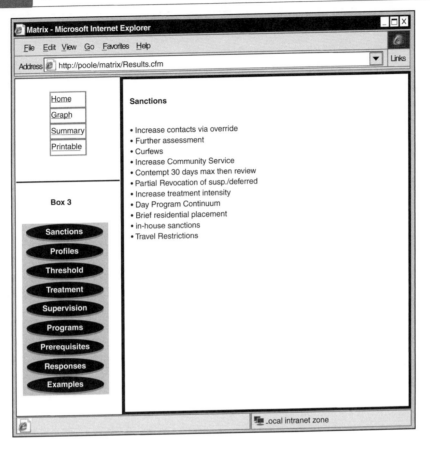

SOURCE: Hinzman, G. (2000). The Matrix: Matching the offender with treatment resources. *Topics in Community Corrections,* 2000 annual issue, 17–22.

placements over substantial time periods. Using data from 1,132 placements, court staff have plotted client placements separately by control axis and by treatment axis.

The Matrix system also has a three-dimensional placement graph (see Figure 8.6). This visual aid allows staff to examine resource needs and identify gaps. From an administrative perspective, it offers a clear look at resource allocation. For example, the graphic in Figure 8.6 shows that those clients who are moderate to elevated in both treatment and control appear to be those on whom the district needs to concentrate significant resources. To address the needs of offenders with high placement levels and those who are in the elevated groups (who together make up a smaller but very significant population), it may be prudent to use the URICA to measure their willingness to change or to engage in programming in a meaningful way.

In addition, community supervision agencies are able to make workload distribution decisions by reviewing the Matrix's information. For example, one can see how many limit setters simply need more structure to successfully complete the conditions of their supervision, and these offenders can then be matched with staff who excel in supervising this type of client.

FIGURE 8.5   Treatment Screen and Readings Supplement for the Matrix System

SOURCE: Hinzman, G. (2000). The Matrix: Matching the offender with treatment resources. *Topics in Community Corrections*, 2000 annual issue, 17–22.

FIGURE 8.6   Clients by Overall Matrix Placement

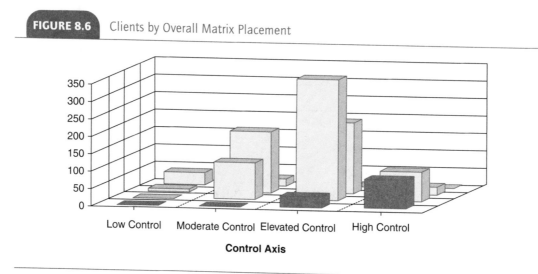

SOURCE: Hinzman, G. (2000). The Matrix: Matching the offender with treatment resources. *Topics in Community Corrections*, 2000 annual issue, 17–22.

It is important to understand that the process of developing the Matrix was not simple. It took this agency several years to develop the Matrix, and without extensive staff involvement, replication of the Matrix by other agencies would be risky. However, this system does demonstrate that serious-minded agency administrators have options in improving the assessment, classification, and case management of the offender population that they supervise. That said, the importance of staff training cannot be understated, as it is crucial to successful case management and to competence with any automated form of technology. The staff must have a fundamental knowledge of effective correctional interventions in order to apply them to case management. Further, they must be fully familiar with any case management software that an agency uses. Both of these areas of knowledge are critical if the agency is to improve security and treatment aspects of its work. Once the initial training for both areas of necessary expertise is completed, a fully automated and integrated method of case management implementation can begin.

> The Matrix is a practical application of the "What Works" literature. It is an excellent teaching tool for new officers who need to learn about practical case management concepts. The Matrix screens actually lead officers through the case planning process by prompting them to match identified client needs to resources that are locally available.
>
> *— Dot Faust,*
> *Director, Fifth District, Des Moines, Iowa*

SOURCE: Hinzman, G. (2000). The Matrix: Matching the offender with treatment resources. Topics in Community Corrections, 2000 annual issue, 17–22.

ASSESSMENT

The principles of correctional intervention indicate that the most effective use of resources is to target your highest-risk offenders. Agencies should use prescreening assessments to identify and divert lower-risk offenders. In the state of Iowa, the Iowa Risk Classification Assessment (modeled after the Wisconsin Risk Assessment) performs this crucial first step in the process. Once this assessment has been done, case management efforts need to be directed to the highest-risk offenders; lower-risk offenders are best managed by low-risk case managers.

Good case management is an integrated system that starts at the assessment interview. This initial interview is critical in setting the tone for the offender's investment in the case management process. For it to be effective, many staff will need to change their approach to conducting an interview. Most are familiar and comfortable with the "interrogation interview"—however, to discover the offender's "reality" and life situation, staff must use motivational interviewing techniques and suspend judgment while gaining insight into how the offender thinks and acts. It is also important to remember the case management plan while interviewing an offender, and to be sure to cover all areas that are critical for completing the plan.

For example, to understand the offender's pattern of behavior, it is important to know what led up to the offense(s), not just the date of the charge and the disposition of the case. If you are going to change behavior, you must have a clear understanding of when the problem behavior is most likely to occur and when the offender is likely to be most vulnerable. Two offenders may have committed the same crime but for very different reasons; exploring the motivation or the need being met by the behavior is a very important aspect of the case management interview. In many ways, this step is analogous to the ABC's (Antecedents, Behavior, and Consequences) of relapse prevention strategies.

In addition to conducting actuarial risk assessments, it is important to obtain data on personality traits, either by performing assessments or by gathering data from outside sources. There are a multitude of assessments, such as IQ tests, the Criminal Sentiments Scale, and Stages of Change, that also reveal pertinent information about an offender. Gathering this information directly or from collateral sources is important in developing programming tailored to the characteristics of the offender. Andrews and Bonta (2003) outline the need to develop interventions and programming in a style and mode that is consistent with the ability and learning style of the offender in order to maximize the effectiveness of the programming; this is known as the "responsivity principle."

Hong Kong Offender Risk/Needs Assessment

In Hong Kong, offender rehabilitation and classification falls under the purview of the Correctional Services Department. In October 2006, a "Risk and Needs Assessment and Management Protocol for Offenders" program was developed with assistance from the Chinese University of Hong Kong and the Correctional Service of Canada in an effort to objectively and scientifically evaluate an offender's specific needs for rehabilitation and risk for committing further crimes after release from custody.

This risk assessment considers seven basic main factors: (1) employment/vocation, (2) marital/family, (3) associates/social interaction or functioning, (4) substance abuse, (5) community functioning, (6) personal/emotional orientation or problems, and (7) attitude/criminal thinking. These factors are evaluated individually to determine the extent of influence on the future of an offender's reintegration into society. In addition, certain types of offenders (juveniles, sex offenders, substance abusers) must be assessed through interviews and psychological tests to determine the type and intensity level of treatment that will be required in order to discourage recidivism. For example, sex offenders are assessed on five additional psychological attributes: (1) rationalization, (2) expectancy, (3) empathy and super-optimism, (4) attitudes toward adult women, and (5) attitudes toward children. This information is entered into a computer program, which automatically determines the offender's risk as high, moderate, or low. Treatment is provided by psychologists, and compliance is monitored by correctional personnel.

The information obtained through the computer's automated system is used to help direct more resources for those offenders who are high risk, to use only those resources needed by the offender, and to develop better profiles of offenders who will recidivate. The Correctional Services Department continues to determine those factors that are the most accurate predictors of recidivism, as most psychological factors used in Western countries have to be modified to suit Hong Kong's social context.

SOURCE: Hong Kong Correctional Services Department. (2006). *Annual review*. Retrieved from http://www.csd.gov.hk/view/2007/index.htm.

Critical Thinking Question

1. Do you believe that a scientific approach to determining an offender's need for treatment is better than a subjective or personal approach? Why or why not?

For more information on Hong Kong Correctional Services, visit the website http://www.csd.gov.hk/view/2007/index.htm.

THE SUPERVISION PLAN

Once the assessments have been completed, the case management plan can be developed. The staff person needs to reflect back to the assessments and use the offender's descriptions of his or her circumstances and behaviors to design a plan that addresses the factors contributing to the problematic behavior. The case management plan should stress the application of new techniques and skills the offender will have learned in appropriate programs. To have the offender participate in cognitive programming is one thing, but having the offender apply what he or she has learned to real-life situations should be the goal, when looking to long-term behavior change. The format of the supervision plan can vary, as long as both agent and offender view the plan as a mutually agreed-upon document.

USE OF TECHNOLOGY

Technology such as the Matrix system developed by the Iowa Sixth Judicial District assists staff in pulling all the results of the various assessments together and then using the results to formulate a case management process. The Matrix will accept input from various risk assessments, including the LSI-R and other specialized assessments. Additional specialized assessments, including substance abuse evaluations, are also factored into the offender's Matrix placement. Offenders are plotted on the risk and need axes based on the results of the assessment materials entered into the matrix. The scores are then weighted and averaged. If the assessment indicates a high score, its impact on the axis placement will be greater. Each entry item affects one axis or both, depending on the item. Once the scores are plotted on the Matrix, the staff user has a menu of options from which to choose in developing a case management plan. The Matrix provides a profile of the offender, supervision strategies, interventions (programming), and sanctions.

The Matrix synthesizes all assessment information and graphically displays the results in an organized and meaningful way. These tools allow staff to use the information to design a consistent case management plan based on risk, needs, and responsivity principles. Technology tools like the Matrix function as quality control mechanisms in that they guide users in matching resources and programming that are consistent with the principles of effective correctional intervention.

Applied Theory — Containment Theory—Outer and Inner Containment Aspects

According to Walter Reckless's (1961) containment theory, there are pushes and pulls upon people that increase and decrease the likelihood of criminal behavior. These influences are due to both outer and inner containments. Outer containments consist of (1) limitations on one's behavior, (2) involvement in meaningful roles and activities, and (3) complementary variables such as reinforcement by groups. All of these issues are important, and the case management process works to address each of these aspects of outer containment when providing offenders with comprehensive services. Further, programs such as the Matrix placement system provide a multifaceted means of identifying the limits on offender behavior (security levels) while also implementing a needs assessment that provides for meaningful activities and group associations that can aid in the treatment process.

The inner containments associated with Reckless's theory are more difficult to ascertain among offenders. As Lilly, Cullen, and Ball (2007) state, "the individual who at one point might be operating in a context of powerful outer containment provided by regulating limits, meaningful roles, and a sense of integration ... might in a short time be operating in another context with few regulations. Inner containment would tend to control the individual to some extent no matter how the external environment changed" (p. 90). This is the precise state that reintegration practitioners hope to achieve when they combine comprehensive case management processes within supervision schemes. Over time, it is intended that offenders will behaviorally comply with various requirements and, at the same time, receive helpful services for their own reintegration. This ultimately will place them in a position where progressively lower levels of supervision are warranted as the offender increases his or her level of connection and involvement with society. It is in this regard that both case management and offender supervision work hand-in-hand, mimicking many of the concepts that have been espoused by Walter Reckless in his theory on outer and inner containments.

SOURCE: Lilly, J. R., Cullen, F. T., & Ball, R. A. (2007). *Criminological theory: Context and consequences* (4th ed.). Thousand Oaks, CA: Sage Publications.

CLIENT CONTRACTING AND SUPERVISION PLANNING

At this point, the case manager will create a design or strategy for intervention. The plan will always include several short-term and long-term goals. The short-term goals are usually designed to be achieved within 1 to 3 months, but the long-term goals will often involve a period of a year or more. These goals will be accompanied by a set of actions or techniques that will typically be written in behavioral terms. It is for this reason that theoretical tenets from behaviorism were presented in Chapters 1 and 2 as being integral to the community supervision process; these are the very building blocks of reform upon which our entire correctional system is built. The student may recall from Chapter 1 that the very use of any form of indeterminate sanction in itself suggests a belief that an offender's behavior can be shaped or modified through the use of incentives (rewards for good conduct or industrious labor). This is exactly what the tenets of operant conditioning contend in regard to human behavior, and this is the precise notion that drives the community corrections system. This particular point is important and warrants further discussion due to the prevalence of this orientation within the criminal justice system. A more extensive review of the basic tenets of operant conditioning is provided in subsequent paragraphs to ensure that students see a clear connection between the behavior-shaping aspects of supervision and the overall treatment planning for the offender as well as his or her reintegration and reformation. While these tenets were discussed in Chapter 1, they were presented more within a context of public safety and security, whereas in this chapter they are shown as being an integral component of the case management process. These processes are so important to the community corrections process that they are worthy of additional exploration. It is hoped that revisiting these concepts will reinforce learning from Chapter 1 while also communicating their importance to this text's approach to community supervision.

The most commonly used mechanisms that underlie behavioral forms of intervention are those associated with *operant conditioning,* as developed by B. F. Skinner (1953). The primary notion is that most behavior is controlled and maintained by the consequences that occur. Essentially, this type of behavior modification relies on four primary and well-known principles; positive reinforcement, negative reinforcement, positive punishment, and negative punishment. A brief overview of each of these concepts will be provided, but students should first understand that all four mechanisms are designed to aid in the *shaping* of desired behavior. **Shaping** is when behaviors are taught by reinforcing successive approximations of a desired behavior until the behavior is fully learned by the client. All aspects of behavior planning, modification, and contracting center on this primary objective as a means of altering family functioning and the performance of individual members.

Reinforcement essentially refers to the use of consequences that immediately follow a behavior and are contingent upon that behavior in order to increase the likelihood of the behavior occurring again. In most all treatment regimens, positive reinforcement is used. *Positive reinforcement* occurs when a benefit or privilege desired by the client is *presented after* the client engages in a behavior that is consistent with the treatment plan as a means of *increasing* the likelihood that the client will repeat the desired behavior. On the other hand, negative reinforcement, while seeking to increase the likelihood of the repetition of a behavior, does so by removing an unpleasant or aversive stimulus or event immediately after the desired behavior is completed. *Negative reinforcement* occurs when an event or stimulus that is unpleasant to the client is *removed after* the client engages in behavior that is consistent with the treatment plan as a means of *increasing* the likelihood that the client will repeat the desired behavior (see *positive reinforcers* and *negative reinforcers* in the Glossary).

While most treatment plans do tend to emphasize the use of reinforcement rather than punishment, behavioral psychology or behavioral therapy integrates the use of punishments as well. Essentially, the use of punishment is intended to decrease a behavior, but punishment has been found to be much less effective than the reinforcement of desired behavior. In fact, it is generally held that if one does not reinforce a behavior, it will eventually become extinct. Thus, **extinction** occurs when a behavior ceases due to a lack of reinforcement. The use of extinction is generally preferred to the use of punishment, but nonetheless the use of punishment is widespread throughout society and is a definite reality in the criminal justice system. As such, operant conditioning principles are important to understand, since many of the case management and supervision approaches operate from such a perspective. Positive punishment results from any stimulus that, when applied after an undesired behavior, reduces the likelihood of that behavior being repeated. Thus, as noted in Chapter 1, **positive punishment** occurs when an event or stimulus that is aversive to the client is *presented after* the client engages in a behavior that is not consistent with the treatment regimen, as a means of *decreasing* the likelihood that the client will repeat the undesired behavior. On the other hand, **negative punishment** (also covered in Chapter 1) occurs when an event or stimulus that is desired by the client is removed after the client engages in a behavior that is not consistent with the treatment regimen, as a means of decreasing the likelihood that the client will repeat the undesired behavior.

These principles of operant condition, reinforcement (both positive and negative), extinction, and punishment (both positive and negative) lie at the heart of behavioral forms of offender management and are the main structure upon which case management with offenders is built. One may recall that *social casework* (see Chapter 1) is the primary mode of offender case management in probation and parole. This process starts with theory and extends into the very skills and professional training helping professionals (case managers, social workers, counselors, and so forth) must have. As noted in Chapter 1, these skills include effective interviewing, fact-finding in the offender's background, and the ability to identify and distinguish surface from underlying problems. These are all skills that are important for the individual case manager to posses, being useful from both a treatment and a supervision standpoint. Likewise, during the process of goal setting, it is critical that case managers have the ability to distinguish between minor and major problems, as this will (as discussed earlier in this chapter) aid in prioritizing needs for the offender, which will translate to goal setting for offenders. These principles also lie at the heart of the supervision process, since offenders will often be punished for offenses committed while on community supervision. Conversely, they are rewarded if their behavior keeps them out of trouble. Though perhaps simplistic, it is a preferred modality in many criminal justice systems because of its straightforward approach and because it results in outcomes that are easily measured.

The key for most criminal justice agencies is that offender progress must be measured. This is consistent with the evidence-based trend in supervision where agencies seek data-driven programs that can be quantified and compared against one another. Further, when a client's progress and activities are listed in behavioral terms, they are easy to identify and tally. This adds a particular appeal to behavioral approaches. Moreover, as noted earlier, clients and the case manager set short- and long-term goals. These goals are usually termed in clear and easily marked and measured form. This again works well with the needs of the criminal justice system, since the specificity associated with well-defined goal setting makes progress easy to observe. Finally, as one may recall from Chapter 1, treatment planning (and case management) intervention involves activities, assignments, and routines that are designed to bring about behavior change in a systematic manner that ultimately results in goal-directed behavior toward the desired community supervision outcome. This last statement demonstrates that treatment planning, case management, goal setting, supervision strategies, and outcome evaluation are all interrelated in effective behavior-shaping models of offender reintegration.

At this point, the client must contract with the program or regimen, indicating compliance with the terms and conditions. Behavioral methods of case management are useful here because offenders, in many cases, do not have effective critical thinking skills, reading capabilities, or retention of what is desired from the process. Behavioral terms, with their clear and specific meaning, appeal to clients since they remove any ambiguity that the client may perceive in the terms and conditions. The more specific the terms and conditions, the better the behavior intervention plan is likely to be, and the better understood by the offender it is likely to be.

While the case management and supervision plan will tend to focus on these basic behavioral concepts, the goals and actions that they must adhere to should be tailored to each of the parolee or probationer's social or psychological problems. Thus, while many clients' supervision will have some similarities, the effective case management system will vary by offender to maximize the security and treatment functions available. This also ensures that the offender's needs are adequately met and helps to improve the prognosis of the offender through the recidivism reduction of offenders on the agency caseload.

ADDRESSING OFFENDER NEEDS HOLISTICALLY

As you may recall from the earlier definition of case management, the goal of case management calls for comprehensive services that address all aspects of the offender's needs, including basic medical, housing, and food accommodations. Such a goal is obviously well beyond the scope of a community supervision agency. This is one primary reason that this text has emphasized the use of community collaboration in both the security functions and the treatment functions associated with offender supervision. However, many agencies (at both the county and state level) are often financially strapped, and this creates a scarcity of resources, time, and ability to afford to case management issues.

When addressing the offender's needs holistically, it is important to again discuss the use of volunteers. Chapter 2 provides a good discussion on the use of volunteers in community corrections and demonstrates how such volunteers can fulfill a number of needs that are associated with offenders. As with the examples that were given toward the end of that chapter, volunteers are able to assist offenders in obtaining their basic needs, but they are also able to do so much more. Volunteers may develop an informal bond with the offender, providing social capital that may prevent that offender from recidivating or relapsing during low emotional points in his or her supervision. This is not to say that the case management process should simply be delegated to volunteers. Obviously, this would not be practical nor would it likely be effective. However, this point is meant to underscore the fact that a good volunteer network can fill in the gaps in the agency networking that occurs throughout the case management process.

The main point to this section of the chapter is to simply demonstrate that once a need is assessed, the offender must be connected with the source agency or person that is tasked with providing the service to fill that need. However, many aspects of case management are often overlooked, and, as some might say, the devil is in the details. For instance, transportation problems may occur—the offender may not be able to find public transportation. Problems with other general and mundane services may occur that most other people take for granted on a daily basis. Offenders may have difficulty finding friends and socializing, since their own prior friends may have all come from criminogenic backgrounds. In such cases, volunteers can help increase the range of possibilities that are offered by county and state agencies.

Nevertheless, when we talk about case management, we typically refer to the interconnected system of official agencies that are designed to provide services to offenders. Some such agencies may provide health services, others may provide specialized housing programs, and still others may provide food assistance. All of these are basic needs that do not even begin to address more complicated concerns related to treatment or recovery from substance abuse issues (a very common issue among the offender population). As with basic needs, the offender will of course need to be connected with those agencies and professionals that provide more detailed or specialized needs. While most issues of basic medical and other specialized information may go beyond the public safety concern that is at the heart of community corrections, they are not beyond the concern of the offender. Such services, when and where available, must be provided. Although such services are typically not related to the security or safety of the public, they must still be attended to so that the offender can function productively (thereby translating to a lower likelihood of recidivism). Mental health concerns, particularly those related to substance abuse issues (which incidentally include medical issues as well), will often require specialized screening or additional assistance.

Many laypersons may view substance abuse issues at a topical level. This is largely due to a misunderstanding of the complex social, psychological, and physiological processes involved with long-term drug or alcohol abuse. To fill the need for comprehensive services, a number of programs have emerged around the nation. The use of drug courts is perhaps the primary example. Their usage is based on a case management model that strives to provide offenders with a comprehensive set of services and interventions. Drug courts have been found to be effective, for the most part, and serve as a good example of the case management model in action within the community supervision context. Because substance abuse is such a widespread problem among the offender population, we now turn our attention to treatment screening and screening tools, while also considering corollary or comorbid issues associated with addiction.

TREATMENT SCREENING AND SCREENING TOOLS

Treatment screening is simply a process where an offender is asked a number of questions, either orally or in written form, and the responses given by that offender determine whether he or she is in need of some sort of treatment. For this text's purposes, **screening** is the process by which an offender is determined to be appropriate for admission to a given intervention program. The means of determining whether the offender is eligible largely depend on the focus of the service, the specific client population that the service is designed to accommodate, and the funding requirements of the particular agency. All of these factors have been discussed throughout this chapter as being part and parcel of the case management approach where the offender's needs are matched with appropriate agency services, being likewise impacted by the level of funding that exists for those services. Thus, screening is a natural component of the case management process. In fact, case management could not even exist if screening were not conducted.

As noted earlier, one of the key services relevant to offenders on community supervision is that of substance abuse intervention. In many cases, offenders may not have an arrest or formal charge against them that is related to alcohol or drugs, but this does not necessarily mean that they lack the need for services related to drug and alcohol abuse. In fact, roughly 60 to 70 percent of all offenders have some sort of drug or alcohol issue at the point of arrest, many being polydrug users. While this may not be the official charge against them (particularly after the plea bargaining process has been settled), it does highlight the fact that alcohol and drugs are a part of the offender lifestyle. Also keep in mind that there are those who are known to have substance abuse issues, while many others are likely to have such problems but have simply evaded detection. Thus, it is important in community supervision to be able to successfully and accurately screen for drug abuse. Later, in Chapter 13, further discussion will be provided regarding substance abuse and drug testing, particularly with urine and hair samples. However, this testing alone is not effective because the offender may later be in denial or may simply claim to have used illicit substances much less frequently than is true. Keep in mind that of all the services available through case management, this is one that most offenders wish to avoid, if they can.

Indeed, offenders typically tend to avoid both substance abuse and mental health interventions, if possible, due to both the stigma and the offender's desire to remain free from scrutiny. With this in mind, how does one go about screening offenders (who are known to be deceptive and often manipulative) for the eligibility of services that they actually do not want? Moreover, how does one use any information gleaned to aid in the intervention process? One instrument that is well-suited to address these questions is the **Substance Abuse Subtle Screening Instrument (SASSI)**, which provides interpretations of client profiles and aids in developing hypotheses that clinicians or researchers may find useful in understanding persons in treatment. The SASSI is a brief and easily administered psychological screening measure that helps identify individuals who have a high probability of having a substance use disorder. What is unique about this screening tool is that the SASSI is designed to identify substance-dependent offenders who may be unable or unwilling to acknowledge relevant substance-related behavior. In other words, the SASSI is able to detect deception and provides indicators of defensive responding by the person answering the questions. This instrument accomplishes this by asking a variety of questions that are only obliquely related to substance abuse and appear to the layperson to have little or nothing to do with such use. However, these questions have been tested statistically (time and again) and have been found to strongly correlate with responses to other questions pertaining to drug abuse. This means that the test is able to detect likely drug-abusing profiles from a range of questions that do not ask about drug or alcohol abuse. In fact, the Adult SASSI-3 identifies substance dependence with an overall empirically tested accuracy of 93 percent. This aspect of the SASSI makes it ideal for the offender population. Further, when the SASSI is used in combination with other available assessment information, SASSI profiles facilitate later treatment planning considerations.

Another instrument that is likewise used for substance abuse screening, intake, assessment, and evaluation is the **Maryland Addictions Questionnaire (MAQ).** This instrument is an excellent treatment planning tool, but it is also an effective screening and assessment tool that takes into account many of the factors related to assessment that were presented earlier, in Chapter 3. The MAQ is typically administered at intake, and it provides the evaluator with an idea of the severity of the addiction, the motivation of the client offender, and the likely risk of relapse. The MAQ also screens for cognitive and affective difficulties (anxiety and depression) that may complicate the treatment regimen. While all of these benefits are certainly great for the case manager and the treatment provider, the MAQ has one other dimension that is particularly well-suited for an offender population of clients—its validity scales, which detect inconsistent responding and defensiveness among persons completing the scale. Thus, similar to the SASSI, the MAQ is able to detect when offenders may be deceptive or unwilling to truthfully provide details necessary for successful intervention. This instrument, like the SASSI, is quick and easy to administer and thus does not require clinicians with extensive and costly licensures or certifications. This makes the MAQ a practical choice for agencies as well.

The last screening or assessment instrument to be discussed is the **Substance Abuse Relapse Assessment (SARA).** The SARA is a structured interview designed as a treatment planning instrument for treatment professionals who work with substance abusers. It is especially helpful in developing relapse prevention goals for clients who tend to use multiple substances and in monitoring the achievement of these goals during treatment. The SARA helps the individual to identify the events that typically precede his or her substance use, as well as the consequences that may reinforce that use. The SARA is designed for use with both juvenile and adult offenders who have a history of drug or alcohol abuse or whose ability to avoid relapse is in question. It is clear from this description that the SARA, unlike the SASSI and the MAQ, utilizes a subjective form of assessment (as described in Chapter 3), namely a structured interview. The SARA tends to be less effective at the initial screening point but instead works well in determining likelihood of relapse, thereby aiding treatment planners in designing interventions aimed at the prevention of relapse.

TREATMENT PLANNING

After the appropriate screening or assessment process has been completed, various treatment staff will typically work to develop a plan of action for the offender's reintegration. This plan of action, usually therapeutic in nature, is often referred to as the treatment plan. Students need to understand that treatment planning is not a one-time occurrence. Rather, it is a continual process that is refined over time as new challenges emerge and as the offender has successes and failures throughout the process. From this statement, it should be clear that offenders are expected to have some failures, and it is up to the treatment staff to aid the client in the difficult transition to reform.

It is important that the treatment staff get a clear picture of the underlying issues relevant to the client. This may not always be what the client overtly states to the counselor. Indeed, the client may be manipulative and may desire to throw the treatment staff off course throughout the treatment process. Treatment providers must identify the needs of a client in an effective and realistic manner. As has been indicated throughout this chapter, it is important that the client's basic needs are met before he or she can be expected to effectively dwell on any meta-needs such as belonging or actualization. Thus, basic needs must first be attended to for most all correctional clients. Keep in mind that when we talk about offender clients, we are typically referring to clients that have a lack of material resources, few job skills, and the social stigma of being an offender working against them, resulting in housing problems, medical issues, and so forth. Any attempt to deliver services amidst this chaotic set of circumstances will likely have dismal results unless effective interventions are in place.

In addition to the needs of the client, the client's strengths and resources must also be considered. In many cases, clients will not necessarily be aware of their own strengths or understand the resources they have available. Sometimes this may be due to esteem issues (not recognizing their own strengths due to a negative self-image), and at other times it may be because they simply have not thought of a given strength or resource as being such.

Naturally, caseworkers will want to ensure that the offender has clear objectives that are written down. These objectives should of course be prioritized, but, just as important, the client should clearly understand why a given order of priority has been assigned to goals and objectives. This teaches and reinforces a valuable skill that many offenders lack—long-term and sequential planning. In addition, a list of steps for each objective should be made. While this may seem mundane and perhaps overly detailed, it is important for clients who may not have had optimal socialization or educational training. Planning and organizing are critical skills for life success, and they should be emphasized when clients are in treatment.

In an ideal case, the correctional client fulfills all of his or her goals and objectives. In the real world, however, this seldom happens, at least initially. This does not mean that overall these clients are not successful with their programs; as pointed out earlier, there will be setbacks and offenders will inevitably experience failures on their road to reintegration. Regardless, once the offender has met the criteria for program completion, he or she should be discharged. At this point, the caseworker will need to, among other things, write a summary of the discharge elements as a means of recording the final outcome for the client while in the treatment program. In addition, the caseworker will need to have additional referrals available in case the offender has other issues or circumstances that he or she may wish to address. These may be corollary to the issues that the offender addressed with his or her counselor, and the offender may not be under any obligation to address such issues. (Often, court-mandated treatment can be very specific, overlooking key areas of needed treatment.) However, some offenders may wish to do so anyway. In such cases, it is important that agencies have an integrated system of services and resources available to aid the offender in his or her post-treatment functions and routines. If the caseworker is successful in arranging this, then it is likely a continuum of care can be achieved for the offender, providing a seamless transition from the role of a criminal justice number to be processed to that of a full-fledged, prosocial member of society.

Progress Notes, Record Keeping, and Connecting the Case Plan With Supervision

One of the most important elements of the case management process, and one that is directly addressed by ethical codes of conduct, is the accurate recording of notes pertaining to the activities of all counseling sessions. Recording and maintaining accurate records is important when guarding against potential liability concerns. In addition, case notes are vital to the process of treatment planning, since they help keep interventions focused on pertinent issues of concern to the offender. To keep treatment planning and intervention work on track, case notes should reflect the offender's progress, or lack thereof, especially as it relates to the particular goals of an offender. Case notes provide one avenue for treatment planners to stay focused on particular issues as well as to verify compliance with legal issues. Accountability is a vital component of the counseling process that must be adhered to. The best way to ensure accountability is to accurately and ethically note all happenings of the treatment process and then record these notes in appropriate files.

Finally, caseworkers must ensure that therapeutic staff and community supervision staff are apprised of the offender's programs, and appropriate insight regarding the offender's progress should be shared. In like fashion, community supervision officers should make certain that treatment staff are informed about noteworthy developments throughout the supervision process. It is in this manner that both supervision and treatment staff can work in tandem, thereby optimizing the offender's likely success. In essence, supervision staff can aid in ensuring offender compliance with attendance at treatment-related functions; caseworkers and treatment staff can likewise provide supervision staff with a more detailed picture of the offender's actual progress in meeting the goals of their supervision. In this way, the casework and security functions of community corrections can aid one another, both being indispensable to achieving successful offender outcomes. Close communication and collaboration between both groups of practitioners and the integration of community assistance make the true ingredients of any successful reintegration program, the result being less recidivism and a safer community.

CONCLUSION

Case management has a history that reaches back to early mental health treatment systems where clients were asked to provide their input into the treatment process. In addition, the use of multiple services led to the need for an organized approach of integration, resulting in the development of case management. However, before case management can be effectively implemented, one must learn the individual needs of a client to know which services are required. This calls for what is known as a needs assessment. The needs assessment compiles all of the different problems and challenges associated with an offender so that a list of needed services can be established. Both the caseworker and the offender provide input into this process, mirroring the early historical notions of case management. Further, these needs are prioritized, following any number of criteria to determine that priority. Once needs are thus identified and prioritized, the treatment plan is constructed to address them, in order of priority, as agreed upon between the caseworker and the offender.

While case management is a process designed primarily for offender reintegration and treatment, it is not entirely separate from the concerns of the community supervision agency. In fact, both work together to provide a coherent process of supervisory and treatment-based contact for the offender. Because case management and caseload management sound similar and both work together, hand-in-hand, they can be confused with one another. Case management, as it pertains to providing basic needs and therapeutic treatment for the offender, is typically associated with social service and mental health practitioners. Caseload management is primarily a process of workload division between community supervision officers so that the supervision of offenders is accomplished with near to equitable levels among officers within the agency.

Classification is important to case management, since it helps to determine priorities with different offender treatment plans and also classifies security levels for offender supervision. However, classification within the case management context is not identical to that conducted for security purposes. Security classification schemes were discussed in depth in Chapter 3, but in this current chapter, case management classification is presented as determining the likely treatment processes. However, this chapter provided an innovative model known as the Matrix, which is a fully integrated classification system that classifies offenders on both security and treatment spectrums. Thus, this model, an automated and high-tech system of data storage and retrieval technology, provides the perfect solution to integrating numerous forms of assessment data in a manner that simultaneously analyzes security, treatment, and agency resource considerations. In short, it is the premier system for multipurpose classification of offenders on community supervision.

Last, screening processes in treatment planning are important, and many are used when considering substance abuse interventions. Several were presented in this chapter, with two providing subtle screening that is designed to surreptitiously detect underlying issues that the offender might not otherwise report if asked directly. Further, these instruments are capable of detecting deceit, defensiveness, and manipulation among offenders. Because of these functions, these tools are considered superior to most screening processes that are overt and excessively face valid. Following appropriate screening, offenders are given a treatment plan for intervention, and it is at that point that actual therapeutic services are provided. Throughout the process, clinicians and supervision practitioners are both tasked with maintaining records to ensure the effective tracking of offender progress.

Key Terms

Assertive community treatment case management

Broker/generalist case management

Case management

Caseload management

Clinical/rehabilitation case management

Conventional model

Conventional model with geographic consideration

Diagnostic and Statistical Manual of Mental Disorders (DSM-IV-TR)

Dispositional needs assessment

Extinction

Intake screening of needs

Intensive needs assessment

Maryland Addictions Questionnaire (MAQ)

Model of caseload delivery

Needs assessment

Negative punishment

Numbers game model

Positive punishment

Screening

Shaping

Specialized needs caseload model

Strengths-based perspective case management

Substance Abuse Relapse Assessment (SARA)

Substance Abuse Subtle Screening Instrument (SASSI)

"What Would You Do?" Exercise

You are a probation officer in a small rural agency. The chief probation officer explains to you that services have not been optimal and that many offenders are having difficulty finding employment. Further, many of them cannot travel the distances that are required to make their appointments. The local jail is full to capacity and the state is not taking low-risk offenders. Your supervisor explains that this issue is not one of failure to meet the conditions of probation but is instead one where the offenders are unable to meet these conditions.

Your supervisor has established a steering committee made up of you, a member of the social services office, a person from city hall, a deputy from the sheriff's office, and another person from the regional hospital. She wants you to come up with some sort of action plan that will allow you to aid persons on community supervision in finding employment, making therapeutic and medical meetings, and meeting the conditions of their restitution requirements. She tells you that this is a very serious task and she knows that it is a difficult one, particularly since your jurisdiction spans a large tri-county area with a total population of only 25,000 people. The local town of Maybury has a population of roughly 8,000 people. Though resources are scant, she encourages you to take this task seriously and notes that she will provide any support possible. In the meantime, she has lightened your caseload to make your new task more manageable.

What would you do?

Applied Exercise

Read each of the four case vignettes below and select one. Explain how you would conduct case management with your selected case. Be sure to address what you might determine from a client needs assessment, and also correctly identify and classify any mental health issues that were presented in this chapter. In addition, from the information presented, provide a GAF Scale rating, using your own best judgment. Provide a rationale for your rating. In addition, explain the various needs that you might wish to address and how you might screen for those needs. This assignment will require that you complete outside research on your own. Each response must be correct and balanced in approach (consisting of realistic possibilities), with anywhere from 300 to 500 words of content being allowed per application.

Students should complete this application exercise as a mini paper that explains the scenario and then addresses each question. Total word count: 1,200 to 2,000 words.

Applied Exercise Case Vignettes

Vignette #1: A male offender who is 57 years old with dementia, who is also an opiate addict due to the need for relief from severe back and neck pain. After the recent death of his wife, he assaulted several family members who were arguing over where he would now stay.

Vignette #2: A female prostitute with substance addiction who has HIV and suffers from depression regarding her plight. She has a 5-year-old son, and it is found that she was a victim of childhood sexual abuse.

Vignette #3: A schizophrenic and paranoid-delusional offender who has been homeless most of his life. He is an alcoholic who suffers from cirrhosis of the liver.

Vignette #4: A mentally handicapped 14-year-old boy who molested his 8-year-old female cousin. He had found some pornography that his older brother had hidden under the couch and he wanted to show his cousin how the pictures worked.

CHAPTER
9

The Viability of Treatment Perspectives

LEARNING OBJECTIVES

1. Compare current evaluations of treatment programs with the outdated Martinson Report.

2. Describe the types of treatment modalities.

3. Understand how different therapist characteristics impact treatment.

4. Demonstrate the importance of agency partnerships and volunteer participation.

5. Know how treatment approaches can be integrated within the community.

6. Describe the various means by which agencies and community volunteers can aid the treatment process.

7. Understand why public knowledge of treatment approaches is important.

INTRODUCTION

Treatment programs for offenders abound all across the United States. The proliferation of treatment programs would lead one to believe that there should be relatively little crime if such programs work well. Often, critics of treatment-oriented policies will note the continued presence of crime as proof that treatment is not effective. However, this is a misleading and misinformed observation on the utility of treatment. Treatment is not prevention, and one cannot simply overlook this point. Prevention programs are designed to eliminate crime *before* it ever has a chance to take place. Treatment programs, on the other hand, are designed to decrease the likelihood of crime *after* a crime or aberrant behavior has been detected and processed. Over generations, one would assume that the reduction in offending would be transmitted to the offender's children and community, but a huge variety of sociological variables impede and undermine treatment effects once a person leaves the structure of a treatment program.

Further, treatment is not a panacea for all criminals and all criminal behavior. There are indeed some offenders who are simply not amenable to treatment. Extremely hardcore offenders (i.e., psychopaths, certain types of serial murderers and serial rapists, and perhaps some hardened gang members) may simply be beyond the reach of current treatment techniques and processes. In short, treatment cannot work with everyone all of the time, and no truly knowledgeable treatment professional would claim otherwise.

Treatment is one of a variety of responses to criminal offending, but it should not be viewed as the *only* response.

Punishment schemes that do not integrate treatment have been tried extensively throughout correctional history, but these approaches do not "work" very well either. Indeed, if punishment was working well, criminal behavior would likely have been eradicated long ago. However, crime continues to occur around the globe, regardless of how stiff the penalties may be. Though certainty of detection may reduce some crime, it does not reduce it all, and even organized criminals may "factor in" some prison time throughout their career as part of the overhead in doing business within the criminal world. Given that prisons are full and that death penalty–prone jurisdictions tend to have high crime rates, it is clear that punishment is not working well.

In that light, one must ask why treatment should not be integrated into the correctional response. After all, it just might work, and, given that state budgets are completely drained by expensive criminal justice budgets, it appears that we have little choice. Though this last point may seem to be a pessimistic means of justifying treatment, it is nonetheless a possible truth. But another question should also be asked: What would society be like if we had no treatment at all? Would it be safer? From the research during the past decade, it is evident that our society would be in worse hands with no treatment programs. Though skeptics in the 1970s might have believed that they had a legitimate claim in eschewing treatment, it has become clear since then that they were misled by faulty research, by faulty reporting, and by personal biases that essentially disavowed the true effectiveness of our correctional system.

THE MARTINSON REPORT—REVISITED

The effects of the Martinson Report have been quite detrimental to those who support a treatment approach. Much of this is because Martinson's report was largely misquoted. Martinson did not actually say that treatment does not work; rather, he noted that no single treatment modality works in every single circumstance. To a large extent, Martinson (1976) was misquoted throughout the professional world. Since the time of that report, a number of studies have been conducted, and treatment success has been found to depend on the offender, the type of treatment used, and the person delivering the treatment. We now turn our attention to some of the research that demonstrates how and under what circumstances treatment programs have been found to be effective.

According to Janet Firshein (1998), treatment does indeed work. Drug treatment is a particularly important area of research, since the majority of the offender population presents with drug or alcohol issues. In examining drug treatment programs, Firshein notes that data released from the National Institute on Drug Abuse (NIDA) makes it quite clear that treatment works, stating that

> NIDA tracked 10,000 drug abusers in 100 treatment programs around the U.S. from 1991 to 1993 and found that methadone treatment cut heroin use by 70 percent. Only 28 percent of patients in outpatient methadone treatment programs reported weekly or more frequent heroin use, down from 89.4 percent prior to admission. The study also found that long-term abstinence-based treatment resulted in 50 percent reductions in weekly or more frequent cocaine use after one year of follow-up. (p. 1)

This is especially good news because it also means that other corollary crimes (such as theft, assault, and prostitution) may also decrease with lowered rates of drug addiction. Further, this study is obviously large in scale and therefore can legitimately be used to refute the earlier research presented by Martinson in his fateful report. However, while the results reported by Firshein (1998) are indeed promising, it is important to look at a number of treatment programs and orientations when determining the efficacy of treatment perspectives.

Consider the research by Babcock (2006), who conducted a meta-analytic review that examined the findings of 22 studies evaluating treatment efficacy for domestically violent males. The outcome literature of controlled quasi-experimental and experimental studies was reviewed to test the relative impact of the Duluth model, cognitive-behavioral therapy (CBT), and other types of treatment on subsequent recidivism of violence. Babcock tested study design and type of treatment as moderators, and she found that treatment design tended to have only a small influence on effect size. Her overall conclusion was that the effects due to treatment were small, meaning that the current interventions have a minimal impact on reducing recidivism beyond the effect of being arrested. In addition, Babcock presents analogies to treatment for other populations for the purpose of comparison.

Other researchers have examined the efficacy of programs that provide therapeutic interventions for sex offenders. One research project examined the effectiveness of treatment by summarizing data from 43 studies with a combined total population of 9,454 sex offenders (K. R. Hanson et al., 2002). These researchers found that most forms of treatment operating prior to 1980 appeared to have little effect. However, when averaged across all studies, the sexual offense recidivism rate was lower for the treatment groups than for those sex offenders that remained untreated. Program modalities and data reflective of the year 2000 and beyond were associated with reductions in sex crime recidivism and general recidivism. In these cases, the recidivism rates for treated sex offenders were lower than the rates for untreated sex offenders. Studies comparing treatment completers with those that did not complete the therapeutic program consistently found higher recidivism rates for the dropouts, regardless of the type of treatment provided (K. R. Hanson et al., 2002).

From the research presented by K. R. Hanson et al., it would appear that treatment programs for sex offenders have improved over the years. This is not surprising since these offenders have drawn considerable attention during the past two decades. Also interesting is the fact that research methodology (and especially statistical applications) has improved during the past two to three decades, and these improvements are likely to effectively differentiate between programs. Nevertheless, the fact that sex offenders do have some success in treatment demonstrates that, at least on some occasions, therapy can and does work.

Further, when considering specialized populations, it would again seem that treatment does work, but making such a determination is complicated. For instance, a study examining treatment programs for female offenders was conducted by Andrews and Dowden (2002). They note the following:

> Although little has been understood about "what works" for female offenders, the findings of this meta-analysis outline a theoretically based and empirically validated set of guidelines for delivering effective correctional treatment to this population. Subject to additional research, we conclude now that the principles of case classification, integrity and core correctional practice are highly relevant to program design and delivery with female offenders. (p. 22)

These researchers found that, in general, hardcore female offenders benefited more from highly structured and tightly supervised forms of intervention. On the other hand, less serious female offenders tended to do better when the treatment regimen was more flexible in orientation. This again shows that treatment can and does work, particularly when the appropriate type of intervention is matched with the appropriate type of offender. Further still, there is abundant evidence that female offenders have better prognoses when they have contact with their children. Thus, we can conclude that female offenders are receptive to treatment. If the treatment is implemented correctly, it is likely to yield successful outcomes that clearly identify "what woks" for female offenders.

With juvenile offenders, it has been widely shown that therapeutic interventions can and do work. Lipsey, Wilson, and Cothern (2000) note that research indicates intervention programs can reduce overall recidivism rates among juvenile offenders, but they examine this further by evaluating treatment outcomes with serious juvenile offenders. These authors conducted a meta-analysis of programs under the banner of the Office of Juvenile Justice and Delinquency Prevention. Their research sought to address two key questions: (1) Can intervention programs reduce recidivism rates among serious delinquents? and (2) If so, what types of programs are most effective? These two questions cut to the chase when considering the widely noted slant of the ill-fated Martinson Report that was previously discussed. While there were many details to this study (as there are with any meta-analysis), Lipsey et al. found that "effects measured across the 200 studies reviewed varied considerably; there was an overall decrease of 12 percent in recidivism for serious juvenile offenders who received treatment interventions" (p. 1). Further, these researchers were able to pinpoint aspects of programs that tended to make them particularly successful. They found that the most effective interventions included interpersonal skills training, individual counseling, and behavioral programs for noninstitutionalized offenders, and interpersonal skills training and community-based, family-type group homes for institutionalized offenders. Thus, even with serious juvenile offenders, there has been clear and solid research that demonstrates the efficacy of treatment.

Even more recently, Hanser and Mire (2008) studied treatment programs of juvenile sex offenders, these offenders having all of the complicated treatment characteristics of hardcore juvenile offenders as well as the characteristics of adult offenders. They examined this specialized and difficult group of offenders in both the United States and Australia. From their research, it is clear that juvenile sex offending can be effectively treated. To be sure, not all such offenders can be effectively treated, but the majority benefited from interventions in the research by Hanser and Mire.

While the previous discussion on treatment intervention effectiveness is by no means exhaustive, it does demonstrate one key point: treatment can indeed work, if it is allowed to. This is quite clear from the research presented, and it should also be noted that each of the studies presented was a meta-analysis (as was Martinson's study in the 1970s). This is significant because it means that each of the studies examined a number of other studies. Therefore, the results presented are likely to be robust, being grounded in the research of numerous other researchers. It would appear that over time, the quality of treatment services has indeed improved, resulting in lowered rates of recidivism—the ultimate litmus test of effectiveness in the criminal justice system. It is because of improved intervention and evaluation techniques that the pendulum of correctional policy has swung in the direction of a "what works" rather than a "nothing works" orientation. The contemporary emphasis, as pointed out in the preceding discussion, is grounded in years of research that has emerged since the seminal study conducted by Martinson (1976). Figure 9.1 provides an illustration of the back-and-forth views on treatment and rehabilitation in correctional policy over the past few decades.

THE NEED FOR COMMUNITY-BASED TREATMENT AND THE PITFALLS OF TREATMENT PROGRAMS IN INSTITUTIONAL SETTINGS

Obviously, the slant of this text is one in favor of the use of community corrections. Likewise, this text favors the use of offender treatment programs for a number of logical reasons. The use of community corrections

FIGURE 9.1   Pendulum Shifts and Swings in Correctional Policy

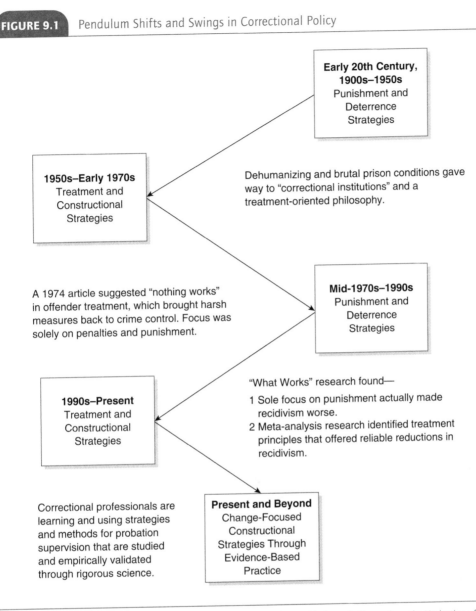

Early 20th Century, 1900s–1950s
Punishment and Deterrence Strategies

1950s–Early 1970s
Treatment and Constructional Strategies

Dehumanizing and brutal prison conditions gave way to "correctional institutions" and a treatment-oriented philosophy.

A 1974 article suggested "nothing works" in offender treatment, which brought harsh measures back to crime control. Focus was solely on penalties and punishment.

Mid-1970s–1990s
Punishment and Deterrence Strategies

1990s–Present
Treatment and Constructional Strategies

"What Works" research found—

1 Sole focus on punishment actually made recidivism worse.
2 Meta-analysis research identified treatment principles that offered reliable reductions in recidivism.

Correctional professionals are learning and using strategies and methods for probation supervision that are studied and empirically validated through rigorous science.

Present and Beyond
Change-Focused Constructional Strategies Through Evidence-Based Practice

SOURCE: Walters, S. T., Clark, M. D., Gingerich, R., & Meltzer, M. L. (2007). *A guide for probation and parole: Motivating offenders to change.* Washington, DC: National Institute of Corrections.

is conducive to better treatment outcomes, and this alone makes it a preferred method of supervising offenders in treatment when compared with programs within the institution.

To begin with, students should understand that most treatment programs in the community, as opposed to jails or prisons, tend to have more face-to-face contact between treatment providers and participants. This is true for a number of reasons. First, the offender has more options in making contact with helping professionals, and helping professionals have more latitude in aiding offenders since they are able to maintain contact at scheduled and unscheduled points of the day or night. The typical administrative limitations associated with the institutional environment are not present in community-based settings. Though ethical constraints and professional decorum always apply, treatment providers can typically be available in a more flexible manner when they are in the community and when the offender has suitable mobility to access assistance at different times of the day or night. While it might intuitively seem that inmates in prison would have more contact with treatment providers, this is usually not the case. In fact, they tend to have very limited contact that is highly structured, being limited by the physical facilities and security.

Further, prison treatment staff tend to be overloaded with demands from heavy caseloads and are hampered by the restrictions associated with the custodial environment. In addition, the security culture that is attributed to prison institutions often undermines any true treatment orientation. Thus, the prison environment is less than ideal. Add to this the fact that the inmate subculture tends to look down on those who disclose to or trust others (such as therapists), and it becomes clear that the environment in prisons works in opposition to treatment strategies. These same restrictions and negative perceptions of the treatment process do not exist at the same magnitude, if at all, within community programs. Because of this, community-based treatment programs usually have better results than those within a secure facility.

In addition, if the offender is not located within a criminogenic region of the community, he or she is less likely to have routine contact with other offenders. In prison facilities, inmates are in constant contact with other criminals and this tends to contaminate the efforts of treatment staff. Thus, existence within the community can aid in separating the offender from other problematic friends or criminal associates, improving the effectiveness of treatment programs. While separation between the offender and old associates is not guaranteed, community supervision officers can aid in observing contacts that the offender makes and providing the appropriate structure that eliminates much of the opportunity for the further commission of crime.

Finally, case managers generally have more options in the community when addressing offender needs. There is often a wider variety of services that caseworkers can coordinate with (e.g., job placement services, transportation services, treatment provider services, etc.), and there are also many more choices for the client to select from with respect to each service that is provided. This alone aids greatly in the treatment process. The end result is a comprehensive set of services that, while not all collected within one single facility, allow for choice and specificity in the selection of various services. Add to this improved access to one's therapist, improved opportunities for corollary services (job placement, medical services, and so forth), and removal from noxious social influences, and it is clear that the community-oriented process of intervention is a superior choice in many cases. While there are certainly some offenders that simply cannot be released into the community due to their level of dangerousness, most are able to make much better use of intervention programs located in the community than those located in the institution. For all of these reasons, this text presents community interventions as superior to those offered within the custodial institution.

Photo 9.1 Southern Oaks Addiction Recovery is a drug treatment facility that is well integrated with the surrounding community. This facility addresses addiction issues within the offender population and routinely coordinates treatment services with the local probation and parole office and the local courthouse.

COMMUNITY SUPERVISION STAFF AND
TREATMENT STAFF: EFFECTIVE ALLIANCES

The main point to this section is to further emphasize that community supervision officers have a strong impact on the ultimate outcome of the offender's supervision process. Students may recall from Chapter 7 the various dynamics that are likely to be experienced during the first encounter between a parole officer and an offender. As noted, this can be a time of serious discomfort for the offender who will likely be anxious during this encounter and will have a difficult time trusting the parole officer. These dynamics are actually true between community supervision officers and those offenders who are new to the community supervision process. This mutual appraisal process, though quite informal, is an important first step in the process of relationship building.

Community supervision officers who build a good rapport with offenders on their caseloads are in a much better position to guide offenders toward effective reform. Since resistance will not likely exist between the officer and the offender in such a relationship, the community supervision officer can better aid in encouraging the offender to actually apply techniques learned while participating in treatment programs. While community supervision officers have the authority to coerce attendance, they typically have a difficult time ensuring that offenders participate in earnest while attending various treatment services. If the community supervision officer can encourage the offender to earnestly participate in treatment, all the while with the understanding that the officer could resort to coercive mechanisms (yet chooses not to force the offender into compliant participation), this is likely to build trust and compliance between the two. This also increases the likelihood that the offender's prognosis will be positive. It is in this manner that community supervision officers can aid treatment providers in maximizing success of the intervention programs available to offenders.

Further, treatment staff who work in unison with supervision officers also provide effective insight into the supervision process. This allows supervision officers to track the behavior of offenders and also to determine if their reintegration extends beyond the mere elimination of recidivism. This is a critical point since there may be a number of other measures that are important regardless of recidivism rates. For instance, an offender that engages successfully in a job training program might recidivate by committing a minor crime, but rather than using restrictive methods to punish the offender, a fine could be given or some other such sanction that does not preclude the offender's continued supervision and participation in the program. In fact, officers could even strive to have sanctions dovetail and complement attendance in treatment by assigning community services in treatment agencies. Constructive use of sanctions can improve offender participation while also utilizing the treatment service provider with the ability to observe the offender's progress, thus increasing the amount of human supervision that the offender is given. This is even truer in many group counseling or group treatment programs where participating members are also expected to maintain contact with one another. It is in this manner that treatment providers and supervision officers can work hand-in-hand to improve security standards (through increased human contacts) and treatment outcomes, by motivating both attendance and actual participation.

Table 9.1 provides an overview of some of the primary functions associated with the reintegration process, demonstrating that these functions often overlap between community supervision personnel and treatment personnel. Likewise, Figure 9.2 illustrates the interface between treatment staff and community supervision personnel during the reintegrative process.

Before proceeding further, students should understand that the idea of treatment-based personnel and supervision personnel working in concert is actually quite consistent with the overall emphasis of this text. Throughout this text, it has been stressed that it is important for community supervision agencies to have interrelationships with individuals within the community and with a variety of professions. In addition to

TABLE 9.1	Functions of Both Community Supervision Personnel and Treatment Personnel in Offender Reintegration		
Primary Functions in Offender Reintegration		*Community Supervision Officer*	*Treatment Specialist*
Build collaborative relationships that both motivate and hold offenders accountable for their actions.		X	X
Target supervision and treatment resources to offenders who are at a higher risk of reoffending.		X	X
Target factors that predict crime and that can be changed.		X	
Help improve the offender's self-control by encouraging natural talents and interests, talking about what worked for an offender in the past, and identifying or role-playing difficult situations.		X	X
Enlarge the offender's connections to other parts of the community through employment, faith communities, and other types of civic participation.		X	
Encourage an offender to change "playgrounds and playmates"—that is, to stay away from criminal friends and criminal behaviors.		X	X
Tailor interactions and interventions to offender characteristics such as motivation, learning style, and intelligence.		X	X

SOURCE: Walters, S. T., Clark, M. D., Gingerich, R., & Meltzer, M. L. (2007). *A guide for probation and parole: Motivating offenders to change.* Washington, DC: National Institute of Corrections.

FIGURE 9.2 The Interface Between Treatment and Supervision Staff

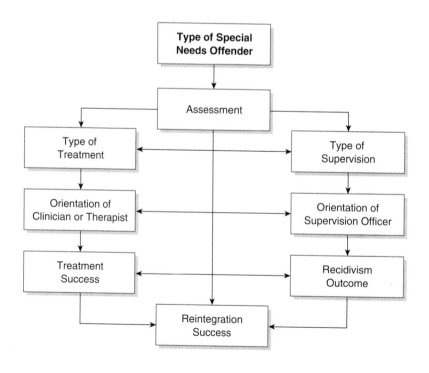

SOURCE: Hanser, R. D. (2006b). *Special needs offenders.* Upper Saddle River, NJ: Pearson/Prentice Hall.

the inclusion of volunteers, there has been an emphasis on networking with other agencies such as was presented in Chapter 8 on case management planning and implementation. Thus, the true means by which offenders are to be reintegrated into the community resides with a multivariate set of circumstances that require assistance from a variety of persons. The reintegration of the offender, as it turns out, is not a task left to the supervision agency alone. This was made clear in Chapter 2 and has been noted throughout this text. True offender reintegration requires supervision personnel, treatment personnel, case managers to coordinate the resources throughout various agencies, a number of personnel from multiple agencies, and involvement from community members themselves. It is clear that reintegration must include comprehensive and varied services that are systematic in their implementation. Any failure to observe this is likely to leave critical offender needs unattended to, thereby increasing the likelihood of criminal activity in the future.

Cross-National Perspective

South Australia's Mental Health Courts

Recognizing that a disproportionate number of mentally ill citizens encounter law enforcement officers, South Australia established a special Magistrate Court Diversion Program to help defer those persons determined to have a mental illness from the regular criminal court system.

The Magistrate Court Diversion Program was initially implemented in 1999, and due to a positive impact on reducing offender recidivism, it became a government-funded program in 2001. The program was designed to assess and treat offenders who have a mental illness or disability and prevent further criminal behavior, help the court system identify and manage mentally ill persons, and divert those persons with mental illness from the regular court system.

In order to participate in the diversion program, the offender must have been charged with a minor offense and have impaired mental functioning caused by mental illness, mental disability, personality disorders, traumatic brain injury, or a neurological disorder. Once impaired mental functioning has been assessed by a clinician, usually a psychologist, the offender's criminal charge may be deferred for up to 6 months, as long as the charge can be shown to have been related to the mental illness or disability. The offender must voluntarily enter the program, but may be referred to the program by a third party, such as a relative, police officer, or social worker. Every 2 months, a magistrate reviews the offender's progress

to ensure compliance and program effectiveness, and should the offender not show sufficient improvement or commit another criminal act, the magistrate may choose to order the offender to serve the original sentence for the crime committed.

In 2005–2006, the Magistrate Court Diversion Program received 395 referrals and accepted 259 offenders, of which 212 completed the program. Of the offenders accepted, almost 74 percent were diagnosed with a mental illness, with schizophrenia and major depressive disorder the most common mental illnesses. The most common offense committed by those accepted by the diversion program was larceny, and less than 1 percent of the offenders who successfully completed the program received prison sentences.

SOURCE: Courts Administration Authority, South Australia. Retrieved from http://www.courts.sa.gov.au/courts/magistrates/index.html

Critical Thinking Question

1. Do you believe that a similar mental health diversion program would help reduce the court caseload in your area? Why or why not?

For more information about the Magistrates Court Diversion Program, visit the website www.courts.sa.gov.au/courts/magistrates/index.html

DIFFERENT TYPES OF TREATMENT MODALITIES/ORIENTATIONS IN THERAPY

There are a multitude of treatment modalities that exist among treatment providers. Many of these modalities are grounded in their own distinct theoretical bases, while others are grounded in theoretical frameworks that are similar to those discussed in earlier chapters (e.g., cognitive-behavioral modalities). Further, the existence of this variety of modalities makes it difficult to assess the efficacy of treatment because there are a number of different approaches to be assessed. This was a major challenge to Martinson's (1976) research and is another reason that meta-analyses of treatment programs are preferable to other forms of evaluation; they allow for comparisons between various studies that may use any number of different modalities for their service delivery. With this in mind, it is important that the student have at least a minimal exposure to these modalities to better understand how some fit quite well within the realm of correctional treatment while others do not seem to fit at all.

The purpose of this section is to orient the student to the basic modalities and theoretical orientations associated with therapeutic interventions. As the main emphasis of this text is on the supervision of offenders and their reintegration into society, the following list of treatment modalities or orientations includes those that are most likely to be used in the criminal justice system. While not an all-encompassing list, it does provide a fairly good overview of what practitioners might encounter among treatment agencies that network and collaborate with community corrections agencies. The most common types of correctional therapy are listed below:

Cognitive Therapy—This approach is based on the belief that faulty thinking patterns and belief systems cause psychological problems and that changing our thoughts improves our mental and emotional health and results in changes in behavior. Cognitive therapy challenges all-or-nothing thinking and overgeneralizations. This type of therapy is particularly appropriate with adult sex offenders and domestic batterers due to their entrenched rationalizations.

Behavioral Therapy—The theory behind this therapy holds that long-term change is accomplished through action and that disorders are learned means of behaving that are maladaptive. The premise to this method of intervention is that if the offender practices the new behavior long enough, then feelings will begin to change as well. In addition, this type of therapy may incorporate elements of social learning theory and models in learning new behavior. This mode of therapy is used extensively and is a preferred modality among criminal justice agencies because it can be easily observed and measured.

Reality Therapy—This modality uses forms of involvement between counselor and client to teach the client to be responsible. The therapist rejects irresponsible and unrealistic behavior and insists that the client assume responsibility that is free of denial or excuse making. Last, the therapist teaches and instructs the offender-client how to fulfill his or her needs within the limits set by reality.

Solution-Focused—This treatment begins from the observation that most psychological problems are present only intermittently. This type of therapy helps the client to notice when symptoms are diminished or absent and to use this knowledge as a foundation for recovery. If a client insists that the symptoms are constant and unrelieved, the therapist works with him or her to find exceptions and make them more frequent, predictable, and controllable.

Less Common Types of Therapy

Family Systems—This is therapy that looks at the entire family as a system with its own customs, roles, beliefs, and dynamics that affect and impact the offender more than any other group. Each family member plays a part in the system, and family systems therapy helps the client discover how his or her family operates, the client's role in that system, and how this affects his or her relationships inside and outside that family system. This type of intervention has been found to be particularly effective with alcoholics and other substance abusers and should be a mandatory form of therapy for families of early childhood offenders and juvenile offenders. Family systems therapy should augment individual counseling and is very effective in getting the family involved in the offender's treatment. It is likewise effective with female offenders, particularly those with children.

Feminist Therapy—This therapy focuses on empowering women. It often aids in strengthening women's communication skills, sense of assertiveness, self-esteem, and relationships. This is useful with female offenders since so many were themselves victims at an early age (childhood sexual abuse) or during adulthood (domestically abusive relationships).

Faith-Based—These forms of therapy are often a blend of cognitive and behavioral techniques that are grounded in scriptural instructions on the appropriate form of cognition or behavior. These types of programs are becoming increasingly popular and have been particularly effective with substance-abusing clients.

Note that in addition to each of the above modalities, most every therapist will utilize the basic techniques associated with **client-centered therapy,** though the full, undiluted version of this type of therapy is not usually used with the offender population. The main point is that client-centered techniques maintain that the therapist must be genuine, accepting, and empathetic to the offender-client. The therapist attempts to create a safe environment where the offender-client feels free to talk about his or her issues and is free to gain insight from them.

It is clear that there are numerous types of therapy that can be used, and they all have a set of characteristics that make them more useful in one situation as opposed to another. Further, some therapists may have a certain therapeutic orientation, or they may have specialized training with one type of offender population but not with another. Thus, a "one-therapist-fits-all" approach is not likely to be effective at integrating offenders. It is with that in mind that we again find that an effective case manager is critical to success, since this individual is the primary official responsible for connecting an offender to an appropriate treatment program.

DIFFERENT TYPES OF TREATMENT PROGRAMS

Numerous types of treatment programs exist for a wide variety of offenders. From a community corrections standpoint, it is first the courthouse that sets the tone as to the particular programs that operate within a given jurisdiction. It is also the courthouse where many community supervision officers will have their initial interface with the offender, including treatment-related aspects of the offender's sentence. Therefore, this section begins with two of the more common court-based treatment programs that exist throughout the United States. These are the drug courts and the mental health courts that typically involve community supervision of offenders processed within their jurisdictions.

The term *therapeutic jurisprudence* is often used to describe court-based programs and their orientation toward case processing. **Therapeutic jurisprudence** is the study of the role of the law as a therapeutic agent. Essentially, therapeutic jurisprudence focuses on the law's impact on emotional life and on psychological well-being (Wexler & Winick, 1998). In this regard, therapeutic jurisprudence focuses on the human, emotional, and psychological side of law and the legal process. Specific examples would include mental health courts and drug courts that were discussed in previous chapters. This is important because it demonstrates a treatment-minded approach to jurisprudence, and this provides additional justification for a reintegrative approach to offender supervision.

Miller (2007) provides a thorough analysis of therapeutic jurisprudence and notes that there are two distinct means of viewing this type of court operation. First, there is the managerial mode, where a court will seek to "identify the range of problems facing its target clientele and ameliorate those problems by matching clients with the available social resources" (p. 127). This perspective is very similar to the case management model described previously in Chapter 8. This is a point worth noting because it demonstrates that most all aspects of community supervision tend to follow a case management method of operation, regardless of whether this consists of courthouse programs or the supervision agency (which is typically a corollary to the court). Second, Miller describes an interventionist mode of therapeutic jurisprudence whereby "the court seeks to intervene to change the way in which ex-offenders perceive themselves as responsible agents, as a means to preclude socially disfavored conduct" (p. 127).

For the most part, court programs engaged in therapeutic jurisprudence have borrowed and adapted their ideas from the drug court model. According to Miller (2007), "drug court judges often point to intervention in the offender's antisocial lifestyle as its core therapeutic feature" (p. 128). As an example, in drug court, the judge may be the informal leader of a team of professionals that are committed to the rehabilitation of the drug-addicted offender. In this respect, the judge utilizes a dynamic, personal relationship with each offender that holds the offender accountable, yet also ensures that the offender is placed in treatment whenever this is a feasible option. In essence, the judge plays the role of a high-powered treatment team leader, or perhaps an authoritative case manager of a sort. This follows the same theme that has been presented throughout this text in regard to offender reintegration.

Much of the therapeutic jurisprudence movement has occurred in response to specialized types of offenders since they are in need of detailed treatment resources. Neubauer (2002) speaks to this, noting that there are now numerous specialized courts that deal with specialized types of offenses and offenders. Common examples include the widely touted drug court, but also innovations such as domestic violence courts, drunk driving courts, elder courts, and so on. These specialized courts are often tailored with a therapeutic justice orientation in mind. Neubauer indicates that there are **five essential elements of specialized courts,** as follows:

1. Immediate intervention

2. Nonadversarial adjudication

3. Hands-on judicial involvement

4. Treatment programs with clear rules and structured goals

5. A team approach that brings together the judge, prosecutors, defense counsel, treatment provider, and correctional staff

Some court applications are better known than others. This section will provide brief discussions on drug courts and mental health courts. As noted previously, drug courts are one of the best-known applications of therapeutic justice. Drug courts vary widely in structure, target populations, and treatment programs. One common way of creating a drug court is to establish one section of court that processes all minor drug cases; the primary goal is to speed up case dispositions of drug cases and at the same time free other judges to expedite their own dockets. Another type of drug court concentrates on drug defendants accused of serious crimes who also have major prior criminal records. These cases are carefully monitored by court administrators to ensure that all other charges are consolidated before a single judge, and no unexpected developments interfere with the scheduled trial date. Still other drug courts emphasize treatment. The assumption is that treatment will reduce the likelihood that convicted drug abusers will be rearrested. These courts will often mandate extensive treatment plans that are to be supervised by the probation officer.

However, it is the sentencing judge, as opposed to the probation officer, who monitors the offender's behavior. All in all, drug courts are thought to be a relatively successful method of combining both the punitive and rehabilitative components of the criminal justice system.

Mental health courts, on the other hand, are designed to ensure that nonviolent mentally ill offenders are not warehoused in prisons, yet at the same time the goal of these courts is to ensure that these offenders are not being a nuisance in the community. Often, these offenders commit petty crimes and are homeless. Because of this, and because the vast majority of mentally ill offenders are not violent, informal interventions such as mental health courts are considered a much more effective method of intervention than jail or prison. These courts provide the offender with treatment and also provide the police and other community responders a venue to utilize when processing these offenders. Mental health courts are adept at working with local agencies to both address the needs of the offender and protect the public's safety. Intervention and treatment specialists work with the judge to make certain that services are effectively delivered to the offender. This, like other previous examples, reflects an integrative casework model of intervention.

While drug courts and mental health courts are created for specific offender issues (i.e., substance abuse and mental health concerns, respectively), there are other types of courts that have been implemented to specifically address the offender population that faces release from prison. These are called reentry courts. **Reentry courts** provide comprehensive services to offenders that return from prison to the community, by utilizing comprehensive services offered by a network of agencies in the surrounding area (see Focus Topic 9.1 for additional details). Importantly, these courts address the needs of *all returning offenders,* not just those that have drug abuse or mental health issues. Also, these types of programs are very important because they address those offenders that are perhaps in the most profound need, going through a transition from prison to release that is often much more difficult to navigate than is the adjustment for offenders placed on probation.

Photo 9.2   The Ouachita Parish Courthouse runs a large drug court program. Local facilities such as Southern Oaks Addiction Recovery (see Photo 9.1) and Rays of Sonshine (see Photo 8.2) routinely coordinate with this courthouse.

Though these court-based treatment models are comprehensive and provide a unique blend of criminal justice and therapeutic responses, there are several other approaches that can serve the reentry management role. The structure of such a program is limited only by one's imagination. Further, various agencies or components of the criminal justice system can and should work in tandem to optimize potential outcomes. For example, the Office of Justice Programs has tested the use of law enforcement, corrections, and community partnerships to manage reentry. Such partnerships have proven central to the reentry court, as well. The issue of partnerships continues to be a recurring theme throughout this text, being specifically mentioned in Chapters 2 and 8 as critical to the supervision and treatment of offenders, and this chapter will discuss the use of partnerships in more detail in a later section. For now, students should note that again, in the current chapter, the forging of agency and community partnerships is integral to the success of specialized programs such as drug courts, mental health courts, and reentry courts. Beyond this point, communities that wish to establish reentry courts will find that collaborative work on the part of agencies and concerned community members can lead to creative methods of drawing upon existing resources and may even lead to additional funding sources. Likewise, collaborative efforts aid in providing a range of essential reentry support services for offenders and mechanisms for ensuring easy access to them. As has been noted earlier in this chapter and in Chapter 2, volunteers and other collaborators can effectively fill in the gaps by assisting with transportation and other informal services that ensure that services are realistically reachable for offenders that may have limited resources. This is a particularly relevant concern for offenders returning from periods of incarceration.

FOCUS TOPIC 9.1

REENTRY COURTS

Reentry courts recognize that offenders need to be held strictly accountable, but at the same time are in serious need of assistance as they return to communities. Importantly, the concept of the reentry court does not envision any change in the timing of decisions regarding a prisoner's release. In other words, reentry courts are not used as leverage tools to obtain offender compliance. They are instead tools to ensure public safety, on one hand, and that offenders receive the necessary case management services, on the other. These courts address the conflict between public safety and offender reintegration, acting as the moderator between the two competing interests. Further, the use of reentry courts acknowledges that most offenders eventually return to the community. These courts focus on the work of prisons in preparing offenders for release, and presume that a reentry court will actively involve the state corrections agency and others, as outlined below.

The core elements of a reentry court are the following:

1. Assessment and Planning. It is envisioned that correctional administrators, ideally with a reentry judge, would meet with inmates prior to release to explain the reentry process. The state corrections agency and, where available, the parole agency, working in consultation with the reentry court, would identify those inmates to be released under the auspices of the reentry court to assess the inmates' needs upon release and begin building linkages to a constellation of social services, family counseling, health and mental health services, housing, job training, and work opportunities that would support successful reintegration.

2. Active Oversight. The reentry court would see prisoners released into the community with a high degree of frequency—probably once a month—beginning right after release and continuing until the end of parole (or other form of supervision). It is critical that the judge see offenders who are making progress as well as those who have failed to perform. The judge would also actively engage the parole officer or other supervising authority and the community policing officer responsible for the parolee's neighborhood in assessing progress. In the drug court experience,

acknowledgment of the successful achievement of milestones by participants provides encouragement to others who observe them.

3. Management of Supportive Services. The reentry court must have at its disposal a broad array of supportive resources, including substance abuse treatment services, job training programs, private employers, faith institutions, family members, housing services, and community organizations. These support systems would be marshaled by the court, drawing upon existing community resources where possible. At the core, the court would again actively engage the parole officer or other supervising authority, as well as the community policing officer responsible for the parolee's neighborhood. In the drug court experience, judges and others have become very effective service brokers and advocates on behalf of participants. An important lesson from the drug court experience is that this brokerage function requires the development of a case management function accountable to the court. To be successful, a reentry court would have to develop a similar case management capacity.

4. Accountability to Community. A jurisdiction might consider creating a citizen advisory board to work with the reentry court to develop both community service and support opportunities, as well as accountability mechanisms for successful reentry of released inmates. Accountability mechanisms might include ongoing restitution orders and participation in victim impact panels. It may also be appropriate to involve the crime victims and victims' rights organizations as part of the reentry process. The advisory board should broadly represent the community. Other mechanisms for drawing upon diverse community perspectives should also be considered.

5. Graduated and Parsimonious Sanctions. The reentry court would establish and articulate a predetermined range of sanctions for violations of the conditions of release. These would not automatically require return to prison; in fact, this would be reserved for new crimes or egregious violations. As with drug courts, it would be important for the reentry court to arrange for an array of relatively low-level sanctions that could be swiftly, predictably, and universally applied. Jurisdictions interested in piloting a reentry court must clearly outline how graduated sanctions would be imposed and the array of sanctions that would be used.

6. Rewards for Success. The reentry court also would need to incorporate positive judicial reinforcement, by rewarding success, perhaps by negotiating early release from parole after established goals are achieved, or by conducting graduation ceremonies akin to those seen in drug courts. The successful completion of parole should be seen as an important life event for an offender, and the court can help acknowledge that accomplishment. Courts provide powerful public forums for encouraging positive behavior and for acknowledging the individual effort in achieving reentry goals. Jurisdictions are required to outline milestones in the reentry process that would trigger recognition and an appropriate reward.

SOURCE: National Criminal Justice Resources. (1999). *Reentry courts: Managing the transition from prison to community.* Washington, DC: Author.

Aside from the courtroom components of different treatment programs, there are various types of other programs. Some treatment programs may require offenders to stay at a facility, while others may simply require the offender to attend for a prescribed number of hours per week. In most cases, these types of treatment programs are designed for substance-abusing offenders. Indeed, with most other forms of mental health intervention, the offender will be required to simply meet his or her therapist for a set number of sessions for a set amount of time, as prescribed by the courts (as has been discussed in prior chapters). Since these different programs have been made most widely available to offenders with substance abuse problems, several examples of treatment programs for drug abusers are presented in the following paragraphs. It should be pointed out that some of these programs (the short- and long-term programs noted below) will appear again in Chapter 10 as community residential treatment centers. This is intentional and demonstrates some degree of overlap between concepts, types of programs, and treatment modalities that are encountered in the field of community corrections. At the risk of being redundant, it is thought that these and other facilities should be presented again in the next chapter as a means for further clarifying the dual nature and purpose of these facilities. The programs presented below have been adapted from the National

Institute on Drug Abuse because they provide clear examples of the general categories of treatment programs and because these are the most relevant types of programs to community corrections agencies in the United States. The examples of various treatment programs are as follows:

Outpatient Drug-Free Treatment: This treatment costs less than residential or inpatient treatment and often is more suitable for individuals who are employed or who have extensive social supports. Such low-intensity programs may offer little more than drug education and admonition. Other outpatient models, such as intensive day treatment, can be comparable to residential programs in services and effectiveness, depending on the individual patient's characteristics and needs. In many outpatient programs, group counseling is emphasized. Some outpatient programs are designed to treat patients who have medical or mental health problems in addition to their drug disorder.

Short-Term Residential Programs: These provide intensive but relatively brief residential treatment based on a modified 12-step approach, patterned after the Alcoholics Anonymous programs. These programs were originally designed to treat alcohol problems, but during the cocaine epidemic of the mid-1980s, many began to treat illicit drug abuse and addiction. The original residential treatment model consisted of a 3- to 6-week hospital-based inpatient treatment phase followed by extended outpatient therapy and participation in a self-help group, such as Alcoholics Anonymous. Reduced health care coverage for substance abuse treatment has resulted in a diminished number of these programs, and the average length of stay under managed care review is much shorter than in early programs.

Long-Term Residential Treatment: This type of treatment provides care 24 hours per day, generally in nonhospital settings. The best-known residential treatment model is the therapeutic community (TC), but residential treatment may also employ other models, such as cognitive-behavioral therapy. TCs are residential programs with planned lengths of stay of 6 to 12 months. These programs focus on the "resocialization" of the individual and use the entire "community," including other residents, staff, and the social context, as active components of treatment. Treatment is highly structured and can at times be confrontational, with activities designed to help residents examine damaging beliefs, self-concepts, and patterns of behavior and to adopt new, more harmonious and constructive ways to interact with others. Many TCs are quite comprehensive and can include employment training and other support services onsite. Compared with offenders in other forms of treatment, the typical TC resident has more severe problems, with more co-occurring mental health problems and more criminal involvement.

Finally, NIDA notes that research has shown that a combination of criminal justice sanctions and treatment (particularly drug treatment) can be an effective means of delivering treatment to the offender population. According to NIDA (2005), "individuals under legal coercion tend to stay in treatment for a longer period of time and do as well as or better than others not under legal pressure" (p. 1). This is important because it demonstrates the efficacy of programs such as drug courts, mental health courts, and other forms of innovative judicial and mental health intervention. Significantly, this also speaks to the discussion regarding Martinson's findings, presented at the beginning of this chapter. From current research, it would appear that "something" does indeed work when providing treatment to offenders.

DIFFERENT TYPES OF TREATMENT PROFESSIONALS

Earlier, in Chapter 4, students were provided an explanation of the different types of treatment professionals that are encountered in the field of community corrections. In addition, the student was made aware of distinctions between licensure and certification. This was meant to demonstrate the differing levels of expertise as well as the different focus that each may have on the treatment process. Rather than my presenting a repetitive discussion on the various treatment professionals in community corrections, the student is simply referred back to that chapter if a review of treatment professionals is necessary.

However, there are some points that need to be added or reinforced in this current chapter. First, as was noted in Chapter 4, the more trained and educated the clinician, the more costly he or she is likely to be. Because of this, agencies must be careful to make fiscally sound decisions, avoiding the possibility of paying an overqualified professional to do work that another, equally qualified but less expensive professional could effectively complete. Further, as noted earlier in this chapter, the key to successful reintegration is to get the right treatment modality matched with the correct offender, a match with the correct treatment being the last key ingredient to therapeutic success. Likewise, it is also important to get the correct type of treatment personnel matched with the type of offender receiving treatment. All of these factors contribute to agency effectiveness (to be discussed later, in Chapter 15) and individual treatment success.

Aside from types of expertise, treatment professionals may vary in the modality they use. Some may be cognitive-behavioral in orientation while others may identify with other theoretical bases of service delivery. This is another important consideration when networking with treatment providers. In some cases, theoretical differences between treatment providers may seem only a topical issue, but in others it may be quite significant. For example, while one therapist may use cognitive-behavioral approaches, another might be more inclined toward solution-focused methods. Each of these is a valid treatment perspective, but each has a different set of strengths and weaknesses. Indeed, solution-focused methods are ideal for short-term therapy, whereas cognitive-behavioral methods might be better suited for long-term therapy.

Moreover, the age of the treatment provider can be very important. With juvenile probationers in treatment, there is typically a stronger rapport if the therapist is younger and closer to the youth's age. This is particularly true and is even further accentuated if the therapist has grown up in an area common to the other youths. A prime example might be juvenile street gang members on community supervision. Gang-exit counseling programs are particularly well-suited for this population when the treatment providers are near to the age of the offenders or if the treatment provider is a former gang member. Understanding the vernacular, music, fashion, and other characteristics can be critical to developing an effective rapport with these types of offenders; a better rapport is directly linked to good treatment outcomes.

Likewise, the gender of the therapist can be important, particularly when considering female offenders. Many of these offenders have challenges that are connected to their status as females within their own subculture as well as the role prescribed to them by broader society. Further, many female offenders have themselves been the victims of sexual assault or other forms of abuse (particularly domestic abuse), and they may feel awkward or anxious talking with male therapists about these and other issues. In addition, feminist therapy (discussed in the last section) may be an effective modality for these offenders; it is typically the female therapist that is most skilled with this type of intervention, and thus, female therapists tend to be better able to leverage the social plight of women as a mechanism for empowerment and change.

Last, the race of the treatment provider may prove important. Considerable research has demonstrated that clients in therapy tend to identify better with therapists from similar backgrounds. Given that much of the offender population is classified as minority status, it may be that therapists from minority groups should be specifically identified and solicited to provide assistance. In fact, client-therapist racial/cultural matching can be seen as a sign of cultural competence among treatment agencies. Thus, the ability to provide treatment providers from similar racial and cultural groups to the offender caseload can be a definite advantage. This issue will be discussed at length in Chapter 14 where the value of diversity and cultural competence is presented in detail. Focus Topic 9.2 provides an example of how culturally competent programs can provide services that are more suitably matched to their target populations, resulting in improved recidivism and treatment outcomes.

CULTURALLY COMPETENT SERVICES FOR AFRICAN AMERICAN OFFENDERS

Using Afrocentric techniques has recently emerged as a promising way of delivering services to African Americans. A study by King, Holmes, Henderson, and Latessa reports an evaluation of an Afrocentric treatment program for juvenile male felony offenders in one city. This evaluation used a two-group, quasi-experimental design to compare the 281 African American youths in the Afrocentric treatment program (called the Community Corrections Partnership) with a group of 140 African American probation youths. Overall, the youths assigned to the Afrocentric treatment program performed slightly better than the probationers on 4 out of 15 measures of juvenile and adult criminality.

SOURCE: King, W. R., Holmes, S. T., Henderson, M. L., & Latessa, E. J. (2007). The Community Corrections Partnership: Examining the long-term effects of youth participation in an Afrocentric diversion program. *Crime and Delinquency, 47*(4), 558–572. Copyright © Sage Publications.

It is clear from the above examples that there are several different types of therapists and that each may have any number of distinct characteristics. Some therapists may specialize, while others may simply vary by racial or ethnic background. Others may utilize differing therapeutic interventions and perspectives, and still others may have different types of licensure or certification. Regardless, it is evident that one element of the equation for obtaining successful outcomes is to ensure that the treatment provider matches the various criteria that are needed within a community supervision agency's caseload. This again speaks directly to the Martinson Report since at the time that Martinson did his research, it was found that the therapist-client relationship was an important factor in obtaining successful treatment outcomes for community supervision agencies. This was true in the past and continues to hold true today.

COMMUNITY PARTNERSHIPS AND AGENCY ALLIANCES

As far back as Chapter 2 of this text, it has been emphasized that the community must be considered a partner in the offender supervision process. Likewise, Chapter 8 and its overview of the case management process make it clear that agency alliances in community supervision are part and parcel of any comprehensive reintegration program. Thus, community corrections not only happens *in* the community; it also happens *with the aid of* the community. This theme is once again brought up in this chapter for two reasons. First, it provides further clarity and a reminder of the integral nature of the community partnerships that are maintained with the community supervision agency. Second, the treatment perspective presented in this chapter benefits from a social environment that is conducive to reintegration; often this requires adequate "buy-in" from community members.

Indeed, the point regarding partnerships is important for additional reasons not noted in Chapters 2 and 8. These reasons are related to the nature of the environment to which many offenders return. In many cases, offenders may return to criminogenic communities and neighborhoods. When this occurs, treatment program benefits are diminished and the likelihood of offender recidivism is increased. From a theoretical perspective, these neighborhoods may be socially disorganized. As noted in Chapter 2, social disorganization theory holds that "disorganized communities cause crime because informal social controls break down and criminogenic cultures emerge" (Cullen & Agnew, 2003, p. 6). In these cases, the community does not have the proper support and cohesion that is required to prevent criminal activity in the area.

While elements of the community or neighborhood are law-abiding and wish to be rid of the criminal actors in their location, they tend to lack the social capital to keep crime at bay. In this regard, social disorganization theory is important to understand for two reasons. First, while these neighborhoods are not ideal areas for offenders to return to, offenders often do return to these types of neighborhoods because their family or friends are located there. This creates a situation of dual and competing interests: on the one hand, the offender is near to family and friends that may be conducive to his or her reintegration, while on the other hand, the offender is likely to once again be within close proximity of other criminal offenders, some of whom the offender might have known prior to his or her own placement on community supervision. Second, social disorganization demonstrates how preventative efforts and neighborhood improvement programs can aid in reducing initial criminal offending, the development of enmeshed subcultures in the area, and recidivism among returning offenders. As noted in Chapter 2, students should understand that neighborhood variables greatly impact the outcome of community supervision programs and, in addition, they also impact the outcomes of many treatment programs within the community.

Having a healthy neighborhood environment helps to ensure that offender treatment outcomes are reinforced. Such environments are necessary if truly comprehensive forms of treatment are to be administered within a given community. Further, it is clear that agencies must network and collaborate on a routine basis if the case management process is to be adequately administered. In previous chapters, students have seen how various partnerships are integral to the case management process and to the effective reintegration of offenders on supervision. A variety of agencies have been considered, most dealing with treatment-related issues or some form of corollary service. However, there is one agency partner that does not immediately come to mind when considering the reintegration of the offender: the police.

Inclusion of the police in a reintegrative model of offender supervision may at first seem counterintuitive because the police are naturally identified with enforcement and with the booking and extraction of offenders from the community. However, such a view of the police is limited in scope and completely ignores other elements of policing that serve to prevent crime and deter offending. These elements can actually aid both the supervision and the treatment process. While agency partnering with the police might be effectively placed in other areas of this text, it is hoped that students will see that any form of partnership can have a positive impact on the efficacy of treatment programs, even those that involve partnerships with the police, who are typically equated with a pure enforcement role. In fact, the Bureau of Justice Assistance (BJA) created a publication entitled *Building an Offender Reentry Program: A Guide for Law Enforcement* (2005), in which the police were specifically identified as effective partners in the reintegration process with offenders. Importantly, this document was drafted by a number of professional members of the International Association of Chiefs of Police (IACP).

This BJA publication is full of useful suggestions for practitioners in policing, and it illustrates that unlikely partnerships can emerge to be fruitful for the community, victims, and offenders. One example, the use of COP Houses, is particularly relevant to the prior discussion on socially disorganized communities presented earlier in this chapter. The use of Community-Oriented Policing (COP) Houses has been implemented in high-crime, low socioeconomic areas of Racine, Wisconsin. These neighborhoods were chosen as focal points because a high number of offenders return to them. The houses serve as an extension of the collaboration already started between police and community corrections. Representatives of police and community corrections are located in the houses to serve as both a resource and a crime deterrent in the community. This demonstrates how collaborative partnerships between the police and community corrections personnel can help to stabilize communities, providing environments that are more productive for offenders who are in the reintegration process. In this manner, COP Houses provide a two-part function, as a deterrent to recidivism and a source of support that gives offenders a social resource. In addition, the community as a whole benefits as crime is reduced and problematic areas are provided stability.

In further demonstration of the interlocking nature of these partnerships, consider that this same publication, oriented to policing agencies, provides narrative to police administrators on the importance of needs and risk assessments. According to this document, criminal justice research has

> revealed that a large amount of crime is committed by a small percentage of the population in a community. Therefore, many offender reentry programs implement needs and risk assessment components to more precisely target how best to help offenders transition. The most common risk and needs assessment tools currently in use are the Level of Supervision Inventory—Revised (LSI-R) or diagnostic tests designed to uncover co-occurring and other mental health disorders. These tools are most helpful to corrections officials in determining the offender's level of supervision and to guide staff in making treatment decisions. (BJA, 2005, p. 12)

The above quoted information is significant because it ties in with earlier discussions in Chapter 3 that addressed the importance of assessment and risk prediction in community corrections. As students may recall, the LSI-R was particularly praised in Chapter 3 as a premiere instrument, and these claims are further validated by disparate sources that include policing organizations such as the IACP and federal agencies such as the BJA. This again demonstrates the interconnected nature of various components and ideas within the criminal justice system. These interlocking components and programs serve to further strengthen the environment in which treatment programs must operate.

Police agencies can be very good partners in transitional/reentry planning. This is a logical extension of the assessment process and also dovetails well with partnerships that seek to stabilize communities that tend to draw prior offenders into their region. In this case, police personnel will be consulted so that they can provide input into the post-release supervision conditions of offenders. Police meet with corrections officials to share information on the offender's criminal history in the community and discuss their concerns for the offender's future. Some law enforcement officials make recommendations of which neighborhoods offenders should (or should not) be permitted to enter and which associates offenders may be restricted from seeing. While it may not be immediately apparent, this can actually have a substantial impact on treatment programs. Moreover, it is likely to be beneficial for treatment professionals to also attend such reentry planning functions and directly collaborate with law enforcement. While guidelines and restrictions on confidentiality would need to be honored by treatment professionals, an initial meeting at the onset of the offender reintegration process can help to build agency rapport and ensure that all parties approach the process in a similar manner.

This idea is further reinforced by the fact that both the IACP and the BJA note that policing agencies should be included in the operation of reentry courts. This again demonstrates that a variety of agencies and methods of intervention may be interlocked to provide a seamless continuum of supervision and treatment services. In this regard, reentry courts can be envisioned as another crime prevention tool in that the court has the ability to order sanctions beyond the existing supervision conditions. Law enforcement experiences with these types of partnerships have been positive and are viewed as effective accountability tools. This again illustrates the overlap between supervision and treatment objectives. Each of these perspectives is necessary to maximize the reintegration process, and the seasoned treatment provider will realize that reinforcers and punishments in the community, when logically and skillfully utilized, help to augment therapeutic outcomes within the treatment program itself. In essence, agency partnerships provide the needed "training wheels" for offenders' behavior as they seek to implement the requirements of their treatment regimen.

In addition, treatment providers that have an effective rapport with local law enforcement will be privy to informal observations that police make when conducting their routine patrol activities. This can often be useful information for treatment providers that may wish to challenge manipulative offenders who are not fully honest or who may not be meeting aspects of their therapeutic contract. This again demonstrates that enforcement functions can augment case management functions in the process of maintaining agency partnerships. The key to integrated partnerships is to have all parties involved as much as possible, and police agencies should not be left out of this picture.

One other recommendation worth mentioning is the often touted idea of incorporating all community resources, specifically noting the need to tap into the policing, community, and partner volunteer programs. Volunteers can be used to support program activities and to spread the word about these programs. This naturally harkens back to the various points made in Chapter 2, including the ancient notion of the hue and cry, where citizens were involved in policing activities. This same point comes back full circle as we now consider notions of reintegration and treatment, but do so from a different perspective. In this case, the emphasis is on integrating the policing agency into the background fabric of the treatment and reintegration process, with citizens again being the backbone of such interlocking community-based programs. As noted in Chapter 2, the use of Neighborhood Watch programs should consciously be solicited. Members of these groups are often more than willing to observe and visit various locations to ensure that their locality is safe.

All of these mechanisms demonstrate that volunteers, employers, families, and probation departments can provide supervision that is comprehensive yet receptive to the reintegration of the offender population. This is important because the components of both care and supervision must be maintained. It is clear from the preceding examples that this obviously requires participation from the community. This is a pivotal point to this entire text. Without support from the community, the likelihood of reintegrating the offender is greatly impaired.

Naturally, a variety of agencies related to employment placement, medical services, educational attainment, and other such services should also be included in any reintegration network. This should be clear from the prior discussion in Chapter 8 related to case management processes with the offender population. Indeed, these partnerships can be effective in offender reintegration as well as treatment programs for victims of crime. This can then ensure a total and comprehensive response to crime and can further provide a community environment that is conducive to offender treatment and reintegration. Focus Topic 9.3 provides an example of one such program that offers comprehensive services to offenders while also providing services to victims. In some cases, such as with family violence issues and juvenile offenders, this may be a particularly viable method of service delivery.

FOCUS TOPIC 9.3

REDHOOK COMMUNITY JUSTICE CENTER

This multiservice site, located in Brooklyn, New York, allows defendants to move expeditiously through the criminal justice system, while enabling them to access a wide range of services to assist in preventing further criminal action. In addition to adjudicating cases, defendants, victims, and community members are able to access a range of services offered at the Redhook Community Justice Center. Some services that are offered include job training, medical care, legal services, family violence counseling, drug treatment, mediation, and victim services. The Justice Center also works with the AmeriCorp Project to assist in community development. It is important to note that this center provides a broad range of case management services to *both* offenders and victims. This then adds further utility to the program's efforts and also allows for increased community support and partnership. Indeed, centers such as these are ideal for healing communities that are impacted by crime, and they also lend themselves to restorative justice applications.

SOURCE: Hanser, R. D. (1999). *Reentry courts: Managing the transition from prison to community.* Washington, DC: National Criminal Justice Resources and Statistics.

Finally, in many cases, treatment services may not be provided by a single individual or agency. Consider, for example, an offender that is a domestic abuser and who has a substance abuse problem. This offender is likely to see a separate therapist for his or her domestic abuse issues while also seeing another service provider for his or her addiction issues. In fact, it is quite common that clinicians will not address a substance abuse issue in addition to other serious clinical issues. Rather, they will refer out or will require that the offender be referred to a substance abuse specialist. Because so many offenders have substance abuse issues, it is actually quite common for them to have two separate therapists, particularly when they are dually diagnosed. This is an important point because it means that these practitioners and their agencies must stay in contact with one another so that comprehensive services can be provided. While this may seem to make intuitive sense, it does not always occur. In fact, in many states, addictions professionals may be licensed and regulated under a board that is entirely different from those of other mental health providers, meaning that each will have its own emphases, board of ethics, and standards or regulation of practice. This can be quite problematic.

Though it may not be new to many seasoned clinicians, community supervision personnel may make the surprising discovery that a schism frequently exists between clinicians and addictions treatment providers. Often, the standards for treatment providers in the addictions field are less stringent than those in other areas of service delivery. Because of this, some degree of conflict, elitism, and sense of authority convolutes the process when clinicians from both camps attempt to work in a collaborative fashion. Indeed, it is not uncommon for addiction treatment providers to have been prior addicts, sometimes referred to as "wounded healers." Because of this, other helping professionals may be skeptical about the field of addiction counseling, thereby increasing the gap between these providers and the rest of the clinical community. Though this may seem to be a superficial or corollary problem, it is actually quite debilitating to the overall treatment process with a large proportion of the offender population. This is particularly true when one considers that over 60 percent of all offenders have some type of substance use at the point of arrest (Hanser, 2007b). Thus, addictions professionals are involved with the majority of the offender population.

Obviously, if addictions professionals are involved with more than half of the offender population and if they operate at odds with many members of the remaining circle of clinical professionals, a problem of considerable magnitude emerges. It is important that agencies look for these types of biases among treatment professionals. It is of course ironic that practitioners that are supposed to be associated with mental health and maturity would allow such differences to constrain their professional effectiveness, but this is nonetheless a frequent reality. The current author is himself a therapist who is licensed for general clinical work and is also separately licensed as an addictions counselor. When speaking on this issue, there is a degree of firsthand experience and knowledge that exceeds a mere academic understanding. In short, this author has worked in this field

Photo 9.3 The Monroe office for state probation and parole coordinates supervision efforts with various treatment facilities in the area such as Rays of Sonshine (see Photo 8.2) as well as the local courthouse of Ouachita Parish (see Photo 9.2).

of treatment extensively and can verify that this hindrance exists within the treatment field in at least three different states, if not more. With this noted, it is important that collaborative partnerships resolve any differences that impair outcome effectiveness. A failure to do this only results in further risk to the community and also makes a mockery of the notion that actors in a given field of work are to be considered professionals—professionals whose goal should be to make society safer in the future, regardless of ideology, theoretical orientation, or their chosen areas of expertise.

TREATMENT STAFF, REFERRALS, AND INCREASED HUMAN SUPERVISION

While correctional treatment professionals are responsible for the actual treatment and rehabilitation of the offender, the efforts of treatment professionals can be enhanced by the active involvement of various community members. The integration of the community and therapeutic service providers can work to provide offenders with treatment opportunities that might not otherwise exist. For example, consider that in some cases, treatment professionals might decide to assign "homework," requiring the offender to accomplish certain tasks that put him or her in contact with a variety of personnel in the community. An exercise in building self-esteem might require the offender to negotiate with a salesperson at a used car lot, or engage in another environment where the offender must apply interaction skills that he or she has learned in therapeutic sessions.

In substance abuse treatment, the treatment specialists might work in tandem with self-help groups, such as Alcoholics Anonymous or Narcotics Anonymous. These groups typically include the use of a "sponsor" that acts as a mentor for the addicted person in recovery. Such a person is a community member who can be available to augment the treatment process, enhancing and supporting the goals decided upon in the official therapeutic setting between correctional treatment staff and the offender. Another example might be the use of clergy members to support the offender. This is particularly useful for those offenders that note spiritual and religious beliefs as being important to them personally. When and where appropriate, religious institutions and the members of these institutions can provide a sense of integration for the offender, and they can assist the offender in meeting agreed-upon treatment objectives. This can also aid offenders of a variety of cultural backgrounds. If offenders request such integration of treatment services, the use of religious support mechanisms can improve the overall treatment outcomes that might be realized.

In addition, treatment professionals may use family counseling perspectives to aid the offender in reintegration, with family members taking a variety of roles in the offender's reformation. For instance, a juvenile offender might benefit from family counseling with his or her parents present. A substance abuse offender might benefit from having his or her spouse and children involved in the treatment process. This goes beyond the mere contact and reporting process the family members might provide to probation agencies. Rather, family members are openly invited to assist in the treatment process, learning about the agreed-upon goals and objectives of the offender's treatment plan and participating in routines that aid the offender between therapeutic sessions. Caring family members can engage in exercises throughout the week that assist the offender in practicing prosocial skills and routines. Family members can also give input to the offender and to the therapist regarding treatment processes, providing an informal support system for the therapeutic process. This can result in a sense of seamless support throughout the week so that the offender is reminded of his or her treatment objectives in between treatment sessions with the counselor. Inviting family members and friends of the offender to actual treatment sessions can help to further strengthen their integration into the treatment program.

Moreover, the use of family and friends in the treatment process means yet another layer of human contact and accountability for the offender. This also helps to augment other partnerships between agencies and volunteers in the community. In all cases, the offender becomes enmeshed in the social system, the resulting support typically improving treatment outcomes. Family and friends will understand the offender's treatment plan and will be in a better position to aid the offender than will most other persons within the offender's network. Further, family and close friends will be around the offender during more personal points of the day and will have more in-depth understanding of the offender's personal characteristics, temperaments, habits, and tendencies. This helps to fill in any gaps that may exist among agency partnerships and the use of community volunteers. With internal family support, the external support of community volunteers, and coordination of agency partnerships for services, the offender has both private and public assistance for his or her treatment regimen. This means that there are numerous layers of support throughout the weeks and months of the offender's participation in treatment. It also means that the offender will have a variety of human contacts throughout that time, in addition to those typically provided by the community supervision agency. This increase in informal human supervision results in a better treatment prognosis while also providing additional leverage for offender compliance with treatment and supervision requirements. The two objectives, treatment and supervision, work together once again, but they do so from the vantage of the treatment provider rather than from a supervision perspective.

Consider also that treatment specialists can use other forms of community involvement that may include "corollary" forms of therapy that are not necessarily central to the offender's crime or even his or her special need, but are nonetheless adaptive activities that the offender can benefit from. For example, the offender may smoke cigarettes or may be overweight. In such cases, the strong urging at the behest of the therapist to join a group for smoking cessation or weight control may not be directly relevant to the crime, but nonetheless is more beneficial than harmful for overall social integration purposes. Further, more community members would be supervising the offender, and the leaders of these programs can report progress to the treatment specialist. This again results in an increased number of weekly human contacts that the offender has. Thus, from a treatment perspective, the offender is constantly under the watchful eye of various persons who are tasked with addressing corollary treatment needs of the offender.

It should be clear by now that treatment specialists can provide another effective link with the community that simultaneously enhances both therapeutic objectives and supervision objectives. This is consistent with the notion of reintegration that was presented in earlier chapters of this text. In fact, the therapeutic process is not unlike the human contact between the offender and another person, as it requires that offenders engage in prosocial activities while also being under the observation of a clinician. This aids in the supervision of an offender but also provides depth in that supervision while requiring a degree of transparency for the offender who must engage in the treatment process. The outcome is one where the activities of different persons (therapists, community volunteers, and community agency staff) serve as interlocking mechanisms to keep the offender's thoughts and behaviors routinely focused on his or her reintegration, providing a comprehensive treatment and supervision strategy.

PROGRESS IN TREATMENT PROGRAMS AND THE LIKELIHOOD OF RECIDIVISM

The title of this section may seem to make intuitive sense and may not warrant additional discussion. For persons working in treatment circles, this might be true, but for laypersons, the implications of treatment progress for recidivism rates might not be so clear. In fact, it could be said that progress in some areas of treatment may have little or no impact on future recidivism of offenders. The point is that the interconnections can be complicated and are not always obvious. To make this clear, some brief explanations are required.

First, when offenders successfully complete treatment programs, this often indicates a likelihood of prosocial behaviors and a corresponding reduction in criminal behavior. Consider, for example, an offender in a halfway house. While in the halfway house and even upon completion of the halfway house's treatment program, it is likely that the offender will experience a reduction in criminal activity. However, this would be true even if no real treatment intervention were applied due to the fact that the offender is under closer control than he or she would be if freely released to the community. Offenders in such a case may "fake good" in their behaviors and responses, knowing that their act is only temporary until they return to the community. This is, of course, where the public skepticism lies in regard to the treatment of the offender population. Concern with manipulation throughout the treatment regimen leads many members of the public to scoff at the validity of treatment perspectives.

On the other hand, even if offenders are genuinely committed to such programs, their return to their families or communities of origin may place them at risk of further offending. A lack of services during the reentry process or insufficient aftercare can ensure that over time, the beneficial gains of treatment are diminished. Thus, the program itself can be quite effective but may only have residual effects when the props and support are removed. In fact, this is one shortcoming of a supervision-only approach to community corrections: once punitive leverage is removed, the offender has no incentive to remain crime free. Effective treatment programs seek to build a sense of internal regulation in offenders through personal insight and a variety of exercises and activities that reinforce that insight.

Likewise, negative treatment outcomes can be indicative of potential recidivism, even if the treatment regimen is corollary to the criminal behavior. Thus, even though the offender may have actually completed a specified number of treatment program sessions, this may not be a good marker of offender reform. In many court sentencing programs, offenders are required to participate for a defined number of weeks or months, and the offender's success is based more on attendance than on actual effort or progress in the treatment program. Court relationships with treatment providers must instead ensure that the input from those providers serves as the defining factor in the offender's completion of his or her therapeutic requirements. When this leverage is provided, offenders are more likely to commit to treatment programs, and overall outcomes in recidivism are destined to be improved.

Finally, a variety of assessment scales that are used in constructing treatment agendas can be used to predict the offender's likely treatment outcome by looking at corollary issues. For instance, some scales may measure the offender's likelihood of relapse for a mental health– or treatment-related issue but may also take additional measures of the offender's cognitive, motivational, or emotional characteristics. Some instruments may even measure the defensiveness and likely honesty of the offender that completes the instrument. Though these predictive mechanisms may be intended for therapeutic outcomes, these same measures are sometimes consistent with likely recidivism. Indeed, offenders that are defensive or manipulative in therapy are also more likely to have such characteristics in regard to their likely criminal behavior. Thus, it may be that indirect measures intended for therapeutic purposes can also lead to effective prediction of recidivism among offenders, even though the intent of these items remains otherwise. While it would not be prudent to utilize instruments beyond their intended purposes, clinicians may find that they can provide additional insight and analysis of offender profiles so that community supervision officials will be better informed about the offender. This demonstrates that therapeutic orientations can include a public safety component, over and above that which occurs when offenders are provided therapeutic services.

EDUCATING THE COMMUNITY ABOUT TREATMENT BENEFITS AND INTEGRATING CITIZEN AND AGENCY INVOLVEMENT

Since treatment is recommended for so many offenders and because community treatment programs are often much more flexibly designed, community partnerships serve to fill the gaps that may emerge in various treatment strategies. As has been continuously emphasized throughout this text, community involvement improves the level of "human supervision" of the offender while also providing a much larger support network. This means that community support is greatly needed in the reintegration of the offender population, and therefore community education is critical. Many community members may have no idea how specific treatment needs can directly impact the likelihood of offender reintegration. Further, these same people may not truly understand that offender recidivism, and the future crime rate, is directly impacted by the successful rehabilitation and reintegration of the offender.

Thus, the education of community members and their recruitment for the treatment process can be very important. As described in Chapter 2, one benefit for society when including community members is the fact that they have the opportunity to make a direct contribution to the justice system by working with victims and offenders. This helps to ensure that volunteers are being used in a significant way and should show them that their contribution is important. A good example of how volunteers can be effective in the reintegration process for juveniles is described in Focus Topic 9.4.

FOCUS TOPIC 9.4

JUVENILE REINTEGRATION

The Office of Juvenile Justice and Delinquency Prevention has collaborated with the Boys and Girls Clubs of America to implement a pilot project called "Targeted Reintegration." This project is designed to provide Boys and Girls Club services to youth in residential placement using trained Boys and Girls Club staff. The goal of the project is to encourage youth, upon reentry into the community, to become involved in Boys and Girls Club–sponsored activities. The initiative has been piloted in three sites—St. Paul, Minnesota; Jacksonville, Florida; and Clark County, Nevada. Services to youth in residential care provided by Boys and Girls Club staff include recreation, life skills, job readiness training, tutoring, and other services. Club staff build relationships with the youth and encourage them to attend the club upon their release. The staff also work closely with institutional staff and probation officers to stay informed and share information about the youth's progress.

SOURCE: Office of Justice Programs. (2001). *Reentry courts: Managing the transition from prison to community.* Washington, DC: Author. Retrieved from http://www.ncjrs.org/pdffiles1/ojp/sl000389.pdf

Many people in the community may not understand basic issues related to criminal offending, and public service campaigns can work toward resolving this lack of understanding. Indeed, basic knowledge of different types of crime, their frequency, and the dynamics associated with each may not be widely known. Such knowledge can provide insight as to the conditions that lead to crime-prone behavior, and this also can lead to public awareness of interventions that can prevent future behavior among persons likely to engage in criminal activity. Aside from prevention, the successful reformation of persons and family systems can eliminate future offending, and it is this aspect that should be emphasized in community awareness campaigns. Treatment groups and even criminal justice agencies must actively advertise this point to the public consumer. Lobbying actions in state legislatures, the use of media campaigns, community newsletters, and word of mouth can all aid in increasing awareness of treatment programs and their effectiveness in reducing criminal activity.

Further, when citizens are involved in reintegration activities, such as the program noted in Focus Topic 9.4, it is important that these activities be publicly showcased. This further demonstrates the need for public commitment and develops a sense of "buy-in" in regard to treatment perspectives. In many cases, it may be best to first showcase juvenile programs since many communities may be more empathetic to the plight of adolescent offenders than they are to that of adult offenders. By first promoting awareness and understanding of juvenile issues and the efficacy of treatment approaches, treatment advocates can gain a "foot in the door," so to speak. This can be the first step in shifting the public mind-set from one that is skeptical of treatment orientations to one that is both understanding and supportive. As part of this change process in community perceptions, it is also important that key community personnel be educated on the complexities involved in determining "what works" in treatment programs. This single issue is perhaps most important because it provides insight to community leaders as to why the beneficial effects of treatment approaches may not be immediately visible to the casual observer. Indeed, this is equally true for successful prevention programs—consider for a moment what the crime rate might look like if one did not engage in prevention at all. This same rationale should be presented for treatment approaches, noting that the social, economic, and personal costs of crime would be much higher than they currently are.

Building social awareness of treatment programs and their efficacy can be very difficult, particularly in areas where criminal offending is pronounced or in regions of the United States that tend to be punitive in their approach to offenders. Nevertheless, this is an important area of focus if one genuinely desires to improve current community supervision strategies. The simple reality is that we cannot afford to incarcerate the majority of our offender population, and added to this is the reality that the majority of offenders will commit crimes that do not warrant incarceration. Thus, offenders will remain in the community regardless of the modality that is utilized by agencies. While improvements in offender supervision are important, this is only one element of reducing recidivism. Such aspects are based on external, compliance-based tactics. However, exclusive attention to these approaches completely ignores and overlooks internal incentives that may exist for many offenders. If community supervision processes are to be optimized, agencies and the community must also ensure that treatment approaches are given adequate focus and attention.

Applied Theory | **Social Disorganization, Collective Efficacy, and Community Supervision**

The work of Robert Sampson, Stephen Raudenbush, and Felton Earls (1997) has found that crime and recidivism are much lower in communities that have their fair share of *collective efficacy*. Collective efficacy refers to a concept where communities that experience disorderly conduct or criminal behavior possess citizens that have the cohesiveness to act in an "effective" way to solve the crime problem in their area. Thus, collective efficacy is a resource in which the community acts as a "self-starter," so to speak. Rather than waiting on formal means of thwarting criminal behavior, the community itself is actively involved in the process of fighting crime.

This concept of collective efficacy is important since it reflects a healthy community, and since this describes the specific characteristics that community supervision agencies seek within communities where partnerships are formed. Communities with high levels of collective efficacy are ideal for aiding agencies in providing additional human supervision of offenders. Further, offenders that might otherwise reoffend are less likely to do so because of the high level of collective efficacy in a neighborhood, the result being that the offender is watched much more carefully by members of that community.

Communities with strong collective efficacy have well-developed informal social control. In other words, non–law enforcement controls from churches, schools, civic groups, and other such informal social institutions will be in place. Further, these communities will tend to have a high degree of social cohesion and trust, both with each other and (ideally) with their community supervision agency. What this means for community supervision agencies is that in addition to educating citizens on the effectiveness of treatment programs, agencies must engage their communities so that the citizens are involved in the reintegration process. Doing so will enhance the collective efficacy that exists. In cases where communities do not exhibit strong collective efficacy, it should be the first order of business among criminal justice agencies to instill this in communities through various public outreach campaigns and initiatives. Doing so will produce benefits and rewards that will positively impact the agency and the community alike, while also reducing likely recidivism rates in the future.

SOURCES: Lilly, J. R., Cullen, F. T., & Ball, R. A. (2007). *Criminological theory: Context and consequences* (4th ed.). Thousand Oaks, CA: Sage Publications; Sampson, R. J., Raudenbush, S. W., & Earls, F. (1997). Neighborhoods and violent crime: A multilevel study of collective efficacy. *Science, 277,* 918–924.

CONCLUSION

This chapter demonstrates several points that further refine the reintegrative orientation of this text. First, it is clear that the widely touted conclusions from the Martinson Report are likely to be outdated, the results of that report no longer being true to the circumstances of today. It is not clear if Martinson's findings were completely accurate to begin with, and it is also true that many persons have distorted the study's findings. This demonstrates that more effective forms of research on treatment programs should be conducted and, as it turns out, an abundance of meta-analyses have examined treatment efficacy in a much more careful, systematic, and rigorous manner. The result of this more contemporary research is that treatment programs do indeed work, depending on the objectives that are desired, the nature of the treatment, and the specific research questions that are asked. To say that "nothing works" is now an outdated, archaic, and incorrect assumption regarding treatment programs in corrections.

This chapter also demonstrates the need to have treatment programs in the community. This should be the first option when reintegration is the desired outcome. The use of institutional treatment programs tends to have drawbacks that can be avoided with programs that are set within the community. Because a treatment perspective is emphasized throughout this text and because treatment programs are best administered in the community, community partnerships between agencies and volunteers become critical to the offender's overall reintegration process. The integration of treatment professionals, community agencies, and community volunteers provides help in reforming offenders and also provides more human contact and interaction. In an indirect sense, this alone creates a process of seamless supervision as the offender remains in close proximity to one person or another. Since the offender is in contact with a variety of persons who are supportive of treatment, there is a chain of custody within the offender's daily interactions, leaving little time or possibility for offending that will go unnoticed. It is this aspect of increased human supervision that improves the treatment prognosis of the offender while also utilizing the community itself to maintain more effective supervision of the offender's behaviors and activities. Thus, treatment staff and community members work together, hand-in-hand, to improve offender treatment outcomes.

Key Terms

Behavioral therapy

Client-centered therapy

Cognitive therapy

Faith-based

Family systems

Feminist therapy

Five essential elements of specialized courts

Long-term residential treatment

Outpatient drug-free treatment

Reality therapy

Reentry courts

Short-term residential programs

Solution-focused

Therapeutic jurisprudence

"What Would You Do?" Exercise

Jimmy is a domestic batterer who is in group counseling for domestic abuse that meets on Monday evenings at 6:30. He is also in an additional group for anger management that meets at 7:00 on Wednesday evenings.

Finally, he is in another group for substance abuse issues at 7:00 on Thursday evenings. On Tuesday and Thursday mornings, he visits a local educational agency for GED preparation. In addition, Jimmy completes roughly 8 hours of community service a week, attends AA meetings on Tuesday evening, and is also required to see you, his probation officer, 5 times per week since he is on intensive supervised probation.

One day, Jimmy's addiction therapist calls you and explains that he is concerned. It seems that Jimmy is violating the bounds of confidentiality by leaking information regarding other members of his batterers' group. During the substance abuse group meeting on Thursday evenings, he routinely refers to clients in his Monday evening batterers' group by name and provides details regarding their relationships and their treatment progress.

The therapist explains that he talked with Jimmy about this, and Jimmy got a bit angry. He was not volatile, but irritated, and exclaimed, "Here I am trying to participate in the group session and you are downin' me, man! What gives with this, dude?"

When you ask Jimmy about this issue, he points out that he is so busy with therapy and meeting the conditions of his supervision that he cannot remember who is in what group and how to sort things out. He claims that he slips up by accident and that he just cannot keep up.

You screen his records and notice that the GED preparation and testing agency conducted a number of tests of cognitive functioning. They found that Jimmy has fairly significant cognitive deficits that affect his concentration. Whether this is substance abuse induced is not clear, but it has been noted in his record (though Jimmy does not seem to be aware of this). On the other hand, the therapist for the batterers' group explains that batterers are very clever (though not necessarily smart academically), are manipulative, and tend to be passive-aggressive by nature. In short, the therapist for the batterers' group believes that Jimmy is manipulating his various treatment challenges to sabotage the therapy so that he can get reassigned. This therapist informs you that Jimmy has noted he does not like the therapist for his addiction group and has been wanting to leave that group for some time.

What would you do?

Applied Exercise

Using the same four case vignettes from Chapter 8 (presented below), select one and this time discuss the various treatment implications involved for the offender that you selected. Be sure to select the specific treatment modality that you would use (type of therapy) and explain why you would choose it. Next, identify the type of treatment professional that you believe is best suited for your chosen case. Provide an explanation for this and be careful not to pick a professional that is overqualified or underqualified for the challenges associated with your chosen vignette. Finally, explain how you might use a variety of community partnerships to enhance the likelihood for treatment success with your chosen vignette. This assignment will require that you complete outside research on your own. Each response to the questions must be correct and balanced in approach (consisting of realistic possibilities), with anywhere from 450 to 900 words of content being allowed for application 1 and 250 to 500 words of content for applications 2 and 3.

Students should complete this application exercise as a mini paper that explains the scenario and then addresses each question. Total word count: 950 to 1,900 words.

Applied Exercise Case Vignettes

Vignette #1: A male offender who is 57 years old with dementia, who is also an opiate addict due to the need for relief from severe back and neck pain. After the recent death of his wife, he assaulted several family members who were arguing over where he would now stay.

Vignette #2: A female prostitute with substance addiction who has HIV and suffers from depression regarding her plight. She has a 5-year-old son and it is found that she was a victim of childhood sexual abuse.

Vignette #3: A schizophrenic and paranoid-delusional offender who has been homeless most of his life. He is an alcoholic with cirrhosis of the liver.

Vignette #4: A mentally handicapped 14-year-old boy who molested his 8-year-old female cousin. He had found some pornography that his older brother had hidden under the couch and he wanted to show his cousin how the pictures worked.

CHAPTER 10

Community-Based Residential Treatment Facilities

LEARNING OBJECTIVES

1. Understand the challenges facing jail facilities and the need for jail diversion programs.

2. Know the history of the development of halfway houses in the United States.

3. Be aware of the various types of community residential treatment programs that exist.

4. Understand the benefits of using community residential treatment programs.

5. Be cognizant of the various offender needs and problems that residential facilities may address.

INTRODUCTION

Jail facilities are typically the first point at which an offender is officially classified as being in the correctional component of the criminal justice system. However, this is a bit deceptive since most people are only being detained after they have been arrested. This detainment, or detention, occurs at a local detention facility that is usually administered by the county and operated by the sheriff's office. This detention facility is what is generally thought of when we use the term *jail.*

In simple terms, a **jail** is a confinement facility, usually operated and controlled by county-level law enforcement, that is designed to hold persons charged with a crime who are either awaiting adjudication or serving a short sentence of one year or less after the point of adjudication. Similarly, the Bureau of Justice Statistics (2008) defines jails as "locally-operated correctional facilities that confine persons before or after adjudication. Inmates sentenced to jail usually have a sentence of a year or less, but jails also incarcerate persons in a wide variety of other categories." This means there is quite a bit of flow in and out of a jail facility for two reasons. First, persons that are arrested are automatically held within the jail facility, but many are released within 2 or 3 days due to the placement of bond or a judge releasing the person on his or her own recognizance. Second, offenders that serve jail terms do so for one year or less, as longer sentences are most often reserved for those serving true prison sentences. Thus, even among those serving a jail sentence, the turnover tends to be rapid because most sentences are only for a few months to a year.

INITIAL OFFENDER PROCESSING IN THE JAIL SETTING

While there is a significant amount of turnover, the jail population is not nearly as large as the population of offenders on community supervision. However, the jail population is still substantial. Indeed, from 2000 to 2006, the jail population increased from 621,149 to 766,010. This is a rate increase of 220 per 100,000 to 256 per 100,000 persons. Thus, the number of persons jailed, per capita, has continued to grow over time. Table 10.1 illustrates both the growth in numbers and the increasing rate of offenders who have been jailed from 2000 to 2006. During the year 2006, the vast majority of jail inmates were male, numbering 661,329, while female offenders in jail numbered 98,577. Juvenile offenders in jail facilities consisted of 6,104 total offenders at midyear in 2006. Thus, it is clear that when we talk about jailed offenders, the majority are male and adult. Though the rate of female offenders in jail is higher than that of male offenders, it is still true that males greatly outnumber females in jail facilities.

As mentioned before, there are far fewer people in jail facilities than there are on community supervision, and this might suggest that jails are a minor component of the criminal justice system. This is of course untrue, and it should be noted that the average daily population data on the number of persons in jail does not adequately portray the important role of the jail and its expanded importance to the correctional and judicial arms of the justice system. While the population of jail facilities may be less than 800,000 persons nationally on any given day, "between 10 and 15 million persons pass through the jail systems during a calendar year" (Wallenstein, 1999, p. 49). This statistic suggests that jail facilities around the nation essentially process roughly 10 times the number of persons that are reflected in a count taken on any given day of the year. Thus, there is clearly a substantial amount of turnover among the jail population. In many cases, a similar group of offenders may recycle in and out of the jail facility, perhaps going through intake and exit from jail at a variety of points throughout the year. The fact that these inmates recycle through the jail facility creates a number of challenges and difficulties for jail staff who must contend with this constantly changing offender population. This also means that jail facilities have a substantial impact on the public safety of communities that surround them. Therefore, jail administrators have a very big responsibility, both to the jail staff and to the community at large, as the jail agency is pushed and pulled by the ingress and egress of inmates as well as the demands of and concern for the community.

With this ingress and egress of persons in mind, it becomes clear that the most critical area of a jail is the admission point, commonly known as the booking area. There are many potential security risks in the booking areas because so many people enter and exit the jail facility from this point. Persons arrested and brought into the booking area are often under the influence of drugs, alcohol, or both, and this naturally creates health, safety, and security problems. Further, these individuals are likely to be anxious or depressed or have some other form of negative affect (including anger, of course). Kerle (1999) notes that many persons that are first booked are potentially assaultive, willing to strike out at staff who are nearby. In fact, according to Kerle's research, many jail altercations tend to occur in the booking area.

Jails also book a large number of persons with mental disturbances (see Chapter 13 for more detail), as these are often comorbid with drug and alcohol problems. For this reason, jail facilities should have mental health personnel and substance abuse specialists on staff and available 24 hours a day to diagnose and manage the array of problems with which these offenders may present (Kerle, 1999). The reality is, such services are often only routinely available in larger jail facilities, with smaller jails in rural areas perhaps having no such staff at all. Even with larger jail facilities, these staff may be so overworked as to hardly be available during times that are not considered peak hours for intake. In cases where such staff are not available, the booking officer must identify unusual behavior, perhaps having been trained through in-service processes to observe sudden shifts in mood or personality, hallucinations, intense anxiety, paranoia, delusions, and loss of memory (Kerle, 1999). Further, the risk of suicide is greater in jail facilities than in prisons, particularly during the first 48 hours and especially if the person is under the influence of alcohol or drugs. The booking officer and other staff must be quick to screen for potential suicide in all circumstances, noting mental health, substance abuse, or other factors that might exacerbate its likelihood.

As noted earlier, jails may commonly house persons that cycle in and out of their confines. The reason for this is that the bulk of criminal activity is committed by a small group of the overall offender population. These offenders, roughly 10 percent of the total offender population, commit well over half of all the crime in a local jurisdiction (Cullen & Agnew, 2006). While much of this crime may be petty, these repeat offenders tend to cycle in and out of jail in between charges, with no long-term prison sentences due to the low priority of the criminal activity. Further, these offenders tend to know each other. Indeed, many are drug users that may sell, share, or use drugs with one another. Others may be partners in criminal activity, and, even more disturbing, some may be mutual members of a street gang. The point is that there tend to be interconnections among the criminogenic population due to chance meetings that occur on the streets or their periodic contact while in prison. Thus, in many larger jurisdictions, this offender population often maintains contact, both in and out of jail, revolving back and forth from the community to the jail and back again.

Among these petty and small-time offenders may be some who are homeless. The homeless population is a particular problem for larger jurisdictions, with most beat cops knowing these individuals by name, so frequent is their contact with them. Many homeless people have substance abuse issues, problems with trauma and anxiety, or other mental health disturbances. All of these factors are further worsened by an unstable lifestyle that consists of poor nutrition, inadequate health maintenance, and drug or alcohol use. Further still, communicable diseases may be more common among these individuals due to poor personal maintenance and risky lifestyle choices. This is particularly true for female offenders who may resort to prostitution either to pay for their drug habit or to pay for their basic needs. In such cases, these offenders are likely to be "regulars" for police officers in those jurisdictions and for jail staff that will book these nuisance offenders multiple times throughout the course of a year. In fact, it is even common among the homeless population for offenses to coincide with colder months of the year, such persons committing petty crimes so that they may spend the winter indoors within the jail facility rather than outside on the streets during the cold of winter.

TABLE 10.1   Number of Jail Inmates per 100,000 U.S. Citizens

Year	Number of Jail Inmates	Jail Incarceration Rate*
2000	621,149	220
2001	631,240	222
2002	665,475	231
2003	691,301	238
2004	713,990	243
2005	747,529	252
2006	766,010	256

SOURCE: Bureau of Justice Statistics. (2007). *Prison and jail inmates at midyear 2006.* Washington, DC: U.S. Department of Justice.

*Number of jail inmates per 100,000 U.S. residents on July 1 of each year.

THE USE OF JAIL DIVERSION PROGRAMS TO ALLEVIATE JAIL CROWDING

Photo 10.1 The Caddo Correctional Center is a large jail facility with numerous types of programs for offenders. This facility houses gang offenders, violent offenders, and a number of other types of offenders who are provided different kinds of in-house programming. The Caddo Correctional Center is well integrated with external agencies, including probation and parole offices.

Jail diversion programs have become a popular type of program when processing many offenders that have already been discussed. The use of such programs helps to prevent overcrowding of a jail system, but this should not be misunderstood—considerations are not made simply based on the population of the jail itself. Rather, jail diversion programs are designed to divert mentally ill offenders from the jail facility. In addition, many jail diversion programs that have emerged are structured for substance abuse treatment. This is important because it underlines the desire to provide treatment to these troubled populations. Thus, **jail diversion programs** are programs that are designed to divert mentally ill offenders and offenders with drug abuse issues from the jail facility as a means of enhancing therapeutic treatment aspects related to the challenges that face these offenders. In addition, many jail diversion programs have benefited from substantial federal funding, with most grants coming from the Substance Abuse and Mental Health Services Administration (SAMHSA) and the National Institute of Corrections (NIC).

Therefore, jail diversion programs seek to identify those persons that are in need of mental health interventions or substance abuse treatment, the premise being that they will be given superior treatment services in environments other than the jail. Further, the jail facility is able to operate more effectively since it is not bogged down with offenders that have serious mental health problems. Thus, these programs are designed for both the welfare of the jail facility and the offender's own welfare and safety. Likewise, the community stands to benefit since offenders are likely to be given more careful and deliberate supervision while in treatment, and this is more likely to reduce their recidivate behavior.

Before proceeding further, it would be good to define what is meant by the term *diversion*. So far in this chapter, definitions for *jails* and *jail diversion* have been provided, but no clear working definition has been offered for the term *diversion*. Understanding its meaning is important since diversion can occur at many points in the offender's jail experience. In addressing this term, a definition will be adapted from Ronald Jemelka (2000) and his monograph contribution entitled *The Mentally Ill in Local Jails: Issues in Admission and Booking*. Jemelka notes that diversion has been used to describe

> virtually any contact between a mentally ill person and any member of the criminal justice community, including diversion activities by police, diversion activities at the point of admission and booking into a jail, mental health services offered in jails, programs to facilitate re-entry into the community when a detainee is released from jail, and community-based programs which have as their goal the prevention or reduction of contact with the criminal justice system by mentally ill persons. (p. 35)

In the case of this text, **jail diversion** refers to any process designed to reduce the contact between the criminal justice system and mentally ill or substance-addicted persons, with the goal being to facilitate reentry of the offender into the community while also avoiding risk of public endangerment. These programs can consist of both pre-booking and post-booking interventions, so long as the primary nexus of intervention occurs during a time frame when the offender makes contact with the jail facility. With the purpose and parameters of jail diversion set, the question that then remains is whether these types of programs actually "work" better than the current "revolving door" system that exists in many jails. In a study by Steadman and Naples (2005), findings were obtained from six jail diversion programs that were federally funded to serve offenders with co-occurring disorders (having both mental health and substance abuse challenges). After a 12-month period, diverted offenders were compared with non-diverted offenders on self-reported outcomes. Steadman and Naples found that jail diversion does indeed reduce time spent in jail without leading to further public safety risks. In addition, these programs were found to be effective in linking offenders with community-based services. Naturally, this last finding is directly relevant to the main tenets of this text; release to the community can improve offender outcomes, thereby lowering public safety risks in the longest of terms.

The jail diversion programs examined in this study included three pre-booking and three post-booking jail facilities, from a variety of areas in the United States. Specifically, the pre-booking jail diversion programs were from Memphis, Tennessee; Montgomery County, Pennsylvania; and Multnomah County, Oregon, while the post-booking facilities were from Phoenix/Tucson, Arizona; Bridgeport, Connecticut; and Lane County, Oregon. The fact that the study compares both pre-booking and post-booking approaches to jail diversion in programs from diverse geographical areas in the United States ensures that the results of this research are generalizable to other parts of the nation. Further, the study by Steadman and Naples (2005) is important because it is one of the few systematic evaluations of jail diversion programs that exists in the literature. It is also one of the most recent studies to provide such a systematic view of these programs.

Steadman and Naples (2005) found that those selected for diversion were significantly different from those not selected when measured at baseline. According to Steadman and Naples,

> Diverted participants were *more likely* to be female; have a primary diagnosis of schizophrenia or a mood disorder with psychotic features; receive Supplemental Security Income or SSDI; have higher Colorado Symptom Inventory scores indicating better mental health; and report higher life satisfaction. The diverted group was *less likely* to live with a spouse or partner; have substance use problems; and have been arrested and spent time in jail. The two groups were similar on measures of physical health, age, race/ethnicity, education level, previous employment, previous treatment/victimization and violent acts. (p. 166)

From the findings just noted, it is clear that those who were diverted tended *not* to be substance abusers and tended predominantly to have mental health issues. Further, the majority were female. The implications are that these agencies were essentially picking those offenders that already had a prognosis for treatment and reintegration that was better than those not selected. Indeed, the fact that females were more often selected tends to verify that these agencies diverted less serious offenders who, in most cases, do not commit violent crimes. Also, these female offenders did not seem to (at least at the point of measurement) be entwined in the domestically abusive relationships common to many female offenders (discussed in detail in Chapter 14). Thus, those female offenders with fewer aggravating family dynamics tended to be selected for diversion; this was likely to skew the outcome in favor of success. Add to this the fact that those with substance abuse problems were less commonly diverted and this again makes the outcomes of these six diversion programs less applicable (or generalizable) to much of the offender population. Indeed, most offenders have at least some sort of substance abuse problem or experience, and alcohol and drug use is very common among the female offender population. But in the case of the female offenders diverted to these programs, alcohol or drug abuse was *less likely,* thus indicating that these programs were essentially selecting safer candidates for success when diverting them to the community.

Further proof of this skewed selection process is evident when considering that the non-diverted group was found to be significantly more likely to report residential treatment for substance abuse problems. The existence of untreated substance abuse issues further complicates treatment prognoses and therefore makes it less likely that such offenders will succeed in reentry, at least during their first attempt. In addition, the diverted participants were significantly more likely to report receiving three or more counseling sessions, hospitalization, taking prescribed medications, and emergency room visits. This suggests that among those that were diverted, there was a higher likelihood this group would seek out help and that they would utilize this help. Again, this is a positive attribute that points toward likely success in any treatment program, especially one centered on the diversion of such offenders.

To be clear, the selection processes used by these six agencies may have been a prudent approach. After all, one does not want to release offenders into the community who have a high likelihood of recidivism. Thinking back to Chapter 3, such a means of selecting offenders for diversion is less likely to result in false negatives when predicting who will and who will not reoffend. This is of course important for any jail administrator, since continual release of offenders that continue to reoffend is likely to cause serious community backlash. Thus, the best cases available are selected for diversion because they are the safer bets and they are less likely to end in a negative reflection on the program. This helps to ensure community support of the program, or it at least avoids the possibility of community resistance emerging. So, to some extent, this skewed selection of offenders is understandable and, one might argue, quite prudent on the part of jail facilities. On the other hand, this demonstrates that positive outcomes from such programs need to be observed with a skeptical eye since the argument could be made that those selected for diversion were likely to reform on their own anyway, at some point or another.

FOCUS TOPIC 10.1

THE PHOENIX PROJECT: MARYLAND'S JAIL DIVERSION PROGRAM FOR WOMEN WITH CO-OCCURRING DISORDERS

The Division of Special Populations of the Mental Hygiene Administration of the Maryland Department of Health and Mental Hygiene oversees programs for individuals with mental illness who may also have co-occurring substance abuse disorders, be homeless, have hearing disabilities, have HIV/AIDS, or be in the criminal justice system. As the number of women in jails has increased nationwide, there has been a corresponding increase in female inmates in the detention centers in Maryland. Although Maryland detention centers have been providing mental health services to inmates of both sexes since 1992, female inmates have not been the focus of specialized treatment until recently.

The Maryland Community Criminal Justice Treatment Program (MCCJTP) was begun as a pilot program in four counties in 1992. Since that initial program, the Division of Special Populations has developed the program in 22 of Maryland's 23 counties. In 1995, the Division focused on

treatment programs for women in response to the concerns of wardens about the special problems that incarcerated women presented to correctional staffs. These problems included increased suicide threats; reclusive behaviors in which women refused to be involved in activities, resulting in a lack of concern for personal hygiene and medical care; and an inability to cope with their situation as inmates. Many of these behaviors resulted in institutional infractions.

The Diversion Process

When police respond to a complaint, the Mobile Crisis Unit (MCU) is called if a woman exhibits signs or symptoms of mental illness or a substance abuse disorder. The disposition of the case is a joint effort between the MCU and the police, depending on multiple factors, including the nature and severity of the offense, the mental status of the woman, her criminal history, and her behavior and conduct. If she is eligible, she is diverted into the Phoenix Project instead of being taken to the detention center.

Women eligible for the services of the Phoenix Project must be 18 or older and have a severe mental illness as evidenced by a *DSM-IV* Axis I clinical diagnosis as well as a substance abuse disorder. The woman must also face arrest for a misdemeanor or a non-violent felony. A woman who is eligible for Phoenix and agrees to participate in the project will at that point be diverted into emergency crisis housing where she will be further evaluated and stabilized, or she will receive intensive case management and clinical interventions in her home. Her children will also be with her. She and the children will be moved to transitional housing as soon as she

is ready. In addition, if she is homeless, she will also be eligible to access the Shelter Plus Care rental assistance available through the Division of Special Population's HUD grant. A key component of the services available to the woman is a case manager who specializes in mental health and substance abuse. The case manager provides direct mental health/substance abuse treatment services and brokers other community services for the woman and her children, as needed. With Maryland's entry into a managed public mental health fee-for-service care system, community services are most often reimbursable.

SOURCE: Quoted verbatim from Gillece, J. (2000). *The Phoenix Project: Maryland's jail diversion program for women with co-occurring disorders.* Washington, DC: National Institute of Corrections.

When examining the costs associated with jail diversion programs, Steadman and Naples (2005) found that, overall, the diverted group incurred higher community-based treatment costs, and the non-diverted group incurred higher jail costs. In relating outcomes to costs, Steadman and Naples found few statistically significant differences. Of those observed, they noted the following:

In each of the sites, diversion was associated with differences in only one of the outcomes. In Lane County, OR, diversion reduced the probability of drug use by 80 percent at no greater net cost. In Tucson, AZ, diversion raised the Colorado Symptom Inventory scores by 4.5 points at a cost of $190 per point of improvement (a non-statistically significant difference). In New York, diversion reduced the odds of nonviolent victimization by nearly 70 percent. In Memphis, TN, diversion raised the Colorado Symptom Inventory scores by 2.4 points at three months at a cost of $1,236 per point of improvement. (p. 168)

From the above, it is clear that jail diversion programs do not necessarily save money, but they do seem to have at least some effect on overall treatment outcomes. These researchers note that the data taken from these six SAMHSA jail diversion programs suggest the following:

1. Jail diversion does "work," at least in terms of reducing time spent in jail, with many offenders spending more time in the community than in and out of jail facilities.

2. Jail diversion does not increase public safety risk.

3. Jail diversion programs more effectively link diverted offenders to community-based services.

4. For the most part, jail diversion offenders had lower criminal justice costs, but this was offset by higher treatment costs. In fact, this additional treatment cost is often higher than the criminal justice savings in the short run.

Taken together, results from these six sites provide mounting evidence that jail diversion results in positive outcomes for individuals, systems, and communities (Steadman & Naples, 2005). While these programs are apparently a bit more expensive in the short term, they do seem to "work" when the correct offenders are selected for such programs and when the appropriate services are utilized. The extent to which these outcomes can be sustained on a long-term basis will determine whether these programs are ultimately considered effective. It is clear that these programs select those more likely to succeed. This selection criterion indicates that the emphasis of these programs is on actual likelihood of treatment success rather than simply easing jail population issues related to overcrowding. Naturally, the actual prognosis for treatment is precisely what should be given priority, with budgetary concerns being subordinate (within reason, of course) to decisions to divert or not divert offenders into the community.

HISTORICAL DEVELOPMENTS OF HALFWAY HOUSES

The use of halfway houses has been traced back to the early 1800s in England. In the United States, the first use of a halfway house is thought to have occurred in 1817 when the Massachusetts Prison Commission recommended establishing a temporary residence for offenders that had just been released from prison (Latessa & Allen, 1999). The commission made this recommendation in the belief that offenders would need a supportive environment immediately after release to assist in the process of establishing a prosocial and law-abiding existence. Among other concerns was the fact that the community itself was (especially during the early 1800s) biased and unforgiving toward prior offenders. Even at this time, the difficulty for offenders in finding employment upon release was noted as a specific problem (Cohn, 1973).

During the early 1800s, a type of penal system had been in practice, commonly referred to as the Pennsylvania System. This model of prison management was first established by the Quakers and emphasized the need for prisoners to experience a sense of penitence and reflect on the errors of their ways. In this model of imprisonment, offenders were kept in single cells and were given the Holy Bible to read as they reflected on their sins, transgressions, and crimes. Offenders were held in their cells and not allowed to interact with other offenders that were similarly housed. These inmates did not work, talk, or recreate with one another. It was thought that if inmates were allowed to communicate, they would essentially "contaminate" one another with their various negative influences and learned experiences. Interestingly, this is similar to the beliefs held by many of today's criminologists that prisons are actually schools of crime, thus lending possible validity to these concerns among prison workers in the early 1800s. As we will see later, in Chapter 15, there is some truth to this, as that chapter will show that the longer offenders are incarcerated, the more likely they are to recidivate upon release.

Unfortunately, recidivism rates were very high in Massachusetts during the early 1800s, and community corrections approaches were not effective in lowering recidivism. Further, the influences of the Pennsylvania model of prison operations impacted the operation of halfway houses in Massachusetts. As a result, the Massachusetts legislature feared that those offenders released to halfway houses might "contaminate" one another if they were allowed to be housed together. This would, it was thought at that time, reverse their prosocial learning and resistance to criminal behavior, thereby making their experience in prison all for naught. As a result, the use of the halfway house was discontinued in that state.

However, the concept did find a warm reception in other correctional systems. For instance, in 1845 the Isaac T. Hooper Home in New York City was opened (also by the Quakers), and it is still in operation today as a home for female offenders seeking reentry into the community (Latessa & Allen, 1999). In 1864, the Temporary Asylum for Discharged Female Prisoners was opened in the Boston area (Champion, 2002; Cromwell, del Carmen, & Alarid, 2002). This halfway house received less community opposition than did homes for men. According to Cromwell et al., the "reason for this difference was an underlying belief that, unlike male prisoners, women prisoners did not associate for the purpose of talking about criminal activity. Women prisoners were believed to contribute to their own rehabilitation" (p. 258). This is interesting because in many respects, modern treatment providers note that female clients do tend to respond to therapeutic interventions in a more effective, trusting, and genuine manner than do male clients, particularly in the offender population. Though halfway houses during the early 1800s did not provide therapeutic services (only basic services such as food and shelter), it is fascinating that observations of differences between the sexes were just as distinct as they are today.

In 1896, Hope House was established in New York City by Maud and Ballington Booth. The Hope House design spread to other cities such as Chicago, San Francisco, and New Orleans, being financially funded by philanthropic groups such as Volunteers of America (Latessa & Allen, 1999). Hope House was considered a premier program for its time and was among the first to provide additional services that went beyond food and lodging. Nevertheless, Hope House would not last due to the emergence of parole within many states. The use of parole in the early 1900s was implemented as a "means for controlling and helping ex-inmates after release from prison" (Latessa & Allen, 1999, p. 373). Parole systems across various states reduced or eliminated the need for halfway

Photo 10.2   This residential treatment facility is informal in appearance and is located among other residences in a low-income area of the community. Its décor is fairly relaxing. Also notice the metal stairs that serve as a fire escape. Refurbished facilities such as these must still meet state fire code and health regulations to remain open.

houses, and given that such facilities were underfunded and not given substantive public support, it was only a matter of time until their demise would be witnessed. Latessa and Allen indicate that as funding became more difficult to obtain during the Great Depression, and as public sentiment toward offenders became more skeptical during such economically hard times, halfway houses began to shut their doors. It was not until the 1950s that the halfway house again emerged in the field of corrections. According to Cromwell et al. (2002), only one halfway house ultimately remained open throughout the Great Depression, namely the Parting of the Ways in Pittsburgh. This was a church-based program funded by donations and contributions of religious followers during that time. Otherwise, from about 1930 to the mid-1950s, halfway houses nearly disappeared from the correctional landscape.

In the mid-1950s, growing dissatisfaction with prisons began to occur in the mind of the American public. This was further intensified by findings that parolees faced challenges in the transition from prison to free-world living, and an understanding that supportive services and gradual integration were necessary if recidivism was to be reduced. In 1954, halfway houses began to reappear in various areas of the United States. Further, private religious organizations again surfaced to provide assistance to the offender population. During this "revival" of the halfway house concept, the use of individualized treatment, counseling, employment referral, and substance abuse counseling emerged as part of the services offered (Latessa & Allen, 1999). In 1961, halfway houses received governmental assistance for the very first time when Attorney General Robert F. Kennedy implored Congress to provide funds to open federal-level halfway houses for young offenders (Champion, 2002; Cromwell et al., 2002; Latessa & Allen, 1999). These developments eventually led to the passage of the Prisoner Rehabilitation Act of 1965, which authorized the Federal Bureau of Prisons to establish community-based facilities for the reintegration of young offenders. Further financial support continued due to the emphasis that was placed on reintegration during this period in community corrections history. (Students should refer back to Chapter 1 for specific historical time periods in community corrections.) In 1968, the Law Enforcement Assistance Administration provided additional funding for the establishment of non-federal halfway houses, and the monetary support for these types of services lasted for over a decade, coming to a close in 1980 (Latessa & Allen, 1999).

Although government funding and support has decreased since the 1980s, private halfway houses continue to emerge as alternatives to prison. More information will follow on the use of various private organizations and facilities to offer halfway house services. As with the earliest of times in the history of corrections (again, see Chapter 1), religious institutions continue to be instrumental in the role of many halfway house services. It would seem that religious institutions and organizations have been the primary sources of forgiveness and sincere reintegration for those persons transitioning from prison to the community at large. It is then ironic that an emphasis on the separation of church and state became a potential impediment to providing services for offenders and for protecting the public from future increases in recidivism.

The year 1964 witnessed one of the most widespread and important developments in the history of halfway houses—the rise of the International Halfway House Association (IHHA) in Chicago. The fact that this organization is discussed, in detail, in other leading texts on community corrections underscores the importance of this organization within the developmental scheme of the halfway house concept. According to Latessa and Allen (1999), the IHHA was motivated by the absence of state and local support for halfway houses and sought to develop a voluntary and professional organization of halfway house administrators and personnel (p. 374; see also Wilson, 1985). The name of this organization was eventually changed to the **International Association of Residential and Community Alternatives (IARCA)** in 1989, reflecting the ambiguity in definitions of halfway houses and other forms of offender residential programs, the distinctions among these being more a matter of semantics than the actual operational function of such facilities. According to Cromwell et al. (2002), the IARCA represents roughly 250 private agencies operating nearly 1,500 programs around the world. Champion (2002) notes that even though halfway house programs were privately funded from the 1980s onward, the growth in their numbers was quite amazing during the decades that followed. As an example, he points out that (as of 2002) in the United States and Canada, some researchers report that nearly 2,300 halfway house facilities are in operation with over 100,000 beds available.

Regardless of how widespread these types of programs are, two things are for certain: the halfway house concept is alive and well in the field of community corrections, and these facilities are operating exclusive of government support in many cases. Though some of these facilities may obtain governmental grants, they are left to their own devices when stewarding their own future and the particular services that they provide. Though this can cause managerial challenges, it also provides for a great deal of flexibility, as private halfway houses can make their own determinations as to whom they will house. This and other areas of pliability in the decision-making process allow these programs to maximize their service delivery and also fill critical gaps that exist in state- and county-level governmental community corrections programs.

At this point, much discussion has transpired in regard to halfway houses, but no true definition has been offered. This is because these facilities have often defied specification as to what does and does not constitute a halfway house. For this text, a **halfway house** is defined as a residential facility for offenders that are either nearing release from prison or already in the initial stages of return to the community. In addition, halfway houses also consist of residential facilities that are designed as an intermediate sentencing option in lieu of prison, typically being applicable to serious probationers. Thus, halfway houses can be defined as being either halfway-out or halfway-in in the scope of their function and operation.

It is this last point of the definition that has not been addressed so far in this chapter. During the last few decades, innovations in the operation of halfway houses have established such facilities as alternatives to jail or prison incarceration. Thus, it becomes clear that these facilities can actually be tied to jail diversion programs, particularly if the halfway house is designed for substance abuse treatment, co-occurring disorders, or primary diagnoses for mental illness. Indeed, many such facilities do specialize in such interventions, and this leads to further blurring of the distinctions between halfway houses and other residential facilities that house the offender population. In fact, Champion (2002) goes so far as to add that these are sometimes referred to as community residential facilities. The fact that the IHHA changed its name to reflect residential and community alternatives underscores much of the blurring that exists within this component of community corrections. Nevertheless, the distinctions between halfway-in and halfway-out houses is important for students to remember since the severity of criminal behavior is typically different. Where one attempts to prevent further drift into an incarceration environment (halfway-in), the other attempts to increase drift from the incarceration environment and, with corresponding social "pulls and tugs," back into the community.

Cross-National Perspective

Canada's Halfway Houses

In 2001, there were approximately 175 halfway houses in Canada. These halfway houses are designed to be a "medium" option between prison incarceration and release into the community. Halfway houses also provide rehabilitation services and reintegration programs to assist an offender's reentry into society. Usually, the offenders are subject to constant supervision while they attempt to find employment, attend school, or engage in other activities necessary for successful reintegration.

Halfway houses may be operated either by the Correctional Service of Canada or by contracted voluntary agencies. Generally, there are four types of halfway houses in Canada: houses that provide only room and board, houses that have minimal intervention by authorities, houses that have a strict schedule of counseling and services, and houses designed to assist those with special needs (mental health, substance abuse, etc.). Every halfway house, regardless of what agency operates the facility, must adhere to minimum standards set by the Correctional Service of Canada. These minimum standards include proper staff training, accurate record of departures and arrivals of residents, and proper reporting procedures to the Correctional Service of Canada.

Most residents of halfway houses have been granted "day parole," which allows the resident to engage in most community activities during the daytime hours, subject to certain conditions, and requires that they return to a supervised facility at night. Day parole is usually granted 6 months before the eligibility date for full parole.

Residents of halfway houses do not enjoy the same privileges as other members in society. Residents may be subject to strict conditions including curfew, reporting regularly to a parole supervisor, remaining drug and alcohol free, mandatory substance abuse counseling or other treatment, and strict adherence to house rules. If residents do not follow the conditions of their release, they may be remanded to custody and subject to serve the remainder of their sentence incarcerated.

Halfway houses and day parole, compared with statutory release and full parole, have proven to be consistently the most successful form of conditional release. Recidivism rates are lowest among those who are gradually released back into society, and of those who successfully complete a gradual release program, only a small percentage committed a new crime.

SOURCE: John Howard Society of Alberta. (2001). *Halfway house*. Alberta, Canada: Author. Retrieved from http://www.johnhoward.ab.ca/PUB/halfway.htm#need.

Critical Thinking Question

1. Do you believe that the general conditions of residence at a halfway house are too strict or not strict enough? Explain your answer.

For more information about halfway houses in Canada, visit the website www.johnhoward.ab.ca/PUB/halfway.htm.

VARIOUS COMMUNITY RESIDENTIAL TREATMENT CENTERS

Community residential treatment centers are non-confining residential facilities for adjudicated adults or juveniles who are not appropriate for probation or who need a period of readjustment after imprisonment. Most of these facilities serve the juvenile population, and some may specialize in either a type of offender (e.g., women) or a type of treatment modality. The distinction between a community residential treatment center and a halfway house may not be clear. The main characteristic of residential treatment centers is that they are designed for those who are not good risks for probation, whereas halfway houses (at least halfway-*out* houses) are specifically designed for offenders that are expected to be released to the community. Halfway-*in* houses could be considered community residential treatment centers, but even in these cases the person is still likely to be classified as being on probation.

With respect to community residential treatment centers, many have been created to address drug or alcohol problems. They can be either short-term or long-term in nature. Students may recall from Chapter 9 that different types of treatment programs were presented in relation to reentry courts. The use of reentry courts was shown to be integrated with various treatment approaches, particularly in regard to substance abuse issues. Among these treatment approaches was the use of drug treatment programs in short-term and long-term residential facilities. This information is provided here in the context of community residential treatment facilities. This is not meant to be redundant but instead is intended to demonstrate the interlocking nature of many community corrections programs and processes. The courts, treatment modality, and type of facility are all interconnected in a means that reflects both treatment and security considerations. The length of term of the residential program, the type of halfway house (i.e., halfway-in versus halfway-out), and the type of jail program all reflect the seriousness of the offender and his or her prior behavior, this being a security consideration in most cases. The particular type of treatment program used may reflect either clinical issues or the type of offender. For instance, consider the use of diversionary treatment programs for mental health or drug treatment programs (type of clinical issue) versus those designed for sex offenders, female offenders, and juvenile offenders (types of offenders). Thus, a great degree of variability and overlap exists when one takes into account both the security and the treatment aspects of offender processing.

FOCUS TOPIC 10.2

SEDGWICK COUNTY'S TEAM CONCEPT FOR RESIDENTIAL PROGRAM MANAGEMENT

Sedgwick County Community Corrections opened a residential program in Wichita, Kansas, in July 1983. Since then, the program has grown to a capacity of 108 clients and a staff of thirty-six. It is highly structured and emphasizes client supervision, rehabilitative referrals, and accountability. Residents of the program are expected to maintain full-time employment and/or enrollment in an educational or vocational program in the community. Clients must budget their personal income to meet court-ordered and program-related financial obligations, complete therapeutic program goals, and master daily living skills, all toward eventual reintegration in the community. The average length of stay is four months.

For six years, the program operated with rigid divisions of labor and lines of authority. However, in order to improve overall program effectiveness while increasing staff involvement and motivation, the agency has begun to encourage teamwork at all levels. It also is attempting to provide training for all staff in program management and client supervision. Staff then have the opportunity to put that training into practice through a system of self-managing treatment teams.

There are four such treatment teams in the program, each providing day-to-day security and supervision. Each team includes a case manager and five to six corrections technicians. Teams work under the preexisting management team of a senior case manager, facility manager, and residential supervisor. Under the new system, team members have opportunities for taking on additional responsibilities and for professional growth. The case manager is the designated team leader and supervises five to six corrections technicians.

Specific responsibilities include scheduling shifts, leading weekly team meetings, hiring and training new team personnel, and evaluating technicians' performance. The case manager also performs daily security/control functions while technicians are absent or performing case management functions. Newly assigned team leaders receive training, technical support, and guidance from the management team. Corrections technicians provide twenty-four hour security, document observations and investigations of client behavior, and facilitate client accountability. In addition to being trained in security/control techniques, corrections technicians also receive training in case management.

The traditional corrections model for running a residential facility, in which "security" and "treatment" staff are separated, has been scrapped. Providing corrections technicians and team-leading case managers with greater involvement and autonomy has improved our staff's morale, sense of ownership, and accountability. Contributions of the corrections technicians to client security and supervision have increased dramatically, and the experience, knowledge, and enthusiasm gained by our entire staff have made this challenging approach worthwhile. One of the program's four treatment teams addresses drug and alcohol abuse education and the rehabilitation needs of clients. The team can treat up to twenty-four offenders from the U.S. Department of Justice.

This co-ed program lengthens the active treatment process through pre-treatment, post-treatment, and relapse prevention components. Clients are evaluated upon admission to the residential facility and, if identified as appropriate for the program, are included as space becomes available. The treatment program makes an allowance for the discharge of clients who are unwilling to recognize and address their substance use disorders during pre-treatment. If discharged from the treatment program, clients are placed in the general residential population for a minimum of thirty days and may reapply for the program after that time. Specific recovery-related treatment tasks are assigned to the client during the interim period. Security, treatment, and reintegration of clients are monitored by a specialized team comprising two certified drug/alcohol counselors, one case manager, and five to six corrections technicians.

For further information, contact Darryl A. Stamp, Interim Director, Sedgwick County Community Corrections, (316) 383-7003, or Mike Yearty, Director, Program Development, Parallax, Inc., (316) 263-5809.

SOURCE: Stamp, D. A. (1994). *Sedgwick County's team concept for residential program management.* Washington, DC: National Institute of Corrections. Quoted verbatim from http://www.nicic.org/pubs/1991/period17.pdf.

As noted at the beginning of this subsection, many residential treatment facilities have been designed for drug treatment. This is one of the most common uses of residential treatment facilities, though other types exist, particularly for juvenile offenders (see Chapter 12 for these particular types of programs). Since the 1980s, there has been an increased connection between drug courts and many community residential treatment facilities. The connection between these two functions (again, refer back to Chapter 9) demonstrates how different components of the criminal justice system may work in unison to provide a comprehensive means of processing. In these partnerships, **short-term residential programs** typically offer intensive but relatively brief residential treatment based on a modified 12-step approach. In most cases, offenders are kept in the program for no more than 90 days; often, their stay is for a period that is considerably less lengthy. On the other hand, **long-term residential programs** provide housing in what are typically non–hospital-like settings.

Within the field of addictions treatment, the most widely utilized form of residential treatment is the *therapeutic community.* These programs tend to house drug offenders for anywhere from 6 to 12 months. One example of the use of long-term, residential, therapeutic community treatment would be the Federal Bureau of Prisons' Residential Drug Abuse Treatment Program, which attempts to identify, confront, and alter the attitudes, values, and thought patterns that lead to criminal behavior and drug or alcohol abuse. This model program consists of three stages. First, there is a unit-based treatment program that exists within the confines of a prison where inmates undergo therapy for up to 12 months. Second, upon completion of the residential portion, offenders continue treatment for up to 12 months while in the general population of the prison, through monthly group meetings with the drug abuse program staff. In the third phase, inmates are transferred to community-based facilities prior to release from custody and are provided with regularly scheduled group, individual, and family counseling sessions (Inciardi, 1999a).

FOCUS TOPIC 10.3

RAYS OF SONSHINE—A FAITH-BASED RESIDENTIAL TREATMENT FACILITY FOR WOMEN

Rays of Sonshine is a residential treatment facility that is tailored to female drug abusers. What is particularly interesting about this facility is that it is faith-based in its modality, meaning that religious conviction and spiritual beliefs are interwoven into the treatment. This treatment program is unique among faith-based programs because it has implemented a very rigorous evaluation component, leaving itself open to research scrutiny. Empirical and data-driven research is rare among these types of interventions, and this makes Rays of Sonshine something of an unusual find, even in an age when faith-based interventions have become more common among programs being funded by federal grant dollars.

This treatment group has developed its own unique 12-lesson curriculum, based on Christian Bible scripture, as a means of directing the client toward a closer relationship with God. Within this orientation of Christian religious precepts, Rays of Sonshine employs typical case management techniques that are found in most other treatment programs, adhering to the standards set forth by the International Certification and Reciprocity Consortium (ICRC), a recognized authority on standards and procedures for administering drug treatment services. The ICRC's established 12 core functions are used and even mandated in a number of states and are thus common to many drug treatment providers. Through a combination of their own unique curriculum, the 12 core functions of the ICRC, and a set of cognitive-behavioral intervention strategies, Rays of Sonshine provides female drug offenders with a compelling intervention program that has proven to be quite successful.

In addition to the curriculum and core practices, Rays of Sonshine maintains a busy lifestyle for its clients, with a series of mandatory group counseling sessions, psychoeducation

related to relapse prevention, life skills training, basic literacy and secondary education, GED classes, physical fitness training, job placement assistance, and a number of other services that reflect a total wrap-around service agency. Between these various activities, Rays of Sonshine offers clients a number of group outings and also has routine "family nights" where family and friends of clients visit and are also trained on various aspects related to addictions, codependence, and other important factors related to substance abuse treatment. Whenever possible, Rays of Sonshine encourages the support of family and friends in a client's recovery.

Last, Rays of Sonshine is committed to research evaluation and transparency in its operational policies and procedures. For instance, the evaluation component used at Rays of Sonshine consists of a battery of standardized instruments available from such well-known manufacturers as Western Psychological Services, Psychological Assessment Resources, and the SASSI Institute. Instruments from these corporations were selected due to their proven validity and reliability. When taken in total, these instruments will assess clients on their severity of substance abuse while also screening or assessing for several comorbid issues. In particular, symptoms related to anxiety, depression, cognitive deficits, and antisocial personality disorder will be specifically examined. The combination of instruments used also has a variety of subscales designed to detect defensiveness and deceit in client responses. Further, these instruments have a variety of strengths that complement one another, with some being targeted for drugs other than alcohol, some targeted for alcohol abuse, and others assessing the use of both. This evaluative project was made possible through funding from the Substance Abuse and Mental Health Services Administration (SAMHSA).

As of this writing, Rays of Sonshine is only at the 4-month point of a 3-year funding period. Throughout the duration of this grant-funded research, measures will be taken using these instruments at intake, and then at 3-month, 6-month, 9-month, and 12-month intervals, when and where feasible. Though true randomization of the client subjects will not be achieved since clients will be determined by their own self-selection into this faith-based program, it is expected that very good data will be provided that can accommodate a variety of statistical applications. This means that Rays of Sonshine will be one of the few faith-based, residential treatment facilities in the United States to have standardized instrumentation and empirically sound evaluative processes. The initial wave of results is expected to be released after the first year of this study.

SOURCE: Rays of Sonshine. (2008). *Rays of Sonshine program description and evaluation program.* Monroe, LA: Author. Funded by the Substance Abuse and Mental Health Services Administration (SAMHSA).

It is interesting to note that social reactions to long-term residential treatment centers, including those operating as therapeutic communities, have ranged from negative to positive, with community reactions often being negative. In many cases, communities have expressed concern over having these types of treatment programs within their locale due to the perceived threat that members pose, and due to effects on local real estate value fluctuations. This is unfortunate since it has been made clear throughout this text that the participation of the community itself is critical to the effectiveness of community corrections programs. While it is of course understandable why community members would be averse to having their property values diminished, it is perhaps the negative perception itself that ultimately results in the reduction of value. Though the process may be complicated, work with various local forms of government to ensure that zoning and home owner's insurance agencies do not penalize communities that work with residential treatment facilities might be one effective means of offsetting community concerns. Further, employers in the area stand to gain from substantial tax breaks when they hire ex-offenders. These offenders seldom take jobs that would actually displace the non-offending community member, particularly when considering the stigma that follows them in the hiring process. Thus, such offenders, while at residential facilities or immediately upon release, can fill an employment gap that may exist in a community. The point is that if done in an innovative, comprehensive, and coherent manner, the negative impact of integrating residential facilities into a community can be mitigated, and, in some cases, the introduction of such facilities can even be a boon to that community.

Another type of residential treatment facility is the **restitution center.** This is a type of facility designed primarily for first-time offenders and property offenders. These offenders are required to pay victim restitution and/or provide community service as a means of fulfilling their sentence. While restitution centers may network with other treatment agencies, when such services are required for a given offender, their primary focus is on employment that allows the offender to provide economic amends to the victims of his or her crimes. This once again demonstrates that residential facilities can provide benefits to the community, especially if the victim is in the very community in which the restitution center exists. In this respect, the offender has to make reparations for the damage that was done to the victim—a much more productive use of the offender's time than sitting in a jail or prison cell. One good example of the use of restitution centers at the state level is provided by the Mississippi Department of Corrections (2007). According to that state's website on restitution centers, the Mississippi Department of Corrections restitution program provides

an alternative to incarceration for minimal risk offenders who are in need of a more structured environment. Residents serving time in a restitution center are referred to as residents. Residents who qualify for the restitution center program are required to work and pay full or partial payments to crime victims. Residents also have to

Photo 10.3 Buildings such as this one demonstrate that residential facilities can be quite large in some cases. Such facilities come in all shapes and sizes, this one being brick and having a much different appearance from the facility illustrated in Photo 10.2.

pay room and board fees ($10 per day), court fees, and establish a savings account. Residents are required to serve a minimum of 40 hours of free community service. (p. 1)

Many of these types of programs exist around the nation, and the above description clearly and succinctly demonstrates that offenders are held accountable to the community. Currently, the state of Mississippi has four such centers, located in the cities of Jackson, Pascagoula, Greenwood, and Flowood. The example provided from this state illustrates that, when such programs are done with deliberation, economic benefits for the local community and the entire state economy can be realized.

As can be seen, there is much variation among residential facilities. For example, some may be privately operated, whereas others are part of an entire state system. Some residential programs may be privately based but funded by federal or state money. In most cases, residential facilities do receive some type of reimbursement for services at either the local county level or the state level. These facilities naturally tend to work in tandem with the local courthouse and the probation agency, as they are designed for offenders that are not suitable for probation. Residential facilities are also impacted by the region and socioeconomic characteristics of their area. In fact, this can have a very important bearing on how such facilities operate and the services that they provide. In particular, centers may find that they face differing challenges depending on whether they are located in a rural area, a midsized area, or a metropolitan area of the nation. It is with this in mind that we now turn our attention to contrasting the challenges faced by rural and urban residential centers.

RURAL AND URBAN RESIDENTIAL CENTERS

Community residential centers in rural areas often deal with many challenges that are not necessary to consider in most urban areas. The towns have smaller populations, and this means that offenders have fewer educational or vocational options when compared with those in urban areas. Transportation may be a serious impediment, as jobs may be far from the residential facility. The rural nature of these areas often requires that offenders travel greater distances to programs, services, and employment opportunities. Moreover, in small towns, the offender may be known to most of the people in the area. This lack of anonymity can also be an impediment, resulting in further challenges for the offender since stigmatization is more likely. In many cases, the offender may find it very difficult to overcome the obstacles that exist in such areas. Further, these residential facilities tend to be limited by budget, making the provision of comprehensive services even more difficult.

Conversely, urban residential centers have many advantages over those located in rural areas. These facilities will have a much wider array of social services to draw from. This alone serves as a very important benefit since it is the ultimate aim of these programs to reintegrate those offenders that are deemed safe for such approaches. Though offenders in residential treatment facilities are not necessarily appropriate for probation, these offenders do eventually reenter the community, whether this be on probation or on some other form of modified sentence. This means that full casework services are important for these offenders just as they are for those on community supervision. In many cases, all of these services are not available to residential facilities located in rural areas, but they are more frequently available in midsized or metropolitan areas. This results in a distinct advantage that these programs have over smaller, rural-based operations. Further, transportation issues are often dealt with through mass transit availability. This makes various employment opportunities within easier reach of offenders since they have the benefit of more flexible mobility in urban areas.

WORK RELEASE AND STUDY RELEASE PROGRAMS

Work release programs are those designed to equip offenders with the opportunity to seek and maintain employment, while also engaging in educational or vocational training, as well as other treatment services that might be available at the facility. These programs are often used to replace jail sentences. They most often provide day and night supervision, job referral services, and counseling for residents (Latessa & Allen, 1999). In many cases, offender unemployment or difficulties in maintaining substantive employment can be major issues behind offender recidivism. Research throughout the United States clearly shows that offender employment tends to reduce recidivism (Champion, 2002; Latessa & Allen, 1999). Because the basic needs of offenders must be met, it is critical that they obtain income that can accommodate those needs. It is this issue, specifically, that work release facilities seek to ameliorate.

The state of Washington has recently (2007) completed a study of its own work release program, examining a total of 15 work release centers that are operated by the state (see Focus Topic 10.4 for more information on those findings). The fact that Washington has conducted recent research on the effectiveness of these programs is important because it illustrates several points that are germane to this chapter and to this text as a whole. First, these programs have been implemented at the state level, demonstrating that, like community restitution centers in Mississippi (discussed earlier), there is widespread use of community corrections alternatives. Second, these programs are being put to the test with very reliable and competently designed forms of research evaluation. Third, this use of community corrections alternatives and the resulting research evaluations are occurring in the modern day, making the information all the more relevant to an argument on behalf of offender reintegration. These three points demonstrate that community residential programs are not just options utilized by private companies, faith-based groups, and other such independent actors, but are often utilized by state correctional programs themselves. This adds to the credibility of these interventions, particularly if the research indicates recidivism reduction as well as other benefits such as lowered costs.

In the state of Washington, work release centers tend to be used with inmates that have already served some time in either a jail or prison facility. The work release program in Washington was first implemented in 1967 and was designed to enable selected offenders to serve up to 6 months of their prison sentence in a residential facility while employed in the community. Currently, Washington has 15 such centers that house roughly 700 offenders throughout the state (Washington State Institute for Public Policy, 2007). While the state has its own criteria as to the types of offenders that may participate in work release, each facility has its own local criteria as well. As an example, some work release facilities may house both male and female offenders, while others are specific to one gender. Likewise, some may be structured as therapeutic communities (as discussed earlier in this chapter) with substance abuse issues being an additional focus beyond employment considerations. Further, this state may also allow certain categories of sex offenders to enter work release programs, though specific forms of careful screening are implemented, identifying those that are not at the upper likelihood of recidivism.

WORK RELEASE PROGRAMS IN THE STATE OF WASHINGTON

Work release facilities enable certain offenders under the jurisdiction of the Washington State Department of Corrections (DOC) to serve up to 6 months of their prison sentence in a residential facility while employed in the community. Today, there are 15 work release facilities that house about 700 offenders statewide.

In 2007, the state legislature began to evaluate whether participation in Washington's work release facilities impacts recidivism. Our time period of study includes offenders who [were] released from DOC between January 1998 [and] July 2003. Findings from the study indicate participation in Washington's work release facilities:

- Lowers total recidivism, by 2.8 percent
- Has a marginal effect on felony recidivism; by 1.8 percent; and
- Has no effect on violent felony recidivism.

Of the 15 facilities operating in 1998 to 2003, the state of Washington found that participation in some facilities was more effective than others in the reduction of recidivism. An economic model was utilized to determine if the marginal benefits of work release outweigh the cost. Based upon the felony recidivism findings, participation in work release generates $3.82 of benefits per dollar of cost. The benefits (about $2,300 per work release participant) stem from the future benefits to taxpayers and crime victims from the reduced recidivism.

For more information, please contact Elizabeth Drake at (360) 586-2767 or kdrake@wsipp.wa.gov.

SOURCE: Washington State Institute for Public Policy. (2007). *Does participation in Washington's work release facilities reduce recidivism?* Olympia, WA: Author. Quoted verbatim from http://nicic.org/Library/022723.

Interestingly, this state uses private contractors to provide security for these facilities, as well as food service, maintenance, and clerical functions. The actual state staff will typically consist of the work release supervisor, the case management staff, and their immediate administrative support (Washington State Institute for Public Policy, 2007). Thus, these facilities utilize a fusion between public and private employees to operate at maximal level while also ensuring accountability to the state's department of corrections. This results in fiscal advantages while at the same time making sure these facilities are given appropriate public oversight.

While in these facilities, offenders are responsible for finding their own employment and are given roughly 10 days to do so once they arrive in the facility (Washington State Institute for Public Policy, 2007). Offenders are required to work 40 hours a week. In many cases, facilities have established informal agreements with local employers as a means of ensuring that offenders are able to obtain employment. In an effort to provide comprehensive employment services, these facilities sometimes have job specialists among the staff who are tasked with teaching offenders résumé design, interviewing techniques, and job preparation. These specialists often are personnel that come from the state's employment services, or they are contracted professionals. The point to this is that offenders are given guidance on techniques for obtaining employment. Thus, these facilities link with outside employers while simultaneously providing a series of services that aid offenders in their job search and their ability to acquire a job. Further, employers get federal tax credits for hiring offenders, and, when the employment is appropriate, the community benefits from the offender's work. When combined with restitution programs, this can provide money for specific victims or victim funds that are operated by the state. Thus, the community as a whole and victims throughout the state, as well as the offender, can benefit from these programs when they are run successfully.

As just noted, work release and restitution centers may have simultaneous functions and, in many cases, may be one and the same. This is not always true, however, as some programs may have limited areas of focus, but when possible, it is recommended that facilities incorporate as many of these various objectives as possible. An emphasis on employment obviously has a logical connection to the offender's ability to provide restitution. Likewise, it was noted that in the state of Washington, many work release programs provide additional focus on treatment issues, such as with substance abuse recovery. This is important because many of these offenders will have problems with substance abuse, such challenges being extremely common among the offender population. Likewise, an emphasis on female offenders would necessitate services such as child care and even perhaps issues related to hiring disparity between men and women, with additional networking necessary to provide women with suitable employment in some industries. This can be particularly important in rural areas where much of the work may be male dominated or geared toward heavy labor. Thus, challenges facing locales and the type of offender involved can be quite diverse. Because of the variety of challenges that are likely to be encountered, it is probably most appropriate for work release centers to be multivaried in their services. This again demonstrates the overlap that exists within community corrections programs and provides further indication of the blurring in distinctions between one type of program and another.

FOCUS TOPIC 10.5

COMCOR, INC., A PRIVATE, NONPROFIT, COMMUNITY CORRECTIONS PROGRAM IN COLORADO SPRINGS

ComCor's Transition program provides correctional and treatment services for Colorado Department of Corrections inmates who have served a prison sentence and then been placed in a community corrections program prior to being placed on parole by the State Board of Parole or being released from custody. These individuals are under the jurisdiction of the Colorado Department of Corrections, Division of Adult Parole, Community Corrections and Youthful Offender System, and the El Paso County Community Corrections Board.

According to the state of Colorado, Division of Criminal Justice, approximately 59 percent of Transition offenders statewide successfully complete their residential placement before being placed on parole or intensive supervision parole.

Individuals participating in ComCor's Transition program are assigned a case manager, and a thorough assessment process is conducted utilizing the state's Standardized Offender Assessment—Revised assessment battery. A vocational needs screen is conducted on each individual to determine if a more thorough vocational assessment needs to be done. A mental health screen is also conducted on each program participant at the time of

admission to identify any immediate mental health issues that need to be addressed.

The case manager collaborates with ComCor's mental health [staff], treatment staff, and vocational staff to develop an individualized supervision plan for each offender, outlining the program outcomes and behavioral expectations for the individual. This supervision plan is based on each individual's unique criminogenic needs and risk factors.

Individuals are required to participate in treatment groups and life skills classes, including vocational classes, while they are at ComCor. Each offender in the Transition program is monitored for alcohol and drug use, utilizing a well-established system of substance abuse testing. Program participants are required to be accountable 24 hours per day, seven days per week, through ComCor's established system of accountability monitoring. Program participants are required to meet regularly with their assigned case manager to discuss progress toward objectives identified in their individualized supervision plans and to address problems that may be impinging on the individual's reintegration within the community.

Individuals are required to maintain employment while in the Transition program and are responsible for paying

(Continued)

restitution, court-ordered costs, child support and other legal obligations along with their program room and board fees. Each participant develops an individualized budget with the case manager that is used to track their employment and financial obligations while in the program.

Individuals will have a thorough orientation process, which gives information on locations of ComCor facilities and programs, mental health, treatment and vocational services available, rules and regulations, accountability requirements (including signing in and out of the facility each time), passes (including work- and job-hunting passes), monitoring and testing requirements for drugs and alcohol, prohibited contraband items, daily facility chores and room inspections, safety procedures, food services system, room and board requirements, employment requirements, personal responsibility for medical care, and other information that is relevant to the individual's participation in ComCor's program.

Individuals are expected to pay $17 per day for room and board (subsistence fees) plus a one-time assessment and testing fee of $50. Individuals can bring their own linens or pay a one-time linen fee of $10. A padlock will be issued and a $5 deposit will be collected and returned at sentence completion.

SOURCE: ComCor, Inc. (2007). *Transition facilities.* Colorado Springs, CO. Quoted verbatim from http://www.comcor.org/correctional/transition.htm.

A less-known and less-used variant of the work release program is the study release center or program. The **study release program** is similar to a work release program but is designed to allow the offender to pursue educational goals. In fact, some states, such as Arkansas, may classify the criteria and the formal request process for study- and work-release options in the same category and require the same paperwork. Thus, these two programs work somewhat hand-in-hand and should be viewed as complementary.

The various types of study release can actually be quite relevant to the offender's ability to ultimately reintegrate effectively and to obtain employment. Study release programs may exist for basic adult education such as high school completion or high school equivalency (GED), technical or vocational education, and even college. Such programs are fairly rare since many prison systems offer similar educational opportunities. Nevertheless, study release may be a service that is offered in tandem with work release functions, thereby providing the offender with even more opportunities within the community.

COST-EFFECTIVENESS AND ACTUAL PROGRAM EFFECTIVENESS

The general body of evidence clearly demonstrates that halfway houses and other community residential facilities are much more cost-effective than prisons, while also meeting the goals of reintegration by providing offenders with the ability to maintain community ties and to access community resources. Further, recent research from the Washington State Institute for Public Policy (2007) offers one of the most systematic and methodologically sound means of examining community-based residential centers in existence. The institute's researchers conducted a cost-benefit analysis to determine the monetary benefits of offender placement into community residential treatment facilities. They factored into their model of evaluation that crime reductions would result in economic benefits to both the taxpayers and crime victims. Overall, this group found that participation in work release generated $3.82 of benefits per dollar of cost. While most of this gain was due to future benefits to the community and potential victims from recidivism reductions, it is nonetheless clear that these programs provide an economic incentive for society as a whole. Further, this does not even count the monetary considerations for restitution to victims. Thus, residential centers were shown to provide cost-effective services that are superior to the increased use of prisons.

In regard to recidivism, it would appear that in most cases, recidivism rates for those in residential treatment facilities are typically no higher than for offenders that remain in prison and are later released directly into society. Latessa and Allen (1999) point out that issues related to determining recidivism are complex to address due to the variety of facilities, the diversity of offenders they service, and the differing regions of the United States (the external community being important to offender outcomes). Because of this variability, it is difficult to develop equivalent comparison groups. Citing 1990s research, Latessa and Allen note that recidivism rates for offenders in residential treatment facilities are low, being from 2 to 17 percent. When considering halfway houses in particular, they note that "on the whole, follow-up recidivism studies indicate that halfway house residents perform no worse than offenders who receive other services" (p. 393).

Even better results were found by more rigorous and more recent research by the Washington State Institute for Public Policy (2007). This group found that in the state of Washington, work release programs reduced overall recidivism (for misdemeanor and felony offenders combined) by about 2.8 percent and reduced recidivism for felony offenders by 1.8 percent. Though these reductions in recidivism are not great, this is still much better than if recidivism outcomes had gone in the other direction. When taking into consideration that these outcomes were achieved while also providing an economic benefit to society, it becomes clear that these programs are superior to pure forms of incarceration and that they do not place the public in jeopardy.

This same research found that these programs did not have any effect on recidivism for violent offenders. This is important for two reasons. First, even with felony offenders, no raising or lowering of recidivism was detected as being statistically significant. Thus, these types of programs do not exacerbate the problem, meaning that primary benefits may come in the way of financial savings rather than reductions in crime. While this in not an ideal outcome, it is still acceptable since violent offending did not increase. Second, this research demonstrates why it is important to appropriately assess and classify offenders before placing them in these programs. It is clear that one would desire to include misdemeanant and felony offenders that are not violent, since these offenders provide the greatest gains in monetary savings as well as slight reductions in recidivism. While violent offenders did not become more serious, they also do not provide the same gains that other offenders do, and therefore should not be considered as candidates for such programs, particularly in agencies that wish to optimize their outcomes and the use of their resources.

Finally, the Washington State Institute for Public Policy (2007) conducted a comparison of research work release programs and recidivism. They found that, in general, programs are effective in reducing recidivism. Table 10.2 demonstrates that, overall, these programs have been successful when they have been evaluated based on recidivism. This is determined by the effect size found in each study. The effect size measures the degree to which a program has been shown to change an outcome for program participants relative to the comparison group. A negative effect size indicates a decrease in recidivism and a positive effect size indicates an increase. While it was determined that 3 of the 4 studies found that work release programs reduce recidivism, the fourth study that implemented more rigorous methodological approaches failed to find any significant differences in outcomes. The researchers noted

TABLE 10.2 Rigorous Studies Evaluating the Impact of Participation in Work Release on Recidivism

	Jeffrey & Woolpert	LeClair & Guarino-Ghezzi	Turner & Petersilia	Waldo & Chiricos
Study Information				
Year published	1974	1991	1996	1977
Research design level[a]	3	3	3	5
Program information				
State	California	Massachusetts	Washington	Florida
Number in work release	109	212	112	188
Number in comparison	92	211	106	93
Adjusted effect size	−0.172	−0.049	−0.049	0.021

Citations:

1. Jeffrey, R., & Woolpert, S. (1974). Work furlough as an alternative to incarceration. *The Journal of Criminology, 65*(3), 405–415.

2. LeClair, D. P., & Guarino-Ghezzi, S. (1991). Does incapacitation guarantee public safety? Lessons from the Massachusetts furlough and prerelease programs. *Justice Quarterly, 8*(1), 9–36.

3. Turner, S. M., & Petersilia, J. (1996). Work release in Washington: Effects on recidivism and corrections costs. *Prison Journal, 76*(2), 138–164.

4. Waldo, G. P., & Chiricos, T. G. (1977). Work release and recidivism: An empirical evaluation of a social policy. *Evaluation Quarterly, 1*(1), 87–108.

SOURCE: Washington State Institute for Public Policy. (2007). *Does participation in Washington's work release facilities reduce recidivism?* Olympia, WA: Author. Retrieved from http://nicic.org/Library/022723.

[a]Studies are rated based upon the Maryland scale of rigor: 1 is the lowest quality and 5 is the highest quality, random assignment. In our analysis of the literature we only report findings of studies rated a 3 or higher.

that there is a dearth of current research on these programs and cite the need for further research in this area.

From the comments made by Latessa and Allen (1999) regarding halfway houses and the research by the Washington State Institute for Public Policy on work release, it is clear that states are finding that, in general, community residential centers do "work," in terms of both saving money and reducing recidivism. Though the reductions in recidivism are often slight, the outcomes are nonetheless improvements that should not be ignored. It cannot be said that "nothing works" in the field of residential treatment, and practitioners that make such claims are simply not educated on current outcomes that exist across the nation. Even when recidivism is not reduced, these programs do not increase recidivism rates. Yet in all cases, there are substantive economic benefits that are realized among these programs, regardless of the impact on recidivism; thus, these programs do indeed work, regardless of what might be otherwise contended by skeptics and laypersons.

Differential association serves as the precursor to many other types of criminological theory based on social learning elements. First postulated by Edwin Sutherland, this theory was researched, tested, and modified by a number of scholars that followed. In describing this theory, Cullen and Agnew (2006) provide a clear and effective explanation:

> Crime is learned through associations with criminal definitions. Interacting with antisocial peers is a major cause of crime. Criminal behavior will be repeated and become chronic if it is reinforced. When criminal subcultures exist, many individuals can learn to commit crime in one location. (p. 6)

The above notion that criminals teach one another how to engage in criminal activity is an important one in the field of corrections. Indeed, a number of studies have found that the longer an inmate spends in prison, the more likely he or she is to recidivate. The general notion is that prison breeds criminals and does not actually work to rehabilitate them. Thus, our nation's prisons encourage the development of inmate subcultures that ensure that crime will continue. This explains, at least in part, the high recidivism rate among parolees and those released from prison.

It is for this reason that community-based residential treatment facilities are considered a much better option than prison, whenever such options are available and feasible for public safety. These facilities generate definitions that are conducive to treatment, not crime. Further, peers selected for such programs will be in them for reintegrative purposes, thus diminishing the impact of pro-criminal peers that one is much more likely to find in prison. The environments associated with residential treatment facilities are designed to specifically counter those associations that are related to criminality. This is the specific charge of any effective treatment program, and staff at such facilities know to look for attitudes and behaviors among residents that might indicate a lack of recovery.

Thus, at their base, residential treatment facilities utilize the concepts of differential association. Indeed, Sutherland contended that pro-criminal and anti-criminal definitions from other persons work to counteract one another. When an excess of pro-criminal influences exists, the individual is more likely to engage in criminal behavior. Likewise, when an excess of anti-criminal definitions exists, the individual will be less likely to engage in criminal acts. This is the precise premise that is used in community-based residential treatment facilities. The offender is given gradual levels of freedom, but is also surrounded by a regimen and group of staff and peers that support prosocial activities, eschewing further criminal activity. As has been noted, these programs have been found to be effective, and this is not surprising since differential association and its protégé, social learning theory (by Ronald Akers), have also received a great deal of empirical support.

SOURCES: Cullen, F. T., & Agnew, R. (2006). *Criminological theory: Past to present* (3rd ed.). Los Angeles: Roxbury; Lilly, J. R., Cullen, F. T., & Ball, R. A. (2007). *Criminological theory: Context and consequences* (4th ed.). Thousand Oaks, CA: Sage Publications.

COMPLEX OFFENDER CASES IN RESIDENTIAL FACILITIES

Just as there are a variety of community-based residential treatment facilities, there are also a variety of offenders that may be encountered in those facilities. While the types of criminal offenses may vary, it is the recommendation of this author that these facilities should generally exclude those offenders that have committed more than one violent crime. While some offenders may have had an isolated incident where violence occurred, those with repeat offenses of simple assault, sexual assault, and more serious assaults pose too great a risk to the community to be trusted in such facilities. Further, these types of offenders are likely to have a negative impact on the informal culture and operations within a residential treatment facility, contaminating the positive effects that other offenders might otherwise realize. However, given that offenders in this category make up such a small percentage of the overall offender population, this should not even be an issue. Thus, community-based residential facilities can and should focus their attention on nonviolent, property, and drug-related offenders. While this means ignoring a portion of the offender population, it still leaves a very large offender base that can benefit from such services.

Even though careful selection is warranted, particularly with violent offenders, facilities will still find themselves challenged with a variety of issues associated with complex offender concerns. As noted previously with jail diversion programs, offenders are often selected based on problems with substance abuse or mental health issues. (This is actually a recurring issue in many residential facilities, whether as a result of jail diversion or not.) Some offenders may simply present with serious bouts of depression, and this obviously will affect their motivation levels when employed in the community, and it may affect their ability to follow through with requirements. These offenders are also likely to require some sort of antidepressant medication, and unless medical staff are available at the facility, accommodations must be made to allow these offenders to have access to such medications. Naturally, this opens up a whole set of difficulties for the facility, in terms of both the offender's welfare and the security of the drugs within the facility.

Other offenders may present with a variety of personality disorders. These offenders will tend to have a number of intractable thought processes that are maladaptive and difficult to work with. The attitudes and personalities may reflect pervasive problems with adjustment, self-perception, and understanding of the social environment around them. Some offenders may have challenges associated with intelligence—a common occurrence, since offenders in prisons tend to score roughly one standard deviation lower on IQ tests than persons in the general community (Hanser, 2007b). Often, this may be due to a lack of educational access, but it also can be the result of neurological deficits that were inherent or even caused by long-term drug use. In addition, other offenders may have problems with anxiety, trauma, or another disorder. The point is that the variety of mental health challenges can be great, and just as jail staff must be prepared to address these issues, so too should persons working at residential facilities.

Beyond mental health issues, there are a number of other factors related to adjustment and cognitive ability that are also relevant. For instance, some offenders may simply have low tolerances for frustration and ambiguity. This is often a sign of lower cognitive functioning, as ambiguity in social situations is more difficult to work with and interpret, and it also leads to stress. Moreover, offenders coping with new adaptations may find it hard to meet demands placed upon them and may act out in both criminal and noncriminal ways. This is particularly true with substance-abusing offenders who may have depleted neural functioning, damage to their nervous systems, or negative social learning experiences that have affected their ability to deal with stressful and undefined circumstances. As a result, these offenders will likely require more attention from residential staff and will also be prone to social problems within the facility. While these behaviors may not be criminal, they still place burdens on staff and other offenders in the facility.

The age of the offender may also present certain challenges. For instance, juveniles are typically kept in separate programs and facilities, away from adult offenders. These offenders present an array of problems that are unique to adolescence and maturation. (Chapter 12 will focus exclusively on this group of offenders.) On the other hand, offenders may be elderly, and thus may be more prone to needing medical services on a routine basis. Further, occupational options may be limited for these offenders since their health may restrict their ability to perform certain duties. In addition, it is common for elderly offenders to lack a support network since many of the persons to whom they were connected may have since given up on them or moved on in life without the inclusion of the offender who has spent years behind bars; this is particularly true for offenders that are returning to the community after a long stint in prison.

Unlike probation and parole, in residential facilities that house elderly offenders or persons with impediments, it is the facility that must take into account these various needs because the offender is in that facility's custody. Thus, staff in these facilities must attend to day-to-day issues associated with these offenders' livelihoods and well-being. While probation and parole staff may have to consider the challenges associated with such offenders, they typically are not charged with providing for their daily needs; it is not usually within the scope of duty for most community supervision officers. Thus, residential staff must contend with the various complex needs of these and other offenders in a much more personal manner. This is one of the key distinctions between care for specialized offenders in residential facilities and supervising offenders in the community. Students should refer to Chapter 14 for more information on elderly offenders.

Finally, some offenders may have medical challenges that impair their ability to function. Some may be physically disabled, while others may have communicable diseases. Still others may have common medical problems such as hypertension, whereas other offenders may have a variety of health issues due to extensive prior addictions. Indeed, it is commonly true that offenders age more rapidly than persons in the general community due to the ravages of their lifestyle on the streets as well as that experienced when in prison. In fact, prior inmates will often appear as if they were 10 years older than they actually may be chronologically, with their physiological functioning being impacted just as much as their appearances are likely to be. In cases of health impairments, accommodations must be made, and legal issues associated with the Americans with Disabilities Act may emerge as a consideration for residential staff and management.

TYPICAL STAFF IN RESIDENTIAL TREATMENT FACILITIES

Typically, within residential facilities, staff will play one of three roles: the security role, the treatment role, or the auxiliary or support role. Each of these areas of operation is critical to residential facility operations. Though all of these individuals act within their own sphere of understanding, their functions may overlap with security or treatment staff fulfilling other functions that are typically associated with auxiliary staff or other personnel. The point is that these facilities often require that staff work in a supportive manner and that the roles and functions may overlap, just as the roles and functions of various community residential treatment programs overlap throughout the United States. Nevertheless, these three types of residential staff are briefly presented in the following paragraphs to provide students with a general idea of the operations within many community residential treatment facilities.

Among staff, there are typically some that will fulfill a security role with offenders in the facility. As noted earlier, some residential facilities are privately operated while others may be overseen by the state or the county. In either event, the role of the *security staff* will typically be very similar. These staff will often be involved in the intake of new offenders by completing the proper paperwork, conducting inventories of the offender's personal property, and explaining the rules of the facility to new residents. These staff will enforce rules by monitoring offender progress via telephone checks to ensure offender compliance while in the community. These same staff will also monitor activities at the facility through physical security checks. These are also the staff that will be tasked with collecting specimens for drug testing, as well as conducting random inspections of offenders and their living quarters to ensure that clients do not have contraband within the facility. In addition, these staff write reports, monitor medications, and perform a sundry array of duties that encompass the day-to-day operations of the facility. These staff positions typically only require a high school diploma or GED, but they also require persons who have good judgment and the ability to work in flexible rotating shifts that are necessary for facility operations.

Other staff might include *correctional treatment staff* or *clinical staff*. Regardless of the specific title that is given to these staff, they typically engage in various forms of case management (as discussed in Chapter 8) and will perform many of the same functions that correctional treatment specialists do (see Chapter 4). These staff will conduct group counseling and individual counseling sessions and will perform a number of other tasks that are clinical in nature. Typically, these individuals will have graduate education at the master's or doctoral level and will be able to complete clinical work such as assessments, evaluations, and a variety of mental health interventions. These individuals may fulfill various functions, providing substance abuse classes, psychoeducational classes, and anger management counseling, as well as individual sessions.

Finally, there are the many auxiliary staff who provide a variety of services such as educational or vocational training, food service, religious programs, transportation, and a wide range of others. Though these staff may not be central to the primary areas of interest in community supervision—security and treatment—they nonetheless provide services that are important and integral to the smooth functioning of the facility. Without their assistance, residential treatment options would likely be impossible to provide.

CONCLUSION

The term *community residential treatment* includes a variety of facilities that all have differing areas of focus. From this chapter, we have found that these facilities exist at different points on the community corrections spectrum, with jail diversion programs existing at pre-booking and post-booking points of offender processing, halfway houses being categorized as halfway-in and halfway-out, residential facilities being designed for persons that are not safe enough to release on probation, and other residential facilities being used as integrated treatment operations to transition offenders back into the community. The fact that different types of facilities provide very similar services and perform similar functions results in a blurring of the distinctions among the different types of programs. In addition, some facilities may be privately operated (as the ComCor example demonstrates), while others may be state run. Some programs may be small in operation, whereas others may be part of an entire state's network (such as the restitution facilities in Mississippi). Thus, when we talk about community residential treatment, we actually refer to a number of different options that are available for offenders.

From the research that has been presented, it is clear that community residential treatment programs are, at least in a marginal sense, effective in reducing recidivism. Further, it is quite obvious that these options are much less expensive than the building of prison facilities to deal with overcrowding. With these two points in mind, it can then be said that these options are considered generally successful in serving their intended purpose: reintegration of the offender while avoiding the ravages and criminogenic effects of prison. In addition, much of the research presented in this text is more recent than that which may be found in many other texts and thus is more relevant to programs in operation today. Further, this demonstrates that "something works" in community residential treatment, and that proponents of Martinson's outdated research are simply that—outdated. The weight of the research illustrates the overall efficacy of these programs. When taken with research that also shows prisons to be criminogenic, breeding worse recidivists than community-based programs do, it becomes clear that alternatives to prison facilities just make good sense. It is on this note that we now close as we look toward the spectrum of intermediate sanctions that are available, many of which may dovetail or be used in tandem with the residential programs that have just been discussed.

Key Terms

Community residential treatment centers

Halfway house

International Association of Residential and Community Alternatives (IARCA)

Jail

Jail diversion

Jail diversion programs

Long-term residential programs

Restitution center

Short-term residential programs

Study release program

Work release programs

"What Would You Do?" Exercise

Meet Tom; he is homeless and an alcoholic. He is known by all of the local police that patrol his area of the community because they see him on the streets almost daily. When on the streets, Tom exhibits heightened states of anxiety from time to time and is also a bit paranoid, but is otherwise considered harmless. Tom is on your supervision caseload as a repeat misdemeanant. It seems that he reoffends each year, engaging in some minor form of criminal behavior that requires his arrest by police. He tends to do this just before the winter months of the year. Police officers and jailers know that he does this to avoid the harsh cold winters in your city, and as noted before, they all consider him quite harmless, though he is much more crass and mean when detoxifying from the alcohol. It seems that there are several other offenders just like Tom—generally harmless, but nuisances to the public and violators of city ordinances. The police know them all by name and generally ignore them until they begin to commit minor acts that require arrest.

The problem is that multiple offenders like Tom seem to be collecting throughout the city. You have several on your caseload, and the city jail is getting quite full due to drug sweeps by area police. The mayor has contacted the judges and asked them to work something out to alleviate the problems with the drunken, mentally disordered homeless in your area. You have been appointed to a community panel where you must help to address this issue. You are required to provide a brief proposal outlining your own thoughts on this issue and how it can be resolved for little or no money.

What would you do?

Applied Exercise

Consider the case of Tom, just presented in the "What Would You Do?" exercise. For this applied exercise, pretend that you are a case manager and Tom is on your caseload. You have been asked to help out with his case by the community supervision agency, some local judges, and the city mayor's office. This group wants to determine a model case management program for Tom and for others like him. You must explain how you would conduct case management with Tom, making sure to address what you might find from a client needs assessment. You should also correctly identify and classify any mental health issues that affect Tom. (Students may need to refer back to Chapter 9.) In addition, provide a GAF Scale rating for Tom, using your own best judgment. Provide a rationale for your rating. In addition, explain if there is a type of residential treatment facility that might work better than jail placement when meeting Tom's needs.

This assignment will require that you complete outside research on your own. Each response to the questions must be correct and balanced in approach (consisting of realistic possibilities), with anywhere from 300 to 500 words of content being allowed per application.

Students should complete this application exercise as a mini paper that explains the scenario and then addresses each question throughout. Total word count: 1,200 to 2,000 words.

CHAPTER 11

Intermediate Sanctions

LEARNING OBJECTIVES

1. Know the definition and purpose of intermediate sanctions.

2. Identify the various types of intermediate sanctions and their placement within the continuum of sanctions.

3. Analyze the various means of ensuring compliance by substance abusers and sex offenders.

4. Compare the various ways intermediate sanctions are used in a variety of states around the nation.

5. Understand both the security and treatment functions associated with intermediate sanctions.

INTRODUCTION

Currently, there is no single definition of intermediate sanctions, nor is there any ironclad agreement about what ought to be included within such a definition. Some researchers contend that almost anything that falls between "regular" probation and a full prison term is an intermediate sanction; others deny inclusion in this category to any sanction that involves incarceration. However, the growing popularity of residential facilities like restitution centers, work release centers, and probation detention facilities, some with capacities in the hundreds, makes this distinction important (McGarry, 1990).

What intermediate sanctions do have in common is the presence of features designed to enhance the desired sanctioning purpose. Regardless of whether the intent is to achieve punishment, incapacitation, rehabilitation, or specific deterrence, intermediate sanctions provide more options than does simple probation. These sanctions also tend to vary in severity, leading to a continuum of sanctions that progress from the most restrictive (prison) to the least restrictive (suspended sentences, deferred adjudication, and so forth). This can lead to increased surveillance and tighter controls on movement, while enhancing the integration of more intense treatment to address a wider assortment of maladies or deficiencies. The integration of supervision and treatment has been discussed in prior chapters (Chapters 8 and 9), and it is the use of intermediate sanctions that optimizes the mix between the two. Indeed, the use of intermediate sanctions should be perceived as a linking pin that integrates elements of both the security and the treatment spectrums, providing the glue between both orientations.

It was during the 1990s that intermediate sanctions truly came into vogue. Even before these sanctions became commonly known by the public, the reasons for their use were described by McGarry (1990) in a report produced by the National Institute of Corrections. According to this report, overcrowding was not the only reason for the interest in intermediate sanctions. Their rise was also fueled by

- Public concern over the adequate supervision of probationers and parolees;
- The demands of victims and their communities to be made whole again following a crime;
- Changing and more available technologies that were challenging our notions of what is possible;
- The continuing desire of judges to tailor sentences to the offense and the offender;
- The rising failure rates of offenders on probation and parole; and
- The impact of the drug abuse crisis around the United States.

As was true then, it is still true now that communities suffering from the results of illegal drug use have little choice but to turn to the criminal justice system, particularly probation, to solve an immense societal problem. The community corrections section of the criminal justice system, often saddled with these offenders, was forced to adopt innovative options for processing large volumes of drug offenders. This was especially true during the War on Drugs of the 1990s, as more and more drug offenders appeared on community supervision officer caseloads. At this time, probation and other forms of community supervision were viewed as being weak on crime, and the use of intermediate sanctions was thought to be a means of bringing respectable public perceptions to the field of community supervision (Hanser, 2007b). Though the suggestions provided by McGarry (1990) were made almost 20 years ago, they offer unusually insightful guidance on the proper use of these approaches. Even today, these suggested actions serve as a good policy basis for agencies that implement intermediate sanctions.

While these sanctions are now used by nearly every community supervision agency across the country, the effective evaluation of these sentences is often questionable. Agencies that follow the actions suggested by McGarry (1990) will find that outcomes associated with intermediate sanctions will be more predictable, more effective, and easier to measure. Thus, there are actions that administrators can take to increase the chances of success for intermediate sanctions in their jurisdictions. The benefit is that, in most cases, implementing these actions does not require additional funding from budget-strapped community supervision agencies. Rather, improvements in job design and other considerations are all that are required.

The first of these suggested actions is *to articulate precisely why a jurisdiction needs intermediate sanctions.* Upon questioning, most stakeholders in the sentencing process tend to indicate dissatisfaction with the choice of options available. The key is to get each stakeholder to specify precisely which offenders are now sentenced inappropriately and what would represent a more appropriate sanction. Typically, responses will range from those of presiding judges who want more restrictive, treatment-oriented programs for offenders they are now putting on probation, to those of chief probation officers who may contend that their staff cannot provide appropriate control in the community for the many offenders that are in the local or regional jail. McGarry (1990) notes that "unless a jurisdiction has unlimited resources, any effort to implement intermediate sanctions must begin with the actors finding the areas of common agreement, whether types of offenders or categories of offenses, and building from there" (p. 4).

A second suggested action is *to establish clear sanctioning goals*—referred to as the "why" of sentencing. The individual actors and agencies within the criminal justice system commonly operate from different and unexamined philosophies of sentencing. The need for understanding of the different sentencing philosophies was discussed earlier in this text (see Chapter 2), and this is conceptually revisited when considering intermediate sanctions. The individual goals of different court actors during the sentencing process may be different from case to case and may be directly contradictory to those of their peers or of another agency. McGarry (1990) notes that this divergence causes a number of problems, providing the classic example scenario below:

> Consider the judge who sentences the young, drug-dependent property offender to intensive probation so that the offender can get treatment for his addiction. The judge's goal in this case is rehabilitation. However, the probation agency does not include treatment in its intensive probation program because, with limited resources, the probation agency believes its primary responsibility is to provide supervision that limits his ability to steal again. Believing that this program's purpose is incapacitation, therefore, the probation department is frustrated that the judge has sentenced a low-stakes offender to a program designed for more serious cases. The agency lacks drug treatment resources because the legislature, sensitive to past charges of "mollycoddling," has eliminated funds for it. It has instead targeted funds for the close supervision of offenders to deter them from committing another offense. (p. 4)

McGarry (1990) goes on to say that in addition to resolving these contradictory efforts, choosing and defining goals is critical in the creation of either an individual sanctioning option or an entire sanctioning continuum. Further, the clarity in definition provides a better means of evaluating the program—an important element when attempting to refine services that are provided. However, regardless of evaluative considerations, the sanctioning goal should determine the features that will characterize the program; a day reporting center designed to offer rehabilitative services, for example, will look very different from one intended primarily to incapacitate or deter offenders (McGarry, 1990). The sentencing purpose should be the primary element in the continuum of sanctions and defines

Photo 11.1 Two attorneys approach the bench to discuss negotiations regarding an offender's case. The process of plea bargaining and settling on specific community supervision requirements between the prosecution and the defense is fairly commonplace in the U.S. justice system.

success for any individual program. The evaluative process, while best factored into the beginning planning stages of the program, should be secondary to ensuring that sentencing is carried out in a meaningful and balanced manner.

A third action in implementing effective and appropriate intermediate sanctions is *to make available a continuum of sanctions scaled around one or more sanctioning goals.* For example, the goal of incapacitation may be implemented through varying levels of surveillance or control of movement. Such a continuum permits the court or corrections authority to tailor sanctions that are meaningful with respect both to their purposes and to the kinds of offenders that come before them.

A current practice is to unload the complete list of sanctions on all offenders, setting up both offenders and the program for failure. A typical offender who is supporting two children, for example, is not likely to be able to pay restitution, perform extensive community service, and participate in frequent drug counseling. Targeting specific sanctions to specific offender profiles, on the other hand, increases the chances of success for both the program and the offender. This kind of policy-directed system can also be responsive to differing and changing behavior on the part of offenders.

The fourth action, as noted by McGarry (1990), is *to collect and use good information about the jurisdiction's criminal justice system,* including offender flow data; offender profiles; and information about sentencing practices, about programs, and about what works and for whom. The availability of this kind of information makes possible much of the other action already described. It is impossible, for example, to create a program for a specific offender population if you do not know the characteristics of that population, the usual disposition for that group, or how many offenders fitting that profile pass through the court in any given period. In many jurisdictions, the problem does not lie in the information technology but rather with the awareness of how to use it.

Currently, as an alternative to the rising costs of incarceration, convicted offenders are being sentenced to community supervision with increasing frequency (Glaze & Palla, 2005). Despite supervising an overwhelming majority of offenders, community supervision (probation) departments have experienced budget cuts, which in turn have led to a reduction in staff and resources, regardless of the drastic increases in caseload sizes. Given the increased caseloads and decrease in program funding, the need for alternative means of supervision and treatment are at a premium. To this end, intermediate sanctions have became the order of the day.

When it comes to finding alternatives to punishment and rehabilitation for offenders, there is no shortage, particularly in terms of community-based rehabilitation. On a simplistic level, intermediate sanctions could be defined as alternatives to traditional incarceration that consist of sentencing options falling anywhere between a standard prison sentence and a standard probation sentence. Reflecting the versatile nature of intermediate sanctions, the National Institute of Corrections (1993) has also defined intermediate sanctions as "a range of sanctioning options that permit the crafting of sentences to respond to the particular circumstances of the offender and the offense; and the outcomes desired in the case" (p. 18). For this text, the definition of these sanctions will consist of a blend of both definitions. Thus, **intermediate sanctions** are a range of sentencing options that fall between incarceration and probation, being designed to allow for the crafting of sentences that respond to the offender, the offense, or both, with the intended outcome of the case being a primary consideration. Table 11.1 provides an examination of the various intermediate sanctions, their philosophical underpinnings, and their intended purposes, while Table 11.2 offers an illustration of the scaling along a continuum of options for intermediate sanctions. This second table also demonstrates how sanctions can meet numerous objectives such as public satisfaction and recidivism reduction.

TABLE 11.1	Summary Listing of Coercive Intermediate Sanction Measures and Sentencing Options		

Warning Measures (Notice of consequences of subsequent wrongdoing)	Admonishment/cautioning (administrative; judicial) Suspended execution or imposition of sentence		
Injunctive Measures (Banning legal conduct)	Travel (e.g., from jurisdiction; to specific criminogenic spots) Association (e.g., with other offenders) Driving Possession of weapons Use of alcohol Professional activity (e.g., disbarment)		
Economic Measures	Restitution Costs Fees Forfeitures Support payments Fines (standard; day fines)		
Work-Related Measures	Community service (individual placement; work crew) Paid employment requirements		
Education-Related Measures	Academic (e.g., basic literacy, GED) Vocational training Life skills training		
Physical and Mental Health Treatment Measures	Psychological/psychiatric Chemical (e.g., methadone; psychoactive drugs) Surgical (e.g., acupuncture drug treatment)		
Physical Confinement Measures	Partial or intermittent confinement	Home curfew Day treatment center Halfway house Restitution center Weekend detention facility/jail Outpatient treatment facility (e.g., drug/mental health)	
	Full/continuous confinement	Full home/house arrest Mental hospital Other residential treatment facility (e.g., drug/alcohol) Boot camp Detention facility Jail Prison	

(Continued)

TABLE 11.1 (Continued)

Monitoring/Compliance Measures (May be attached to all other sanctions)	Required of the offender	Mail reporting
		Electronic monitoring (telephone check-in; active electronic monitoring device)
		Face-to-face reporting
		Urine analysis (random; routine)
	Required of the monitoring agent	Criminal records checks
		Sentence compliance checks (e.g., on payment of monetary sanctions; attendance/performance at treatment, work, or educational sites)
		Third-party cheeks (family, employer, surety, service/treament provider; via mail, telephone, in person)
		Direct surveillance/observation (random/routine visits and possibly search; at home, work, institution, or elsewhere)
		Electronic monitoring (regular phone checks and/or passive monitoring device—currently used with home curfew or house arrest, but could track movement more widely as technology develops)

SOURCE: National Institute of Corrections. (1993). *The intermediate sanctions handbook: Experiences and tools for policymakers.* Washington, DC: Author.

TABLE 11.2 Illustration of Scaling Possibilities for Criminal Sanctions; Type of Sanction, by Scaling Dimensions and Units of Measurement

	Scaling Dimensions					
Type of Sanction	*Retributive Severity*	*Crime Reduction[a]*	*Recidivism Reduction[b]*	*Reparation*	*Economic Cost*	*Public Satisfaction*
Sanction A Sanction B Sanction C Sanction D Etc.	Value in terms of pain and suffering[c]	Value in terms of impact on crime rate	Value in terms of impact on reoffense rate	Value in terms of compensating aggrieved parties[d]	Value in terms of cost efficiency	Value in terms of public approval ratings

SOURCE: National Institute of Corrections. (1993). *The intermediate sanctions handbook: Experiences and tools for policymakers.* Washington, DC: Author.

a. General deterrence effects

b. Specific deterrence, incapacitation, rehabilitation effects

c. Or in terms of units of onerousness, intrusiveness, or deprivation of autonomy/liberty

d. Direct victims and possibly indirectly affected individuals, groups, or entities [e.g., family members, insurers, taxpayers, community, society]

The definition of intermediate sanctions, as just presented, provides a perspective that is highly consistent with the emphasis on reintegration that is found in this text. It is clear that these types of sanctions allow for a great deal of flexibility that can be adjusted to accommodate treatment and supervision considerations. These sanctions are guided by the intent of the sentencing body but allow for consideration of the various needs, challenges, and issues associated with the offender and the type of offending that he or she is prone to committing. This permits the calibration of sentences so that specific details are a better fit with the type of offense considered as well as the individual variables associated with the offender. Such flexibility is what provides the field of community corrections with its greatest source of leverage among the offender population, in terms of both treatment and supervision.

This chapter will discuss the most commonly implemented and researched intermediate sanctions of intensive supervision, day reporting centers, day fines, home detention, electronic monitoring, shock incarceration, boot camps, community service, and various methods of compliance assurance. When considering the overcrowding problems in prison systems around the nation, it is clear that there is simply a pragmatic need for more space. As a result of the public's outcry for increased traditional sentencing of offenders, coupled with legislative action as a response to the public, the use of intermediate sanctions has grown. Recent reports indicate that many parolees and probationers are supervised under some form of intermediate sanctioning (Camp & Camp, 2003). It must be remembered as we discuss intermediate sanctioning that the applicability of such programming is dependent upon the potential for harm in local communities and the ability of intermediate sanctions to reduce recidivism.

FINES

Most offenders convicted of a criminal offense are assessed a fine as a punishment for committing the offense. A **fine** can be defined as a monetary penalty imposed by a judge or magistrate as a punishment for having committed an offense. In most cases, the fine is a certain dollar amount established either by the judge or according to a set schedule, depending upon the offense committed. The logic behind the fine is that it will deter the offender from committing another offense in the future for fear of being fined again. In most jurisdictions, the fines are assessed and paid in monthly installments to the receiving agency. In contemporary community supervision agencies, offenders are now able to pay their fines via credit or debit cards. The feelings are mixed regarding allowing an offender to pay in this manner. Officers sometimes feel that by delaying the effect of the monetary fine, it does not allow the offender to accept personal responsibility.

As the offense seriousness increases from misdemeanor to felony, presumably the fines increase as well. This assessment of fines is totally dependent upon judicial discretion. Gordon and Glaser (1991) have demonstrated that most offenders are more likely to pay their fines in totality, and that the likelihood of recidivism for these offenders is significantly less than for those who are sentenced to traditional institutional incarceration after controlling for offender type and type of offense committed.

At both the federal and state level, fines are imposed. Traditionally, there was one set fine for certain offenses regardless of the financial standing of the offenders. As time has passed, many judiciaries are beginning to understand that one set fine is more punishing to the offender who happens to earn the least amount of money and a "cakewalk" to those offenders who happen to be financially blessed. Given this, there has been a push for graduated fines that are dependent upon the income of the offender at time of sentencing. In this day of drastic budget cuts and pushes for alternatives to incarceration, fines are the order of the day. They allow the offender an opportunity to pay for his or her treatment and punishment as opposed to the traditional method of placing the financial burden on the state.

As community corrections becomes more contemporary, agencies are beginning to experiment with alternative ways to pay fines. Today, there are a host of private, for-profit companies that have contracted with community supervision agencies to handle their fee payments. There are those companies that now allow offenders to pay their fines online or anywhere there is Web access. For several years in New York City, offenders have been able to pay fines at kiosks around the city as opposed to having to travel to a centralized location that may be miles from their residence or place of employment.

COMMUNITY SERVICE

Perhaps the most widely known yet least likely to be used form of intermediate sanctioning is that of community service. **Community service** is the work that one conducts in hopes of repaying his or her debt to society after being found at fault for committing a criminal or deviant offense. In most cases, community service is ordered by the sentencing judge and supervised by the community supervision officer. Most judges prefer that offenders sentenced to complete community service do so at a not-for-profit agency within their local jurisdiction. Types of community service range from trash pickups to caring for animals at an animal shelter or participating in menial labor jobs at the local public facilities.

It is said that community service was created as an alternative to paying fines for female offenders who could not otherwise make their fee requirements. Due to the fact that many offenders are economically challenged, community service options began to spring up all around the country, particularly as an option for younger and less violent offenders. To date, community service is mostly used as an integral condition of probation or parole. In most cases, offenders are required to complete a set amount of community service hours a month.

Community service serves a dual purpose: to both rehabilitate and punish offenders. In terms of rehabilitation, community service affords the offender time to participate in something constructive, all the while providing him or her with an opportunity to build "sweat equity" in something that is beneficial to the community. Community service is punitive, too, in that the offender is forced to give up his or her own time to work off a criminal debt without being paid.

At latest count, most U.S. states had some form of community service at either the juvenile or adult offender levels. Most offenders placed on probation are required to complete some specified amount of community service, in addition to various other conditions of probation. Though there may be statutorily prescribed amounts of community service ordered, the amounts typically given out are very subjective, the appropriate amount being determined by the presiding judge.

Thus, the amount of community service required varies, and in most cases the offenders must find time to complete their hours within the confines of their normal workweek. For those offenders without employment, officers often require that they perform as many as 40 hours of community service per week until they have completed their total hours. In certain jurisdictions, offenders are allowed to work off some of their fines by completing additional hours of community service. Most cases call for a subjective determination of the value of an hour of community service by the directors of the agencies. The standard has been that the offenders are given at least minimum wage credit for each hour of community service.

The question remains as to how effective community service is at meeting its intended objectives of rehabilitation and punishment. The reality is that no matter how effective or ineffective such a sanction might be, numerous nonprofit agencies are grateful for the massive amount of assistance they receive from community service workers. For example, after Hurricane Katrina, one of the five costliest and deadliest hurricanes in American history, community service offenders were responsible for putting in hours of assistance in local shelters, feeding, clothing, and filling other emergency needs of recently evacuated citizens of the Gulf Coast region.

Anderson (1998) has demonstrated that most offenders complete their community service conditions as directed by the court. Those offenders who are least likely to complete their hours have been shown to have an officer who does not stress the completion of their community service. However, judges are very reluctant to provide an offender additional time to complete community service unless there is proof of extenuating circumstances such as significant health and transportation concerns.

Due to the low cost of overhead in funding community service programs, coupled with the added use of much-needed labor in communities, community service options will continue to be well utilized. One of the most pressing problems in evaluating community service is that such opportunities vary so widely, and often offenders participate in multiple community service sites and types throughout their time under supervision. In most cases, community service is completed anywhere the offender can get the hours. For example, an offender may begin community service at the local courthouse and complete his or her hours at the homeless mission. Despite the lack of research in this area, community service is clearly an integral part of intermediate sanctioning and provides a positive avenue through which offenders and the community can learn the rehabilitative and punitive ideals.

INTENSIVE SUPERVISION PROBATION/PAROLE (ISP)

Perhaps the most commonly known form of intermediate sanction is that of intensive supervision. **Intensive supervision** is the extensive supervision of offenders who are deemed the greatest risk to society or are in need of the greatest amount of governmental services (e.g., drug treatment). In most cases, intensive supervision is the option afforded to individuals who would otherwise be incarcerated for felony offenses. The early forms of intensive supervision operated under the conservative philosophy of increasing public safety via strict offender scrutiny. Today's ISP's are focused on a host of components.

In the early days, ISP's operated under the assumption that increasing an offender's contact with his or her supervising officer would increase public safety and simultaneously the offender's chances of rehabilitation. As an example, the California Special Intensive Parole Unit of the 1950s was created with an emphasis on increased supervision and a special interest in offender rehabilitation. A short time later, the field began to seek the optimal offender–officer ratio in terms of effectiveness. As a result of the inability to find that optimal ratio, intensive supervision suffered in credibility during the 1960s and 1970s.

If you were to examine today's intensive supervision units, it might seem that ISP's are focused more on public safety, punishment, and ultimately offender control, and not so much on the offender's rehabilitation. Within the last 10 to 15 years, that has been the trend in the use of intensive supervision programs. Perhaps this may be a result of the massive number of offenders incarcerated in the United States, with the most recent numbers reflecting over 2.2 million prisoners (Sabol, Minton, & Harrison, 2008).

In their early years, intensive supervision was afforded the luxury of smaller caseloads, mostly as a result of the smaller number of offenders being processed through the criminal justice system. Despite the enviable officer-to-offender intensive supervision ratio, the rates of offender rearrests and reconvictions remained significantly high. Given the old adage that history repeats itself, today's intensive programs have begun to decrease the offender–officer ratio, while at the same time focusing on offender control and supervision. It should be noted that despite reverting to the old days of intensive supervision as described above, the U.S. prison population continues to rise.

When examining the various facets of intensive supervision, one finds that they are quite diverse. Some ISP's focus on specific offense and offender types (e.g., sex offending and younger offenders, etc.), while others vary in their level of supervision, which may range from 5 days per week to once every 2 weeks. The types of supervising officers vary from untrained community supervision officers to specialized officers who have been well trained in the supervision of at-risk offenders. In most cases, officers are afforded a lighter than normal caseload of approximately 10 to 20 offenders. Placement into intensive supervision is dependent upon the sentencing judge, the supervision officer, the parole board, or some combination of these. In today's agencies, the decision to place an offender on intensive supervision is made based on the level of assessed offender risk of rearrest.

Much of the literature regards ISP's as cost savers of public funds when compared with institutional incarceration. However, this is difficult to prove because in order to determine the amount of money saved by ISP's as opposed to prison, one would have to actually decrease the prison operating cost, which would never happen. Research has demonstrated that ISP's are not significant predictors of a lowered rate of recidivism(Champion, 2002; Latessa & Allen, 1999). This lack of influence may be a result of the reality that the ISP offenders are put under increased scrutiny, which ultimately leads to increased chances of arrest because more infractions are likely to be detected, whether they be minor or major in nature. No research has been examined, to date, which studies the influence of ISP's on offenders' chances of recidivism. However, Petersilia and Turner (1993a) found that ISP offenders who took part in a rehabilitative component of ISP were more likely to desist from criminal or addictive behavior.

Photo 11.2 Officer Jared Steward examines an electronic ankle bracelet. These types of devices are used with high-risk offenders, including sex offenders. Officer Steward is currently a graduate student in one of the author's courses.

ELECTRONIC MONITORING

Perhaps the most widely used but least understood intermediate sanction is that of electronic monitoring. It was Ralph Schwitzgebel who first proposed the use of some form of monitoring apparatus for supervising offenders in the community, with the first type developed and utilized in 1968. The legal liability of such monitoring was argued in the *Harvard Law Review* in 1966. California has been credited with the first use of electronic monitoring (Schwitzgebel, 1969). In the 1970s, the use, effectiveness, and liability associated with electronic monitoring often found debate among the legal and scholarly community (Ingraham & Smith, 1972; Szasz, 1975). Renzema (1992) conducted an analysis of the states that use electronic monitoring and found that 44 states were utilizing the monitors. The National Institute of Justice (1999) revealed that there were over 100,000 offenders being supervised via electronic monitoring in 1,500 programs.

Electronic monitoring includes the use of any mechanism that is worn by the offender for the means of tracking his or her whereabouts through electronic detection. Electronic monitoring includes both active and passive monitoring systems. Active systems require that the offender answer or respond to a monitoring cue (such as a computer-generated telephone call), whereas passive forms of monitoring emit a continuous signal for tracking. With both types of electronic monitoring devices, offenders are required to wear an ankle bracelet with a tracking device. The active types are used in conjunction with the local telephone line. At random times throughout the day, the offender's home phone will ring, and the offender has a certain amount of time to answer. Once the offender answers the phone, a signal is transmitted via the tracking device, which validates that the offender is at home. With the passive type, the ankle bracelet transmits a continuous signal to a nearby transmitter, which transmits the signal to a monitoring computer. With each type, the supervising officer is sent a readout each morning of the offender's compliance.

If an offender attempts to alter the connection, most devices have alarms that will sound and send an immediate alarm to the monitoring device. It is also not uncommon for an offender to be at home, not having tampered with the ankle bracelet, and yet it appears that he or she is noncompliant. Of the two electronic monitoring types, the active system has the lower rate of false alarms. Even though the passive system has the higher rate of false alarms, it is the fastest in determining noncompliance because it assesses the offender's whereabouts much faster.

In a rare analysis of the effectiveness of various electronic monitoring programs, Baumer, Maxfield, and Mendelsohn (1993) demonstrated that the effectiveness of such programming is dependent upon the administrative philosophy and the offender types placed under supervision. Of all offenders, the pretrial offenders were the most likely to violate the conditions of electronic monitoring but the most likely to be diverted from jail as a result of electronic monitoring. Electronic monitoring devices have cost close to $50,000 to purchase, with additional daily operating costs. Some jurisdictions have required that the offenders assist in paying for the use of GPS systems (described further below). This has raised concerns because the less well-to-do offenders are not afforded an opportunity for independence from direct supervision, unlike the more financially blessed offenders.

Those who are in favor of electronic monitoring are basing their argument on the ability to increase public safety due to the knowledge of the whereabouts of each offender. Simply knowing they are being personally tracked may deter offenders from committing crime. Proponents also argue that electronic monitoring provides the least punitive alternative to incarceration, as it allows for offenders to be supervised in the community.

Undoubtedly, electronic monitoring is a viable intermediate sanction in terms of diverting offenders from incarceration. However, questions remain as to the ability of electronic monitoring to assist offenders in the desistance from criminal behavior, whether supervision officer discretion helps or hurts the outcome, and the effects of community and family involvement on electronic monitoring. Focus Topic 11.1 provides an example of an electronic monitoring system in action.

FOCUS TOPIC 11.1

ELECTRONIC MONITORING: A NEW APPROACH TO WORK RELEASE

The telephone was ringing as electronic detention participant Jones returned home from work. Jones was half an hour late according to his approved movement schedule, and community correctional center staff had initiated response procedures to locate him. This scenario could be played out at any Illinois community correctional center on any given day, because the centers have a central role in the operation of the Department of Corrections' electronic detention (E.D.) program.

Working cooperatively with parole agents assigned to the Special Intensive Supervision Unit, the centers have served 1,540 E.D. participants between June 1989 and 1991. Of those 1,540 participants, 645 have successfully completed the program, and 384 have been returned to prison for technical program violations. There have been eight arrests

for new crimes, but only two have led to prosecution by local law enforcement officials. The primary reason for this success is the personal involvement of the community correctional center staff in client screening, programming, and monitoring.

Program Requirements

The E.D. program is for offenders in work release status, and they are required to abide by the same guidelines as those who live at a center. These guidelines require participants to be involved in employment, education, and/or vocational training for more than 35 hours per week. Those not actively participating in programming must demonstrate that they are trying to become involved in it.

(Continued)

(Continued)

Offenders being considered for the E.D. program are initially screened by a center counselor who also orients them to the program. After conducting a needs assessment, the counselor helps the offender develop an individual program contract that defines specific goals. Prospective participants also sign an agreement to abide by the program rules—counselors clearly inform them that failure to abide by the agreement will result in their being returned to prison with the possible loss of good conduct credits.

Once in the program, the E.D. participant reports weekly to the center to meet with his or her counselor for 30 to 45 minutes. During these meetings, counselors review participants' progress in accomplishing their program goals. The counselor also approves the next week's itinerary, which includes specific times for each activity so that the participant's movements can be monitored. Participants are aware that they may be tested for drugs or alcohol at any time.

They may be required to submit to urinalysis either during their weekly visits to the center or at any other time that their counselor determines that testing is necessary. Participants also must turn in their paychecks and work with the counselor to budget their incomes for living expenses.

Like center residents, E.D. participants must pay maintenance to the department at a rate of 20 percent of their earnings to a maximum of $50 per week. The most important result of the weekly counseling sessions is that they give E.D. participants an opportunity to identify with their counselors and the counselors a chance to know them.

Security

The role of the E.D. agent is to be a watchdog, acting as the community corrections center's eye in the community. Although center staff spot-check E.D. participants' movements by telephone, there are insufficient staff to allow physical visits or to follow up on those missing. E.D. agents are required to make face-to-face contact with their clients at least twice a week. Agents are on call 7 days a week, 24 hours a day to respond to alarms sounded when E.D. participants are missing. In these instances, the agent visits the host site and other areas where the offender might be, such as with other family members. If all efforts to locate the participant fail, he or she is placed on escape status. Department rules permit revocation of up to 1 year of good

conduct credits for escape, and local law enforcement may prosecute as well.

Mr. Jones was fortunate. He was just a little late, but he made a mistake by not phoning the center to tell staff that he was late leaving work and would be late returning home. Since this was the first time it has happened and he hasn't had any other problems, Mr. Jones will probably just receive a lecture. But if it becomes a habit or he is unavailable for longer periods, he won't be allowed to stay in the program.

Accountability

Electronic monitoring fosters accountability. Participants are forced to schedule, plan ahead, and budget their earnings. This structured environment provides a support base that allows them to gradually reintegrate into their home communities. It is important to convince the public that safety is actually improved when participants learn to take on more responsibility at the same time they are being held accountable. The alternative, "cold turkey" release to both the freedom and responsibilities of the outside world, is often too much for the releasee to handle. The result may be a return to crime, reliance on drugs or alcohol, and ultimately another prison term.

Cost Savings

Agencies considering implementation of electronic monitoring programs must be careful not to be misled by dollar signs and promises of an easy and inexpensive way to solve a population crunch. However, electronic monitoring is economical. In Illinois, prison incarceration requires an estimated $16,200 per year per inmate, compared with an estimated $7,034 for electronic monitoring. This includes the cost of the monitor at about $3,285 and another $3,849 per participant for staff salaries and overhead costs.

For further information, contact Anthony Scillia, Logan Correctional Center, R.R. 3, Lincoln, Illinois, 62566; (217) 735–5581.

SOURCE: Scillia, A. (1994). *Electronic monitoring: A new approach to work release.* Washington, DC: National Institute of Corrections. Retrieved from: http://www.nicic.org/pubs/1991/period17.pdf.

Electronic Monitoring in Sweden

In Sweden, approximately 13,000 people are under some type of noncustodial care, compared with only 5,000 sentenced to prison. Probation is the most common form of noncustodial care, but offenders may be sentenced to intensive supervision with electronic monitoring.

An offender may serve the sentence at home rather than in a correctional facility while under intensive supervision with electronic monitoring. In order to qualify, the offender must submit an application for electronic monitoring and have been sentenced to less than 2 months in prison. A local probation authority reviews the applications submitted and decides whether or not to recommend intensive supervision with electronic monitoring. Once approved, a transmitter is fastened around the offender's ankle, which sends signals to a receiver attached to the telephone line in the offender's home. A computer receives these signals and compares these signals with activities planned and registered by a probation officer. The probation officer prepares a timetable, which includes the exact time an offender may leave for work and return to his or her residence. Other activities may be allowed, such as community service programs or treatment programs, but must be preplanned as well. Should the offender fail to follow the timetable set by the probation officer, an alarm is triggered and the offender may be subject to serve the remainder of the sentence in prison.

Offenders sentenced to intensive supervision with electronic monitoring must meet certain criteria, which include a residence equipped with electricity and phone line, being employed or a student, participating in rehabilitation programs, and remaining drug and alcohol free. If employed, a portion of the offender's income goes into a fund established for crime victims. Offenders are also subject to frequent residence checks and drug tests to ensure compliance with the conditions set by their probation office.

SOURCE: Swedish Prison and Probation Service. (2008). *Kontakt.* Stockholm: Author.

Critical Thinking Question

1. Do you believe that a similar intensive supervision with electronic monitoring program would be effective in your area? Why or why not?

For more information about the Swedish Prison and Probation Service, visit the website www.kriminalvarden.se.

GLOBAL POSITIONING SYSTEMS

In this new millennium, community supervision is beginning to utilize military capabilities to keep track of offenders. A **Global Positioning System (GPS)** receiver uses 24 military satellites to determine the exact location of a coordinate. By using the satellite monitoring and remote tracking, offenders can be tracked to their exact location. The GPS tracking system utilized with offenders is used in conjunction with an ankle or wrist device that sends a signal to a tracking device, that sends a signal to the GPS tracking system. The tracking device can be placed in an offender's bag, and the offender must remain within 100 feet of the tracking device. After receiving the signal, a continuous report is sent to a computer, which tracks the whereabouts of the offender. The GPS tracking device for offenders allows supervising officers to place location restrictions on the offenders so that certain places can be off limits. For example, sex offenders may be excluded from being within the vicinity of a school yard or church. If the offender enters a prohibited area, an alarm will sound. On the flip side, an officer can program the offender's schedule for work and religious services and regular day-to-day activities so that it can be easier to detect and verify where the offender is and what he or she is doing. In some cases, the system can send notification via pager or telephone that the offender is near the victim or any other excluded location. The advantage of such a program is that the offender's whereabouts are known in a more real-time manner.

Given all of the new advances that the GPS has provided for community corrections, there are also obvious disadvantages such as expense and loss of signal. Just as with any other satellite device, the GPS offender tracking systems often lose their signal during bad weather or when in an area densely populated with trees. Of the disadvantages, the most often noted one is the monetary concern. GPS tracking is complex and very costly, and in this day of drastic budget cutbacks in community corrections, many agencies are not willing to designate funding for such contemporary and often unnecessary devices. Some have suggested that a way to cut back on the operational costs of GPS devices is to have agencies request the offender's whereabouts every 30 minutes or so as opposed to every minute. Others have suggested that GPS devices should be reserved for the most serious offenders within the community such as child molesters and rapists. Across the United States, approximately 150,000 offenders are being supervised by electronic monitoring devices. Among them, there were only 1,200 offenders being monitored with Global Positioning System devices (Greek, 2002).

HOME DETENTION

Also known as house arrest, **home detention** is the mandated action that forces an offender to stay within the confines of his or her home or on the property until a time specified by the sentencing judge. It is the "Father of Modern Science," Galileo, who provides the example of the first offender who was placed on home detention, after he proposed that the earth rotated around the sun. However, it wasn't until the late 20th century's "War on Drugs" that home detention gained notoriety. As a result of the massive numbers of drug offenders being sentenced to jail or prison, officials were seeking an alternative to supervision that would allow an offender to be supervised prior to trial or just before being placed into a residential treatment facility.

Many offenders sentenced to home confinement are required to complete community service and pay a host of fines, fees, and victim restitutions, while others are forced to wear electronic monitors or other detection devices to ensure that they are remaining in their residence during the specified time. In many cases, home detention is used for offenders during the pretrial phase or just prior to an offender being let out of prison on a work or educational release program. If an offender leaves his or her residence without permission or against the policies set forth, the offender is seen as having technically violated the conditions of his or her supervision (Government Accounting Office, 1990).

Given the fact that home detention was designed as an alternative to incarceration, its initial use was very minimal, mostly as a result of the amount of work involved in supervising an offender under these conditions. Home detention is advantageous for those offenders who are not well-suited for incarceration, such as those with health concerns or pregnant offenders within days of delivery. Electronic monitoring devices are used to increase the level of offender surveillance for many offenders while on home detention. The issue of "net widening" is the most damning argument against the use of home detention programs (Rackmill, 1994). This argument holds that since home detention programs are available, those offenders who would otherwise be ordered to pay a host of fines and complete community service are instead placed on home detention because the option is now available.

It should be noted that there is a lack of empirical research examining the effects of home detention in terms of recidivism, overall effectiveness, process evaluations, and outcome evaluations. In an evaluation of the Florida Community Control Program, the National Council on Crime and Delinquency (Smith & Akers, 1993) demonstrated that home detention programs are effective in reducing prison overcrowding, correctional funding allocations, and offender recidivism. Overall, the use of home detention has emerged as another viable intermediate sanction in many jurisdictions throughout the United States. Most home detention sentences are used in the juvenile court system where the youth are placed under the custody of their parents, and for adult low-risk offenders.

DAY REPORTING CENTERS

Day reporting centers are treatment facilities where offenders are required to report, usually on a daily basis. These facilities tend to offer a variety of services, including drug counseling, vocational assistance, life skills development, and so forth. The offenders that are likely to be required to report to day reporting centers may be one of two types: either those that are placed on early release from a period of incarceration, or those that are on some form of heightened probation supervision. For those that are released early from a jail or prison term, the day reporting center represents a gradual transition into the community in which they are supervised throughout the process.

The advantage of day reporting centers is that they do not require the use of bed space and therefore save counties and states a substantial portion of the cost in maintaining offenders in their custody. Focus Topic 11.2 provides a very good example of a day reporting center, this one operated by Hampden County, Massachusetts. This example demonstrates the various facets of day reporting centers and also dovetails well with the discussion in Chapter 9 regarding police and community corrections partnerships for offender treatment. The Hampden County facility is operated by that county's sheriff's department and therefore provides a strong integration of law enforcement efforts and those of community supervision agencies.

FOCUS TOPIC 11.2

AN EXAMPLE OF A DAY REPORTING CENTER

The Hampden County Day Reporting Center: Three Years' Success in Supervising Sentenced Individuals in the Community

By Richard J. McCarthy, Public Information Officer,
Hampden County, Massachusetts, Sheriffs Department

In Massachusetts, the county correctional system incarcerates both those in pre-trial detention and those sentenced to terms of 2 ½ years or less for crimes such as breaking and entering, larceny, driving while intoxicated, and drug possession. Thus, each county facility is both a jail for pre-trial detainees and a

> *Total contacts under the Hampden County program range from fifty to eighty per participant, per week.*

house of correction for sentenced individuals. The sheriff of each county, an elected official, is the administrator of the jail and house of correction.

Sheriff Michael J. Ashe, Jr. has been in charge of the Hampden County Jail and House of Correction in Springfield, Massachusetts for more than 15 years. One of his early

actions as sheriff was to choose not to live in the "Sheriff's House" that went with the job, but to turn it instead into a pre-release center. Inmates in residence at the center are within 6 months of release and are able to work and participate in community activities. These activities range from Alcoholics Anonymous and Narcotics Anonymous groups to individual counseling, religious services, "work-out" regimens at the YMCA, and community restitution.

In October 1986, faced like many other correctional administrators with worsening overcrowding, Sheriff Ashe instituted what the Crime and Justice Foundation refers to as the first day reporting center in the nation. The day reporting center was located in the country's pre-release center, so that the new operation could draw on the pre-release center staff's experience in supervising offenders in the community. In

(Continued)

(Continued)

addition, pre-release center staff member Kevin Warwick was selected to direct the day reporting center.

Program description. The Hampden County Day Reporting Center supervises inmates who are within 4 months of release and who live at home, work, and take part in positive activities in the community. Participants' behavior is monitored in several ways:

- They must report into the center daily to be observed by staff,
- They must call in daily at several specified times,
- They must be at home when scheduled to be there, to receive random computer calls from an electronic monitoring system, and
- They must pass frequent random urinalysis tests that detect alcohol or drug use.

Participants also are monitored randomly by "community officers." Under this system, each participant is contacted between 50 and 80 times per week.

Day reporting center participants meet with their counselors at the beginning of each week to chart out a schedule of work and attendance at positive community activities. They are responsible for following this schedule to the letter.

It is important to note that the Hampden County day reporting center is not a "house arrest" program; participants spend a good deal of time out of their homes, re-entering the community. Day reporting is also not a diversion program. Sheriff Ashe was concerned that, if used as a diversion program, day reporting would just "widen the net," so that

> Day reporting is the ultimate "carrot" in our incentive-based program participation philosophy; inmates who behave well in jail can serve the end of their sentences at home.

offenders who would not have otherwise gone to jail would be sentenced to day reporting.

Day reporting participants are still on sentence, in the custody of the sheriff, and have earned their way into the day reporting program by positive behavior and program participation. Some participants "graduate" from pre-release center in-house status to day reporting. Others, on shorter sentences, come right from the main institution to day reporting. All have been assessed for entrance into the program based on the likelihood of their being accountable for their behavior in the community.

Program success. Nearly 500 individuals have participated in the day reporting center program to date, and, because of the program's close supervision, none has committed a violent crime in the community while in the program. Eighty percent of participants have successfully completed the program. Twenty percent have been returned to higher security, usually for lack of accountability (e.g., not following the required schedule) or a failed urinalysis test. Under the program, one "dirty" urine (testing positive for either alcohol or drugs) results in a return to higher security. This strict policy was established because of the pre-release center's experience that alcohol or drug use was the primary reason that program participants caused problems in the community.

Pre-trial participants. During the past year, the day reporting program has expanded to provide some supervision of pre-trial individuals, who are released by the court on personal recognizance with the provision that they report daily to the day reporting center, even though they are not in the custody of the sheriff. These individuals do not receive the full services or supervision of day reporting, but their daily reporting is seen by the court as preferable to a release on personal recognizance with no stipulations for reporting at all.

Benefits. Advantages of the day reporting center to our department are numerous. Cell and bed spaces are saved for those who need them the most. Costs of supervising participants in the day reporting program are considerably less than costs for 24-hour lock-up. Day reporting is also the ultimate "carrot" in our institutional incentive-based program participation philosophy; inmates who behave well in jail can serve the end of their sentences at home.

We have also found that individuals who earn the opportunity for home and community participation at the end of their sentences have an improved chance of successful community re-entry. When sentences are a continuum of earned lesser sanctions, the final step to productive and positive community living is much easier than when inmates are released from a higher-security setting. Day reporting also benefits the community because participants work, pay taxes, and perform community service.

We in Hampden County would be happy to share information about our experience in implementing and operating the day reporting center with any interested jurisdictions. For more information, write to Richard McCarthy, Public Information Officer at the Hampden County Sheriffs Department, 79 York Street, Springfield, Massachusetts 01105, or call (413) 781-1560, ext. 213.

SOURCE: National Institute of Corrections. (2006). *The Hampden County Day Reporting Center: Three years' success in supervising sentenced individuals in the community*. Washington, DC: Author. Retrieved from http://www.nicic.org/pubs/1990/period74.pdf. Reprinted with permission.

Day reporting centers are similar to residential treatment facilities except that offenders are not required to stay overnight. In some jurisdictions, the regimen of the day reporting center is designed so that offenders attend 8- to 10-hour intervention and treatment classes. This is an important element of the day reporting center since it provides added human supervision. As noted previously in Chapter 9, the implementation of creative and versatile forms of human supervision serve to optimize both treatment and security characteristics of offender supervision, and day reporting centers facilitate this concept. Indeed, one staff person conducting some form of instruction class (e.g., a life skills class, a psychoeducational class on effective communication, or perhaps a parenting class) can essentially watch over several offenders at the same time. Further, the offender's time is spent in prosocial activities with little opportunity to engage in any form of undetected criminal activity. Thus, day reporting centers

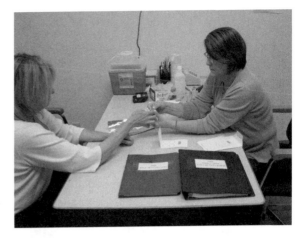

Photo 11.3 A community supervision worker takes a DNA sample. The use of DNA samples to identify whether criminals are recidivists at various crime scenes is becoming common practice in many state probation and parole systems.

enhance security processes while filling up the leisure times in an offender's day or evening with activities that are constructive and beneficial to the offender and to society; little time is left for distractions or unregulated activity.

Effective day reporting centers will tend to be those that have a variety of classes, such as relapse prevention, educational development, individual counseling, and group counseling (Hanser, 2007b). In addition, these programs may include structured *bibliotherapy* (expressive therapy that uses the person's relationship to the content of books and other written words) that requires clients to complete assignments as homework, returning each day to discuss their assignment in a classroom or group counseling setting. Naturally, this serves to keep the offender on track while he or she is at home, and the staff person supervising the bibliotherapy component will be able to detect if the offender is working toward effective reform based on the time and quality that the offender seems to put into the assignments. This allows for another measure or observation of the offender's genuineness and motivation to reform.

While such a system is not failsafe, the use of multiple mechanisms and techniques provides a multilayered collection of interventions that keep the offender constructively busy, well supervised, and on task. As part of their participation in the day reporting center program, offenders might also be subject to electronic monitoring or even GPS tracking, depending on the offender and his or her offense history. The point is that the day reporting center is used in tandem with other sanctions, providing an interlocking set of tools to monitor the offender. At the same time, the day reporting center provides an environment that facilitates the ultimate reintegration of the offender into the community. Thus, the offender is immersed into a treatment regimen that accomplishes three key tasks:

1. The offender is supervised on a face-to-face basis.

2. The offender is kept busy and thus cannot be out on the street offending.

3. The offender is forced to comply with treatment, and regardless of any resistance, a certain amount of this treatment will eventually be processed by the offender.

SHOCK INCARCERATION/SPLIT SENTENCING

For certain offenders, the subjection to a loss of freedom is all that is needed to get their lives in order. As a result, the mechanism used for its stunning value is that of shock incarceration. **Shock incarceration** is a short term of incarceration followed by a specified term of community supervision in hopes of deterring the offender from recidivating. Because the brief stint of incarceration is meant to provide a sense of punitive reality to the offender, most shock incarceration programs are designed for juvenile offenders and those who have never been incarcerated before. Given the basic tenets of shock incarceration, it is mostly used in the form of mixed sentencing. In this case, offenders are given a short term of confinement and then placed on community supervision to complete their term of probation or parole.

Under shock incarceration (sometimes called split sentencing), offenders are sentenced to a term of confinement only to be released after a set time and ordered to serve the remainder of their time on probation. The logic behind such action is that the offender will develop a natural dislike of incarceration and will seek to abstain from criminal behavior in hopes of avoiding such an unpleasant experience. Vito and Allen (1981) hold that shock incarceration should be viewed as a viable intermediate sanction because it (1) allows offenders the opportunity to realistically reintegrate into the community, (2) continues positive connections with existing family, (3) decreases the amount of time spent in prison, (4) decreases prison populations, and (5) decreases the amount of funding spent on prisons. Research has demonstrated that at least three-quarters of all shock incarceration programs have shown some effectiveness.

METHODS OF ENSURING COMPLIANCE—DETECTING DRUG USE AMONG OFFENDERS

The detection of offender drug use is accomplished through a number of testing procedures that use a variety of body samples. The most common are those obtained from the offender's urine, blood, hair, sweat, or saliva. According to Robinson and Jones (2000), urine testing is the most cost-effective, reliable, and widely used drug testing procedure. Nevertheless, it is important that staff understand the drug use demographics of their own region or jurisdiction so that they can determine the most appropriate drug testing strategy to employ. This will vary according to the type of drug use that is most common among drug abusers in the region as well as other considerations. In general, there are five sources from which samples are drawn for drug testing. The descriptions of these sources are taken from the U.S. government document written by Robinson and Jones and published by the Office of Justice Programs, and they are as follows:

1. **Urine Testing:** Due to price and accuracy of the testing process, urinalysis is considered the most suitable method for drug courts and most criminal justice agencies for detecting the presence of illegal substances. Generally, urine testing methods fall into two types: instrumental and noninstrumental (or "point-of-contact") testing (both defined further below). Both methods use some form of immunoassay technology to provide an initial determination of the presence of a drug (p. 3).

2. **Blood Testing:** Blood tests can provide discrete information regarding the degree of an individual's impairment, but the invasiveness of the procedure and the potential danger of infection make blood testing inappropriate for drug court programs (p. 3).

3. **Hair Testing:** The introduction of new, powerful instruments for hair analysis has increased interest in hair testing. Despite its increased popularity among agencies, caution should be used because hair analysis is subject to potential external contamination. Indeed, there are indications that hair analysis can produce tainted results, depending on the type of hair as well as the type of drug that is analyzed. For example, dark pigmented hair absorbs drugs more readily than blond or bleached hair. Male African American hair (black/brown) appears

to absorb drugs more readily than hair of other groups, such as female African Americans (black/brown), male Caucasians (black/brown), and female Caucasians (black/brown and blond) (p. 3).

4. **Sweat Testing:** Sweat samples, which are obtained from patches that can be placed on a person for a number of days, have the advantages of a longer time frame for detection and the fact that they are difficult to adulterate. They do not, however, provide a correlation regarding the degree of impairment, and they are subject to individual differences in sweat production (p. 3).

5. **Saliva Testing:** Saliva samples permit a correlation with the degree of impairment and can be easily obtained. They are, however, subject to contamination from smoking or other substances (p. 3).

Photo 11.4 The multi-drug screen test allows community supervision officers to find a variety of drugs that may have been used by offenders.

Testing Technologies—Immunoassay and Chromatography

The most widely used technology for testing the presence of drugs in the human system is the immunoassay. This system is typically used as a screening mechanism, with immunoassays using antibodies that bind to drugs and their metabolites (the chemical compounds that result after the body has metabolized a drug) in urine and other fluids. The immunoassay drug-screening procedures have been widely used due to the fact that they are relatively inexpensive, provide rapid results, and are highly accurate when performed properly (Robinson & Jones, 2000).

Gas chromatography/mass spectrometry (GC/MS), on the other hand, is an analytical technique that can be used to confirm a positive initial drug screen. Chromatography testing provides a method that is specific to a particular drug of interest and can distinguish a specific drug from other substances that may have similar chemical properties, such as a prescription medication (Robinson & Jones, 2000). This advanced technology allows technicians to identify and quantify atoms, isotopes, and the chemical composition of a given sample. Gas chromatography/mass spectrometry can be used to analyze urine, blood, hair, and other samples to determine the presence of drugs and other substances. Robinson and Jones note that this process is currently the most definitive procedure available when attempting to pinpoint the use of specific types of drugs.

Testing Methods—Instrumental and Point-of-Contact Testing

Urine testing methods fall into two types: instrumental and noninstrumental. Both methods of analysis use some form of immunoassay technology to provide an initial determination of the presence of a drug, while chromatography is used to confirm the presence and quantity of a given drug. It is critical that the integrity of the collection, testing, and reporting process is maintained to (a) ensure that the specimen is from the named defendant, (b) detect adulteration, and (c) ensure that no contaminants have been introduced that would affect the validity of the results (Robinson & Jones, 2000). Evidence of drug use may be present in the urine in the form of the parent drug or metabolites. According to Robinson and Jones, **instrumental testing** is analysis that involves instrumentation (a machine) that will sample, measure, and produce a quantitative result that is given as a numeric amount on a scale. Instrumental analysis has the advantage of being automated, providing precise and accurate documentation, and lending itself to convenient storage of samples in the event that subsequent retesting may be required. Instrumental methods for testing urine rely on immunoassay technology for initial detection. These analyses have increased accuracy and precision in testing results and provide data printouts for review and courtroom presentation.

According to Robinson and Jones (2000), **point-of-contact testing** is analysis that involves devices that require manual sampling and manual observation to produce a qualitative result that includes negative and/or positive values. Point-of-contact testing utilizes a noninstrument device to analyze a sample at the point of collection. Noninstrumental test devices have improved significantly in recent years and can be useful if handled by properly trained staff. Although noninstrumental testing does not provide the detailed analysis that is obtained with instrumental readouts, these tests provide quick and relatively accurate results (Robinson & Jones, 2000). Last, staff training is essential to ensure that test results are interpreted correctly. Relying on a visual detection of a color result can lead to misinterpretation for a number of reasons, including mistaken readings of color acuity, color perception, and lighting. Care must also be taken to ensure that staff are not color-blind. In particular, skill in interpretation is required for those circumstances where positive indication of drug use is weak because of the sample that is utilized, requiring greater judgment from the person interpreting the outcome (Robinson & Jones, 2000).

METHODS OF ENSURING COMPLIANCE—SEX OFFENDER NOTIFICATION PROGRAMS AND COMMUNITY PARTNERSHIPS

Currently, every state has some type of notification process when sex offenders are released into the community. This is true regardless of whether the sex offender is on probation (having not been incarcerated) or has been released on parole (after serving a prison term). Commonly, these requirements fall under **Megan's Laws**, which were passed as a result of the brutal rape and murder of a 7-year-old New Jersey girl named Megan Kanka. The victim's parents pushed for legislation in the state of New Jersey to mandate reporting of sex offenders that are released into the community, and in 1994, New Jersey was the first state to pass such legislation. The following year, the federal government passed similar legislative requirements. Since that time, other states have followed suit, with these laws often being informally referred to as Megan's Laws out of respect for the crime victim who served as the catalyst for this reporting requirement.

The Center for Sex Offender Management (CSOM) is operated by the U.S. Department of Justice and is perhaps the leading national warehouse for training on sex offender–related issues and training. This organization is a federally operated program that provides a vast array of curricula, which are available to the general public and are ideal for community training. The CSOM (2008) notes that in addition to the typical notification programs that exist throughout the United States, there are many occasions where public agencies (such as police, prosecutors, and community supervision agencies) are required to provide specific information pertaining to individual sex offenders. This is conducted through a variety of means, including door-to-door citizen notification, public meetings, and the distribution of written and printed notices.

Further, the CSOM notes that as more comprehensive and collaborative approaches to the management of sex offenders emerge, community members, victims, the victim's family, the offender's family, and others are invited to become partners in the sex offender management process. This dovetails nicely with this text's emphasis on community partnerships and citizen involvement with the offender supervision and treatment process. Students may recall that similar discussion was provided in Chapters 2, 8, and 9 of this text, noting that community partnerships are the key to filling in gaps in both supervision and treatment objectives.

At this point, it should be clear to the student that there are a number of sources—particularly federal sources—that constantly refer to this same theme of using the community as a means of improving offender reintegration, in terms of both security and treatment. Indeed, this text draws from a substantial array of federal publications and documents as source material because these sources are generally considered valid by both practitioners and academic communities, and thus they add legitimacy to this text. It is against this backdrop that we note CSOM's following point:

> As knowledge about the extensive occurrence of sexual assault becomes more widespread, the agencies responsible for sex offender management are beginning to recognize that community notification meetings and interactions with individual community members become opportunities to engage in sexual abuse prevention activities; to connect sexual assault victims with services; and, generally, to advance a community's ability to understand and protect itself from sexual abuse and its trauma. (p. 1)

Naturally, the ability of agencies to collaborate with community members will be specific to that region or location, as some areas are more amenable to such forms of notification and offender tracking than others. Such agency-community programs require that staff exercise sensitivity to the context and needs of individuals, families, and communities that are involved (CSOM, 2008). This process, while entailing a very important community education component, also requires a great deal of care since victim reactions can be quite varied.

Thus, this aspect of ensuring compliance consists of two parts. First is the notification process by which the community is made aware of the existence of a sex offender. Second is the community's involvement in ensuring that the offender is monitored by human observation, interaction, and general community awareness. This provides a strong preventative component for the offender and also ensures that other potential victims are vigilant regarding the possible threat that exists within their community. Nevertheless, these programs must also educate community members on the dynamics of sex offending and the likelihood of recidivism. For instance, in most cases, sex offenders do not recidivate; the majority of all sex offenses are actually not committed by an offender with a prior sex-offending history. This is important for community members to understand because it will increase the efficacy of reintegrative approaches while improving overall supervision of the offender. According to the CSOM (2008), community supervision staff tasked with establishing community partnerships should

- Inform community members about their state's sex offender registration and community notification laws, and about local supervision and treatment efforts to safely manage these offenders.
- Acknowledge community members' interest in their own safety and the safety of their neighborhoods. Explain that stability is a key ingredient in preventing reoffense. If the offender is intimidated, harassed, or threatened because of citizen overreaction, it can lead to the offender "going underground" or hiding from the criminal justice professionals charged with his or her supervision; avoiding helpful therapeutic opportunities; and even disengaging from other positive activities, such as work.
- Explain the potential consequences of abuse of the law such as harassment of the offender. Explain that vigilantism is against the law and that if citizens take matters into their own hands, they can be prosecuted.
- Provide a brief description of the specific efforts that are under way to safely manage the offender, emphasizing the supervision methods, special conditions, and therapeutic interventions being employed with this offender.
- Provide contact information for community members if they have further questions about the offender.
- Provide information about the sex offender subject to community notification as required by statute and policy in the agency's jurisdiction. This probably will include a general description (or photograph) of the offender, the address at which the offender will reside, and the crime of conviction.

It is with these mechanisms in place that compliance of sex offenders can be optimized. This also can be effective in providing a sense of control and empowerment within the community: as members become more aware and proactive, they then have a sense of control or influence over their community environment. Further, the legal parameters that apply to citizens in regard to offender supervision will be clarified, and this can yield productive results in terms of citizen confidence and understanding of their own role in the partnership as well as that of the community supervision agency. In this manner, citizen involvement aids in ensuring that sex offenders comply with various intermediate sanctions imposed upon them, such as community service requirements or requirements associated with house arrest.

INTERMEDIATE SANCTIONS IN DIFFERENT STATES

This section will describe a series of programs that are offered in a variety of states around the nation. It is interesting to see that the use and application of intermediate sanctions can vary quite considerably by the type of offender being supervised, the type of program delivery, and the particular state that is examined. The key point in showcasing these various programs is to illustrate the utility of intermediate sanctions and the flexibility that is associated with their implementation. This is an important selling point for the increased use of intermediate sanctions, since it gives agencies a set of diverse responses that address a diverse array of challenges. We now turn our attention to a number of different programs from various states. The write-ups for these programs have been adapted from the public domain document entitled *NIC Focus: Intermediate Sanctions,* a government publication released by the National Institute of Corrections.

Connecticut Alternative Incarceration Centers

An **alternative incarceration center (AIC)** is a highly structured, community-based program that saves prison or jail beds for more serious offenders. Before this type of facility was added to the system, judges' only option was to sentence offenders to either prison or probation. These centers offer a high level of supervision and service to assist four types of criminal justice system clients who previously would have been placed in prisons or jails:

- Accused individuals in pretrial status;
- Individuals sentenced to the AIC program in lieu of incarceration;
- Individuals assigned to AIC supervision and services as a condition of early release from a correctional facility; and
- Individuals requiring AIC supervision as an alternative to reincarceration following failure on community supervision.

The AICs in Connecticut are jointly planned and managed by the state Department of Corrections and the Connecticut Judicial Department, with consultation from the privately run Connecticut Prison Association. All AICs are operated under contract by private agencies with long histories of working with criminal justice agencies. An AIC serves as a day supervision and treatment center and is open from 8:30 AM to 9:00 PM, 5 days per week, and from 9:00 AM to 2:00 PM on Saturdays. Most of the clients' needs are met in-house by a variety of trained AIC personnel. Clients have immediate access to job developers, crisis intervention workers, substance abuse staff, community service restitution coordinators, family caseworkers, and onsite Alcoholics Anonymous meetings.

Most AICs have supervised transitional housing (limited to 30 days) for clients in need of a residence. Leisure activities are monitored by AIC staff. Clients are encouraged to spend significant blocks of otherwise unstructured time at the center, participating in group discussions, viewing educational videotapes, and planning their week's activities under the supervision of AIC staff. Clients' progress is reported to the appropriate referral agency (bail commission or probation or corrections department). A key element to the program's credibility has been the staff's ability to understand that accurate reporting of noncompliance is paramount to continued support of the program, even though the ultimate consequence is often reincarceration. Although providing social services to AIC clients is certainly vital, community safety dictates that strict monitoring and reporting should be the highest priority. Close to 50 percent of the clients fail the program and therefore do some time behind bars. This tough, no-nonsense approach builds confidence between the private-sector vendors and the criminal justice system.

AIC locations are chosen for their proximity to the courts and each region's social service network. Staff go to court daily and attempt to become a part of the court routine, thereby increasing their credibility as members of the corrections team. Being located close to the court is also important because most clients lack dependable transportation.

Kansas (Sedgwick County) Home Surveillance Program

The Sedgwick County Community Corrections Home Surveillance Program (HSP) provides an additional, restrictive level of intensive supervision in the community for identified high-risk offenders. This house-arrest program represents the most intensive supervision currently available short of placement in the residential programs. The county's residential center provides in-house, 24-hour supervision and could be compared to a work release facility. It offers residents self-help classes during their off-work hours. Because the residential center is usually full, the HSP becomes an even more important part of the agency's range of sanctions. Clients are sentenced to the HSP by the court, if recommended by community corrections evaluators, or are placed there after their graduation from the residential center or by other case managers who have experienced difficulty with them during intensive supervision.

The daily schedule at the HSP is explained to the offender prior to intake acceptance. All clients must agree to the HSP rules and regulations, which are explained in detail. Clients are required to keep a daily itinerary or agenda of their activities. They must sign out from their residence, stating where they are going and for what reason, and they must sign in upon their return. Each daily agenda is approved by the case manager. Offenders are also required to keep other records, such as Alcoholics Anonymous attendance forms and, in some cases, job search forms. Every client also must submit to a minimum of one urinalysis/drug screen or breath analysis per week.

Offender contacts are preferably made at the place of residence, place of employment, or other field sites. Staff conduct a minimum of four personal field contacts per week for each client, and daily contacts are attempted as time permits. Many contacts are made during the evening, usually after 10:00 PM because all clients have a 10:00 PM curfew. The HSP has two levels. Level I restricts clients to their homes with the exception of visits to their doctors or attorneys, which must be approved by the case manager. Clients who comply with Level I rules for 14 days progress to Level II, where they are allowed four 4-hour furloughs per week away from their residence, plus two 8-hour furloughs per week on their days off. All furloughs must be approved by the case manager. At the end of a 90-day period, staff review the case to decide whether the client will be placed on regular supervision. Clients not in full compliance or reasonably close to it will remain in the HSP.

Many offenders are placed in the program because they have failed to comply with the basic conditions of probation, such as reporting to their case manager and making regular payments on their court obligation.

Frequent contacts in the HSP increase understanding of each client's needs and encourage clients to make their regular monthly payments. Because all HSP clients are considered high-risk to some degree, staff use a two-way portable radio assigned to the sheriff's channel. The radio provides a direct link to the dispatcher, who can summon any services that may be needed in the event of a field emergency or a threat to the staff. In addition, HSP clients use a voice 10-second pager to contact the staff when necessary. The pager has proved to be an invaluable means of communication, since staff are usually in a vehicle while on duty.

The HSP seems to be effective because staff get to know clients and their habits in a very short time. Frequent contacts help build rapport between clients and staff very quickly. In fact, clients have requested to stay in the program when it was time for their discharge. The cost of home surveillance obviously exceeds the cost of regular field services supervision. However, it is a more economical alternative than placement in a residential program or prison. In the future, the department may expand the HSP without increasing the number of staff, by adding electronic monitoring devices for higher-risk clients.

Iowa Diversion Program for Sentenced Drunk Drivers

In response to treatment needs and prison overcrowding concerns, an innovative intermediate sanction was implemented in Iowa in 1986 to divert drunk drivers sentenced to imprisonment. The program targets all offenders sentenced to the Department of Corrections for a second or third offense of operating a vehicle while intoxicated (OWI). Effective October 1, 1986, these offenders are processed through the Iowa Medical and Classification Center and then placed in a community residential substance abuse treatment program within a few weeks. An intensive public policy debate preceded this legislative initiative. The debate revolved around implementing either one centralized institutional program or numerous community-based corrections programs to address the chronic substance abuse problems of this population. On the one hand, these offenders were identified as a relatively low-risk population that could be managed in structured settings without undue risk to the community. Furthermore, therapeutic value could be obtained from family involvement and the creation of reentry support networks if offenders remained in the community. On the other hand, it was argued that the community expected repeat drunk-driving offenders to be punished by removal from the community. Economies of scale could also be realized with one efficient program structure. Because some community corrections beds were available to partially offset capital costs, it was ultimately decided that the value of family support and community involvement outweighed the merits of punishment by banishing offenders and the limited cost savings of centralization. Interestingly, the involvement of family or significant others in the treatment process is frequently cited as a major factor in successful program completion.

The OWI population served by the OWI residential treatment programs is unquestionably made up of chronic substance-abusing offenders. Of these, 83 percent have been convicted of OWI offenses three or more times, 60 percent have been using alcohol for more than 10 years, and more than 75 percent have had prior substance abuse treatment admissions. In addition, nearly half have been discharged from a prior treatment program within one year of admission to an OWI program. The OWI residential treatment programs are required to supervise offenders 24 hours per day, provide 220 hours of licensed substance abuse treatment programming, and meet applicable standards of the American Correctional Association. Besides completing the substance abuse treatment program and complying with facility rules, offenders in the program are required to maintain 90 days of stable employment and establish an aftercare treatment plan prior to their release. Successful program completion takes from 4 to 6 months.

Although the OWI residential treatment programs in each district comply with the foregoing specifications, each operates quite differently. Programs range in size from five to forty beds and contract with both private and public substance abuse treatment agencies for at least some of the required services. Contractual services range from problem assessment only to the entire residential and treatment phase of the program. Some districts have developed two-phase programs characterized by 30 days of intensive primary treatment, following which the offender obtains employment. In other programs, employment is required throughout the program, with treatment provided outside of work hours. The cost of these programs ranges from $38 to $56 per day, with an average cost of $46.49. Offenders pay a minimum of $10 per day to help offset program costs.

Missouri: A Control and Intervention Strategy for Technical Parole Violators

In an effort to effectively manage its offender population, the Missouri Department of Corrections has focused on a group that represents a significant number of prison commitments: technical parole violators. The department found that a large number of recommitments were offenders whose parole was revoked for technical violations rather than new convictions. Realizing that many of these violators were being returned to prison due to their inability to address alcohol and drug problems, the department, in concert with the Board of Probation and Parole, instituted a new concept in dealing with them.

The program's treatment center is designed for technical parole violators whose behavior has demonstrated their need for control and intervention. This facility offers more structure than other intermediate sanctions, such as intensive supervision, house arrest, or traditional halfway house placement, because offenders are confined to the facility with no passes during their 90-day stay. Offenders are screened by local field staff in conjunction with a coordinator from the facility to determine eligibility. Offenders must be technical violators who have not been charged with new law violations.

Further, it must be demonstrated that traditional strategies have been implemented and the offender has been unresponsive to them. Finally, the violation must be serious enough to warrant revocation and commitment to the Department of Corrections. This program facility is the final stop before recommitment to prison. Because the offenders in this program have been unable to remain on supervision within the community, they are placed on a vigorous treatment schedule. This program consists of three phases that are dedicated to building offender responsibility through a cognitive approach in a structured, didactic, interactional, and confrontational manner. The program follows a logical progression from problem awareness to skill building to relapse prevention and follow-up. The model relies on an Alcoholics Anonymous (AA) methodology, with study and work groups that enhance the daily education and therapy classes. Counseling groups help violators apply the class material to their own needs.

Phase I, which lasts 3 weeks, consists of intake, assessment, orientation, and intensive classes on the disease concept of chemical dependency. This work lays a foundation for violators to begin problem solving, using the tools furnished by AA and the 12-step recovery process. The skills violators learn through this general approach can be applied to their lives in the community, whether they have found chemicals to be a way of life or a component of an overall criminal lifestyle. Phase II makes up the next 6 weeks of the program. One topic is covered each week to bring about meaningful skill development. Topics include problem solving, understanding emotions, managing stress, assertiveness, relapse prevention, and the role of the family and others. The final 4 weeks, designated as Phase III, focus on vocational and job readiness, along with follow-up and placement planning sessions to provide the violator with a practical application of the techniques learned previously. All of these sessions are conducted by department staff, including psychologists, parole officers, and caseworkers. Custody personnel also receive training to help them adapt to the treatment approach as opposed to the traditional prison milieu.

Arizona (Maricopa County) Community Punishment Program

The state of Arizona has enacted numerous legislative initiatives for enhancing probation programs, with the provision that the enhancements be targeted at diverting probation clients from prison and jail. Among these initiatives, there are three programs in particular that are of interest. These three programs are intended to meet the specific supervision and therapeutic needs of substance abusers, sex offenders, and mentally ill probationers. The three proposed "community punishment programs" (CPPs) are probation specific and do not compete with community treatment programs. Rather, they are stopgap measures to bring services to populations previously underserved because of lengthy waiting lists, economic demands, offenders' geographic location, or their inability to meet other eligibility criteria. The programs make no financial requirements of the probationer for participation. All programming is imposed in addition to the requirements of probation, thus increasing offender supervision and accountability for behavior.

Each program component is intended to serve nonviolent offenders who are at risk of being directly sentenced to long-term incarceration and offenders under community supervision whose probation is in jeopardy due to behaviors not associated with the filing of new criminal charges. Essentially, the program attempts to target the defendant who is teetering on the edge of incarceration but who can be safely managed in the community with increased levels of supervision and treatment. The goal of the *chemical dependency component* is to provide services for defendants who, due to chemical abuse, are unstable and in need of immediate treatment. It provides most of the diversions from prison, because the vast majority of initial sentences and probation revocations involve chemical abuse and related allegations. The 12-week outpatient program is staffed by six chemical dependency counselors, who each carry a core caseload of 30 offenders. The counselors are probation department employees who directly interact with the supervising probation officers to ensure clients' participation. Offenders receive 4 to 5 hours of counseling weekly.

Resources available to the counselors include public transportation passes for clients, urine testing, and job referral services; job referrals are provided by a specialist who also assists in educational placement. The program allows for a spouse or significant other to be involved in therapy. All defendants participate in counseling groups, which are limited to 15 clients. Individual counseling is also available on a limited scale, as needed.

Sex offender treatment is another component of this program. These probation cases fall into three general categories: incest offenders, offenders with a history of indecent exposure ("hands-off" offenses), and defendants with low mental functioning. Counseling for these offenders includes group therapy, as well as psychological, physiological, and polygraph testing as required. (Examples of these types of supervision/treatment techniques will be provided in Chapter 13 of this text.) Victims of the offense are also afforded counseling through this program to aid their recovery. The program will pay for offenders' spouses to participate in the therapy when children are in the home. Costs for therapy range from $50 to $100 per session, and the program subsidizes whatever the defendant cannot afford. In addition to this specialized, offense-specific counseling, sex offenders are subject to surveillance similar to that used in intensive supervision probation/parole (ISP). Defendants are also placed in a specialized caseload, supervised by a seasoned probation officer specially trained in the area of sexual deviance. Probationers are not allowed to return to any living environment where children are at risk. The third component of this program addresses *mental health issues.* The program's Transitional Living Center, or TLC, is a 25-bed inpatient facility specifically designed to assist mentally ill probationers in crisis. Offenders may stay in the program for up to 45 days. During that time, defendants participate in individual and group counseling, psychiatric intervention, stabilization via medication (if appropriate), and vocational and educational planning. Financial assistance and treatment programs are pursued for the defendants, and staff seek community resources to provide the most appropriate environment upon offenders' stabilization and release. Admission requirements specify that defendants must have a documented history of mental illness and that they be sentenced to supervised probation. Defendants cannot be overtly violent or suicidal at the time of admission. During the vendor selection process, it was found that services could be provided to this population at a savings of 25 to 50 percent over rates paid to current treatment providers. Naturally, this savings helps to illustrate why treatment in the community tends to have more benefits than treatment within a prison or jail setting.

Tennessee GPS Tracking of Sex Offenders

In 2007, the state of Tennessee published an evaluation of their experience utilizing GPS tracking of sex offenders. This detailed report provided a multifaceted examination that produced some fairly surprising results. Among the beneficial findings, it was found that community supervision officers were better able to establish inclusion zones, which are locations where the offender must be located during specified time periods, such as work or home during certain times of the day or evening. Further, GPS tracking aided in monitoring exclusion zones for places where the offender was not permitted to enter. Thus, the use of GPS tracking aided the overall supervision quality and monitoring of the offender. However, these same types of monitoring are able to be conducted using other methods. A key distinction with GPS tracking is the fact that it allows officers to see specific patterns of activity and then follow up on frequently visited locations. Because the supervision officer can track total movement of the offender, suspicious areas or those frequently visited by the offender can be more readily investigated. Further, it was held by most officers that GPS tracking seemed to deter sex offenders from engaging in other forms of deviant or criminal activity, simply due to the fact that these offenders were cognizant of the monitoring that they were under. In addition, when offenders did violate their community supervision requirements, officers were more likely to determine the specific violation that occurred. Thus, the overall supervision ability was enhanced, and the ability to pinpoint specific offense behavior improved the effectiveness of officers who sought to revoke or modify community supervision parameters.

Moreover, GPS tracking helped to cultivate better partnerships between local law enforcement agencies, since this tool helped to more accurately confirm or eliminate allegations of potential criminal activity. This serves as an aid to both community supervision agencies and law enforcement agencies, as accuracy in detection allows for better placement of resources. Law enforcement is also provided an added benefit when attempting to resolve cases in their jurisdiction. Likewise, GPS data provides officers with information to investigate and verify citizen claims of inappropriate offender activity. This function would be likely to aid in further cementing partnerships between the agency and the wider community, a primary goal that has been noted throughout this text.

However, it was noted that GPS tracking had several limitations or challenges, both in implementation and in maintenance of the program. First, officers that used this system pointed out that it is not necessarily the best approach for all sex offenders. This is consistent with prior research. In some cases, false positives may occur (remember Chapter 3), resulting in excessive forms of supervision that also create resentment among those offenders that are making genuine efforts toward reform. In these cases, the offenders perceived the use of GPS as a punishment. It should be pointed out that research does indicate that lower-risk offenders who are supervised by strict levels of supervision recidivate more frequently and have overall higher recidivism rates than similar offenders supervised at less stringent levels (Champion, 2002; Tennessee Board of Probation and Parole, 2007). Much of this recidivism is thought to be due to the negative impact on offender motivation and the contrast between increased supervision and positive, reintegrative efforts (Hanser, 2007b).

In addition, evaluative research by Middle Tennessee State University (MTSU: 2007) produced statistically significant descriptive and demographic results using subjects from both treatment and control groups. Briefly, the treatment group was administered GPS tracking while the control group was given some form of supervision that did not include GPS tracking. This allowed the evaluators to determine the impact of the GPS tracking itself, since other aspects of the supervision sentence were kept roughly equal or comparable between the groups. (For further discussion of evaluative research and the use of treatment and control groups, see Chapter 15 of this text.)

The evaluative research by MTSU found that offenders younger than 40 years old were more likely to commit new offenses (though not necessarily sex offenses) while under GPS supervision than were offenders that were over 40 years old. In addition, it was found that offenders in the 30- to 40-year-old age range were statistically more likely to gain new criminal charges than were offenders in any other 10-year age category investigated. Thus, it is clear that this group is perhaps most in need of enhanced supervision. Further, offenders that had less than a high school education were more likely to commit a new offense than were those that had a background that included high school or higher levels of educational attainment. Findings such as these are useful since they can be used to avoid false negatives (recall Chapter 3) to more accurately determine which offenders are most suitable for additional security through GPS tracking devices. This is particularly useful when only a finite number of tracking devices exists within an agency.

Aside from the issues noted, there were also some serious issues regarding officer workload when supervising clients on GPS monitoring. This issue of course harkens back to our prior discussion in Chapter 4 related to workload and stress for community supervision officers. It would appear that officers with GPS caseloads must count on doing much more work than other officers with no such offenders on their caseload. For instance, the research by MTSU found that GPS officers would receive alerts or violation reports requiring immediate response much more frequently and during the day, evening, and weekend hours. This of course included holidays and those days that the officer was off duty from the agency. Thus, the reality of being "on call" was far more relevant for these officers (Tennessee Board of Probation and Parole, 2007). Further, this evaluative report noted that the continuous on-call status and increased workload had a significant, negative impact on GPS officers' personal lives; the sporadic alert responses infringed on officers' quality time with their families and increased stress in their daily routine (Tennessee Board of Probation and Parole, 2007).

Moreover, with respect to the actual job function itself, GPS officers noted that supervision required significantly more time and attention, including substantial time working on equipment problems. Thus, this type of supervision is much more labor-intensive than other forms of supervision, and potential malfunctions can impair effectiveness of the program. In addition, it was a concern among some officers that when they received alerts during the night, law enforcement backup was not always available. This meant that responding to alerts late at night presented safety issues for these community supervision officers who were not armed (MTSU, 2007).

From this discussion, it is clear that GPS tracking has many pros and cons. The detailed study conducted by MTSU, on behalf of the Tennessee Board of Probation and Parole, clearly provides a very detailed picture of the implementation of this intermediate sanction. This is important because GPS tracking is hailed as one of the most modern and sophisticated innovations. While it certainly has its place and while it does indeed provide a contribution to the range of supervision strategies, there are pitfalls that agencies must consider. Often, the balance between the pros and cons can be delicate when considering intermediate sanctions, and the use of GPS technology is no different.

For the most part, the tenets of routine activities theory, by Cohen and Felson, reflect the general premise behind most intermediate sanctions. Cullen and Agnew (2006) provide a clear and effective synopsis of this theory in the following statement:

> Crime occurs when there is an intersection in time and space of a motivated offender, an attractive target, and a lack of capable guardianship. People's daily routine activities affect the likelihood they will be an attractive target and will encounter an offender in a situation where no effective guardianship is present. (p. 7)

Intermediate sanctions work to eliminate the likelihood that offenders will not have effective guardianship. In other words, an effective guardian will protect potential victims. This guardian is the use of surveillance devices and supervision programs utilized by community supervision agencies. Further, when agencies keep the community informed and when the community is encouraged to volunteer and partner with the agency, an additional layer of guardianship is added to the offender's supervision.

When the offender is released into the community, members of an informed and involved community are able to modify their routines to reduce the likelihood of victimization. Further, the offender is deterred from likely recidivism due to the understanding that he or she is being supervised by a number of different persons and through a variety of potential mechanisms. Thus, heightened community vigilance and increased controls placed on the offender work to augment one another, providing an ethereal prison, of a sort, when implemented correctly.

During this process, it is hoped that the offender learns to modify his or her own activities. While under supervision, many are restricted from certain areas of the community (e.g., an alcoholic may be restricted from bars and nightclubs, a sex offender may be restricted from approaching an elementary school, and so forth). Over time, graduated sanctions are lessened as the offender demonstrates that he or she is able to maintain his or her own behavior within the constraints of prosocial behavior. It is in this way that the reinforcement of routine activities theory leads to a form of internal social learning, being operantly reinforced upon the offender, whether the offender realizes it or not.

SOURCE: Cullen, F. T., & Agnew, R. (2006). *Criminological theory: Past to present* (3rd ed.). Los Angeles: Roxbury; Lilly, J. R., Cullen, F. T., & Ball, R. A. (2007). *Criminological theory: Context and consequences* (4th ed.). Thousand Oaks, CA: Sage Publications.

CONCLUSION

This chapter has provided an overview of several types of intermediate sanctions that are used around the country. In addition, specific examples have been offered to demonstrate the variety of sanctions that exist and their flexibility in being utilized. The flexibility of intermediate sanctions gives community supervision agencies a range of potential responses to offender criminal behavior. This range falls along a continuum according to the amount of liberty that is denied the offender. These various penalties are interchangeable with one another and vary by level of punitiveness to allow community supervision agencies to calibrate the offender's punishment with the specific offense severity or tendency toward recidivism. In addition, intermediate sanctions help to connect the supervision process with the treatment process. Various intermediate sanctions, such as community service and the payment of fines, create a system of restoration, while the use of flexible supervision schemes such as electronic monitoring and GPS tracking allow the offender to engage in employment activities. Other programs, such as day reporting centers, ease the transition of offenders from incarceration to community membership and provide a series of constructive activities to ensure that the offender remains on task with respect to his or her reintegration process. Each of these sanctions can be used in conjunction with others to further augment the supervision process, all the while being less expensive and more productive than a prison term.

Finally, as has been noted consistently throughout this text, the use of community partnerships is again emphasized. In this case, the community partnerships come by way of citizens monitoring the offender who is tasked with completing various activities to fulfill his or her sentence. The use of human supervision is again shown to be important, and intermediate sanctions are well-suited to citizen involvement when ensuring offender compliance. It is in this manner that intermediate sanctions are yet an additional tool that provides an external incentive for offenders to work their regimen within the community. These sanctions, when administered in a social vacuum, would not be expected to be effective. But when utilized against a backdrop of community involvement, agency collaboration, and solid case management processes, intermediate sanctions serve as another interlocking supervision mechanism that improves the overall prognosis of offender reintegration.

Key Terms

Alternative incarceration center (AIC)

Blood testing

Community service

Day reporting centers

Electronic monitoring

Fine

Global Positioning System (GPS)

Hair testing

Home detention

Instrumental testing

Intensive supervision

Intermediate sanctions

Megan's Laws

Point-of-contact testing

Saliva testing

Shock incarceration

Sweat testing

Urine testing

"What Would You Do?" Exercise

You are the executive director of a new day reporting center. You own this center and have invested a significant portion of your own time and money into this project. You have extensive experience as a case manager but have always dreamed of having your own place to run. The county-level jail and the state probation/parole department have agreed to send offenders to your center, and you have networked well to ensure that you are able to maintain a steady flow of clients. Further still, you recently completed a grant proposal for homeless drug abusers from the Substance Abuse and Mental Health Services Administration (SAMHSA). Thus, money seems to exist to ensure that you are able to maintain your facility.

However, the state department of probation/parole and the local jail facility want to know about the different types of services that you will provide to offenders that visit your facility during the day. You are asked to write a comprehensive outline of the different services that you plan to offer to clients.

In addition, SAMHSA informs you that they have a number of requirements for their grant recipients. They are asking that you explain how you will demonstrate that your services are effective in the community. Though they do not require a statistical evaluation for this project at this time (not until after a year of funding), they do still want to know how you will ensure that your services are working.

What would you do?

Applied Exercise

Read each of the case scenarios below and select the type of intermediate sanction that you think is best suited for each offender. The list of intermediate sanctions is presented after the scenario. Once you have made your selection, write a 50- to 150-word essay for each scenario that explains why you chose a particular intermediate sanction or combination of sanctions.

Students should remember that intermediate sanctions operate on a continuum, and students will need to avoid false positives (overpredicting—refer to Chapter 3 for more details) or false negatives (underpredicting—refer to Chapter 3 again) when making their decisions. Total word count for this assignment is approximately 500 to 1,500 words.

Grading Rubric (This assignment is worth a maximum total of 100 points.)

1. Student provides a reasonable match between scenarios and intermediate sanction. (Each scenario is worth 3 points.)

2. Student provides adequate justification for each match between scenarios and intermediate sanction. (Each essay justification is worth 7 points.)

Applied Exercise Case Scenarios:

_____ Scenario #1: A male juvenile who constantly sneaks out of the house despite parent's attempts to prevent him. He leaves home at night to meet friends, use drugs, and commit acts of vandalism.

_____ Scenario #2: A female offender who "keyed" the car of a neighbor that kept parking on the curb nearest to her own side of the street.

_____ Scenario #3: A male delivery driver who is on community supervision for failing to appear in court for court proceedings related to thefts in a neighborhood.

_____ Scenario #4: A male gang offender who physically assaulted a man who smarted off to him.

_____ Scenario #5: A female drug addict who has been busted for prostitution.

_____ Scenario #6: A young male who has been committing petty acts of vandalism.

_____ Scenario #7: A woman convicted of writing hot checks.

_____ Scenario #8: A male teenager who made threatening prank calls to various people in the community.

_____ Scenario #9: A middle-aged male who continues to drive while drunk. This is his second DWI offense. He has never been to prison.

_____ Scenario #10: A bunch of youth who were playing pranks on elderly people in the community. They egged multiple homes and caused some light property damage to porch lights and other such components of victims' homes.

Applied Exercise Intermediate Sanction Choices:

A. Intensive supervised probation/parole
B. GPS tracking and probation
C. Standard probation and restitution
D. Home detention and electronic monitoring
E. Standard probation and community service
F. Shock incarceration, probation, and community service
G. Restitution
H. Community service
I. Day reporting center and the use of ISP
J. Standard probation
K. Home detention, electronic monitoring, and ISP
L. Drug court with ISP

NOTE: Students may use any of the above options more than once to apply to the scenarios provided. Likewise, there is no requirement that students use every one of the choices presented above.

CHAPTER 12

Juvenile Offenders

LEARNING OBJECTIVES

1. Know the early origins of juvenile probation.

2. Know and understand the processes involved in juvenile probation.

3. Demonstrate knowledge of the juvenile court system and its effect on community corrections with juvenile offenders.

4. Understand how risk factors and protective factors affect the likelihood for continued offending among juveniles.

5. Identify the different forms of residential and nonresidential programs that exist in juvenile corrections and the types of therapy they each employ.

6. Be aware of the basic dynamics associated with juvenile gang offenders, and understand the difficulties in getting youths out of gang life.

7. Be aware of the informal and alternative approaches to juvenile processing, including restorative justice, family conferences, and teen courts.

INTRODUCTION

The juvenile justice system is complicated and quite different from the adult criminal justice system. It is also a major component of the work involved in community supervision. Since young people tend to commit more crime than those who are older, and since most juveniles are not incarcerated for long periods of time (if at all), this means that there is a substantial population of juvenile offenders on probation throughout the United States. Therefore, the juvenile population must be given specific attention and consideration when discussing various aspects of community supervision. Though it is impossible to fully describe and detail the entire juvenile justice system in one chapter of a text, this chapter seeks to fill in some of the gaps in information that might otherwise exist, thereby integrating information specific to juvenile offenders with the whole scheme of this text. In this manner, the information in this chapter augments the other information so that the student will be fully aware of community supervision issues when dealing with both adult and juvenile offender populations.

THE EARLY HISTORY OF JUVENILE PROBATION

As with most issues pertaining to juvenile justice, juvenile probation traces its roots back to those precepts that were established in England during the Middle Ages under the principle of *parens patriae*. **Parens patriae** is a Latin term that denotes that the king, as father of his country, is empowered and obligated to protect the welfare of the country's children. However, it is John Augustus, a shoemaker in Boston, Massachusetts (1785–1859), who is revered as the father of juvenile probation, just as he is held to be the father of adult probation. During the first quarter of the 1800s, Augustus voluntarily supervised offenders who had committed minor infractions. Many of these offenders were drunkards, but the offenders Augustus informally supervised also included women and children from time to time. John Augustus often did this for humanitarian purposes, working out the informal terms and conditions with the judge of the court. Indeed, it was not uncommon for Augustus to supervise juvenile offenders. This is particularly true when one considers that laws back then were different from today in relation to adulthood, child protection, and the general coming of age into the "age of majority" (the threshold of adulthood recognized by law). Thus, even the "adult" offenders that John Augustus might have supervised were probably juveniles by today's standards. John Augustus's work was instrumental in prompting legislation that established probation for juveniles in 1878. During this same time period, the Society for the Prevention of Cruelty to Children (1875) was also established. Later, in 1899, this group would be central to the formation of the first juvenile court, in Cook County, Illinois.

The Cook County Juvenile Court emerged from the concerns of a group of compassionate and wealthy women in Chicago who advocated for the rights of disadvantaged children that were found errant regarding the law. These women, commonly referred to as the "child savers," fought for these needy children to have the same care, custody, and treatment as their natural family would have presumably provided. The creation of the juvenile court was one project that was thought to help toward this objective, integrating individualized treatment approaches, serving needs of the youth, and providing guidance to avoid the children engaging in further deviant behavior. It was at this time that the concern with stigmatization of youth emerged within the treatment of juveniles, a concept that is still alive and well today. In order to avoid the negative effects of labeling, informal court proceedings were utilized where the full gamut of constitutional safeguards would not be necessary; the goal of the court was reintegration rather than punishment.

Thus, juvenile court proceedings were informal and conducted without any of the typical constitutional protections secured by adults, with the goal being to protect and serve the "best interests" of the child. Interestingly, juvenile court records were sealed as a means of ensuring that youth were not negatively labeled as a result of their contact with the court, the whole idea revolving around the notion that youth, unlike adults, were not yet lost and that reintegrative efforts would tend to have optimal likelihoods of success. This line of thought also considered youth to be more impressionable and open to positive change, if only given the appropriate guidance. The use of constitutional safeguards was thought to be an impediment to the informal helping approach that was desired, since these safeguards were rooted in an adversarial mentality that juvenile advocates sought to avoid.

After the first juvenile court was established, these courts spread throughout the United States until, in 1927, all but two states had enacted legislation for both juvenile courts and juvenile probation. It is important to point out that probation is an extension of the courts in many respects, even though it is presented in this text (and in others) as a branch of corrections. Thus, any developments in the juvenile court also transferred to eventual changes in the nature of juvenile probation. Juvenile probation quite naturally implemented the helping approach with youth, just as did those courts that processed juveniles. According to Latessa and Allen (1999), "the theoretical assumption of juvenile probation was that providing guidance, counseling, resources, and supervision would assist low-risk juveniles to adapt to constructive living," and in the process these youth could avoid the detrimental effects of institutionalization.

THE NATURE OF JUVENILE PROBATION

Juvenile probation is a judicial disposition under which youthful offenders are subject to certain conditions imposed by the juvenile court while being allowed to remain in the community for the duration of their sentence. Probation is the most widely used judicial disposition in juvenile courts around the country. The three primary functions of juvenile probation are intake, investigation, and supervision. During the intake stage of the court proceedings, the probation officer will typically decide whether or not to file a petition on a child referred to the court. Investigation consists of the compilation of a social history of the juvenile to assist the judge in making decisions. Finally, supervision focuses mainly on crime control elements to ensure that juveniles do not reoffend.

During the *intake stage* of the juvenile process (see *intake screening of needs* in the Glossary), the probation officer screens youth that are referred to the court and conducts a preliminary investigation, which includes an interview where the probation officer will advise the youthful offender of his or her rights. If the parents or legal guardians have not yet been notified of the juvenile's status, the probation agency will inform them and will ensure that they are advised of their legal options and their right to secure an attorney. In addition, the probation officer conducting the intake may find it useful to interview the family, witnesses, victims, and others to determine if detention or other considerations may be necessary for the youthful offender. Naturally, the juvenile's school will likely be contacted to gain information and to also make appropriate educational arrangements for the youth while he or she is being processed. Finally, if the youth has been in court before or is already on probation, the intake officer will find it necessary to update himself or herself with the previous reports that are on file.

The *investigation stage* (see *social study* in the Glossary) is roughly 60 days in length, but if the courthouse combines the adjudicatory and disposition stages, it may be required that the officer finish the investigation prior to the youth's appearance in court. This investigation is often referred to as the **social study**, which details the youth's personal background, family, educational progress, previous violations, employment, and so forth. This social study will end with the probation officer's diagnosis and treatment plan, as well as the officer's ultimate recommendation to the court. With this report, the probation officers provide a final determination regarding whether the youth should be returned to the community as well as the specific conditions for the recommended probation sentence.

The **supervision stage** includes the casework, surveillance, and various aspects of security management to track the behavior of the juvenile. This stage is, at least in the most basic terms, a key function of the probation department. In the process of performing this function, it is common for juveniles to actually develop a strong connection with their juvenile probation officer. Despite the fact that juvenile probation officers may be responsible for supervising the security elements of the youth's sentence, the other functions of juvenile probation often mitigate the relationship and provide for a blend between mentor and rule monitor. The strong focus on rehabilitation tends to carry the most weight and reflects the general operational focus of the juvenile probation officer.

Probation supervision is used in the majority of cases where juveniles are adjudicated. This form of sentence is considered appropriate for youth who are not violent and are not seen as being in serious need of intensive services, such as might be encountered with drug-addicted youth or those with serious mental health concerns. In such cases, these youth would be sent to residential community treatment centers, most of which will be designed for youthful offenders. Even though the youth may have emotional or behavioral problems, they can still end up on probation due to a lack of effective in-patient services being available in a given area. This might be true in some rural communities where there are no residential facilities. In such cases, youth are typically required to participate in a number of activities or treatment-related functions as a means of accommodating their corollary (but important) issues. Further, during the supervision of the youth, there are often added requirements that the youthful offender obey his or her parents/guardians, that the offender attend school, that the youth return home at a specified time during the day, and that he or she avoid other known youthful offenders. During this process, the probation officer will often work with the youth, attempting to dialogue about problems facing the young offender, including the pushes toward crime and the potential lack of pulls to keep the youth from returning to crime.

There are many theories that speculate on the causal factors associated with delinquency, but nearly all agree that the presence of adult supervision is important and that the existence of family influences is perhaps the most instrumental form of socializing element available. Thus, probation officers that oversee juveniles will likely be engaged in a number of functions that also involve the families of the juvenile offender. Addressing these factors can become quite complicated, since it may be that the parents themselves are not high functioning or may be ill-equipped to handle the youth's behavior, both at home and in the youth's school or community. Indeed, some parents may be in need of parenting classes and may be misguided on effective parenting techniques to aid their child. In these cases, it may seem that the entire family is on probation, particularly if family therapy is warranted or it is determined that the parents have been neglectful or abusive of the youth. It is common for many juvenile offenders to report abuse in their past histories, leading researchers to conclude that abusive experiences aggravate the likelihood of offending and compound the likelihood of recidivism. Thus, returning youth to these homes may not be the best option. However, many youth must be returned to homes that are not the best option due to a lack of resources. Though juvenile probation officers will tend to monitor the family system's progress, this can still have negative effects on the youth and their overall ability to break out of criminal behavior. This is particularly true when the juvenile does not wish to be separated from his or her family, regardless of how toxic that family might be.

On the other hand, it may be that the parental system functions quite well and that the youthful offender engages in delinquent actions due to other factors. One primary factor can be the peers that are selected. The impact of a teen's friends is great, and if the youth befriends other youngsters that are delinquent, a certain pull toward criminogenic behavior is likely. The impact of delinquent peers is actually a commonly studied phenomenon (Cox, Allen, Hanser, & Conrad, 2008; Hanser, 2007b). In fact, as youth progress from early childhood to adolescence, they tend to place more importance on the judgment of their peers than that which they receive from their parents; that is a natural process of autonomy seeking, a process common to youth that are maturing into adults. This then means that some may go through periods of storm and stress where parents seem to have lost much of the influence and impact that they once had in guiding their child's life. Add to this the various physiological changes that occur during the teenage years, and it becomes clear that these individuals can be inherently challenging for even the best of parents. Thus, it cannot be said that youthful delinquency is simply a product of poor parenting.

Other problems that result in juveniles on probation stem from an inability or unwillingness to relate in a constructive manner with authority figures (Abadinsky, 2003). Abadinsky claims that "parents, school officials, and others who have represented authority to the young person have caused him or her to develop a negative, even hostile, attitude toward authority in general" (p. 143). While it is true that many youth on juvenile probation may have a natural distrust of authority (particularly adult authority), the general claim that school officials and parents serve as the cause of these problems is something that should be refuted. Indeed, some youth will present with a variety of behavioral disorders, such as oppositional defiant disorder, hyperactivity disorder, or the even more serious conduct disorder (Hanser, 2007b). These disorders tend to appear with disproportional frequency among those youth processed through the juvenile justice system relative to youth not processed. Often, when youth present with these types of diagnosable disorders, the fault does not lie with parents or school officials. In such cases, the causal factors are complicated and often due to personal characteristics of the young person that are biopsychosocial in nature.

Even in such cases where treatment-resistant diagnoses are involved, probation officers can have an overall positive impact by role modeling healthy reactions to the youth's aberrant behavior while also enforcing consequences for illegal behavior. Further, other role models that are important to the young person should be utilized, when feasible. In some cases, juvenile probation officers may incorporate such persons into the overall supervision plan, and this helps to provide a meaningful bond for the young person as well as offer an additional source of human supervision that is based in well-intended purposes for the youth. Throughout the course of the helping process, the probation officer will often involve the family and will meet the juvenile probationer at different times and places. The juvenile probation officer is likely to network with school officials (counselors, teachers, and administrators) and may even serve as an advocate for the child to secure public school placements (Abadinsky, 2003).

In fact, many youth processed through the juvenile justice system present with learning disabilities and other challenges, and this can add to the list of problems that they face. In most cases, the worse these youth do at school, the more likely they are to engage in problematic behaviors. In frustration and perhaps due to diagnosable problems, these youth may exhibit disruptive behavior, making school administrators hesitant to accommodate them. Thus, the juvenile probation officer may find that he or she is indeed the youth's most passionate advocate when resolving problems that face the individual. In some cases, probation officers may have to arrange for placement of juveniles into a foster home or adoption. This is particularly true if the family conditions are deplorable. Thus, juvenile probation officers find themselves often working in tandem with other social service agencies. The partnerships between these agencies and the probation officer are often critical to ensuring that the young person receives the appropriate help.

THE JUVENILE COURT SYSTEM

Neubauer (2002) notes that while all states today have juvenile courts, their organizational relationship to other judicial bodies varies greatly, and that only a few states have created juvenile courts that are completely separate from other judicial bodies in their jurisdiction. In fact, juvenile courts have a great deal of difference from state to state, falling within one of three general categories: that of a separate court, a part of the family court, or a component of the local trial court system.

When a juvenile court operates as its own separate statewide entity, it has its own administrators, judges, probation officers, clerks of the court, and other personnel. This type of system is actually rare, existing only in the states of Connecticut, Rhode Island, and Utah. However, in a few large metropolitan areas of other states, the juvenile court is kept completely separate from other court systems. Most jurisdictions do not separate juvenile courts because their operation is thought to be more expensive when administered separately. It is thus more common for such courts to be connected to other court systems or functions.

A second and more common form of juvenile court organization is to include juvenile courts within the broader scope of the family court system. Family courts have jurisdiction over most all family matters, which are often civil in nature. Further, since family issues include those pertaining to children, the integration of juvenile court proceedings into these services is even more pragmatic in nature. In many cases, family courts oversee matters concerning delinquency, status offenses, and child-victim or child abuse cases (a topic that follows this subsection).

The most common means for juvenile courts to operate is as part of the broader trial court system. Though this is the most common means of administration, it is also a very interesting means of handling juvenile justice. Indeed, when going beyond the legal considerations of the jurisdiction, the question of where juvenile cases are heard tends to be more a function of the courthouse caseload within a given jurisdiction. Neubauer (2002) states that "in rural areas with few cases, they most often are a type of case on the judge's calendar much like tort and contract cases" (p. 506). This demonstrates that juvenile cases may be "worked in" with the common court caseload in a rather informal and potentially haphazard manner. The quality of such proceedings is perhaps questionable, at best. In most other areas, there tend to be sufficient cases to warrant one or more specific judges who devote themselves fully to the juvenile caseload. While this separation of the juvenile court is grounded in the need to more effectively process the volume of juvenile cases in these jurisdictions, it is also rooted in the fact that juvenile cases can in this way be better shielded from the public eye. In other words, it is easier to keep juvenile proceedings from public view or scrutiny when they are conducted in separate sections of the court or (even better) in an entirely separate courthouse.

JUVENILE RECORDS

Juvenile records include various types of information. Among these records there is likely to be a composite of the criminal history, family and personal information, abuse history, and truancy records, as well as other identification information such as fingerprinting or photographs. Other information, such as driving records, HIV/AIDS testing, status offense records, substance abuse history, and so forth may also be included. In addition, if the juvenile has committed a violent crime, there is likely to be information regarding the victim and the witness notification process as a means of protecting those persons from the juvenile offender.

Importantly, some states, such as Texas, may have a central repository for juvenile records, whereas other states may have local jurisdictions maintain the records of juveniles that are processed within their jurisdiction. Obviously, the more centralized the records, the more likely they are to be useful for public safety purposes. However, juvenile records tend to be confidential in nature, and only the juvenile offender, the juvenile's parents or legal guardian(s), or the attorney of record is typically given access. State social service or various law enforcement agencies also typically have the right to access these records, given appropriate justification. The general public, however, is not given access.

It is clear that centralized record systems are superior to those maintained by far-flung jurisdictions, particularly when agencies must share information in the interest of public safety. Given the recent concern with violent juvenile offenders in general and juvenile sex offenders in particular, issues related to interagency information sharing have become an increasing area of concern. Effective information systems on juvenile offenders tend to be fingerprint-based systems. This helps to address issues related to the reliability and accuracy of juvenile records. Since fingerprints are the biometric standard for identification of persons that are classified in criminal justice computerized systems, this basis makes good sense.

ADJUDICATION PROCESSES AND DIFFERENCE FROM ADULT COURTS

The juvenile court system consists of unique legal characteristics that are reflected in the very terms that are used. Where adults are arrested, tried, and sentenced to prison, juveniles are summoned, have a hearing, and are committed to residential placement (Neubauer, 2002). According to Neubauer, juvenile courts differ from adult courts in four important ways: These courts are informal in nature, their legal basis is in civil law, they tend to have closed proceedings, and they do not usually have jury trials. These differences provide for more fluid options, in terms of both processing and sentencing, reflecting the desire of the juvenile courts to reform the juvenile, when practical.

In helping the child, the juvenile courts emphasize informality which, as noted earlier in this chapter, contrasts with the formal and adversarial nature of the adult court. Although some elements of due process have been added to juvenile proceedings in recent years, they continue to rely on less formal proceedings. As a result, the rules of evidence and procedural laws have little relevance in many juvenile proceedings (Neubauer, 2002). As an extension from the premise that juvenile courts are designed to help the child, the early shapers of the juvenile court system viewed procedural safeguards as unnecessary, and, even more important, they viewed these safeguards as harmful to the outcome for most juveniles. The concern was that a legal technicality might keep a child from receiving the appropriate help or assistance that he or she might need: "In essence, the substance of the decision (helping the child) was more important than the procedures used to reach that decision" (Neubauer, 2002, p. 504).

Further highlighting the differences between adult and juvenile courts is the fact that while adult prosecutions are conducted in criminal courts, juvenile court proceedings are handled in civil court. This is the main reason for the differences in terminology that exist between the two types of proceedings. A primary premise behind the use of civil law is that the notions of rehabilitation would be emphasized instead of those associated with punishment. As Neubauer (2002) points out, it is for this reason that a child's juvenile court record is not admissible in adult court: "Regardless of the frequency or severity of the offenses committed by a juvenile, once he or she becomes an adult in the eyes of the criminal law, the person starts over with no prior record" (p. 504). This demonstrates how earnest the intent is within the juvenile court system to ensure that youth are not permanently stigmatized by the effects of their actions that are committed during an early phase of their life. This also is thought to aid in reducing the likelihood of recidivism, since these youth will be able to avoid the negative impact of a public recording of their crimes.

In what seems to be a recent trend, the U.S. Supreme Court and various state courts and legislatures have modified various procedural due process aspects of the juvenile court, resulting in a blend between both courts. The intent in these cases has been benevolent, providing safeguards to juveniles while still attempting to maintain the informal nature of much of the court process. Given the fact that juveniles are being tried in adult courts with more frequency, this latest development is perhaps expected. The hope is that juveniles can be afforded more safeguards in juvenile court while simultaneously ensuring that the pro-treatment aspect of juvenile courts is maintained.

This pro-treatment characteristic of juvenile courts is further reflected in the fact that juvenile court proceedings are typically closed from public view. Essentially, this means that crime victims and ordinary citizens wishing to view these proceedings are restricted from doing so. Thus, public audiences within the juvenile court are not a usual occurrence as they are within adult courts. Further, most jurisdictions prohibit law enforcement and juvenile court personnel from releasing the identity of juvenile offenders to the media (Neubauer, 2002). Moreover, even when media personnel are able to find out the identities of juvenile offenders, the ethics governing bodies within the journalism industry prohibit the revealing information from being printed, broadcast, or otherwise disseminated (Neubauer, 2002). There are of course both advocates and critics of the closed nature of these proceedings. Advocates tend to view it as being necessary for effective interventions, while critics contend that such secrecy prevents public scrutiny— something that most critics believe would work to deter juveniles from future crime while also providing victims with rights to information regarding the juvenile perpetrator that has victimized them.

Photo 12.1 The Center for Children and Families provides therapeutic services for youth and their families of origin. Family Foundations (see Focus Topic 12.1) is a subdivision of the center that provides aftercare services for youth who are released from state custody. Note the Family Justice Center sign further back in the photo. This center provides services for victims of domestic violence. The two agencies are adjacent to one another and represent the partnering emphasized in this text. The author of this text is on the steering committee for the Family Justice Center and is also involved in the preliminary stages of a research evaluation project with Family Foundations.

On another front, juvenile courts also differ in the manner by which the offender is tried. While offenders in adult court have the right to trial by a jury of their peers, juveniles have no such constitutional right. This is to ensure that juvenile proceedings remain informal in nature. The absence of jury trials also strengthens the control and flexibility that juvenile court personnel have when maintaining supervision of the offender. This greatly aids both judges and probation officers in juvenile courts who are entrusted to act in the best interests of the child.

THE ROLE OF CHILD PROTECTION

In many cases, juvenile youth are victims of various forms of neglect or abuse. This is a very important aspect of juvenile offending, particularly in community corrections. Thus, community supervision officers will find themselves networking with child protection agencies, and they will likewise tend to have offenders on their caseloads who are in need of parenting assistance, whether the offender realizes it or not. Further, one must consider that over 70 percent of female offenders on community supervision are also the primary caretakers of their children. This is an important observation, especially when one considers that the proportion of female offenders on community supervision is much higher than those that are incarcerated. This means that community supervision officers are likely to come across issues related to the welfare of children on a fairly frequent basis. Further still, among a high number of delinquent youth, disproportionate rates of abuse and neglect occur. This further demonstrates that community supervision officers that supervise juvenile offenders are likely to contend with neglect and abuse issues with young offenders on their caseload. Child neglect and abuse can thus be relevant to community supervision officers who supervise either adult or juvenile offenders.

In discussing these issues, we first turn our focus to child neglect because such maltreatment is often a precursor to later forms of abuse, and neglect also often occurs in conjunction with abusive treatment. **Child neglect** occurs when a parent or caretaker of the child does not provide the proper or necessary support, education, or medical or other remedial care that is required by a given state's law, including food, shelter, and clothing. Child neglect also occurs when adult caretakers abandon a child that they are legally obligated to support (Cox et al., 2008). Neglect is typically divided into three types: physical, emotional, and educational. **Physical neglect** includes abandonment, the expulsion of the child from the home (being kicked out of the house); a failure to seek or excessive delay in seeking medical care for the child; inadequate supervision; and inadequate food, clothing, and shelter. **Emotional neglect** includes inadequate nurturing or affection, allowing the child to engage in inappropriate or illegal behavior such as drug or alcohol use, as well as ignoring a child's basic emotional needs. Last, **educational neglect** occurs when a parent or even a teacher permits chronic truancy or simply ignores the educational or special needs of a child (Cox et al., 2008).

The impact of neglect is not as readily observable as that of abuse. Over time, however, the long-term effects to the child can be just as damaging as they are when a child is overtly abused. Among the offender population, child neglect is not at all uncommon. In cases where either the male or female parent is a serious drug abuser, it may be common for the child to be neglected. In fact, there are some circumstances where the oldest child may be *parentified* and delegated the responsibility of caring for younger siblings while also taking care of the parent. **Child parentification** occurs when the child is placed in a position within a family system where he or she must assume the primary caretaker role for the family, often taking care of both children and adults within that family system. This is common in single-head-of-household families where the adult caretaker is an alcoholic or drug abuser, and even in some dual-adult household families, particularly those that are criminogenic in nature.

Interestingly, children that are neglected, including those that are parentified, often do not realize that they are being mistreated. Even if they do, many have no recourse, and when coupled with the emotional bonds that they may have with their siblings, they are unlikely to leave or report such maltreatment on their own. These inappropriate family circumstances lead to very poor socialization in many cases, with children observing negative behaviors and developing criminogenic mind-sets. Thus, these toxic family systems help to breed a new generation of persons that are susceptible to further perpetuation of the criminal lifestyle. It is because of this that community supervision officers overseeing juvenile offenders must take into account the family situation, encouraging family involvement when the family is functional and recommending interventions when the family is not functional.

Beyond child neglect, acts of abuse are even more serious forms of maltreatment and include both physical and psychological forms of harm. **Child abuse** occurs when a child (being a youth under the age of 18 in most states) is maltreated by a parent, an immediate family member, or any person responsible for the child's welfare. Child maltreatment can include physical, sexual, and emotional abuse as well as physical, emotional, and even educational neglect from the caretaker (Cox et al., 2008). There are varying degrees of abuse, and, in many cases, multiple forms of abuse may have been inflicted against the child. Further, these youth may also come from homes where there is domestic abuse between spouses or significant others. Research has shown that the existence of child abuse is a common characteristic among juvenile sex offenders in the United States as well as in other countries (Hanser & Mire, 2008). The presence of abuse in a youth's background is an important observation to attend to, since aberrant behaviors are likely to have been learned from other dysfunctional family members. In some cases, the youth's behavior may be a form of acting out against the stress and frustration of the toxic family environment.

According to Cox et al. (2008), **physical abuse** "can be defined as any physical acts that cause or can cause physical injury to a child" (p. 266). These authors go on to describe child abuse as a vicious cycle that involves parents who have unrealistic expectations of their children, and thus get easily frustrated with the shortcomings they perceive their children to have. It is not uncommon for such parents to have themselves been abused as children, resulting in an intergenerational transmission of violence through their abusive behavior. The extent of the harsh discipline tends to depend on the level of frustration that the parent feels, the ability to regulate his or her own emotions, and the parent's views on appropriate parenting and discipline practices. The level of parenting skills and the age of the child often affect the type of abuse and frequency of abuse that is inflicted, since younger children are less able to defend themselves or run away.

Further, this type of treatment can greatly exacerbate any potential diagnoses that the young person might have (such as those just discussed in prior subsections), and this further complicates any treatment approaches for that child. In fact, the adult family members themselves may have a number of mental health issues, and this adds further difficulty to the family situation. Within such family environments, it is unlikely that the youth will be able to ever achieve any sense of normalcy or positive support. The parent's own challenges will tend to aggravate those problems facing the youth, and the youth's behavior will in turn serve as a further aggravating factor for the parent's own maladaptive parenting. The two will therefore continually fuel the dysfunction within the family system, thereby ensuring that the maladaptive system continues. In such cases, it is usually not a good idea for the juvenile to remain within the family system, and it should be considered that the youth's behavior is perhaps a symptom of an unhealthy family grouping.

Psychological abuse is the third most frequently reported form of child abuse, with physical abuse and child neglect being the first and second most common types. Psychological abuse is somewhat vague and hard to define. Definitions that are too narrow are not likely to capture the various aspects of psychological abuse that might exist within an adult–child relationship that is abusive. On the other hand, definitions that are too broad may be nearly impossible to clearly identify in quantitative terms for research or in a legally substantive manner that could aid law enforcement and prosecutors. For these reasons, this is the most difficult form of abuse to prosecute, being somewhat elusive when put to rigorous examination. Further, much of this abuse likely goes unreported because it is so difficult to detect, prove, and document.

Psychological abuse is also sometimes referred to as emotional abuse and includes actions or the omission of actions by parents and other caregivers that could cause the child to have serious behavioral, emotional, or mental impairments. In some instances of psychological abuse, there is no clear or evident behavior of the adult caregiver that provides indication of the abuse. Rather, the child displays behavior that is impaired or has emotional disturbances that result from profound forms of emotional abuse, trauma, distance, or neglect. This is an issue that should be seriously considered when children present with diagnosable disorders, particularly those that are obsessive/compulsive, dissociative, anxiety-based, or oppositional/defiant in nature.

When considering children with disorders such as those just previously indicated, it should not necessarily be taken to mean that the caregiver is the cause of the disorder, though that likelihood can certainly exist as well. Rather, it may well be that the child presents with these disorders and, due to frustration, the parent resorts to punishments that are bizarre or unorthodox. For example, parents of a strongly oppositional child may resort to locking him or her in a dark closet as a means of containing the child and also depriving the child of stimuli that may heighten his or her emotionality. While this may have a basis of logic to it, this type of punishment is not appropriate, and yet it may occur for long periods of time. In the process, the child's short-term behavior may be adjusted, but his or her sense of long-term maladjustment is further aggravated; in short, the parents contribute to the emotional disturbances that the child exhibits. On the other hand, a parent that is psychologically abusive may also actually be a causal factor in a child developing any of a variety of emotional or adjustment disorders. Children who are psychologically abused may present as depressed, anxious, dissociative, and so forth. In such cases, the abusive treatment from the caregiver negatively impacts that child's ability to thrive, resulting in an emotionally impaired child.

When neglect or abuse is detected within the home of a juvenile on a community supervision officer's caseload, or when an adult offender is thought to be neglecting or abusing his or her children, the officer is under a legal obligation to report these actions to child protective services within that state. In reality, most citizens are required to report this activity anytime that they observe it occurring, but community supervision officers are especially liable and required to make such reports when they encounter child maltreatment. In essence, the community supervision officer is required to intervene. Intervention officially begins when the officer reports the neglect or abuse and the child protection agency proceeds to the investigatory stage. This stage usually involves a home visit and interviews with all parties involved in the behavior or who know about the circumstances. Child protection officials typically then generate a risk assessment and make a decision regarding the best type of action to take that reflects the best interests of the child.

If it is determined that abuse has indeed occurred, the police and the investigator for the child protection agency will take the case to the local prosecutor so that it can be charged. Even with the official determination of neglect or abuse, these proceedings can be difficult and challenging. First, the juvenile may be quite ashamed, unable or even afraid to leak information regarding his or her abuse. Cox et al. (2008) note that "in many cases, even though they are being regularly and severely abused, children will not tell others because of the fear (sometimes instilled by their abusers) that their parents will be taken away from them if they do seek help" (p. 274). This is a very important observation—since these children often know no other way to live, their current abusive situation is seen as a "normalized" part of their life. Among some cases that do go to court, the child may be unable to effectively testify due to fear, trauma, and anxiety that impedes his or her ability to provide information effectively to the court. Moreover even in those cases where the child is able to provide effective testimony, judges or family protection agencies may still be hesitant to remove the youth from a home due to objections from the family members, often including objections from the very juvenile that has been abused.

When youth are enmeshed in such toxic systems and when their socialization is such that they are not even personally aware that they should, in fact, seek refuge from their abusive family system, it is important that states exercise the right that was mentioned earlier in this chapter, the right of *parens patriae*. The state should protect the welfare of the juvenile, both as a moral obligation and as a public safety obligation. In this way, the state protects the welfare of the child while aiding in future crime prevention within the community, since a reduction in maltreatment of these youth will translate to a reduction in future delinquency. In such cases, intervention simply makes good sense.

When maintenance of the family is not a viable option and it is not in the juvenile's best interest to remain with the family, the juvenile probation officer may place the juvenile in a foster home. Typically, foster homes are used for children who have been victims of abuse or neglect. For those youth that are persistently delinquent, the use of residential treatment facilities is generally more appropriate (Cox et al., 2008). Foster homes are intended to provide the appropriate supervision and care that, in the case of juvenile offenders, is likely to have been missing from their own family life. The care and attention provided by foster homes naturally go beyond that which the probation officer can provide, and therefore these homes are critical resources for youth that truly have nowhere else to turn.

Though juvenile courts are careful when selecting foster home placements, it is inevitable that some juveniles will simply be too difficult to control. This places a hardship on the foster parents that attend to such youth, and this also can negatively impact other youth staying at the foster home. In some cases, difficult juveniles may victimize the other children staying at the home, and this then creates a risk that makes further placement unlikely, resulting in the youth's placement in residential treatment. It is clear that the complexities involved with raising these needy youth can be quite challenging and stressful for foster parents, so careful screening is typically conducted of those persons that apply. As Cox et al. (2008) note, "assuming responsibility for a delinquent, abused, or neglected juvenile placed in one's home requires a great deal of commitment, and many juveniles who might benefit from this type of setting cannot be placed due to the lack of available families" (pp. 246–247).

FAMILY SERVICES AND FAMILY INTERVENTIONS

In many communities, a number of programs exist that provide family services; community supervision officers that have juvenile offenders on their caseloads will likely become familiar with these agencies over time. Such services can be important in reducing delinquency and in providing the juvenile probationer with some degree of grounding since these agencies tend to have a variety of healthy and prosocial programs for youth. This range of services can include recreational activities, after-school programs, access to therapeutic services for families, services for domestic violence victims (adult and juvenile), Planned Parenthood or teenage pregnancy services, and a number of other important functions and activities. Focus Topic 12.1 provides an excellent example of an agency that offers multiple family services for youth at risk of delinquency and their families.

FAMILY FOUNDATIONS—A MODEL AGENCY FOR ADOLESCENT SERVICES

Family Foundations in Monroe, Louisiana, is a pragmatic and goal-oriented treatment program that specifically targets those factors that contribute to an adolescent's problematic behavior. This agency's interventions primarily seek to improve caregiver discipline practices; decrease the youth's association with deviant peers; increase the youth's association with prosocial peers; engage youth in prosocial recreational activities; enhance school or vocational performance; and develop a support network of extended family, neighbors, and community to aid parents and caregivers in implementing desired changes.

Family Foundations uses a variety of family therapy approaches and delivers services in the family's natural environment(s), such as the home, school, and areas of the community. Treatment plans are designed in collaboration with family members and are, therefore, family-driven rather than being directed primarily by the counselor. This is an important component of the program's intervention style, as it empowers the family to address issues and work together at problem solving. The typical duration of home-based services is approximately 10 weeks, with multiple staff-to-family contacts occurring throughout each week. The services at Family Foundations are more intensive than traditional forms of family counseling, requiring multiple hours of treatment per week rather than the typical 50-minute sessions once per week that are used in many other programs.

Family Foundations provides a complete initial family assessment that is used as a baseline for the treatment team. During this process, treatment staff integrate information obtained from family members, teachers, referral sources, and others to determine the factors that are contributing to the youth's problems. Further, this agency provides case management for the entire family for a full year, with family advocates/case managers identifying specific services that are needed to strengthen the family. Other services include the use of paraprofessionals to aid in family skill building.

Skill-building aids may consist of parenting classes, activities to strengthen the parent–child bond, reduction of social isolation, and trust-building approaches. Additional services include high-quality counseling with master's level therapists. Teens are seen weekly for individual counseling sessions in their school environment, integrating treatment planning processes with educational planning. Parents are seen separately by a family counselor to allow them the opportunity to address marital conflicts and improve the health of both the marriage and the family as a whole.

Last and most interesting, this program provides a 3-hour, in-home family counseling session, once per week, with all family members and the counselor being present. This is perhaps one of the most unique, comprehensive, and effective aspects of the treatment program, making this program much more intensive than others throughout the nation. Family Foundations chose this particular approach based on published research that demonstrates that higher proportions of time spent by therapists with client families in the home equated to higher rates of treatment success. Further, their approach is based on findings that comprehensive services delivered in the home tend to have improved treatment outcomes.

Family Foundations has made a point to design its program based on research findings throughout the literature. In addition, this agency has adopted an evidence-based orientation, subjecting its own services to careful assessment and evaluation. In this way, the agency seeks to continually improve its services to the community, refining reintegration efforts of juveniles while improving the family circumstances that these youth encounter. Family Foundations thus provides measurable contributions to the overall welfare of the Northeast Louisiana region, with these important contributions occurring one family at a time.

SOURCE: Family Foundations. (2007). *Family Foundations program descriptions.* Rayville, LA: Author.

RISK FACTORS AND PROTECTIVE FACTORS FOR JUVENILES

When implementing any program for treating juvenile offenders or preventing juveniles from offending, the risk factors that lead to juvenile delinquency must be understood. Risk factors may be found in the individual, the environment, or the individual's ability to respond to the demands or requirements of the environment.

Research has indicated a number of factors that have a high likelihood of leading to delinquent behavior (McCall, 1994; Moffitt, 1993). Further, all of these factors, when added together, can have a cumulative effect on the likelihood of future delinquency. For instance, while poor parenting is a risk factor, this becomes more pronounced when it is coupled with a child's poor academic performance. Moreover, the environment can serve to compound this, such as when a child attends a school where rules of conduct are lax and teachers are dissatisfied; in these cases, the chances of the child engaging in delinquency increase (McCall, 1994).

Risk factors are many and occur along a continuum within the child's development. Table 12.1 shows some risk factors that could be used to predict the onset of juvenile offending. It should be pointed out that these risk factors simply serve to increase the likelihood of future delinquency; they do not *cause* delinquency. As Table 12.1 demonstrates, these risk factors fall within one of five primary domains:

Photo 12.2 The Caddo Parish Juvenile Complex consists of a number of courtrooms and offices that provide services for adjudicated youth. This complex works in tandem with many other local agencies and facilities for juvenile reform.

individual, family, school, peer group, and community. If youth are found to possess certain risk factors within these domains, it can help to determine the likelihood of future juvenile offending.

Protective factors, on the other hand, serve to counter the effects of risk factors that may exist for the individual within the family, school, peer group, or community. In essence, protective factors are variables that are the opposite of risk factors. For instance, a community risk factor might be the existence of crime and drugs within a neighborhood. In contrast, a protective factor would be a program implemented to teach youth to avoid crime and drugs, providing alternate activities for youth to engage in. While both the risk factor and the protective factor may exist within that same community, each works against the other in the young person's environment.

Amidst these community-level risk and protective factors, the individual domain and the family domain might also either mitigate or aggravate the likelihood of juvenile offending. Using Table 12.1, we can consider "Janice" as an example, where Janice is a young person who is female and has a high I.Q. (both of which are protective factors in the individual domain) but also has a negative social orientation (a risk factor in the individual domain). Further adding to the equation is the fact that Janice's family uses harsh forms of punishment (a risk factor in the family domain) but also provide a good degree of parental monitoring (a protective factor in the family domain). Last, when examining Janice's school and peer group domains, it is discovered that she engages in conventional school activities (a protective factor in the school domain) while her friends also tend to engage in conventional behaviors (a protective factor in the peer group domain). As with this example, students should understand that there are many factors at play that impact the potential for delinquent behavior in youth; essentially, risk factors push youth into delinquent activity, whereas protective factors pull them away from the same activity. The exact combination of each tends to determine both the *amount* of juvenile offending and the *severity* of that offending that is likely to occur.

In regard to protective factors, there is some disagreement among experts that attempt to specifically define and identify them. This is because protective factors have been viewed both as the absence of risk and as something conceptually distinct from risk (Wasserman & Miller, 1998). The former view typically places risk and protective factors on the opposite ends of a continuum. For example, good parent–child relations might be considered a protective factor because it is the opposite of poor parent–child relations, a known risk factor. This is similar to how risk and protective factors were presented using our example of Janice. However, a simple linear relationship of this sort (where the risk of juvenile delinquency decreases as parent–child relations improve) blurs the distinction between risk and protection, making them essentially the same thing.

From all of the factors that span the gamut of individual, family, school, peer group, and community domains in Table 12.1, it becomes clear that there are more protective factors than there are risk factors that affect Janice. Thus, Janice would be less likely to engage in juvenile offending. While this is an oversimplification of how offending may take place (as Table 12.1 is not all-inclusive), this should provide the student with a clear understanding of how there are various factors that work with and against one another across a variety of domains. Throughout this interplay between risk factors and protective factors, a final analysis is derived in which the likelihood of future juvenile delinquency can be estimated.

On the other hand, the view that protection is conceptually distinct from risk defines protective factors as characteristics or conditions that interact with risk factors to reduce their influence on juvenile offending (Stattin & Magnusson, 1996). For example, low family socioeconomic status is a risk factor for juvenile offending, and a warm, supportive relationship with a parent may be a protective factor. The warm relationship does not improve the child's economic status, but it does buffer the child from some of the adverse effects of poverty. Protective factors may or may not have a direct effect on juvenile offending, but they can moderate or buffer the effects of risk that are likely to increase the likelihood of juvenile offending (Davis, 1999). Thus, protective factors offer an explanation for why children and adolescents who face the same degree of risk may be affected differently.

The concept of protective factors is familiar in the field of public health. However, identifying and measuring the effects of protective factors is relatively new in juvenile research, and information about these factors is limited. Because they buffer the effect of risk factors, protective factors are an important tool in the prevention of juvenile offending. Like risk factors, proposed protective factors are grouped into individual, family, school, peer group, and community categories. Just as risk factors do not necessarily cause an individual child or young person to become violent, protective factors do not guarantee that an individual child or young person will not become violent. They reduce the *probability* that young people facing a risk factor or factors will engage in juvenile delinquency.

| TABLE 12.1 | Risk Factors for Juvenile Offending |

Domain	Risk Factors	Protective Factors
Individual	1. Antisocial attitudes 2. Low I.Q. 3. Being male 4. Negative social orientation 5. Willingness for risk taking 6. Substance abuse	1. Intolerant attitude to criminality 2. High I.Q. 3. Female gender 4. Positive social orientation 5. Sanctions/punishment taken seriously
Family	1. Harsh or lax discipline 2. Poor adult supervision 3. Low parental involvement 4. Low socioeconomic status 5. Abusive home	1. Warm relationship with adult caretaker 2. Peer group accepted by parents 3. Parental monitoring
School	1. Poor attitude or performance 2. Academic failure	1. Commitment to school 2. Engages in conventional school activities
Peer Group	1. Antisocial peer group 2. Weak social ties	1. Friends engage in conventional behavior
Community	1. Neighborhood crime and drugs	1. Crime and drug-free neighborhood

SOURCE: U.S. Public Health Services. (2002). *Youth violence: A report of the Surgeon General.* Available online at http://www.mentalhealth.org/youthviolence/surgeongeneral/SG_Site/chapter4/sec1.asp.

The use of family, school, and community factors actually entails elements of **social bond theory**, developed by Travis Hirschi, which consists of two basic propositions. First, juvenile offending and social bonds are inversely related, meaning that youth are less likely to offend as social bonds are strengthened. Second, social bonds have four elements: attachment, commitment, involvement, and belief (Cullen & Agnew, 2006). These elements may work independently or together as protective factors that help to restrain juvenile offending. **Attachment** is a form of psychological influence over the youth's behavior such that when temptation to offend appears, the youth will consider the wishes of his or parents and prior socialization. Attachment involves an emotional connection to another person in which the youth is concerned with how that person will view him or her. **Conformity** is the concept of youth being committed to social prospects and therefore complying with expectations. Thus, a youth with good school or job prospects in the future is not as likely to commit acts of deviance as those that do not have similarly bright prospects. **Involvement**, on the other hand, entails the notion that if youth are involved in conventional (prosocial) activities, they will be less able and less likely to engage in delinquent behavior. The last element is **belief**, which refers to beliefs that counter delinquent behavior. In essence, delinquent behavior results not from the possession of pro-delinquent beliefs as much as from a lack of beliefs regarding the inappropriateness of delinquency.

All of the previously mentioned elements of social bond theory—attachment, conformity, involvement, and belief—are essentially factors that protect against delinquent behavior. Attachment is equivalent to the family-based protective factor of having a warm relationship with adult caretakers, as listed in Table 12.1. Conformity might be equated to the individual factor where sanctions/punishments are taken seriously. Involvement would be related to the school-based risk factor where the youth is involved in conventional, school-based activities, with the peer group protective factor entailing the group's tendency to engage in conventional activities as well. Finally, belief might be equated to the individual risk factor where the youth is intolerant of criminal activity. From these examples, it is clear that the elements of Hirchi's social bond theory are very similar to the protective factors and risk factors that have been presented in this chapter. Thus, the social bond is particularly relevant to this chapter as we explore the various factors that may lead to juvenile offending.

Finally, it is important to note that this interplay among the individual, family, school, peer group, and community domains offers important possibilities for community supervision agencies. When considering the previous examples and discussion, it becomes clear that juvenile community supervision agencies are well served to maximize their partnerships with local schools, family social services, and community programs that provide youth with healthy and prosocial activities. One primary theme throughout this text has been the need for community supervision agencies to maximize the use of partner agencies and community volunteers when providing comprehensive supervision and treatment services. The current examination of risk and protective factors further supports this concept when providing services to juveniles at risk of offending and to those that have committed some offense. Thus, programs that include family interventions or support activities are actually responding to the various and complex interplays between risk factors and protective factors within the family domain. At the same time, after-school programs respond to this interplay within the school domain, while community recreational services may do so at the community level. Taken together, these various programs can enhance the ability of community supervision agencies to better supervise juvenile offenders and to provide better alternative options for these youth, all with the intent of countering the likelihood of future juvenile offending.

JUVENILE INTENSIVE PROBATION SUPERVISION

As was noted previously, probation is generally the most common sanction given to juvenile offenders. While this may be true, there are those juvenile offenders on probation that do not necessarily require institutionalization but are still in need of stricter forms of supervision. It is with this in mind that juvenile intensive supervision is often utilized for certain juvenile offenders. Intensive supervised probation has become more widely used as a result of a desire to keep juveniles out of institutions and a broader acceptance of community corrections programs and processes. **Juvenile intensive probation supervision (JIPS)** is a regimented program that requires much greater supervision contact than regular probation and also serves as an alternative to incarceration while maintaining acceptable levels of public safety. Currently, JIPS is used in roughly half of all programs around the nation. Though JIPS is a tool for any juvenile probationer that requires strict forms of supervision, it is typically only used with those youth who have residential placement as their only other alternative.

The main distinction between JIPS and standard probation is the number of supervision contacts throughout the week that the juvenile is required to make and the location and circumstance associated with those contacts. For instance, contacts may occur at home with the family, at school and with teachers, or even in other social settings that the youth might frequent. In addition, most community supervision officers who have JIPS caseloads usually network with other agencies and services as a means of providing the child with needed assistance while further increasing the number of human contacts that occur. This of course harkens back to discussions in past chapters where adult probation programs employ similar techniques to ensure that offenders are well supervised. However, JIPS will have services that in many cases are more readily available or are more specific to juvenile issues. For example, groups such as Big Brothers/Big Sisters may be involved, foster grandparent programs may be utilized, and alternative education programs may be part of the services delivered. These types of services would not likely exist in most adult supervision programs.

Juvenile intensive probation supervision typically requires nearly daily supervision by a juvenile probation officer. At a minimum, six face-to-face contacts per month should occur between the probation officer and the juvenile offender. In addition, it is recommended that juvenile probation officers make at least three face-to-face contacts with the youth's parents, and at least two contacts with school officials. With such intensive contact and with other requirements added to the probation sentence, the juvenile probation officer is clearly quite busy maintaining his or her caseload and tracking the various corollary activities that may be mandated by the court. Likewise, the juvenile offender is also kept busy, with additional requirements for community service, drug and alcohol counseling, anger management classes, educational services, restitution activities, and psychoeducational programs placing high demands on these probationers. Research indicates that this type of supervision is best used with serious, hardcore offenders rather than younger offenders that have committed only petty crimes. The regimen is simply not necessary among less serious offenders.

In some cases, such as in the state of Arizona, juvenile offenders on JIPS are supervised by teams of probation personnel. Typically, one probation officer will be utilized, and other staff, called surveillance officers, will also be included. These are often either two-person or three-person teams. For two-person teams, the state of Arizona sets the caseload at no more than 25 juvenile offenders, while three-person teams may supervise no more than 40 juveniles at a time. According to the Arizona State Supreme Court website (2008), JIPS probation officer teams are tasked with the following duties:

1. Keep complete identification records for each youth supervised.
2. Meet with each probationer at least four times a week, and make weekly contact with the juvenile's parents or guardian, school, employer, and treatment program.
3. Closely monitor each juvenile's conduct, including evening and weekend activities.
4. Monitor the juvenile's payment of restitution.

Generally speaking, JIPS has been found to be fairly effective. For instance, a study by Wiebush (1993) was conducted that examined the 18-month recidivism of juvenile felony offenders who were placed into an intensive supervision program as an alternative to institutionalization. This study compared the outcomes of JIPS participants with other juveniles who were institutionalized and then released to parole, as well as a third group that was given standard probation. The results of this study were promising, as it was found that recidivism rates for youth were lower in the JIPS program than for those who were institutionalized, and this type of supervision provided better controls than did standard probation. However, it was found that JIPS was not necessarily cost-effective unless large-scale diversion programs were implemented. Apparently, the reduction in recidivism was not so great as to offset the added expense except in cases where substantial numbers of juveniles were diverted (Wiebush, 1993).

FOCUS TOPIC 12.2

CALIFORNIA'S 8% SOLUTION

The prevalence of serious juvenile delinquency could be reduced significantly by identifying and treating the small percentage of juveniles who are at risk of becoming chronic offenders when they first come into contact with the juvenile justice system. [One state-level program that has used this knowledge to maximize program effectiveness is] the California 8% Solution study and the 8% Early Intervention Program, which assesses the needs of and provides treatment services to these youth.

The 8% Solution: Preventing Serious, Repeat Juvenile Crime describes efforts begun by the Orange County (CA) Probation Department in the latter part of the 1980s to "make a dent in the long-term crime problem" by focusing its resources in the most effective way. The Probation Department's research staff tracked two groups of first-time offenders for 3 years and found that a small percentage (8 percent) of the juveniles were arrested repeatedly (a minimum of four times within a 3-year period) and were responsible for 55 percent of repeat cases.

The characteristics of this group of repeat offenders (referred to as "the 8% problem") were dramatically different from those who were arrested only once. These differences did not develop after exposure to the juvenile justice system, as some might expect; they were evident at first arrest and referral to juvenile court, and they worsened if nothing was done to alleviate the youth's problems. Unfortunately, in wanting to "give a break" to first-time offenders, the juvenile justice system often pays scant attention to those at greatest risk of becoming chronic offenders until they have established a record of repeated serious offending.

The good news is that most of the small group of potentially serious, chronic offenders can be identified reliably at first contact with the juvenile justice system. The "8%" offenders enter the system with a complex set of problems or risk factors, which the study identified as (1) involvement in crime at an early age and (2) a multi-problem profile including significant family problems (abuse, neglect, criminal family members, and/or a lack of parental supervision and control), problems at school (truancy, failing more than one course, or a recent suspension or expulsion), drug and alcohol abuse, and behaviors such as gang involvement, running away, and stealing.

Armed with the study's results, Orange County created its 8% Early Intervention Program to serve first-time offenders who were no older than 15 and who exhibited at least three of the four risk factors in the multi-problem profile. The program focuses on high-risk youth and their entire families. Its goals are to increase structure, supervision, and support for families; make potential "8-percenters" accountable; ensure that youth and families understand the importance of school; and promote prosocial values, behavior, and relationships. The program also works to develop intervention strategies and services for youth in the community and to instill a strong commitment to teamwork by all partners, including representatives from other youth-serving agencies.

The program's pilot phase began in July 1994 with youth from Anaheim and Buena Park in northern Orange County but offered only limited assistance from outside agencies. Since June 1998, full services for youth and their families, augmented by State funds through California's legislatively established Repeat Offender Prevention Program (ROPP), have been provided through a collaborative team of public and private agencies. These services were provided first at the North Orange County Youth and Family Resource Center in Anaheim. By early 1999, four additional Youth and Family Resource Centers had opened in Orange County: a second site adjacent to the first one in Anaheim but tailored for older youth under the State-funded 8% Challenge Program; a central site in Santa Ana; a western site in Westminster; and a southern site in Aliso Viejo.

SOURCE: Office of Juvenile Justice and Delinquency Prevention. (2001). *The 8% solution.* Washington, DC: Author. Quoted verbatim from http://www.ncjrs.gov/pdffiles1/ojjdp/fs200139.pdf.

RESIDENTIAL TREATMENT PROGRAMS

Residential treatment programs are facilities that offer a combination of substance abuse and mental health treatment services while youth are kept under 24-hour supervision in a highly structured and secure environment. These programs typically are designed for youth with significant psychiatric or substance abuse problems and who are not otherwise appropriate for foster care services, day treatment programs, or other less secure programs. Although these treatment centers must be licensed by their respective states, they are frequently owned and operated by private companies, with treatment approaches and admissions criteria varying widely among institutions throughout the nation.

The specific modalities of treatment may vary, but they all tend to include various forms of therapy, psychoeducational counseling, behavioral management, group counseling, and other such services. Settings come in a variety of types, including hospital-like environments, group homes, and even halfway houses (see Chapter 10). Though there are many different approaches, research regarding the effectiveness of these facilities is quite mixed; yet these facilities continue to be an important component of the juvenile correctional process. It is for this reason that they are presented in this chapter.

Wilderness camps (sometimes called challenge programs) are residential programs where juveniles engage in a series of physically challenging outdoor activities, such as backpacking, canoeing, or even rock climbing. These programs vary considerably in their settings, types of activities, and therapeutic goals, but their treatment perspectives are usually based on an experiential learning approach that is designed to stimulate personal growth and build a sense of self-efficacy (Office of Juvenile Justice and Delinquency Prevention [OJJDP], 2007). Such programs raised a number of concerns during the 1980s and early 1990s due to the risks that youth encountered and a number of incidents around the country where youth either were injured or died accidentally. Since that time, programs have been designed to be less physically intensive and extreme while still allowing youth to engage in activities intended to build personal confidence.

One researcher conducted a meta-analysis of 29 different studies that examined wilderness programs (Lipsey, 2000). This study involved over 3,000 juvenile offenders and found that youth in these programs have recidivism rates that are about 8 percent lower than juveniles in other programs. However, this study was not able to adequately account for the various differences in programming among the programs in the various studies, leaving much open to speculation. However, Lipsey did find that programs that included intense physical activity as well as therapeutic interventions such as individual counseling, family therapy, and group counseling were more effective than those that involved little or no therapeutic content.

Perhaps one of the most widely known wilderness programs in the United States is VisionQuest. This program provides alternatives to incarceration for serious juvenile offenders. Youth in this program spend from 12 to 15 months engaged in a variety of challenging outdoor activities coupled with various therapeutic treatment programs. A normal treatment course often includes a 3-month stay at a wilderness orientation program where participants typically camp outdoors; a 5-month adventure program during which time juveniles participate in activities such as wagon train journeys, cross-country biking, or ocean voyages; and a 5-month stay in a community residential/therapeutic program (OJJDP, 2007). Interestingly, this program also includes an aftercare program called HomeQuest that offers support to youth and families upon reentry. This follow-up care helps to make the entire process one that is transitional in nature, providing support for the juvenile that is transitioned back into the community. Controlled studies of VisionQuest have consistently demonstrated its effectiveness in lowering juvenile recidivism rates (OJJDP, 2007).

Juvenile **boot camps** are residential facilities that are run in a military fashion with drill instructors and other staff using a strict regimen and intensive interventions over a relatively short period of time, usually between 90 and 120 days. These programs were widely touted as innovative treatment programs during the 1990s but since that time have consistently failed to demonstrate any positive impact on juvenile offenders' recidivism rates (Clear & Cole, 2003). Further, these programs tend to be much more expensive to operate than simply incarcerating youth in secure facilities. Thus, these programs, though intuitively seeming to make good sense, are actually failures at treatment and in terms of fiscal considerations.

Group Homes

Group homes are residential placement facilities for juveniles that operate in a homelike setting with unrelated children living together for varied periods of time, depending on their individual circumstances. Group homes usually serve 5 to 15 youth, who are placed there as result of a court order or through interactions with public welfare agencies (OJJDP, 2007). These homes may utilize a single set of "house parents" or they may have rotating staff. The primary treatment approach used in group homes today is the *teaching family model*. This model relies heavily on structural behavior interventions and highly trained staff who act as parents and live in the group homes 24 hours a day (OJJDP, 2007). Other group homes rely more on individual psychotherapy and group interaction (U.S. Public Health Services, 2002).

Studies suggest that adolescents placed in group homes experience positive treatment effects while they are in these

Photo 12.3 This juvenile detention center is new and modern in appearance. Many such buildings may not even seem like detention facilities. Indeed, if the sign at the entry did not note the purpose of this building, it might be difficult to know the true purpose of its existence. To some extent, this may be reflective of the fact that the juvenile system seeks to avoid the labeling of delinquent youth in the community.

homes, but little evidence exists to suggest that treatment outcomes are sustained over time (OJJDP, 2007). When compared with foster homes, research has demonstrated that foster homes offer several advantages over group homes. For example, foster homes require lower costs, have less recidivism, and result in more frequent reunifications between the juvenile and his or her family (OJJDP, 2007). One reason for the difference in outcomes between these two programs is that group homes are frequently used as the last stop before juveniles are placed in secure detention. Thus, youth referred to these facilities often suffer from more serious mental or behavioral problems than those who are referred to foster homes (OJJDP, 2007).

Nonresidential Programs

Home confinement, or house arrest, is an intermediate community corrections sanction where offenders are restricted to their residence except during specifically designated times when they are authorized to attend vocational, educational, treatment-based, or social functions. This sanction allows offenders to remain in their homes, go to work, run errands, attend school, and maintain other responsibilities (OJJDP, 2007). However, their activities are closely monitored (either electronically or by frequent staff contacts) to ensure that they are complying with the conditions set by the court. Offenders placed under home confinement are restricted to their residence for varying lengths of time and are required to maintain a strict schedule of daily activities (OJJDP, 2007).

Day treatment facilities are highly structured, community-based, nonresidential programs for serious juvenile offenders. The goal of day treatment is to provide intensive supervision to ensure community safety while exposing the juvenile offender to a wide range of services that he or she might not otherwise access. The intensive supervision is fulfilled by requiring the offender to report to the facility on a daily basis at specific times for a specified length of time. In most cases, these programs are open throughout the week during both the day and evening, with special weekend activities often included to ensure that youth are

Photo 12.4 The Ouachita Parish Juvenile Court is a smaller facility than the Caddo Parish Juvenile Complex in Photo 12.2. Nevertheless, this facility provides court, detention, and aftercare services to youth who are processed through the juvenile justice system.

kept busy while completing their sentence (OJJDP, 2007). Treatment services in day treatment facilities tend to be fairly comprehensive and may include individual and group counseling, recreation, education, vocational training, employment counseling, education, life skills and cognitive skills training, and substance abuse treatment, as well as community resource referrals (OJJDP, 2007).

Aftercare can be defined as reintegrative services that prepare juveniles released from an institution for reentry into the community by establishing collaboration among agencies, the community, and available resources to maximize reintegrative processes (Altschuler & Armstrong, 2001). Aftercare requires the creation of a seamless set of systems across formal and informal social control networks as well as the creation of a continuum of community services to prevent the reoccurrence of antisocial behavior. It can also involve public–private partnerships to expand the overall capacity of youth services. Effective aftercare is very important due to the stigmatizing effect that institutionalization can have upon youth. As was noted previously with the VisionQuest program, the use of effective aftercare can greatly reduce any recidivism rates that an agency encounters within its jurisdiction.

TREATMENT PROGRAMS AND TYPES OF THERAPY

Wrap-around services form a complex, multifaceted intervention strategy designed to keep delinquent youth at home and out of institutions whenever possible. As the name suggests, this strategy involves "wrapping" a comprehensive array of individualized services and support networks "around" young people, rather than forcing them to enroll in predetermined, inflexible treatment programs (OJJDP, 2007). Although one of the central features of the wrap-around approach is individual case management, wrap-around interventions should not be confused with traditional case management programs. Conventional case management programs merely provide youth with an individual case manager (or probation officer) who guides them through the existing social services or juvenile justice system (OJJDP, 2007). Numerous public agencies and research organizations, including the U.S. Surgeon General's Office and the Substance Abuse and Mental Health Services Administration (SAMHSA), have offered their own definitions of what constitutes a wrap-around program. While these definitions vary slightly, the OJJDP (2007) notes that true wrap-around services feature several basic elements, including the following:

A collaborative, **community-based interagency team** that is responsible for designing, implementing, and overseeing the wrap-around initiative in a given jurisdiction. This team usually consists of representatives from the juvenile justice system, the public education system, and local mental health and social service agencies. In most cases, one specific agency is designated the lead agency in coordinating the wrap-around effort.

A **formal interagency agreement** that records the proposed design of the wrap-around initiative and spells out exactly how the wrap-around effort will work. At a minimum, this agreement should specify who the target population for the initiative is, how they will be enrolled in the program, how services will be delivered and paid for, what roles different agencies and individuals will play, and what resources will be committed by various groups.

Care coordinators who are responsible for helping participants create a customized treatment program and for guiding youth and their families through the system of care.

From the above basic elements of wrap-around services, it is clear that this concept mirrors the same premise that has been presented throughout this text, namely, that interagency partnerships are needed that are community-based in orientation. The use of formal interagency agreements helps to ensure that there is accountability within these partnerships. Further, the use of care coordinators helps to organize the various programs and services, reflecting many of the concepts that were initially presented in Chapter 8 on case management. However, as previously noted, wrap-around services are not just the utilization of typical case management processes but are much more comprehensive, interlaced, and multidimensional in scope. This is considered superior to many other forms of intervention and is particularly suitable for juveniles due to the fact that they are thought to be at an impressionable point in their lives and therefore are more amenable to the treatment programming.

Perhaps the most widely used form of therapy in the criminal justice system is **cognitive-behavioral therapy (CBT)**, a problem-focused approach designed to help people identify and change the dysfunctional beliefs, thoughts, and patterns of behavior that contribute to their problems. Its underlying principle is that thoughts affect emotions, which then influence behaviors. This type of therapy combines both cognitive and behavioral approaches into one of the most empirically validated treatment orientations in existence. Cognitive therapy concentrates on thoughts, assumptions, and beliefs. With cognitive therapy, offenders are encouraged to recognize and to change faulty or maladaptive thinking patterns. It is a way to gain control over inappropriate, repetitive thoughts that often feed or trigger various presenting problems.

Behavioral therapy, on the other hand, concentrates on specific actions and environments that either change or maintain behaviors. Behavioral interventions target behavior on a mechanistic level with a more direct training approach using observable reinforcements, punishments, and stimuli (Van Voorhis, Braswell, & Lester, 2000). Behavioral interventions may also incorporate elements of social learning theory and models in learning new behavior (Hanser, 2007b) and will utilize techniques such as role-playing, performance feedback, and imitation. This type of therapy is used extensively with almost all types of offender-clients and is one of the favorites in criminal justice agencies because it can be easily observed and measured (Hanser, 2007b). The empirical evidence shows that CBT is associated with significant and positive changes, particularly when therapy is provided by experienced practitioners (Waldron & Kaminer, 2004). According to the OJJDP (2007),

> Cognitive Behavioral Therapy has been successfully applied across settings (e.g., schools, support groups, prisons, treatment agencies, community-based organizations, churches) and across ages and roles (e.g., students, parents, teachers). It has been shown to be relevant to people with differing abilities and from a diverse range of backgrounds. The strategies of CBT have been successfully used to forestall the onset, ameliorate the severity, and divert the long-term consequences of problem behaviors among young people. Problem behaviors that have been particularly amenable to change using CBT have been (1) violence and criminality, (2) substance use and abuse, (3) teen pregnancy and risky sexual behaviors, and (4) school failure. Across the range of continuum-of-care, many model programs have successfully incorporated the strategies of CBT to effect positive change. (p. 3)

Cognitive-behavioral treatments for juvenile offenders are designed to correct dysfunctional thinking and behaviors associated with delinquency, crime, and violence. Cognitive-behavioral therapy has been successfully implemented in a host of correctional systems such as residential juvenile facilities and boot camps and in numerous other venues such as schools and job training programs. Further, meta-analyses of various treatment programs for criminal offenders have consistently shown cognitive-behavioral treatment modalities to be highly effective in reducing recidivism rates (Little, 2005; OJJDP, 2007).

Another common form of treatment that is often very effective with juvenile offenders is family therapy, which consists of therapeutic approaches that include the juvenile's family members in the treatment plan through ongoing counseling sessions (OJJDP, 2007). Students should look to Focus Topic 12.1 for an example of a community-based, family therapy treatment program for juvenile offenders and their families. Among the various family therapy approaches, one in particular has been shown to be highly effective with juvenile offenders; this is multisystemic family therapy (MSFT), which targets chronic, violent, or substance-abusing juvenile offenders (ages 12–17) who are at risk for out-of-home placement (OJJDP, 2007). This type of family therapy is delivered in the home, school, and community rather than in a clinic or residential treatment setting. (Again, students should refer to the Family Foundations example in Focus Topic 12.1.) Emphasis is placed on promoting behavior change in the youth's own environment as well as on the behaviors and interactions of other family members. Services are more intensive than traditional family therapies and include several hours of treatment per week rather than the traditional 50 minutes (OJJDP, 2007). With this type of therapy, "the emphasis is on developing a support network for the family in which the family is empowered to handle difficulties with the offending youth, and the youth is empowered to cope with family, peer, school, and neighborhood problems" (OJJDP, 2007, p. 3).

Cross-National Perspective

Japan's *Bosozoku*

Japanese police usually approach juvenile delinquency with a "strong and kind" philosophy, but with juveniles 6 times more likely to commit a crime than their adult counterparts, this approach has gradually changed. Juveniles account for 30 percent of the entire offender population and are responsible for 60 percent of all street crimes. Juveniles also have a considerably higher recidivism rate than their adult peers at 30 percent.

Juvenile offenders, with 94.1 percent of all arrests, almost exclusively commit motorcycle theft. This may be linked to juvenile involvement in motorcycle gangs called *bosozoku*. Data from 1999 reported by the National Police Agency estimate that *bosozoku* were responsible for an overwhelming 80 percent of all serious youth crimes. At the end of 2006, there were 847 known *bosozoku* with an estimated 54,434 involved riders, of which 54 percent were juveniles under the age of 20. The National Police Agency also reports that violent group runs are increasingly more frequent, with 4,730 incidents reported in 2006.

Bosozoku violence escalation may be related to their involvement with the *yakuza*, a Japanese organized crime syndicate. As police continue to crack down on the *yakuza*, the *yakuza* pressure the *bosozoku* for "protection" payments and road taxes for riding motorcycles on the roadways, causing more violent gang turf wars by the *bosozoku* gangs.

Police have responded to the rise in *bosozoku* violence by collaborating with community residents, schools, and businesses to curb *bosozoku* activities. Police also cooperate with juvenile police volunteers, juvenile guidance officials, and school authorities to target juveniles prone to involvement in *bosozoku* gangs and to improve the two factors believed to influence involvement in delinquency: an invalidating school system and the growing instability of many Japanese homes.

SOURCES: National Police Agency. (2007). *Overview of Japanese police and information from the National Police Agency*. Tokyo, Japan: Author. Retrieved from http://www.npa.go.jp/english; Sato, I. (1991). *Kamikaze biker: Parody and anomy in affluent Japan*. Chicago: University of Chicago Press.

Critical Thinking Questions

1. What else do you believe may influence juveniles to join *bosozoku* motorcycle gangs?

2. How would you discourage juvenile involvement in *bosozoku* motorcycle gangs?

For more information on Japan's National Police Agency, visit the website http://www.npa.go.jp/english/.

THE JUVENILE GANG OFFENDER

According to the OJJDP (2007), the average age of gang members is 17 to 18 years old, with members being older, on the average, in cities where gangs have existed longer. The typical range in age for juvenile gang offenders tends to be from 12 to 24 years (OJJDP, 2007). The median age at which youths start hanging around gangs is roughly 13 years old, and the median age for joining a gang is 14 (OJJDP, 2007; Valdez, 2005). Although female gang membership is increasing, male gang members outnumber females by a wide margin. Certain offenses are related to different racial/ethnic gangs, though all groups tend to be involved in the drug trade due to its being so lucrative. It is important to point out, however, that the disproportionate representation of minority groups in gangs is not a result of a predisposition toward gang membership, but rather the fact that minorities tend to be overrepresented in areas overwhelmed with gang activity (Valdez, 2005).

There are other ways to classify gangs in addition to ethnicity. One way is by viewing gangs along a continuum of their level of organization (Valdez, 2005). Gangs in the community tend to have one of two forms of organizational structure: the vertical/hierarchical organization and the horizontal organizational structure (Bureau of Justice Assistance [BJA], 1999; Valdez, 2005). Gangs with a vertical/hierarchical organizational structure are likely to indulge in group as opposed to individual violence; however, these gangs generally avoid using violence at all. This type of gang tends to focus on making money, which typically overrides individualistic acts of violence. It is a fairly high functioning gang, and when juvenile members are involved, they tend to work under the leadership of adult gang leaders. Because of the intermix between adult and juvenile gang members, these gangs are able to exert greater control over their members (older veteran gang members maintaining power over younger, less acclimated members). In contrast, gangs that have a horizontal structure tend to have less control over their members. While some of these gangs may include cliques or subgroups that can be very organized and able to control their members, the gang as a whole is a loose collection of factions with limited organizational coordination (BJA, 1999).

Gang members commit a disproportionate number of offenses and commit serious and violent offenses at a rate several times higher than non–gang members (Hanser, 2007b). Further, gang members are much more likely than their non-gang peers to commit certain types of crime, such as assault; carrying concealed weapons in school; auto and other theft; intimidating or assaulting victims and witnesses; participating in drive-by shootings and homicides; and using, selling, and stealing drugs, even when the two groups have grown up under similar circumstances (OJJDP, 2007). Thus, the nature of gangs and their involvement in serious crime and violence produces many risk factors for youth. Likewise, the greater the number of risk factors to which youths are exposed, the greater their risk of joining a gang (Hanser, 2007b). It should be noted that many young gang offenders report that they view their gang as their actual family. This should not be surprising since earlier in this chapter it was made clear that many of the more serious juvenile offenders come from homes that are chaotic, neglectful, and abusive. It is only natural, then, that these youth would turn to others like themselves as a source of support and protection and become gang members.

Establishing an Effective Youth Gang Exit Program

According to Sawdon (Evans & Sawdon, 2004), anti-gang programs should not just include law enforcement sweeps and gang suppression efforts, but should also include community advocacy to facilitate cohesive neighborhoods that are not intimidated by gang threats and activity. In Toronto, Canada, a program does just that and is targeted toward young gang members. This gang-exit program strategy has three components: (1) assessment and intake, (2) intensive training and personal development, and (3) the case management process.

Gang member assessment and intake is the phase that identifies interest and motivation of the gang member, the amount of gang involvement, and the member's family and social history (Evans & Sawdon, 2004). During this phase, members are provided an orientation to the program. The next phase is *gang member intensive training and personal development.* This phase implements two separate curricula, one for male and another for female gang members. Each curriculum involves up to 60 hours of intensive training. Topics include anger management, aggression, sexism, racism, homophobia, and bullying. Communication skills training is also given during this phase. The last phase is *gang member case management,* which involves individual support for the member but also requires ongoing group meetings for the ex–gang member. The intent is to reinforce what was learned at the intake and to provide a proactive intervention when life takes some unforeseen turn for the prior gang member.

This program utilizes prior members that successfully complete the exit program as future facilitators with future members of the program. These prior gang members are tasked with being active in establishing community contacts and outreach. Participants visit local community centers and other youth services to provide information about the program. At this point, many prior members will engage in community presentations to help generate support (financial and otherwise) for the anti-gang program. This program trains these prior members who are "passing the word" with leadership skills training; empathy building; counseling; and the development of their own "personal stories," which are stories that explain how they became involved in gangs and why they have chosen to cease their involvement. This "story" is told in schools and other areas where the ex–gang member tries to warn against joining the gang life.

If it is possible to extract youth from the gang-oriented environment, then this option should be given priority. Indeed, the youth is much less likely to recidivate when away from the adverse peer group. In the absence of such an intervention, the next-best strategy is to inoculate him or her from the effects of the gang world and to also replace the prior peer group with a new prosocial peer group. This is specifically what the gang-exit program attempts to do, all the while working against the backdrop of the prior gang family's pressure to return. This is what makes the task so difficult for the offender and the community supervision officer, as it is the strong tug of a subculture that eschews any attempt at reform made by the prior member.

RESTORATIVE JUSTICE TECHNIQUES, FAMILY CONFERENCES, AND TEEN COURTS

Restorative justice, as discussed in Chapter 7 regarding parolees, seeks to restore the victim and the community to its state of functioning prior to the criminal act, often involving numerous persons in the community in the reintegration of offenders and holding them accountable for their behavior. By bringing together victims, offenders, families, and other key stakeholders in a variety of settings, restorative justice helps offenders understand the implications of their actions and provides an opportunity for them to become reconnected to the community. Thus, restorative practices, while emphasizing the need for victim compensation and community healing, are essentially reintegrative approaches for the offender. Some programs typically associated with restorative justice include restitution, community service, and family group conferences.

The most common and well-established types of restorative justice are restitution and community service programs. These programs hold offenders personally accountable for their crimes and require that they make reparations to victims (either directly or indirectly). According to Schneider and Finkelstein (1998), there are three major types of restitution programs: community service, monetary restitution, and direct service to victims. **Community service** is work performed by an offender for the benefit of the community as a component of the offender's sentence. Community service is one means by which the offender is held accountable and required to provide amends for the harm caused by his or her criminal conduct. **Monetary restitution** is a process by which offenders are held partially or fully accountable for the financial losses suffered by the victims of their crimes. Restitution is typically ordered for property crimes or crimes in which something of value was stolen or procured, such as with fraud, forgery, or theft. Restitution payments may also be used to reimburse victims of violent crime for expenses related to their physical and mental health recovery (Schneider & Finkelstein, 1998). Students may recall from earlier readings in Chapter 10 that some states utilize restitution centers (as does the Mississippi Department of Corrections) where the primary focus of the facility is on restitution. The programs discussed in this current chapter are similar in nature but are more directly aimed at the needs of juveniles that are supervised in the community. Last and most rare is the use of restitution from the juvenile directly to the victim. According to Schneider and Finkelstein, this is a type of reconciliation in which the offender and the victim meet in a supervised setting to determine how the offender can make restitution directly to the victim through the performance of some type of service. In some states, this may be referred to as *victim–offender dialogues.*

Family group conferences are discussions that are facilitated and bring the victim, the victim's family, the offender, and the juvenile offender's family together to discuss the impact of a crime committed by the juvenile so that the group can decide how the juvenile is to be held accountable (Hanser, 2007b; OJJDP, 2007; Umbreit, 2000). Family conference groups originated in Australia and Oceania, and were eventually adopted in various areas of the United States. Today, they are used as a formal juvenile sanction in Indiana, Florida, Maine, Minnesota, Montana, New Mexico, Pennsylvania, Vermont, and Virginia (OJJDP, 2007). Group conferencing is consistent with the theoretical concepts of reintegrative shaming (see the Applied Theory box). This approach to offender reintegration contends that youth are generally deterred from committing crime by two informal forms of social control: fear of social disapproval and conscience (Braithwaite, 1989; OJJDP, 2007). Braithwaite argues that the consequences imposed by family members, friends, or other individuals important to an offender are more meaningful and therefore more effective than those imposed by the legal system. Further, Braithwaite contends that once shamed, the effects can be stigmatizing unless specific efforts are made by persons in the community to draw the juvenile back into the mainstream. The key is to eliminate the behavior, not the offending person.

Applied Theory   Juvenile Offending, Labeling, and Reintegrative Shaming

It is clear that early juvenile advocates were concerned that juvenile offenders' initial acts of offending might negatively affect their future possibilities in adulthood, even when they might otherwise have stopped offending. This is also true today, and it serves as one primary basis for having youths' records sealed and for preventing public view of the proceedings. These concerns reflect the general ideas of labeling theory. Labeling theory, as defined and discussed in Chapter 2, holds that when individuals are labeled as criminals, they will become stabilized in those roles, developing criminal identities that separate them from the mainstream population and exclude them from conventional roles. It should be obvious to the student that engagement in conventional activities or roles is a protective factor from further juvenile offending. If youth are excluded from such activities due to labeling, then it is clear that labeling does, in fact, further enmesh the youth into further lifestyles of offending. In short, labeling can be a risk factor for further juvenile offending.

The work of John Braithwaite provides an alternate view of labeling that is perhaps more balanced in approach. Basically, Braithwaite's primary point is that criminal behavior will be higher when shaming is stigmatizing and lower when shaming is reintegrative. This helps to explain why some persons reoffend more than others. Further, Braithwaite notes that shaming has the most profound impact on individuals with few social bonds to conventional society. (Students should

(Continued)

(Continued)

recall the discussion of social bond theory earlier in this chapter when discussing risk factors and protective factors.) Braithwaite notes that this is especially true for young, unmarried, unemployed males. This naturally describes many juvenile offenders in today's society.

While labeling theorists claim that no labeling should occur, Braithwaite offers another view to the shaming and offending connection. Essentially, he holds that a degree of shaming is useful for social control but that it should also include some form of reintegrative process. Offenders should be connected back with society; the key issue is what follows after they have been shamed by the community for their actions. Reintegration is essential because shamed youth are at a turning point in their lives. This is a time when they will either become reconnected with society or further entrenched into criminal behavior. The reactions of the community are quite instrumental to the final outcome. Thus, restorative forms of justice serve to fulfill this process of reconnection. When a degree of forgiveness is coupled with accountability to the victim and to the community, there is then the possibility of *reintegrative shaming*. The use of restorative justice therefore closely mirrors the underlying concepts of Braithwaite's version of labeling theory. Through this process, repentant offenders are given a chance to be forgiven after taking public responsibility for their actions, a process that then allows them and even encourages them to reconnect with their friends, family, and community. This makes the entire justice experience one that is productive rather than destructive—a primary desire in the field of juvenile corrections.

SOURCE: Lilly, J. R., Cullen, F. T., & Ball, R. A. (2007). *Criminological theory: Context and consequences* (4th ed.). Thousand Oaks, CA: Sage Publications.

A typical conference begins when the victim, the offender, and each of their supporters are brought together with a trained facilitator to discuss the incident and the harm it has caused. This proceeds with the offender describing the incident and each participant describing the impact of the incident on his or her life (OJJDP, 2007; Umbreit, 2000). The purpose of this process is for the offender to acknowledge the human impact of his or her crime (Umbreit, 2000). From this point, victims are then given the chance to express feelings, ask questions about the offense, or explain their own desired outcomes from the conference. At the end of the conference, all participants must reach a mutual agreement on how the juvenile should make amends to the victim, and the juvenile offender must sign a reparation agreement (OJJDP, 2007; Umbreit, 2000). The reparation agreement most often includes an apology as well as an outline of the specific type of restitution that must be made to the victim (OJJDP, 2007).

Teen courts are much like traditional courts in that there are prosecutors and defense attorneys, offenders and victims, and judges and juries, but other youth rather than adults fill these roles, and these youth even determine the disposition of the case (OJJDP, 2007). Similar to restorative justice precepts, the primary goal of teen courts is to hold young offenders accountable for their behavior while requiring reparation for the harm inflicted against the victim and the community (OJJDP, 2007). "The basic theory behind the use of young people in court is that youths will respond better to prosocial peers than to adult authority figures" (OJJDP, 2007, p. 3). This peer justice approach assumes that, similar to the way in which an association with delinquent peers is highly correlated with the onset of delinquent behavior (U.S. Public Health Services, 2002), peer pressure from prosocial peers may serve as a protective factor that pulls youth away from antisocial behavior and toward prosocial behavior (Butts, Buck, & Coggeshall, 2002; OJJDP, 2007). The primary function of most teen courts is to determine a fair and appropriate disposition for a youth who has already admitted to the charge (Butts et al., 2002; OJJDP, 2007). Teen courts utilize a number of innovative dispositions that allow those to be chosen that best fit the case and the crime committed by the processed juvenile. Resulting dispositions may include paying restitution, performing community service, writing formal apologies, or serving on a subsequent teen court jury (OJJDP, 2007). Teen courts may also require that sentenced juveniles attend classes to improve decision-making skills, enhance victim empathy, or deter them from future recidivism (Butts et al., 2002; OJJDP, 2007).

CONCLUSION

Juvenile offenders are a large subgroup of the community corrections population and therefore warrant specific and detailed coverage. In addressing the juvenile offender population on community supervision, it is important to understand the historical background and philosophical basis behind the juvenile justice system in general and the use of community sanctions with juveniles in particular. The concept of *parens patriae* serves as an ancient and fundamental principle behind juvenile supervision and ensuring the welfare of youth processed by the state. In cases where youth are acting outside of the scope of the law or where parents or guardians fail to maintain adequate supervision of their children, the state has an obligation to intervene and take charge of the juvenile. In many (but certainly not all) cases, the juvenile youth that are processed through the courts also have issues at home or may come from criminogenic family systems, which requires criminal justice intervention with the young offender and his or her family. Often, serious juvenile offenders come from abusive or neglectful family systems, making family interventions all the more important.

Juvenile probation, though similar to adult probation, does have some fundamental differences that are interlaced with the juvenile court's concern with stigmatization. Basically, the goal is to ensure that youth are accountable for their actions, but, at the same time, permanent stigmatization is to be avoided. Often, the relationship between the probation officer and the youngster may have much more depth than the mere supervision of the youngster. In some cases, the probation officer may be a mentor or even a counselor to the youth, the desire for reintegration of the youthful offender being an important component of juvenile community corrections. The juvenile probation officer will conduct a social investigation and, similar to a PSI, will provide this inquiry to the judge prior to disposition of the case. The very use of different terminology in juvenile court (from that used in adult court) echoes the difference in orientation and underscores the fact that juvenile courts are civil in nature, not criminal.

The effects of risk factors on a juvenile's likely recidivism are very important. Effective prevention programs will address these issues in advance, when possible. Intervention programs will likewise attempt to reduce the severity of risk factors as a means of lowering the likelihood of future recidivism. Further, protective factors tend to be at the other end of the spectrum. These factors tend to insulate the youth from delinquent or criminal acts. Treatment programs often work to specifically improve or develop these protective factors to make youth resistant to likely recidivism. By working on both ends of the spectrum, it is hoped that youth will be discouraged from further acts of criminality.

There are a number of residential and nonresidential programs for juvenile offenders. Residential programs may include day residential treatment facilities, boot camps, group homes, or wilderness programs. Each of these has its own specific focus, but all are based on the premise that youth can change, if given the appropriate guidance to do so. Nonresidential programs might include home confinement, day treatment centers, or aftercare. All of these are more intensive than the basic probation sentence, but each allows the juvenile to return home each evening and maintain his or her own domicile that is separate from the treatment program. Each of these types of programs utilizes a variety of therapeutic methods, with cognitive-behavioral therapy and family systems therapy being two of the most effective and most commonly used therapeutic orientations. Further, the use of effective gang-exit strategies is important when dealing with juveniles in gangs. Each of the prior discussed treatment programs and therapeutic orientations should be used, but the integration of gang-exit techniques is imperative if this specific group of juvenile offenders is expected to avoid future criminality.

Finally, juvenile community corrections uses a number of alternate means of processing juvenile cases. Among these are restorative justice principles, family conferences, and teen courts. Restorative justice approaches ensure that the victim and the community are made whole and that the offender is held accountable to the victim and the community for his or her actions. Family conferences follow a similar method of processing offender-victim issues but integrate the family members of both the victim and the offender, as well as other community members. Each of these approaches is moderated and supervised by trained personnel. Last, teen courts are similar to common juvenile courts except other youth actually fill the roles of the typical adult courtroom actors. The disposition itself is decided by these youth, and thus the juvenile is truly tried by his or her own peers. Each of these approaches demonstrates the unique orientation of the juvenile justice system and of juvenile community supervision, a system that is quite distinct from the adult system of justice.

Key Terms

Aftercare

Attachment

Belief

Care coordinators

Child abuse

Child neglect

Child parentification

Cognitive-behavioral therapy (CBT)

Community-based interagency team

Community service

Conformity

Day treatment facilities

Educational neglect

Emotional neglect

Formal interagency agreement

Group homes

Home confinement

Involvement

Juvenile boot camps

Juvenile intensive probation supervision (JIPS)

Juvenile probation

Juvenile records

Labeling theory

Monetary restitution

Parens patriae

Physical abuse

Physical neglect

Psychological abuse

Residential treatment programs

Restorative justice

Social bond theory

Social study

Supervision stage

Teen courts

Wilderness camps

Wrap-around services

"What Would You Do?" Exercise

Chuck is a 16-year-old male who has had numerous encounters with law enforcement. He is currently on juvenile probation and is in an alternative school. Chuck has had a long history of attention-deficit/hyperactivity disorder and has also been diagnosed with conduct disorder in his early childhood. He is presently in counseling for bullying, anger management, and substance abuse (he consumes methamphetamine from time to time as well as ecstasy). Further, Chuck's parents have brought him to your office because even they feel that the requirements of his probation are not stringent enough. In short, they want you, his probation officer, to do something about Chuck. In fact, you get the idea that they want to get rid of him.

Chuck has constantly been in trouble at school and in the community. He surrounds himself with a number of younger youth who look up to his acts of violence and intimidation. Chuck is also fond of taking risks, such as jumping in the street to force cars to veer aside while he throws eggs at the windshield to blind the driver.

Chuck also loves to fight and bully others. He gets mad easily and when he does, he becomes a real "loose canon," hurling verbal insults and often simply attacking people who "piss him off."

Chuck is likewise a skilled liar. He lies to everyone about his whereabouts and is difficult to locate. He is fond of going from house to house and friend to friend. When he gets caught for something, even if the person actually *sees* him do it, he will vehemently deny his involvement.

He stays out late despite his parents' directions, and breaks the city ordinance curfew for juveniles. In fact, 2 nights ago Chuck was reportedly out in a neighborhood at 2:00 AM with some other youth, drinking beer and beating mailboxes with an aluminum bat. One of the girls that was with the group told him that he was immature and he should stop. Chuck called her a number of inappropriate names and then threw a brick at the girl; luckily, he missed.

When Chuck was 10 years old, he was diagnosed with conduct disorder. He exhibited acts of cruelty toward pets and other animals from time to time, and he seemed indifferent to the pain they suffered. In fact, he indicated a bizarre and morbid fascination with their death. At the age of 13, Chuck reportedly tried to coerce one of his cousins into sexual intercourse but was stopped just before the act could be committed.

Chuck's parents are not naive about Chuck's behavioral problems. In fact, they are very worried because he is now 16 and they feel as if they have completely failed as parents. Chuck has been on probation with you for nearly 3 months without incident. However, his parents claim that he threatens kids in the neighborhood and gets one of his friends to do his dirty work, all so he does not get caught fighting. You look to Chuck, and he just says that his parents are out to get him.

What would you do?

Applied Exercise

Consider the case of Chuck, just presented in the "What Would You Do?" exercise. For this applied exercise, pretend that you are a youth counselor and Chuck has been referred to you by the local community supervision agency. You must correctly identify and classify any mental health issues that affect Chuck (students may need to refer back to Chapter 9). In addition, be sure to select the specific treatment modality (type of therapy) that you would use and explain why you would select that type of therapy. Likewise, indicate if you would consider placing Chuck in some type of residential treatment facility. Explain why or why not and provide a thorough rationale. This assignment will require that you complete outside research on your own.

Each response to these questions must be correct and balanced in approach (consisting of realistic possibilities), with anywhere from 400 to 700 words of content being allowed per application. Students should complete this application exercise as a mini paper that explains the scenario and then addresses each question. Total word count: 1,200 to 2,100 words.

CHAPTER 13

Specialized and Problematic Offender Typologies

LEARNING OBJECTIVES

1. Identify different types of adult sex offenders.

2. Understand various methods of supervision for sex offenders as well as common treatment techniques.

3. Identify and understand substance abusers.

4. Understand the concept of co-occurring disorders.

5. Identify and discuss different types of treatment programs for substance abusers.

6. Understand and discuss the mentally ill offender.

7. Identify different types of mental illness common to the offender population.

8. Understand various classifications of mental retardation.

INTRODUCTION

This chapter is composed of three main sections, each of which covers a specialized and problematic offender. The first type that will be introduced is the sex offender. Sex offenders pose special problems due to the nature of their actions and the severe consequences suffered by their victims. Sexual offenses are often characterized as possessing a heightened sense of heinousness that is difficult for most to understand, especially when one considers that some sex offenders are drawn to children or the elderly. In the next few sections of this chapter, we will explore sex offenders whose victims are adults as well as those whose victims are children. In addition, we will look at the number of sex offenders in community supervision and the various mechanisms related to recidivism. Finally, we will discuss the different functions of the community supervision officer charged with working with this type of offender as well as some of the treatment techniques commonly employed.

The second type of offender that often poses specific challenges for community corrections is the substance abuser. What makes this group of offenders difficult to maintain is the fact that substance abuse is often accompanied by other psychological and emotional disorders. In fact, substance abuse is best viewed as a symptom of repressed emotion. In other words, the offender who engages in the consumption of mind-altering substances is likely to be someone whose emotional landscape is barren. This type of offender would likely have difficulty describing events or activities that he or she would consider "fun." In relation to the substance abuser, we will explore different types of substance addiction as well as various treatment programs. In addition, we will describe 12 core functions in addictions treatment that seem to be critical components of successful interventions.

Finally, we will explore the difficult challenge of effectively managing offenders suffering from mental illness. The mentally ill offender usually presents a complex set of circumstances that can be hard to decipher and successfully manage within the community. This is because there are various types of mental illness that may be further complicated by the coexistence of personality and mood disorders. In this section, we will pay particular attention to some of the more common disorders and various methods of response commonly employed by community corrections.

Prior to moving into the main content of this chapter, a critical note is offered, the essence of which should be kept in mind by the reader throughout the duration of this material.

FOCUS TOPIC 13.1

SPECIALIZED AND PROBLEMATIC OFFENDERS

Specialized and problematic offenders often suffer from symptoms, disorders, and illness not commonly or fully understood by most employees of community corrections agencies. As a result, it is critical that these employees identify resources within their communities that offer the expertise and capabilities of providing needed services to certain offenders. In order for community corrections agencies to maximize their ability to effectively supervise specialized offenders, supervision efforts should coincide with appropriate psychological and emotional counseling provided by licensed professionals within the community.

SEX OFFENDERS

This section addresses the issue of sexual assault against adult (as opposed to child) victims. Before proceeding, however, it is necessary to define sexual assault. First, the reader should understand that it is used as a blanket term to refer to a number of sexually related forms of offending. **Sexual assault** includes all types of sexual offenses that involve touching or penetration of an intimate part of a person's body without consent. Thus, sexual assault includes forced sodomy, forced oral copulation, child molestation, and any form of undesired sexually related touching (LeBeau & Mozayani, 2001). For purposes of this chapter, *sexual assault is the act of forced penetration of any bodily orifice (vaginally, anally, or orally), or forced cunnilingus or felatio, involving violation of the survivor's body and psychological well-being.* The assault is accomplished by the use of force, the threat of force, or without force when the victim is unable to physically or mentally give his or her consent.

Sex Offender Typologies: Victim Chosen Is Adult

Throughout North America, sex offenders make up an increasing proportion of persons that are convicted and later incarcerated. In some states, it has been found that the largest group of offenders is that of sex offenders (Morris & Tonry, 1990). The most common demographic feature is that rapists tend to be young. When examining the Uniform Crime Reports (UCR) data, over half of rapists arrested are under 25 years of age, and a full 80 percent are under the age of 30. Further, the National Crime Survey estimates that roughly one-fourth of all combined rapes and attempted rapes that occur at any point in the year are committed by offenders who are between the ages of 12 and 20. Further, it has been shown that a high number of rapes of adult victims have been committed by juvenile offenders. This underscores the finding that roughly half of all adult sex offenders report that their first sexual offense occurred during their teens (Bartol, 2002).

Bartol (2002) notes that roughly half of all men arrested for rape tend to be employed in working-class occupations, with another approximate third being unemployed. Of the convicted rapists, only 20 percent had a high school education and the overwhelming majority came from labor-oriented occupations (Bartol, 2002). Thus, few white-collar or professional workers are convicted of rape. There is substantial evidence that most charges for rape are dropped or pleaded out of court to a lesser charge for those men who are more affluent.

The majority of these offenders are not under correctional supervision before their initial arrest for their sex offense, and most are established to some degree within the community. Further, it has been found that sex offenders do not share the same tendency to "age out" of their crimes as do offenders who commit other types of offenses (Abel & Rouleau, 1990). Thus, one can deduce that sex offenders start their offending at a young age and they are likely to continue offending throughout their life span if some form of intervention is not successful.

It should also be noted that most sex offenders do not present with a serious mental illness. Although a diagnosis of antisocial personality disorder is very common among sex offenders, it is generally not considered sufficient to justify classifying the offender as mentally disordered (Rice, Harris, & Quinsey, 2002). Moreover, despite sensationalism from the media, most sex offenders do not have a major mental disorder such as schizophrenia or some other psychosis (Sturgeon & Taylor, 1980).

Many researchers have attempted to classify various kinds of rapists (Holmes & Holmes, 2002). However, the chosen typology that will be used for this text and for this chapter was originally devised by Knight and Prentky (1990). This typology divides rapists into four categories: power reassurance, anger retaliation, power assertive, and sadistic. In addition, two more categories have been provided to more adequately discuss the various types of adult-on-adult sex offenders and their motives for committing their crimes. These two additional categories are the opportunistic rapist and the sexual gratification rapist.

Power Reassurance Rapist

The **power reassurance rapist** is probably the least violent of the types that will be considered. These offenders are typically not socially competent and may be quite introverted in thought and behavior. These individuals typically have a low sense of self-esteem and suffer from profound feelings of inadequacy, both socially and sexually. With this group of sex offenders, aggression is not a key factor of motivation; rather, these offenders seek to prove their sexual prowess and adequacy. They are likely to have fantasies in which they imagine eagerly yielding victims who succumb to their sexual coercion and who enjoy the experience so much that they actually begin to desire further sexual intercourse. Such fantasies are soothing to the offender's sense of insecurity and incompetence.

Knight and Prentky (1990) point out that many of these offenders come from single-parent homes. They also do not tend to do well in school and have an average educational level of 10th grade. They are typically single and may be adults that continue to live with their parents. This offender is not likely to be athletic; he is likely to be passive, and will generally have few if any friends. He is, however, likely to be a stable and reliable worker but is typically employed in a menial occupation due to his lack of desire for achievement.

Power reassurance rapists are not likely to be mentally ill, but they may have other sex disorders such as transvestism (cross-dressing) or fetishism. They may engage in exhibitionism, voyeurism, and so on, as this may be part of the method by which they select victims in their own neighborhoods for future sexual assaults. These offenders may watch their victim intensely over time until they feel secure in their decision to assault. They typically will case the home of their victims and are most likely to commit the act within the home of the victim when the opportunity presents. The main purpose of rape for this type of offender is to improve his sense of self-respect. The primary aim is sexual in nature and is not necessarily about power over his victim.

Sexual Gratification Rapist

For the **sexual gratification rapist,** aggression is simply instrumental and is used to gain compliance. However, unlike the power reassurance rapist, this offender is not necessarily withdrawn or reclusive. Rather, this offender may simply desire sex and may be in a situation where he feels that force or coercion could successfully get him the sexual intercourse that he wants. This type of rape is most reflected by date rape and similar forms of sexual assault. It may or may not be a repetitive behavior, depending on how any previous attempts at coercion have ended. It is unlikely that this type of offender will allow the coercion or aggression to escalate to the point to serious injury to the victim.

This type of offender may have a high degree of social and interpersonal competence, and the sexual offense is likely to reflect more sexualization in both activity and interaction. Further, the offender is likely to express his interest in the victim as a sex object. He may use any means of cajoling, flattery, or pleading while employing the gentlest of force necessary to encourage the victim to submit to his desire. Within this group of offenders are those who drug their victims (e.g., with Rohypnol or excessive alcohol, or by providing the drug ecstasy), and there is often no use of physical violence against the victim. The offender simply has sex with the victim without the person's consent. This is still clearly rape, but it is also not based on attempting to cause pain to the victim as much as it is designed to gratify the sexual urges of the offender.

The offender who is successful in this type of rape is likely to repeat the act with other victims as well. Further, it should be noted that many victims will fail to report the act because they know the offender personally (perhaps very well), or the victim may experience a sense of guilt or shame. In addition, the intoxicated or drugged state of the victim does not help her sense of credibility, in her mind if nothing else. Thus, the act tends to go unreported. This method of rape is a primary tactic used on many college campuses and among individual students as well as student groups that may rape, such as members of fraternities or athletic groups or teams.

Opportunistic Rapist

The **opportunistic rapist** demonstrates neither strong sexual nor aggressive features, but engages in spontaneous rape when an opportunity presents that makes it look like an easy prospect. This form of rape is usually conducted during the commission of another crime, such as robbery or burglary. The victim simply happens to be at the scene, or the victim of the crime resists and this provokes the idea of assaulting the victim. In most cases, this offender is likely to have a history of criminal offenses (not necessarily all of the crime being detected by police, however) besides rape. In fact, the offender may never have committed a prior rape and may not even rape again after the isolated opportunity that had presented itself. In order to fall within this category, the offender must both show callous indifference to the welfare and comfort of the victim and use no more force than would be necessary to obtain compliance from the victim.

Power Assertive Rapist

With the **power assertive rapist**, rape is an attempt to express the person's virility and sense of dominance over the victim. This offender has a sense of superiority that is based on "hypermasculinity" in which he believes he is entitled to sexual access simply because he is a man. For this offender, rape is an impulsive act of predatory victimization that the female deserves because she is female and is fair game for subjugation (Holmes & Holmes, 2002). The aggression exhibited in the rape is intended to secure the compliance of the victim rather than necessarily cause harm to the victim. To be sure, the power assertive rapist is not concerned with whether the victim is injured in the process, but this is not his primary motivation when using force against a victim. The primary motivation is simply to obtain and maintain control over the victim. Thus, unlike the power reassurance rapist, this rapist is indifferent to the comfort of his victim; he simply is concerned with ensuring compliance from the victim. The power assertive rapist commits sexual assault so as to feel a sense of dominance and control over a female victim due to heightened beliefs regarding the roles and rights of men and women (Holmes & Holmes, 2002).

Holmes and Holmes (2002) note that about 70 percent of these rapists have been raised in single-parent households and roughly a third of these offenders have stayed in foster homes. In addition, the majority (three-fourths) have suffered from prior abuse as children (Holmes & Holmes, 2002; Knight & Prentky, 1990). This type of rapist generally has many domestic problems and has often been involved in numerous failed marriages. Obviously, these marriages are replete with negative incidents, including (or especially) domestic violence.

The attack of the power assertive rapist consists of a mixture of verbal and physical violence. If he is resisted, he will physically overpower his victim. The level of aggression of these rapists tends to escalate as their raping continues. Power assertive rapists are not typically considered to be amenable to treatment. In fact, Holmes and Holmes (2002) clearly point out that the power assertive rapist is likely to be the most difficult of rapists to interview and interrogate. These rapists are unlikely to provide any cooperation even when intimidation, pleas for aid, or appeals for the victim's welfare are used.

Holmes and Holmes (2002) contend that "the power assertive rapist . . . may be considered to be close to the clinical evaluation of having a character disorder" (p. 153). In fact, these authors state that this category of rapist is likely to be psychopathic in nature. Further, power assertive rapists feel no remorse for their actions (reflective of their common underlying antisocial personality disorder, narcissism, and tendencies toward psychopathy) or the victim's welfare (Holmes & Holmes, 2002). They simply care about having power over the victim or the situation. With investigators, the fact that they have information desired by the investigators itself becomes a form of power that they are likely to relish.

Anger Retaliation Rapist

The **anger retaliation rapist** strongly desires to harm women. This offender seeks to "get even" with women who have embarrassed or humiliated him in his past. These causes for embarrassment or humiliation may be real or imagined, but this type of offender essentially views women as bad, even evil, and thus deserving of harm. Unlike the power reassurance rapist, the anger retaliation rapist is socially competent (Holmes & Holmes, 2002). This type of rapist usually comes from a noxious family of origin where abuse or neglect was commonplace. There is a high likelihood that male role models were abusive to the mother of the offender and that the mother was, in turn, abusive to the offender when he was a child (Holmes & Holmes, 2002). These abusive mother–child interactions may be a substantial part of why this category of offender harbors resentment toward women.

For this type of offender, the act of rape is meant to humiliate the victim, especially when the victim is chosen because she seems to be promiscuous or because she is seen as deserving of the abuse (Holmes & Holmes, 2002). When acting alone, this rapist is likely to use verbal insults toward the victim and he is likely to rip off her clothing in a demonstration of force. This type of offender will also be likely to use weapons of opportunity to assault the victim. This rapist will tend to commit his crimes near home and will usually stalk victims that are of his own race and near to his own age. It should also be noted that this type of offender is not likely to attempt further contact with the victim after the assault is over (Holmes & Holmes, 2002).

It should not be surprising that most of these offenders present with co-occurring disorders, with antisocial personality disorder being the most frequent in conjunction with sexual sadism. Sadistic rapists will often use restraint, blindfolding, paddling, spanking, whipping, pinching, beating, burning, electrical shock, cutting, strangulation, mutilation, and any other imaginable act of torture and abuse to rape their victim (American Psychiatric Association, 2000). Among this group of offenders are a high number that present with the classic traits for psychopathy. It cannot be understated that this offender has so strongly paired aggression and sexual gratification that he has eroticized it, and this type of offender is likely to be incapable of having sex that does not have violent overtones.

Sadistic Rapist

The **sadistic rapist** is the most dangerous and the most likely to kill or permanently maim his victim. The primary desire of this offender is to cause pain to the victim. This offender will seek to express sexually aggressive fantasies that have formed from an extended history of the classically conditioned pairing of sexual excitement and violence. Indeed, graphic pairings such as that presented in "snuff" pornographic films are an integral part of the offender's day-to-day thoughts and lifestyle in many cases. This offender derives ultimate pleasure when inflicting pain and psychological terror upon his victim. In fact, he has difficulty obtaining sexual satisfaction without inflicting harm upon the object of his desire.

When sexual sadism is severe, and especially when it is associated with antisocial personality disorder, these individuals are likely to kill their victims. According to the American Psychiatric Association (2000), the diagnostic criteria for the mental disorder of *sexual sadism* are as follows:

A. Over a period of at least 6 months, recurrent, intense sexually arousing fantasies, sexual urges, or behaviors involving acts (real, not simulated) in which the psychological or physical suffering (including humiliation) of the victim is sexually exciting to the offender. (p. 573)

B. The person has acted on these sexual urges with a non-consenting person, or the sexual urges or fantasies cause marked distress or interpersonal difficulty. (p. 573)

Because it is unlikely that this type of crime can go unreported by the victim due to the nonsexual injuries that would require hospitalization, this offender is more likely than any other to murder his victim so that the person will be silenced. As with the power assertive rapist, the prognosis for this group of offenders is extremely poor. These types of offenders are also not good security or treatment risks for community supervision programs.

Sex Offender Typologies: Child as Victim

According to the *DSM-IV-TR*, **pedophilia** involves sexual activity with a prepubescent child (generally age 13 and younger). The individual with pedophilia must be at least 16 years of age and at least 5 years older than the child who was the victim. Pedophiles most often report a stronger attraction to children within a certain age range. Those most attracted to females usually prefer 8- to 10-year-olds. Those attracted to males usually prefer slightly older children. Pedophilia involving female victims is reported more often than pedophilia involving male victims.

These offenders may limit their activities to their own children, stepchildren, or relatives, or they may victimize children outside their families. Some individuals with pedophilia threaten the child to prevent disclosure. Others, particularly those who routinely victimize children, develop complex techniques for obtaining access to their victims, which may include winning the trust of a child's mother; marrying a woman with an attractive child; trading children with other individuals with pedophilia; or, in some rare cases, adopting children from underdeveloped countries or even abducting the children from strangers.

The pedophile may be attentive to the child's needs in order to gain the person's affection, interest, and loyalty and to prevent the child from reporting the sexual assault. Pedophiles start to notice their urges in adolescence in most cases, but some report that they did not become aroused by children until middle age. The recidivism rate for those having a preference for males is roughly twice that for those who prefer females (American Psychiatric Association, 2000).

While there is considerable variability in the age of child molesters, most who are convicted are between the ages of 36 and 40. This is in stark contrast to the rapists who choose adult victims where, as mentioned, about 75 percent are under age 30. Despite the statistical finding that child molesters tend to be older than most other sex offenders, there seems to be a pattern of victim preference that is based on the age of the pedophile (Bartol, 2002). It has been found that older pedophiles (over the age of 50) seek immature children who are 10 years old or younger. On the other hand, younger pedophiles (under the age of 40) tend to select girls who are between the ages of 12 and 15 years (Bartol, 2002). These latter pedophiles are referred to as *hebophiles*, which simply denotes a type of pedophile that prefers preteen and teenaged children rather than prepubescent children. Most child molesters do not present with mental illness of any sort other than the pedophilia disorder as listed in the *DSM-IV-TR*. Pedophiles typically do not finish high school, and most have poor work histories in unskilled employment.

Adult Sex Offenders in the Community

When addressing sex offenders on community supervision, the first concern that comes to mind is public safety. This concern is the overriding and understandable priority when considering the suitability of community supervision for sex offenders. Thus, understanding the true recidivism rates for sex offenders, and understanding recidivism rates for different types of sex offenders, is critical if an agency is to make effective and safe decisions about early release. In 2003, the U.S. Department of Justice published a study that examined recidivism among sex offenders released in 1994 and tracked their reoffending rates during the subsequent 3 years. This study looked at prison systems in 15 states that had released a total of 9,691 male sex offenders. These offenders comprised two-thirds of all the male sex offenders released from state prison systems throughout the United States in 1994 (Bureau of Justice Statistics [BJS], 2003). The 9,691 offenders were divided by type of sex offender, and the breakdown was as follows:

3,115 released rapists

4,295 released child molesters

6,576 released sexual assaulters

443 released statutory rapists

It should be noted that the study included the "big four" among state correctional systems (California, New York, Texas, and Florida). The remaining states were selected due to their representativeness of the overall U.S. correctional population. These states together released a total of 272,111 prisoners in 1994, meaning that the 9,691 sex offenders consisted of about 3.6 percent of all those released on community supervision. On average, the 9,691 sex offenders served 3.5 years of an average 8-year sentence before being released in 1994 (BJS, 2003).

This study found that within the first 3 years following their release from prison, 5.3 percent (517 of the 9,691) of released sex offenders were rearrested for a sex crime. The rate of reoffending for the 262,420 released non–sex offenders was lower—1.3 percent. For sex offenders, it was found that in the first 12 months following their release from a state prison, roughly 40 percent recidivated. In comparison, an average of 4,295 child molesters were released after serving about 3 years of an approximate 7-year sentence. With child molesters, the first 3 years following release from prison resulted in 3.3 percent (141 of 4,295) of released child molesters being rearrested for another sex crime against a child (BJS, 2003).

While recidivism studies typically find that the older the prisoner is when released, the lower the rate of recidivism, this was not the case with sex offenders. Overall, of the 9,691 released sex offenders, 3.5 percent (339 of the 9,691) were reconvicted for a sex crime during the 3-year follow-up period. From these results, it can be seen that sex offenders have a higher likelihood of recidivism (3.5 percent) than do non–sex offenders (1.3 percent).

Thus, many community supervision programs utilize what is referred to as the *containment approach*, which has been publicized by the American Probation and Parole Association. The **containment approach** is based on the idea that multiple dimensions of supervision are necessary to optimize public safety, and this therefore requires numerous actors within the criminal justice and community setting. When utilizing the containment approach, the supervision team will consist of at least three persons, each with his or her own specific role in the process (Center for Sex Offender Management, 2001). The Center for Sex Offender Management points toward three personnel who are commonly involved with the containment approach in supervision:

Community Supervision Officer: The community supervision officer monitors the offender's behavior in the community and assesses his or her compliance with court mandates. These officers of the court maintain regular contact with the offender (usually through some form of intensive supervision coupled with electronic monitoring) and have routine conversations with the treatment therapist. These agents represent the authority of the court and are responsible for initiating court action if the offender does not comply with the terms of supervision.

Sex Offender Therapist: The therapist usually sees the offender once a week in a group counseling setting. These therapists are highly trained and experienced in working with the sex offender population. Advance training is usually required in most states before a therapist can provide such services. The therapist maintains close contact with the community supervision officer, and both work collaboratively to identify potential problems in the offender's compliance with community supervision requirements. When the sex offender therapist and the community supervision officer work together, the offender is less able to hide relevant issues from the therapist or the treatment group.

Polygraph Examiner: Sex offenders are generally very manipulative and superficially compliant. They are very adept at withholding information and keeping secrets. The expertise of the polygraph examiner is very useful in detecting deception in sex offenders. The information gained from polygraph examinations is forwarded to the therapist and community supervision officer.

Photo 13.1 This community supervision officer is assigned solely to a sex offender caseload. He holds a miniature tracking device, typically referred to as an MTD in the field. This piece of equipment works in conjunction with GPS surveillance technology.

In essence, these three supervising agents work together to "contain" the offender's risk to the community.

Further, depending on the type of sex offender, there may be conditions regarding their potential contact with children. Most sex offenders are initially restricted from having contact with children. This is of course clearly the case with pedophiles. However, some offenders may be allowed to have supervised contact with their own children if they had not been victims and if the offender does not seem to be a risk to the children. As the offender's progress in treatment continues, the conditions of this restriction may be modified as seems practical with that offender. Further, these offenders are almost always restricted from residing near a school or day care center, and they cannot go to places commonly known to have children present. Finally, sex offenders are often restricted from purchasing pornography or frequenting sexually oriented businesses. Restrictions on Internet use are becoming common as well.

One community supervision program in Hunt County, Texas, utilizes an approach that is known as the Sex Offender Accountability Program (SOAP), which offers a good example of what a community supervision program should entail when sex offenders are the primary client caseload. This program utilizes the treatment team approach for supervision of sex offenders endorsed by the American Probation and Parole Association. Offenders in this program are required to attend sex offender treatment. This treatment is cognitive-behavioral in orientation, and offenders often have their views and beliefs challenged with intense confrontation. Group therapy is utilized most frequently because offenders are expected to challenge one another as well, while under the guidance of the group facilitator. The offenders are taught such things as predictable indicators in their offense cycle, victim empathy, and relapse prevention. Further, offenders are required to state and behaviorally model their accountability for their offense. Last, to ensure public safety, and as a backup to ensure offenders' compliance with the treatment program, this program uses the polygraph, the penile plethysmograph, random field visits, and electronic monitoring to ensure that offenders are committed to the treatment regimen and that they are adequately supervised.

Many of the instruments mentioned in this program of supervision are common to most treatment programs throughout the nation. Our current discussion has also summarized some recently published research on recidivism rates of sex offenders released from prison and has also presented a number of characteristics that are common to community supervision programs around the country. From our example chosen from the Hunt County Community Supervision and Corrections Department, it is clear that supervision and treatment become almost "one and the same." In fact, it seems difficult to talk about one without including the other dimension. With this in mind, we now turn our attention to some treatment techniques and orientations beyond those that we have already discussed.

South Africa's HIV/AIDS-Infected Offenders

According to the World Health Organization, 6 million of South Africa's 47 million residents are currently infected with HIV. What's even more alarming, prison officials report prevalence rates for HIV-infected offenders that are 5 times the rates found in the general population. In 2007, there were 163,049 people incarcerated in South Africa's prisons; 25,271 of these were sex offenders. Although the HIV infection rate of these sex offenders is still unknown, community supervision options for these offenders are a major concern for prison officials. Not only must prison officials assess the level of risk for the offender committing new crimes, but also the risk to the community for further spreading HIV.

To address this issue, in 2002 the Minister of Correctional Services approved an HIV and AIDS policy directed to educate offenders regarding the prevention of spreading HIV while incarcerated and after release. This policy includes placing condoms at accessible locations to promote safer sex practices and teaching precautions in how to handle bodily fluids. Social workers and peers provide counseling services to HIV-infected offenders, and offenders are encouraged to participate in special events such as World AIDS Day and the International Candlelight Memorial Day. In addition, offenders are treated for opportunistic and sexually transmitted infections.

HIV-infected offenders may be allowed to serve their sentence in the community. Conditions of community supervision may include house arrest, community service, victim's compensation, remaining drug and alcohol free, and participation in treatment programs. Should the offender violate these conditions, he or she would face an additional sentence of up to 10 years.

SOURCE: Department of Correctional Services. (2008). *White paper.* Johannesburg, South Africa: Author.

Critical Thinking Question

1. What other measures could be taken by the Correctional Department to help prevent the spread of HIV/AIDS by infected offenders?

For more information on South Africa's Department of Correctional Services, visit the website www.dcs.gov.za.

TREATMENT STRATEGIES FOR SEX OFFENDERS

While most readers (particularly students of criminal justice) are aware that a variety of offenders may be given treatment, they are not typically aware of how these treatment techniques are utilized. This last section offers a brief overview of some of the techniques used in sex offender treatment. Specifically, the reader will be given a list of various methods of intervention that are used with the sex-offending population to enable a more direct understanding of how interventions are applied. The primary types of treatment fall under three categories: (1) cognitive-behavioral therapy, (2) interrogation-oriented, and (3) drug administrative treatment.

Cognitive-Behavioral Techniques

These treatments are geared toward reducing or eliminating the deviant sexual arousal. There are many techniques commonly used by clinicians, each with a different rationale. The first group of interventions teaches impulse control, the second teaches arousal reduction, and the last group teaches empathy to the offender. Table 13.1 provides a quick listing of these three categories and their corresponding techniques.

1. Impulse-control forms of cognitive-behavioral techniques include the following:

    Thought-stopping: This is used to disrupt a deviant thinking pattern. The offender is given pictures of arousing images and is forced to stop his thoughts when the image is seen. The use of group confrontation, observation, and journaling assists in ensuring that this is accomplished (Knopp, 1989).

Thought-shifting: This requires that the offender shift his thoughts to aversive imagery. The sex offender may be allowed to view or think about some arousing image, but then is trained to immediately think about something aversive, like an approaching police officer. Again, the use of group confrontation, observation, and journaling assists in ensuring that this is accomplished (Knopp, 1989).

Impulse-charting: This is a method used to track points and times when certain thoughts or desires seem more intense. The time of day, location, and number of times per week are all important. The offender will usually also be required to report the level of intensity of the impulse (i.e., on a 1-to-10 scale), and this will be tracked through a journaling process with the therapist (Knopp, 1989).

2. Arousal-reduction forms of cognitive-behavioral techniques include the following:

   Scheduled overmasturbation: This intervention requires that the client routinely masturbate on a progressively more frequent schedule throughout the week. This is intended to reduce sexual drive and to make control easier for the offender. This exercise also teaches that the client does have some measure of control over his sexual arousal and use of sexual energy (Knopp, 1989).

   Masturbatory reconditioning: This technique involves having the client masturbate to an appropriate fantasy, until he has an ejaculation (Knopp, 1989).

   Aversion therapy: This behavioral technique is used in varying degrees in several sex offender programs. The aim of aversive techniques is to teach offenders to associate unpleasant stimuli with presently desirable yet unacceptable behaviors (Van Voorhis, Braswell, & Lester, 2000). A wide range of physical or overt aversive stimuli have been used to treat sex offenders. Most notable are electric shock, foul odors and tastes, drugs that temporarily paralyze, and drugs that induce vomiting. Because of ethical and constitutional considerations, some of the more extreme forms of aversive stimuli are not used as frequently as they were some 20 to 30 years ago.

   Spouse monitoring: This involves supervision on the part of the spouse (if and when available, though other family members may be able to assist) or significant other to complete a daily checklist on the offender's compliance with the treatment and to ensure that any therapeutic homework given to the client is being completed at the prescribed times in the week. This increases the overall supervision of the offender (Knopp, 1989).

   Environmental manipulation: This helps to get the offender out of situations that are a high risk for him and his potential victims. The offender should train himself to move out of the house and find a new location, rather than the victim having to leave, if the offender perceives a risk of reoffending (Knopp, 1989).

3. Empathy training forms of cognitive-behavioral techniques include the following:

   Victim counselors: Victims are invited to attend the group meeting. In fact, the victim may even co-lead the group. Offenders may be required to visit a victim advocate center and, at their own expense, ask the victim counselor to explain his or her feelings on sex crimes.

   Cognitive restructuring: The offender constructs scenes that cast him or significant others in the role of the victim. The offender then focuses on typical rationalizations he uses to justify the assault (Knopp, 1989). Scenes are constructed in which he utilizes and internalizes the rationalization. These scenes are then paired with aversive imagery. Finally, alternate scenes are constructed where the offender catches himself in the distortion and counters with a reality-grounded message in which it is acknowledged that these actions do not end in the way that the offender hopes (Knopp, 1989).

   Role-playing: The offender reenacts his own crime scene(s) with another offender, and they take turns playing the role of their victim. The remaining offenders in the group observe and later critique the role-play and allow for group processing of the effects on the victim.

Interrogation-Oriented Techniques

Interrogation-oriented techniques are designed to ensure that the offender is being honest in the feedback he is providing to the program treatment staff. This is important in that sex offenders are notorious for lying and manipulating. These tools assist the therapist and community supervision staff in determining whether

TABLE 13.1	Cognitive-Behavioral Techniques Used With Sex Offenders
Intervention Grouping	*Specific Technique*
Impulse Control Methods	Thought-stopping
	Thought-shifting
	Impulse-charting
Arousal-Reduction Methods	Scheduled overmasturbation
	Masturbatory reconditioning
	Aversion therapy
	Spouse monitoring
	Environmental manipulation
Empathy Training Methods	Victim counselors
	Cognitive restructuring
	Role-playing

progress is being made in the program. The two techniques presented require the use of mechanical instruments to ensure compliance with the program. The techniques are as follows:

Polygraph: This is the standard lie detector used to measure biological responses to deception. The polygraph is used in sex offender supervision for three primary reasons: (1) to break through offender denial of the offense, (2) to assess honesty in sexual history, and (3) to monitor the offender's compliance with probation conditions (Hunt County CSCD, 2004).

Penile Plethysmograph (PPG): This technique uses a cup or band that is placed around the penis while the offender is in a private room. The offender is shown non-pornographic pictures of different categories of stimuli, and auditory stimuli are also provided. A computer records the degree of arousal experienced by the offender (Hunt County CSCD, 2004).

Drug-Administered Techniques

Chemical Castration: With chemical castration, sex offenders are injected with drugs (most commonly Depo-Provera) to reduce the amount of testosterone in their body. This achieves the sex-drive reduction of surgical castration but does not require the controversial surgery. Some side effects include fatigue, weight gain, loss of body hair, and depression. Sex offenders typically regard this as the least preferred intervention (Rice et al., 2002).

The use of these drugs has been found to generally work, but only if the offender dutifully maintains the schedule for taking them. Programs can monitor this by having the offender report to a clinic that works with the community supervision agency to receive the injection. Nonetheless, this drug will not be effective for all sex offenders. For instance, sadistic rapists and pedophiles are not necessarily motivated by sex alone. Rather, the infliction of pain is their primary source of arousal. Thus, this treatment would not be effective with this group of offenders.

SUBSTANCE ABUSERS

American culture promotes high consumption of legal and illegal drugs. This high rate of drug use factors into the rate of criminal behavior. To illustrate this fact, consider that in 1999, it was reported that more than 50 percent of adult male arrestees tested positive for at least one drug. In fact, as much as 64 percent of all arrested adult males and 67 percent of all arrested adult females tested positive for the use of drugs. It would appear that marijuana was the drug of choice among most male arrestees, with cocaine being the next-highest choice. With arrested adult females, cocaine, marijuana, and methamphetamines were found to be the most common. The use of multiple drugs was also common, with more than a quarter of the adult male arrestees testing positive for two or more drugs (Bartol, 2002).

With respect to the connection between drug use and criminal activity, there are three broad commonalities that can be stated. First, drug abusers are more likely to commit crime than non–drug abusers; second, many arrestees are under the influence while committing crimes; and third, drug use and violence tend to occur together in many reported violent incidents (Hanson, Venturelli, & Fleckenstein, 2002).

Photo 13.2 Mental health interventions are becoming more frequent as community corrections is tasked with supervising mentally unstable offenders. The sign in this photo refers to a local mental health facility that routinely works with local courts and state facilities.

Other demographics on drug abusers are not always easy to determine. Of those that exist, most are based on either arrests or admissions into detox or treatment programs. One such variable is age. The age of the drug offender often shapes the dynamics of the person's drug abuse, including the offender's drug of choice. For children under the age of 12, experimentation with drugs is found with those who are neglected, abused, or isolated, as well as those with undiagnosed behavioral or learning disorders. The abuse of inhalants and vapors from glues, paints, and solvents is of particular concern at this age (Myers & Salt, 2000). For adolescents, the individual risk factors for substance abuse are compounded by the confluence of developmental conflict and demands that occur during adolescence, as well as a number of other risk factors for general delinquency that may covary with the substance abuse risk factors. For middle-aged and elderly drug offenders, issues surrounding body image, loss of friends and family, and other normal life span losses may be pertinent. Further, elderly offenders may not necessarily have drug abuse problems with illegal drugs but are more likely to present with dependencies on prescription drugs that have resulted in usage levels that violate federal drug laws (Myers & Salt, 2000).

The gender of the drug offender is also an important consideration. When assessing female drug offenders, it is particularly important to explore relationships with significant others, support systems, and issues related to domestic abuse and prior childhood sexual abuse. Female drug abusers are prone to being involved with a male drug-abusing spouse or boyfriend. They tend to stay with their addicted partners, and the most important reason for their use and increase in use is the intimate relationship to which they belong (Myers & Salt, 2000). This is a particularly relevant issue when one considers that female offenders tend to become involved in crime with a romantic partner who is typically the primary active criminal.

Considerable research demonstrates that some social, racial, or cultural groups have *drugs of choice* in their drug-using habits. A **drug of choice** is a one that is consistently used with greater frequency than other types of drugs by a certain identifiable demographic group. For instance, crack cocaine is typically considered a drug of choice among the urban poor African American underclass, whereas heroin is more often associated with Latino Americans. Perhaps equally intriguing is the fact that the majority of drug offenders using methamphetamine or ecstasy tend to be Caucasian Americans who are most often of middle-class status (Hanson et al., 2002). Likewise, Latino American women (Latinas) are more likely than Latino American men (Latinos) to be shamed within their own cultures for substance abuse. Also, while African American males do not seem to differ from other ethnic groups in their symptoms of drug abuse, during the 1980s, black males convicted of drug offenses as a group experienced the largest increase in incarceration rates (Van Voorhis et al., 2000). Figures 13.1 through 13.3 illustrate racial group use of crack cocaine, methamphetamine, and powder cocaine, respectively.

FIGURE 13.1 Crack Cocaine Use by Racial Group

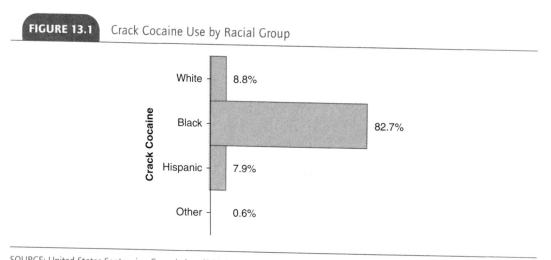

SOURCE: United States Sentencing Commission. (2007). *2007 sourcebook of federal sentencing statistics.* Washington, DC: Author.

FIGURE 13.2 Methamphetamine Use by Racial Group

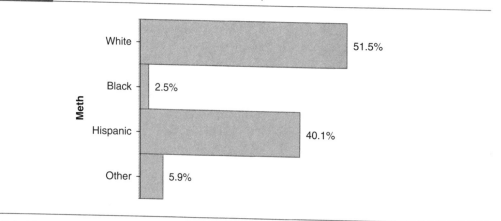

SOURCE: United States Sentencing Commission. (2007). *2007 sourcebook of federal sentencing statistics.* Washington, DC: Author.

FIGURE 13.3   Powder Cocaine Use by Racial Group

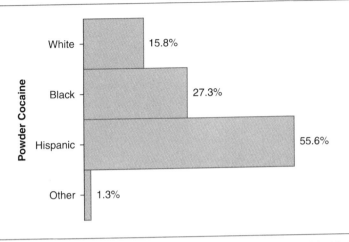

SOURCE: United States Sentencing Commission. (2007). *2007 sourcebook of federal sentencing statistics.* Washington, DC: Author.

Regardless of public concern over hard drugs, it is the use of alcohol that is the most problematic for society. In fact, alcohol is responsible for more deaths and violence than all of the other drugs combined (Bartol, 2002; Hanson et al., 2002). Roughly one-third of all offenders who commit a violent crime were drinking at the time of the offense, and many were highly intoxicated (Bartol, 2002). Despite the fact that alcohol is so debilitating and that alcohol is the most common drug to be associated with violent crime, there is still widespread cultural support for the continued social use of alcohol (Hanson et al., 2002). This makes the screening and assessment of such use all the more difficult.

Screening and Placement Criteria for Treatment Programs

Every form of treatment program involves some sort of screening. According to Myers and Salt (2000), screening serves two major purposes:

1. It attests to the presence of a condition that may go unrecognized if not detected.

2. It provides data to help decide whether a client is appropriate for a specific treatment program and vice versa.

In the first use of screening, social, health, and criminal justice workers determine if there are sufficient grounds for referral of a client to a particular drug/alcohol treatment program. This screening is very important because the earlier that the intervention takes place, the better the prognosis for the client. Obviously, the likelihood of reform is much better when treating a drug experimenter (as described previously) than when treating a compulsive user. The second use of screening is to determine client appropriateness for a given treatment modality. Keep in mind that the decision regarding placement may not only consider the client's individual characteristics but also take into account the ability of a given agency to provide these services (e.g., fiscal constraints may be a factor despite the fact that the treatment program may be ideal for the client). In either case, it is this use of screening that provides the placement criteria for drug offenders in the criminal justice system.

Placement criteria are vital when processing drug offenders. The initial placement is important for both public safety and treatment-oriented concerns. When deciding upon placement criteria, a match must be made between the severity of the addiction and the level of care needed, ranging from medical inpatient care, to nonmedical inpatient care, to intensive outpatient care, to outpatient care (Hanson et al., 2002). Further, also matching the client's profile to a treatment modality is more likely to achieve lasting success, translating to enhanced program effectiveness. For example, a client with attention-deficit/hyperactivity disorder might be unsuited for the regimentation of a therapeutic community. Likewise, a person with low self-esteem, insecurities, and a fragile sense of self-worth would not be appropriate for a highly confrontational style of intervention.

Substance Abuse Treatment Programs

The primary modality of treatment implemented in most jails is chemical detoxification. **Detoxification** is designed for persons dependent on narcotic drugs (e.g., heroin, opium) and is typically found in inpatient settings with programs that last for 7 to 21 days. The rationale for using detoxification as a treatment approach is grounded in two basic principles. The first is a conception of "addiction" as drug craving accompanied by physical dependence that motivates continued usage, resulting in a tolerance to the drug's effects, and a syndrome of identifiable physical and psychological symptoms when the drug is abruptly withdrawn. The second is that the negative aspects of the abstinence syndrome discourage many addicts from attempting withdrawal, which makes them more likely to continue using drugs (Hanson et al., 2002; Myers & Salt, 2000). The main objective of chemical detoxification is the elimination of physiological dependence through a medically supervised procedure.

While many detoxification programs address only the addict's physical dependence, some provide individual or group counseling in an attempt to address the problems associated with drug abuse. Many detoxification programs use medical drugs to ease the process of overcoming the physical symptoms of dependence that make detoxification so painful for the addicted substance abuser. For drug offenders in jails or prisons, the mechanism of detoxification varies by the client's major drug of addiction. For opiate users, methadone or clonidine is preferred. For cocaine users, desipramine has been used to ease the withdrawal symptoms. Almost all narcotic addicts and many cocaine users have been in a chemical detoxification program at least once (Inciardi, 1999a). However, studies show that in the absence of supportive psychotherapeutic services and community follow-up care, nearly all are certain to suffer from relapse (Ashford, Sales, & Reid, 2002).

In all detoxification programs, success depends upon the addict following established protocols for drug administration and withdrawal. In a recent assessment of research literature on the effectiveness of detoxification, there appear to be promising rates of program completion (Ashford et al., 2002). Yet many clinicians note that mere detoxification from a substance is not drug abuse "treatment" and does not help people stay off drugs. It in no way ensures that relapse will not occur, and thus it is important for any program to provide much more than a simple detoxification process. In essence, detoxification should be viewed as an initial step, after the intake, of a comprehensive treatment process.

The Therapeutic Community

After the detoxification phase of treatment, the residential therapeutic community is the next full-service form of treatment provided to incarcerated substance abusers. The therapeutic community is a total treatment environment in which the primary clinical staff are typically former substance abusers—"recovering addicts"—who themselves were rehabilitated in therapeutic communities (Inciardi, 1999a; Myers & Salt, 2000). The treatment perspective of the therapeutic community is that drug abuse is a disorder of the whole person—that the problem is the person and not the drug, and that addiction is a symptom and not the essence of the disorder. In this view of recovery, the primary goal is to change the negative patterns of behavior, thinking, and feeling that predispose a person to drug use. The overall goal is a responsible, drug-free lifestyle. Recovery through this form of treatment depends on positive and negative pressures to change. This pressure is brought about through a self-help process in which relationships of mutual responsibility are built. In addition to individual and group counseling, this process has a system of explicit rewards that reinforce the value of earned achievement. In this way, privileges are earned. Therapeutic communities have their own rules and regulations that guide the behavior of residents and the management of their facilities. Their purposes are to maintain the safety and health of the community and to train and teach residents through the use of discipline.

Societal reactions to therapeutic communities have ranged from negative perceptions from the local community to highly supportive views by various governmental programs. Many communities frown upon these types of treatment programs being located in their area due to the perceived threat that members pose and the potential effects on local real estate value fluctuations. Despite this, some organizations have maintained that therapeutic communities hold an irrefutable value to society. For instance, the Ford Foundation Drug Abuse Survey Project has held therapeutic communities in high regard. Further, there are hundreds of treatment programs around the United States that follow the therapeutic community model (Myers & Salt, 2000).

The Use of Drug Courts

Established as a result of court and prison overcrowding, special drug courts have proven popular. In 1989, a special drug court was established by judicial order in Miami, Florida. This high-volume court expanded on traditional drug-defendant diversion programs by offering a year or more of court-run treatment; defendants who complete this option have their criminal cases dismissed. Between 1991 and 1993, Miami influenced officials in more than 20 other jurisdictions to establish drug courts as well (Abadinsky, 2003). Within a decade, drug courts moved from the experimental stage to being recognized as well-established programs. The government now lists over 325 drug courts across 43 states (Neubauer, 2002).

Although they vary widely, common features of drug courts include a nonadversarial approach to integrating substance abuse treatment with criminal justice case processing. The focus is on early identification of eligible substance abusers and prompt placement in treatment, combined with frequent drug testing.

In discussing the objectives of drug courts, Ashford et al. (2002) illuminate eight key objectives:

- Drug courts integrate alcohol and other drug treatment services with justice system case processing.
- Using a nonadversarial approach, prosecution and defense counsel promote public safety while protecting participants' due process rights.
- Eligible participants are identified early and promptly placed in the drug court program.
- Drug courts provide access to a continuum of alcohol, drug, and other related treatment and rehabilitation services.
- Abstinence is monitored by frequent alcohol and other drug testing.
- A coordinated strategy governs drug court responses to participants' compliance.
- Ongoing judicial interaction with each drug court participant is essential.
- Monitoring and evaluation measure the achievement of program goals and gauge effectiveness.

These features are among those that are thought to constitute an "ideal" model of a drug court, though few courts meet these requirements (McNeece et al., 2002). In general, an offender is placed in a drug court program for 9 to 12 months. On successfully completing that program, the offender continues on probation for another year. In some jurisdictions, the offender's criminal record may be expunged if all of the court's conditions for treatment are satisfied (McNeece et al., 2002).

The role of the judge is crucial in a drug court. Judges are free to openly chastise or praise clients for their behavior during the courtroom proceedings. Beyond that, judges may issue court orders requiring that a client attend treatment, submit to urinalysis, seek employment, meet with a probation officer, avoid associations with drug-abusing friends, or meet any other condition that seems appropriate (McNeece et al., 2002). Failure to comply with these judicial determinations may place the offender in contempt of court, put the offender in jail, or cause the offender to be transferred to a regular criminal court. Judges are provided with continuous feedback on the offender's performance by the other drug court participants. Because of this, there is little room for the offender to evade accountability within the program.

Substance Abusers on Community Supervision

The main method of monitoring offenders who have been released to the community is probation. With regular probation, an offender lives at home and receives periodic monitoring. Many offenders with substance abuse problems are sentenced to intensive supervision probation (ISP), a more restrictive type of probation (discussed in Chapter 11). ISP requires that the offender and probation officer keep in close contact, which generally includes random home visits to ensure the offender is meeting the minimum criteria of the program.

In addition, drug offenders on probation may be required to submit to drug screens to ensure compliance with treatment. Court and corrections officials will generally want to know if the offender is complying with treatment and remaining abstinent from drugs. In programs in which access to treatment may be limited by available space or funding, those who do not comply may be discharged from treatment. Those who do not successfully complete treatment and continue to have positive drug screens may be sent back to court for further sentencing. While drug testing does appear to serve a useful purpose in monitoring offenders with substance abuse problems, this testing alone is not sufficient to keep offenders from using drugs and reoffending. The best approach may be to combine random drug testing with forms of rehabilitative drug treatment to address the addiction and minimize the likelihood that the individual will engage in future criminal behavior.

Drug offenders on probation are placed in what are termed "outpatient" treatment programs, which usually include individual and group therapy, and some programs offer family therapy and relapse prevention support. An increasing number of drug-free outpatient treatment programs are including case management services as an adjunct to counseling. The basic case management approach is to assist clients in obtaining needed services in a timely and coordinated manner. The key components of the approach are assessing, planning, linking, monitoring, and advocating for clients within the existing nexus of treatment and social services.

Evaluating the effectiveness of drug-free outpatient treatment is difficult because programs vary widely, from drop-in "talk" centers to highly structured arrangements that offer counseling or psychotherapy. Some likewise include a strong "faith-based" element to their intervention that represents a blend between therapy and religious instruction. A number of studies have found that outpatient treatment has been moderately successful in reducing daily drug use and criminal activity. However, the approach appears to be inappropriate for the most troubled and the antisocial users.

The number of rigorously designed studies of corrections-based "outpatient" programs is quite small. One of the few examples involves a relatively well-funded and -designed program know as "Passages"—an 8 hours per day, 5 days per week, 12-week nonresidential program for women incarcerated in the Wisconsin correctional system. Although the treatment staff and correctional administrators agreed that the program improved clients' self-esteem, subsequent reduced drug use and criminal activity was not seen to occur (Ashford et al., 2002).

Self-Help Groups

Self-help groups, the vast majority of them 12-step programs, are composed of individuals who meet regularly to stabilize and facilitate their recovery from substance abuse. The best known is Alcoholics Anonymous (AA), in which sobriety is based on fellowship and adhering to the 12 steps of recovery (Hanson et al., 2002; Inciardi, 1999a; Myers & Salt, 2000). The 12 steps stress faith, confession of wrongdoing, and passivity in the hands of a "higher power." These steps are studied and learned one at a time, as they move group members from a statement of powerlessness over drugs and alcohol to a resolution that they will carry the message of help to others and will practice the AA principles in all affairs. In addition to AA, other popular self-help 12-step groups are Narcotics Anonymous, Cocaine Anonymous, and Drugs Anonymous. All these organizations operate as stand-alone fellowship programs but are also used as adjuncts to other modalities. Although few evaluation studies of self-help groups have been carried out, the weight of clinical and observational data suggest that they are crucial to recovery.

Research has failed to demonstrate that anonymous fellowship meetings by themselves are effective with heavy drug users. According to Inciardi (1999a), there are few known evaluations of prison-based self-help programs, for a variety of reasons: Prison administrators tend to prefer other types of programs, the model contains variables that are extremely difficult to operationalize and measure, members and leaders often view scientific studies of their groups as intrusive threats to anonymity and therapeutic processes, and evaluation research funding is more often available for innovative programming than for such well-established services. Nonetheless, self-help programs are widely used in community correctional agencies. There is a widely held belief that they work. The meetings are organized and run by volunteers at no cost to the prison authorities, and the meetings appear to help inmates make the transition from correctional to community-based settings (Inciardi, 1999a).

The success of self-help programs in general, and AA in particular, may be explained by their comprehensive network, which supports abstinence and recovery; frequent attendance at AA meetings where role modeling, confession, sharing, and support take place; and participation in the member network between meetings, including obtaining and relying on a senior member or sponsor. Al-Anon, a fellowship for relatives and significant others of alcoholics, was founded in 1951, although it did not take off as a movement until the 1960s. Narcotics Anonymous (NA), the third of the three major 12-step fellowships, was founded in 1953. It was relatively small throughout the 1950s and 1960s but obtained a great deal of popularity during the 1970s and 1980s. The atmosphere of NA meetings is more emotional than AA, and this is likely due to the fact than many members attended drug treatment programs that emphasize interpersonal interaction in group sessions (Myers & Salt, 2000).

Cullen and Agnew (2006) note that research has suggested that genetic factors and biological harms of a nongenetic nature, such as head injuries, may increase the likelihood that individuals will develop traits that make them more prone to criminal activity. Among these are traits such as impulsivity or sensation-seeking behaviors. David Rowe (2002) argues that physiological factors account for a substantial amount of criminal activity due to the effects of genetics or injury to various segments of the central nervous system.

In particular, Rowe has focused on the chemical messengers, called neurotransmitters, that exist within our nervous systems and transmit electronic signals between the billions of neurons in our brain. The neurotransmitters are many, but serotonin and dopamine are particularly important because they affect our mood and emotional stability, and because even slight changes in the amount of each in our bloodstream can lead to different levels of emotional response or behavior. Further, Rowe (2002) and others have examined critical hormones such as testosterone that help to regulate various impulses such as our sex drive and reaction to stressors that are presented.

This research is not just important from a mental health perspective; it also ties in with many of the substance abuse issues presented in this chapter. Indeed, most illicit drugs impact our serotonin and dopamine levels of release. In fact, it is this release of neurotransmitters that actually gives people their sense of "high" or release when using the substance. This provides direct reinforcement to the cerebral areas that are affected. Moreover, many drug users experience additional social reinforcers due to social contact with other drug users and acceptance within that crowd.

Though it may seem far-fetched, substantial research has demonstrated a connection between nervous system functioning and criminal activity (Bartol, 2002). This is true for both juvenile and adult offenders as well as for both nonviolent and violent offenders. Numerous cases exist where offenders were found to have various forms of imbalance in their neurochemistry. Andrea Yates, a female offender who drowned her own children during a serious bout of postpartum depression, is one classic example. Others abound throughout the literature, particularly in regard to the study of the classic "psychopath" whose central nervous system does not process anxiety-related impulses, making the person less able to acquire empathy for his or her victims. Indeed, brain imaging with MRI's and PET scans has pinpointed specific biological deficits involved in criminal dispositions among a variety of offender types; these deficits appear to be in the frontal cortex area of the brain, an area that regulates higher-order functioning.

Given the confluence of these physiological factors—mental illness, substance abuse, and criminal activity—the *individual trait theories* are important to consider. These theories are grounded in medical science and study specific physiological effects, producing results that are much more valid and reliable than the survey-based research attributed to most social-based theories. In effect, these theories seem to point toward inherent risk factors that are possessed by the person before any social learning takes place. Naturally, these theories hold serious implications for society and also impact how we might assess offenders in the future.

SOURCES: Cullen, F. T., & Agnew, R. (2006). *Criminological theory: Past to present* (3rd ed.). Los Angeles: Roxbury; Rowe, D. (2002). *Biology and crime.* Los Angeles: Roxbury.

MENTALLY ILL OFFENDERS

There are special challenges involved with addressing mental disorders within the offender population. Often the problems associated with mentally disordered offenders have less to do with their actual threat to society and more to do with the bizarre nature of their behavior. Most mentally ill people do not commit crimes, especially when intent is considered. However, many mentally ill people may act strangely by public standards or may act in a manner that would be considered "irresponsible" from a common citizen's standpoint.

Bartol (2002) notes that the media have portrayed mentally ill people as not only criminal, but outright violent. This is often the case on television and in newspapers and magazines. Most violent crime (particularly murder), however, is impulsive and committed by non–mentally disordered persons who are simply stressed to the point of using violence among their repertoire of behavioral responses (Bartol, 2002).

Mental disorders are manifested in a variety of behaviors, ranging in severity from what many might refer to as "crazy behavior" to conduct that is simply unusual. Crazy behavior is defined as that which is obviously strange and cannot be logically explained (Bartol, 2002). The concept of mental disorder includes behaviors that are bizarre, dramatic, harmful, or mildly unusual, and the classifications for individuals exhibiting these behaviors can be found in the *Diagnostic and Statistical Manual of Mental Disorders IV—Text Revision (DSM-IV-TR)*. For the purposes of this chapter, **mental illness** is defined as any diagnosed disorder contained within the *DSM-IV-TR*, as published by the American Psychiatric Association. Mental illness causes severe disturbances in thought, emotions, and ability to cope with the demands of daily life. Like physiological forms of illness, mental illness can be acute, chronic, or under control and in remission.

Common Types of Mental Disorders in the Offender Population

Specific types of disorders have been found to be more problematic than others among the offender population. Among these are the mood disorders, schizophrenic disorders, and personality disorders. A backdrop to these disorders is the reality that a high number of offenders also have addiction or substance abuse disorders that are comorbid with the primary diagnosis (Sacks, Sacks, & Stommel, 2003). This is commonly referred to as a "dual diagnosis" within the treatment community, denoting the fact that the offender has two or more disorders. In most cases, when an offender is said to have a **dual diagnosis,** the clinician is referring to a primary disorder accompanied by a substance abuse–related disorder. The frequency of the dual diagnosis among the offending population is the reason for the eventual development of mental health courts.

Mood Disorders

Mood disorders are those such as major depressive disorder, bipolar disorder, and dysthymic disorder. Major depressive disorder is characterized by one or more major depressive episodes (i.e., at least 2 weeks of depressed mood or loss of interest accompanied by at least four additional symptoms of depression). Major depressive disorder is the most common mood disorder associated with the offender population. Bipolar disorder is characterized by one or more manic episodes, which are usually accompanied by major depressive episodes. The individual afflicted with bipolar disorder will have mood swings that go back and forth between manic and depressive states. Dysthymic disorder is characterized by at least 2 years of depressed mood for more days than not, accompanied by additional depressive symptoms that do not meet the criteria for a major depressive disorder.

According to the *DSM-IV-TR*, the degree of impairment associated with **major depressive disorder** varies, but even in mild cases, there must be either clinically significant distress or some interference in social, occupational, or other important areas of functioning. The afflicted person will likely have decreased energy, tiredness, and fatigue without physical exertion. Even the smallest tasks may seem to require substantial effort. Further, these individuals often have a sense of worthlessness or guilt that may include unrealistic negative evaluations of their worth or guilty preoccupations or ruminations over minor past failings. Such individuals often misinterpret neutral or trivial day-to-day events as evidence of personal defects and have an exaggerated sense of responsibility for untoward events (*DSM-IV-TR*, p. 350). The

National Institute of Mental Health (2002) notes that a person experiencing major depression is likely to present with the following:

- Persistent sad, anxious, or "empty" mood
- Feelings of hopelessness, pessimism
- Feelings of guilt, worthlessness, helplessness
- Loss of interest or pleasure in hobbies and activities that were once enjoyed, including sex
- Decreased energy, fatigue, a sense of being "slowed down"
- Difficulty concentrating, remembering, making decisions
- Insomnia, early-morning awakening, or oversleeping
- Appetite and/or weight loss or overeating and weight gain
- Thoughts of death or suicide; suicide attempts
- Restlessness, irritability
- Persistent physical symptoms that do not respond to treatment, such as headaches, digestive disorders, and chronic pain

In those persons presenting with bipolar depression, manic symptoms will also typically occur, alternating with depressive symptoms. The manic symptoms listed below are taken from the National Institute of Mental Health (2002):

- Abnormal or excessive elation
- Unusual irritability
- Decreased need for sleep
- Grandiose notions
- Increased talking
- Racing thoughts
- Increased sexual desire
- Markedly increased energy
- Poor judgment
- Inappropriate social behavior

Schizophrenic Disorders

According to the *DSM-IV-TR,* **schizophrenic disorders** have five characteristic symptoms, and at least two must be present before the diagnosis can be made. These symptoms are as follows: (1) delusions, (2) hallucinations, (3) disorganized speech, (4) grossly disorganized behavior, and (5) inappropriate affect. Further, the social, self-care, or occupational life of the individual must show signs of being well below the level achieved prior to the onset of the illness. Last, these symptoms must have existed for 6 months or longer.

Personality Disorders

Personality disorders are characterized by an enduring pattern of inner experience and behavior that deviates markedly from the expectations of the individual's culture, is pervasive and inflexible, has an onset in adolescence or early adulthood, is stable over time, and leads to distress or impairment (American Psychiatric Association, 2000). The focus of this section will be on specific personality disorders that are most frequently seen as problematic within the offender population. Descriptions of these disorders follow, with the exception of antisocial personality disorder. This disorder is so problematic and is encountered so frequently among the offender population that an entire section is devoted to it and its link with violent actions by offenders.

The first personality disorder we will discuss, **borderline personality disorder,** manifests in a pervasive pattern of instability of interpersonal relationships, self-image, and affects, as well as a marked impulsivity beginning by early adulthood and present in a variety of contexts as indicated by five (or more) of the following:

- Frantic efforts to avoid real or imagined abandonment
- A pattern of unstable and intense interpersonal relationships characterized by alternating between extremes of idealization and devaluation
- Identity disturbance: markedly and persistently unstable self-image or sense of self
- Impulsivity in at least two areas that are potentially self-damaging (e.g., spending, sex, substance abuse, reckless driving, binge eating)
- Recurrent suicidal behavior, gestures, or threats, or self-mutilating behavior.
- Affective instability due to a marked reactivity of mood
- Chronic feelings of emptiness
- Inappropriate, intense anger or difficulty controlling anger
- Transient, stress-related paranoid ideation or severe dissociative symptoms

Histrionic personality disorder is a pervasive pattern of excessive emotionality and attention seeking, beginning by early adulthood and present in a variety of contexts, as indicated by five or more of the following:

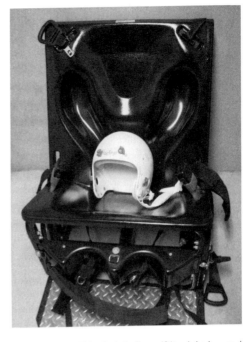

Photo 13.3 This chair looks as if it might be used for punishment, but, in reality, it is used in some jails to safeguard a detainee from harming him- or herself. The risk of suicide for arrested offenders on drugs is high during the first 48 hours. Equipment such as this actually is intended to save the life of the offender.

- Is uncomfortable in situations in which he or she is not the center of attention
- Interaction with others often characterized by inappropriate sexually seductive or provocative behavior
- Displays rapidly shifting and shallow expression of emotions
- Consistently uses physical appearance to draw attention to self
- Has a style of speech that is overly dramatic and attention-getting, with a corresponding lack of detail
- Shows self-dramatization, theatricality, and exaggerated expression of emotion
- Is suggestible, i.e., easily influenced by others or circumstances
- Considers relationships to be more intimate than they actually are

Among the offending population, this disorder is seen among female offenders most frequently. This is not surprising because female offenders often engage in criminality while under the guidance or due to the influence of a male partner. Because of the "codependent" nature of their relationships and the often-noted low self-esteem found among female offenders, it appears that this disorder develops from the need to have attention. Likewise, as noted in the list above, these offenders are easily suggestible. This works well for their male counterparts such as drug runners using the female to carry drugs, the pimp involving the female offender in prostitution, or the male offender who implicates the female by asking her to provide alibis and other peripheral support.

Narcissistic personality disorder is characterized by a pervasive pattern of grandiosity (in fantasy or behavior), need for admiration, and lack of empathy, beginning by early adulthood and present in a variety of contexts, as indicated by five (or more) of the following:

- Has a grandiose sense of self-importance (e.g., exaggerates achievements and talents or expects to be recognized as superior without commensurate achievements)
- Is preoccupied with fantasies of unlimited success, power, brilliance, beauty, or ideal love
- Believes that he or she is "special" and unique and can only be understood by, or should only associate with, other special or high-status persons or institutions
- Requires excessive admiration
- Has a sense of entitlement, i.e., unreasonable expectations of especially favorable treatment or automatic compliance with his or her expectations
- Is interpersonally exploitative, i.e., takes advantage of others to achieve his or her own ends
- Lacks empathy: is unwilling to recognize or identify with the feelings and needs of others
- Is often envious of others or believes that others are envious of him or her
- Shows arrogant, haughty behaviors or attitudes

Prevalence rates for this disorder within the clinical population range from 2 to 16 percent. Since most offenders are given clinical screening and are more frequently diagnosed than the general population, the expectation is that the offender population will present with higher percentages of this disorder. Possession of narcissistic personality disorder will result in a person who is likely to be tough-minded, glib, superficial, exploitative, and unempathetic. However, such persons are not likely to have characteristics of impulsivity, aggression, or deceit that are associated with antisocial personality–disordered individuals. The *DSM-IV-TR* notes that vulnerability in self-esteem makes the narcissistic individual very sensitive to "injury" from any form of criticism or defeat. Such responses may not be apparent outwardly, but these individuals are likely to feel humiliated, degraded, hollow, and empty. Reactions may range from disdain to rage, and to defiant counterattack. Violent offenders occasionally present with this disorder and may note that their violence was sparked by a display of insult from the other party. Family violence batterers also have a tendency to present with this disorder.

Anxiety and Stress-Related Disorders

Generalized anxiety disorder is characterized by excessive anxiety and worry (apprehensive expectation), occurring more days than not for at least 6 months, about a number of events or activities. The individual also must report that it is difficult to control the worry to the point that it causes clinically significant distress or impairment in social, occupational, or other areas of functioning. To be diagnosed with this disorder, the anxiety and worry must be associated with three (or more) of the following six symptoms (with at least some symptoms present for more days than not for the past 6 months):

- Restlessness or feeling keyed up or on edge
- Being easily fatigued
- Difficulty concentrating or mind going blank
- Irritability
- Muscle tension
- Sleep disturbance (difficulty falling or staying asleep, or restless unsatisfying sleep)

A number of offenders may present with this disorder, though it may be difficult to determine because many of them will have objectively sound reasons for their anxiety. The hallmark of this disorder is when the individual worries, but there is no specific reason for this worry. This is not necessarily a common disorder among offenders; it tends to present mostly in those who have particularly difficult backgrounds (i.e., abuse) or who have had difficulty adjusting to their experiences within the criminal justice system. This disorder is most prevalent in female offenders because it is more common among females in the general population. In addition, this disorder tends to coexist with mood disorders or with addiction disorders. Often, the addiction disorder may be a direct attempt to medicate the sense of anxiety.

Antisocial Personality Disorder, Psychopathy, and Other Mental Disorders With High Risks of Violence

The offender with **antisocial personality disorder** is the one of most concern to the criminal justice system and to the public at large. This is the offender that is likely to be violently dangerous and is almost certain to reoffend. It is this type of offender that makes it hard to plead mercy and leniency for other offenders presenting with other forms of mental disorder. The essential feature of antisocial personality disorder is a pervasive pattern of disregard for, and violation of, the rights of others that begins in childhood or early adolescence and continues into adulthood. Diagnosis of this disorder occurs if the individual presents with three (or more) of the following symptoms:

- Failure to conform to social norms with respect to lawful behaviors as indicated by repeatedly performing acts that are grounds for arrest
- Deceitfulness, as indicated by repeated lying, use of aliases, or conning others for personal profit or pleasure
- Impulsivity or failure to plan ahead
- Irritability and aggressiveness, as indicated by repeated physical fights or assaults
- Reckless disregard for safety of self or others
- Consistent irresponsibility, as indicated by repeated failure to sustain consistent work behavior or honor financial obligations
- Lack of remorse, as indicated by being indifferent to or rationalizing having hurt, mistreated, or stolen from another

Additional symptoms, as outlined in the *DSM-IV-TR*, include stealing, truancy, and resisting authority, which are typical childhood symptoms. An individual with antisocial personality disorder (ASPD) lacks empathy and tends to be callous, cynical, and contemptuous of the feelings, rights, and sufferings of others (Bartol, 2002). Furthermore persons with ASPD frequently engage in precocious and aggressive sexual behavior, excessive drinking, and the use of illicit drugs. These individuals also seem to lack the ability to maintain lasting and meaningful relationships with family, friends, or intimate partners.

For the most part, persons with ASPD rarely become independent and responsible adults. They spend much of their lives in some form of institutional setting or dependent on family members. It should be noted that this disorder is much more prevalent in males versus females, with base rates in the community being roughly 3 percent for males and 1 percent for females (Gacono, Nieberding, Owen, Rubel, & Bodholdt, 2001). However, it is estimated that up to 30 percent of all males in secure correctional facilities suffer from ASPD, with it being progressively more common as the level of institutional security increases (Gacono et al., 2001).

Mentally Ill Offenders in the Community

Long-term inpatient care or hospitalization of mentally disordered people has largely ceased to occur. As a result, the mentally disordered individual has become more prevalent within society. This trend from hospitalization to community release was first set in motion in 1959 when nearly 559,000 mentally ill patients that were housed in state mental hospitals were progressively released over time due to a shift to "deinstitutionalize" mentally ill persons (National Institute of Corrections, 2004). By the late 1990s, the total number of persons housed in public psychiatric hospitals dropped considerably. This is despite the fact that the United States population (and the mentally ill population as well) has grown considerably since 1959. Thus, more people are mentally ill but fewer and fewer of them are placed in secure facilities. Rather, these individuals are returned to the community. Some mentally ill persons experience difficulty adjusting to life in the community and, as a result, may come into increasing contact with the criminal justice system.

Mental Health Courts

According to Watson, Hanrahan, Luchins, and Lurigio (2001), "the mental health court movement emerged out of recognition of inequities in the experiences of mentally ill offenders and two converging developments in the legal arena: therapeutic jurisprudence and the drug court movement" (p. 3). Since the 1980s, therapeutic jurisprudence has developed into an approach for examining a wide range of legal issues pertaining to mental health and the criminal court process. At heart is the notion that the two systems, those of psychotherapeutic and criminal court services, can work together hand-in-hand to achieve a common interest that is best for both systems, the offender, the victim, and society alike.

In Ohio and Florida, mental health courts have emerged to help local courts handle the growing number of disturbed persons in their criminal justice system. Judges in these two states have specifically noted their desire to have these types of courts, as they find themselves loaded with revolving-door dockets of minor offenders in their courthouses (McNutt, 1999). Butler County, Ohio, and Broward County, Florida, have specific budgets for nonviolent, mentally ill, petty offenders that seem to overwhelm the court docket. In addition to modifications in court processing of the mentally ill, a coordinated police response has been established with specific training in handling mentally ill people in order to improve police response. Prior to this, most police agencies simply jailed the mentally ill individual if he or she presented a community nuisance. The problem for police as well as traditional court systems is that there has not been any specific agency with legal jurisdiction over mentally ill offenders that is adequately suited to address their specific needs. The established mental health courts have stepped in to manage this jurisdiction, and they integrate both therapeutic and criminal justice strategies.

Trial and Sentencing

More specific to the court process is the issue of trial and sentencing. Jurisdictions utilizing either mental health courts or their own hybrid system should ensure that certain factors are taken into account within the court system. Specifically, judges and other parties involved in the court process should be cognizant of the effects that mental illness can have on a person's behavior, particularly when criminal behavior is at issue. Such an understanding should go beyond merely determining competency to stand trial. Other factors should be considered as well. The Sentencing Project (2002) makes note of the following factors and suggestions that should be considered when promoting such awareness among courthouse parties involved in the sentencing process:

1. The defense bar needs training on mental health issues, including the following:
   - Interviewing techniques
   - Use of social worker and staff trained in mental health issues
   - Practice of obtaining records and tracking down discharge summaries or physicians' evaluations for a client with a mental health history
   - Staff that have familiarity with treatment issues, especially medications and their various impacts

2. Mentally ill individuals should be given timely access to counsel, preferably with attorneys who have experience in working with individuals with mental illnesses.

3. Judges must have information on offenders' mental health status available to them so that they can make a determination regarding the defendant's competence to stand trial, whether medication is needed in order to achieve competency, and the viability of developing specific plans to address offenders' mental health needs and establish referral mechanisms.

4. State criminal codes should authorize or permit judges to divert nonviolent offenders with mental illness away from incarceration to appropriate treatment, including granting authority for judges to defer entries of judgment pending completion of treatment programs and to dismiss charges and expunge records of individuals who successfully complete treatment programs (p. 19).

Probation and Parole

Services for mentally ill probationers can be most effective when they are provided through special programs staffed by officers with specialized training and experience (The Sentencing Project, 2002). For probation services to be successful with the mentally ill, they must address the broad range of offenders' needs and work in collaboration with other agencies and services to ensure that these needs are met. Specifically, community service agencies should

- Increase access to mental health professionals.
- Provide specialized cross-training to parole and probation officers pertaining to characteristics of mental illness, the effects that these illnesses have on daily functioning, and the goals of treatment programs. Also, core functions of the therapeutic process such as crisis intervention, screening, counseling, discharge planning, and community follow-up in case management are very helpful.
- Fully understand the requirements of confidentiality statutes and mental health law.
- Ensure increased communication among community supervision and other provider agencies. This should result in a collaborative effort between the therapist/treatment facilitator and the client's probation officer. They should know each other on a "first name" basis.
- Provide training for culturally competent community corrections services.
- Ensure that caseloads for individual probation officers are reasonable.

The last recommendation is critical, as this is one of the primary complaints of individual probation officers. Lurigio (1996) notes that probation officers struggling with large caseloads are likely to avoid mentally disordered probationers because of their problematic or bizarre behavior. Further, officers often do not feel equipped to address the problems associated with emotional instability. Because of this, specialization among probation and parole officers is becoming a common strategy for handling probationers and parolees with particular needs or elevated risk for continued criminality (Lurigio, 1996).

CONCLUSION

In this chapter, we have examined various types of sex offenses and their typologies. The method of perpetration is important, as this can tell us a great deal about the offender and his or her motivation. We also noted important distinctions and characteristics between those offenders who choose adults as their victims and those who choose children. Research shows that sex offenders have a higher recidivism rate when compared with other types of offenders, but this rate has not been determined to be high enough to preclude their ultimate release into the community. Some sex offenders (those with sadistic sexual disorders or psychopathic characteristics) are perhaps untreatable, and it is recommended that they be incarcerated indefinitely. Finally, methods of supervision in the community need to be collaborative in nature to ensure compliance from these offenders.

Substance abuse offenders require numerous special services if the addiction is to be successfully overcome. Regardless of personal or professional viewpoints on treatment efficacy, it is clear that alcohol and drugs are strongly correlated with other criminal behavior. This correlation is so common that it could well be argued that substance abuse offenders are in fact not "special" needs offenders but are instead "common" needs offenders. Thus, any program that overlooks drugs or alcohol is ignoring a primary component behind most offenders' repertoire of behaviors. Substance abuse programs have been shown to work for both court-mandated and voluntary clients.

Regarding mentally ill offenders, it should be clear that they are somewhat misunderstood by the general public, particularly when the effects of the media on public perception are considered. For the most part, offenders who are mentally ill either exhibit bizarre behaviors (if they have some form of psychosis) or present with extremes in mood or personality development. Though this is the case, a select group of offenders with antisocial personality disorder do pose an elevated risk to society, and they are particularly resistant to treatment. With all mentally ill offenders, a secondary problem with substance abuse exacerbates the illness, and it is this dual diagnosis that creates the truly dangerous mentally ill offender.

The ability to distinguish between those mentally ill offenders who are violent and dangerous and those who are simple nuisances and not dangerous is critical, both for public safety and when planning methods of intervention within the institution and the community. Various jurisdictions around the United States are becoming more aware of this need within the criminal justice and mental health systems and are thus retailoring various criminal justice responses to better address the specialized needs of the mentally ill offender. It becomes clear that these offenders have a multiplicity of problems and that a "one size fits all" approach to mental illness is not appropriate for treatment, nor is it effective for public safety.

Key Terms

Anger retaliation rapist	Containment approach	Impulse-charting
Antisocial personality disorder	Detoxification	Major depressive disorder
Aversion therapy	Drug of choice	Masturbatory reconditioning
Borderline personality disorder	Dual diagnosis	Mental illness
Chemical castration	Environmental manipulation	Mood disorders
Cognitive restructuring	Generalized anxiety disorder	Narcissistic personality disorder
Community supervision officer	Histrionic personality disorder	Opportunistic rapist

Pedophilia

Penile plethysmograph (PPG)

Personality disorders

Polygraph

Polygraph examiner

Power assertive rapist

Power reassurance rapist

Role-playing

Sadistic rapist

Scheduled overmasturbation

Schizophrenic disorders

Self-help groups

Sex offender therapist

Sexual assault

Sexual gratification rapist

Spouse monitoring

Thought-shifting

Thought-stopping

Victim counselors

"What Would You Do?" Exercise

You are a probation officer, and you have a client name Suzie who comes to your office for routine probation contact. Suzie is a misdemeanant offender who is in trouble for shoplifting. She is 23 and is quite attractive. Her probation ends in 2 months, and she has made it clear that she would like to date you once she is finished with her probation.

One night, while out at the grocery store, you find yourself turning the aisle and your cart hits another person's cart. You look up to see that it is none other than Suzie, apparently shopping at the same store and at the same time. You give her an apology and begin to go the other way when she stops you and says, "Look, I know that you are following me, and that's okay," at which point she walks up very close to you and says, "I remember all of those sexual remarks that you made a few months ago. That's why I love going to your office."

You have no idea what she is talking about because sexual innuendo has never been exchanged between the two of you. Suzie has been sexually suggestive at times, but you have never responded. However, now she is contending that you have made overtures toward her and she adds, "I know that you have been hanging out near my house, watching me through the window," followed with, "I promise that I will not tell anyone, if you just agree to come over when my probation is finished. If not, I am going to tell everyone what a lecherous man you are."

It is clear that Suzie is making up her allegations, but there is no way to disprove her. You can go to your supervisor about this, but you know that your supervisor is a very skeptical person and the agency will want to investigate this situation. You know that going to Suzie's house is out of the question, but you are not sure how to handle this.

What would you do?

Applied Exercise

Read the case vignette below and then explain how you would design a "mini" treatment plan for the offender. This assignment will require that you complete outside research on your own. In addition, you must specifically explain the types of treatment orientations you might use with this offender, and you should also provide a clear and well-designed supervision strategy for this client. Each response to the questions below must be correct and balanced in approach (consisting of realistic possibilities), with anywhere from 300 to 750 words of content being allowed per application.

Students should complete this application exercise as a mini paper that explains the scenario and then addresses each question. Total word count: 1,000 to 2,200 words.

Applied Exercise Case Vignette

Nathan is a 39-year-old Caucasian male. He lives alone in his rented home and is on intensive supervision probation.

Nathan is a pedophile and the whole neighborhood knows it. Nathan is also divorced; his previous wife left him after discovering that he had been molesting her 7-year-old son, Mark, for nearly 2 years. Prior to this, Nathan had been suspected of inappropriate relationships with other children when he was a substitute teacher at a local elementary school. Nathan's previous wife did not know of the dropped allegations that had been made against him, nor did she know that he had lived with another woman, Sherry, who had two kids and suspected that Nathan was not to be trusted around her children.

Nathan is depressed because he really did care for Mark and did not want to hurt him. He thought Mark was special and believed he was very attentive to Mark's needs. In addition, Nathan explains to you that "deep down inside, I know Mark cared about me, too. I just do not know why he would tell his mom otherwise. I feel so betrayed!"

Nathan disclosed this during your last session with him. Instead of expressing remorse, he seems to be sorrowful over his loss of the "relationship" with Mark. Indeed, Nathan feigns commitment to treatment, but sometimes his comments indicate that he saw his molestation as consensual activity with Mark.

When Nathan was ultimately arrested, he was found with excessive amounts of pornography, but none of it included children as subjects. Further, his two prior adult female partners both noted that Nathan was capable of normal sexual activity, but would go through periods of seeming "distracted" and uninterested in a normal sexual routine. This might last for weeks.

You can tell that Nathan genuinely does not desire to physically harm children, but his overpowering attraction to children is obvious. What is more, he acts as if he *genuinely* cared about these children as if they were some legitimate adult love interest. Further, he does not seem to have any deep-seated issues with adult women, and in fact, he is capable of at least faking his relationships with women, though Sherry did note that Nathan always seemed a bit disinterested in their adult relationship and frequently found ways to involve the kids as a topic in their private discussions. As his probation officer, you can tell that Nathan is not really interested in treatment, but he goes along with it.

Nathan currently has a night job stocking freight at a local warehouse. He has numerous restrictions on his movement. His prognosis does not seem great, and he seems to be keeping to himself. He has no real friends, and you notice that he seems to spend an exorbitant amount of time at home alone.

Questions for the Student

1. What might be effective and appropriate supervision techniques or strategies for this type of offender?

2. What are likely to be some effective treatment options for Nathan?

3. Incorporate case management practices from Chapter 8 and outside research into a treatment plan for Nathan. Be sure to explain why and how you incorporate this information into your treatment plan.

Diversity Issues and Cultural Competence in a Changing Era

INTRODUCTION

Culture, diversity, ethnicity, and race are interconnected concepts that are commonly found within the criminal justice literature. However, these terms tend to be elusive in nature because they are similar in focus but do not always address the same specific point of interest. Indeed, there is even a lack of consensus among authors in the criminal justice fields in terms of the concepts' definitions and their respective relationships to one another. Further, there are occasional circumstances where authors may use the term *ethnicity/race* when it is clear that only one or the other term should apply. Harper and McFadden (2003) note quite correctly that persons who have a specific culture of origin tend to have an ethnic identity and, in a broader, more sociopolitical sense, a racial identity that may be separate from their sense of culture. In addition, Harper makes a far-reaching point in noting the discrepancy in identity when persons define ethnic or racial identity for themselves versus when others define it for them, based on the law or perception of their appearance or location of origin.

Before going further, it is important to distinguish between the two terms *race* and *ethnicity*. First, race is a concept that is used to describe a social category. Often different cultures will classify individuals into racial groups based on certain characteristics that have significant social meaning. However, as Clear, Cole, and Reisig (2006) note, **race** is traditionally considered "a biological concept used to distinguish groups of people by their skin color and other physical features" (p. 555). While some authors disagree with the concept of biological factors constituting race, this is not of consequence to the current definition since social characteristics of a person are likely to be matters of ethnicity, culture, or even personal differences between people individually. The social meanings attached to certain characteristics are important because these meanings, when based on characteristics of the individual, are often the basis for disparity and discrimination within society. Thus, race has its grounding in the physiological differences that can be observed as well as the perceptions that others have of those physiological differences. The term **ethnicity,** on the other hand, refers to a "concept used to distinguish people according to their cultural characteristics—language, religion, and group tradition" (Clear et al., 2006, p. 553). Further, ethnicity includes a common heritage shared by a particular group; it is a concept used to describe a person's origin of birth or descent (Zenner, 1996).

It is important to clearly distinguish between race and ethnicity. Further, it is essential to understand that one is not necessarily inclusive of the other. For instance, consider two persons, one from Nigeria and the other from Jamaica. While both are of African racial origins, their *ethnic* backgrounds are completely different. Likewise, consider two persons, one from China and the other from Japan. While both are of Asian origin, their ethnic backgrounds are quite different, and both ethnicities have histories of hostility with one another. Thus, even though they are located in the same area of the world, and even though they are both of Asian racial origin, their ethnic groups have had plenty of animosity toward one another. Consider again two people, one from Finland and the other from Italy. Both may indeed be Caucasian in racial origin, but their ethnic characteristics are obviously quite different.

Even with the previous examples being given, there is still blurring that takes place in regard to the classification of racial orientations. For instance, one might wonder how biracial persons (those whose parents each come from a different racial group, such as one being African in descent and the other being Native American) might be classified. Likewise, some persons of African descent have physical features that are often attributed to areas of African origin while others do not. Even more confusing for some is the fact that Hispanic (or Latino) persons may have very similar features to Native Americans, particularly due to intermarriage between the two groups over centuries. Likewise, some persons of Middle Eastern descent may appear similar to persons of Hispanic origin or Native American origin.

The 2000 United States Census defined racial groups in a manner that broke precedent with previous governmental definitions. For instance, the term **white** or **Caucasian American** refers to persons whose origins are with any of the original peoples of Europe, the Middle East, or North Africa. The term **black** or **African American** (for this text's purposes) refers to persons having origins in any of the black racial groups from the continent of Africa. The term **Asian** or **Asian American** (for this text's purposes) refers to persons having origins among any of the original peoples of the Far East, Southeast Asia, or the Indian subcontinent. The term **American Indian** or **Native American** (for this text's purposes) refers to people whose origins are with any of the original peoples of North, Central, or South America and who maintain tribal affiliation or attachment. The term **Hispanic** or **Latino American** refers to those persons having origins with any of the original peoples of North, Central, or South America, but who also do not maintain tribal affiliations. Last, the term **Native Hawaiian** or **Other Pacific Islander** (Asian Pacific American, for this text's purposes) refers to a person having origins with any of the original peoples of Hawaii, Guam, Samoa, or other Pacific Islands.

WHY IS DIVERSITY SO IMPORTANT IN COMMUNITY CORRECTIONS?

Because there is a great deal of diversity among the offender population, it is important that criminal justice personnel be well versed on various issues related to race, gender, and other forms of diversity. Among the offender population, minorities are proportionally overrepresented, and this includes both probation and parole (see Table 14.1). Consider that in 2006, the Bureau of Justice Statistics announced that roughly 29 percent of all probationers were African American (compared with a national average of 12.3 percent African Americans in the general population) and 13 percent were Latino American (compared with a national average of 12.5 percent). Though the amount of Latinos that are on probation may not seem out of proportion, this should be compared with the fact that only 55 percent of the population on probation are Caucasian American, even though the Caucasian American community constitutes 75.1 percent of the entire United States population. Thus, an overrepresentation of minorities exists among probationers, with the main area of disparity lying with the African American population, accompanied by a full representation of Latino American offenders and an underrepresentation of Caucasian American offenders, based on their presence in the general population.

Among the offender population on parole, the statistics are even more telling. In this case, minorities are even more proportionally overrepresented, as 39 percent of all parolees in 2006 were African American and 18 percent were Latino American. Only 41 percent of parolees were Caucasian American. Thus, in this case, the offender population is overrepresented by African American and Latino American offenders, while at the same time the Caucasian American population is substantially underrepresented. Though the parolee population is quite small compared with the probation population, it still stands as an oddity that roughly 59 percent of that population are either African American or Latino American when the two combined only account for about 26 percent of the broader United States population.

The reason for the pronounced disparity among parolees has to do with the even more pronounced disparity that exists for minorities among the incarcerated population. In 2007, it was reported by Glaze and Bonczar that 37.5 percent of the nation's prison inmates (combining both state and federal) were African American, 20.5 percent were Latino American, and 5.7 percent were of another race or were biracial. The same data indicated that only 35.1 percent of the nation's prison inmates were Caucasian American. Thus, when it comes to prisons, Caucasian Americans are *underrepresented* by 50 percent of their proportion in the broader population, while African Americans are *overrepresented* by almost 300 percent of their proportion in the broader population, and Latino Americans are overrepresented by nearly 150 percent of

TABLE 14.1	Racial Composition of Offenders on Probation in the United States	
Race		*Percentage*
White		55
Black		30
Hispanic		13
American Indian/Alaskan Native		1
Asian/Native Hawaiian/Pacific Islander		1

SOURCE: Glaze, L. E., & Bonczar, T. P. (2007). *Probation and parole in the United States, 2005*. Washington, DC: U.S. Department of Justice.

their proportion in U.S. society. Taken in total, nearly 64 percent of the entire prison population in the United States belong to a minority group.

Given that minorities are overrepresented throughout the entire correctional population, it should be very clear that issues addressing minority groups are relevant to community supervision personnel. It is because of the diverse racial, cultural, and ethnic backgrounds of offenders that this chapter has been included. This issue is relevant to 45 percent of all probationers, 59 percent of all parolees, and 64 percent of all prison inmates. The racial disparity among prison inmates is relevant to community supervision because it is clear that the majority of these offenders will ultimately be released back into the community. Therefore, issues pertaining to racial diversity are very important for community supervision personnel since they will come into frequent contact with persons from these various backgrounds.

As noted, minority offenders are represented among the offender population in much greater proportions than are Caucasian Americans, and their numbers are disproportionate to their representation in the overall population. Often, this is attributed to the intertwining effects of low socioeconomic status, undercurrents of discrimination in the criminal justice system, and greater exposure to violence in the community (Healey, Smith, & O'Sullivan, 1998; Williams & Becker, 1994). Community supervision personnel should not ignore these factors because they are relevant to the client, their sense of motivation, and their experiences of the world.

Further, some minority communities may contend that the criminal justice system is nothing less than a form of **institutionalized racism**—a term that indicates that a society is, at its base, racist in nature as an entire institution; this is regardless of whether such racism is deliberate or accidental among members of that society. The disproportionate incarceration rates, the fact that Caucasian American offenders get prison sentences less often and for shorter periods of time, the saturation of the policing presence in most poor minority communities, the media attention to racial profiling, and other aspects of the racialized justice system serve to confirm this notion among many minority communities. It is important that community supervision officers be aware of these beliefs and dynamics because this can affect the supervision relationship. In many cases, supervision officers may simply be perceived as "the man" and may find it difficult to maintain a rapport. Further, community supervision officers visiting areas with urban poor minorities are not likely to get a warm reception. Indeed, it is not uncommon for officers to feel out of place and even in danger due to the negative outlook that is cast upon their presence and the role that they play. This situation is aggravated when community–police relations are strained in such a neighborhood, thereby impairing effective reintegration of minority offenders into mainstream society. This also tends to reflect many of the characteristics that are associated with institutional racism, an issue that may be perceived as pervasive in some minority communities, and in some cases, these perceptions may be materially correct.

The issues associated with institutional racism are important to understand and appreciate, particularly in regard to the African American population within the United States. For this group, a prior heritage of slavery cuts at the very core and fabric of that community's initial development and identity within the United States. Much of the history specific to the African American experience in the United States has been one where the pursuit of equality and true citizenship has been a recurring (if not constant) theme. As noted, this has its roots in the initial and fundamental imbalance that was set in motion during the slavery era and the discrimination that continued well past emancipation. The Civil Rights Era is still etched in the minds of many in the African American community with the distinct understanding that more work still needs to be done. Naturally, just as these issues affect the African American community as a whole, so too do they affect the African American correctional population. This is again very important for practitioners to understand because of the disproportionate representation of African American offenders in most state correctional systems and because the supervision process is one that is, by its very nature, oppressive to the desires of the individual under observation.

The dynamics of institutionalization tend to exacerbate the potential difficulties in developing a rapport between a criminal justice practitioner and an offender within the community corrections context. Thus, offenders released from jail or prison and placed on community supervision will have their views further affected by the noxious experiences associated with incarceration. Aside from the fact that inmate prison culture is not conducive to "opening up," there is the inherent distrust among many minority communities of most social services, as they are often provided by state agencies that are seen as being in league with "the man," or the authority figure that consists of a predominantly Caucasian agency which, by extension, further validates the sense of institutionalized racism. All of these factors are important for the supervision officer to understand and be receptive to. If the supervision officer is unable to incorporate this into his or her understanding of the client dynamics within the offender population, it is likely that the officer will not be very effective.

Photo 14.1 Community supervision officers may have clients from a variety of diverse backgrounds and communities. In some communities, ethnic and cultural identity is important. Probation and parole officers conducting home visits in these communities must understand the importance of cultural identity among offenders on their caseload.

Finally, a bit of clarity must also be provided for two terms that are often used synonymously—*disparity* and *discrimination*. Definitions for these terms are either borrowed or adapted from Clear and Cole (2003). **Disparity,** in the context of this text, refers to the unequal treatment of one group by the criminal justice system, compared with the treatment accorded other groups. **Discrimination,** on the other hand, refers to differential and negative treatment of an individual or group without reference to the behavior or qualifications for that treatment. These two terms are important to understand. They are both relevant to minority clients in the offender population because there is substantial disparity in the treatment between the poor and the wealthy as well as between minorities and the Caucasian American population. Naturally, as one might guess, the poor minority offender is even worse off in terms of the type of sentence typically given, the length of the sentence, and other factors.

Further, discrimination has been a problem that minorities have often faced. Discrimination can be covert (such as a business that fails to hire minorities yet makes no official policy to refrain from hiring them) or overt (such as the banning of a specific racial group from a given premises). The point to this is that minorities tend to experience discriminatory practices from the broader culture, and this, coupled with the disparity in treatment, provides much of the background experience that forms the client's self-concept. Community corrections professionals must understand this and be receptive to these experiences in a manner that is beneficial to the therapeutic process. By the same token, it is important that the counselor not allow the client's prior experiences to serve as a crutch or justification for aberrant behavior. This can be a difficult and delicate balancing act to maintain, but it is imperative that the counselor do so with the offender population, since many of these issues will be sources of underlying trauma and will also place offenders' actions in perspective. At this point, we now turn our focus to some basic issues regarding minorities in the United States.

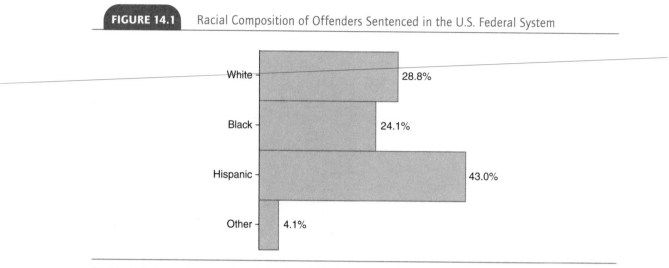

White — 28.8%

Black — 24.1%

Hispanic — 43.0%

Other — 4.1%

SOURCE: United States Sentencing Commission. (2007). *2007 sourcebook of federal sentencing statistics.* Washington, DC: Author.

THE NOTION OF CULTURAL COMPETENCE

The idea of cultural competence is one that has come into vogue during the last 10 to 15 years. Prior to this, it was more common that cultural *sensitivity* be noted as important among practitioners. Cultural competence goes beyond mere sensitivity or awareness and focuses on the need to have actual knowledge and skills related to interactions with persons from cultures that are different from our own. **Cultural competence** requires the possession of knowledge and information pertaining to individuals and groups that is integrated with service delivery and case management processes; this entails using skills, services, and techniques that match the individual's culture and improve the relevance of services to the person in question. The New York State Office of Mental Health (NYSOMH) provides a good explanation of the components of cultural competence. The following list, adapted from the NYSOMH (2008), demonstrates what cultural competence typically should achieve among agencies that provide services to the community:

1. A continual developmental process to provide culturally relevant services

2. Promotion of community-based treatment that is consumer driven and family oriented

3. Addressing of access to services, cultural adaptation of services, and equity in service benefit

4. An active process to encourage treatment and services that are effective across cultures

5. Integration throughout the service delivery system—needs assessment, information exchange, service design and development, hiring practices, staff development and supervision, outcome supervision, and policy and governance

Each of the above five listed points is both important to cultural competence and relevant to most of the chapters that have been presented so far. First, it has been made clear throughout this text that agencies must continually seek to improve their services using community members and agency networks. Much of the integration of community participants will then provide a broad range of actors that allow agencies to provide services that are more likely to be culturally relevant. This is consistent with point 1 (above). Further, this text obviously holds that community-based interventions are more desirable than those administered in institutional settings. The emphasis on family members, community members, mental health providers, and case management systems of coordination addresses the needs of the offender from a multivaried perspective, thereby addressing point 2.

Points 3 and 4 are both issues that agencies must contend with. Again, the emphasis on volunteers to fill in service gaps and the networking of various agency interventions can address issues related to access and to cultural appropriateness. This will require that agencies make a concerted and deliberate effort to do so, but the tools and mechanisms exist for those that integrate community members and partnerships into the process. Last, the need for agencies to assess their own jurisdictions and their service delivery resonates with issues related to Chapter 15 where evaluation of agency effectiveness will specifically be addressed. Naturally, agencies will want to evaluate their effectiveness regarding service provision to offenders from a variety of backgrounds. In addition, the hiring practices and the development of staff should reflect the need for diverse personnel within an agency. This allows for a better goodness of fit between service providers and those that receive services.

Cultural competence is an aspect of agency operation that is best infused throughout the entire process of service provision, as these considerations are relevant to community supervision agencies, case management specialists, and other agencies that network with the community supervision agency. This is important because offender reintegration can be directly impacted by these considerations. If practitioners truly wish to lower recidivism and to make their community safer for its citizens, they must understand that consideration of cultural competence issues will help to ensure that interventions are more relevant and effective. This is then likely to improve supervision and treatment outcomes.

According to the NYSOMH (2008), agencies should meet the following objectives when implementing culturally competent services to offenders:

1. Develop a written strategic plan to address disparities.

2. Know and understand the various cultural groups present in the community served.

3. Recruit and retain a diverse array of staff that are representative of the community.

4. Plan to include readily accessible bilingual/bicultural staff or translators.

5. Provide language assistance at all points of contact as needed.

6. Provide translated vital service documents, program documents, and rights and grievance information.

7. Provide ongoing training about the cultural groups served, and assure strategies employed are effective across cultures.

8. Include assessment of cross-cultural interactions as part of the employee evaluation and supervisory processes.

9. Consider various methods and media for information exchange, education, and awareness of offender needs.

10. Adapt service environments, practices, and delivery to match the individuals and families served.

11. Collect demographic data about the community at large and service recipients to determine future directions for program development.

12. Develop partnerships with community leaders, cultural brokers, and natural networks to facilitate increased service access and to provide feedback that will guide service design.

13. Examine agency and individual outcomes to determine whether specific groups within the service population are over- or underrepresented, to track consumer satisfaction, and to promote consumer-driven services.

Students should understand that this list is not topical, but actually addresses the various components of a culturally competent program. If agencies make a good-faith effort toward completing each of these objectives, they will be sure to deliver appropriate services that are recordable and accountable. Further, this will invariably improve rapport with communities and can have a healing effect upon communities that have not typically been the focus of improved service delivery. In addition, it is clear that this text's emphasis on community partnerships and collaborative efforts matches up well with the recommendations above. Thus, these objectives easily tuck into the grand scheme of this text—creating an agency that provides services that are ideally suited for its surrounding community. It is important that other agencies within the case management network also adopt these objectives or principles. This will provide a seamless sense of service delivery for the minority population, which constitutes a large proportion of the agency caseloads that will likely be encountered.

Effective integration of these objectives will improve the rapport that develops between the supervision personnel and offenders on their caseload. Indeed, it is likely to improve the general experiences of supervision officers who enter communities where a large number of citizens are on supervision. The easing of this social tension can be good for the individual offender and the community. This also allows for more effective integration of community members and further reinforces partnerships with community groups that may be influential in the area. All of this can be instrumental in impacting the recidivism outcome for offenders—the treatment prognosis for offenders is improved, thus reducing the likelihood of future recidivism as well as the severity of crime that occurs in the region.

Finally, there is of course a need to demonstrate whether such practices do indeed reach the appropriate clientele and whether they have the intended effects. Thus, some form of accountability and measurement is required. The NYSOMH again speaks to this issue in a very clear way. According to the NYSOMH (2008), the process of connecting cultural competency with evidence-based practices entails the following objectives:

1. Cultural competence activities need to be imbedded within all stages of development, implementation, and evaluation of evidence-based practices.

2. Implementation should ensure that clinical and administrative practices are tracked in a manner that yields a rubric or other evaluation scheme that can produce clear outcomes.

3. Attention should be paid to the effectiveness of evidence-based practices across cultural groups with data tracking maintained throughout.

4. Cross-culturally relevant strategies should be identified and defined in measurable terms, whenever possible.

5. Dissemination of "what works" should be a priority, with performance measures taken to determine how well interventions seem to be working.

The above objectives provide guidance so that culturally competent approaches may impact on the overall success rates in treatment and in regard to recidivism. This is actually a very important component of any culturally competent program, since it ensures that agencies are refining the process and that they are conducting their day-to-day operations in a manner that integrates such approaches to service delivery. Over time, agencies can use their outcome data to continually refine their approach, just as they would with any other issue of importance where a measurement of one sort or another is necessary. It is important that cultural competence not escape similar measurements lest it ultimately be ignored and forgotten over time.

AFRICAN AMERICAN, LATINO AMERICAN, AND ASIAN AMERICAN OFFENDERS IN METROPOLITAN AREAS

African Americans

One of the most important components of providing effective services to minority offenders is to appreciate the historical context of their particular race. As of 2001, there were approximately 34 million African Americans—roughly 12 percent of the population—living in the United States (U.S. Census Bureau, 2001). Most, if not all, African Americans currently residing in the United States can trace their ancestry to the slave trade from Africa. It is estimated that millions of Africans, over a period spanning two centuries, were kidnapped or purchased to be brought to the United States in order to perform manual labor. These African slaves were considered personal property of their owners. According to Thernstrom and Thernstrom (1997), even after the 14th Amendment extended citizenship to African Americans, many continued to live in poverty due to a continued dependence upon those who held power while they were also made to remain largely uneducated.

Currently, many African Americans still live in poor neighborhoods that are largely segregated and clearly delineated from other nonminority settlements. In these neighborhoods, there are few resources and high rates of unemployment, homelessness, crime, and substance abuse (Jones & Hanser, 2005). Practitioners need to understand that due to these circumstances, many African Americans experience prolonged perceptions of personal vulnerability. These perceptions and attendant psychological and emotional consequences that originate at the community level will often overpower individual control (Shusta, Levine, Wong, & Harris, 2005). In essence, it is important to appreciate the environments and conditions of many African Americans and understand how these factors affect their coping process, which in turn impacts their effective completion of community supervision requirements.

Although poverty rates are decreasing, many African Americans are still relatively poor. African Americans are much more likely than whites to live in severe poverty, with a rate of more than 3 times that of whites (Joiner, 2006). Currently, sufficient evidence indicates that poverty is one of the most frequent correlates in relation to criminal behavior (Joiner, 2006; Shusta et al., 2005). In order to be effective, practitioners need to be aware of the effects of poverty and how these effects manifest themselves into cognition and behavior. The historical adversity experienced by African Americans through slavery, and through exclusion from educational as well as social and economic resources, is largely responsible for many of the socioeconomic disparities they face today. Socioeconomic status is linked to mental health. In essence, poor mental health is more common among the impoverished than among those who are more affluent (McGoldrick, Giordano, Pearce, & Giordano, 1996). Poor mental health will often translate into criminal behavior, especially for those who are homeless or have substance abuse problems. These factors coalesce in a manner that aggravates the prognosis for many African American offenders, particularly those who live in disadvantaged communities and have few resources.

Reflecting this lack of material resources, African Americans make up a large portion of the homeless population. In fact, according to Jencks (1994), almost 44 percent of the homeless population in the United States consists of African Americans. This is 3 times the percentage of whites who are homeless. What makes these figures particularly disturbing is the fact that mental illness is found at much higher rates among the homeless population. Even more disturbing is the fact that among the homeless populations, the most serious mental disorders are among the most common. For example, approximately 13 percent of homeless people suffer from schizophrenia as compared with 1 percent of the general population; 30 percent of those classified as homeless suffer from mood disorders as compared with 8 percent of the general population (Substance Abuse and Mental Health Services Administration [SAMHSA], 2001). *What makes this information so important is that those who are homeless are more likely to come into contact with the criminal justice system, and a large percentage of the homeless are African Americans.* Therefore, it is likely that community corrections professionals will work with a substantial number of African American offenders, which requires an understanding of the socioeconomic, cultural, and contextual intricacies of this population.

Latino Americans

The term *Latino American* refers to Americans who are of Mexican, Central American, South American, or Caribbean descent, who are most often of Spanish origin, and who tend to speak Spanish. Before discussing the central components related to Latino Americans, it is first necessary to distinguish the different groups commonly classified as Hispanic. Currently, the U.S. Census Bureau recognizes four different groups described as Hispanic: Mexicans, Puerto Ricans, Cubans, and Central Americans. It should be pointed out that the term *Latino American* is a much broader term than is *Hispanic*. In the literature, there may be a degree of overlap when using the terms. Officially, the U.S. Government uses the term *Hispanic* to designate the four categories noted previously. However, these designations do not encompass persons from all of Latin America, and thus *Latino American* is the more inclusive term. As will be demonstrated in the discussion that follows, Latino Americans are a heterogeneous group in most circumstances, including those that led to or contributed to their migration. The Latino American population is rapidly expanding. According to the U.S. Census Bureau, projections indicate that by 2050, the number of Hispanic Americans will be roughly 97 million, or one quarter of the U.S. population.

Mexicans

There are several important factors (both historical and therapeutic in nature) to consider when counseling Mexicans or Mexican Americans. First, it is useful to remember that after the Mexican–American War (1846–1848), large territories of Mexico became part of the United States. This included land from Texas to California on which many Mexican citizens chose to stay, thereby becoming U.S. citizens. In addition to the Mexican war, and as noted by McGoldrick et al. (1996), there are a myriad of both push and pull factors that heavily influence the flow of Mexicans into the United States. Poor economic conditions in Mexico contribute to the push factor, and the need for laborers in the United States influences the pull factor. It is important to note that the origins of migration among all of the Hispanic groups are closely tied to economic factors. In essence, the overwhelming majority of Hispanics who choose to migrate to the United States do so in hopes of improving circumstances for themselves and their families. The one factor, however, that is largely responsible for the vast majority of Hispanic Americans being Mexican is the fact that the two countries border each other. Logistically, it is usually easier for Mexicans to come to the United States than other Hispanic groups simply because they do not have as far to travel, especially in light of the fact that migrant travel is often over land, much of which is often covered on foot.

It is important for community corrections professionals to understand that many of their clients may come from families that are illegally in the United States. This naturally puts members of the Latino community in a defensive position, particularly when community supervision personnel may visit neighborhoods on a home visit or some other supervision function. The cultural variables associated with this type of extra-legal existence should be understood by community supervision personnel; this is a common dynamic among the offender population. Further, this also means that the offender's family may have illegal status, even if the offender does not. This then impacts the overall schema of reintegration for the offender, and it must be taken into account when creating supervision plans. Likewise, the levels of acculturation and assimilation may vary from one Mexican client to another. In a similar vein, the inability to speak the English language or to speak it well can be a barrier unless the practitioner speaks Spanish sufficiently well.

Puerto Ricans

One of the characteristics that distinguishes Puerto Ricans from other Hispanic groups is that, as of 1917, by way of the Jones Act, Puerto Ricans are automatically American citizens. Therefore, they can enter and exit the mainland of the United States at their will. After World War II, many Puerto Ricans began migrating to the mainland in order to find work. Rising populations on the island of Puerto Rico contributed to the high unemployment there and made it difficult to find meaningful work. As the workforce began to age, many Puerto Ricans who had come to the United States began to return home to retire, creating a circular pattern beginning in the early to mid-1980s (SAMHSA, 2001).

Cubans

The most significant migration of Cuban immigrants to the United States began in 1959 after Fidel Castro toppled the Batista government and assumed control of the country. Many of the initial Cuban immigrants were well-educated professionals who have since become well established in America. Other immigrants who were not as well established in Cuba also attempted the trip and are commonly referred to as *Balseros*. Balsero is a concept that describes less-than-secure and often makeshift watercraft that have been used by many Cuban immigrants because of their poor economic situations. Finally, many of the Cubans who have come to the United States have received full rights to citizenship due to their declared status as political refugees.

Central Americans

Central Americans are generally considered to be those immigrants whose country of origin is El Salvador, Guatemala, or Nicaragua. Central Americans are thought to be the newest Hispanic subgroup in the United States, as their distinction is relatively recent. Many of the Central Americans who have come to the United States have done so due to political turmoil and massive atrocities carried out by rival political factions in their homeland. A large number of Central Americans arrived in the United States during the 1980s to escape the bloody revolution happening in Nicaragua. As with all of the subgroups, however, it is important to understand that migration is a constant process with ebbs and flows. There have been historical and political events over the past decades that have contributed to spikes or shifts in the flow of immigrants, but underneath this is the relatively stable fact that large numbers of individuals travel toward and often into the United States each year.

Important Points to Consider With Latino Americans

One key reason for at least briefly describing the characteristics of each group's circumstances causing their migration is because we are able to glean valuable insight into their experiences and possible mental health needs. In addition, how these groups have been received once in the United States is also important. For example, Puerto Ricans, regardless of whether they were born in the United States or Puerto Rico, are considered U.S. citizens. This is important to note because citizenship allows access to government programs and sponsored services aimed at providing needed support. Similarly, many Cuban immigrants have achieved citizenship due to their declared status as political refugees.

Mexican and Central American immigrants, however, are much less likely to be granted citizenship. Many of the Central American immigrants were fleeing war-struck countries mired in political turmoil. Despite these circumstances, Central American immigrants are not considered political refugees. Therefore, many Hispanics migrating to the United States arrive without documentation that would make them legal immigrants. Those immigrants who are undocumented live with the constant fear of deportation. This reality makes it difficult to find and sustain meaningful employment, let alone advance in one's career. In addition, due to their illegal status, immigrants are rarely able to establish permanent homes due to the risk of losing their property if deported. Therefore, adjustment to migration can often be difficult, especially for Mexicans and Central Americans. Current trends indicate, however, that migration is difficult for all groups of Latino Americans, largely because many of the immigrants are unskilled laborers. They work long, hard hours, often for meager pay.

Asian Americans and Pacific Islanders

Asian Americans and Pacific Islanders are extremely diverse groups. Shusta et al. (2005) report that as many as 43 different ethnic groups are classified as Asian Americans or Pacific Islanders. Asian immigrants now account for approximately 4 percent of the U.S. population and are rapidly increasing. By 2020, the Asian American and Pacific Islander population is expected to reach 20 million, accounting for approximately 6 percent of the U.S. population.

The first Asians to arrive in the United States were from China. The first groups of Chinese consisted of small numbers of immigrants who began arriving in the late 1700s. The numbers quickly increased, as an additional 300,000 Chinese immigrants arrived between 1848 and 1882 (Huang, 1991). The increase was in response to the discovery of gold in California, and most Chinese immigrants were indentured to work in the mining and railroad industries.

A substantial portion of Asian Americans are born outside of the United States, collectively comprising more than 25 percent of all its foreign-born citizens (Bennett, 2002; Shusta et al., 2005). Indeed, throughout the United States, over 60 percent of all Chinese Americans, 70 percent of all Asian Indian Americans, and a full 90 percent of all Vietnamese Americans were not born in the United States. There has been a vast amount of literature on the immigration and acculturation of these groups, particularly in the social science research. However, Shusta et al. (2005) provide one of the clearest and most pragmatic descriptions of this process by describing several categories or points of acculturation that Asian Americans may fall within. These categories apply equally well to any Asian American group, whether they be Chinese American, Vietnamese American, Asian Indian, or of other Asian backgrounds. The following categories are adapted from Shusta et al.:

Surviving—This includes individuals that have recently immigrated to the United States (within the last 5 years), and the majority of their socialization and experience will have been in their own nation of origin.

Preserving—This includes immigrants or refugees that have been in the United States for more than 5 years but who had the majority of their socialization in their nation of origin.

Adjusting—This groups includes the second-generation offspring of Asian American immigrants.

Changing—This group includes immigrants, but these immigrants will have had the majority of their experiences within the United States.

Choosing—This category consists of third-generation (or later) Asian Americans.

When considering each of these categories, it is important to understand the individual perspective from which these groups view the world. For instance, those in the "surviving" category are typically in a survival mode and may have come from areas where police and other authority figures were oppressive and abusive. This will then tend to shape their frame of reference when dealing with police in the United States. Likewise, individuals in the "preserving" category seek to preserve their home culture and identity. Their own values and customs are preserved, and this can be the source of intergenerational conflict within their family as youth become more "Americanized" and lose contact with their culture of origin. Among the remaining categories (adjusting, changing, and choosing), the homeland is valued, but there is also a realistic understanding that changes will need to be made (Shusta et al., 2005). This is particularly true for those in the "changing" and "choosing" categories, where decisions to include aspects of the old culture or to integrate aspects of the new

Photo 14.2   Officer David Jackson points to his zone of supervision on a map of the local community. Officer Jackson, a prior student of the author, now works full time with Probation and Parole in Louisiana.

culture are made. These individuals tend to be truly bicultural, and many will use English as their primary language, allowing their proficiency with their native language to lapse. For these individuals, contact with law enforcement may be no different from that occurring with other citizens of the United States.

Lack of proficiency with the English language is a particular hindrance that can cause serious misunderstandings between police officers and Asian American citizens. This issue is somewhat tied to the generational status of the individual Asian American, since those groups that have immigrated most recently tend to be those with large percentages that do not speak English. This is particularly true among the Southeast Asian groups. For example, nearly 38 percent of all Vietnamese Americans do not speak English. In addition, it has been determined that approximately 23 percent of Chinese Americans also do not speak English (Shusta et al., 2005). On the other hand, this is not typically an issue for Asian Indian Americans due to the fact that most all speak English as a result of prior subjugation during the reign of the British Empire (Almeida, 1996).

MINORITY CASELOADS, MINORITY GANG AFFILIATIONS, AND TRAINING FOR COMMUNITY SUPERVISION STAFF

As was pointed out earlier, the proportion of minority offenders on community supervision is much higher than their proportion among the broader community. Thus, it is quite commonplace for community supervision officers to have a wide range of minority offenders on their caseloads. This will naturally vary from region to region in the United States, in terms of both the overall number of minority offenders and the range of different racial or ethnic groups that may be encountered. For instance, in some areas of the southern United States (e.g., Alabama, Louisiana, Arkansas), a large number of minorities may be encountered on community supervision caseloads, but most of them are likely to be African American. On the other hand, in areas such as the Southwest, minority offenders may again be very common, but they are likely to be Latino American or perhaps Native American. In areas such as New York, Illinois, and California, minority offenders will be commonplace on caseloads, but they are likely to be quite diverse in both race and ethnicity. The impact of minority offenders is so important that some jurisdictions, such as New York, have created specialized positions among the ranks of probation and parole officers. Focus Topic 14.1 provides a job announcement from New York that illustrates this fact.

FOCUS TOPIC 14.1

MINORITY GROUP SPECIALIST PROBATION OFFICER

Distinguishing Features of the Class:

The work involves responsibility for the application of modern social work techniques in making social case studies of minority probationers and carrying out probation treatment. This position is similar to Probation Officer with the additional responsibility of identifying and relating to the specific problems encountered by minority probationers. The caseloads for these positions may, to a significant extent, be composed of individuals who need special attention due to the sociocultural environments from which they come. Incumbents of these positions may provide insight that could enhance and increase county probation departments' special sensitivities, experiences, and knowledge necessary to operate and to assist in the evaluation of local programs and service delivery to make them more responsive to the diverse and pluralistic populations which county probation departments serve. Assignments are received as cases from the Probation Supervisor or higher-level professional and reviewed through conference and narrative status reports on the probationer's readjustment in a guided environment. Supervision is exercised over trainees, paraprofessionals, and clerical support staff. Does related work as required.

Typical Work Activities:

- Develops and maintains relationships with groups and organizations providing services to young ethnic minorities
- Supervises probationers and advises and assists them in their rehabilitation
- Makes probation investigations of persons coming before the courts to ascertain previous criminal and delinquent records; social history; and physical, mental, and psychiatric data. Submits written reports of probation investigations to supervisor or directly to the court
- Interprets conditions of probation to probationers
- Enforces conditions of probation
- Reviews case histories to determine degree of adjustment and advisability of referral or court action
- Prepares reports and recommendations, such as, status of probationer, impact of department's sanctions, decisions and requirements on service delivery to ethnic minorities, etc.
- Maintains probation supervision and financial records
- May carry a firearm on some assignments

SOURCE: New York State. (2003). *Probation officer–Minority group specialist.* Retrieved from http://www.ongov.net/Employment/jobs/specs/sp43050.pdf.

In addition, it should be understood that most gangs in jails and especially prisons are based on racial lines of loyalty. In other words, gangs are frequently composed of one predominant racial group. Some may even harbor animosity against persons of other racial groups. Since gang members tend to cycle in and out of facilities, gangs tend to recruit members within and outside the prison that also maintain racial lineages of loyalty. It is beyond the scope of this chapter to give an overview of the various gangs, but suffice it to say that anyone conducting an examination of prison gangs will find that most consist of a predominant racial orientation in membership. Further, there has been increased friction among groups of inmates in some areas of the United States, such as that encountered in the state of California, where race wars occurred during 2006 in that state's prison system between Latino American and African American gang members. The dynamics between gang membership and racial affiliation can vary from state to state, but community supervision officers should understand those dynamics and be aware of them. Naturally, this is particularly true in cases where both minority representation and gang membership are common within a given jurisdiction.

Because of the variability in racial and ethnic issues that may be encountered with the offender population and because perceptions and motivations of some offenders are based on race, it is prudent for community supervision officers to be provided suitable training on a variety of issues dealing with diverse populations. This is an important consideration that will continue to grow in importance in the future. The offender population, like the broader United States population, is becoming more diversified with each passing year. Community supervision officers must be acclimated to the various racial and ethnic groups in their area. This is important when developing rapport with individual offenders on their caseload, and it is important from a community relations standpoint for the agency as a whole. This will automatically occur if agencies follow the objectives set forth by the New York State Office of Mental Health when crafting agency policies and procedures related to culturally competent services for minority clients. For those agencies that do not, repercussions will not only affect the agency but also impact the community through increased recidivism and victimization rates.

FEMALE OFFENDERS

We now turn our attention to another issue related to diversity, that of gender. This section will familiarize the student with the common problems associated with the female offending population. For this text, **female offenders** are defined as both juvenile and adult offenders who have committed a criminal offense that has been either adjudicated or criminally processed; these offenders include women in facilities as well as those in community corrections settings. It should be pointed out that while female offenders make up a small minority of the incarcerated population (about 8 percent), in 2006 they constituted a full 24 percent of the nation's probationers and 12 percent of the nation's parolees. This means that community supervision officers will have roughly a fifth to a quarter of their caseload consist of female offenders.

As will be seen in subsequent pages, women offenders have several physiological and psychological characteristics that set them apart from the male offending population. Some of these characteristics are present in the female population in broader society, whereas others are unique to females that find themselves involved in the criminal process. Of the offending population, no more than 8 to 10 percent are women, depending on whether one is talking about jails, prisons, community supervision, or a combination of these. This number is small enough to appropriately categorize them as a specialized type of offender, particularly since it will become clear that female offenders have numerous considerations that are not relevant to the remaining nine-tenths of the offending population. On the other hand, the number of female offenders in the United States correctional system and the higher rate of growth of this offending population (as compared with male offenders) ensure that we cannot overlook this group. Indeed, considerations regarding the female offending population will become an increasingly important variable for the police, courts, corrections, and treatment specialists for some time to come.

When discussing female offenders, it becomes clear that the majority of female offenders are minority members, thereby further attesting to the importance of the prior section of this chapter on minority offenders. In addition, these women typically have few options and few economic resources. Thus, many of these offenders are marginalized in multiple ways from the access to success and stability commonly attributed to broader society. In 2002, roughly 176,300 women were incarcerated in a state prison, federal prison, or local jail. Of these female inmates, about 76,100, or 44 percent, were Caucasian American; 66,800, or 38 percent, were African American; and 28,300, or 16 percent, were Latino American (Harrison & Beck,

2003). Of those women that are incarcerated, approximately 44 percent have no high school diploma or GED and 61 percent were unemployed at the point of incarceration (Bloom, Owen, & Covington, 2003). In addition, roughly 47 percent were single prior to incarceration, while an approximate 65 to 70 percent of these women were the primary caretakers of minor children at the point that they were incarcerated (Bloom et al., 2003). Finally, over one-third of those incarcerated can be found within the jurisdictions of the federal prison system, or the state prison systems of Texas and California (Harrison & Karberg, 2004). With the above demographic characteristics in mind, we now will turn our attention to several subcharacteristics that have been found to be commonalities among the female offending population. The remainder of this section will consider each subcategory in an attempt to demonstrate the multitude of difficult problems that confound effective intervention for many female offenders.

Domestic Violence

The research on the prevalence of domestic violence and its impact on women in the United States is so abundant and extensive that it goes beyond the scope of this chapter to discuss. However, when limiting the discussion to female offenders and their experiences with domestic violence, it appears that they are at greater risk for physical abuse than are women in the general population. One survey of female offenders shows that incarcerated women are very likely to have histories of physical abuse (American Correctional Association, 1990). This study indicated that 53 percent of incarcerated adult women and nearly 62 percent of incarcerated juvenile girls had been victims of physical abuse. Nearly half of both these groups (49 percent of adults and 47 percent of juveniles) reported experiencing multiple episodes of physical abuse. Furthermore, this study found that this violence is most likely to have been perpetrated by a boyfriend or husband in the case of adult women offenders (50 percent) or by a parent in the case of juvenile girls (43 percent).

Photo 14.3 A courthouse bailiff fingerprints a female court employee in a training exercise. Fingerprinting is also done with offenders who are placed on community supervision.

For juvenile girls, most episodes of domestic violence occur between the ages of 10 and 14. Adult incarcerated women report having been subjected to the most violence at ages 15 to 24 (Bloom et al., 2003). Thus, this abuse tends to follow the female offender into adulthood, indicating that these offenders return to a lifestyle that is self-damaging. Because the women on probation and parole are likely to be somewhat socially isolated from common social circles, their peer network is likely to be limited (Bloom et al., 2003). At best, it will include other women in a similar situation, or perhaps coworkers (keep in mind the educational level, unemployment rate, and vocational skills of these women). More likely, these women are likely to continue to associate within their subculture of origin, meaning that many of the friends and family that they return to are likely to be, or have been, criminal offenders (Hanser, 2007). This is evidenced by the fact that many women who offend do so as accomplices to a male primary offender who is often a husband or boyfriend. Thus, these women are not likely to have many resources to rely on and may find themselves quite dependent on a man, even an abusive man.

Physical and Sexual Abuse

A study on self-reported prior abuse, conducted by the Bureau of Justice Statistics in 1994, found that female offenders are abused more frequently than male offenders. State prison inmates reported both physical and sexual abuse experiences prior to their being sentenced. The results found that 57.2 percent of females had experienced abusive treatment compared with 16.1 percent of males. Of this same group, 36.7 percent of the female offenders and 14.4 percent of the male offenders reported that the abuse occurred during their childhood or teenage years. Other findings from this study were as follows:

- Males tend to be mistreated as children, but females are mistreated as both children and adults.
- Both genders reported much more abuse if they had lived in a foster home or other structured institution.
- Higher levels of abuse were reported among offenders that had a family member who was incarcerated.
- Offenders reporting prior abuse had higher levels of drug and alcohol abuse then those that did not report abuse. Further, female offenders who were abused used drugs or alcohol more frequently than did male offenders.

Sex Industry Activity and Sexually Transmitted Diseases

A large amount of research shows that female criminals often have some history of prostitution, although the causal factor(s) and the order of these factors are not very clear. A debate, indeed a schism, exists among researchers as to whether this is the case due to economic necessities or whether prior sexual victimizations are at the root of this common form of female offense. Many researchers contend that prior victimization (especially sexual) is at the root, pointing toward the high incidence of sexual abuse among female criminals and the high rate of female criminals' involvement in prostitution.

The rate of HIV infection is higher for female offenders than for male offenders. According to the Bureau of Justice Statistics (Snell, 1994), among state prisoners tested for HIV, women were more likely to test positive. An estimated 3.3 percent of the women reported being HIV positive, compared with 2.1 percent of the men. Among prisoners who had shared needles to inject drugs, more women than men were likely to be HIV positive (10 percent vs. 6.7 percent).

Applied Theory   **Feminist Criminology and the Female Offender**

Feminist criminology offers a variety of propositions regarding female criminality that are different from other theoretical perspectives. Among other points, feminist criminologists argue that traditional schools of criminology fail to account for the various issues that are specific to women, the female experience, and the causal factors associated with female criminality. If this is indeed true, then it means that traditional criminological theory has failed to be *gender competent*, a derivative of cultural competence. This is an important point for both academics and practitioners alike; any failure to understand and appreciate the specific factors relevant to women means that causal factors tend to be misunderstood, and this also means that supervision and treatment programs will be misdirected and ineffectual. Thus, it behooves practitioners to heed the call of feminist criminologists when designing and implementing their programs for female offenders. In summarizing feminist criminology, Cullen and Agnew (2006) state,

(Continued)

Crime cannot be understood without considering gender. Crime is shaped by the different social experiences of and power exercised by men and women. Patriarchy is a broad structure that shapes gender-related experiences and power. Men may use crime to exert control over women and to demonstrate their masculinity—that is, to show that they are "men" in a way that is consistent with societal ideas of masculinity. (p. 7)

From the reading thus far in this chapter and when considering the description of feminist criminology presented by Cullen and Agnew (2006), it should be clear to the student that there is a great deal of similarity between these two portrayals of female offending. From this chapter, it is evident that much of female crime is shaped by gender-related experiences and power. Activity in the sex industry, a prime area of involvement for female offenders, seems to indicate that much of the activity related to female criminality is indeed rooted in gender-related experiences.

Further, when one considers the fact that the overwhelming majority of domestic violence victims are female and that female offenders experience higher rates of domestic violence perpetrated against them, this lends further credence to feminists who contend that men use crime to exert control over women and to demonstrate their power over them. Naturally, acts of sexual abuse directed at young girls would also back up this theory, and, as this chapter demonstrates, female offenders generally have higher rates of prior childhood sexual abuse.

Finally, the effects of this abuse and the corresponding ravages associated with being raised in a criminogenic family environment tend to manifest themselves through various mental health symptoms and maladaptive coping mechanisms. It is perhaps for this reason, as well as other factors related to a poor sense of self-efficacy (common among many female offenders), that substance abuse may be so high among these offenders. The use of drugs, as well as comorbid problems with depression and anxiety, put female offenders at further risk of having difficulties. Nevertheless, women do tend to be more verbally communicative than men, and this means that they also tend to do better in treatment regimens that utilize talk therapy. As a result, these offenders often have a better prognosis when in treatment than do their male counterparts. Perhaps, then, treatment programs for female offenders should continue to be intensified, with a continued focus on female-specific factors and theoretical frameworks that are consistent with feminist criminology. To fail to do so essentially puts the female offender, her children (as most female offenders have children), and the rest of society at risk for future criminality. In short, it simply makes good sense to integrate this theoretical perspective into the various supervision and treatment regimens designed for female offenders.

SOURCE: Cullen, F. T., & Agnew, R. (2006). *Criminological theory: Past to present* (3rd ed.). Los Angeles: Roxbury.

Drugs

Drug use is a major contributor to female criminality. Female offenders use drugs more often than male offenders, though differences are not extreme, and research focuses mostly on arrested and incarcerated subjects. However, between 1985 and 1994, women's drug arrests increased 100 percent, whereas men's drug arrests increased only by about 50 percent. The point here is that when dealing with female offenders, addressing drug use is critical if you are to prevent recidivism. Further, female offenders engage in riskier drug habits than male offenders, as they report higher levels of needle usage and needle sharing (Snell, 1994). This social problem is further compounded because a high number of female offenders who are intravenous drug users likewise engage in prostitution and sex industry activity to support their habits.

Violent Crime

It is important to note that when it comes to violent crime, there is a huge disparity between male and female offenders. Simply put, female offenders do not commit violent crimes with great frequency. Most of their crimes revolve around property offenses, fraud, larceny, or theft. Of those women who do commit homicides, the vast majority involve the killing of intimates, usually in self-defense or in retaliatory response to long-term abusive relationships (Hanser, 2007).

Female chronic offenders are similar to male chronic offenders in that they are likely to be minority group members, single, and substance abusers, with a history of spouse abuse. But they differ in that they show disparities in years of education (women typically have more), tend to paradoxically score lower on IQ tests, are more likely to come from homes of divorce, and are more likely to come from criminogenic families. When both genders are compared, men are likely to be sentenced to prison for violent, property, and drug offenses, while women are more likely to be sentenced to prison for drug offenses and property crimes. Only about one-fifth of all prison sentences for female offenders are due to violent offenses (Clear et al., 2006).

Female Crime

Most female offenders engage in some form of property offense, with nearly half being convicted of some form of fraud and another quarter being convicted of larceny. On the average, women are sentenced to probation more often than men, and this is largely thought to be true because of the differences in offense patterns. With respect to parole, female offenders are generally found in numbers that are proportionate with their offending patterns, and this tends to be true at both the state and federal level. Thus, most female offenders on parole are drug or property offenders. Further, female parolees have a lower recidivism rate than men, making them much better suited for most forms of community supervision (Latessa & Allen, 1999).

Female Offenders as Mothers

In 1998, female offenders in the criminal justice system were mothers to approximately 1.3 million children. Many female offenders under criminal justice supervision face losing custody of their children. Some female offenders have relatives or friends who will care for their children while they are incarcerated, but many do not. For those who are able to arrange placement with relatives, the likelihood of permanent separation between mother and child is significantly reduced. It has been observed that maternal grandmothers most often care for the children of female prison inmates (Bloom et al., 1996). If a mother is unable to place her children with relatives or friends, the local child welfare agency will most likely place the child in foster care. When children of imprisoned mothers are placed in foster care, caseworkers are expected to make concerted efforts to sustain family ties and to encourage family reunification (Bloom et al., 1996). Most incarcerated mothers, particularly those who are mentally ill, do not have access to the resources they need to meet other reunification requirements imposed by the court such as parent education, counseling, drug treatment, and job training. Upon release from custody to community corrections, mothers face numerous obstacles in reunifying with their children. They must navigate through a number of complex governmental and social service agencies in order to regain custody of their children. Although differences exist across jurisdictions, in many cases, it is considered to be beyond the purview of probation and parole agencies to intervene in child custody cases.

When fathers are incarcerated, there is usually a mother left at home to care for the children. However, when mothers are incarcerated, there is not usually a father in the home. This situation is further exacerbated by the fact that there are fewer women's prisons, and this means they tend to be great distances from one another and from the likely location where the female offender lived prior to incarceration. Because of this, there is a greater risk that female offenders will be incarcerated far away from their children than there is for males. Indeed, an average female inmate is more than 160 miles further from her family than a male inmate, and at least half the children of imprisoned mothers have not seen or visited their mothers since they were incarcerated (Bloom et al., 1996).

Due to the fact that many female offenders are primary caretakers for children, their crimes tend to be less serious, and they have lower recidivism rates than male offenders, alternative forms of sentencing have been considered as highly suited for female offenders. One example exists in the state of Missouri, where House Bill SB720 was passed in 1998 to establish the Children of Incarcerated Parents Task Force in 1999. This special task force noted that while Missouri is only the 17th most populous state in the United States, it was among the top 10 for the number of persons behind bars. Further, in 2001 there were 2,077 female inmates in the state, leading the Midwest in the number of incarcerated female offenders. It was noted that approximately 61 percent of the female inmate population had committed nonviolent offenses and that nearly 50 percent had no previous criminal history. This stands in stark contrast to most male inmates who typically have prior convictions before a prison sentence (Clear & Cole, 2003). More alarming is the fact that over 78 percent of the female inmate population had dependent children. Between the daily cost of incarcerating the female offender ($36 per day in 2002) and the cost to the Missouri Department of Family Services for the foster care of the children (between $227 and $307 per month per child), it was found that incarcerating women was counterproductive to the appropriate sentencing (when considering the offense) and rehabilitation, and it was too costly to be of much utility to the state. This was further compounded by the fact that female offenders on probation and parole have been found to be an equal (probation) or better (parole) risk for recidivism when compared with male inmates.

The Children of Incarcerated Parents Task Force specifically noted many alternatives to incarceration because alternative services were found to be the best approach to breaking the generational cycle of incarceration. Added to this were the fact that the majority of incarcerated women were found to be the primary custodian of at least one child under the age of 18 and the task force's desire to keep the family intact if this proved to be in the best interest of the child. The task force's specific recommendations were very similar to community-based sanctions noted in this text's previous chapters (Chapters 8 and 9 in particular). Among these recommendations were the following:

1. **The use of drug courts** as an effective alternative to incarceration. Offenders in Missouri were offered a stay of prosecution if they agreed to participate in a court-supervised treatment program. Upon successful completion of the program, the participant may be discharged without a criminal record, whereas failure to complete the program results in the filing of criminal charges. Under this program, mothers who are charged with drug offenses would be able to maintain the caregiver role while receiving treatment for their addictions.

2. **The use of mental health courts** to serve offenders with co-occurring disorders (mental disorder and substance abuse disorder), developmental disabilities, or head injury. The goal of the Mental Health Court program is to reduce the number of offenders with co-occurring disorders committed to the Department of Corrections while still providing for public safety. Successful completion of the program may result in deferred prosecution for the offender.

3. **The use of restorative justice** to address offenses (particularly property offenses that are common to female offenders) through direct restitution to the victim (financially or through services provided by the offender) or indirect restitution via community service. The use of victim–offender mediation in particular was noted because this has been shown to be an effective approach for dealing with crime and for reviving the community. More important, this form of intervention allows the female offender to make amends while at the same time keeping the family intact within the community.

Ideal Treatment Programming for Female Offenders

Based on the research presented and the specific treatment needs of female offenders, it is evident that treatment considerations for female offenders can be quite complicated. Indeed, it is plausible that a female offender could have the sundry challenges outlined in this chapter as well as numerous others included in various other chapters of this text. Thus, many female offenders can be viewed as being "special needs plus" when considering the various issues that may be present. With this in mind, Dolan, Kolthoff, Schreck, Smilanch, and Todd (2003) make specific recommendations regarding treatment programs for female offenders. Their recommendations are outlined as follows:

Treatment plans must be individualized in structure and include

- Clear and measurable goals.
- Intensive programming with effective duration.
- Appropriate screening and assessment.

Female offenders must be able to acquire needed life skills:

- Parenting and life skills must be taught; these are both critical.
- Anger management must be addressed.
- Marketable job skills are important because female offenders typically have few job skills and, unlike male offenders, have more difficulty obtaining jobs in the manual labor sectors that pay higher wages (e.g., construction, plant work, etc.).

Victimization issues must be addressed:

- Programs should address self-esteem, which is typically tied in to previous abuse issues, which in turn increase likelihood of substance abuse and prostitution, two main segments of female crime.
- Programs must address domestic violence issues. These are highly common among female offenders, both from their family of origin and from previous boyfriends or spouses; often, this is intergenerationally transmitted.

Dolan et al. (2003) discuss the importance of having gender-specific treatment programs for correctional clients with co-occurring disorders. Their insights are important for a couple of key reasons that should be emphasized in this chapter. First, it is becoming increasingly clear within the treatment literature that therapists, caseworkers, and the curriculum that they use must be able to address diverse populations. Many persons do not consider that women, elderly people, and disabled individuals are part of most diversity programs just as much as ethnic and racial groups are. This is important because correctional programs must increasingly address issues related to these groups as well.

The program by Dolan et al. (2003) is an excellent example of how most programs for female offenders should be structured, and it should be considered a model program. The reasons for this are because it is comprehensive and demonstrates how the multitude of issues pertinent to female offenders can be addressed within a single facility while utilizing a wide array of services within the community. This program falls well within the theme of this text, demonstrating how integration of community resources and public and private agencies can address complicated social ills in cost-effective ways. Because of this, it is the contention of this text that other areas of the nation should look toward this program when designing treatments for their female offending client population.

GERIATRIC OFFENDERS

Having now covered race and gender, the last category related to diversity issues that will be addressed is that associated with age. In this section, the emergence of elderly offenders will be illustrated, as they provide a new set of conditions and challenges for community supervision agencies. For this text's purposes, **geriatric/elderly offenders** are defined as those persons who have committed a criminal offense and are serving a sentence while being 50 years of age or older. It should be noted that Chapter 12 provided an in-depth discussion on youth offenders and that an age spectrum of offenders will not be addressed in this current chapter.

With this preliminary introduction out of the way, it is noteworthy that geriatric offenders have the lowest rate of recidivism (Morton, 1992). One study reported that 45 percent of offenders age 18 to 29 commit a new crime after release from prison, while only 3.2 percent of those over the age of 55 commit a new crime. In the state of New York's prison system, statistics that correlate age and recidivism show the following for each age-group:

Age	Likelihood of Recidivism
16–18	70.0 percent
45–49	26.6 percent
50–64	22.1 percent
65 and older	7.4 percent

According to Morton (1992), one option to consider with elderly offenders is an early release program that targets elderly prisoners who no longer pose a threat to society. Low-risk inmates may be suitable for special parole. Inmates having a moderate level of risk to the community might be able to be released but could be required to stay under electronic supervision. It is of course important that such electronic monitoring be carefully planned and implemented, as this is in the interest of both the community and the offender.

Challenges With Elderly Offenders

In addressing challenges associated with elderly offenders, consider that the nation's population of Alzheimer's patients is skyrocketing. In 1980, an estimated 2.9 million seniors had the disease. Today, the total is about 4 million, according to the Chicago-based Alzheimer's Association. The disease strikes about 1 in 10 who are older than 65 and nearly half of those older than 85. The association anticipates the number of Americans suffering from Alzheimer's will double by 2030 and reach 14 million by 2050. Though some advocates may contend that violence among Alzheimer's patients is rare, it is more likely that this rarity is due to the fact that the violence is simply not reported. Given the likely family dynamics, the seriousness of the offense (not usually very serious), and the overall contextual view of elderly people committing crime, it is likely that the rate of violence among those afflicted with Alzheimer's is underreported. Further, if individuals with Alzheimer's are widowed or living alone, their mental disorders may simply evade detection and diagnosis. The symptoms of Alzheimer's, paranoia, hallucinations, and delusions, can all work to predispose these individuals to violence. According to Price (2000), as many as 70 percent of those diagnosed with dementia develop significant behavioral problems in the first 6 or 7 years of their illness.

It is also very likely that other factors will become important in dealing with elderly offenders. Family dynamics and racial/ethnic diversity among this group are likely to become increasingly important. In general, the elderly are more heterogeneous than any other age-group (Morton, 1992). This fact makes it even more difficult for correctional agencies because more attention must be given to individualized assessment, programming, planning, and monitoring to meet the needs of this diversified and growing group of offenders (Morton, 1992).

Cross-National Perspective

England's Aging Prison Population

Like many countries, England faces the inevitable challenges of dealing with an aging prison population. In England, the geriatric offender is defined as an offender who is 50 to 55 years or older. This age bracket may not be typical of the definition of a geriatric person as far as the general population is concerned, but correctional authorities agree that an offender within the 50 to 55 age bracket usually exhibits the physical appearance and health problems of a person 10 years older than his or her numerical age.

In 2005, women over 50 constituted 4 percent and men over 50 accounted for 8 percent of the total prison population. Between 1995 and 2003, the number of women incarcerated who were over 50 rose 87 percent and the number of men incarcerated over 50 rose 113 percent. This makes the geriatric male offender the largest growing age-group of male offenders.

Geriatric offenders require medical services and have social care needs that can burden the prison system. Medical costs for caring for geriatric offenders are considerably more than the cost for younger offenders, due in part to the rising cost of health care, chronic medical problems of the offenders, and vulnerability to infectious diseases prevalent in prisons.

Prisons have attempted to accommodate geriatric offenders by designating special wings and units for them. These units provide programs and activities designed for geriatric offenders, offer an environment less brutal than the prison environment in general, modify facilities to accommodate wheelchair access, and ensure that medical staff—including nurses and occupational therapists—are available.

There is, to date, no comprehensive policy or strategy for dealing with this increasing segment of the prison population. However, the prison system is working with other government and social institutions to evaluate and meet the needs of geriatric offenders by addressing their physical and mental health, providing educational and vocational opportunities, developing rehabilitative programs, and offering long-term or terminal care.

SOURCE: Wahidin, A., & Aday, R. (2006). *The needs of older men and women in the criminal justice system: An international perspective.* London: Her Majesty's Prison Service.

Critical Thinking Question

1. Do you believe age should be a factor when considering an offender's potential for rehabilitation after release from prison? Why or why not?

For more information on Her Majesty's Prison Service, visit the website www.hmprisonservice.gov.uk.

Pre-prison Community Supervision (Probation)

Because most elderly offenders do not commit serious crimes and because their rate of recidivism is low, they are perhaps good candidates for probation. This may even be true if they have committed a nonsexual violent crime that is in the "heat of passion," since these types of offenders are not likely to recidivate and these offenses do not usually reflect the true nature of the offender's psyche. This is important since it basically confirms that at least one subgroup of elderly offenders are good candidates for reintegration.

It is likewise true that first-time elderly offenders are likely to have immediate family support. This is particularly true if the offender did not commit a sex crime (particularly pedophilia, which has been noted as a problem among male geriatric offenders). It is the recommendation of this author that elderly offenders that have committed an act of pedophilia should be given incarceration because they have a poor treatment prognosis and they are also the least likely to have family support.

For elderly offenders convicted of other types of crimes, the use of community supervision is an ideal way to process this group of offenders. This is true due to their lack of institutional dependency, since they have ostensibly not been in jail long enough to have internalized the coping mechanisms associated with elderly offenders that have been incarcerated for long periods of time. Also, as mentioned above, these offenders are more likely to have family support of one type or another. Thus, their less serious offending, their lack of being institutionally dependent, and their likelihood of family support make the elderly first-time offender a better-than-average risk for release on probation.

Applied Theory | **Life Course Criminological Theories and Elderly Offender Typologies**

Though this chapter presents the geriatric offender population as a separate category of offenders, it is important to point out that a "one-size-fits-all" approach will not adequately address this entire population of offenders. Indeed, the elderly offender population has different levels and types of criminal history that are important when making assessments related to public safety risks. From the offending patterns of elderly offenders, three basic typologies emerge: the *elderly first-time offender*, the *habitual elderly offender*, and the *offender-turned-elderly-in-prison*. The rise in numbers of *habitual elderly offenders* and *offenders-turned-elderly-in-prison* has to do largely with the advent of "three strikes" felony sentencing in many states (Anno, Graham, Lawrence, & Shansky, 2004). These sentences require that third-time felony offenders serve mandatory sentences of at least 25 years to life. It should be noted that the felony record does not necessarily mean that the offender is violent in nature. Also adding to these statistics are the punitive sentencing measures associated with the War on Drugs of the 1980s and 1990s where the rate of drug-using offenders being locked up was at an all-time high, regardless of whether the crime involved violence or any form of drug trafficking (Anno et al., 2004).

Thus, the *habitual elderly offenders* and the *offenders-turned-elderly-in-prison* are the result of a confluence of social factors and criminal justice policies. These offenders, for various reasons, have been given enhanced penalties that preclude their release into the community. This greatly distinguishes them from the *elderly first-time offender* who does not share a similar criminogenic background. Though they may appear to be the same at first glance, they are usually quite different from one another, and the public would be well-served to keep this squarely in mind.

The reasons for these differences in typologies have generated numerous criminological debates during the past two decades. Indeed, some theorists, such as Terrie Moffitt, contend that the early backgrounds of most of these offenders were troubled, even as far back as early childhood. She argues that one would find if one were able to go back in time, that this group of offenders went through a variety of causal sequences that began during critical formative years and "are dominated by chains of cumulative and contemporary continuity" (Moffitt, cited in Cullen & Agnew, 2006, p. 510). Moffitt further contends that personal characteristics such as poor self-control, impulsivity, and "inability to delay gratification increase the risk that antisocial youngsters will make irrevocable decisions that close the doors of opportunity" (cited in Cullen & Agnew, 2006, p. 510). Thus, Moffitt would say that most of the people that we see now as geriatric offenders were destined to be in their current plight from a very early age due to a variety of personal characteristics that set them apart from other young children. Indeed, these offenders, as juveniles, were even different from other juvenile offenders who eventually *aged out* of criminal activity. The reason for this is due to the personal characteristics that Moffitt notes, which are synonymous with the risk factors discussed earlier, in Chapter 12, that were related to juvenile offenders.

Thus it is that Moffitt would contend that the *habitual elderly offender* and the *offender-turned-elderly-in-prison* were what she calls life course persistent (LCP) offenders, meaning that they commit crimes persistently throughout their life span. Those juveniles that aged out of crime or responded to treatment would be termed adolescent limited (AL) offenders by Moffitt, since their offending was restricted to adolescence or young adulthood.

Moffitt's contentions are quite interesting because they demonstrate a life course connection between juvenile offending discussed in Chapter 12 of this text and geriatric offenders examined in this current chapter. Her theory provides an explanation for the two more serious geriatric offender typologies that are encountered by the criminal justice system. The interconnections between early offending and later-life offending are explained by her *life course persistent* offender category. In many ways, Moffitt provides the missing link between juvenile offenders that fail to reform and the persistent adult offender that ultimately turns gray within the criminal justice system. Incidentally, the *elderly first-time offender* is not addressed by any specific criminological theory. This is largely due to the fact that these offenders tend to engage in criminal activity that is isolated in nature and typically due to spurious causal factors.

SOURCES: Cullen, F. T., & Agnew, R. (2006). *Criminological theory: Past to present* (3rd ed.). Los Angeles: Roxbury; Anno, B. J., Graham, C., Lawrence, J. E., & Shansky, R. (2004). *Correctional health care: Addressing the needs of elderly, chronically ill, and terminally ill inmates.* Washington, DC: National Institute of Corrections.

Post-prison Community Supervision (Parole)

It is suggested that community supervision agencies work closely with the Social Security Administration to ensure that elderly offenders on community supervision are certified as eligible to draw benefits in a timely manner upon release. Referrals to long-term care and assisted-living facilities and eligibility determinations for Medicaid should also be conducted. Last, the task of finding a job is particularly difficult for the nonoffending elderly population, so this will naturally be problematic for offenders just released. Community supervision agencies should develop a community-based program that attempts to link these offenders with jobs so that subsistence is at least moderately covered.

However, problems with motivation often emerge with geriatric offenders. It is thought that older offenders are often hard to motivate due to their bleak perceptions of their future prospects. Further, many elderly offenders have few support systems (as discussed earlier), have no permanent place to live, have serious health problems, and are typically harder to employ (Hanser, 2007a). Because of these drawbacks, they are often considered poor prospects for most comprehensive reintegration programs, since these offenders are viewed as being beyond assisting. Rather, these offenders are seen as being inclined to simply wait for their ultimate demise, watching one day pass into the next with a depressive mood that undermines their ability to perform any of the necessary functions required by community supervision programs. Elderly offenders that have spent long periods behind bars tend to have fewer living friends or family members that can lend assistance to their transition within the community. Many of these friends or family may have since died or moved on with their lives, leaving the elderly offender on his own. Thus, these offenders may be very difficult to reintegrate.

Also, parole from prison is usually contingent upon good institutional adjustment, which is often demonstrated by participation in various programs within the prison institution. This type of participation is associated with improvements in risk management, improvements in behaviors and attitudes, and so forth. Since the majority of elderly offenders do not take active part in many prison programs, they may not be readily eligible for community release. Due to these and other reasons, elderly offenders have a less favorable prognosis and therefore do not obtain community release from prison more often than the average inmate; they may in actuality receive it less. The result is that many elderly offenders do not even bother to apply for parole and instead consign themselves to ultimately dying within the institution.

Because of this, Uzoaba (1998) states that the parole system should recognize that elderly offenders are burdened with a double disadvantage, having a criminal record and an advanced age. Bias or ageism against elderly workers is itself a stigma difficult to overcome. Add to this a criminal conviction on record and it makes it very difficult for elderly offenders to gain economic stability while in the community. Indeed, for some offenders with serious health care costs, prison may become the preferred domicile. In fact, it may be speculated that just as the homeless have been known to commit petty crimes so that they can stay in jail during the winter months, elderly offenders may commit crimes later in life as a means of obtaining at least minimal medical care without enduring the financial burden. This may be particularly true if they have been unable to afford medical insurance, and this is likely to be the case for many of those offenders that have been recidivists. Though this may sound far-fetched, prison may be considered a feasible option for persons who are involved in a criminogenic subculture, particularly if they have been incarcerated in their past.

CONCLUSION

This chapter has discussed three different offender categories, each of which addressed a different aspect of diversity. These three groups included minority racial and ethnic groups, female offenders, and elderly offenders, and the discussion thus addressed issues related to race, gender, and age among the offender population. Racial minorities are overrepresented among the offender population on community supervision, and this alone makes it important for community supervision staff to be well-versed in the dynamics impacting different racial and cultural groups. In other words, agencies must emphasize the need for cultural competence among their employees, and this requires specific effort, training, and exposure when developing such competence. The many challenges facing different racial and cultural groups should be taken into account, both in regard to rapport between the supervision officer and the offender and in regard to recidivism and treatment outcomes.

Female offenders are impacted by a number of specific social ills, many of which are fairly unique. Among these are domestic violence, sexual abuse, drug use, prostitution, sexually transmitted diseases, and child custody issues. Since these offenders represent a sizable portion of the community supervision population, it is important that community supervision professionals become accustomed to the challenges facing the female offender. Further, this offender population is likely to continue to grow in number, making this all the more relevant. Many of the problems associated with female offenders have hidden costs that affect the rest of society in a multifaceted manner. Any failure to improve services to this offending population will simply ensure that future generations likewise adopt criminogenic patterns of social coping. This is specifically the case given that female offenders tend to be primary caretakers of children in the majority of cases. In the long term, it is advisable that agencies work to improve services and ensure that accommodations are made for female offenders.

Elderly offenders are the fastest growing group of offenders in the nation, and this group is a virtual microcosm of the "graying" that is occurring throughout the rest of the nation. It should also be recognized that elder offenders are a diverse group. This presents an even more difficult challenge in providing services to this group. This also makes it difficult to decide on housing considerations for these offenders within prison settings (see the Cross-National Perspective box in this chapter). Community supervision agencies are not as challenged if family networks are in place, but the ability of community supervision agencies to ensure adequate reintegration services is severely impaired with elderly offenders.

Typically, correctional programs are designed for younger offenders who have time in their life span to overcome some of the stigma associated with a criminal conviction. However, even beyond the concerns with stigma is the deviance from societal expectations of the elderly. Society, simply put, does not expect the elderly to commit crimes, and thus society is often ill-equipped to address issues surrounding such offenders. Both institutional and community corrections will need to increase and refine their services to the elderly or run the risk of creating either legal liability to the inmate or some form of public safety error with the community. Neither of these is a desirable option, making services for elderly offenders an ever greater priority.

Key Terms

Adolescent limited (AL) offenders

American Indian or Native American

Asian or Asian American

Black or African American

Cultural competence

Discrimination

Disparity

Ethnicity

Female offenders

Geriatric/elderly offenders

Hispanic or Latino American

Institutionalized racism

Life course persistent (LCP) offenders

Native Hawaiian or Other Pacific Islander

Race

White or Caucasian American

"What Would You Do?" Exercise

On a late Tuesday night, you get a call from one of your probationers named Linda. She is female, 30 years old, and has been sexually abused in her childhood. She was put on probation for a drug possession charge but has also been active in prostitution and drug smuggling. Typically, she smuggles drugs for her husband, a man that has been known to "pimp" her out to friends and associates on occasion. Further, she has acted as a "mule," carrying drugs across state lines for her boyfriend by hiding them in internal body cavities.

Linda has been doing well during this current sentence of probation. She is not on home confinement or intensive supervision, nor is she on electronic monitoring. She has two children, and she has recently been awarded custody of both. She has been working in a retail store and has been doing fairly well in meeting the conditions of her probation.

However, the call that you receive lets you know that Linda is not okay. She tells you that her boyfriend, a citizen of both Mexico and the United States, is very jealous and has been upset with her because he believes that she is flirting with someone at the retail store. She explains that her boyfriend does not mind sharing her with friends and associates since that is business and money is being made. But he does not want her getting involved with other men, because she will then be likely to leave.

While on the phone, she explains to you that her boyfriend has threatened to take her kids to Mexico and go into hiding if she does not do what he says. She explains that he knows many dangerous men in this area and that he is connected with a number of gang members, though he is not himself a gang member. She says that she cannot go to a shelter, even a domestic violence shelter, because she knows that he will be able to find her; the gangs have female spies in all of the abuse shelters throughout the state.

Finally, she tells you that if he is arrested, he has arranged to have members of the Bandidos (a Mexican biker gang) take her kids. They will leave and flee to Mexico, and Linda will never see her kids again.

Linda does not know what to do and asks you, her community supervision officer, for help.

What would you do?

Applied Exercise

For this exercise, pretend that you are a correctional treatment specialist (students may recall these types of practitioners from Chapter 4). Read the case vignette below regarding Duane and then explain how you would design a "mini" treatment plan for the offender in this vignette. This assignment will require that you complete outside research on your own. You must specifically explain the types of treatment orientations you might use with this offender, and you should also provide a clear and well-designed supervision strategy for this client.

Students should complete this application exercise as a mini paper that explains the scenario and what you would do to aid Duane. Total word count: 900 to 2,100 words.

Applied Exercise Case Vignette

Duane is currently on probation for voyeurism and indecent exposure. He has been arrested and convicted of both. The community supervision department has decided to send him to your office for mental health services. From the records given to you, it is obvious that Duane also suffers from dementia. His records note a gradual onset and continuing cognitive decline over the past few years. Duane is 64 years old and has numerous respiratory health problems related to heavy smoking. He has been diagnosed with dementia of the Alzheimer's Type, with early onset.

Duane has been exhibiting bizarre behavior lately, including uncontrollable and unpredictable bursts of cursing and screaming, petty shoplifting in retail stores, and a concurring total loss of memory of the incidents.

Duane is beginning to demonstrate problems with spatial perception and has injured himself numerous times while in his own home. He has two daughters, Jenny (age 28) and Tina (age 25), both of whom refuse to talk with him. He has exposed himself to one of his granddaughters (Jenny's 5-year-old daughter), and he was caught spying on Tina when she was in bed with her husband. Both Jenny and Tina have had strained relationships with their father in the past and left home early. Incidentally, Duane is a widower and was retired early by the chemical plant at which he had worked.

Duane is often morose and sullen, and has actually brought up doing something "crazy." One of his friends told a senior-care worker that Duane has thought about "going out with a bang" and described notions that Duane had been considering (e.g., committing bank robbery, a mass shooting, bombing some popular cite, etc.). Duane alludes to these possibilities as if they were a joke. You are not so sure.

You will be seeing Duane later this afternoon. It is not really clear if anything can, in fact, be done to "fix" these problems. What do you do?

CHAPTER 15

Program Evaluation and Future Trends in Community Corrections

LEARNING OBJECTIVES

1. Identify the process of evaluative research and distinguish between process and outcome measures.

2. Understand the basics of cost-effectiveness studies.

3. Know and apply the assessment-evaluative cycle.

4. Be able to explain how evaluative research contributes to public safety.

5. Be aware of likely future trends in community supervision programs.

INTRODUCTION

One of the first questions asked by politicians, policy makers, program administrators, and government officials is, "Is the program working?" That is, they want to know, "Is the money that we are spending on a particular program yielding positive results and accomplishing the goals set forth?" As will be illuminated in this chapter, the question of whether a program is effective is often a very difficult issue to decide. The number of variables impacting such results is legion. When one considers the enormous complexity of human beings and the various motivations driving behavior, it becomes clear that researchers need a framework from which to operate.

Effective research and evaluation of community corrections programs is critical if we are to begin to understand what treatments are capable of producing lasting change in offenders. Failing to effectively research and evaluate such programs is, in essence, resigning our efforts to chance. Chance is not acceptable, however, when huge amounts of money and many individuals' lives are at stake. Therefore, the question becomes, how do we effectively evaluate community corrections programs charged with administering habilitating or rehabilitating services to offenders? How do we know what is working? How do we know which

463

treatments are most effective? Finally, how do we know if the treatment is flawed, or if the method in which the treatment is administered is flawed?

These important questions provide the foundation on which this chapter is constructed. The most effective way to begin to identify "what works" is through research and evaluation driven by principles of scientific investigation. *Science is a concept that describes the process of observing, identifying, describing, experimentally investigating, and theoretically explaining natural phenomena.* This chapter begins with an explanation of scientific investigation and the necessary steps in attempting to arrive at the truth. We will also briefly look at various research designs with an aim toward identifying those most capable of producing results that are valid and reliable. In addition, we will discuss the specific function of evaluation research, which can be described as a form of explanatory research. Finally, the chapter concludes with a discussion of ethical principles related to conducting research.

SCIENTIFIC INQUIRY

One of the questions that often accompany results of research endeavors is, "Are the results based on science?" In fact, for any consumer of research this should be an important concern. Only through the process of scientific research can we be reasonably confident that our findings accurately depict the phenomenon under scrutiny. Scientific inquiry can be described through the following steps, which should be viewed as a cycle:

1. We formulate a theory about some phenomenon.

2. By the process of deduction, we develop a hypothesis about the possible relationship among the constructs of the theory.

3. We design a test of this hypothesis.

4. We use this test to gather and analyze the data.

5. We then interpret the data.

6. Through an inductive process, we confirm, modify, or reject the original theory (Friel, 2008).

Viewing this process as a cycle is very important, especially within the social sciences. The goal of scientific research is to understand how things work through establishing scientific laws about relationships among variables. Examples of scientific laws include pendulum motion and gravity. Another example is the mathematical equation of $2 + 2 = 4$. These are facts and do not change. Within the social sciences, however, scientific facts are very difficult to produce. For example, we cannot say that murder is the result of poverty, or that murder is the result of anger, or that murder is the result of neglect. Some murders may be the result of power, or greed, or a feeling of having been disrespected, whereas others may be the result of mental illness. As mentioned above, human behavior is very complex. There are myriad reasons why someone might commit murder, theft, or assault. Therefore, the process of scientific investigation might best be thought of as a circular process that never ends.

From Theory to Hypothesis to Acceptance/Rejection of the Theory

A **theory** is a concept that describes the process of developing a set of interrelated constructs that purport to explain some phenomenon (Friel, 2008). Friel notes that theory serves as both a means and an end in the process of scientific inquiry. In the form of a means, a theory provides direction and organization in attempting to predict or explain some phenomenon. For example, a criminal justice official may theorize that a person suffering from high rates of trauma is more likely to be involved in criminal behavior. This is an example of a theory that is based on the observations of a particular individual. The two interrelated constructs contained within our hypothetical theory consist of trauma and criminal behavior. Once tested, our theory could serve as an end in the form of providing scientific information regarding the impact of trauma on criminal behavior. The real value of theory is that we are able to focus on specific constructs and ultimately determine if they are significantly related. What if we wanted to test our hypothetical theory? How would the process work?

It is important to understand that a theory on its own cannot be tested. A theory contains broad, interrelated constructs that must be defined before they can be tested. A hypothesis is the bridge between the theory and its test. A **hypothesis** is an affirmative statement about the relationship between two variables. Therefore, in order for our theory to be transformed into a hypothesis, we must define trauma and criminal behavior. Through the process of defining these terms, we will take two constructs and turn them into variables via *operationalization*. For example, we could operationalize trauma through the use of a trauma scale. Criminal behavior may be operationalized as any action that is forbidden through statutory law. As a result, through the process of defining our constructs, we can develop a hypothesis consisting of variables that could read as follows: Persons with higher trauma scores are more likely to be involved in behaviors forbidden by statutory law. It is now possible to create a test of this hypothesis.

First, we could select a trauma scale used to measure trauma. This would provide quantitative data regarding perceptions of different events that may have resulted in trauma. Second, we could review court records to see how often a person has been arrested by law enforcement. Together, we have the necessary information to gather and then analyze our data.

The method we choose to analyze the data depends on the specific research question and the specifics of our hypothesis. For example, our hypothetical research question is, do higher rates of trauma increase the likelihood of criminal behavior? Therefore one way to analyze our data using a method with which we are able to answer our research question would be correlational analysis. Through a correlational analysis, we could determine if there is a correlation (relationship) between trauma scores and number of arrests. Obviously, we are not able to determine causality with this method, but we would be able to ascertain whether there is a relationship and also the direction of the relationship.

Interpreting the data is a very important step, and one must use caution to ensure the interpretations stay within the scope of the information provided. Continuing with our hypothetical research question, we might find that there is in fact a correlation between trauma and criminal behavior. We might even find that those who score higher on the trauma scale are more likely to be involved with criminal behavior and have been arrested more times than those who have lower scores on the trauma scale.

Based on the interpretation of the data, we can confirm, modify, or reject our original theory that trauma is related to criminal behavior. The real message, however, is that scientific inquiry does not end here. The only time scientific inquiry ends, in relation to a specific research question, is if our results produce a scientific law. As was mentioned above, in the social sciences this is rarely the case. Therefore, the process is best viewed as ongoing, with additional pieces of the puzzle constantly being added and other incorrect pieces being discarded. Once we have concluded that trauma is likely to be related to criminal behavior, we may expand our research question to include the variable of poverty. For example, it seems as though those individuals who suffer higher rates of trauma and are also exposed to poverty might be more likely to be involved with criminal behavior. To test this theory, the process of scientific inquiry begins anew.

Reliability and Validity in Evaluative Studies

The specific design a researcher chooses to evaluate a research question depends on many different factors. For example, how much time, money, and assets are available? How important are the potential findings? Are these findings going to be used to determine policies and procedures, or are the results primarily intended for personal use? These initial questions are very important and drive many of the critical decisions involved with identifying the appropriate research design. For criminal justice purposes, the results of research projects are often critical and frequently determine if programs will continue to exist. For example, much research has been conducted in relation to the viability of juvenile boot camp programs. The results have generally shown that juvenile boot camps are not able to sustain lasting change in the behavior of juveniles (students may recall this from Chapter 12). In essence, the research showed that many of the juveniles returned to criminal behavior once back in their original environments.

The question, however, is, are the results accurate? How do we know if our findings accurately depict the phenomenon under scrutiny? For example, is it the structure of juvenile boot camps that is flawed, or is it that juvenile boot camps could be well-designed and successful if there was a reentry component that helped offenders adjust to going back to their original neighborhoods? All of these questions are primarily hinged on two central constructs, first introduced in Chapter 3: (1) the reliability and (2) the validity of a study.

Reliability is a concept that describes the accuracy of a measure, which in turn describes the accuracy of a study. Students may recall that this same concept was presented earlier, in Chapter 3, when addressing risk prediction and assessment. In that case, reference was made to the reliability of measurement scales, whereas in this case, we refer to the reliability of measures in a study. In both cases, the general concept is the same. For example, let's assume we are attempting to measure whether a person is experiencing depression. Reliability describes how accurate our measure is in capturing the person's true level of depression. Is the person mildly depressed; moderately depressed; or experiencing major, debilitating depression? Our measure is said to be reliable if it is able to assess the person's true level of depression. Our measure would not be reliable if results show only minor depression when in fact the person is moderately or majorly depressed.

Some of the literature describes reliability as a measure's ability to yield consistent results. Certainly, this is an important component, but it should not be the sole indicator of whether a measure is reliable. For example, a measure may consistently show a moderately depressed person as only mildly depressed. In this case, our measure could be described as consistent but not reliable. Keep in mind that reliability describes accuracy. The best way to describe a measure that consistently shows a moderately depressed person to be only mildly depressed is consistently inaccurate and therefore not reliable.

Validity is a concept that describes whether the chosen instrument is measuring what it is intended to measure. This concept was also addressed in Chapter 3, where it was noted that instruments must be valid if one wishes to measure the actual phenomenon of interest (such as recidivism predictors, treatment success, and so forth). In order for a study to be valid, it must measure the intended variable. Continuing with the example of depression, our study would be said to be valid if we are in fact measuring depression as opposed to anxiety or some other disorder. Therefore, if we are truly able to answer a research question, our methods must yield results that are both reliable and valid. If our results cannot be characterized as reliable *and* valid, our best answer becomes, "We don't know." That is, the only true response our study supports is, "It appears as though there is a connection, but we are not really sure." Obviously, such determinations are nothing more than guesswork and do not aid administrators in making effective and future-oriented decisions for their agencies.

Therefore, reliability and validity are crucial components within the domain of evaluative research that generates data for administrative planning. Research concerning the discipline of criminal justice is among the most important because of the nature and implications of its findings, such as a person's freedom or whether a person is administered a treatment that has the ability to better his or her quality of life. How, then, do we ensure that our results are both reliable and valid? The answer is that it is impossible to ensure complete reliability and validity. Then how do we ensure that our results are as reliable and valid as possible? The answer to this question is directly related to whether the researcher strictly adhered to the principles of scientific inquiry. In the following subsections, several research designs available to researchers are described. Much of the information is borrowed from a document published by the National Institute of Justice (NIJ; 1992), as these designs have an emphasis on criminal justice applications.

Experimental Designs

One investigative technique that provides the analyst maximum control, so that the relationship between a particular element of a project and the desired outcome can be isolated from other causal forces and measured accurately, is the laboratory experiment. If all factors are held constant, and an effect is observed after one factor changes, the researcher is in the strongest position to say that the manipulated factor caused the observed effect. Branches of science that have been able to impose laboratory conditions upon the matters they investigate have thus developed powerful explanations for complex phenomena.

Outside the laboratory, one can approximate lab conditions in field experiments (Campbell & Stanley, 1963). If one were in the laboratory studying the effects of a treatment regime, one might be able to control not only environment but also individual differences among subjects. (Laboratory mice, for example, are bred from a common genetic stock expressly for the purpose of experimentation.) In the field, however, such control over subjects and their environments cannot be gained. The strategy for approximating this control is to assign at random equally eligible subjects (cases, arrestees, addicts, and so forth) to two groups. The subjects in one group (the "experimental group") are then exposed to or given the "treatment"—be it a drug treatment project, enhanced prosecution, or whatever else the project is designed to do—while the other group (the "control group") is not. Random assignment provides optimal assurance that any differences in the outcomes observed in the two groups can be attributed to the experimental treatment, and not to preexisting differences or to chance.

While it may seem difficult to undertake experiments in criminal justice settings, several studies with experimental designs have been carried out with much success, yielding powerful findings (Lempert & Visher, 1987). Unfortunately, such studies are complicated, often vulnerable to a number of threats that may spoil the ability to draw strong conclusions, and generally very costly and time-consuming.

Quasi-experimental Studies

Where random assignment of participants to treatment or control groups is not feasible for practical, ethical, or legal reasons, the evaluator may choose **quasi-experimental evaluation designs** to approximate the advantages of random selection. One such design involves identifying a comparison group that is similar to the treatment group in those characteristics thought to be capable of influencing the outcome under examination (Campbell & Stanley, 1963). The strength of this design rests on the extent to which all the influential characteristics are accounted for in selecting the control group. The analyst can then account statistically for differences between groups that might influence the observed outcomes. The only requirements are that no differentiating characteristic belong uniquely to one group, and that such competing factors be measured in both groups.

Because the use of a nonrandom comparison group does not eliminate all alternative explanations for the relationship between treatment and outcome, this type of design requires much more complicated analysis and yields less certain results than true experiments. Nonetheless, quasi-experimental designs can at times produce findings that are much stronger than other types of evaluation methods that impose fewer controls (e.g., case studies, before/after comparisons, descriptive models).

Some treatment programs are not well-suited to either experimental or quasi-experimental evaluation designs because their operations fluctuate too much due to their newness. Both evaluation designs require that treatment be constant and uniform throughout the time that the data are collected. If programs have not reached a state of relative stability in operations, the expense and time required for an experiment are likely to be wasted. In such instances, a focus on program implementation is likely to be more fruitful.

Before/After Studies

When the evaluator is asked to assess the impact of a project (program), or to assess its effectiveness in accomplishing its goals, methods for testing cause-and-effect hypotheses are called for. One such method compares the target population or conditions before and after the project begins its operations. This "bargain basement" approach seeks to establish that participation in, or implementation of, the project is at least associated with the desired change. This design, termed a **before/after comparison study,** requires obtaining data about the conditions that prevailed before the project intervention was initiated. (The researcher may find it possible to rely on data that another agency collected before the project's intervention occurred.) If the desired changes are shown to occur after the intervention, support is given to the assertion that the project *caused* the change to happen.

Photo 15.1   During the evaluation process, it is important to have cooperation from the courthouse and from those persons affiliated with courtroom operations. Attorneys and other courtroom actors, whether intentional or otherwise, ultimately contribute to the overall evaluation outcome that occurs in our justice system.

Confidence in the findings of such before/after comparisons depends, however, upon whether factors other than the project's interventions changed as well. Was the observed change really due to another force that operated independently of the project? Many of the conditions targeted by criminal justice projects are influenced by demographic, social, legal, and economic forces that operate independently of a project's intervention. Any increase or decrease in the observed outcomes may be affected by these outside factors and may therefore be unrelated to the project. To rule out these other possible explanations, the analyst/researcher must devise strategies for testing them. One such method is to collect data on these other possible causes and to impose statistical controls to isolate their effects from the project's operations (NIJ, 1992).

EVALUATION RESEARCH

In the past several years, a massive effort on behalf of the United States government has been aimed at enhancing evaluation practices and services. As a result, various documents have been published and placed in the public domain to help community corrections programs better understand the impact of various treatment services. Much of the following information comes from the Center for Substance Abuse Treatment (2005), a government agency responsible for implementing and evaluating many treatment programs attempting to better serve offenders suffering from mental illness and co-occurring disorders.

Research and evaluation are critical dimensions of community corrections programs in the criminal justice system. Evaluations are needed for program monitoring and for decision making by program staff, criminal justice administrators, and policy makers. These evaluations provide accountability, identify strengths and weaknesses, and create a basis for program revision. In addition, evaluation reports are useful learning tools for others who are interested in developing effective programs. Many treatment programs in the criminal justice system have operated without evaluations for many years, only to find out later that key outcome data are needed to justify program continuation.

Conducting an adequate evaluation requires the evaluator to clearly formulate the treatment model and reasonable program goals and to specify objectives related to client needs. General goals must be translated into measurable outcomes. The evaluator generally works closely with program administrators to translate their evaluation guidelines into operational components. For example, general goals of helping program participants become drug and crime free can be operationalized into intermediate goals of changing behavior (e.g., reductions in rule infractions and fewer positive drug test results) while in a program. In essence, scientific principles for conducting research should be carefully adhered to in order to enhance the viability of findings.

There are three basic components of evaluation:

1. Implementation

2. Process

3. Outcome

An important note before we discuss the three main parts of evaluation research is that while implementation and process evaluations can begin when the program is initiated, outcome evaluation should not begin until the program has been fully implemented. Outcome evaluations are generally more costly than other types of evaluation and are warranted for programs of longer duration that are aimed at modifying lifestyles (such as therapeutic communities), rather than for drug education interventions that are less intensive and less likely to produce long-term effects.

Implementation Evaluation

While programs often look promising in the proposal stage, many fail to materialize as planned in the security-oriented correctional environment. Other programs are rigidly implemented as planned, but lack adjustments for the realities of community corrections, often rendering them less effective. **Implementation evaluations** are aimed at identifying problems and accomplishments during the early phases of program development for feedback to clinical and administrative staff. Such evaluations involve informal and formal interviews with correctional administrators, staff, and offenders to ascertain their degree of satisfaction with the program and their perceptions of problems. In order to initiate an implementation evaluation, in addition to having a clear, detailed proposal that describes the planned program, evaluators should be familiar with the model or theory the program is based on:

- Criteria for participation
- Program components

- Planned treatment duration
- Staff qualifications
- Plans for staff orientation and training
- The schedule for implementation

These elements provide the basis for assessment. Periodic implementation feedback reports to program administrators can be very useful in identifying problems and planning corrective measures prior to services being disrupted.

Process Evaluation

Traditionally, **process evaluation** refers to assessment of the effects of the program on clients while they are in the program, making it possible to assess the institution's intermediary goals. Process evaluation involves analyzing records related to the following:

- Type and amount of services provided
- Attendance and participation in group meetings
- Number of clients who are screened, admitted, reviewed, and discharged
- Percentage of clients who favorably complete treatment each month
- Percentage of clients who have infractions or rule violations
- Number of clients who test positive for substances (This can be compared with urinalysis results for the general prison population.)

Effective programs produce positive client changes. These changes initially occur during participation in the program and ideally continue upon release into the community. The areas of potential client change that should be assessed include the following:

- Cognitive understanding (e.g., mastery of program curriculum)
- Emotional functioning (e.g., anxiety and depression)
- Attitudes/values (e.g., honesty, responsibility, and concern for others)
- Education and vocational training progress (e.g., achievement tests)
- Behavior (e.g., rule infractions and urinalyses results)

Within community corrections, it is also important to evaluate program impact on the host institution. Well-run treatment programs often generate an array of positive developments affecting the morale and functioning of the entire institution. Likewise, poorly run programs will yield negative developments in these same areas. Some areas to examine for program impact include the following:

- *Offender behavior.* Review the number of rule infractions, the cost of hearings, court litigation expenses, and inmate cooperation in general prison operations.
- *Staff functioning.* Assess stress levels, which may manifest in the number of sick days taken and the rate of staff turnover. Generally, the better the program, the lower the stress, and the better the attendance, the involvement, and the commitment of staff.
- *Physical plant.* Examine the physical properties of the program. Assess general vandalism apparent in terms of damage to furniture or windows, as well as the presence of graffiti. Assess structural damage, for example, to walls and plumbing.

FIGURE 15.1 Commonly Used Measures in Reentry Program Performance

Process Measures

- Substance abuse treatment services received
- Employment services received
- Housing assistance received
- Family intervention and parent training received
- Health and mental health services received

Outcome Measures

- Rearrest rates
- Reincarceration rates
- Proportion employed
- Rates of drug relapse
- Frequency and severity of offenses
- Proportion that is self-sufficient
- Participation in self-improvement programs

SOURCE: Bureau of Justice Assistance, Center for Program Evaluation. (2007). *Reporting and using evaluation results.* Washington, DC: Author. Retrieved from http://www.ojp.usdoj.gov/BJA/evaluation/sitemap.htm.

Outcome Evaluation

Outcome evaluations involve quantitative research aimed at assessing the impact of the program on long-term treatment outcomes. Such evaluations are more ambitious and expensive than implementation or process evaluations. They are usually carefully designed studies that compare outcomes for a treatment group with outcomes for other less intensive treatments or a no-treatment control group (e.g., a sample of offenders who meet the program admission criteria but who do not receive treatment). Outcome evaluations may include complex statistical analyses and sophisticated report preparation.

Follow-up data (e.g., drug relapse, recidivism, employment status) are the heart of outcome evaluation. Follow-up data can be collected from criminal justice records and face-to-face interviews with individuals who participated in certain programs. Studies that use agency records are less expensive than locating participants and conducting follow-up interviews. Outcome evaluations can include cost-effectiveness and cost-benefit information that is important to policy makers. Because outcome research usually involves a relatively large investment of time and money, as well as the cooperation of a variety of people and agencies, it must be carefully planned. A research design may be very simple and easy to implement, or it may be more complex. In the case of more complex studies, it is usually advisable to enlist the assistance of an experienced researcher.

There is a hierarchy of evaluation approaches ranging from simple outcome monitoring to nonrandom or quasi-experimental designs to experimental research studies that use random assignment. As mentioned, the selection of a research design depends on available funding and assets, as well as whether comparison groups are available. Any claims to a program's effectiveness rest on comparisons that demonstrate that outcomes for the treatment group are superior to those for nontreatment groups or groups that have received another type of treatment. The power of a research design is related to how defensible study results are against potential criticisms. Usually, criticisms will be in the form of challenges regarding reliability and validity issues. Although simple outcome monitoring studies are relatively

Photo 15.2 In many instances, evaluators may use a variety of standardized tests and assessments to monitor client or offender progress. The selection of these instruments and the maintenance of their data can be very important, especially for agencies that seek grant funding. In this photo, the evaluator works late at night making decisions regarding assessment tools and the type of data that is desired for a prospective research and evaluation project.

economical to conduct, they lack the comparison groups needed to show the specific effects of a program. While specific program outcomes can be compared with national and state norms or with published outcomes of another program, such comparisons are limited because of the many uncontrolled potential differences between the program group being monitored and the comparison groups.

The defining characteristic of a **pure research design** is random assignment of offenders to treatment and control groups. Random assignment may be done by using a lottery-type procedure that ensures there are no systematic pre-treatment differences between the groups (such as motivation or background characteristics). The concern is that any important pre-treatment difference in program and control groups may bias the results and compromise any claims for program effectiveness. Random assignment is difficult to implement in community corrections programs because of ethical and legal implications of denying offenders treatment. If a program has a substantial waiting list, it may be feasible to implement a lottery procedure as a fair method to control program admission, thus creating a random assignment situation.

Nonrandom assignment is an attempt to approximate the power of the pure experimental design. A popular quasi-experimental design uses a comparison group that is matched to the program group on as many pre-treatment factors as possible. Statistical methods are frequently employed to control pre-treatment group differences that might influence outcomes. Large samples are needed in outcome studies to demonstrate significant results and to study the effects of multiple variables. For example, an analysis of the role of ethnicity (African American, Caucasian, and Hispanic/Latino) reduces group size by a third. When reporting results, it is generally best to use less complex statistics such as percentages and averages so that they are clear and understandable to nonstatisticians. Often, showing results in figures and charts is helpful. It is advisable to keep reports concise and clear for policy makers who may have little time or patience to study complex material. Finally, the credibility of outcome studies is often enhanced when conducted by outside researchers who have fewer vested interests in the outcomes.

STAFFING COMMUNITY CORRECTIONS PROGRAMS

Training and professional and workforce development issues are of paramount concern in implementation of treatment programs within the criminal justice system. Because the criminal justice system affects the environment in which treatment occurs and provides the structure to which the client must respond, community corrections staff need to become familiar with the criminal justice system, its unique terminology, and methods of balancing client treatment needs with safety issues. Treatment professionals working with criminal justice clients should be knowledgeable about criminogenic risk factors, the most effective strategies and approaches for use with offender populations, and the need for professional boundaries.

By the same token, criminal justice staff should understand the goals of substance abuse treatment, the effects of frequently abused drugs, and the various types of treatment that are available. In addition, staff should have a working knowledge of various emotional and psychological disorders that often accompany substance abuse. Treatment knowledge is particularly important for criminal justice staff, since treatment is increasingly affecting all aspects of diversion, community supervision, court monitoring, and incarceration. Cross-training activities can encourage employees to work together. Training is also needed to address the wide variety of "special needs" populations under criminal justice supervision and the impact of managed care systems and tiered placement criteria (e.g., American Society of Addiction Medicine criteria) on publicly funded treatment systems.

Given that the rapid growth of treatment programs within the criminal justice system has not been matched by equal growth in organizational and staff resources, the system has been strained. Staff turnover, burnout, and other occupational hazards can be addressed through efforts to increase professionalism, such as developing

- A clear hierarchy of staff positions with increasing responsibilities at each level.
- Clear requirements for advancement in the hierarchy.
- Incentives for additional training, made readily available.
- Incentives for working on units that are considered more difficult or are higher security.
- Merit pay (Center for Substance Abuse Treatment, 2005).

An Example: Evaluating a Jail Diversion Program

Jail diversion programs generally operate to divert offenders away from jail or prison and into community service programs able to address their needs (Mire, Forsyth, & Hanser, 2007). There are a variety of different diversion programs currently in existence, as described in Chapter 10. Drug court, for example, could be considered a derivative of diversion since the emphasis is on better addressing the needs of offenders suffering from substance abuse through the use of services provided in the community. The diversion program used here, as an example, is one that is funded through the federal government and is aimed at identifying and diverting offenders suffering from mental illness and co-occurring disorders.

The essence of this diversion program is to identify those offenders suffering from mental illness and co-occurring disorders who have been arrested for nonviolent offenses and provide them with appropriate community services aimed at addressing their psychological and emotional problems. Therefore, a possible theory to guide an evaluation of this program could be something similar to the following:

Offenders suffering from mental illness and co-occurring disorders are less likely to engage in crime if their needs are identified and addressed in community settings as opposed to being placed in a jail or prison.

The next step would be to begin the process of turning theoretical constructs into variables that can be measured. For example, what do we mean by mental illness and co-occurring disorders? Also, how do we define crime? These questions must be answered as we progress from theory to hypotheses. As mentioned above, a hypothesis consists of an affirmative statement about the relationship between variables. In order to transform a theoretical construct—mental illness—into a variable, we must define the construct through the process of operationalization. An example of operationalization could consist of the following:

Mental illness is a concept that describes the process of a person suffering from a diagnosable disorder such as depression, anxiety, trauma, bi-polar disorder, schizophrenia, etc. A co-occurring disorder is a concept that describes the process of a person suffering from more than one disorder such as substance abuse and depression, or substance abuse and trauma, etc. Crime is a concept that describes the process of a person engaging in activity that is prohibited by law, i.e., any action that is defined as a criminal offense.

Now we have risen from the theoretical domain into the operational domain of hypotheses. The difference between a theory and a hypothesis is that the hypothesis can be tested. Two possible hypotheses follow:

Hypothetical hypothesis 1:

Crime will be reduced if a nonviolent offender suffering from trauma and substance abuse receives counseling and education in the community, as opposed to being placed in jail.

Hypothetical hypothesis 2:

Counseling and education will improve the offender's quality of life, reducing the offender's participation in crime.

At this point, we have two potential hypotheses that consist of variables that can be measured. The next step is to design a test that is able to measure each variable in a manner that allows us to answer the research question: Are nonviolent offenders who suffer from mental illness and co-occurring disorders less likely to engage in crime if treated in the community as opposed to being placed in jail? There are a variety of research designs available to test the hypotheses. The question that researchers will have to answer is, how do we ensure maximum reliability and validity with the amount of money and assets available for the project? Currently, government-funded jail diversion programs are evaluated using a before/after design in which offenders are interviewed within 7 days of being accepted into the diversion program and again at 6 and 12 months. The purpose of this design is to obtain a baseline status of each offender and then determine if the program interventions are achieving the desired outcomes.

For many jail diversion programs, the process begins when an offender charged with an offense is arrested by police and brought in for booking (as students may recall from Chapter 10). In this example, the offender is assessed and found to be suffering from substance abuse and trauma. As a result, the offender is accepted into the jail diversion program. At this point, the first step is to obtain baseline information. This baseline information is likely to be related to a series of process and outcome variables that we might wish to measure. The idea is to generate sufficient information so that an effective measure can be obtained for specific areas of evaluative inquiry. When determining what our baseline data will consist of, it is useful to first have a clear idea of the types of process and outcome measures we wish to examine. The kinds of outcome information that might be collected can be found in Table 15.1, which demonstrates how general outcome measures as described in Focus Topic 15.1 can be expanded and tailored to a more specific area of evaluation—in this case, evaluation of a jail diversion program.

The **baseline interview** consists of gathering data related to each variable we are attempting to measure at the time of entry into the program. As was made clear in Chapter 3, it is important that we use valid and reliable survey or assessment instruments. Typically, *those instruments that are standardized are preferred to those that are not since their validity and reliability have been established by prior researchers.* After the point of the initial assessment, classification, and data collection of the offender, program offenders begin consuming services. The primary services offered include counseling, education, assistance with housing, and help finding employment. Counseling is a concept that describes the process of a trained and licensed professional attending to the psychological and emotional needs of the offender in an effort to improve

TABLE 15.1   Potential Outcome Measures for Jail Diversion Programs

Drugs	• Urinalysis results • Drug-related parole infractions • Drug-related arrests
Crime	• Parole rule infractions • Time until parole rule infraction • New misdemeanor arrests of any type • New felony arrests for non-drug-related crimes • New felony arrests for drug-related crimes • New felony arrests for violent crimes • Time until arrest • Reincarceration
Social adjustment	• Employment and education • Family (e.g., support, child rearing, marital, etc.) • Substance abuse treatment • Community involvement (e.g., community service)
HIV risk behaviors	• Intravenous drug injection • Sexual behavior • HIV test results
Cost information	• Cost estimates of substance use • Cost estimates of crimes • Cost estimates of social services to family (e.g., welfare) • Criminal justice processing and detention costs
Tracking information	• Tracking locator information (e.g., social security and license numbers, addresses of family and friends, etc.)

SOURCE: Center for Substance Abuse Treatment. (2005). Substance abuse treatment for adults in the criminal justice system. *Treatment Improvement Protocol (TIP) Series 44*. DHHS Publication No. (SMA) 05-4056. Rockville, MD: Substance Abuse and Mental Health Services Administration.

cognitive and behavioral processes. Education usually consists of a broad range of topics that include, but are not limited to, factors related to substance abuse, obtaining a GED, healthier methods of handling stress, and recognizing symptoms.

The 6- and 12-month interviews consist of surveys that are very similar to the baseline. The purpose of the interviews is to obtain data from each offender that accurately captures their perceptions of each variable and to begin the process of gauging the impact of the services being provided. Once we have conducted the 6- and 12-month interviews, the evaluation begins to focus on analyzing the data. Through the process of analyzing and interpreting our data, we can begin identifying whether the interventions have had an impact on the offender's overall quality of life and whether this seems to be correlated with reduced criminal behavior. It is important to note that our methods of analyzing and interpreting the data should be driven by the construction of our hypotheses. Finally, based on our results, we are able to modify, confirm, or reject our original theory.

A final note regarding this example is that researchers must be careful with the language they use in describing their results. For example, our hypothetical research design using a jail diversion program implemented a before-and-after study. There are many limitations to such a design. For example, we do not have a control group, we are not able to employ random sampling, and we are not able to control all variables that may be impacting the consumers. Because of this, we must be sure to phrase all findings as correlations and not causal factors of any change in the offender's behavior.

Program Quality, Staffing Quality, and Evaluation of Program Curricula

Aside from outcome and process measures, there are a number of other areas that agencies may wish to evaluate. These may or may not require the input of the offender, and they may or may not be dependent upon the offender population's outcome results. Some examples would be when agencies wish to assess the quality of their program, their staff, or their curricula. Each of these three components is very important, but may require something beyond simple outcome evaluation measures. In some cases, such as with program curricula, there may be a connection to the general process measures used to evaluate the program. However, it is important when agencies evaluate curricula that they keep this separate and distinct from the blurring effects of staff who may modify the general process with their own therapeutic slant or means of implementing aspects of a job requirement. In other words, the individual preferences of different persons employed in the agency are not what you hope to observe in a curricular assessment; rather, it is the uniform and written procedures that are of interest.

From the example with curricular assessment just noted, it is clear that evaluations can be quite complex and detailed, depending on the approach taken by the agency. The key to an effective and ethical evaluation is evaluative transparency. **Evaluative transparency** is when an agency's evaluative process allows an outside person (whether an auditor, an evaluator, or the public-at-large) to have full view of the agency's operations, budgeting, policies, procedures, and outcomes. In transparent agencies, there are no secrets, and confidential information is only kept when ethical or legal requirements mandate that the information not be transparent, such as with a client's treatment files or a victim's personal identity. In such cases, the intent is a benevolent safeguarding of the client's welfare, not the agency's own welfare.

If one is to evaluate the quality of a program, it stands to reason that the program must be transparent to the evaluator who is tasked with observing that program. Agencies that seek to meet high ethical standards must be transparent. This is a core requisite to ensuring the quality of the program that is implemented. Further, programs of quality are accountable to the public, and this is, in part, an element of transparency. Public accountability is a matter of good ethical bearing, and this is consistent with the reason that ethical safeguards are put into place—to protect the public consumer. In the case of community corrections agencies, the product that is "sold" to the public is community safety, and it is the obligation of the agency to be accountable and transparent to the public when providing services to its jurisdiction. Thus, in community corrections, the quality of the program should be appraised based on its ability to deliver ethical, open, and honest services that hold community safety paramount.

In regard to staffing quality, agencies should make a point to evaluate their standards as well as the support that they provide to their staff. Naturally, recruitment and hiring standards should be evaluated routinely, but it is also important that agencies examine their own support services for staff. Some examples might include the existence of an effective human resources division; sufficient budgeting for equipment to effectively do their job; and the nature of the job design, particularly in regard to caseload. As one might guess, this is related to the overall quality of the program as well.

Of course, agencies should also evaluate their hiring standards and should examine factors such as the number of complaints generated by the community regarding staff functioning. Grievances or complaints by offenders can also be examined if it should turn out that there is some legitimacy to such complaints. Likewise, employee standards of conduct are important, as are incidents where employees do not meet the standards expected by the agency. Further, staff should be consulted, and evaluators should consider whether the line staff feel prepared and whether they consider their work environment to be on a par with other agencies. All of this staff-related information provides a richer analysis of agency operations and also yields additional transparency in the day-to-day routines that occur.

Evaluation of the agency's curriculum is also needed. In treatment programs, this is an especially important consideration. Indeed, the curriculum of a treatment program forms the basis upon which the interventions will be implemented with offenders and also sets the tone for treatment services within the agency. As an example, a treatment program such as Family Foundations (an agency previously presented in Chapter 12) will have a curriculum that emphasizes family-based interventions that are common to most family therapists around the nation. On the other hand, a program like Rays of Sonshine (previously presented in Chapter 10) has a curriculum that is faith-based, being a unique modality unto itself. Incidentally, as was mentioned in Chapter 10, this program also adheres to the 12 core functions listed by the International Certification and Reciprocity Consortium (ICRC), functions that are an internationally recognized set of treatment curricula in their own right.

The point to the previous examples is that curriculum development is not a cosmetic issue or one that is of minor significance. Rather, the agency curriculum determines the entire approach used by case managers, correctional treatment specialists, and even administrators. The assessment of agency curriculum requires methodical processes that must be subject to replication. Often, when examining the curriculum, policies, or procedures of an agency, evaluators will utilize what is referred to as a content analysis of the written curriculum, policies, and procedures that exist within the agency. **Content analysis** is the "systematic analysis and selective classification of the contents of mass media. This technique is excellent for comparative and historical studies or for discerning trends in existing phenomena" (Hagan, 2000, p. 250). Content analyses occur at two levels, the manifest and the latent. *Manifest analyses* include the identification of key words and phrases, with a simple counting of their frequency. *Latent analyses* go beyond this to address the underlying intent behind written procedures and policies, rather than relying on mere word counts or the appearance of a given topic or subject matter. Obviously, the use of content analysis requires a great deal of expert judgment, and this requires that the evaluator be conversant on a given agency's goals, objectives, and mode of operation.

As an example, the author of this textbook employed content analysis to determine the degree of multicultural competence within the curriculum of state-approved agencies that delivered batterer intervention services. Through the counting of identified words and topics (e.g., multiculturalism, diversity, Latino American, Hispanic, Native American, African American, Asian American, cross-cultural, interracial, and so forth), a manifest analysis was conducted of the curricula throughout the targeted agencies. In addition, specific policies and their intent to serve diverse groups were analyzed, regardless of the specific wording. Instead, they were assessed based on intent and appropriateness of the surrounding multicultural population for that agency. This evaluation was able to determine whether agencies were, in fact, in tune with the needs of their region and whether their curricula served as an appropriate foundation to provide services to minority-status batterers within their jurisdiction. Thus, the use of content analysis is able to examine treatment orientations, agency operations, or policies as a means of determining the baseline appropriateness of agency services in relation to the needs of the service area in which they are located.

Cost-Effectiveness and Cost-Benefit Analyses

Another critical area in program development is that of program costs, including cost savings and cost-benefit/cost-offset information. Program administrators are routinely required to provide evidence that monies are being spent effectively. The literature indicates that treatment has cost benefits in certain settings. Positive cost-offset results (savings down the road) have been demonstrated to accrue from treatment through specific approaches such as drug courts (Belenko, 2001). Similar results have been shown for treatment in prison settings (McCollister & French, 2001). A **cost analysis** is important in determining how to allocate funds within a program and for understanding the relationship between costs and outcomes. Examining costs for the program as a whole (or for parts of it) is a basic form of cost analysis. Cost analyses can be provided as a monthly or quarterly report, as costs generally vary over time. Costs to evaluate at several levels include

- Total cost of the program for the average treatment.
- Cost of each part of the program each day.
- Total monthly or annual cost per offender.

According to the Center for Substance Abuse Treatment (2005), the major types of cost analyses include "cost," "cost-effectiveness," and "cost benefit," and these are described below:

Cost analysis	A thorough description of the type and amount of all resources used to produce substance abuse treatment services
Cost-effectiveness analysis	The relationship between program costs and program effectiveness—that is, patient outcome
Cost-benefit analysis	The measurement of both costs and outcomes in monetary terms

Some treatment program evaluations measure direct monetary outcomes, such as a reduction in the use of health services. Other treatment program evaluations can measure indirect costs and benefits, such as reduction in crime-related costs, reduced recidivism, and the costs of incarcerating offenders. Other ways to report the relationship between costs and benefits include the following:

- The *net benefit* of a program can be shown by subtracting the costs of a program from its benefits.
- The *ratio* of benefits to costs is found by dividing total program benefits by total program costs.
- The *time to return on investment* is the time it takes for program benefits to equal program costs.
- The *present value* of benefits takes into account the decreasing value of benefits attained in the distant future.
- Because neither net benefits nor cost-benefit ratios indicate the size of the cost *(initial investment)* required for treatment to yield the observed benefits, it is important to report this as well (Center for Substance Abuse Treatment, 2005).

Feedback Loops and Continual Improvement

In evaluating community corrections agencies, the information obtained from the evaluation should serve some useful purpose. The Bureau of Justice Assistance's Center for Program Evaluation (2007) elaborates on the need for evaluations to be constructed in a manner that is useful to the stakeholders of the evaluation. **Stakeholders** in community corrections evaluations include the agency personnel, the community in which the agency is located, and even the offender population that is being supervised. According to the Bureau of Justice Assistance (BJA), evaluators need to be clear on what agency administrators wish to evaluate, and evaluators must also ensure that administrators understand that evaluative efforts are to remain objective and unbiased in nature.

Beyond the initial understanding between administrators and evaluators, it is always important that evaluators provide recommendations for agencies, based on the outcome of the evaluation (BJA, 2007). It is through these recommendations that agencies can improve their overall services and enhance goal-setting strategies in the future. Indeed, evaluation information can be a powerful tool for a variety of stakeholders. Program managers can use the information to make changes in their programs that will enhance their effectiveness. Decision makers can ensure that they are funding effective programs. Other authorities can ensure that programs are developed as intended and have sufficient resources to implement activities and meet their goals and objectives (BJA, 2007).

Agencies that are adept at assimilating evaluative information and recommendations are sometimes referred to as learning organizations. **Learning organizations** have the inherent ability to adapt and change, improving performance through continual revision of goals, objectives, policies, and procedures. Throughout this process, learning organizations respond to the various pushes and pulls that are placed upon them by utilizing a continual process of data-driven, cyclical, and responsive decision making that results in heightened adaptability of the organization. The ideal community corrections agency is a learning organization—one that can adjust to outside community needs and challenges as well as internal personnel and resource issues. Finally, in its ideal state, evaluation is an ongoing process that is embedded in the process of program planning, action setting, and later improvement. The BJA (2007) notes that evaluation findings can be used to revise policies, activities, goals, and objectives (see Focus Topic 15.1) so that community supervision agencies can provide the best possible services to the community to which they are accountable.

FOCUS TOPIC 15.1

WHAT ARE POLICIES, ACTIVITIES, GOALS, AND OBJECTIVES?

Policy: A governing principle pertaining to goals, objectives, or activities. It is a decision on an issue not resolved on the basis of facts and logic only. For example, the policy of expediting drug cases in the courts might be adopted as a basis for reducing the average number of days from arraignment to disposition.

Activities: Services or functions carried out by a program (i.e., what the program does). For example, treatment programs may screen clients at intake, complete placement assessments, provide counseling to clients, etc.

Goal: A desired state of affairs that outlines the ultimate purpose of a program. This is the end toward which program efforts are directed. For example, the goal of many criminal justice programs is a reduction in criminal activity.

Objectives: Specific results or effects of a program's activities that must be achieved in pursuing the program's ultimate goals. For example, a treatment program may expect to change offender attitudes (objective) in order to ultimately reduce recidivism (goal).

SOURCE: Bureau of Justice Assistance, Center for Program Evaluation. (2007). *Reporting and using evaluation results.* Washington, DC: Author. Retrieved from http://www.ojp.usdoj.gov/BJA/evaluation/sitemap.htm.

This again reflects many of the points made in earlier chapters, particularly Chapter 2. In fact, students may notice that Focus Topic 15.1 is actually a reprinted version of Focus Topic 2.1. This is to demonstrate the importance of policy making as well as the setting of goals and objectives that guide a community supervision agency into the future. This cyclical pattern of going from assessment to implementation to evaluation demonstrates a continual circle of development that uses past data to better face future challenges.

This is the most effective means of utilizing real-world research to tailor-fit programs to the challenges within a jurisdiction. With this in mind, we once again look to the work of Van Keulen (1988), who roughly 20 years ago noted that

> Goals and objectives also play a critical role in evaluation by providing a standard against which to measure the program's success. If the purpose of the program is to serve as an alternative to jail, the number of jail-bound offenders the program serves would be analyzed. If the program's focus is to provide labor to community agencies, the number of hours worked by offenders would be examined. Last, having a statement of goals and objectives will enhance your program's credibility by showing that careful thought has been given to what you are doing. (p. 1)

As pointed out in Chapter 2, Van Keulen (1988) demonstrates the reasons why clarity in definition, point, and purpose behind a community corrections program is important. Clearly articulated goals not only help to crystallize the agency's philosophical orientation regarding the supervision process but also provide for more measurable constructs that lend themselves to effective evaluation. Clarity in the goals and objectives allows the agency to perform evaluative research to determine if its efforts are actually successful or if they are in need of improvement. This then facilitates the ability of the agency to come "full circle" as the planning, implementation, evaluation, and refinement phases of agency operations unfold.

COMMUNITY HARM WITH INEFFECTIVE PROGRAMS: SEPARATING POLITICS FROM SCIENCE IN THE EVALUATIVE PROCESS

As we near the close of this text, it is important to reflect on the potential consequences that might be incurred if agencies are allowed to operate ineffectively. As was noted back in Chapter 2, public safety is "job one," so to speak. This is the main priority for community supervision staff, and agencies bear a responsibility to ensure that the public's welfare is safeguarded. However, as has been made clear throughout this text, the best long-term approach to improving public safety is through the use of effective reintegration efforts for offenders. Thus, programs that fail to adequately supervise offenders on community supervision run the risk of allowing the community to be harmed. Likewise, programs that fail to implement effective treatment approaches also put the community at risk.

Multiple means of maintaining supervision over offenders have been provided in this book. From the broad and progressive continuum of intermediate sanctions to the use of residential treatment facilities, community corrections interventions can be implemented in a manner that is a "best-fit" scenario for the offender and his or her likely level of risk. This comes back to one of the most critical aspects of community supervision: the assessment and classification process. As was noted in Chapter 2, the assessment and classification process sets the stage for everything else that follows. It is also at this point where correctional resources can be optimized by ensuring the best fit between supervision resources and offender risk as well as between treatment resources and offender needs. The importance of effective intake assessment cannot be overemphasized here.

The evaluation of community supervision agencies is directly tied to the assessment component that occurs as the offender is first processed. Indeed, the assessment of the offender typically serves as the baseline measure when examining evaluation processes. Both process and outcome evaluations tend to examine data during the initial assessment against the data that is received when the offender exits a particular program or sentencing scheme. It is in this manner that the evaluation of correctional supervision programs serves to reinforce the initial assessment process. The initial assessment and classification process will be considered effective if, at the end of the offender's involvement in a given supervision program, the evaluation of the program demonstrates

Photo 15.3 This open space is called Cabrini Green, an area of Chicago's gangland once known for extreme gang-related violence. Today, due to grassroots community organizations, this area has become tame and gang violence has subsided. Evaluations of programs in the area demonstrate that their efforts have been a strong contributing influence to this decrease in violent activity.

that the offender is indeed less likely to recidivate, particularly if this likelihood falls below that experienced at other agencies in the area and throughout the country. Thus, the evaluation process is a feedback loop into the initial assessment process, demonstrating to agencies that their programs are (or are not) working. If they are found to be in need of improvement, evaluators can then determine if this is due to the initial intake assessment or if the deficiency is due to some process issue further along in the program's service delivery. Checking the initial assessment and ensuring that this process is adequate follows a "garbage in–garbage out" philosophy; that is, the outcome will only be as good as the process leading up to it.

Such a process creates a systemic loop whereby the agency is constantly assessing and evaluating itself. This is the sign of a high-functioning agency, the type of agency that is less likely to commit *false positives* (thereby losing resources on an offender who is less likely to recidivate than others) or *false negatives* (placing the community at risk with an offender that is more likely to recidivate). The process of interrelated evaluation (at the back end of offender processing) and assessment (at the front end of offender processing) helps to link or loop the two concepts in a manner that results in continual self-improvement. This is known as the **assessment-evaluation cycle,** which is the process whereby assessment data and evaluation data are compared to determine the effectiveness of programs and to find areas where improvement of agency services is required. Agencies that successfully implement the assessment-evaluation cycle tend to use public resources more effectively and also are not prone to placing the community at risk for future criminal activity. In other words, agencies using the assessment-evaluation cycle will operate at an optimal level, avoiding harm to the community and the mismanagement of resources. On the other hand, those agencies that do not successfully implement the assessment-evaluation cycle will be more likely *both* to waste agency resources and to place the community at a level of risk that otherwise would be preventable.

Last, the assessment and evaluation process should be neutral and objective. This is why the evaluator should ideally be a person who is outside of the agency. In many cases, agencies have a great deal to gain by having a positive evaluation. Indeed, future funding and salaries may be dependent upon meeting grant-funding objectives; a failure to obtain these funds could impair an agency in future years. Thus, there are occasionally some agencies that may attempt to exert influence over the evaluator. This must not be allowed to happen. Otherwise, it is the community that is likely to suffer from the tainted evaluation that will then be used as the basis for further supervision of offenders.

In addition, some advocacy groups and other persons with special agendas have been known to exert influence in the community. The evaluator should be careful not to allow his or her information to be misconstrued or presented in a false manner. This may be done by local politicians who wish to use the criminal justice system as a springboard for their own specific and ulterior reasons. Other criminal justice persons, such as judges or local district attorneys, might be seeking reelection, and some of these individuals might attempt to "cozy up" to the evaluator. They might even attempt to hire the evaluator as a means of influencing outcome data. Though these are all unethical circumstances, such situations can and do happen. The wise evaluator will keep his or her integrity closely guarded, remembering that scientific stewardship is invaluable and that the public's safety should always be within the evaluator's purview of concern and consideration.

Lilly, Cullen, and Ball (2007) note that differing theories simply present different methods of reducing crime. This is precisely true, and it is one key reason that evaluative research is so important to criminal justice in general, and community corrections in particular. As has been pointed out throughout this text, there are a variety of theoretical bases for punishment or intervention that exist. These theories provide criminal justice agencies with a direction or framework from which policies are formulated, depending on the particular goals of the jurisdiction and the effectiveness of a given approach in reducing crime. Thus, the evaluation of different treatment perspectives, supervision approaches, case management systems, and other aspects of community corrections is critical to the development and improvement of the community corrections process.

It is through the constant generation of theories that hypotheses are generated, tested, refined, and retested to provide for continual improvement in the community corrections process. Naturally, as discoveries are made, policies are then formulated to reflect these discoveries. Through this process of theory generation, testing, and policy application, standards in community supervision are formulated and disseminated throughout the United States. Thus, theory lies at the basis of everything that occurs in the community corrections arena in particular, as well as in the criminal justice system as a whole.

Lilly et al. (2007) provide an excellent synopsis of this concept by stating the following:

The very changes in theory that undergird changes in policy are themselves a product of transformations in society. Explanations of crime are linked intimately to social context—to the experiences people have that make a given theory seem silly or sensible. Thus, it is only when shifts in societal opinion occur that theoretical models gain or lose credence and, in turn, gain or lose the ability to justify a range of criminal justice policies. (p. 6)

The above quote holds true for policies on community corrections as well. Indeed, it is true that attitudes toward offender reintegration have been going through a state of change as the pendulum seems to be shifting back to a more reintegrative approach to offender reentry. This apparent shift in national policy makes this text's approach very timely and provides a strong basis for the suggestions and recommendations contained herein. Quite naturally, then, theories that emphasize treatment and reintegrative aspects are those that are consistent with this text and the current public perceptions of crime, punishment, and rehabilitation. Whether these reinvented approaches will prove to be effective in the future will be determined by the use of methodologically sound evaluative data processes. Thus, in many respects, the future of community corrections lies in the hands of agency evaluators who, on an individual basis, contribute to the collective determinations regarding the efficacy of reintegrative efforts. In due time, it will become clear if these current winds of change have been successful in improving our society or if they have instead led to additional uncertainty regarding our response to criminal behavior.

SOURCE: Lilly, J. R., Cullen, F. T., & Ball, R. A. (2007). *Criminological theory: Context and consequences* (4th ed.). Thousand Oaks, CA: Sage Publications.

THE FUTURE OF COMMUNITY CORRECTIONS

It is perhaps fitting that this chapter concludes with a section on future trends in community corrections for two reasons. First and quite obviously, this is the last chapter of the text, and it is the typical location where such a section is placed. Second, this chapter addresses evaluation, research, and the connection between assessment and evaluation. This last point is most important because it is through the use of our evaluative research that we predict future trends in agencies and in the community as a whole. Thus, research methodology allows us to formulate additional theories that generate hypotheses, which in turn are tested for accuracy. It is on this note, and with much trepidation, that some speculations regarding future trends in community corrections will be provided. Before doing so, it should be noted that many psychologists, particularly behavioral psychologists, claim that the best predictor of future human behavior is past human behavior. In fact, empirical research has shown this to be generally true. It is with this in mind and with the inclusion of prior research from the field of community corrections that some general observations and predictions will be made.

In providing some insight into future outcomes that we are likely to observe, it should be noted that this text has been addressing two key themes that are likely to continue for the foreseeable future: the use of collaborative efforts between agencies and the community and the emphasis on reintegration as a key to effective offender processing. These two trends are likely to continue for a variety of practical rather than theoretical reasons. Evidence of this already exists throughout the correctional literature, and, as this text clearly demonstrates, many agencies around the nation have already set a course for these two themes to be part of their long-term mission.

First, agencies are strapped for resources, and there are serious limits to what they can do to enhance public safety. Simply put, there are just too many offenders for the current system to effectively supervise them all. Without public support and assistance, police and community supervision officers find themselves caught in a revolving-door system of justice that never seems to slow down. Without the addition of other external resources, it would seem that the justice system is essentially doomed to continue repeating "more of the same."

Second, prisons are full, and community supervision officers already experience significant stress due to high caseloads. Continuing along with a "stuff 'em and cuff 'em" mentality will simply not work for a system that is already quite overstuffed. If something different cannot be introduced to alleviate the continued overcrowding of prisons and the already overloaded case management approaches that exist, then either correctional systems will need much larger budgets or offenders will have to simply be set free without any form of supervision. Obviously, the latter possibility is simply too dangerous to consider, and the former will just result in more of the same problems that already face the criminal justice system. With this in mind, a discussion of the likely trends in community supervision programs will follow.

Community Involvement, Community Corrections, and Community Justice

From a variety of developments around the nation, it is becoming increasingly clear that the community will need to be involved in the community corrections process. This means that the average citizen must know of both the offender and any programs in which the offender may be involved. This is important, and it requires that the agency provide aggressive advertisement and community awareness campaigns. Community supervision agents should visit not just the offender's home, but also other homes in the neighborhood to increase the informal social controls and human supervision that are in place.

As has been made clear throughout this text, community supervision has seen partnerships emerge among police agencies, faith-based organizations, civic associations, social service agencies, and a wide range of other specialized organizations. In this emerging collaborative schema, community supervision agencies are looked at as the leader in addressing crime as a community-based social problem. Thus, community supervision agencies will need to continue spearheading conjoint community action in the supervision of offenders. This is best achieved through the implementation of a community justice orientation. According to Clear and Cole (2003), **community justice** should be thought of as simultaneously being a philosophy of justice, a strategy of justice, and a combination of justice programs. When creating a community justice orientation within a given community, Clear and Cole (2003) note that there are three essential components: community policing, environmental crime prevention, and restorative justice. This discussion will focus on two of those elements—community policing and environmental crime prevention.

Community policing employs methods of creating partnerships between the police and the community. This means that programs such as Neighborhood Watch, Citizens on Patrol, and so forth are utilized to create a working relationship between citizens and the police. Further, community policing is intended to make the police the friends of the community and will often be decentralized in nature so that individual officers can mill about the community to build more personal and individualized relationships with citizens. This form of policing is likewise effective when dealing with diverse communities. Indeed, the community policing model has been found to be particularly effective in fighting problems of gang infestation within racially or ethnically diverse communities. Often the gang members will victimize weaker members of their own racial group (such as with Chinese gangs or Latino gangs and protection or extortion rackets), making it difficult for officers to detect such crime. Officers who are fluent in the primary language of such a community will have more informal exposure to community members and will often be in a better position to detect such subversive victimization. According to Shusta, Levine, Wong, and Harris (2005),

> Law enforcement agencies adopting the community policing strategy have not only become partners within a community but advocates for public well-being. As a result, the role of the peace officer, especially at the line level, changes dramatically. In addition, with increased contact between community members and police, there will be opportunities to educate the public as to the difficult practices and decisions that police have to make continually. (pp. 486–487)

Shusta et al. (2005) further note how police will not only need to coordinate with the community citizen on a more effective level; it will also be in their mutual best interests for police and community supervision officers to routinely collaborate. For community supervision officers, rising caseloads place an ever-growing burden on individual officers, and any supervisory assistance they can get makes their job, and the stress of that job, much easier to handle. Further, this makes the supervision process much more effective in detecting offender noncompliance. For police, the advantage is in the intensive background tracking that probation departments are able to provide, as well as the ability to keep an eye on the homes, significant others, and lives of those who are most likely to be repeat problems while they patrol their neighborhood beats. This eliminates much of the headache associated with policing, particularly in communities that have a disproportionate offender population. Thus, community police officers and community supervision officers work hand-in-hand quite naturally and with little extra effort needed to substantially improve the quality of oversight of the special needs offender.

The **environmental crime prevention** component of a community justice orientation will determine why certain areas of a jurisdiction are more crime prone than others (Clear & Cole, 2003), an approach that combines elements of routine activities theory (discussed extensively in Chapter 2). This is important in the prevention of crime, and it is specifically important when attempting to supervise offenders who are likely to visit prior cohorts and criminal associates. Areas rampant with drugs are vital to locate so as to deter drug offenders from recidivism. In addition, areas of town where prostitution is known to occur should be monitored and supervised by community supervision officers and police officers to deter female offenders from engaging in the business of illicit sex services. Finally, areas known to have gang problems should be saturated by an agency presence and citizen groups as a means of deterring gang influence in that community and to improve the odds of prior gang members who are trying leave their previous lifestyle.

Mental Health Issues Will Remain Important

The Martinson Report (recall Chapter 9) is now dead. It no longer holds true with today's correctional system nor with the offenders that are currently processed. The recognition of co-occurring disorders among offenders has led to a wide variety of new and innovative treatments that have been shown to work based on numerous studies. The research showing that psychotherapy (especially when accompanied by appropriate medication) is both useful and effective is overwhelming. Orientations such as family

Photo 15.4 Dr. Kuanliang is a researcher and evaluator who specializes in juvenile research. In this photo, he is investigating potential causal factors for some of the outcomes that he has noted in the data displayed on his computer.

interventions have also added social factors and influences, demonstrating that treatments can effectively focus on both internal characteristics of the offender and external relationships that they have with others, to enhance likely outcomes. Simply put, offenders need mental health assistance, and mental health treatment programs work. A better fit between needs and services could not exist; the only thing missing is a vigorous and wholehearted devotion to these efforts.

It will become important for agencies to focus on both paraprofessional and professional forms of mental health intervention training. Indeed, this has already come into vogue and, as will be seen in future years, it will be impossible to provide too much of such training. Staff will need to be conversant on various issues related to mental disorders, cognitive deficits, and access to social services. Case management aspects of the community supervision officer's job will continue to be important, as offenders continue to require multivariate services. Addictions recovery will continue to be central to offender reformation, and reintegration will be dependent on addictions and corollary mental health issues being addressed in a suitable manner.

An Emphasis on Cultural Competence Will Continue to Be Important

Chapter 14 of this text addressed cultural competence and the increasing representation of minority offenders in the criminal justice system. It is clear that the United States is becoming more racially and culturally diverse. Indeed, the need for multilingual skills and understanding of differing religious beliefs, lifestyle orientations, and other matters of diversity will become mandatory for future employees in the area of community corrections. The continued diversity among the offender population, along with other challenges (such as mental health needs), means that caseloads for officers are likely to become much more complicated in the future. Naturally, this can add to the already stressful conditions under which supervision officers work and will mean that agencies will need to find the means to mitigate these challenges and their associated stress.

Assessment Methods Will Need to Be Continually Refined

In 1999, Maghan noted that inmates that were incarcerated were becoming more dangerous because of their unpredictability both before and during their incarceration. This points toward the need for refined methods of assessment and classification. This also denotes the importance of effective evaluation to gauge whether assessment processes are working effectively. According to Maghan, the new generation of inmates is committing detected crimes at ever-younger ages of initial arrest. Further, these offenders tend to be learning disabled and suffer cognitive challenges. It would appear that these impairments affect their ability to learn academically as well as behaviorally. This is so much the case that they are seemingly impervious to punitive sanctions and unmotivated by reinforcements or rewards for prosocial behavior. Maghan describes the following characteristics as those likely to exist with future offenders:

- Members of racial minority groups
- Not healthy (appearing to be an average of 10 years older than physical age)
- Have sexually transmitted diseases, HIV, or tuberculosis
- Overly emotional and lack impulse control
- Children that are having children
- Gang affiliated
- Unmarried
- Children of single-parent households

Thus, offenders are likely to have a number of problems that impact and intensify one another. Further, the climate of today's society is one that is becoming more and more tolerant of diverse lifestyles, further increasing the likelihood that alternative lifestyles and mores will impact the types of offenders that are seen. This also will undermine the effectiveness of traditional treatment approaches based on a traditional middle-class American worldview. Assessment and treatment planning will simply require a more varied approach that allows for multiple challenges that stem from various negative life course choices and the consequences of those choices.

An Emphasis on Employment Programs Will Be Necessary

Research is showing that offenders simply need jobs if they are to be able to make ends meet while paying restitution, fines, and other obligations to society. Programs such as Project Rio in the state of Texas are finding that vocational programs that aid in job placement are quite effective in reducing recidivism. The results around the nation are very clear, and it would seem that since employers are able to secure tax incentives for hiring offenders, these programs also benefit society as a whole. Such programs ensure that society is compensated for property crimes, and, when used within a restorative justice or victim compensation framework, they can heal damage that is done from nonviolent crimes. This is important because the victim, society, and the offender all benefit from such programs. Thus, vocational training will be critical, and the use of work release and restitution programs will continue to be necessary.

Geriatric Populations Should Be Shifted to Community Supervision Schemes in the Future

The entire population is graying in the United States and in other industrialized countries. In addition, the prison population in the United States is graying at a faster rate than is the general society beyond prison walls. This issue has been given considerable attention in recent years, with Texas, California, Florida, New York, and Louisiana all experiencing a rise in per capita elderly inmates that are incarcerated. The states just mentioned either have the largest prison population or have the highest rates of incarceration in the United States. In all cases, the costs that are associated with the elderly inmate are exponentially higher than those associated with younger inmates. This leads to other issues for administrators, such as the possibility of early release of inmates that are expected to die soon and the implementation of human caregiver programs such as Hospice, as well as accountability to the public. It is this accountability that places prison administrators in a dilemma, since public safety is the primary concern for all custodial programs. The sobering reality is that, like it or not, society will, one way or another, pay the expenses of keeping elderly inmates.

It is with this point in mind that state-level correctional systems will need to increase their use of community supervision programs for elderly offenders, including those that are chronically ill. This may seem to be an oversimplified recommendation, but it is one that has not truly been implemented by many states. Most states do have programs designed for the early release of elderly inmates, but these programs are not used extensively. The recommendation here is that community supervision be *automatically implemented* when an inmate reaches the age of 60, unless the offender is a bona fide pedophile or child molester. In the case of pedophiles, the typical risk assessment methods should remain intact, since these offenders have such poor prognoses for reform. However, all other elderly inmates should be automatically placed on community supervision, since this would reduce costs of upkeep significantly.

Further, elderly inmates, when they are automatically released, should be given intensive supervision that uses the latest and greatest forms of human supervision and electronic gadgetry. Though this adds to the cost, the outcome is much cheaper than that of prison alternatives. With routine weekly contact by probation/parole officials, frequent electronic phone monitoring, the use of GPS tracking devices, house arrest, and other such innovations, the risk to public safety can be greatly minimized. Further, it is a simple fact that recidivism for these offenders is very low, and of the crimes that are committed, few are assaultive in nature. Thus, public safety is not compromised. In fact, this is the safest population to place on community supervision, as long as such a policy is not used for the pedophile population.

Equally important is the benefit that elderly inmates will receive. The medical services are generally better in the community than they are in jails or prisons, even those that are state-run services. Thus, the standard of care would be greatly improved and would actually entail no difference in cost since the state would be providing such medical services in both instances. Further, elderly offenders on community supervision could be gainfully employed, would have exposure to prosocial activities outside of the corrupt prison environment, and would even be able to benefit from better conditions (e.g., they could have domestic pets, could have plant life within their living spaces, etc.). The physical and psychological conditions would be improved, and this could actually augment any reform efforts that might occur, particularly if such offenders still have positive contact with their own families. Such offenders could even have the opportunity to make amends to the victims of their crime(s), depending on the circumstances and the desires of the victim. In total, this is a win–win situation for all parties involved, entailing lower costs, better health services, and reintegrative opportunities for the elderly offender, while avoiding any increased risk to the public.

Sentencing May Become More Indeterminate in Nature

It has historically been the case that the criminal justice system operates on a spectrum, with punitive philosophies at one end and reformative philosophies on the other. Chapter 1 clearly illustrated that there has been an ebb and flow related to the acceptance of reintegrative approaches. Nevertheless, an argument was presented that initial correctional thought revolved more around reintegration than the alleviation of overcrowded prison facilities or overworked jailers. In many respects, we are likely to see correctional thought go "back to the future," so to speak, with a return to more acceptance of reintegrative efforts. Indeed, the previous 10 to 15 years have been reflective of a crime control model of criminal justice that has had an emphasis on mandatory minimums for sentencing as well as purely determinate sentencing schemes. Historically speaking, the pendulum may begin to swing toward less restrictive prison sentencing, thereby increasing the use of community corrections sanctions.

However, the public perception of community supervision still remains negative due to misunderstanding as well as the failure of many agencies to provide clear evaluative data on their programs, or to publicize this data, especially in the media. Paparozzi states that "the absence of clear and convincing program evaluation data establishes the foundation for ideologically driven, as opposed to the more preferred evidence-based policies, programs, and practices" (2003, p. 47).

This is a very good point because criminal justice policy is often driven by ideology and by media portrayals of the justice system. Paparozzi (2003) contends that when using a research-based analysis that is more objective in nature, it is more likely that treatment-based approaches will be found to reduce crime than punitive approaches. Research abounds that supports this, and, to make matters more certain, there is also research that demonstrates that criminal offending is worsened when offenders are sent to prison. Thus, prisons breed crime and reintegrative efforts reduce crime. The only thing left is to get the news out, once and for all, that correctional systems and practices no longer have to be held captive by the bindings of the Martinson Report. Our civilization has evolved, and we are all capable of producing a better answer than a simple "nothing works" approach to our correctional system and the community that it serves.

THE MEDIA AND COMMUNITY CORRECTIONS

The media can prove pivotal in the success or failure of any program's ability to effectively deal with offenders under their supervision. Because community supervision agencies will need to establish community-based partnerships when establishing effective supervision over offenders, the media stands as a potential tool toward facilitating that process. Further, the media can also make the agency more visible so that community members will be apprised of programs that are being implemented. Indeed, the media can aid the agency in finding volunteers and agencies that are willing to lend a helping hand, thereby establishing a truly effective sense of community justice.

However, certain groups of offenders, such as sex offenders, have drawn public attention and concern. This is of course understandable, but if it is not presented in the appropriate light, the public will tend to make erroneous conclusions regarding the offender population, and this can completely undermine an agency's ability to implement an effective supervision scheme that is integrated with the community. **Media effects** are an important consideration in community supervision and refer to the impact that the media has upon the public perception of offender supervision programs in the community. How the media reports specific incidents can affect this. Further, when programs are successful or innovative, the media can provide effective coverage of these as well, to ensure that the public is getting the most accurate information possible regarding both special needs offenders and community supervision.

Garrett (1999) notes certain points to consider when deciding upon the involvement of the media in corrections. These questions have been adapted for community supervision agencies and demonstrate the potential concerns when the media is involved:

- To what extent will the media representatives disrupt the day-to-day operations of supervision personnel in the community? Will schedules and routine activities be hindered?
- How are offenders likely to react to the media coverage, and how is this likely to impact their ability to reintegrate within the community at large?

- How are people in the community likely to react to the coverage? Will this impair the ability of the offender to reintegrate within the community at large?
- To what extent can coverage impair public safety, particularly for prior victims?
- Will the coverage be likely to cause further trauma for previous victims or families of victims or the offender? (Garrett, 1999, p. 441)

Thus, agency administrators who are attempting to build collaborative partnerships must foster good relations with the media and must always be aware that the media can be a double-edged sword when presenting coverage on special needs offenders. This is particularly true with those offenders who may be bizarre or unusual in appearance or mannerisms.

CONCLUSION

Research and assessment of community corrections programs is vital. It is through this process that we are able to identify program strengths and weaknesses that serve to inform the literature. The ultimate question that should guide research and assessment projects is, "So what?" In other words, if we choose to conduct a research project, will the results provide a meaningful contribution to what is known about some phenomenon? From another standpoint, if we did not conduct the research project, would there continue to be a significant gap in the literature hindering our ability to make optimal decisions regarding community corrections programs? In essence, a quality research program is able to answer the question, "So what?"

Further, the best way to construct research programs that are capable of producing meaningful information is to strictly adhere to the principles of scientific investigation. Research designs should be guided by a theory, informed by the literature, from which hypotheses are constructed and are capable of being measured. In addition, the methods of analyzing and interpreting the data should comport with the basic research question in order to maximize reliability and validity of the findings. Good scientific research is not easy to conduct. At every decision point, there are obstacles and limitations. This reality, however, must not be cause for significant deviation from scientific principles of research; one's mental and emotional health, as well as individual freedoms, are at stake.

It is important to keep in mind that the assessment process is an integral component of the evaluation of any agency. This means that what agencies put into their program will be reflected in their final output. Thus, assessment can be seen as a measure of what goes into a program, and evaluation can be seen as a measure of what comes out. The two work hand-in-hand with one another. Because of this, students should be familiar with the assessment-evaluation cycle, since this is the primary means by which community supervision agencies measure their performance, and since this is what ultimately determines if an agency is meeting its goals and objectives. For agencies with unfavorable evaluations, an examination of their policies and activities may be in order or, in some cases, a reassessment of the goals and objectives.

Finally, this chapter reflects on some of the themes that have emerged throughout this text. These themes are important to contemporary community corrections and were also presented as being the direction that community corrections agencies will need to take in the future. A number of likely trends were noted, and recommendations were given for agencies that will face challenges that loom on the horizon. Community corrections is a field that is both dynamic and demanding; practitioners that work in this field will have their work cut out for them. However, the work of community corrections personnel is critical, and it warrants support from the various funding sources as well as the public at large. Without this support, the entire public is likely to pay dearly for such negligence.

Key Terms

Activities

Assessment-evaluation cycle

Baseline interview

Before/after comparison study

Community justice

Community policing

Content analysis

Cost analysis

Environmental crime prevention

Evaluative transparency

Goal

Hypothesis

Implementation evaluations

Learning organizations

Media effects

Objectives

Outcome evaluations

Policy

Process evaluation

Pure research design

Quasi-experimental evaluation designs

Reliability

Stakeholders

Theory

Validity

"What Would You Do?" Exercise

This is an extension of the "What Would You Do?" exercise in Chapter 8. In that prior exercise, you were a probation officer in a small rural agency. Your supervisor had established a steering committee made up of you, a member of the social services office, a person from city hall, a deputy from the sheriff's office, and another person from the regional hospital. You were to come up with some sort of action plan that would allow you to aid persons on community supervision in *finding employment, making therapeutic and medical meetings,* and *meeting the conditions of their restitution* requirements. This task was difficult, but you successfully implemented the needed program in a jurisdiction that spans a large tri-county area with a total population of only 25,000 people. The largest town in your region, named Maybury, had a population of roughly 8,000 people. Though resources were scant, you took this task seriously and did well with its implementation. In fact, you did so well that you were given a pay raise and a small promotion.

Since that time, the state capitol has noticed your efforts and has offered to provide some additional state monies to supplement your program. This would be a very good benefit for you since resources are so scarce in your jurisdiction. You are asked to meet several policy makers at the state capitol and showcase your new program. However, you are told that they will want to see how you would evaluate your program, once given state funding. Essentially, they want to see that their money is going to good use. Your supervisor asks you to put together an evaluation plan for your fairly new program. Specifically, she asks that you identify process and outcome measures that you would utilize and be ready to explain why you have selected those measures.

What would you do?

Applied Exercise

For this exercise, you will need to consider your readings in this chapter as they apply to prior readings in Chapter 13 on sex offenders. Your assignment is as follows:

You are a researcher that has recently been hired by the community supervision system of your state. You have been asked to design and evaluate a new sex offender treatment program for adult pedophiles that has been implemented in one of the larger cities in your state. Specifically, you are asked to examine how various aspects of social learning theory may lead to pedophilia, and then you must explain how various treatment options might best address those issues with this population. The program that you will evaluate uses all of the interventions listed in Chapter 13 of this text, including those techniques/approaches that are listed under *cognitive-behavioral interventions, empathy-building interventions,* and *interrogation-oriented techniques.* Last, you will need to provide a clear methodology for testing and evaluating your proposed program, including such factors as validity and reliability of your study and the validity and reliability of your instruments (if any), the use of control and experimental groups, and distinctions between process and outcome measures, as well as ethical issues that might be involved with conducting such research.

Students should complete this application exercise as a mini paper that explains the scenario and then addresses each question throughout the content of the discussion. Total word count: 900 to 2,100 words.

Glossary

Absolute immunity: Exists for those persons that work in positions that require unimpaired decision-making functions. Judges and prosecutors have this type of immunity.

Activities: Services or functions carried out by a program (i.e., what the program does). For example, treatment programs may screen clients at intake, complete placement assessments, provide counseling to clients, etc.

Adolescent limited (AL) offenders: Includes those juveniles that age out of crime or respond to treatment since their offending is restricted to adolescence or young adulthood.

Aftercare: Reintegrative services that prepare juveniles released from an institution for reentry into the community by establishing collaboration among agencies, the community, and available resources to maximize reintegrative processes.

Alternative incarceration center (AIC): A highly structured community-based program that saves prison or jail beds for more serious offenders.

American Indian or **Native American:** Refers to people whose origins are with any of the original peoples of North, Central, or South America and who maintain tribal affiliation or attachment.

Anger retaliation rapist: This rapist desires to harm women. This offender seeks to "get even" with women who have embarrassed or humiliated him in his past.

Antisocial personality disorder: A personality disorder characterized by pervasive antisocial tendencies, excessive risk-taking behaviors, and a lack of empathy or remorse.

Asian or **Asian American:** Refers to persons having origins among any of the original peoples of the Far East, Southeast Asia, or the Indian subcontinent.

Assertive community treatment case management: An intensive case management model with low caseloads and frequent, community-based contact with clients.

Assessment-evaluation cycle: The process whereby assessment data and evaluation data are compared, one with the other, to determine the effectiveness of programs and to find areas where improvement in agency services is required.

Attachment: A form of psychological influence over a youth's behavior such that when temptation to offend appears, the youth will weigh heavily the wishes of his or her parents and the youth's prior socialization.

Augustus, John: A cobbler and philanthropist of Boston, often recognized as the father of modern probation.

Aversion therapy: Behavioral technique often used in varying degrees within sex offender programs. The aim of aversive techniques is to teach offenders to associate unpleasant stimuli with presently desirable yet unacceptable behaviors.

Baseline interview: Consists of gathering data related to each variable we are attempting to measure at the time of entry into the program.

Before/after comparison study: A process where data is collected on conditions that prevailed before the project intervention was initiated, followed by a comparison with data that is collected after the project intervention has been completed.

Behavioral therapy: Holds that long-term change is accomplished through action and that disorders are learned means of behaving that are maladaptive.

Belief: This refers to a general *lack* of beliefs that counter delinquent behavior. In essence, it is not the possession of pro-delinquent beliefs as much as it is a lack of beliefs regarding the inappropriateness of delinquency.

Benefit of clergy: This benefit was the pardoning of a person from the commission of a crime. The benefit of clergy was originally implemented for members of various churches, including clerics, monks, and nuns who might be accused of crimes.

Black or **African American:** Refers to persons having origins in any of the black racial groups from the continent of Africa.

Blood testing: A highly invasive procedure that can provide discrete information regarding the degree of an individual's impairment. However, the invasiveness of the procedure and the potential danger of infection make blood testing inappropriate for many drug programs.

Boot camps: Short-term forms of incarceration in an environment that is similar to basic training in the military. This sanction is primarily used with youthful offenders and is intended to have an emphasis on disciplining the offender.

Borderline personality disorder: A disorder characterized by a pervasive pattern of instability of interpersonal relationships, self-image, and affects, and a marked impulsivity beginning by early adulthood.

Broker/generalist case management: Narrow in scope of action, the broker/generalist model focuses primarily on rapid linkage and referral. The case manager provides limited direct services, other than the initial assessment to determine service needs, service referrals, and occasional monitoring of service provision.

Care coordinators: Those responsible for helping participants create a customized treatment program and for guiding youth and their families through the system of care.

Case management: The process whereby an offender is provided fully comprehensive and coordinated services that address the offender's vocational, social, educational, and mental health functions. The goal is to address the offender's needs so that he or she can be a fully functioning member of society.

Caseload management: The process we use to assign supervision workloads to community supervision officers. This takes into account the number of offenders, the security risk of those offenders, and the specialized needs that those offenders may have. The more serious the security risk or the more profound the needs, the more intensive that offender is to supervise, resulting in fewer offenders in a caseload, under a balanced system of caseload management.

Certification: Implies a certain level of oversight in that a minimum standard of competency exists. This is particularly relevant to mental health professionals, such as counselors.

Chemical castration: Method of reducing violent behavior in which sex offenders are injected with drugs (most commonly Depo-Provera) to reduce the amount of testosterone in their bodies.

Child abuse: Maltreatment of a child (being a youth under the age of 18 in most states) by an immediate family member, or any person responsible for the child's welfare.

Child neglect: Occurs when a parent or caretaker of the child does not provide the proper or necessary support, education, or medical or other remedial care that is required by a given state's laws, including food, shelter, and clothing.

Child parentification: Occurs when a child is placed in a position within a family system in which he or she must assume the primary caretaker role for the family, often taking care of both children and adults within that family system.

Client-centered therapy: Therapy technique whose central point is that the therapist must be genuine, accepting, and empathetic to the offender-client.

Clinical/rehabilitation case management: Approach to case management in which those providing case management services deliver the clinical treatment as well, providing both in an integrated manner.

Cognitive-behavioral therapy (CBT): A problem-focused approach designed to help people identify and change the dysfunctional beliefs, thoughts, and patterns of behavior that contribute to their problems.

Cognitive restructuring: Therapy technique in which the offender constructs scenes that cast him or her or significant others in the role of the victim. The client then focuses on typical rationalizations he or she uses to justify the assault.

Cognitive therapy: Approach based on the belief that faulty thinking patterns and belief systems cause psychological problems and that changing our thoughts improves our mental and emotional health and results in changes in behavior.

Collective efficacy: Refers to a sense of cohesion within a given community whereby citizens have close and interlocking relationships with one another.

Community-based interagency team: The team of people responsible for designing, implementing, and overseeing the wrap-around initiative in a given jurisdiction.

Community corrections: Includes all non-incarcerating correctional sanctions imposed upon an offender for the purposes of reintegrating that offender into the community.

Community justice: Simultaneously a philosophy of justice, a strategy of justice, and a combination of justice programs.

Community policing: Employs methods of creating partnerships between the police and the community. Examples include programs such as Neighborhood Watch and Citizens on Patrol.

Community residential treatment centers: Non-confining residential facilities for adjudicated adults or juveniles who are not appropriate for probation or who need a period of readjustment after imprisonment.

Community service: Work performed by an offender for the benefit of the community as a component of that offender's sentence.

Community supervision officer: A term used to identify persons that work in community supervision agencies and perform the supervision duties that are typically associated with probation or parole officers.

Compensatory damages: Payments for the actual losses suffered by a plaintiff (typically the offender).

Conformity: This is the concept of youth being committed to social prospects and therefore complying with expectations.

Consolidated parole administration model: Model in which the parole board is merely a semiautonomous agency that is connected to (and perhaps subservient to) a larger agency or governmental body.

Containment approach: Based on the idea that multiple dimensions of supervision are necessary to optimize public safety, and this therefore requires numerous actors within the criminal justice and community setting.

Content analysis: The systematic analysis and selective classification of the contents of mass media.

Conventional model: Involves the random assignment of offenders to community supervision officers. This model of case assignment results in officers having a mix of different types of offenders, which has both pros and cons as far as developing equity in workload among officers and in optimizing service coordination for offenders.

Conventional model with geographic consideration: A prime determinant of this model is the amount of time that officers must spend traveling to various locations during their day-to-day routine of checking on offenders. This model takes into account such geographic factors.

Cost analysis: Important in determining how to allocate funds within a program and for understanding the relationship between costs and outcomes.

Counselors: Professionals who typically have training in particular mental health areas, such as a substance abuse counselor. Many counselors have a master's degree and full licensure; in these cases, the counselor is referred to as a Licensed Professional Counselor.

Crime control model of corrections: Model of corrections that seeks to simply incapacitate the offending population with no concern for the reentry issues that will follow for the community or the offender.

Cultural competence: Possession of knowledge and information pertaining to individuals and groups that entails skills, services, and techniques that match an individual's culture and improve the relevance of services to the person receiving them.

Day reporting centers: Treatment facilities that offenders must report to on a daily (or near daily) basis. These are similar to residential treatment facilities except that offenders on intensive supervision are not required to stay overnight.

Day treatment facilities: Highly structured, community-based, nonresidential programs for serious juvenile offenders.

Declaratory judgment: A judicial determination of the legal rights of the person bringing suit.

Defamation: An invasion of a person's interest through his or her reputation. In order for this to occur, some form of slander or libel must have occurred against the aggrieved individual.

Determinate sentencing: Consists of fixed periods of incarceration imposed on the offender with no later flexibility in the term that is served. This type of sentencing is grounded in notions of retribution, just deserts, and incapacitation.

Deterrence: Discouraging people from lawbreaking by example.

Detoxification: Treatment designed for persons who are dependent on narcotic drugs (e.g., heroin, opium). This treatment is typically found in inpatient settings with programs that last for 7 to 21 days.

Diagnostic and Statistical Manual of Mental Disorders (DSM-IV-TR): Manual that allows mental health practitioners to label, or diagnose, an individual (in this case an offender) so that the person can be better categorized for further treatment interventions. This is a necessary process when attempting to match a client with the correct treatment modality.

Discrimination: Refers to differential and negative treatment of an individual or group without reference to the behavior or qualifications for that treatment.

Disparity: Refers to the unequal treatment of one group by the criminal justice system, compared with the treatment accorded other groups.

Dispositional needs assessment: Provides additional information within one or more given need dimensions regarding the specific program or treatment that would benefit the offender.

Drug of choice: A drug that is consistently used with greater frequency than other types of drugs by a certain identifiable demographic group.

Dual diagnosis: A term that denotes the fact that the offender has two or more disorders.

Dynamic risk factors: Those characteristics that can change and are more or less influenced or controlled by the offender, such as employment, motivation, drug use, and family relations.

Educational neglect: Neglect that occurs when a parent or even a teacher permits chronic truancy or simply ignores the educational or special needs of a child.

Electronic monitoring: Includes the use of any mechanism that is worn by the offender for the means of tracking the person's whereabouts through electronic detection. Electronic monitoring includes both active and passive monitoring systems. Active systems require that the offender answer or respond to a monitoring cue (such as a computer-generated telephone call), whereas passive forms of monitoring emit a continuous signal for tracking.

Emotional neglect: This neglect includes inadequate nurturing or affection, allowing the child to engage in inappropriate or illegal behavior such as drug or alcohol use, and ignoring a child's basic emotional needs.

English Penal Servitude Act: Alexander Maconochie lobbied for this act in 1853, which established several rehabilitation programs for convicts in both England and Ireland.

Environmental crime prevention: Component of a community justice orientation that determines why certain areas of a jurisdiction are more crime prone than others.

Environmental manipulation: Getting the offender out of situations that are high risk for him and his potential victims. The offender should train himself to move out of the house, rather than the victim.

Ethnicity: A concept that takes into account cultural characteristics, such as language and religion, as a means of identifying different groups of people.

Evaluative transparency: When an agency's evaluative process allows for an outside person (whether an auditor, an evaluator, or the public-at-large) to have full view of the agency's operations, budgeting, policies, procedures, and outcomes.

Extinction: Pertaining to behavior, extinction occurs when a behavior ceases due to a lack of reinforcement.

Faith-based: Forms of therapy that are often a blend of cognitive and behavioral techniques that are grounded in scriptural instructions on the appropriate form of cognition or behavior.

False negative: Data result implying that the offender is predicted to not reoffend but the prediction turns out to be false.

False positive: When an offender is predicted to be likely to commit a crime but later, despite this prediction, the offender is released to community supervision and is found to never reoffend.

Family systems: Therapy that looks at the entire family as a system with its own customs, roles, beliefs, and dynamics that affect and impact the offender more routinely than does any other group.

Female offenders: Defined as both juvenile and adult female offenders who have committed a criminal offense that has been either adjudicated or criminally processed. These offenders include women in facilities as well as those in community corrections settings.

Feminist theory: Contends that traditional criminology has typically generated theories that are suited for the male population, with little or no regard for the corresponding female offender.

Feminist therapy: Therapy that focuses on empowering women. This type of therapy often aids in strengthening women's communication skills, sense of assertiveness, self-esteem, and relationships.

Fine: Monetary penalty imposed by a judge or magistrate as a punishment for being convicted of an offense.

Five essential elements of specialized courts: Include the use of (1) immediate interventions; (2) nonadversarial adjudication; (3) hands-on judicial involvement; (4) treatment programs with clear rules and structured goals; and (5) a team approach that brings together the judge, prosecutors, defense counsel, treatment provider, and correctional staff.

Formal interagency agreement: Agreement that records the proposed design of the wrap-around initiative and spells out exactly how it will work.

General deterrence: Intended to cause vicarious learning whereby observers see that offenders are punished for a given crime and therefore are discouraged from committing a like-mannered crime due to fear of similar punishment.

Generalized anxiety disorder: Characterized by excessive anxiety and worry (apprehensive expectation), occurring more days than not for at least 6 months, about a number of events or activities.

Geriatric/elderly offenders: Defined as those persons who have committed a criminal offense and are serving a sentence while being 50 years of age or older.

Global Positioning System (GPS): This type of system uses 24 military satellites to determine the exact location of a coordinate. By using the satellite monitoring and remote tracking, offenders can be tracked to their exact location.

Goal: A desired state of affairs that outlines the ultimate purpose of a program. This is the end toward which program efforts are directed. For example, the goal of many criminal justice programs is a reduction in criminal activity.

Good faith defense: Buffers a community supervision officer from liability in Section 1983 cases unless the officer violated some clearly established constitutional or federal statutory right that a reasonable person would have known to exist.

Gross negligence: A failure to exercise the standard of care and attention that is even less than that which would be expected from someone who was already careless in his or her duty.

Group homes: Residential placement facilities for juveniles that operate in a homelike setting with unrelated children living together for varied periods of time, depending on their individual circumstances.

Hair testing: The introduction of new, powerful instruments for hair analysis has increased interest in hair testing. Hair testing is used to detect trace amounts of drugs in the person's body. Despite its increased popularity among agencies, caution should be used because hair analysis is subject to potential external contamination.

Halfway house: Residential setting for offenders who are court-ordered to stay at the facility while on community supervision. Offenders who are exiting prison will often be required to stay at one of these facilities. Also defined as residential facilities for offenders that are either nearing release from prison or in the initial stages of return to the community (*specific to Chapter 10*).

Hearing stage: Stage of disposition of an offender that allows the probation agency to present evidence of the violation while the offender is given the opportunity to refute the evidence offered.

Hispanic or Latino American: Refers to those persons having origins among any of the original peoples of North, Central, or South America but who also do not maintain tribal affiliations.

Histrionic personality disorder: A pervasive pattern of excessive emotionality and attention seeking, beginning by early adulthood and present in a variety of contexts.

Home confinement: An intermediate community corrections sanction where offenders are restricted to their residence except during specifically designated times when they are authorized to attend vocational, educational, treatment-based, or social functions.

Home confinement and Global Positioning System: Form of supervision that uses a series of satellites to monitor and locate offenders.

Home confinement with electronic monitoring: Sanction used instead of incarceration for persons on community supervision. This is the most restrictive form of community supervision.

Home detention: The mandated action that forces an offender to stay within the confines of his or her home or on the offender's property until a time specified by the sentencing judge.

Hypothesis: An affirmative statement about the relationship between two variables.

Implementation evaluations: Evaluations aimed at identifying problems and accomplishments during the early phases of program development for feedback to clinical and administrative staff.

Impulse-charting: Method used to track points and times when certain thoughts or desires seem more intense. The time of day, location, and number of times per week are all important.

Incapacitation: Deprives the offender of liberty and removes him or her from society with the intent of ensuring that society cannot be further victimized by that offender during the offender's term of incarceration. Also, the physical restriction to prevent further opportunities for lawbreaking (*specific to Chapter 2*).

Independent parole administration model: Supervision model in which a parole board is responsible for making release determinations from prison as well as overseeing the supervision processes of offenders that are released on parole (or good time releases).

Indeterminate sentencing: Sentencing that includes a range of years that will be potentially served by the offender. The offender is released during some point in the range of years assigned by the sentencing judge.

Injunction: A court order that requires an agency to take some form of action(s) or to refrain from a particular action or set of actions.

Institutionalized racism: A term that indicates that a society is, at its base, racist in nature as an entire institution. This is regardless of whether such racism is deliberate or accidental among members of that society.

Instrumental testing: Analysis that involves instrumentation (a machine) that will sample, measure, and produce a quantitative result that is given as a numeric amount on a scale.

Intake screening of needs: Leads to a series of judgments that subdivide offenders into broad categories of basic needs or deficits. This then points case managers in the general direction for referral of offenders to generalized service areas.

Intensive needs assessment: Highly detailed intervention plan within a priority need area. Identifies areas of need that require increased involvement of specialized professionals, such as job placement programs, educational institutions, medical services, or mental health treatment services.

Intensive supervised probation/parole (ISP): Form of sanction usually viewed as the most effective alternative to imprisonment. This type of supervision requires more face-to-face contact between the officer and the offender. In addition, the supervision officer may visit the offender at home and work on a routine basis. The requirements of ISP are much stricter than those for traditional probation.

Intensive supervision: The extensive supervision of offenders who pose the greatest risk to society or are in need of the greatest amount of governmental services. In most cases, intensive supervision is the option afforded to individuals who would otherwise be incarcerated for felony offenses.

Intentional tort: A tort (suit) in which the actor, whether it was expressed or implied, was judged to have possessed intent or purpose to injury.

Intermediate sanctions: A range of sentencing options that fall between incarceration and probation, being designed to allow for the crafting of sentences that respond to the offender or the offense, with the intended outcome of the case being a primary consideration.

Intermittent sentences: A sentence that requires some form of temporary confinement throughout intermittent and partial periods of an offender's sentence.

International Association of Residential and Community Alternatives (IARCA): Established in 1989, this organization advocates for the use of various types of intermediate facilities for offender reentry. The name of the organization reflects the ambiguity in definitions that separate halfway houses and other forms of offender residential programs.

Invasion of privacy: Aside from the commonly understood issue of interfering with a person's reasonable right to privacy (the actual right to privacy itself being fluid in nature), invasion of privacy can also be found if the aggrieved can show that there is some form of encroachment or damage to his or her very personality.

Involvement: Concept conveying that if youth are involved in conventional activities, they will be unable or less likely to engage in delinquent behavior.

Jail: A confinement facility, usually operated and controlled by county-level law enforcement, that is designed to hold persons charged with a crime who are either awaiting adjudication or serving a short sentence of one year or less after the point of adjudication.

Jail diversion: Refers to any process designed to reduce the contact between the criminal justice system and mentally ill or substance-addicted persons, with the goal being to facilitate reentry of the offender into the community while also avoiding risk of public endangerment.

Jail diversion programs: Programs that are designed to divert mentally ill offenders and offenders with drug abuse issues from the jail facility as a means of enhancing therapeutic treatment aspects related to the challenges that face these offenders.

Juvenile intensive probation supervision (JIPS): A regimented program of supervision that requires much greater supervision contact than regular probation and also serves as an alternative to incarceration while maintaining acceptable levels of public safety.

Juvenile probation: A judicial disposition under which youthful offenders are subject to certain conditions imposed by the juvenile court while being allowed to remain in the community during the duration of their sentence.

Juvenile records: Records that include a composite of the youth's criminal history, family and personal information, abuse history, and truancy records, as well as other identification information such as fingerprinting or photographs.

Labeling theory: Contends that individuals become stabilized in criminal roles when they are labeled as criminals. As a result, they are stigmatized, develop criminal identities, are sent to prison, and are excluded from conventional roles.

Learning organizations: Organizations that have the inherent ability to adapt and change, improving performance through continual revision of goals, objectives, policies, and procedures.

Level of Supervision Inventory—Revised (LSI-R): A well-regarded, quasi-objective clinical inventory that is used to determine offender likelihood of recidivism and suitability for community supervision.

Licensure: Professional certification that provides the legal right to see clients and receive third-party billing. Third-party billing is when insurance companies, employment assistance programs, or state programs are billed to reimburse the therapist. Licensure is important for the therapeutic practitioner working in private practice or in a nonprofit but private facility.

Life course persistent (LCP) offender: Offender that commits crimes persistently throughout his or her entire life span.

Long-term residential programs: Treatment programs that provide care 24 hours per day, generally in nonhospital settings. The best-known residential treatment model is the therapeutic community (TC), but residential treatment may also employ other models, such as cognitive-behavioral therapy. These programs tend to house drug offenders for anywhere from 6 to 12 months.

Major depressive disorder: The afflicted person will have decreased energy, tiredness, and fatigue without physical exertion. Even the smallest tasks may seem to require substantial effort. Further, these individuals often have a sense of worthlessness or guilt that may include unrealistic negative evaluations of their worth or guilty preoccupations over minor past failings.

Malicious prosecution: When a criminal accusation is made by someone that has no probable cause and when the person generates such actions for improper reasons.

Mark system: Created by Alexander Maconochie, a system whereby "marks" were provided to the convict for each day of successful toil. Under this plan, convicts were given marks and moved through phases of supervision until they finally earned full release.

Martinson Report: A landmark report released in 1974 that noted that with few and isolated exceptions, the rehabilitative efforts that had been reported thus far had had no appreciable effect on recidivism. This report generated substantial controversy in the field of corrections.

Maryland Addictions Questionnaire (MAQ): A substance abuse assessment instrument that is typically administered at intake. It provides the evaluator with an idea of the severity of the addiction, the motivation of the client offender, and the likely risk of relapse for the offender.

Masturbatory reconditioning: Treatment technique that involves having the client masturbate to an appropriate fantasy, until he has an ejaculation.

Media effects: An important consideration in community supervision, the term refers to the effects that the media have upon the public perception of offender supervision programs in the community.

Megan's Laws: A blanket term used to refer to various state notification laws addressing the release of sex offenders in the community. This term is attributed to the brutal rape and murder of a 7-year-old girl named Megan Kanka. The victim's parents pushed for legislation to mandate reporting of sex offenders that are released into the community. These laws have now been adopted by all states, though each may use different names for its own particular legislation.

Megargee Offender Classification System: System of classification that is known to provide solid empirical support for classification and placement decisions. This system is especially effective in assisting criminal justice practitioners in dealing with an offender population that includes mentally ill or disordered individuals within its ranks.

Mental illness: Defined as any diagnosed disorder contained within the *DSM-IV-TR,* as published by the American Psychiatric Association.

Misrepresentation of facts: Occurs if the community supervision officer provides some sort of false representation of either a past or present fact that is used in a decision-making outcome related to the offender.

MMPI-2: Stands for the Minnesota Multiphasic Personality Inventory-2, an objective personality adjustment inventory test that can be given to large numbers of offenders at the same time or individually as desired.

MMPI-2 Criminal Justice and Correctional Report: Designed to identify those offenders who may suffer from thought disorders, serious depression, and substance abuse problems; identifies those that may need mental health treatment as well as those that are most likely to be hostile, predatory, bullied, or victimized while incarcerated. This report also includes predictor items related to self-injury and suicide.

Model of caseload delivery: Process whereby offenders are initially assigned their community supervision officer. This is often determined by the agency size and the number of offenders under the agency's jurisdiction.

Monetary restitution: A process by which offenders are held partially or fully accountable for the financial losses suffered by the victims of their crimes.

Mood disorders: Disorders such as major depressive disorder, bipolar disorder, and dysthymic disorder. Major depressive disorder is characterized by one or more major depressive episodes.

Narcissistic personality disorder: A pervasive pattern of grandiosity (in fantasy or behavior), need for admiration, and lack of empathy, beginning by early adulthood and present in a variety of contexts.

Native Hawaiian or Other Pacific Islander: Refers to a person having origins among any of the original peoples of Hawaii, Guam, Samoa, or other Pacific Islands.

Needs assessment: Refers to those aspects of offender classification that seek to identify or determine the condition or state of individuals relative to some preestablished functional criteria.

Needs-principled assessment: Type of assessment that deals with the subjective and objective needs of the offender to maximize his or her potential for social reintegration and to reduce the likelihood of future recidivism.

Negative punishment: The removal of a valued stimulus when the offender commits an undesired behavior.

Negative reinforcers: Unpleasant stimuli that are then removed when a desired behavior occurs.

Negligence: Defined as doing what a reasonably prudent person would not have done in similar circumstances, or failing to do what a reasonably prudent person would have done in similar circumstances.

Numbers game model: Caseload model in which the agency defines a desired caseload per officer (such as 40 offenders per officer), and the agency makes its hiring decisions based on this formula.

Objectives: Specific results or effects of a program's activities that must be achieved in pursuing the program's ultimate goals. For example, a treatment program may expect to change offender attitudes (objective) in order to ultimately reduce recidivism (goal).

Official halfway house: See *halfway house*.

Opportunistic rapist: Demonstrates neither strong sexual nor aggressive features, but engages in spontaneous rape when there appears an opportunity that makes the rape an easy prospect. This form of rape is usually perpetrated during the commission of another crime, such as robbery or burglary.

Outcome evaluations: Evaluations that involve quantitative research aimed at assessing the impact of the program on long-term treatment outcomes.

Outpatient drug-free treatment: Treatment option that typically costs less than residential or inpatient treatment and often is more suitable for individuals who are employed or who have extensive social supports.

Parens patriae: Latin term that originally meant that the king, as father of his country, is empowered and obligated to protect the welfare of the country's children. In modern times, this means that the state is empowered and obligated to protect the welfare of children, even when this might result in the removal of a child from the family home.

Parole: Defined as the early release of an offender from a secure facility upon completion of a certain portion of his or her sentence, based on good behavior or other factors.

Parole revocations officer: The officer tasked with the routine holding of preliminary parole revocation hearings by reviewing allegations made by parole officers against parolees.

Passive agent: An officer who views the job as just that—a job. This officer will tend to do as little as possible, and he or she does not have passion for the jobs. Officers who are passive agents do not tend to care about the outcome of their work so long as they avoid any difficulties.

Paternal officers: Officers who use a great degree of both control elements and assistance techniques in supervision.

Pedophilia: Crime involving sexual activity with a prepubescent child (generally age 13 or younger).

Penile plethysmograph (PPG): Treatment technique utilized with sexual offenders that uses a cup or band that is placed around the penis while the offender is in a private room. This instrument is designed to measure sexual arousal, particularly when stimuli such as the pictures of children are presented to the offender.

Personality disorders: Psychological disorders that are characterized by an enduring pattern of inner experience and behavior that deviates markedly from the expectations of the individual's culture, is pervasive and inflexible, has an onset in adolescence or early adulthood, is stable over time, and leads to distress or impairment.

Physical abuse: Any physical acts that cause, or have the potential to cause, some sort of physical injury to children or adults.

Physical neglect: Encompasses abandonment; the expulsion of the child from the home (being kicked out of the house); a failure to seek or excessive delay in seeking medical care for the child; inadequate supervision; and provision of inadequate food, clothing, and shelter.

Point-of-contact testing: Analysis using devices that require manual sampling and manual observation to produce a qualitative result that includes both negative and positive values.

Policy: A governing principle pertaining to goals, objectives, or activities. It is a decision on an issue not resolved on the basis of facts and logic only. For example, the policy of expediting drug cases in the courts might be adopted as a basis for reducing the average number of days from arraignment to disposition.

Polygraph: The standard lie detector apparatus used to measure biological responses to deception.

Polygraph examiner: This individual operates the polygraph machine, which is able to detect the likelihood of untruth through a measure of physiological indicators. Because sex offenders are generally very manipulative, superficially compliant, and adept at keeping secrets, the polygraph examiner is invaluable when interviewing or interrogating the sex offender.

Positive punishment: When a stimulus is applied to the offender in response to the offender committing an undesired behavior.

Positive reinforcers: Rewards for a desired behavior.

Power assertive rapist: A rapist who is characterized by a sense of superiority that is based on "hypermasculinity" in which he believes he is entitled to sexual access simply because he is a man. For this offender, rape is an impulsive act of predatory victimization that the female deserves simply because she is female and is fair game for subjugation.

Power reassurance rapist: The least violent of the types considered in this text. These offenders are typically not socially competent and may be quite introverted in thought and behavior. They typically have a low sense of self-esteem and suffer from profound feelings of inadequacy, both socially and sexually.

Preliminary hearing: Examines the facts of the arrest to determine if probable cause exists for a violation.

Presentence investigation report: File that will typically include demographic, vocational, educational, and personal information on the offender, as well as records on his or her prior offending patterns, and the probation department's recommendation as to the appropriate type of sentencing and supervision.

Prisonization: A process whereby inmates become dependent upon institutional routines and guidance as a means of functioning on a day-to-day basis. This is an over-adaptation to prison life that is dysfunctional among the social community outside of prison.

Private probation: This type of probation is similar to other forms but is administered by privately owned and operated companies that contract with courts to supervise misdemeanor cases.

Probation with community service and restitution: This sanction requires the offender to provide a certain number of designated hours of free labor to a given cause determined by the court.

Probationers: Criminal offenders who have been sentenced to a period of correctional supervision in the community in lieu of incarceration.

Process evaluation: Refers to assessment of the effects of the program on clients while they are in the program, making it possible to assess the institution's intermediary goals.

Prognosis: Refers to the likelihood that an offender will successfully reform and simultaneously refrain from further criminal activity. There is both a treatment component and a public safety component contained within an offender's prognosis.

Programmed contact system: An electronic monitoring system that has randomly programmed times during the day or night when an automated system calls the offender's house to make sure he or she is home.

Psychiatrists: These are medical doctors. Their ability to prescribe medication for anxiety, depression, anger, and other disorders distinguishes them from the other categories of mental health provider.

Psychological abuse: This is sometimes referred to as emotional abuse and includes actions or the omission of actions by parents and other caregivers that could cause a child to have serious behavioral, emotional, or mental impairments.

Psychologists: These professionals have doctorates in psychology and have extensive education in research, theories of human behavior, and therapeutic techniques. In addition, most also specialize in the administration of psychological tests and assessments.

Punitive damages: Monetary awards the court orders the offender to pay as a form of punishment for the particular type of crime committed due to its seriousness.

Punitive officers: Officers who see themselves as needing to use threats and punishment in order to get compliance from the offender.

Pure research design: A design that includes random assignment of offenders to treatment and control groups.

Qualified immunity: Requires that the community supervision officer demonstrate certain key aspects prior to invoking this form of defense against suit.

Quasi-experimental evaluation designs: Used to approximate the advantages of random selection. An example of such a design might be to identify a comparison group that is similar to the treatment group in those characteristics thought to be capable of influencing the outcome under examination.

Race: A concept that is based on biological factors such as skin color and other physical features as a means of distinguishing among different groups of people.

Reality therapy: Uses forms of involvement between counselor and client to teach client to be self-responsible.

Recognizance: This practice involves the use of an obligation entered into by a defendant, who is bound to refrain from engaging in crime for a stipulated period and to appear in court on a specified date for final disposition of the case. In exchange, the defendant is not required to remain in jail while waiting for his or her court date.

Reentry courts: Courts that provide comprehensive services to offenders that return from prison to the community, by utilizing comprehensive services provided by a network of agencies in the surrounding area.

Rehabilitation: Implies that an offender should be provided the means to fulfill a constructive level of functioning in society, with an implicit expectation that such offenders will be deterred from reoffending due to having worthwhile stakes in legitimate society, stakes that the offender will not wish to lose due to criminal offending. Also, changing the offender's behavior or circumstances to reduce the possibility of further lawbreaking *(specific to Chapter 2)*.

Reliability: A concept that describes the accuracy of a measure, which in turn describes the accuracy of a study.

Residential treatment home: Facility designed to house the offender, but the offender is not ordered by the court to stay at the facility. These facilities may also have "day students" who use the facility as a day reporting center (see *day reporting centers*).

Residential treatment programs: Facilities that offer a combination of substance abuse and mental health treatment services while youth are kept under 24-hour supervision in a highly structured and secure environment.

Restitution: Compensation to the victim and/or community for crimes committed.

Restitution center: A type of facility that is designed primarily for first-time or property offenders. These offenders are required to pay victim restitution and/or provide community service as a means of fulfilling their sentence.

Restorative justice: A term for interventions that focus on restoring the health of the community, repairing the harm done, meeting the victim's needs, and emphasizing that the offender can and must contribute to those repairs. Restorative justice considers the victims, communities, and offenders as participants in the justice process.

Retribution: Often referred to as the "eye for an eye" mentality, this term simply implies that offenders committing a crime should be punished in a like fashion or in a manner that is commensurate with the severity of the crime that they have committed.

Risk-principled assessment: For this type of assessment, the main concern revolves around the protection of society. The risk-principled assessment system will ensure that hardcore offenders are not in the same treatment regimen as less serious offenders.

Role identity confusion: Occurs when an officer is unclear about the expectations placed upon him or her as the officer attempts to juggle between the "policing" oriented nature of his or her work and the "reform" orientation.

Role-playing: A therapy technique in which the offender reenacts his or her own crime scene(s) with another offender, and they take turns playing the role of their victim.

Routine activities theory: A theory based on three simplistic notions. First, in order for a crime to occur, a motivated offender must converge with a suitable target. Second, this theory contends that the likelihood of such an occurrence is affected by the routine activities that both victims and offenders engage in. Third, the area of occurrence must be absent of capable guardians that might thwart criminal behavior.

Sadistic rapist: The most dangerous of sex offenders. The primary desire for these offenders is to cause pain to their victim.

Salient factor score: An instrument that measures offender risk along six items, each of which is measured with a value that ranges from 0 (zero) to 3 with inverted indications of risk (i.e., the lower the number, the higher the likelihood that the offender will recidivate).

Saliva testing: Saliva samples permit drug testing and even HIV/AIDS testing to be easily administered. These samples are subject to contamination from smoking or other substances.

Sanctuary: Sanctuary existed historically through the identification of various cities or regions (most often cities) that were set aside as a sort of neutral ground, protected from criminal prosecution. Accused criminals could escape prosecution by fleeing to these cities.

Scheduled overmasturbation: Intervention requiring the client to routinely masturbate on a progressively more frequent schedule throughout the week. This is intended to reduce sexual drive and to make self-control easier for the offender.

Schizophrenic disorders: According to the *DSM-IV-TR,* such disorders have five characteristic symptoms and at least two must be present before the diagnosis can be given to an individual. These symptoms are as follows: (1) delusions, (2) hallucinations, (3) disorganized speech, (4) grossly disorganized behavior, and (5) inappropriate affect.

Screening: The process by which an offender is determined to be appropriate for admission to a given intervention program.

Self-help groups: As the term is used in this text, these are 12-step programs, composed of individuals who meet regularly to stabilize and facilitate their recovery from substance abuse. The best known is Alcoholics Anonymous (AA).

Sentencing stage: When a judge requires either that the offender be incarcerated or, as in many cases where the violation is minor, that the offender continue his or her probation sentence but under more restrictive terms.

Sex offender therapist: This therapist usually sees the offender once a week in a group counseling setting. These therapists are highly trained and experienced in working with the sex offender population.

Sexual assault: Includes all types of sexual offenses that involve touching or penetration of an intimate part of a person's body without consent.

Sexual gratification rapist: For this rapist, aggression is instrumental and is designed to gain compliance. This offender simply desires sex and may be in a situation where he feels that force or coercion could successfully get him the sexual intercourse that he wants.

Shaping: Therapy concept in which behaviors are taught by reinforcing successive approximations of a desired behavior until the behavior is fully learned by the client.

Shock incarceration: Short term of incarceration followed by a specified term of community supervision in hopes of deterring the offender from recidivating.

Shock probation: A process of placing an offender in prison and later releasing him or her on probation at some unknown date and time. The shock of incarceration is expected to have a deterrent impact on the offender, with a corresponding sense of gratitude when the offender is released from the facility to probation.

Short-term residential programs: Programs that typically provide intensive but brief residential treatment based on a modified 12-step approach. In most cases, offenders are kept in the program for no more than 90 days.

Slight negligence: The failure to exercise the standard of care and attention that highly conscientious and attentive persons might use.

Social bond theory: A theory, generated by Travis Hirschi, consisting of two basic propositions. First, juvenile offending and social bonds are inversely related, meaning that youth are less likely to offend as social bonds are strengthened. Second, social bond is impacted by a youth's possession of four elements: attachment to others, commitment to society, involvement in prosocial activities, and belief in legal mores and norms.

Social disorganization theory: Examines issues associated with norms in the community and contends that, for offenders, informal socialization processes (i.e., family, peers, etc.) break down and in their place, criminogenic influences are left unchecked.

Social learning theory: Contends that offenders learn to engage in crime through exposure to and the adoption of definitions that are favorable to the commission of crime.

Social study: Second stage of juvenile supervision, following the intake. Also called the investigation stage. This is similar to a *presentence investigation report* (PSI) and details the youth's personal background, family, educational progress, previous violations, employment, and so forth.

Social workers: Most of these professionals have a master's degree in social work. Their knowledge of social support systems, organizations, and groups, along with their background in psychological interventions, distinguishes their field of competence.

Solution-focused: This treatment begins from the observation that most psychological problems are present only intermittently. Solution-focused therapy assists the client in noticing when symptoms are diminished or absent, and helps him or her to use this knowledge as a foundation for recovery.

Specialized needs caseload model: Pertains to community supervision assignments to offenders who share common specialized needs around such areas as substance abuse, sex offending, a given set of disabilities, and so on.

Specific deterrence: The infliction of a punishment upon a specific offender in the hope he or she will be discouraged from committing future crimes.

Split sentencing: A sentence by a judge that consists of a fixed period of incarceration, which is expected to be followed by an additional fixed term of probation supervision. Felony-level offenders are more likely to receive split sentences than are misdemeanants.

Spouse monitoring: This involves supervision on the part of the spouse (if and when available, though other family members may be able to assist) or significant other to complete a daily checklist on the offender's compliance with the treatment.

Stakeholders: In the context of community corrections evaluations, this group would include the agency personnel, the community in which the agency is located, and even the offender population that is being supervised.

Standard probation: The basic form of supervision that is administered by most agencies. This type of sentence is actually little more than a baseline starting point for sanctioning.

Static risk factors: Characteristics that are inherent to the offender and are usually permanent in nature.

Strain theory/institutional anomie: This theory holds that when individuals cannot obtain success goals (such as money, status, and so forth), they will tend to experience a sense of pressure often called *strain*. Under certain conditions, they are likely to respond to this strain by engaging in criminal behavior.

Strengths-based perspective case management: Case management in the strengths-based model involves assisting clients to examine and identify their own strengths and assets as the vehicle for resource acquisition and goal attainment.

Study release program: Similar to a work release program but designed to allow the offender an opportunity to pursue educational goals.

Subcultural theory: Theory that many individuals tend to simultaneously learn to commit crime in one location, and this results in crime rates becoming disproportionately high in such areas where criminal behavior is learned as a valued norm.

Subjective assessment process: The use of interviewing and observation methods to determine the security and treatment needs of the offender. Professionals use their sense of judgment and experience to determine the offender's possible dangerousness and treatment needs.

Subjective structured interview: A process whereby an interviewer will ask a respondent a set of prearranged and open-ended questions so that the interview seems informal in nature, yet because of the prearranged questions, a structure evolves throughout the conversation that ensures that certain bits of desired data are gathered.

Substance Abuse Relapse Assessment (SARA): A structured interview designed as a treatment planning instrument for treatment professionals who work with substance abusers. It is helpful in developing relapse prevention goals for clients who tend to use multiple substances and in monitoring the achievement of these goals during treatment.

Substance Abuse Subtle Screening Instrument (SASSI): A substance abuse screening instrument that provides interpretations of client profiles and aids in developing hypotheses that clinicians or researchers may find useful in understanding persons in treatment.

Supervision stage: This stage of juvenile supervision includes casework, surveillance, and various aspects of security management to track the behavior of the juvenile. This stage is a key function of the probation department.

Sweat testing: Uses sweat samples obtained from patches that can be placed on a person for a number of days. This type of testing has the advantage of providing a longer time frame for detection of drug use, and it is difficult to adulterate the testing results.

Technical violations: Actions that do not comply with the conditions and requirements of a probationer's sentence, as articulated by the court that acted as the sentencing authority. Technical violations are not necessarily criminal and would likely be legal behaviors if the offender were not on probation.

Teen courts: Much like traditional courts in that there are prosecutors and defense attorneys, offenders and victims, and judges and juries, but youths rather than adults fill these roles, and these youths even determine the disposition of the case.

Theory: A concept that describes a set of interrelated constructs that purport to explain some phenomenon.

Therapeutic jurisprudence: The study of the role of the law as a therapeutic agent. Essentially, therapeutic jurisprudence focuses on the law's impact on emotional life and on psychological well-being.

Thought-shifting: This requires that the offender shift his thoughts to aversive imagery. The sex offender may be allowed to view or think about some arousing image but then is trained to think about something aversive, like an approaching police officer.

Thought-stopping: This is used to disrupt a deviant thinking pattern. The sex offender is given pictures of arousing images and is forced to stop his thoughts when the image is seen.

Ticket-of-leave: A permit that was given to offenders on Norfolk Island and Australia in exchange for a certain period of good conduct. Through this process, convicts could earn their own wage through their own labor prior to the expiration of their actual sentence.

Tort: A legal injury in which the action of one person causes injury to the person or property of another as the result of a violation of one's duty that has been established by law.

True negative: Implies that an offender is predicted to not reoffend, and that prediction turns out to be true.

True positive: Implies that the offender is predicted to reoffend and that this prediction later turns out to be true.

Urine testing: Due to low cost and reasonably high accuracy of the testing process, urinalysis is considered the most suitable method for drug courts and most criminal justice agencies for detecting the presence of illegal substances.

Validity: A concept that describes whether the instrument used is measuring what it is intended to measure.

Victim counselors: These persons are counselors who were prior victims of some type of traumatic crime, such as domestic abuse or sexual assault.

Victim's impact statement: This allows the victim to express his or her own views on the appropriateness of the parolee's release, and it also allows the victim to voice his or her sense of trauma and victimization that resulted from the criminal actions of the offender.

Welfare workers: Name for officers who view the offender more as a client than as a supervisee on their caseload. These officers believe that the best way to enhance the security and safety of the community is by reforming the offender so that further crime will not occur.

White or **Caucasian American:** Refers to persons whose origins are with any of the original peoples of Europe, the Middle East, or North Africa.

Wilderness camps: Residential programs where juveniles engage in a series of physically challenging outdoor activities, such as backpacking, canoeing, or even rock climbing.

Willful negligence: Refers to the committing of an act that flagrantly disregards the consequences that are probable and of which the offender was most assuredly aware.

Wisconsin Risk Assessment System: One of the best-known risk assessment systems, it examines 10 specific factors. This form of structured assessment has become the prototype for many probation and parole systems in the United States.

Work release programs: Programs designed to equip offenders with the opportunity to seek or maintain employment while also engaging in educational or vocational training, as well as other treatment services that might be available at the facility.

Wrap-around services: Complex, multifaceted intervention strategy designed to keep delinquent youth at home and out of institutions whenever possible. Services are provided to offenders transitioning to the community with the aid of a team of support individuals that may include the offender's family, clergy, social service workers, probation and/or parole officers, and other parties.

References

Abadinsky, H. (1993). *Drug abuse: An introduction* (2nd ed.). Chicago: Nelson-Hall.

Abadinsky, H. (2003). *Probation and parole: Theory and practice* (8th ed.). Upper Saddle River, NJ: Prentice Hall.

Abel, G. G., & Rouleau, J. L. (1990). The nature and extent of sexual assault. In W. L. Marshall, D. R. Laws, & H. L. Barbaree (Eds.), *Handbook of sexual assault: Issues, theories, and treatment of the offender* (pp. 9–20). New York: Plenum.

Alarid, L. F., Burton, V. S., & Cullen, F. T. (2000). Gender and crime among felony offenders: Assessing the generality of social control and differential association theories. *Journal of Research in Crime and Delinquency, 37*(2), 171–199.

Almeida, R. (1996). Hindu, Christian, and Muslim families. In M. McGoldrick, M. Giordano, J. Pearce, & J. Giordano (Eds.), *Ethnicity and family therapy* (2nd ed., pp. 395–423). New York: Guilford Press.

Altschuler, D. M., & Armstrong, T. L. (2001). Reintegrating high-risk juvenile offenders into communities: Experiences and prospects. *Corrections Management Quarterly, 5*(1), 79–95.

American Association on Intellectual and Developmental Disabilities. (2008). *Frequently asked questions on intellectual disability and the AAIDD definition.* Retrieved from http://www.aaidd.org/Policies/faq_intellectual_disability.shtml.

American Correctional Association. (1990). *The female offender: What does the future hold?* Washington, DC: St. Mary's Press.

American Probation and Parole Association. (1991). *Issue paper on caseload standards.* Washington, DC: Author.

American Probation and Parole Association. (2006). *Adult and juvenile probation and parole national firearm survey* (2nd ed.). Lexington, KY: Author.

American Psychiatric Association. (2000). *Diagnostic and statistical manual of mental disorders—text revision (DSM-IV-TR).* Arlington, VA: Author.

Anderson, D. (1998). *Sensible justice: Alternative to prison.* New York: New Press.

Andrews, D. A., & Bonta, J. L. (1994). *The psychology of criminal conduct.* Cincinnati, OH: Anderson.

Andrews, D. A., & Bonta, J. L. (1999). *Level of Supervision Inventory—Revised: Screening version user's manual (LSI-R:SV).* Toronto, Ont., Canada: Multi-Health Systems.

Andrews, D., & Bonta, J. (2003). *Level of Supervision Inventory—Revised (LSI-R).* Retrieved from http://www.pearson-uk.com/product.aspx?n=1316&s=1322&cat=2020&skey=3868.

Andrews, D. A., & Dowden, C. (2002). *A meta-analytic investigation into effective correctional intervention for female offenders.* Ottawa, Ont., Canada: Carleton University Press.

Anno, B. J., Graham, C., Lawrence, J. E., & Shansky, R. (2004). *Correctional health care: Addressing the needs of elderly, chronically ill, and terminally ill inmates.* Washington, DC: National Institute of Corrections.

Anthony, W., Cohen, M., & Farkas, M. (1990). *Psychiatric rehabilitation.* New York: Center for Psychiatric Rehabilitation.

Aos, S., Miller, M., & Drake, E. (2006). *Evidence-based adult corrections programs: What works and what does not.* Olympia: Washington State Institute for Public Policy.

Arizona State Supreme Court. (2008). *Juvenile intensive probation supervision (JIPS).* Retrieved from http://www.supreme.state.az.us/jjsd/JIPS/jips.htm.

Arkansas speeds parole to ease jam. (2001, November 30). *Corrections Digest.*

Arkansas to emphasize rehabilitation in drive to curb crowding, cut costs. (2002, July 12). *Corrections Digest.*

Ashford, J. B., Sales, B. D., & Reid, W. H. (2002). *Treating adult and juvenile offenders with special needs.* Washington, DC: American Psychological Association.

Austin, J. (2006). How much risk can we take? The misuse of risk assessment in corrections. *Federal Probation, 20*(2). Retrieved from http://www.uscourts.gov/fedprob/September_2006/risk.html#basics.

Australian Institute of Criminology. (2006). *AICrime reduction matters. Wilderness programs and boot camps—Are they effective?* Canberra, Australia. Retrieved from http://www.aic.gov.au/publications/crm/crm044.html.

Babcock, J. (2006). *Does batterer treatment work? New directions to improve its efficacy.* Paper presented at the Annual Meeting of the American Society of Criminology (ASC). Available at http://www.allacademic.com/meta/p127404_index.html.

Barker, L. (2004). *Learning and behavior: Biological, psychological, and sociological perspectives.* Upper Saddle River, NJ: Prentice Hall.

Barnes, H. E., & Teeters, N. D. (1959). *New horizons in criminology*. Englewood Cliffs, NJ: Prentice Hall.

Bartol, C. R. (2002). *Criminal behavior: A psychological approach* (5th ed.). Upper Saddle River, NJ: Prentice Hall.

Baumer, T., Maxfield, M., & Mendelsohn, R. (1993). A comparative analysis of three electronically monitored home detention programs. *Justice Quarterly, 10,* 121–142.

Bazemore, G., & O'Brien, S. (2002). The quest for a restorative model of rehabilitation: Theory-for-practice and practice-for-theory. In L. Walgrave (Ed.), *Restorative justice and the law*. Portland, OR: Willan Publishing.

Beccaria, C. (1983). An essay on crimes and punishments. In A. Caso (Ed.), *An essay on crimes and punishments* (4th ed; E. D. Ingraham, Trans.) Boston: International Pocket Library. (Original work published 1764)

Begnaud, C. (2007). *Parole and probation in the United States*. New York: Associated Content. Retrieved from http://www.associated content.com/article/151400/parole_and_probation_in_the_ united.html.

Belenko, S. (2001). *Research on drug courts: A critical review. 2001 Update*. New York: National Center on Addiction and Substance Abuse. Retrieved from http://www.drugpolicy.org/docUploads/ 2001drugcourts.pdf.

Bennett, C. E. (2002). *A profile of the nation's foreign-born population from Asia (2000 update)*. Washington, DC: U.S. Census Bureau.

Bloom, B., Brown, M., & Chesney-Lind, M. (1996). *Women on Probation and Parole*. In A. J. Lurigio (Ed.), Community corrections in America: New directions and sounder investments for persons with mental illness and codisorders (pp. 51–76). Washington, DC: National Institute of Corrections.

Bloom, B., Owen, B., & Covington, S. (2003). *Gender responsive strategies: Research, practice, and guiding principles for women offenders*. Washington, DC: National Institute of Corrections. Retrieved from http://www.nicic.org/Library/018017.

Bonczar, T. P. (1995). *Characteristics of adults on probation*. Washington, DC: U.S. Department of Justice.

Bond, G. R., Salyers, M. P., Rollins, A. L., Rapp, C. A., & Zipple, A. M. (2004). How evidence-based practices contribute to community integration. *Community Mental Health Journal, 40*(6), 569.

Boone, H. N. (1994). Recommended outcome measures for program evaluation: APPA's board of directors survey results. *APPA Perspectives, 18,* 19–20.

Braithwaite, J. (1989). *Crime, shame, and reintegration*. Cambridge, UK: Cambridge University Press.

Bureau of Justice Assistance. (1999). *Addressing community gang problems: A model for problem solving*. Washington, DC: Office of Justice Programs. Retrieved from http://www.ojp.usdoj.gov.

Bureau of Justice Assistance. (2005). *Building an offender reentry program: A guide for law enforcement*. Washington, DC: Author. Retrieved from http://www.theiacp.org/profassist/reentry/ReentryProgramGuide .pdf.

Bureau of Justice Assistance, Center for Program Evaluation. (2007). *Reporting and using evaluation results*. Washington, DC: Author. Retrieved from http://www.ojp.usdoj.gov/BJA/evaluation/ sitemap.htm.

Bureau of Justice Statistics. (1994). *Special report: Women in prison*. Washington, DC: U.S. Department of Justice.

Bureau of Justice Statistics. (1997). *Sex offenses and sex offenders*. Washington, DC: U.S. Department of Justice.

Bureau of Justice Statistics. (1999). *Drug and crime statistics*. Washington, DC: Author.

Bureau of Justice Statistics. (2003). *Recidivism of sex offenders released from prison in 1994*. Washington, DC: U. S. Department of Justice.

Bureau of Justice Statistics. (2007). *Prison and jail inmates at midyear 2006*. Washington, DC: U.S. Department of Justice.

Bureau of Justice Statistics. (2008). *BJS home page: Corrections*. Washington, DC: U.S. Department of Justice. Retrieved from http://www.ojp.usdoj.gov/bjs/jails.htm.

Burke, P. B. (1997). *Policy-driven responses to probation and parole violations*. Washington, DC: U.S. Department of Justice, National Institute of Corrections.

Burrell, B. (2006). *Caseload standards for probation and parole*. Lexington, KY: American Probation and Parole Association. Retrieved from http://www.appa-net.org/ccheadlines/docs/ Caseload_Standards_PP_0906.pdf.

Butts, J., Buck, J., & Coggeshall, M. (2002). *The impact of teen court on young offenders*. Washington, DC: The Urban Institute.

Camp, C., & Camp, G. (2003). *The 2002 corrections yearbook: Adult corrections*. Middletown, CT: Criminal Justice Institute.

Campbell, D. T., & Stanley, J. C. (1963). *Experimental and quasi-experimental designs for research*. Boston: Houghton Mifflin.

Carbonnell, J. L., & Perkins, R. (2000). Diagnosis and assessment of criminal offenders. In P. Van Voorhis, M. Braswell, & D. Lester (Eds.), *Correctional counseling and rehabilitation* (4th ed.). Cincinnati, OH: Anderson.

Center for Sex Offender Management. (2001). *Training curricula*. Washington, DC: United States Department of Justice.

Center for Sex Offender Management. (2008). *Training curricula*. Washington, DC: Office of Justice Programs, U.S. Department of Justice.

Center for Substance Abuse Treatment. (2005). Substance abuse treatment for adults in the criminal justice system. *Treatment Improvement Protocol (TIP) Series 44*. DHHS Publication No. (SMA) 05-4056. Rockville, MD: Substance Abuse and Mental Health Services Administration.

Champion, D. (2002). *Probation, parole, and community corrections* (4th ed.). Upper Saddle River, NJ: Prentice Hall.

Clear, T. R., & Cole, G. F. (2003). *American corrections* (6th ed.). Belmont, CA: Thompson/Wadsworth.

Clear, T. R., Cole, G. F., & Reisig, M. D. (2006). *American corrections* (7th ed.). Belmont, CA: Wadsworth/Thomson Learning.

Clements, C. B., McKee, J. M., & Jones, S. E. (1984). *Offender needs and assessment: Models and approaches*. Washington, DC: National Institute of Corrections.

Cohen, L. E., & Felson, M. (1979). Social change and crime rate trends: A routine activity approach. *American Sociological Review, 44,* 588–607.

Cohn, J. (1973). *A study of community-based correctional needs in Massachusetts*. Boston: Massachusetts Department of Corrections.

Colorado Department of Corrections. (2006). *Parole officer job description.* Colorado Springs, CO.

Connolly, M. M. (2003). *A critical examination of actuarial offender-based prediction assessments [electronic resource]: Guidance for the next generation of assessments.* Doctoral dissertation, The University of Texas at Austin. Available online at http://www .ncjrs.org/pdffiles1/nij/grants/202982.pdf.

Cox, S. M., Allen, J. M., Hanser, R. D., & Conrad, J. L. (2008). *Juvenile justice: A guide to theory, policy, and practice* (6th ed.). Los Angeles: Sage Publications.

Cromwell, P. F., del Carmen, R. V., & Alarid, L. F. (2002). *Community-based corrections* (5th ed.). Belmont, CA: Wadsworth.

Cullen, F., & Agnew, R. (2003). *Criminological theory: Past to present* (2nd ed.). Los Angeles: Roxbury.

Cullen, F. T., & Agnew, R. (2006). *Criminological theory: Past to present* (3rd ed.). Los Angeles: Roxbury.

Cumming, J., & Cumming, E. (1962). *Ego and milieu.* New York: Atherton Press.

Davis, L. E. (1999). *Working with African American males: A guide to practice.* Thousand Oaks, CA: Sage Publications.

Del Carmen, R. V., Barnhill, M. B., Bonham, G., Hignite, L., & Jermstad, T. (2001). *Civil liabilities and other legal issues for probation/parole officers and supervisors.* Washington, DC: National Institute of Corrections.

Dolan, L., Kolthoff, K., Schreck, M., Smilanch, P., & Todd, R. (2003). Gender-specific treatment for clients with co-occurring disorders. *Corrections Today, 65*(6), 100–107.

Domurad, F. (2000). So you want to develop your own risk assessment instrument. *Topics in Community Corrections, 2000 Annual Issue,* 11–16.

Dressler, D. (1962). *Practice and theory of probation and parole.* New York: Columbia University Press.

Drummond, R. J. (1996). *Appraisal procedures for counselors and helping professionals* (3rd ed.). Englewood Cliffs, NJ: Prentice Hall.

Emerling, G. (2006, March 20). No more sugar and spice: Girl gangs on rise in D.C. *The Washington Times.*

Enos, R., & Southern, S. (1996). *Correctional case management.* Cincinnati, OH: Anderson.

Evans, D. G., & Sawdon, J. (2004). The development of a gang exit strategy. *Corrections Today, 66,* 76–81.

Fabelo, T., & Nagy, G. (2006). *Better diagnosis: The first step to improve probation supervision strategies.* Washington, DC: JFA Institute.

Family Foundations. (2007). *Family Foundations program descriptions.* Rayville, LA: Author.

Finn, P., & Kuck, S. (2003). *Addressing probation and parole officer stress.* Washington, DC: National Institute of Justice.

Firshein, J. (1998). *Does treatment work?* Retrieved from: http://www .thirteen.org/closetohome/policy/html/treatwork.html.

Friel, C. M. (2008). *Advanced research design.* Retrieved from http://www.shsu.edu/~icc_cmf.

Froland, C., Pancoast, D. L., Chapman, N. J., & Kimboko, P. J. (1981). *Helping networks and human services.* Beverly Hills, CA: Sage Publications.

Gacono, C. B., Nieberding, R. J., Owen, A., Rubel, J., & Bodholdt, R. (2001). Treating conduct disorder, antisocial, and psychopathic personalities. In J. B. Ashford, B. D. Sales, & W. H. Reid (Eds.), *Treating adults and juvenile offenders with special needs.* Washington, DC: American Psychological Association.

Gagnon v. Scarpelli, 411 U.S. 778 (1973).

Garrett, J. S. (1999). Working with the Media. In P. M. Carlson and J. S. Garrett (Eds.). *Prison and Jail Administration: Practice and Theory.* Gaithersburg, MD: Aspen Publications.

Glaser, D. (1964). *The effectiveness of a prison and parole system.* Indianapolis, IN: Bobbs-Merrill.

Glaze, L. E., & Bonzar, T. P. (2007). *Probation and parole in the United States, 2005.* Washington, DC: Bureau of Justice Statistics.

Glaze, L. E., & Palla, S. (2005). Probation and parole in the United States, 2004. *Bureau of Justice Statistics Bulletin* (NCJ 210676). Washington, DC: U.S. Department of Justice.

Goffman, E. (1961). *Asylums: Essays on the social situation of mental patients and other inmates.* Garden City, NY: Anchor Books.

Gordon, M., & Glaser, D. (1991). The use and effects of financial penalties in municipal courts. *Criminology, 29,* 651–676.

Gottfredson, M., & Hirschi, T. (1990). *A general theory of crime.* Stanford, CA: Stanford University Press.

Government Accounting Office. (1990). *Intermediate sanctions.* Washington, DC: Author.

Greek, C. (2002). The cutting edge: Tracking probationers in space and time: The convergence of GIS and GPS systems. *Federal Probation, 66,* 51–53.

Greenholtz v. Inmates of the Nebraska Penal and Correctional Complex, 442 U.S. 1 (1979).

Grinnel, F. W. (1941). The common law history of probation. *Journal of Criminal Law and Criminology, 32*(1), 15–35.

Hagan, F. (2000). *Research methods in criminal justice and criminology* (5th ed.). Needham Heights, MA: Allyn & Bacon.

Hanser, R. D. (1999). *Reentry courts: Managing the transition from prison to community.* Washington, DC: National Criminal Justice Resources and Statistics.

Hanser, R. D. (2002). Inmate suicide in prisons: An analysis of legal liability under Section 1983. *The Prison Journal, 82*(4), 459–477.

Hanser, R. D. (2006a). Restorative justice applications to sex offenders and domestic abusers in Canada. *Crime and Justice International, 22*(90), 31–35.

Hanser, R. D. (2006b). *Special needs offenders.* Upper Saddle River, NJ: Pearson/Prentice Hall.

Hanser, R. D. (2007a). Restorative justice paradigms as applied to nonviolent and violent special needs offenders. *International Journal of Restorative Justice, 3*(1), 54–65.

Hanser, R. D. (2007b). *Special needs offenders in the community.* Upper Saddle River, NJ: Prentice Hall.

Hanser, R. D., & Mire, S. M. (2008). Juvenile sex offenders in the United States and Australia: A comparison. *International Review of Law and Technology, 22*(1 & 2), 101–114.

Hanson, G. R., Venturelli, P. J., & Fleckenstein, A. E. (2002). *Drugs and society* (7th ed.). Sudbury, MA: Jones and Bartlett.

Hanson, K. R., Gordon, A., Harris, A. J., Marques, J. K., Murphy, W., Quinsey, V. L., et al. (2002). First report of the collaborative outcome data project on the effectiveness of psychological treatment for sex offenders. *Sexual Abuse: A Journal of Research and Treatment, 14*(2), 169–194.

Harlow v. Fitzgerald, 457 U.S. 800 (1982).

Harper, F. D., & McFadden, J. (2003). *Culture and counseling: New approaches*. New York: Allyn & Bacon.

Harris, P. (1994). Client management classification and prediction of probation outcomes. *Crime and Delinquency, 40*(1), 154–174.

Harris, P. (2002). *Research to results: Effective community corrections*. Lanham, MD: American Correctional Association.

Harrison, P. M., & Beck, A. J. (2003). *Prisoners in 2002*. Washington, DC: Bureau of Justice Statistics. Retrieved from http://www.ojp.usdoj .gov/bjs/pub/pdf/p02.pdf.

Harrison, P. M., & Karberg, J. C. (2004). *Prison and jail inmates at midyear 2003*. Washington, DC: Bureau of Justice Statistics. Retrieved from http://www.ojp.usdoj.gov/bjs/pub/pdf/pjim03.pdf.

Healey, K., Smith, C., & O'Sullivan, C. (1998). *Batterer intervention: Program approaches and criminal justice strategies*. Washington, DC: National Institute of Justice.

Hill, B. J. (2003). *Four-point strategy reduces technical violations of probation in Connecticut*. Whethersfield, CT: National Institute of Corrections Information Center.

Hinzman, G. (2000). The Matrix: Matching the offender with treatment resources. *Topics in Community Corrections*, 2000 annual issue, 17–22.

Holmes, R. M., & Holmes, S. T. (2002). *Profiling violent crimes* (3rd ed.). Thousand Oaks, CA: Sage Publications.

Huang, K. (1991). Chinese Americans. In N. Mokuau (Ed.), *Handbook of social services for Asian and Pacific Islanders* (pp. 79–96). Westport, CT: Greenwood Press.

Human Rights Watch. (2008). *No easy answers: Sex offender laws in the U.S.* New York: Author.

Inciardi, J. A. (1999a). *Drug treatment behind bars*. In P. M. Carslon & J. S. Garrett (Eds.), *Prison and jail administration: Practice and theory*. Gaithersburg, MD: Aspen Publications.

Inciardi, J. A. (1999b). Prison-based therapeutic communities: An effective modality for treating drug-involved offenders. In K. C. Haas & G. P. Alpert (Eds.), *The dilemmas of punishment* (pp. 403–417). Prospect Heights, IL: Waveland.

Ingraham, B., & Smith, G. (1972). Electronic surveillance and control of behavior and its possible use in rehabilitation and parole. *Issues in Criminology, 7,* 35–52.

Jemelka, R. (2000). *The mentally ill in local jails: Issues in admission and booking*. Washington, DC: National Institute of Corrections.

Jencks, C. (1994). *The homeless*. Cambridge: Harvard University Press.

Joiner, C. T. (2006). An examination of racial profiling data in a large metropolitan area. *Professional Issues in Criminal Justice, 1*(2), 81–93.

Jones, J. (2007). *Pre-release planning and re-entry process: Addendum 02*. Tulsa: Oklahoma Department of Corrections.

Jones, K., & Hanser, R. D. (thesis chair). (2005). *Faith-based treatment: A dual analysis of race and voluntary versus mandatory participation of clients*. Master's thesis, University of Louisiana at Monroe.

Jones, M. (1953). *The therapeutic community*. New York: Basic Books.

Kansas v. Hendricks, 117 S. Ct. 2072 (1997).

Kerle, K. (1999). Short-term institutions at the local level. In P. M. Carlson & J. S. Garrett (Eds.), *Prison and jail administration: Practice and theory*. Gaithersburg, MD: Aspen.

King, W. R., Holmes, S. T., Henderson, M. L., & Latessa, E. J. (2007). The Community Corrections Partnership: Examining the long-term effects of youth participation in an Afrocentric diversion program. *Crime and Delinquency, 47*(4), 558–572.

Knight, R. A., & Prentky, R. A. (1990). Classifying sexual offenders: The development and corroboration of taxonomic models. In W. L. Marshall, D. R. Laws, & H. L. Barbaree (Eds.), *Handbook of sexual assault: Issues, theories, and treatment of the offender* (pp. 9–20). New York: Plenum.

Knopp, F. H. (1989). Northwest Treatment Associates: A comprehensive community-based evaluation and treatment program for adult sex offenders. In P. C. Kratcoski (Ed.), *Correctional counseling and treatment* (2nd ed., pp. 364–380). Prospect Heights, IL: Waveland Press.

Krauss, D. A., Sales, B. D., Becker, J. V., & Figueredo, A. J. (2000). Beyond prediction to explanation in risk assessment research. *International Journal of Law and Psychiatry, 23*(2), 91–112.

Krauth, B., & Linke, L. (1999). *State organizational structures for delivering adult probation services*. Washington, DC: National Institute of Corrections.

Latessa, E. J., & Allen, H. E. (1999). *Corrections in the community* (2nd ed.). Cincinnati, OH: Anderson.

LeBeau, M., & Mozayani, A. (2001). *Drug-facilitated sexual assault*. San Diego Academic Press.

Lehman, J., Beatty, T. G., Maloney, D., Russell, S., Seymour, A., and Shapiro, C. 2002. *The Three "R's" of Reentry*. Washington, DC: Justice Solutions.

Lempert, R. O., & Visher, C. A. (Eds.). (1987). *Randomized field experiments in criminal justice agencies: Workshop proceedings*. Washington, DC: National Research Council.

Lilly, J. R., Cullen, F. T., & Ball, R. A. (2007). *Criminological theory: Context and consequences* (4th ed.). Thousand Oaks, CA: Sage Publications.

Lipsey, M. W. (2000, July 16–19). *What 500 intervention studies show about the effects of intervention on the recidivism of juvenile offenders*. Paper presented at the Annual Conference on Criminal Justice Research and Evaluation, Washington, DC.

Lipsey, M. W., Wilson, D. B., & Cothern, L. (2000). *Effective intervention for serious juvenile intervention*. Washington, DC: Office of Juvenile Justice and Delinquency Prevention.

Little, G. L. (2005). Meta-analysis of moral reconation therapy: Recidivism results from probation and parole implementations. *Cognitive-Behavioral Treatment Review, 14,* 14–16.

Lowry, K. D. (2000). United States probation/pretrial officers' concerns about victimization and officer safety training. *Federal Probation, 64*(2), 51–59.

Lurigio, A. J. (1996). Responding to the mentally ill on probation and parole: Recommendations and action plans. In A. J. Lurigio (Ed.), *Community corrections in America: New directions and sounder investments for persons with mental illness and codisorders* (pp. 166–171). Washington, DC: National Institute of Corrections.

Mactavish, M., & Winter, V. (1991). *The practical planning guide for community corrections managers.* Washington, DC: National Institute of Corrections. Retrieved from http://www.nicic.org/pubs/1991/009018.pdf.

Maghan, J. (1999). Corrections countdown: Prisoners at the cusp of the 21st century. In P. M. Carlson & J. S. Garrett (Eds.), *Prison and jail administration: Practice and theory.* Gaithersburg, MD: Aspen Publications.

Martinez v. California, 444 U.S. 277 (1980).

Martinson, R. (1976). What works? Questions and answers about prison reform. *The Public Interest, 10,* 22–54.

Maximus. (2003). *MAXIMUS Acquires misdemeanor probation outsourcing firm.* Reston, VA: Gale Group. Retrieved from http://www.thefreelibrary.com/MAXIMUS+Acquires+Misdemeanor+Probation+Outsourcing+Firm-a0101341267.

McCall, R. B. (1994). *Preventing school failure and antisocial behavior in the U.S.A.* Pittsburgh, PA: University of Pittsburgh Office of Child Development.

McCollister, K. E., & French, M. T. (2001). *The economic cost of substance abuse treatment in criminal justice settings.* Miami, FL: University of Miami. Retrieved from http://www.amityfoundation.com/lib/libarch/CostPrisonTreatment.pdf.

McCoy, T. (2000). Probation officer safety: The results of the National Association of Probation Executives Probation Safety Survey. *Executive Exchange,* 4–11.

McGarry, P. (1990). *NIC focus: Intermediate sanctions.* Washington, DC: National Institute of Corrections.

McGoldrick, M., Giordano, J., Pearce, J. K., & Giordano, J. (1996). *Ethnicity and family therapy* (2nd ed.). New York: Guilford Press.

McNeese, C. A., Springer, D. W., & Arnold, E. M. (2002). Treating substance abuse disorders. In J. B. Ashford, B. D. Sales, & W. H. Reid (2002). *Treating adult and juvenile offenders with special needs.* Washington, DC: American Psychological Association.

McNutt, R. (1999, November 10). Court for mentally ill offenders advocated: Judicial officials at seminar told that treatment is lacking. *Cincinnati Enquirer.* Available at http://www.enquirer.com/editions/1999/11/10/loc_court_for_mentally.html.

Megargee, E. I. (2004). *MMPI-2 criminal justice and correctional report.* Upper Saddle River, NJ: Pearson. Retrieved from http://www.pearsonassessments.com/tests/mmpi_correct.htm.

Merton, R. K. (1938). Social structure and anomie. *American Sociological Review, 3,* 672–682.

Messner, S. F., & Rosenfeld, R. (2001). *Crime and the American Dream* (3rd ed.). Belmont, CA: Wadsworth.

Middle Tennessee State University. (2007). *Monitoring Tennessee's sex offenders using Global Positioning Systems: A project evaluation.* Nashville, TN: Author.

Miller, E. J. (2007). The therapeutic effects of managerial reentry court. *Federal Sentencing Reporter, 20*(2), 127–135.

Miller, M., & Lane, R. (2002). *A risk assessment model for offender management.* Paper presented at the Probation and Community Corrections: Making the Community Safer Conference convened by the Australian Institute of Criminology and the Probation and Community Corrections Officers' Association, Inc. Perth, Australia. Retrieved from http://aic.gov.au/conferences/probation/maller.pdf.

Miller, W. B. (1958). Lower class culture as a generating milieu of gang delinquency. *Journal of Social Issues, 14*(3), 5–19.

Mire, S. M., Forsyth, C., & Hanser, R. D. (2007). Jail diversion: Addressing the needs of offenders with mental illness and co-occurring disorders. *Journal of Offender Rehabilitation, 45*(1/2), 19–31.

Mississippi Department of Corrections. (2007). *Restitution centers.* Jackson, MS: Author. Retrieved from http://www.mdoc.state.ms.us/restitution_centers.htm.

Moffitt, T. E. (1993). Adolescence-limited and life-course persistent antisocial behavior: A developmental taxonomy. *Psychological Review, 100,* 674–701.

Monchick, R., Scheyett, A., & Pfeifer, J. (2006). *Drug court case management: Role, function, and utility.* Alexandria, VA: National Drug Court Institute.

Morris, N., & Tonry, M. (1990). *Between prison and probation: Intermediate punishments in a rational sentencing system.* Oxford, UK: Oxford University Press.

Morrissey v. Brewer, 408 U.S. 471 (1972).

Morton, J. B. (1992). *An administrative overview of the older inmate.* Washington, DC: National Institute of Corrections.

Myers, P. L., & Salt, N. R. (2000). *Becoming an addictions counselor: A comprehensive text.* Sudbury, MA: Jones and Bartlett.

National Center for Victims of Crime. (1988). *Responding to workplace violence and staff victimization in probation, parole, and corrections: A training and resource manual.* Arlington, VA: Author.

National Institute of Corrections. (1993). *The intermediate sanctions handbook: Experiences and tools for policymakers.* Washington, DC: Author.

National Institute of Corrections. (2004). *Mentally ill persons in correctional settings.* Retrieved from http://www.nicic.org.

National Institute of Justice. (1992). *Evaluating drug control and system improvement projects: Guidelines for projects supported by the Bureau of Justice Assistance.* Washington, DC: Author.

National Institute of Justice. (1998). *What can the federal government do to decrease crime and revitalize communities?* Washington, DC: Author.

National Institute of Justice. (1999, October). Keeping track of electronic monitoring. *National Law Enforcement and Corrections Technology Center Bulletin.*

National Institute of Mental Health. (2002). *Depression.* Bethesda, MD: Author.

National Institute on Drug Abuse. (2005). *Types of treatment.* Washington, DC: Office of National Drug Control Policy. Retrieved from http://www.whitehousedrugpolicy.gov/treat/treatment.html.

National Police Agency. (2007). *Overview of Japanese police and information from the National Police Agency.* Tokyo, Japan: Author. Retrieved from http://www.npa.go.jp/English.

Nelson, K. E., Ohmart, H., & Harlow, N. (1978). *Promising strategies in probation and parole.* Washington, DC: Government Printing Office.

Neubauer, D. W. (2002). *America's courts and the criminal justice system* (7th ed.). Belmont, CA: Wadsworth.

New York State Office of Mental Health. (2008). *NYS OMH fact sheet: Cultural competence, evidenced based practices and planning.* Albany, NY: Author. Retrieved from http://www.omh.state.ny.us/omhweb/ebp/culturalcompetence.htm.

Office of Juvenile Justice and Delinquency Prevention. (2007). *OJJDP model programs guide.* Washington, DC: Author. Retrieved from http://www.dsgonline.com/mpg2.5/mpg_index.htm.

Office of the Auditor. (2007). *Probations services for Athens-Clarke County state and municipal courts: Report to the mayor and commission.* Athens-Clarke County, GA: Unified Government of Athens-Clarke County.

O'Keefe, M. L., Klebe, K., & Hromas, S. (1998). *Validation of the Level of Supervision Inventory (LSI) for community based offenders in Colorado: Phase II.* Colorado Springs: Colorado Department of Corrections.

Paparazzi, M. (2003). Probation, parole and public safety: The need for principled practices versus faddism and circular policy development. *Corrections Today, 65*(5), 46–51.

Parsonage, W. H., & Bushey, W. C. (1987). The victimization of probation and parole workers in the line of duty: An exploratory study. *Criminal Justice Policy Review, 2*(4), 372–391.

Partee v. Lane, 528 F. Supp. 1254 (U.S.D. Ill. 1982).

Payton v. United States, 636 F.2d 132 (5th Cir. 1982).

Peak, K. J. (1995). *Justice administration: Police, courts, and corrections management.* Upper Saddle River, NJ: Prentice Hall.

Perlman, H. H. (1957). *Social casework: A problem-solving process.* Chicago: University of Chicago Press.

Petersilia, J., & Turner, S. (1993a). *Evaluating intensive supervised probation/parole results of a nationwide experiment.* Washington, DC: U.S. Department of Justice.

Petersilia, J., & Turner, S. (1993). Intensive probation and parole. In M. Tonry (Ed.), *Crime and justice: A review of research* (pp. 281–335). Chicago: University of Chicago Press.

Price, J. H. (2000). *Elderly and armed: Aging offenders.* Gale Group. Retrieved from http://www.findarticles.com/p/articles/mi_m1571/is_46_16/ai_72329012.

Providence Service Corporation. (2006). *Providence Service Corporation acquires MAXIMUS Correctional Services Business.* Tucson, AZ: Providence Service Corporation. Retrieved from http://investor.provcorp.com/phoenix.zhtml?c=145700&p=irol-newsArticle&t=Regular&id=912855&.

Quinion, M. (2007). *World Wide Web words.* Retrieved from http://www.worldwidewords.org/qa/qa-hue1.htm.

Rackmill, S. (1994). An analysis of home confinement as a sanction. *Federal Probation, 58,* 45–52.

Rapp, C. A. (1998). The active ingredients of effective case management: A research synthesis. *Community Mental Health Journal, 34*(4), 363.

Reckless, W. C. (1961). *The crime problem.* New York: Appleton-Century-Crofts.

Reilly, E. F., Jr. (2002). *28 CFR Part 2: Paroling, recommitting, and supervising federal prisoners: Prisoners serving sentences under the United States and District of Columbia codes.* Washington, DC: Department of Justice, Parole Commission.

Reinventing Probation Council, The. (1999, August). *Broken windows probation: The next step in fighting crime.* Civic Report # 7. New York: Center for Civic Innovation, Manhattan Institute.

Renzema, M. (1992). Home confinement programs: Development, implementation, and impact. In J. Bryne, A. Lurigio, & J. Petersilia (Eds.), *Smart sentencing: The emergence of intermediate sanctions* (pp. 41–53). Beverly Hills, CA: Sage Publications.

Rice, M. E., Harris, G. T., & Quinsey, V. L. (2002). Research on the treatment of adult sex offenders. In J. B. Ashford, B. D. Sales, & W. H. Reid (Eds.), *Treating adult and juvenile offenders with special needs.* Washington, DC: American Psychological Association.

Richardson v. McKnight, 117 S. Ct. 2100 (1997).

Robbins, S. P. (2003). *Organizational behavior* (10th ed.). Upper Saddle River, NJ: Prentice Hall.

Robinson, J. J., & Jones, J. W. (2000). *Drug testing in a drug court environment: Common issues to address.* Washington, DC: U.S. Department of Justice, Office of Justice Programs. Retrieved from http://www.ncjrs.gov/pdffiles1/ojp/181103.pdf.

Rowe, D. (2002). *Biology and crime.* Los Angeles: Roxbury.

Sabol, W. J., Minton, T. D., & Harrison, P. M. (2008). *Prison and jail inmates at midyear 2006.* Washington, DC: Bureau of Justice Statistics.

Sacks, S., Sacks, J. Y., & Stommel, J. (2003). Modified therapeutic community programs: For inmates with mental illness and chemical abuse disorders. *Corrections Today, 65*(6), 90–100.

Sahagun, L. (2007, June 2). A mother's plight revives sanctuary movement. *Los Angeles Times.* Retrieved from http://articles.latimes.com/2007/jun/02/local/me-beliefs2.

Sampson, R. J., & Laub, J. H. (1993). *Crime in the making: Pathways and turning points through life.* Cambridge, MA: Harvard University Press.

Sampson, R. J., Raudenbush, S. W., & Earls, F. (1997). Neighborhoods and violent crime: A multilevel study of collective efficacy. *Science, 277,* 918–924.

Santos, M. (2000). *Understanding the presentence investigation.* Lompoc, CA: Retrieved from http://www.prisontalk.com/forums/showthread.php?t=271.

Sato, I. (1991). *Kamikaze biker: Parody and anomy in affluent Japan.* Chicago: University of Chicago Press.

Schmalleger, F. (2004). *Criminal justice: A brief introduction* (5th ed.). Upper Saddle River, NJ: Prentice Hall.

Schmidt, A. (1994). An overview of intermediate sanctions in the United States. In U. Zvekic (Ed.), *Alternatives to imprisonment: A comparative perspective.* Chicago: Nelson Hall.

Schneider, A., & Finkelstein, M. (1998). *National directory of restitution and community service programs.* Washington, DC: U.S. Office of Juvenile Justice and Delinquency Prevention.

Schwitzgebel, R. L. (1969, April). A belt from big brother. *Psychology Today 2:* 45–47.

Sentencing Project, The. (2002). *Mentally ill offenders in the criminal justice system: An analysis and prescription.* Washington, DC: Author.

Short, J. F., & Nye, F. I. (1958). Extent of unrecorded juvenile delinquency: Some tentative conclusions. *Journal of Criminal Law, Criminology, and Police Science, 49,* 296–302.

Shusta, M., Levine, D. R., Wong, H. Z. & Harris, P. R., (2005). *Multicultural law enforcement: Strategies for peacekeeping in a diverse society* (3rd ed.). Upper Saddle River, NJ: Prentice Hall.

Siegel, L. J. (2003). *Criminology: Theories, patterns, and typologies* (7th ed.). Belmont, CA: Wadsworth.

Siegel, L. J., Welsh, B. C., & Senna, J. J. (2003). *Juvenile delinquency: Theory, practice, and law* (8th ed.). Belmont, CA: Wadsworth.

Sieh, E. W. (2006). *Community corrections and human dignity.* Boston: Jones & Bartlett.

Singh, D., & White, C. (2000). *Rapua te huarahi tika: Searching for solutions: A review of research about effective interventions for reducing offending by indigenous and ethnic minority youth.* New Zealand: Ministry of Youth Affairs.

Skinner, B. F. (1953). *Science and human behavior.* New York: Macmillan.

Smith, L. G., & Akers, R. L. (1993). A comparison of recidivism of Florida's community control and prison: A five-year survival analysis. *Journal of Research in Crime and Delinquency, 30*(3), 267–292.

Snell, T. (1994). *Women in prison.* Washington, DC: Bureau of Justice Statistics.

Stanton, A. H., & Schwartz, M. (1954). *The mental hospital: A study of institutional participation in psychiatric illness and treatment.* New York: Basic Books.

State of Georgia. (2007). *Sample contract—Private probation services—Georgia courts.* Retrieved from http://www.georgiacourts.org/councils/sample_contract.pdf.

Stattin, H., & Magnusson, D. (1996). Antisocial development: A holistic approach. *Development and Psychopathology, 8,* 617–645.

Steadman, H. J., & Naples, M. (2005). Assessing the effectiveness of jail diversion programs for persons with serious mental illness and co-occurring substance use disorders. *Behavioral Sciences and the Law, 23*(2), 163–170.

Stinchcomb, J. B., McCampbell, S. W., & Layman, E. P. (2006). *Future force: A guide to building the 21st century community corrections workforce.* Washington, DC: National Institute of Corrections.

Sturgeon, V. H., & Taylor, J. (1980). Report of a five-year follow-up study of mentally disordered sex offenders released from Atascadero State Hospital in 1973. *Criminal Justice Journal, 4,* 31–63.

Substance Abuse and Mental Health Services Administration. (2001). *Cultural competence standards in managed care mental health services: Four underserved/underrepresented racial/ethnic groups.* Rockville, MD: Author. Available at http://mentalhealth.samhsa.gov/publications/allpubs/sma00-3457/default.asp.

Swedish Prison and Probation Service. (2008). *Kontakt.* Stockholm, Sweden: Author.

Szasz, T. (1975). The control of conduct: Authority vs. autonomy? *Criminal Law Bulletin, 11.*

Tennessee Board of Probation and Parole. (2007). *Monitoring Tennessee's sex offenders using Global Positioning Systems: An evaluative report.* Nashville, TN: Author.

Texas Board of Pardons and Paroles. (2001). *Parole guidelines score: Offender information system.* Austin, TX: Author. Retrieved from www.reentrypolicy.org/reentry/Document_Viewer.aspx?DocumentID=300.

Thernstrom, S., & Thernstrom, A. (1997, September 3). The real story of black progress. *Wall Street Journal.*

Torres, S. (2005). Parole. In R. A. Wright & J. M. Mitchell (Eds.), *Encyclopedia of criminology.* New York: Routledge.

Travis, J., & Lawrence, S. (2002). *Beyond the prison gates: The state of parole in America.* Washington, DC: Urban Institute Justice Policy Center.

Umbreit, M. (2000). *Family group conferencing: Implications for crime victims.* St. Paul: University of Minnesota, School of Social Work, Center for Restorative Justice and Peacemaking.

Umbreit, M. S., Coates, R. B., & Vos, B. (2002). *The impact of restorative justice conferencing: A review of 63 empirical studies in 5 countries.* St. Paul: University of Minnesota.

United States Sentencing Commission. (2007). *2007 sourcebook of federal sentencing statistics.* Washington, DC: Author.

U.S. Census Bureau. (2001). *The black population in the United States: March 2000* (update) (Report No. PPL-146).

U.S. Public Health Services. (2002). *Youth violence: A report of the Surgeon General.* Available at http://www.mentalhealth.org/youthviolence/surgeongeneral/SG_Site/chapter4/sec1.asp.

Uzoaba, J. H. E. (1998). *Managing older offenders: Where do we stand?* Montreal, Quebec: Research Branch of Correctional Service of Canada.

Valdez, A. (2005). *A guide to understanding street gangs.* San Clemente, CA: Law Tech Publishing.

Van Keulen, C. (1988). *Colorado alternative sentencing programs: Program guidelines.* Washington, DC: National Institute of Corrections. Retrieved from http://www.nicic.org/pubs/pre/007064.pdf.

Van Voorhis, P., Braswell, M., & Lester, D. (2000). *Correctional counseling and rehabilitation* (4th ed.). Cincinnati, OH: Anderson.

Vazsonyi, A. T., Pickering, L. E., Junger, M., & Hessing, D. (2001). An empirical test of a general theory of crime: A four-nation comparative study of self-control and the prediction of deviance. *Journal of Research in Crime and Delinquency, 38*(2), 91–131.

Vito, G., & Allen, H. (1981). Shock probation in Ohio: A comparison of outcomes. *International Journal of Offender Therapy and Comparative Criminology, 25,* 70–76.

Wahidin, A., & Aday, R. (2006). *The needs of older men and women in the criminal justice system: An international perspective.* London: Her Majesty's Prison Service.

Waldron, H. B., & Kaminer, Y. (2004). On the learning curve: The emerging evidence supporting cognitive-behavioral therapies for adolescent substance abuse. *Society for the Study of Addiction, 99,* 93–105.

Walker v. Prisoner Review Board, 594 F. Supp. 556 (U.S.D. Ill. 1984).

Wallenstein, A. (1999). Intake and release in evolving jail practice. In P. M. Carlson & J. S. Garrett (Eds.), *Prison and jail administration: Practice and theory.* Gaithersburg, MD: Aspen.

Walsh, J. (2000). *Clinical case management with persons having mental illness.* Belmont, CA: Brooks/Cole.

Walters, S. T., Clark, M. D., Gingerich, R., & Meltzer, M. L. (2007). *A guide for probation and parole: Motivating offenders to change.* Washington, DC: National Institute of Corrections.

Washington State Institute for Public Policy. (2007). *Does participation in Washington's work release facilities reduce recidivism?* Olympia, WA: Author. Retrieved from http://nicic.org/Library/022723.

Wasserman, G. A., & Miller, L. S. (1998). The prevention of serious and violent juvenile offending. In R. Loeber & D. P. Farrington (Eds.), *Serious and violent juvenile offenders: Risk factors and successful interventions* (pp. 197–247). Thousand Oaks, CA: Sage.

Watson, A., Hanrahan, P., Luchins, D., & Lurigio, A. (2001). Mental health courts and the complex issue of mentally ill offenders. *Psychiatric Services, 52*(4), 477–481.

Weisz, M., & Crane, R. (1977). *Defenses to civil rights actions against correctional employers.* Washington, DC: American Correctional Association.

Wexler, D. B., & Winick, B. J. (2008). Therapeutic jurisprudence. In A. W. Graham (Ed.), *Principles of addiction medicine* (4th ed., pp. 550–552). Chevy Chase, MD: American Society of Addiction Medicine.

Whitehead, J. T. (1986). Job burnout and job satisfaction among probation managers. *Journal of Criminal Justice, 14,* 25–35.

White House, The. (2006). *Fact sheet: The Adam Walsh Child Protection and Safety Act of 2006.* Washington, DC: Office of the Press Secretary.

Wiebush, R. G. (1993). Juvenile intensive supervision: The impact on felony offenders diverted from institutional placement. *Crime & Delinquency, 39*(1), 68–89.

Williams, O., & Becker, R. L. (1994). Domestic partner abuse treatment programs and cultural competence: The results of a national survey. *Violence and Victims, 9*(3), 287–296.

Wilson, D. B., & MacKenzie, D. L. (2006). Boot camps. In B. C. Welsh & D. P. Farrington (Eds.), *Preventing crime: What works for children, offenders, victims and places* (pp. 73–86). Dordrecht, The Netherlands: Springer.

Wilson, G. (1985). *Halfway house programs for offenders.* In L. F. Travis (Ed.), *Probation, parole, and community corrections* (pp. 151–164). Prospect Heights, IL: Waveland Press.

Wilson, S. J., & Lipsey, M. W. (2000). Wilderness challenge programs for delinquent youth: A meta-analysis of outcome evaluations. *Evaluation and Program Planning, 23,* 1–12.

Wolff v. McDonnell, 418 U.S. 539 (1974).

Yacus, G. M. (1998). *Validation of the risk and needs assessment used in the classification for parole and probation of Virginia's adult criminal offenders.* Doctoral dissertation, Old Dominion University, Norfolk, VA.

Zenner, W. (1996). Ethnicity. In D. Levinson & M. Ember (Eds.), *Encyclopedia of cultural anthropology* (pp. 393–395). New York: Holt.

Zhan, X., & La Paz, C. (1990). *The evaluation of the Wisconsin classification system as it applies to the Los Angeles probation population.* Downey, CA: Los Angeles County Probation Department.

Index

About the Author

Robert D. Hanser is a full-time faculty member and the department head of the Department of Criminal Justice at the University of Louisiana at Monroe. He is also a part-time core faculty member of Ellis University. Rob has dual licensure as a professional counselor in the states of Texas and Louisiana, is a certified anger resolution therapist, and has a specialty license in addictions counseling. He has worked as a child and adolescent therapist in an urban domestic violence shelter and has also worked as a secondary educator at an alternative school for troubled youth experiencing emotional and legal challenges.